Matthias Daub

**Coordination of Service Offshoring Subsidiaries
in Multinational Corporations**

GABLER RESEARCH

mir-Edition

Herausgeber / Editors:

Prof. Dr. Andreas Al-Laham
Technische Universität Kaiserslautern,
Prof. Dr. Johann Engelhard
Universität Bamberg,
Prof. Dr. Michael Kutschker
Universität Eichstätt, Ingolstadt,
Prof. Dr. Profs. h.c. Dr. h.c. Klaus Macharzina
Universität Hohenheim, Stuttgart,
Prof. Dr. Michael-Jörg Oesterle
Universität Bremen,
Prof. Dr. Stefan Schmid
ESCP-EAP Europäische Wirtschaftshochschule Berlin,
Prof. Dr. Martin K. Welge
Universität Dortmund,
Prof. Dr. Joachim Wolf
Universität Kiel

In der mir-Edition werden wichtige Ergebnisse der wissenschaftlichen Forschung sowie Werke erfahrener Praktiker auf dem Gebiet des internationalen Managements veröffentlicht.

The series mir-Edition includes excellent academic contributions and experiential works of distinguished international managers.

Matthias Daub

Coordination of Service Offshoring Subsidiaries in Multinational Corporations

With a Foreword by Prof. Dr. Stefan Schmid

GABLER

RESEARCH

Bibliografische Information der Deutschen Nationalbibliothek
Die Deutsche Nationalbibliothek verzeichnet diese Publikation in der
Deutschen Nationalbibliografie; detaillierte bibliografische Daten sind im Internet über
<http://dnb.d-nb.de> abrufbar.

Bibliographic information published by the Deutsche Nationalbibliothek
The Deutsche Nationalbibliothek lists this publication in the Deutsche Nationalbibliografie;
detailed bibliographic data are available in the Internet at http://dnb.d-nb.de.

Dr. Matthias Daub finished his doctorate at ESCP-EAP Europäische Wirtschaftshochschule in Berlin, Chair of International Management and Strategic Management. He now works as a management consultant specializing on topics of strategy, globalization, and technology.

Dissertation ESCP-EAP Europäische Wirtschaftshochschule Berlin, 2008

Abonnenten von mir – Management International Review erhalten auf die in der mir-Edition veröffentlichten Bücher 10% Rabatt.

Subscribers to mir – Management International Review are entitled to a 10 % price reduction on books published in mir-Edition.

1. Auflage 2009

Alle Rechte vorbehalten
© Gabler | GWV Fachverlage GmbH, Wiesbaden 2009

Lektorat: Claudia Jeske | Jutta Hinrichsen

Gabler ist Teil der Fachverlagsgruppe Springer Science+Business Media.
www.gabler.de

Das Werk einschließlich aller seiner Teile ist urheberrechtlich geschützt. Jede Verwertung außerhalb der engen Grenzen des Urheberrechtsgesetzes ist ohne Zustimmung des Verlags unzulässig und strafbar. Das gilt insbesondere für Vervielfältigungen, Übersetzungen, Mikroverfilmungen und die Einspeicherung und Verarbeitung in elektronischen Systemen.

Die Wiedergabe von Gebrauchsnamen, Handelsnamen, Warenbezeichnungen usw. in diesem Werk berechtigt auch ohne besondere Kennzeichnung nicht zu der Annahme, dass solche Namen im Sinne der Warenzeichen- und Markenschutz-Gesetzgebung als frei zu betrachten wären und daher von jedermann benutzt werden dürften.

Umschlaggestaltung: KünkelLopka Medienentwicklung, Heidelberg
Gedruckt auf säurefreiem und chlorfrei gebleichtem Papier
Printed in Germany

ISBN 978-3-8349-1928-1

Vorwort der Herausgeber

Für viele Unternehmen ist es heutzutage unerlässlich, sich auf ausländischen Märkten zu betätigen. Ein erfolgreiches Management der Internationalisierung stellt Unternehmen allerdings immer wieder vor neue Herausforderungen. Die Herausgeber beabsichtigen mit der Schriftenreihe **mir-Edition**, die vielfältigen und komplexen Managementanforderungen der internationalen Unternehmenstätigkeit wissenschaftlich zu begleiten. Die **mir-Edition** soll zum einen der empirischen Feststellung und der theoretischen Verarbeitung der in der Praxis des Internationalen Managements beobachtbaren Phänomene dienen. Zum anderen sollen die hierdurch gewonnenen Erkenntnisse in Form von systematisiertem Wissen, von Erklärungen und Denkanstößen sowie von Handlungsempfehlungen verfügbar gemacht werden.

Diesem angewandten Wissenschaftsverständnis fühlt sich seit nunmehr 50 Jahren auch die in über 40 Ländern gelesene internationale Fachzeitschrift **mir** – Management International Review – verpflichtet. Während in der Zeitschrift allerdings nur kurzgefasste englischsprachige Aufsätze publiziert werden, soll der breitere Raum der vorliegenden Schriftenreihe den Autoren und Lesern die Möglichkeit zur umfänglichen und vertieften Auseinandersetzung mit dem jeweils behandelten Problem des Internationalen Managements eröffnen. Der Herausgeberkreis der **mir-Edition** wurde 2008 um weitere renommierte Fachvertreter des Internationalen Managements erweitert. Geblieben ist jedoch die Herausgeberpolitik für die **mir-Edition**, in der Schriftenreihe innovative und dem Erkenntnisfortschritt dienende Beiträge einer kritischen Öffentlichkeit vorzustellen. Neben Forschungsergebnissen, insbesondere des wissenschaftlichen Nachwuchses, können auch einschlägige Werke von Praktikern mit profundem Erfahrungswissen im Internationalen Management einbezogen werden. Wissenschaftliche Sammelbände, etwa zu Tagungen aus dem Bereich des Internationalen Managements, sind ebenso sehr gerne in der Reihe willkommen. Die Herausgeber laden zu Veröffentlichungen sowohl in deutscher als auch in englischer Sprache ausdrücklich ein.

Das Auswahlverfahren sieht vor, dass die Herausgeber gemeinsam über die Veröffentlichung eines für die Reihe eingereichten Werkes entscheiden. Wir freuen uns auf Ihre Manuskripte und hoffen, mit dieser seit langer Zeit renommierten Schriftenreihe die wissenschaftliche Diskussion und die praktische Lösung von Problemen des Internationalen Managements weiter zu stimulieren.

Andreas Al-Laham, Johann Engelhard,
Michael Kutschker, Klaus Macharzina,
Michael-Jörg Oesterle, Stefan Schmid,
Martin K. Welge, Joachim Wolf

Preface

Nowadays, it is essential for a multitude of companies to engage in foreign markets. However, the successful management of internationalization processes constantly poses new challenges. By publishing the book series "mir-Edition", the editors attempt to provide academic guidance on the manifold and complex requirements of international business activities. The book series' purpose hence is twofold. Firstly, the "mir-Edition" is to provide empirical assessment and theoretical elaboration on the phenomena which can be observed in international management practice. Secondly, the findings obtained are to be made available in the form of systematised knowledge, explanations, thought-provoking impulses as well as recommendations for further courses of action.

For the past 50 years, the international journal "mir – Management International Review", which is read in more than 40 countries, has seen itself committed to promoting an understanding of international management as an applied academic discipline. As of now, the journal only publishes articles in English. The wider range of the existing book series ought to give authors and readers the opportunity to deal with the various problems of international management in a comprehensive and thorough manner. The editorial board of the "mir-Edition" was extended in 2008 through the addition of renowned experts from the domain of international management. Yet, the established editors' policy for the "mir-Edition" of presenting innovative work to a critical audience, which support the scientific advancement, has remained unchanged.

Besides the academic contributions of young scholars, the editors also welcome the relevant works of practitioners, who possess a profound knowledge in the area of international management. Furthermore, edited volumes, collecting for instance presentations held at conferences in the field of international management, are invited for publication. The editors explicitly welcome books both in the English and the German language.

The selection process stipulates that the editors jointly decide on the publication of any book manuscript submitted for the series. As editors of this well established and renowned book series, we are looking forward to receiving your manuscripts and we hope to further stimulate the academic discussion and to provide applied solutions for the challenges in the area of international management.

Andreas Al-Laham, Johann Engelhard,
Michael Kutschker, Klaus Macharzina,
Michael-Jörg Oesterle, Stefan Schmid,
Martin K. Welge, Joachim Wolf

Foreword

Multinational Corporations (MNCs) benefit from their presence in various countries for creating and enhancing their competitive advantage. In the past, many Western MNCs reflected upon the question whether they should transfer some of the activities so far carried out at home to foreign markets in order to guarantee or to increase their competitiveness. While formerly the transfer of activities mainly concerned the production of goods, more recently MNCs have offshored some of their services across borders. Cost reasons are a major factor for service offshoring to countries in Asia or Central and Eastern Europe. However, there are many additional rationales which may bring a Western company to carry out some services in a foreign country, whereby the company has the choice between a foreign subsidiary and a foreign partner.

The present contribution focuses on service offshoring of German MNCs in Central and Eastern Europe. Matthias Daub is not only interested in the question whether we can find different types of service offshoring centres; he also analyses in how far the coordination of a service offshoring centre depends on its respective role. In this way, Matthias Daub interprets service offshoring centres as a specific type of subsidiary. The research on which the publication is based can be linked to the research programme at my department. For some time, at my department, we have been interested in the roles foreign subsidiaries can play and in the management which is appropriate for headquarters-subsidiary relationships.

In his contribution, Matthias Daub develops a typology for service offshoring which is theoretically grounded. He uses the resource-based view on the one hand and network approaches on the other hand to come up with a four-cell matrix, based on two dimensions. This enables him to differentiate four types of service offshoring units, i.e. "Service Factories", "Internal Competence Centers", "Support Centers" and "Specialized Contributors". Matthias Daub's identification of subsidiary roles is not an end in itself. In his contribution, Matthias Daub is interested in the question in how far the four types differ with respect to coordination. He establishes propositions which link the four types of service offshoring units to structural, technocratic, personal and output control. The propositions are confronted with rich empirical data. By using a selective sampling method, Matthias Daub is able to find evidence for each of the four service offshoring types. The empirical data gives him the opportunity to also empirically investigate the relationships to coordination, as suggested by his propositions.

The work done by Matthias Daub is extremely relevant to the business world. Although currently some MNCs re-locate foreign activities to the home country (after negative experiences abroad), the majority of them are using service offshoring in some way or the other. Managers benefit from Daub's work, since it clearly shows that each service offshoring centre requires a different coordination approach. This is due to the strategic relevance of the services carried out, but also due to the specific approach to integration. Furthermore, in his empirical study, Daub is able to find out that additional factors can influence the appropriate coordination. By this, he shows that we should refrain from too simplistic generalizations.

I am convinced that Matthias Daub's work can have an impact on future research beyond its obvious relevance for management practice. Matthias Daub enriches the subsidiary role stream in the International Business field; he also adds value to the general business and management literature by showing applications of the resource-based view and network approaches in empirical settings, and he contributes to the regionally focused literature in business and management by choosing Central and Eastern Europe as his empirical setting. I wish all readers valuable insights when studying the present contribution by Matthias Daub.

Berlin, April 2009   Stefan Schmid

Preface

Service offshoring has not only taken hold in multinational corporations in their attempts to find the best location worldwide for their operations. It has also influenced this thesis, for which providers of transcription services from the US and Bulgaria were used. Though the coordination of one researcher and one transcriber involves relatively little effort, it points in itself to some of the challenges that can occur for corporations in the coordination of offshore operations. These are a source of fascination for me and have laid the foundation for this study (that intends to analyze how companies coordinate their service offshoring subsidiaries).

However, not only does this dissertation build on network theories, it has also been created within a network that merits special mention and thanks. First and foremost, my debt of gratitude is to Prof. Dr. Stefan Schmid from whom I have learned so much during the time I had the possibility to work at his department. His academic rigor, his insistence on delving deeper until a clear picture and results emerge, have made this work successful and I have very much benefited from working with him. I have also enjoyed the time there because of his great sense of humor. My second supervisor, Prof. Dr. Hartmut Kreikebaum, has my deepest respect not only for his academic achievements and his advice on how to advance this thesis but also for his integrity and for all his support throughout my university years.

This work has benefitted from the many excellent contributions by members of the organizations who were interviewed in the empirical parts of the study and who cannot be named for reasons of confidentiality. I am greatly indebted to them for their time and valuable insights.

Projects at my employer McKinsey&Co. initially inspired me to explore the offshoring waters. For their generous support along the way I am especially grateful to my current and former colleagues Detlev Hoch, Dr. Peter Peters, Holger Friedrich, Dr. Markus Löffler, Dr. Ulrich Freking, Tobias Schwarz, Dr. Markus Schaper, and Dr. Timo Meynhardt.

My colleagues from the chair of International Management and Strategic Management at the ESCP-EAP European School of Management Berlin, Monika Dammer, Andrea Daniel, Swantje Hartmann, Thomas Kotulla, Dr. Katharina Kretschmer, Dr. Mario Machulik, Renate Ramlau, and Stephan Schulze, were always willing to brainstorm and discuss new topics with me and go through parts of the thesis in great detail. In addition, Vera Dobreva, Karen Finney-Kellerhoff, Christian Geiselmann, and Dr. Simon Kaja have made the research process much easier for me and I have enjoyed working with them. The support of the Konrad-Adenauer foundation has helped me in many dimensions but especially with regard to the possibility of discussing topics unrelated to my dissertation and getting a fresh perspective on areas of life that are not subject to offshoring.

On a more personal note: I am deeply grateful to my family and my parents who have foregone so much to support my education and help me grow and develop. My further thanks go to my friends Prof. Dr. Michael Behnam, Dr. Stefan Behrens, Dr. Tobias Popović, and Dipl.Kfm. Sascha Stürze for their critical comments, patience in pointing me to flaws in the research design and for being there in need.

Without my wife Mihaela I would not be what I am and where I am today. I do not have the words to express my gratitude for her encouraging words, her great support and her love. The latest addition to our family, my daughter Hanna Katharina, has brought the most joyful moments in my life. Finally, I thank my Lord and Savior Jesus Christ, for richly blessing me, giving a meaning to my life and for making all of the above possible.

Berlin, Summer 2009   Matthias Daub

BRIEF CONTENTS

1 INTRODUCTION – APPROACHING SERVICE OFFSHORING 1

2 THEORETICAL FOUNDATIONS – DEVELOPING BUILDING BLOCKS OF SERVICE OFFSHORING TYPOLOGY 14

3 RESEARCH MODEL AND PROPOSITIONS – DERIVING TYPOLOGY DIMENSIONS FROM ORGANIZATIONAL THEORIES 82

4 A TYPOLOGY OF SERVICE OFFSHORING SUBSIDIARY – COMBINING BUILDING BLOCKS AND DIMENSIONS 132

5 METHODOLOGY – PREPARING AND CONDUCTING QUALITATIVE RESEARCH 149

6 RESULTS – PRESENTING FOUR CASE STUDIES OF SERVICE OFFSHORING SUBSIDIARIES IN EASTERN EUROPE 199

7 DISCUSSION – FINDINGS FROM CROSS-CASE ANALYSIS AND BEYOND 334

8 CONCLUSIONS – WHAT WE HAVE LEARNED, WHAT WE HAVE NOT LEARNED, AND WHAT MIGHT COME NEXT 369

Contents

FIGURES XXIII

TABLES XXV

ABBREVIATIONS XXVII

1   INTRODUCTION – APPROACHING SERVICE OFFSHORING 1

    1.1   Relevance of the Topic 1

    1.2   Research Questions 4

    1.3   Scope, Structure, and Methodology of This Study 7

    1.4   Uniqueness of This Research 10

2   THEORETICAL FOUNDATIONS – DEVELOPING BUILDING BLOCKS OF SERVICE OFFSHORING TYPOLOGY 14

    2.1   The Perspective of International Business Research 15

    2.2   Service Offshoring 19

        2.2.1   Definition of Service 19

        2.2.2   Definition of International Services 23

        2.2.3   Overview of Existing Definitions of Service Offshoring ... 26

        2.2.4   Differentiation of Service Offshoring and Related Practices ... 33

            2.2.4.1   Differentiation of Outsourcing and Offshoring ... 33

            2.2.4.2   Differentiation of Manufacturing and Service Offshoring ... 37

            2.2.4.3   Differentiation of Shared Services Centers and Service Offshoring 42

        2.2.5   Our Service Offshoring Definition 44

        2.2.6   Description of Service Offshoring 45

            2.2.6.1   History 45

- 2.2.6.2 Reasons for Service Offshoring 46
- 2.2.6.3 Barriers to Service Offshoring 48
- 2.2.6.4 Current Size and Expected Growth of Service Offshoring 49
- 2.2.6.5 Industries and Functions 52
- 2.2.6.6 Characteristics of Service Offshoring Centers 53
- 2.2.6.7 Examples of Service Offshoring 54

2.3 TYPOLOGIES OF INTERNATIONAL SUBSIDIARIES 55
- 2.3.1 Typologies in Business Research 55
- 2.3.2 Overview of Subsidiary Typologies 58
- 2.3.3 Typologies and Service Offshoring 63
- 2.3.4 Evaluation of Existing Typologies 65

2.4 COORDINATION MECHANISMS 69
- 2.4.1 Overview of Coordination 69
- 2.4.2 Evaluation of Coordination Mechanisms 73
- 2.4.3 Result of Evaluation and Consequences for This Study 77

3 RESEARCH MODEL AND PROPOSITIONS – DERIVING TYPOLOGY DIMENSIONS FROM ORGANIZATIONAL THEORIES 82

3.1 SELECTION OF ORGANIZATIONAL THEORY 83

3.2 THE RESOURCE-BASED VIEW OF THE FIRM 88
- 3.2.1 Introduction to the Resource-Based View 88
- 3.2.2 Resource-Based View and International Business Research 93
- 3.2.3 Relevance of the Resource-Based View for Service Offshoring 100
- 3.2.4 Strategic Relevance as Dimension of Service Offshoring 104

- 3.2.5 Operationalization of the Resource-Based View 106
- 3.2.6 Propositions Derived from the Resource-Based View 110
- 3.3 THE VIEW OF THE MNC AS A NETWORK 112
  - 3.3.1 Introduction to Network Approaches 112
  - 3.3.2 Network Approaches of the MNC 114
  - 3.3.3 Relevance of Network Approaches for Service Offshoring 117
  - 3.3.4 Network Embeddedness as Dimension of Service Offshoring 120
  - 3.3.5 Operationalization of the MNC Network Approach 124
  - 3.3.6 Propositions Derived from Network Approaches 128
- 3.4 RELATIONSHIP BETWEEN RESOURCE-BASED VIEW AND NETWORK APPROACHES 130

4 A TYPOLOGY OF SERVICE OFFSHORING SUBSIDIARY – COMBINING BUILDING BLOCKS AND DIMENSIONS 132

- 4.1 METHODOLOGY OF TYPOLOGY DEVELOPMENT 133
  - 4.1.1 Application in Current Research 133
  - 4.1.2 Criticism of Typology Research and Possible Answers 136
- 4.2 PRESENTATION OF TYPOLOGY 138
- 4.3 DISCUSSION OF RESULTING TYPES 139
  - 4.3.1 Service Factory 140
  - 4.3.2 Internal Competence Center 141
  - 4.3.3 Support Center 142
  - 4.3.4 Specialized Contributor 143
  - 4.3.5 Summary of Characteristics of Service Offshoring Subsidiaries 144

4.4		EXTENSION OF SERVICE OFFSHORING TYPOLOGY TO OTHER SUBSIDIARIES 146

5 METHODOLOGY – PREPARING AND CONDUCTING QUALITATIVE RESEARCH 149

5.1 Overview of Choices 150

5.2 Typology Illustration and Evaluation 151

5.2.1 Description of the Case Study Method 151

5.2.1.1 Overview of Qualitative Research and the Case Study Method 151

5.2.1.2 Reasons for the Use of Case Studies in This Study 154

5.2.1.3 Types of Case Studies 157

5.2.2 Case Selection 159

5.2.2.1 Alternatives for Case Selection 159

5.2.2.2 Selection Criteria for Cases 161

5.2.2.3 Selection Process and Outcome 162

5.2.3 Data Collection 164

5.2.3.1 Data Collection Methods 164

5.2.3.2 Interview Process 167

5.2.3.3 Interview Design 169

5.2.3.4 Interview Guide and Measures 170

5.2.4 Data Interpretation 182

5.2.4.1 Epistemological Underpinnings of Data Interpretation 182

5.2.4.2 Transcription of Interviews 183

5.2.4.3 Coding of Interviews 184

5.2.4.4 Case Display 190

	5.2.4.5 Generalization of Results 193
	5.2.5 Quality Criteria for Case Studies 194
5.3	REGIONAL FOCUS OF EMPIRICAL RESEARCH 195
5.4	FUNCTIONAL FOCUS OF EMPIRICAL RESEARCH.. 197
6	**RESULTS – PRESENTING FOUR CASE STUDIES OF SERVICE OFFSHORING SUBSIDIARIES IN EASTERN EUROPE 199**
6.1	CASE 1: SERVICE FACTORY ALPHA 200
	6.1.1 Company Overview 200
	6.1.2 Type of Service Offshoring Subsidiary 204
	6.1.2.1 Analysis of Strategic Relevance.. 204
	6.1.2.2 Analysis of Network Embeddedness... 210
	6.1.3 Coordination Mechanisms 212
	6.1.3.1 Overview of Coordination... 212
	6.1.3.2 Structural Coordination Mechanisms... 212
	6.1.3.3 Technocratic Coordination Mechanisms 215
	6.1.3.4 Output-based Coordination Mechanisms 220
	6.1.3.5 Personal Coordination Mechanisms 222
	6.1.3.6 Comparative Analysis of Coordination Mechanisms 230
	6.1.4 Discussion of Case 231
6.2	CASE 2: INTERNAL COMPETENCE CENTER BETA... 235
	6.2.1 Company Overview 235
	6.2.2 Type of Service Offshoring Subsidiary 242
	6.2.2.1 Analysis of Strategic Relevance.. 242

		6.2.2.2 Analysis of Network Embeddedness	250
	6.2.3	Coordination Mechanisms	253
		6.2.3.1 Overview of Coordination	253
		6.2.3.2 Structural Coordination Mechanisms	253
		6.2.3.3 Technocratic Coordination Mechanisms	255
		6.2.3.4 Output-based Coordination Mechanisms	257
		6.2.3.5 Personal Coordination Mechanisms	258
		6.2.3.6 Comparative Analysis of Coordination Mechanisms	265
	6.2.4	Discussion of Case	265
6.3	CASE 3: SUPPORT CENTER GAMMA		268
	6.3.1	Company Overview	268
	6.3.2	Type of Service Offshoring Subsidiary	274
		6.3.2.1 Analysis of Strategic Relevance	274
		6.3.2.2 Analysis of Network Embeddedness	278
	6.3.3	Coordination Mechanisms	280
		6.3.3.1 Overview of Coordination	280
		6.3.3.2 Structural Coordination Mechanisms	281
		6.3.3.3 Technocratic Coordination Mechanisms	284
		6.3.3.4 Output-based Coordination Mechanisms	288
		6.3.3.5 Personal Coordination Mechanisms	288
		6.3.3.6 Comparative Analysis of Coordination Mechanisms	293
	6.3.4	Discussion of Case	293
6.4	CASE 4: SPECIALIZED CONTRIBUTOR DELTA		297

	6.4.1	Company Overview 297
	6.4.2	Type of Service Offshoring Subsidiary 302
		6.4.2.1 Analysis of Strategic Relevance 302
		6.4.2.2 Analysis of Network Embeddedness 308
	6.4.3	Coordination Mechanisms 311
		6.4.3.1 Overview of Coordination 311
		6.4.3.2 Structural Coordination Mechanisms 311
		6.4.3.3 Technocratic Coordination Mechanisms 314
		6.4.3.4 Output-based Coordination Mechanisms 317
		6.4.3.5 Personal Coordination Mechanisms 318
		6.4.3.6 Comparative Analysis of Coordination Mechanisms ... 329
	6.4.4	Discussion of Case 330

7 DISCUSSION – FINDINGS FROM CROSS-CASE ANALYSIS AND BEYOND 334

7.1 OVERVIEW OF FINDINGS 335

7.2 FINDINGS REGARDING COORDINATION MECHANISMS IN SERVICE OFFSHORING CENTERS 335

    7.2.1 Findings for Each Proposition 336

    7.2.2 Findings for Each Coordination Mechanism 340

    7.2.3 Comparative Analysis of Coordination Mechanisms 344

    7.2.4 Implications of Findings for Types of Service Offshoring Subsidiary 346

    7.2.5 Newly Identified Factors Influencing Coordination 349

7.3 ADDITIONAL FINDINGS RELATING TO TYPOLOGY 357

    7.3.1 Application of the Typology to Different Levels of Analysis 357

	7.3.2	Impact of Entry Mode Decision on Coordination 358
	7.3.3	Relevance of the Service Offshoring Subsidiary's Local Network 358
	7.3.4	Perception Gaps between Headquarters and Service Offshoring Subsidiary 360
	7.3.5	Changes of Types over Time 361
7.4		FINDINGS REGARDING TRENDS IN SERVICE OFFSHORING 364
7.5		FINDINGS REGARDING METHODOLOGY 366
8		**CONCLUSIONS – WHAT WE HAVE LEARNED, WHAT WE HAVE NOT LEARNED, AND WHAT MIGHT COME NEXT** 369
8.1		MAJOR CONTRIBUTIONS 369
8.2		IMPLICATIONS FOR MANAGEMENT AND POLICY MAKERS 371
8.3		LIMITATIONS OF STUDY AND AVENUES FOR FUTURE RESEARCH 373
APPENDICES 379
LITERATURE 403

FIGURES

Figure 1-1: Structure of this study 11

Figure 2-1: Categorization of international services by Sampson and Snape (Source: Mößlang (1995), p. 128) 24

Figure 2-2: Categorization of international services (Source: Vandermerwe/Chadwick (1989), p. 82) 25

Figure 2-3: Relationship between offshoring and outsourcing (Source: Based on Ge et al. (2004), p. 30 33

Figure 2-4: Illustration of the definition of service offshoring 45

Figure 2-5: Cumulative number of service jobs (in thousands) moved offshore per region (Source: McCarthy (2003); Parker (2004)) 50

Figure 2-6: Market sizes 2001 in billion USD for offshoring and outsourcing (Source: Slightly adapted from Farrell et al. (2005), p. 15) 51

Figure 2-7: Differentiating levels of findings on the international subsidiary 60

Figure 2-8: Differentiation between behavioral coordination and output control 75

Figure 3-1: Relationship between resources, combination of resources and competitive advantage 91

Figure 3-2: Possibilities for the combination of resource location and mode of gaining control of resource 96

Figure 3-3: Hierarchy of resources (with the example of resources for a logistics company) 103

Figure 3-4: Relationship between firm resources, strategic relevance, coordination mechanisms and sustained competitive advantage (Source: Based on Barney (1991), p. 112) 106

Figure 3-5: Differentiating network levels (Source: Translated from Schmid (2005), p. 240) 115

Figure 3-6: Levels of network analysis (Source: Translated from Schmid (2005), p. 243) 124

Figure 3-7: Examples for low and high degrees of embeddedness (Source: Inspired by Echols/Tsai (2005), p. 222) 126

Figure 3-8: Overview of propositions 130

Figure 4-1: Typology for service offshoring subsidiaries (Source: Previously also in Schmid/Daub (2005), p. 17) 139

Figure 5-1: Initial relationships between codes 189

Figure 6-1: Service delivery within Alpha's network 201

Figure 6-2: Alpha Center's service delivery relationships 203

Figure 6-3: Different configurations of IT service delivery within BetaCorp 237

Figure 6-4: Beta's international delivery network (Source: Based on information from Beta's web site) 237

Figure 6-5: Service delivery within Beta's network 240

Figure 6-6: Organization chart Beta Center 241

Figure 6-7: Beta Center's service delivery relationships 242

Figure 6-8: Gamma's locations in Germany (Source: Gamma's web site) 270

Figure 6-9: Service delivery within Gamma's network 274

Figure 6-10: Coordination between Gamma and Gamma Center 281

Figure 6-11: Service delivery within Delta's network 300

Figure 6-12: Organization chart Delta Center 302

Figure 7-1: Change in factor model 350

Figure 7-2: Enhanced factor model 356

Figure 7-3: Current positions and expected movements of cases in typology 363

TABLES

Table 2-1: Research focus on MNCs from a network perspective (Source: Translated and slightly adapted from Renz (1998), p. 80) 17

Table 2-2: Classification of service characteristics (Source: Based on Lovelock (1983)) 21

Table 2-3: Overview of definitions for service offshoring 26

Table 2-4: Differences between service and manufacturing offshoring (Source: Own table, partially based on UNCTAD (2004b), pp. 152-153) 40

Table 2-5: Differences between shared service centers and service offshoring subsidiaries 44

Table 2-6: Typologies versus taxonomies (Source: Slightly adapted from Bensaou/Venkatraman (1995), p. 1472) 57

Table 2-7: Evaluation of subsidiary typologies for service offshoring (Source: Partially based on Kutschker/Schmid (2005), p. 335) 65

Table 2-8: Coordination mechanisms in use for this study 79

Table 3-1: Journal contributions on embeddedness 122

Table 3-2: Differentiating existing embeddedness research from our contribution 127

Table 4-1: Typical shortcomings of subsidiary typologies and possible solutions (Source: Shortcomings are taken from Schmid et al. (1998), pp. 95-99) 137

Table 4-2: Overview of characteristics of service offshoring subsidiaries 144

Table 5-1: Overview of case population (Source: Press research) 162

Table 5-2: Steps for interview investigation (Source: Based on Kvale (1996), pp. 88-92) 168

Table 5-3: Overview of measures for independent variables 174

Table 5-4: Overview of measures for dependent variables 179

Table 5-5: Codes used for transcript analysis 185

Table 5-6: Structure for case display 190

Table 6-1: Structure of AlphaIT's service catalog (Source: Alpha internal
          document) 202

Table 6-2: Evaluation of suitability of propositions for service factory 231

Table 6-3: Evaluation of suitability of propositions for internal competence center 266

Table 6-4: Gamma's split of activities across locations 271

Table 6-5: Template for project folder in Gamma (Source: Delta internal
          document (translated)) 285

Table 6-6: Evaluation of suitability of propositions for support center 293

Table 6-7: Evaluation of suitability of propositions for specialized contributor 330

Table 7-1: Evaluation of propositions 336

Table 7-2: Overview of coordination mechanisms 341

Table 7-3: Distribution of quotations over coordination mechanisms 345

Table 7-4: Overview of adapted characteristics of service offshoring subsidiaries 347

ABBREVIATIONS

Abbreviation	Meaning
BPO	Business Process Outsourcing/Offshoring
EUR	Euro
ERP	Enterprise Resource Planning
FDI	Foreign Direct Investment
ISO	International Standardization Organization
HQ	Headquarters
IT	Information Technology
KPI	Key Performance Indicator
MNC	Multinational Corporation
MNE	Multinational Enterprise
NIC	Newly Industrialized Country
SO	Service Offshoring
U.S.	United States of America
UNCTAD	United Nations Conference on Trade And Development
USD	U.S. Dollar
R&D	Research and development
RBV	Resource-Based View

1 INTRODUCTION – APPROACHING SERVICE OFFSHORING

1.1 RELEVANCE OF THE TOPIC

Many multinational corporations (MNCs) have started to shift their internal service processes to other, often developing, countries. Especially American corporations have moved many business processes abroad, primarily to India.[1] What started with the establishment of large service centers in India by companies such as General Electric from the U.S. or British Airways from the UK has now also become common practice for companies from Continental Europe: Lufthansa has set up a finance and accounting center in Krakow, Poland, to serve its European subsidiaries. DHL has built up a large IT center in Prague, Czech Republic, to support its operations worldwide.[2]

Politicians and economists alike debate service offshoring – the international relocation of service activities.[3] For instance, it became an issue in the last U.S. presidential election campaign[4] and German corporations use it as a threat in wage negotiations with unions.[5] Developing countries see offshoring as an opportunity to attract foreign direct investment (FDI) and so accelerate economic growth.[6] Developed economies on the other hand feel threatened by the arbitrage possibilities that arise from the large differences in wages and fear job losses. Service offshoring is thus sometimes considered to undermine the job security of highly skilled jobs in the Western world, such as investment research and software programming. Therefore, much of the discussion so far has focused on the effects of offshoring on a nation's economy in more general, macroeconomic terms.[7] Only little attention has been given to the corporate "players" and their motives.[8]

Offshoring – and outsourcing as well[9] - are not new phenomena. A number of companies started to relocate production outside of their home country decades ago.[10] How-

---

[1] Schaaf (2004), p. 8.
[2] Wagstyl (2004), p. 4.
[3] For a detailed discussion and definition of service offshoring see section 2.2.1.
[4] Kerry (2004), p. 611.
[5] Busse/Hennes (2004), p. 2.
[6] Farrell/Zainulbhai (2004), pp. 53-54, Moreira (2004), p. 52, Kshetri (2007).
[7] See Bhagwati et al. (2004), BMF (2004), Colquhoun et al. (2004), Farrell (2004), Samuelson (2004), Levy (2005), Blinder (2006), Harrison/McMillan (2006), Lapid (2006). E.g., Farrell (2004) and BMF (2004), pp. 59-65 discuss the effects of offshoring on the German economy.
[8] For some exceptions see, however, Agrawal et al. (2003), Karmarkar (2004), Ramamurti (2004), Venkatraman (2004), Doh (2005), Mol et al. (2005), Grote/Täube (2007), Maskell et al. (2007).
[9] See section 2.3 for definitions of the terms "outsourcing" and "offshoring".
[10] Burgmaier et al. (2004), p. 21.

ever, the transfer of *services* – often relating to company-internal functions – to another location and/or another owner is relatively new. Service offshoring is motivated by lower factor cost and the desire to access labor markets with highly skilled people in developing countries. In recent years two major advances have facilitated service offshoring:[11]

- Firstly, technological progress is such that data can now be rapidly moved to any place in the world, thus making it possible to have work executed in far-off locations. It is only by this "seamless" technological integration that companies like Tata Consulting from India are able to carry out services for MNCs from the UK and the U.S.

- Secondly, the political stabilization and opening of countries and regions such as India[12] or Eastern Europe have enabled companies from industrialized countries to set up service centers in these emerging markets. Thus, they have not only gained from cost savings but also substantially altered the way that people work and live in these countries.[13]

This work focuses on firms, more specifically on MNCs[14] that mainly drive the offshoring development. This focus was chosen because service offshoring is important for an MNC's (1) organization and (2) strategy; however, currently (3) there is very little documentation of this phenomenon:

(1) Service offshoring seems to have great potential to change *the way companies are organized* today,[15] for instance, by allowing for a fragmentation of many parts of a company that were hitherto considered part of its core. Karmarkar calls this the "industrialization of services"[16]. However, it is not yet clear how offshoring will be integrated into an MNC's organization. Managers are confronted with the offshoring discussion and need to find an answer to the questions if and how their company should offshore

---

[11] Ramamurti (2004), p. 278.
[12] Farrell/Zainulbhai (2004), pp. 51-52.
[13] Slater (2004), pp. 1-2.
[14] In our understanding we follow Kutschker/Schmid (2005), p. 245 who define the MNC as a firm that is involved to a significant degree in international activities, which generally entails regular transactions with foreign entities (see also section 2.1). We consider this general definition to be the most appropriate one for our research. We will later focus our research by concentrating on a specific function and on MNCs with wholly-owned subsidiaries abroad.
[15] Venkatraman (2004), p. 16.
[16] Karmarkar (2004), p. 100.

activities and how they can develop their firm into a "next-generation organization"[17] with an increased international division of labor.

(2) Service offshoring has the potential to affect a *company's strategy and competitive standing*: On the one hand, it can be a threat if competitors gain a much better competitive position, but on the other hand it could allow those companies that embark on it early to become more effective and/or efficient and to generate additional revenues and profits. MNCs from the U.S. and from the UK were the first to engage in service offshoring.[18] Even though some European MNCs have also launched similar projects, they could be at risk of losing competitiveness if they fail to exploit the potential benefits from service offshoring such as cost reduction, higher flexibility and quality enhancement. This makes it necessary to explore the settings in which service offshoring can occur and how MNCs can make the best use of it. Especially now, as more and more companies from Continental Europe are starting to offshore to Central and Eastern Europe, this issue is of high relevance.

(3) Despite the potential impacts on MNCs' organization and strategy, there seems a to be a *need for more detailed description* of how service offshoring works: In a recent survey conducted jointly by Roland Berger Strategy Consultants and UNCTAD, the authors found that only 39 per cent of the 500 participating major European companies were actively engaged in service offshoring. The other 61 per cent of firms have not only so far refrained from offshoring activities but most of them are also not planning to offshore in the future.[19] This hesitance could point to the expected or real difficulties in coordinating a remote service center. Still, the finding of the survey is surprising given that those companies with offshoring experience plan to extend their offshore activities even further.[20] The gap between hesitance on the one hand and contentment on the other could be widened furthered by offshoring failures.[21] Given the newness of the phenomenon and the secrecy with which firms typically deal with failures, one can conclude that there is a substantial management challenge in finding the right approach to service offshoring. Thus, there is a need for an exploration of existing offshoring arrangements and for a detailed assessment of individual setups. As a recent report by

---

[17] Venkatraman (2004), p. 16.
[18] Clott (2004), p. 157.
[19] Roland Berger/UNCTAD (2004), p. 6.
[20] Roland Berger/UNCTAD (2004), p. 6.
[21] For several examples, see Ebstrategy (2005) and Streitz (2005). For an example of the failure of a large outsourcing contract, see Heise Online News (2004).

UNCTAD puts it: "... any assessment of the potential for services offshoring requires a careful analysis of corporate strategies."[22]

To conclude, service offshoring is on the rise and it is extremely relevant for MNCs. How exactly MNCs can use it and are using it, is not yet clear. We will discuss this in more detail and derive our research questions in the next section.[23]

1.2 RESEARCH QUESTIONS

This research addresses two major challenges that the management of an MNC might face when dealing with service offshoring:

(1) Differentiation of service offshoring constellations: First documentation of this relatively new phenomenon indicates that there is not just a single type of service offshoring but rather a host of different ways in which service offshoring centers operate and a multitude of reasons why they are set up.[24] Knowledge of the main differentiating dimensions can be an important stepping stone towards better understanding service offshoring. An often-used instrument to describe and analyze MNC sub-units such as service offshoring centers are typologies of international subsidiaries. However, despite the abundance of typologies that describe the many different types of international subsidiaries and suggest how they can be managed, there is none that fits service offshoring subsidiaries.[25] The main reasons for this are that much of the research on international subsidiaries focuses on the role that the local market plays and that, historically, manufacturing offshoring predominates. However, for service offshoring subsidiaries that send their "products" abroad, the local market is not that important.[26]

---

[22] UNCTAD (2004b), p. 152.
[23] Even though a single author wrote this study, the personal pronoun "we" is used to refer to the author. This approach is in line with the tendency in several recent single-author contributions such as Grandori (1997), Harzing (1999).
[24] Lory (2005).
[25] We will discuss existing typologies in more detail in section 2.3.
[26] Research from other areas does not seem helpful, either. For instance, literature that deals with the division of tasks between different people – such as research on shift work – does not include the factor of different geographies. The literature regarding shift work mainly considers the optimal allocation of people to a given task. However, it fails to describe mechanisms for coordination between different units within an organization. In addition, it does not consider a situation in which the various units are located in different geographic locations. For an overview of the literature on shift work, see Siegel (1982), Mayshar/Halevy (1997). Other contributions consider more specifically mathematical models for shift work optimization (Hung (1997), Keeling (1999b), Keeling (1999a), Winstanley (2004)), another stream of literature evaluates the social effects of shift work (see, for instance, Zedeck et al. (1983), Peterson (1985), Papalexandris/Kramar (1997)).

1 – Introduction

To name but a few, the dimensions that we encountered to differentiate service offshoring subsidiaries comprise the following:

- *Type of activity:* Service offshoring subsidiaries can differ with respect to the service they carry out. Some MNCs might use their subsidiaries to provide services that require a lot of low-skilled manual work but do not add much value to the MNC. Their focus would potentially be on low-cost labor in offshore locations. Other firms, however, may move parts of their product development to offshore locations. In such cases, the services that are provided out of those locations would be very valuable to the firm and the focus would probably be not only on cost but also on the quality of the services.[27]

- *Relationships between the service offshoring subsidiary and the MNC network:* Another dimension which could be used to differentiate service offshoring subsidiaries[28] is the embeddedness of the subsidiary in the MNC's far-flung network of operations. Every new subsidiary represents an additional unit that needs to establish one or more relationships to other units, which increases the international division of labor even further. The coordination of these relationships requires managerial skills.[29] The importance of the management of relationships – be it within or across the boundaries of the firm – has increased in the past and is a crucial factor for the success of the firm.[30] For instance, research on cross-border knowledge transfers shows that the management of dispersed resources is an important source of competitive advantage.[31] This applies equally well to service offshoring, especially given the ease with which services can be transported between provider and recipient of services.[32] This new possibility increases management challenges and thereby the importance of analyzing the relationships of the service offshoring subsidiary in the MNC network. One form of such a unit could deal mainly with the MNC headquarters and the relationship

---

[27] Berry (2006), pp. 32-33, Maskell et al. (2007), pp. 254-255.
[28] We refer to service offshoring subsidiaries and service offshoring centers synonymously.
[29] Dacin et al. (1999), pp. 337-338.
[30] Sydow/Windeler (1994), p. 2.
[31] Jensen/Szulanski (2004), p. 517.
[32] Furthermore, companies are already starting to consider a three-tier approach to service offshoring: Not only does the MNC move part of its service execution to another location, but the provider of the services in turn splits "service production" across two locations, for instance, the more creative tasks to a location in Eastern Europe and the labor-intensive steps of the process to Asia (personal communication with Mr. Steve Keil, CEO of the Bulgarian software provider Sciant that has a subsidiary in Asia; 13.03.2006).

would be rather distant. At the other end of the scale, a service offshoring subsidiary could provide services to the MNC headquarters and to many other international subsidiaries. Thus, a second dimension that seems relevant for the management of a service offshoring subsidiary is the degree of embeddedness within the MNC network.

These considerations lead to our first research question:

1. *If we differentiate centers with respect to the activities they carry out and their organizational setup within the MNC's network, what types of service offshoring subsidiaries can be discerned?*

(2) Coordination of the service offshoring subsidiary: There seems to be a gap between potential benefits and uncertainty about how service offshoring centers are coordinated. Existing research on the management of a subsidiary does not provide answers to these challenges. This is because it is suggested that coordination is different for services than for production units;[33] however, the former have only been infrequently analyzed.[34] As the service offshoring trend continues,[35] the question of how to coordinate these centers becomes ever more critical. While service offshoring is much discussed in the literature, it has been impossible to identify publications that deal with the management of offshoring constellations. Typically, an international subsidiary is specifically established to provide services to the MNC from an offshore location. This change in configuration calls for coordination.[36] However, the management of this kind of subsidiary is no mean task. It has not been elaborated yet how service offshoring centers can be coordinated and managed most effectively and efficiently. Recent failures – most prominently Dell's move to withdraw part of its call center operations from India[37] – suggest that the transfer of capabilities and responsibilities to an offshore location and the resulting coordination requirements are not as easy to accomplish as envisaged at the outset when MNCs were attracted to service offshoring by the large potential for labor cost arbitrage.[38] Nevertheless, offshoring centers are presumed to reach high levels of productivity and

---

[33] Davis (1991), pp. 55-56, Feinberg et al. (2003), pp. 213-214.
[34] For some examples see Bufka (1997), Kriegmeier (2003).
[35] Warner (2005).
[36] Holtbrügge et al. (2004), pp. 162-163.
[37] Willenbrock (2004), p. 71.
[38] Anonymous (2005).

quality within short time frames.³⁹ It can be asked what coordination mechanisms have to be in place for service offshoring centers to deliver the required services right from the start.

Our first question aims at discerning the different types of service offshoring units. We know from research on the international subsidiary that MNCs should treat and coordinate their subsidiaries according to the roles they have.⁴⁰ Building on the first research question and incorporating the considerations on coordination, we derive our second research question:

2. *What coordination mechanisms are needed to support the different types of service offshoring subsidiaries?*

The focus of this study will be how service offshoring works and how service offshoring subsidiaries can be coordinated and integrated into an MNC's strategy to deliver the required services from the start. By answering these questions, we aim to fill a gap in the knowledge of international business research.⁴¹ Our research is in line with that of other authors who have stated that it is not sufficient to analyze the "architectural view of the organization"⁴² but that the underlying processes and tools have to be considered in more detail.⁴³

1.3 SCOPE, STRUCTURE, AND METHODOLOGY OF THIS STUDY

As discussed above, we do not want to examine service offshoring at the level of a nation. Rather, our unit of analysis is the service center that performs those services which MNCs have moved abroad. Our main questions build upon the above-mentioned challenges and lead to the two research goals theory building and theory illustration/theory evaluation:

---

[39] It could be concluded that a fast start for a service offshoring center would be similar to the very fast development of a center of competence. This seems to contradict to current thinking on the development of international subsidiaries. For instance, Schmid/Schurig state that it takes trust and time for international subsidiaries to become centers of competence (Schmid/Schurig (2003), pp. 759-760).
[40] Bartlett/Ghoshal (1986), Ghoshal/Nohria (1989), Gupta/Govindarajan (1991), Martinez/Jarillo (1991), p. 441, Harzing (1999), p. 309, Madureira (2004).
[41] Ramamurti (2004), p. 281.
[42] Doz/Prahalad (1984), p. 71.
[43] Doz/Prahalad (1984), p. 71.

Theory building: The work aims at building a theoretic framework for service offshoring subsidiaries in the form of a subsidiary typology. We have decided to develop a new typology rather than use an existing one. This is because we did not find an existing typology that would be appropriate for our research.[44] Our typology shall serve to categorize and describe different existing and future service offshoring models. Several theories from economics and international business research can help to explain *why* the service offshoring trend is happening[45] but no cohesive framework is available to answer our question *how* the management of service offshoring centers works. Therefore, we will analyze various approaches from organizational theory and select the most appropriate of these to develop a typology that gives answers to our research questions. Based on these theories, we will derive propositions that describe the coordination mechanisms that are used for each of the types. The underlying assumption is that different models will be coordinated differently in the MNC's network. To sum up, we aim to create a typology that describes what types of service offshoring subsidiaries exist and how MNCs coordinate their service offshoring operations for different scenarios.

Theory illustration/theory evaluation: Our theoretical propositions will describe how service offshoring takes place in MNCs. The typology that we evolve will then be evaluated and augmented in selected case studies. Based on the results of the empirical evaluation, advancements of theory will be proposed. Conclusions will then be drawn from the empirical research and suggestions for further research will be formulated. The dissertation will follow an empirical-qualitative approach[46] that will allow us to capture much of the newness of the phenomenon and to analyze a number of cases in more detail.

The case studies will be carried out in German MNCs and their service offshoring subsidiaries in Eastern Europe.[47] We chose all MNCs from one country to make the results more comparable and to avoid a situation where differences of national culture of the headquarters influence coordination mechanisms. We chose Germany as a major economy in Continental Europe whose companies have only recently started to explore service offshoring opportunities more forcefully. So far, U.S. and UK corporations espe-

---

[44] We will discuss reasons for this choice in section 2.3.4.
[45] See section 2.1.
[46] For a discussion of quantitative versus qualitative research approaches see Kutschker et al. (1997).
[47] We concentrate only on company-internal offshoring to subsidiaries and not on international outsourcing. The reasons for this choice are explained in detail in section 2.2.2.1.

cially have been much more active in the cross-border purchasing of services;[48] very often from offshoring subsidiaries they set up in Asia.[49] The decision for Eastern Europe as the location of service offshoring subsidiaries was made because this is the region in which corporations from Continental Europe prefer to locate their offshoring activities, the language barriers and cultural distance to India, for example, being much higher than for their U.S. and UK competitors.[50] Lastly, research in international business has generally concentrated on the traditionally important markets North America, Japan, and Western Europe and has considered Eastern Europe only marginally.[51] With the ongoing integration of Eastern European countries into the European Union, the region is fast becoming more attractive for foreign direct investment and as a service offshoring destination.

The function on which our research focuses is information technology.[52] This function was selected because information technology is one of the most advanced areas for service offshoring[53] and there is a high likelihood of finding suitable case studies. In addition, the IT function can comprise a wide array of activities, from tasks that are mainly focused on the support of the rest of the business (such as the operation of a computer network) to tasks that are closely related to product development for external customers. Our typology is not per se limited to the IT function, but to ensure better comparability of our case results, we have narrowed the focus.[54]

The work is structured as follows: The main building blocks of the research – service offshoring, coordination and subsidiary typologies – are presented in chapter 2. In chapter 3, we then discuss the resource-based view and network approaches as organiza-

---

[48] Roland Berger/UNCTAD (2004), p. 2.
[49] Hagel III (2004), pp. 82-83.
[50] Roland Berger/UNCTAD (2004), p. 4.
[51] Choi et al. (1999), p. 264.
[52] Information technology has been defined as "any form of computer-based information system, including mainframe, as well as microcomputer" (Kulkarni (2000), p 55). The IT function "involve[s] technological resources or the entire infrastructure including hardware, software, and communications systems deployed, and human resources with managers, programmers, system administrators, maintenance and related personnel involved in the design, maintenance and use of the overall IT infrastructure." (Cheon et al. (1995), p. 209). For a detailed definition and discussion of information systems see Weber (1997), pp. 31-67.
[53] Roland Berger/UNCTAD (2004), p. 4.
[54] Some topics of this study have been discussed in previous publications (Schmid/Daub (2005, 2007) such as a first version of the service offshoring typology and an assessment of network embeddedness and its operationalization. Throughout this work we make reference to the specific sections of earlier publications.

tional theories that form the basis of our research. Chapter 4 presents the typology that we developed based on the theories discussed previously. This is followed by a more detailed examination of the methodological questions of the research, namely case study research design (chapter 5). Finally, we evaluate the applicability of our typology in a series of case studies (chapter 6), discuss findings from cross-case analysis (chapter 7), and conclude the dissertation with a summary of the results, a discussion of the limitations of the study, and proposals for future research (chapter 8).

Our research serves to describe and evaluate service offshoring constellations rather than to consider normative aspects. This means that (financial) performance assessments or evaluations of the effects on job markets are not included in our discussions. However, when we turn to our case studies, we might find cases that do not match our expectations. We will then need to discuss whether our original propositions were in fact adequate or whether an adaptation of coordination mechanisms to our propositions might be beneficial for the firm under consideration.

The general approach of our work is summarized in Figure 1-1.

1.4 UNIQUENESS OF THIS RESEARCH

While service offshoring is a new topic, there are of course related subjects (which we will discuss later on). However, we believe that the research questions we are asking are not only new, but also highly relevant. Before we discuss the underlying elements in more detail, we would like to indicate several points in which this research differs from existing research:

1 – Introduction

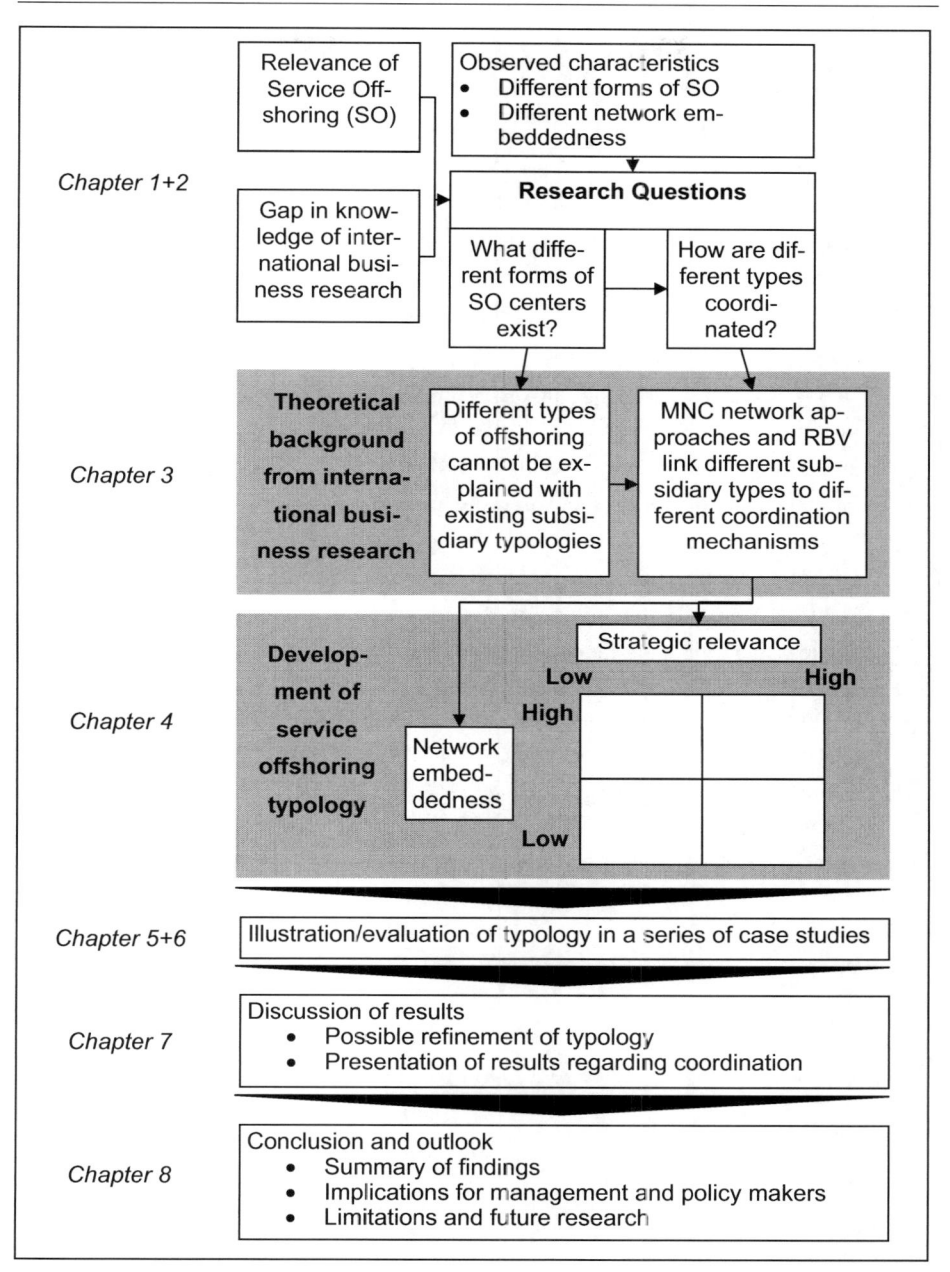

Chapter 1+2	**Relevance of Service Offshoring (SO)** / **Observed characteristics**: Different forms of SO; Different network embeddedness / **Gap in knowledge of international business research** → **Research Questions**: What different forms of SO centers exist? → How are different types coordinated?
Chapter 3	**Theoretical background from international business research**: Different types of offshoring cannot be explained with existing subsidiary typologies → MNC network approaches and RBV link different subsidiary types to different coordination mechanisms
Chapter 4	**Development of service offshoring typology** — Network embeddedness (High/Low) × Strategic relevance (Low/High) matrix
Chapter 5+6	Illustration/evaluation of typology in a series of case studies
Chapter 7	Discussion of results: Possible refinement of typology; Presentation of results regarding coordination
Chapter 8	Conclusion and outlook: Summary of findings; Implications for management and policy makers; Limitations and future research

Figure 1-1: Structure of this study

- *Services:* There have been many calls for service studies,[55] most of them hitherto unanswered. There is reason to believe that companies in the service area deal differently with coordination.[56] The effective coordination of service offshoring centers can be considered an organizational capability that can be understood as "socially complex routines that determine the efficiency with which firms physically transform inputs into outputs"[57] and that can lead to a competitive advantage. However, what particular organizational capability is required, depends on time and industry.[58] Thus, it is important to carry out specific evaluations. Accordingly, our research focuses exclusively on service offshoring and we hope to add to the still insufficient body of knowledge in this area.[59] In addition, our research will show in more detail differences between manufacturing and service offshoring and the specific challenges that result from service offshoring. One possible explanation for the extraordinary demands that service offshoring poses for MNCs is that it represents the next step in the increasing complexity of the global division of labor. While MNCs have by definition distributed activities, they are required to coordinate these operations with ever more precision in the context of a global alignment of service execution.

- *Breadth of coordination mechanisms:* Research on coordination mechanisms between headquarters and subsidiaries has often been very narrow. For instance, some authors have only considered formalization and personal coordination, without further differentiating between the different sub-types.[60] Our qualitative research design allows us to draw a more complete picture.[61]

Some methodological enhancements also help to differentiate our research from existing contributions:

---

[55] See, for instance, Boddewyn et al. (1986), p. 54, Combs/Ketchen Jr. (1999), p. 871, Rugman/Girod (2003), p. 24.
[56] Garnier (1982), p. 897.
[57] Collis (1994), p. 145. The author explicitly distinguishes products and services (Collis (1994), p. 146).
[58] Collis (1994), p. 151.
[59] See also section 1.1.
[60] For instance, Van De Ven et al. (1976) differentiate impersonal, personal, and group coordination modes. Martinez/Jarillo (1991) distinguish between formal and more subtle coordination mechanisms.
[61] Kim et al. (2003), p. 329.

- *Multilateral perspective:* Research on the relationships between headquarters and subsidiaries has often focused on only one part of the relationship. In many cases, the focus has been on headquarters. In other cases, only the subsidiaries have been evaluated.[62] Although sometimes both have been included in a sample, their pairwise relationships have not been considered, but rather the sampling was independent for headquarters and for subsidiaries. The relationships within *one* MNC have rarely been considered.[63] We want to redress this by including both levels in our empirical research following Young's call for coordination research that analyzes both headquarters and subsidiaries.[64] Thus, we approach our unit of analysis, the service offshoring subsidiary, from a multilateral perspective.

- *Pure form of international subsidiary:* Service offshoring subsidiaries seem to concentrate only on the one function for which they were set up. This makes research especially interesting because there are fewer of the distorting effects that occur when a subsidiary has more than one role.[65] In addition and broadly speaking, the service centers are still in their infancy and therefore serve as a "purer" unit of analysis than an older subsidiary that might have taken on additional tasks and potentially developed more independence.

- *Direct access to decision makers:* Our case study research design allows us to analyze the situations in which coordination actually takes place. The identification of appropriate interviewees can hardly be achieved by a mail survey since it is often not enough to discuss with one person only but to gain more contacts and tap additional data sources through referrals.[66]

---

[62] For instance, Roth/Nigh (1992) have asked subsidiary management in the South Eastern region of the U.S. about its relationships with headquarters. Garnier (1982) evaluates and compares the autonomy of subsidiaries of American firms in Mexico and France by a mail survey of the subsidiaries.
[63] Schmid et al. (1998), p. 98.
[64] Young/Tavares (2004), p. 231.
[65] Birkinshaw/Morrison (1995), p. 750.
[66] Macdonald/Hellgren (2004), pp. 267-268.

2 Theoretical Foundations – Developing Building Blocks of Service Offshoring Typology

> *"Many economic historians are concerned about the possibility of large-scale offshoring of jobs from the United States and Europe to China, India, and other countries. They speak of another Industrial Revolution, the third since the 18th century, that will transform commerce and industry and require painful adjustments."*
>
> Hans F. Sennholz

Summary

This chapter introduces the theoretical background on service offshoring. Since service offshoring is a new topic, we first describe it and differentiate it from related subjects such as manufacturing offshoring. Approaches from the realm of international business research can be successfully applied to the service offshoring phenomenon in general. In particular, we show how research on subsidiary typologies can be used to differentiate service offshoring units. However, existing typologies are found to be inappropriate for our purpose and we conclude that we need to develop a new typology. In addition, we discuss coordination mechanisms and present a classification of these mechanisms – structural, technocratic, output-based, and personal – that will be used for the new typology.

2.1 THE PERSPECTIVE OF INTERNATIONAL BUSINESS RESEARCH

As briefly mentioned above, the discussion about service offshoring has so far almost exclusively focused on its broader economic effects or on individual functional areas. Neither the media nor academia have explicitly regarded the setting in which most offshoring deals take place. The discussion has given only little attention to the actual players in the "offshoring game": those companies that offshore activities, mainly from developed countries and those companies that take over these activities and that are located mainly in the developing world or in transition countries. Research hitherto has not analyzed the phenomenon, the driving forces behind it, and how it is going to affect the competitiveness of a company. In short, so far there has not been sufficient consideration of the MNC from which offshoring typically originates.[67]

However, a perspective at the level of an individual firm, often an MNC, is needed to ensure that decisions on offshoring are taken in accordance with the company's overall strategy and not just with a view to optimizing one functional area. International business research as the main perspective of this study can add to the discussion as it deals with multinational companies to which we will frequently refer. There has been lengthy debate about when a firm could or should be considered multinational. We shall follow Kutschker/Schmid (2005) who convincingly argue that a firm is to be deemed multinational when it has international activities. Other criteria, such as the generation of a specific share of profit or revenue from abroad, do not seem to be theoretically well grounded and in our case are not useful. Thus, multinational corporations are considered companies that substantially engage in international activities, especially in regular transaction with other economic actors in other countries.[68]

With an understanding of offshoring as the international transfer of activities, international business research is a discipline that is directly related to offshoring. So far international business scholars have not participated actively and explicitly in the discussion on service offshoring.[69] However, as offshoring directly affects the MNC, they should indeed consider it. To date, no answers have been forthcoming to the challenges and questions that were defined in Section 1.2. International business research is called upon

---

[67] Maskell et al. (2007), p. 254.
[68] Kutschker/Schmid (2005), p. 245. Welge/Holtbrügge use a similar definition in referring to companies that involve two or more countries (Welge/Holtbrügge (2003), p. 37).
[69] One reason for this hesitance might be that a related topic, outsourcing, is not very relevant for international business research as is more domestic in character and does not necessarily involve international aspects.

to analyze the implications for MNCs[70] and to explore the phenomenon not from the economist's broad perspective and not from the narrow vantage point of individual functions such as purchasing or IT.

Of course, approaches from international business research can already explain many facets of service offshoring subsidiaries. To mention only a few of these, existing contributions can show (1) why companies are interested in purchasing services from abroad, (2) why they set up their own centers abroad or purchase from an external vendor, (3) where to set up subsidiaries, and (4) how to distribute activities across locations and how to define products and services:

1. *Trade theories* show that the purchase of goods from abroad is an attractive option if the foreign country has an absolute or relative advantage in its factor costs. The first theories to explain trade – such as those by Smith (1775/1976) and Ricardo (1817/1970) – have often been criticized but they still provide explanations for the initial motivation to purchase from abroad.

2. Approaches that explain the *different forms of internationalization* can contribute to understanding why companies set up service offshoring subsidiaries abroad rather than purchase services from an external vendor. For instance, Buckley/Casson (1991) show which advantages an MNC can gain by setting up its own center. On a more general level, Dunning's OLI paradigm can be helpful in advising companies on the setup of service offshoring subsidiaries, including aspects of ownership, location and internalization advantages.[71]

3. Approaches such as those by Davidson (1980) or Tesch (1980) help to *differentiate between locations* and can explain why an MNC sets up a service offshoring subsidiary in a specific country. Porter's diamond framework could be used to determine why a specific country could be attractive for service offshoring subsidiaries (which could be understood as a specific industry in Porter's sense).[72]

---

[70] Ramamurti (2004), p. 281.
[71] This paradigm is developed in several publications by the author, see for instance Dunning (1973), Dunning (1988), Dunning (1995), Dunning (2000).
[72] Porter (1990). Bunyaratavej et al. (2007) discuss location choices for the specific situation of service offshoring.

4. Other research discusses the consequences of the international concentration or distribution of activities (*configuration strategies*) and the international *standardization or differentiation* of services and products.[73] These approaches can also be used to describe the activities of service offshoring centers in more detail.

Thus, there is a large body of knowledge that can be readily applied to service offshoring. However, the approaches we briefly discussed deal mainly with the reasons for and the forms of internationalization. They are not suitable for finding answers to our questions regarding the management of an existing subsidiary in general terms or the coordination of service offshoring subsidiaries in particular.

A framework that can be helpful when dealing with the analysis of international subsidiaries in an MNC network shows that relevant topics can be clustered in four relevant research perspectives. We use this to indicate the direction in which our research is headed. The framework distinguishes between the focus on headquarters and subsidiaries on the one hand and between the focus on the internal or the external network on the other. The resulting perspectives can be found in Table 2-1.[74]

Table 2-1: Research focus on MNCs from a network perspective (Source: Translated and slightly adapted from Renz (1998), p. 80)

	Focus on internal network	Focus on external network
Focus on subsidiary	Role	Management in networks
Focus on headquarters	Coordination	Knowledge transfer

Traditional research on the subsidiary level has developed several subsidiary typologies, though, sometimes without indicating their management implications. This research takes an internal network focus but discusses both subsidiaries and the resulting effects on the headquarters. Thus, we have both a "role" as well as a "coordination" perspec-

---

[73] For an overview of these approaches see Kutschker/Schmid (2005), pp. 970-986.
[74] One could question this framework, for instance, why knowledge transfer is not important in external networks. Still it helps to structure different research topics around MNC networks.

tive. Specifically, therefore, we will consider approaches that deal with typologies and coordination:

1. *Role typologies of international subsidiaries:* Service offshoring centers that are under control of the MNC (i.e. they are not outsourced) are by definition international subsidiaries. They represent a special type of international subsidiary in the sense that they are focused on the execution of only one or a limited number of processes; in that they do not have strong local networks and that they do not have a specific mandate for the local market in which they are situated. The differentiation and description of different types (roles) of international subsidiaries is a separate stream in international business research and many different dimensions to describe subsidiaries have been developed. These include the dispersion of activities across several units and the specialization of activities (and concentration of one kind of activity in one unit).[75] Concerning the terms dispersion of activities and specialization of activities, service offshoring can be regarded as an increasing dispersion of activities and in many cases an increasing specialization of activities.

2. *Coordination mechanisms:* When activities that were previously carried out in a given country (typically the MNC's home country) are moved abroad, coordination mechanisms are impacted upon. There need to be rules and principles governing the way in which the units and the people within these units will work together in the future when they are no longer located on the same site (and sometimes not even in the same time zone). The coordination mechanisms can depend on the kind of processes that are carried out in the service offshoring center. For very standardized processes, such as bookkeeping, coordination might occur through an initial mutual agreement that defines the number of transactions per unit of time per employee that the service center has to deliver. For more complex processes, such as software programming, the interaction between the unit that orders a certain process and the service offshoring center will most probably take place more frequently and will potentially involve personal discussions and visits between the locations.

We will evaluate the explanatory potential of these topics with regard to the coordination of service offshoring subsidiaries. At the same time, we will outline the research

---

[75] These dimensions and a more complete description can be found in Ghoshal/Bartlett (1993), p. 88.

2 – Theoretical Foundations

gaps which we aspire to fill. However, before discussing these in more detail, we will use the next section to develop a more complete description of service offshoring.

2.2 SERVICE OFFSHORING

While the term service offshoring is often used as an standing expression, we want to analyze its components in more detail. We will first look at services (section 2.2.1) and especially international services (section 2.2.2) before we then report on findings regarding offshoring: Section 2.2.3 provides an overview of existing service offshoring definitions, section 2.2.4 differentiates service offshoring from related practices, section 2.2.5 defines our understanding of service offshoring, and section 2.2.6 concludes with a broader description of service offshoring.

2.2.1 DEFINITION OF SERVICE

Even though there is no common understanding of services,[76] there is a large body of literature and different classification schemes that help to approach the topic. The common distinction between the primary (agriculture), secondary (manufacturing) and tertiary (services) sector can be used as a starting point for defining services. Recent years have seen a constant decrease in the economic activity in the first two sectors (as a percentage of overall economic activity) and a steady increase in the tertiary sector. Also, services can be found within the secondary sector such as, e.g., a manufacturing firm's internal consulting unit. However, the share of services in the secondary sector is decreasing, presumably because of the continuing trend to outsource service activities.[77] Overall, the tertiary sector is growing, confirming the importance of services in developed economies. The total volume of service exports rose from about 0.4 trillion USD in 1980 to 1.9 trillion USD in 2003, increasing its share of total trade from 17 per cent to 20 per cent.[78]

The macroeconomic distinction between different sectors is on a very high level and does not serve the purpose of this work since we are not considering an entire sector or firm, but rather individual service processes that are provided inside a firm. Other definitions specify services in more detail: Some define them by their constitutive characteristics, others by excluding what they are not and a third group simply compiles a list of

---

[76] UNCTAD (2004b), p. 145.
[77] Albach (1989), p. 403.
[78] UNCTAD (2004a).

services. The first approach seems most appropriate for the scope of this thesis since it is the only way to allow new elements to be identified as services.[79]

A common way of defining services is to consider different dimensions of the phenomenon, these typically being the result, the process and the potential. Even though there are some differences, consensus seems to exist with regard to a few constitutive characteristics:[80]

- They have immaterial results, as they are typically considered "intangible, invisible, perishable"[81],
- their production and consumption take place simultaneously,[82] and
- they require interaction with the external entity that demands the service.[83]

Thus, a definition of services – for now unrelated to service offshoring – is as follows:

A service is the immaterial result of a business process whose production requires an external factor which is not under the complete control of the producing entity.[84]

While the definition of services is in itself a daunting task, their categorization proves even more difficult. There is a multitude of approaches to clustering services and differentiating among them.[85] We want to point here to a very comprehensive categorization scheme that can help to better determine our research subject. Lovelock's (1983) work incorporates many of the earlier approaches.[86] The author distinguishes a number of dimensions. We represent these dimensions in Table 2-2 first and then explain what kind of services this work refers to. In the table we highlight in bold letters those entries that describe the understanding of service which we adopt for our research.[87]

---

[79] Bufka (1997), p. 22.
[80] Skaggs/Huffman (2003), p. 776; see also Hatch (1997), p. 132, Maleri (2004), p. 40.
[81] UNCTAD (2004b), p. 145.
[82] Holtbrügge et al. (2004), p. 167.
[83] Bufka (1997), pp. 29-31, Schmid/Gouthier (1999).
[84] This definition is in line with many similar service definitions such as by Mößlang (1995), pp. 15-21, Bruhn (2000), pp. 23-24.
[85] See Mößlang (1995), pp. 118-119 for an exhaustive overview.
[86] Approaches such as Rathmell (1974), Hill (1977), Maister/Lovelock (1982) are explicitly considered, but also later classification schemes such as Maleri (1997) are compatible.
[87] Where no specific value applies to our research, we did not highlight any value.

2 – Theoretical Foundations

Table 2-2: Classification of service characteristics (Source: Based on Lovelock (1983))

Dimension	First possibility	Second possibility
Recipient of service	People	**Things**
Tangibility of service act	Tangible	**Intangible**
Relationship between producer and consumer	No formal relationship	**Membership**
Interaction between producer and consumer	a) Consumer goes to producer or b) producer goes to consumer	**Transaction at arm's length (mail or electronic communication)**
Nature of service delivery	Discrete transactions	**Continuous delivery**
Availability of service outlets	**Single site**	Multiple site
Degree of service customization	Low	High
Degree of judgment of service personnel	Low	High
Degree of supply constraint	Low	High
Degree of demand fluctuations	Low	High

We now want to briefly describe each dimension and indicate the kind of service to which our work refers:

- Lovelock differentiates between situations in which services are performed on people or on things. In our case, services are always performed on things. We exclude personal services such as haircuts from our analysis.

- Services can be tangible or intangible, either being directed at "goods or other physical possessions"[88] or at intangible assets. We refer to intangible services only and exclude those that alter goods.[89]

- Since we analyze service delivery relationships within a company, there is always a membership relationship between the service organization and the recipient. We exclude service delivery situations without formal relationships (such as radio stations or police protection).[90]

- Some services can require physical contact between service provider and recipient (for instance, a taxi service). In our case, we consider services that are delivered at a distance.[91]

- Next, Lovelock distinguishes between discrete transaction and continuous delivery of services. Our analysis focuses on a continuous delivery of services that occur repeatedly and over a longer period of time.

- Services can be delivered from a single site or several sites. In our analysis, we look at services that are delivered from one location (the service offshoring subsidiary).

- There can be a varying degree of standardization of services. Some are special orders, others are standardized. In our case, we consider the entire spectrum of services with regard to this dimension.[92]

- In some cases, the service personnel has to exercise a high degree of judgment to meet the customer's need (such as legal services). In other cases, a very low degree of judgment on the part of the service personnel is involved (such as hotel services). We do not confine our analysis in this regard.

---

[88] Lovelock (1983), p. 12.
[89] See also Hill (1999) for a more detailed discussion of tangibility.
[90] Lovelock (1983), p. 13.
[91] This does not exclude the personal interaction during the visit between service provider and recipient. The distinguishing criteria is whether or not the service delivery requires personal contact. One could argue that there is an overlap between this dimension and the first – services carried out on people or things – but there are services that require personal contact but are not executed on people's bodies or minds (such as mail delivery).
[92] Actually, on aspect of the strategic relevance of a service that we will define later could also be the degree of customization. Thus, we here do not restrict our analysis.

- Finally, Lovelock classifies the degree of supply constraint or demand fluctuation of services. These two dimensions are not relevant for our analysis.

We have now reflected on services in general and classified our work with regard to several, commonly used dimensions. The next section will further differentiate between domestic and international services and show what consequences our focus on international services has.

2.2.2 DEFINITION OF INTERNATIONAL SERVICES

Services that are relevant for service offshoring are international services, since they cross borders when being produced and consumed. Authors from the field of international services emphasize the appearance of the phenomenon because of "the emergence of modern communications and information technologies that facilitate cost-effective international business operations"[93]. In principle, international services share the same constitutive characteristics we have defined above for all services.[94] However, they differ in that they "cross national borders"[95]. Several researchers have addressed the effects of the specific characteristics of international services to structure and analyze the research field. Amongst the most commonly used framework is that developed by Sampson and Snape which is displayed in Figure 2-1.

The authors differentiate services by the mobility of the consumers and producers, respectively. Services that are considered in this study fall into category (a) where both the producer and consumer of a service are not mobile, that is, they do not (need to) move for the production or consumption of the service.[96] In this case, the service is exported by the producer and consumed in the location of the consumer.[97] This requirement limits the export of services to those that can be delivered by telecommunication or data networks or that can be conserved in storage media. One important aspect is that the service needs to be transported quickly over long distances without losing its properties. This can only be achieved through telecommunication networks which require a "digitalization" of the service.[98]

---

[93] Knight (1999), p. 347
[94] Knight (1999), pp. 348-349.
[95] Clark et al. (1996), p. 12.
[96] This is in line with our classification in Lovelock's scheme where we focus on services delivered to a remote location.
[97] Mößlang (1995), p. 132.
[98] UNCTAD (2004b).

		Not mobile	Mobile
Producer	Mobile	(c) Production and consumption in the country of the consumer	(d) Production and consumption in third country
	Not mobile	(a) Production in the country of the producer Consumption in the country of the consumer	(b) Production and consumption in the country of the producer
		Not mobile	Mobile
		Consumer	

Figure 2-1: Categorization of international services by Sampson and Snape (Source: Mößlang (1995), p. 128)

This last implication can also be found in the work of Clark et al. (1996). The authors make an important differentiation amongst international services into "contact-based services" where people who deliver services cross borders, "vehicle-based services" that are transported across communication networks, "asset-based services" which are services industries' foreign direct investments (for instance, banks), and "object-based services" which are services embedded in objects (such as machinery repairs).[99] The services considered here fall into the category of "vehicle-based services", since the services provided by the service offshoring subsidiary are delivered via communication networks.

Another important classification to differentiate international services stems from Vandermerwe/Chadwick (1989).[100] The authors regard the relative involvement of goods and the degree of consumer/producer interaction to be relevant dimensions.[101] The resulting categorization can be found in Figure 2-2.

---

[99] Hill (1999), pp. 12-13.
[100] This framework together with Samson/Snape is often referred to in publications on international services. See, for instance, Bruhn (2005), pp. 11-14.
[101] The authors use this scheme to differentiate between internationalization modes. We rely here only on the classification without referring to forms of internationalization which are not relevant for our research.

2 – Theoretical Foundations

		Lower	Higher
	"Pure" service Low on goods	**Sector 1** Domestic mail Knife sharpening	**Sector 4** Engineering Consulting Management Advertisement Education Insurance Medicine
Relative involvement of goods	Services with some goods or delivered through goods	**Sector 2** Retailing Couriers Fastfood Hotels Shipping Air Freight	**Sector 5** Banking Personal Air Travel Maintenance
	Services embodied in goods	**Sector 3** Music/Compact Disks Software/diskettes Movies/videocassettes Training/books Journals On-line news services	**Sector 6** Teleshopping Electronic mail

Degree of consumer/producer interaction

Figure 2-2: Categorization of international services (Source: Vandermerwe/ Chadwick (1989), p. 82)

The services we consider are located in sector 4. On the "goods involvement" dimension, we refer to services that are the pure form of services, without material content. On the other dimension, the services under consideration require a high degree of consumer/producer interaction. Vandermerve/Chadwick use their classification to determine which form of internationalization is most appropriate for which sector.[102]

We have now described which type of services we consider in our research based on a discussion of services and international services. We will now further specify the topic by moving into literature that explicitly deals with service offshoring but unfortunately sometimes does not refer to the international services literature and thus does not sufficiently connect to existing research. Therefore, we have here provided an overview of this field.

2.2.3 OVERVIEW OF EXISTING DEFINITIONS OF SERVICE OFFSHORING

Service offshoring is mentioned frequently in the print media; however, few scholars from (international) business research have so far addressed the topic. Partially due to the newness of the phenomenon, there is no common definition available. Let us first look at the root of the word: Offshoring stems from "offshore" meaning "from the shore, seaward" or "outside the country, abroad"[103]. "Offshore" is used in the context of the oil industry ("offshore drilling locations") and banking ("offshore banking location"), but also with regard to the relocation of manufacturing activity.[104]

Before we provide our own definition, we want to give an overview of existing definitions in Table 2-3 that we drew from a wide range of sources, from journals of international business research to practitioner's guides. The first column lists the source; the second column cites the definition.

Table 2-3: Overview of definitions for service offshoring

Source	Definition
Agrawal et al. (2003), p. 25	Business-process offshoring is the export of "back-office functions such as data entry, payroll processing and call centers"
Agrawal/Farrell (2003), p. 37	Service offshoring is "moving service industry to countries with lower labor costs"

---

[102] Interestingly, for sector 4 they recommend foreign direct investment in subsidiaries to be the most appropriate (Vandermerwe/Chadwick (1989), p. 84). This is in line with our expectations to have offshore services carried out by a subsidiary.
[103] Merriam-Webster dictionary entry for "offshore".
[104] For manufacturing, see Anderson (1983), p. 31. He uses the term "off-shore assembly".

Source	Definition
Blunden (2004)	Outsourcing is "a practice whereby an external agency is hired to provide services to a company that could normally be performed in-house." (p. 4) "The term *offshoring* is actually short for *offshore outsourcing* [emphasis in original]. ... American corporations have begun to move whole projects, or in some cases entire divisions, overseas to other countries." (p. 13)
Boes/Schwemmle (2005), p. 9 [our translation]; same definition as in Boes et al. (2004)	Often offshoring is understood as a specific form of outsourcing. With this understanding, it is the logical next step of the trend to external processing of previously in-house tasks. This form of outsourcing is more accurately called "offshore outsourcing". It is different from that kind of offshoring where an IT provider establishes its own development capacities in offshore regions and uses capacities within the firm. This often happens when subsidiaries or joint ventures with local IT firms are set up. This is not outsourcing in the original sense because the firm does not hand over tasks to an external party but rather has them executed by subsidiaries in regions with low labor costs.
Bottino (2004)	Offshoring refers to "the practice of sending service jobs overseas"
Carmel/Tjia (2005), p. xviii	Offshoring is "the shifting of tasks to *low-cost* [emphasis in original] nations, rather than to any destination outside the country. Low-cost countries are those that fall into the economic grouping of "developing nations" or "emerging nations." Thus a British software firm does not usually refer to its US software research center as an 'offshore site.'"
Colquhoun et al. (2004), p. 9	Offshoring is "the shift of UK production and employment to other, oversea locations in order to satisfy demand from UK customers.

Source	Definition
Davies (2004), p. 21	Offshoring refers to "outsourcing your processes *offshore* [emphasis in original]". Outsourcing refers to firms' practice to "contract some portion of their IT and business processes to outside organizations."
Doh (2005), p. 696	Service offshoring refers to firms "decoupling their core production and service activities"
Dutta/Roy (2005), p. 16	"[O]utsourcing is turning over selected parts of a firm's IT projects or functions to another provider for a specified period of time, usually at least a few years. … *IT offshoring* [emphasis in original] is used to refer to outsourcing when the provider is in another country such as India, Ireland, Philippines, or China."
Ebstrategy (2005)	"offshore outsourcing is a powerful tool to cut costs, improve performance, and refocus on core business"
Farrell (2005), p. 675	Offshoring refers to the "opportunities for businesses to take advantage of high-skilled, low-wage workers in emerging markets" and the "global division of labor"
Garner (2004), pp. 6-7	"The term 'offshoring' refers to the relocation of jobs and production to a foreign country. The relocated jobs and production could be at a foreign office of the same multinational company or at a separate company located abroad. In contrast, the term 'outsourcing' does not necessarily imply that jobs and production are relocated to another country. Outsourcing of such jobs as janitorial services and payroll accounting by manufacturing firms to domestic service companies has long been an important factor driving the growth of business services employment."

Source	Definition
Jones (2005), p. 94	"'[O]utsourcing occurs when a firm reduces its level of vertical integration and externally accesses (through various means ranging from relational contracting to spot markets) inputs/skills/activities that were formally generated in-house. The provider(s) of the outsourced activity may be geographically proximate, in the same country but at some distance, and/or located overseas." Offshoring refers to "firms not reducing their level of vertical integration but rather relocating (or *spatially restructuring* [emphasis in original]) some of their value-chain activities from the USA to other countries that offer a combination of reliable supply, reasonable quality, and substantial cost savings."
Karmarkar (2004), p. 1	Offshoring is "the movement of labor to foreign countries"
Offshore Outsourcing (2005), p. 673	Offshoring is "the practice of transferring employment to lower cost countries"
Pfannenstein/Tsai (2004), p. 72	Outsourcing is "turning over a firm's computer operations, network operations, software development and maintenance, or other IT functions to a provider for a specified time, generally at least a few years." Offshoring is "outsourcing to another country, most often today to India, Ireland, the Philippines, China, and other countries. However, the terms are also used interchangeably …"
Robinson/Kalakota (2004), p. 2	"[O]ffshoring is the migration of part or all of the value chain to a low-cost location. Offshoring hinges on cost management through labor and skill arbitrage. It is dependent on the dramatic advances in telecommunications technology that have made it possible to locate back-office operations in a variety of locations and to benefit from significantly lower labor costs."
Robinson/Kalakota (2004), p. 4	"Offshore outsourcing is the delegation of administrative, engineering, research, development, or technical support processes to a third-party vendor in a lower-cost location."

Source	Definition
Roland Berger/UNCTAD (2004), p. 2	Offshoring refers to the fact that "various service processes are increasingly being shifted abroad. So far, the focus is on back office services, but most service processes are potential future candidates for offshoring."
Harrison/McMillan (2006), p. 8	"Offshoring refers to a broad range of tasks executed by a firm in another country that could include setting up a foreign subsidiary or outsourcing offshore through an arm's length agreement with another firm."
Venkatraman (2004), p. 14	Offshoring is "the practice among U.S. and European companies of migrating business processes to overseas to India, the Philippines, Ireland, China, and elsewhere to lower costs without significantly sacrificing quality"
Note	Where an exact definition has been provided, it is represented here by "… is …". A more indirect reference is represented by "… refers to …".

Individual definitions focus on a wide variety of aspects. We have identified and summarized below six themes that are repeatedly included in the definitions. We will discuss their relevance for our work and determine whether or not they need to be included in our definition of service offshoring. As the first three topics require a more extensive discussion, we will treat them in separate sections.

1. *Relationship between offshoring and outsourcing:* Some definitions refer to the phenomenon on which our analysis is focused as outsourcing, while most call it offshoring. Still it seems necessary to elaborate further on the differences between these two practices. We will discuss them in more detail below.

2. *Services:* In contrast to earlier relocations of economic activities abroad, the recent offshoring trend focuses primarily on services. Many definitions refer to a specific type of activity that is shifted abroad. Not all activities are included but only those that are computer-readable and computer-transferable. This characteristic is important because not all services can be provided from a distance and there seems to be only a limited set of services for which provision from

outside the country of origin is appropriate. These services, which have been referred to as "vehicle-based services", have been discussed above.[105] In the following, we will address the differences between manufacturing offshoring and service offshoring.

3. *Relationship between receiver and provider of the service:* The receiver of the service stays in its present location.[106] This is implied by the notion that it is back-office processes which are lifted and carried out elsewhere. Thus, service offshoring represents the internationalization of the MNC that is not primarily market-seeking or strategic asset-seeking but more resource-seeking and efficiency-seeking.[107] Service offshoring is not the transfer of responsibility for a sales division to an international subsidiary that would provide these services directly to final customers and no longer under the supervision of the original unit. Rather, service offshoring is similar to shared services centers that emerged about a decade ago and that were also used to concentrate service processes. We will discuss similarities and differences to shared services centers below.

4. *International transfer:* Almost all definitions include a term such as "moving", "turning over", "migrating", or "delegating" some kind of activity to another country. Thus, this aspect seems to be indisputably relevant for service offshoring and will form the basis of our definition. However, we think it is not appropriate to refer to offshoring as job relocation even though it is frequently referred to as such. It is not typically the jobs that are shifted abroad. Nor is it necessarily the same position that is filled with a person in a different country, and very rarely will the original incumbent migrate to the new location to continue executing his tasks from there. We prefer to speak about activities because it can be left open whether or not the firm carries out these activities in the same manner as before or if it reorganizes activities in a way that would no longer require exactly the same job description in the new location.

---

[105] See section 2.2.2. "Vehicle-based services" are relevant for service offshoring since services need to be transported across communication networks.

[106] This implicitly refers to the category a) from the Sampson/Snape categorization where the recipient and the provider of the service are in different countries (see the definition of international services in section 2.2.2).

[107] Dunning differentiates between these four main motives for MNC internationalization (Dunning (1994), pp. 29-31).

5. *Reasons:* Some authors define service offshoring as an activity that companies use to concentrate on their core competencies. Others focus on the potential cost reduction and on the transfer of ownership to external parties.[108] Even though the element of cost reduction is very often an important factor in the decision to offshore, it is not necessary to include it in the definition in our case. Our definition will be intentionally broad, as it does not seem justified to exclude a certain type of economic activity or to include a certain objective as some authors do.[109] There might be other reasons that would warrant such a move and that could result in the same practice. In short, we do not wish to limit the scope of service offshoring unnecessarily.

6. *Geography:* Some authors define service offshoring as a phenomenon that takes place between specified countries. We also do not include references to target and destination countries because the practice of service offshoring does not depend on the country of origin or its destination. Similarly, we also refrain from distinguishing between nearshoring (the move to a geographically not so distant location) versus offshoring (the move to a location further away) because it is very difficult to establish clear criteria for differentiation. Secondly, it can easily become confusing when American corporations use offshoring to send work to Eastern Europe while corporations from Continental Europe use nearshoring when they actually move activities to the same location.

Thus, we have identified six recurring aspects, the first three of which will be discussed in more detail below since they are crucially important for our study. We have also shown that the fourth area – international relocation – is indisputably an aspect of offshoring and is part of our own definition as well. Finally, we have discussed why geographical aspects or the reasons are not relevant for our definition. In order to make the scope of service offshoring more precise we shall now discuss the differences to the related topics identified above – outsourcing, manufacturing offshoring, and shared service centers.

---

[108] For instance, Robinson/Kalakota state: "Offshore outsourcing is the delegation of administrative, engineering, research, development, or technical support processes to a third-party vendor in a lower-cost location." (Robinson/Kalakota (2004), p. 4).

[109] E.g., Robinson/Kalakota include in the definition of offshoring "… to benefit from significantly lower labor costs" (Robinson/Kalakota (2004), p. 3).

2.2.4 DIFFERENTIATION OF SERVICE OFFSHORING AND RELATED PRACTICES

2.2.4.1 DIFFERENTIATION OF OUTSOURCING AND OFFSHORING

"Outsourcing" is a term that has been used for several years in management science. It stems from the words "outside", "resource" and "using" and thus refers to the usage of resources from the outside. More specifically, it refers to the purchase of products and services that had been previously part of a company's own value chain and are now produced or carried out by an external provider.[110] The term *"offshoring"* has appeared only recently and has been frequently used synonymously with "outsourcing" even though this might not be appropriate in all cases. Given the newness of the phenomenon, a standard definition of offshoring has not yet been developed (see also above). Outsourcing typically describes the shifting of an economic activity from one institution to another, thus it contains the element of ownership/control.[111]

Outsourcing has increasingly been used to also describe the moving of an economic activity to another location, more specifically to another country.[112] However, change of location is not a necessary precondition for outsourcing. Thus, the term "offshoring" better describes the relocation of an activity independently of ownership.[113] Both phenomena can occur together or individually. Figure 2-3 gives an overview of the different resulting combinations of offshoring and outsourcing.

Dimension: Location			
	Offshore	1. Captive offshoring	2. Offshore outsourcing
	Onshore	3. In-house execution	4. Onshore outsourcing
		In-house	Outsource

Dimension: Ownership/control

Figure 2-3: Relationship between offshoring and outsourcing (Source: Based on Ge et al. (2004), p. 30

---

[110] For a detailed discussion on the roots of the words "outsourcing" see Nagengast (1997), pp. 47-53.
[111] Cheon et al. (1995), p. 209. For an overview of outsourcing definitions, see Espino-Rodríguez/Padrón-Robaina (2006), p. 51.
[112] Recently "international outsourcing" or "global outsourcing" have been used frequently to describe the shifting of activities to another location independent of ownership/control (see, for instance, Anonymous (2004b), p. 80 and Ge et al. (2004), pp. 6-7).
[113] Ge et al. (2004), pp. 5-6.

The different resulting possibilities are:

1. *Captive offshoring*[114] can be understood as the purchase of products or services from a subsidiary that is located far away (typically in another country or even continent).

2. If products or services are purchased from an external party rather than a subsidiary and the external party is located far away from the acquirer, we speak of *offshore outsourcing*.[115]

3. *In-house execution* is the original situation where the specific task is executed within the boundaries of the firm and within the home country.

4. *Onshore outsourcing* is defined as the acquisition of products or services from an external party that is located relatively close to the acquirer (typically in the same country). Examples include the automotive industry in which outsourcing partners are often located very close to the car manufacturers to reduce stock and delivery times.[116]

The framework from Figure 2-3 can be applied to both products and services.[117] Consequently, the offshoring of services means the shifting of services from an existing to a new location that is outside national borders independent of control.[118] It is important to note the difference between outsourcing and offshoring. Traditional explanations for outsourcing do not necessarily apply to offshoring. It might well be that patterns which were observed during the outsourcing boom, e.g., in the area of information manage-

---

[114] The word "captive" originally means imprisoned, locked up. In business language it is widely used to refer to units that belong to the firm. The Merriam-Webster thesaraus defines it as "owned or controlled by another concern and operated for its needs rather than for an open market". Here it is used in accordance with Agrawal et al. (2003), p. 27 to refer to service offshoring centers in one country that belong to a company in another country.

[115] For a detailed discussion of offshore outsourcing, see Kedia/Lahiri (2007).

[116] See, for example, Kochan (2002), p. 31, for a description of the proximity between MCC (producer of the Smart car) and its suppliers.

[117] It also has to be noted that the different combinations of ownership/control and location might be chosen in different settings and with different goals. However, they are not just four discrete areas. Rather, they should be considered as the extremes of a continuum that also includes configurations such as a joint venture that has elements of both in-house execution and outsourcing (Ge et al. (2004), p. 8).

[118] This understanding is shared by many authors, see, for instance, Burgmaier et al. (2004), p. 21, Schaaf (2004), p. 3, Trampel (2004), p. 5. However, some of these authors do not distinguish further between service and manufacturing offshoring. To better differentiate this work will use the term "service offshoring".

ment systems will not be repeated in offshoring. One indication for this is that many outsourcing relations were concluded within the same national market, therefore, dimensions like cultural, social, and legal differences did not play an important role. In offshoring scenarios, however, they can be crucial. Besides, there are services that can easily be outsourced but not offshored at all.[119]

Whereas outsourcing was often considered as a way of "trimming" a company to the right size and focusing on its core competencies,[120] it seems that offshoring does not follow the same path. Some companies seem to concentrate primarily on cost differences to make their operations more efficient. Others have entered countries where they expect to attract a high share of the best-qualified employees from the local labor market. Yet other companies have transferred critical development activities offshore to benefit from both lower labor costs and to gain access to talent pools. In short, they have not abandoned activities but rather used offshoring to strengthen them. On the other hand, companies relocate activities that create only little value – such as accounting – abroad to gain from lower labor cost. In such cases, the motivation for offshoring comes much closer to the traditional arguments for outsourcing.

The differentiation between these two extremes – offshoring as an alternative to outsourcing on the one hand and offshoring as a way to improve existing competitive advantages – has not been discussed to date. However, it seems critical to distinguish these different models as they supposedly have very different coordination mechanisms.

An MNC can keep service offshoring activities in-house or delegate them to a third-party vendor (outsourcing). In our research, we have selected captive offshoring centers for several reasons that relate to existing research on outsourcing:

- Compared with an outsourced service offshoring center, a wider range of coordination mechanisms can be applied to a captive service offshoring center, i.e. an international subsidiary.[121] This is because the ownership of a subsidiary adds

---

[119] E.g., the on-site management of computer hardware has frequently been outsourced to local providers but cannot be transferred to a remote location as the computer hardware such as a keyboard and monitor are location-dependent.

[120] Prahalad/Hamel (1990), pp. 83-85.

[121] The main coordination elements in an outsourcing contract are the contractual obligations that both parties agree to and that are typically formalized in extensive documentation. There are situations where personal coordination mechanisms and autonomy can also act as coordination mechanisms; however, this is not the case for all outsourcing contracts.

the element of hierarchy to the relationship that is not per se given in a relationship between a provider and receiver of an outsourced service. Thus, to focus on captive service offshoring centers seems more promising with regard to the breadth of expected results on coordination mechanisms.

- Captive offshoring centers can have a larger variety of resources. If the assumption holds that competitive advantage stems from valuable, rare, inimitable and hardly substitutable resources, then the firm will want to keep these resources within its boundaries.[122] Consequently, outsource offshoring will work only for a smaller range of services.[123]

In addition, several methodological considerations also influenced our choice:

- As briefly indicated above, Eastern Europe is a very interesting offshoring destination for European MNCs. However, there are far fewer large service providers in this region than in India. Where such providers are not available, MNCs need to opt for captive offshoring. Considering what is more relevant to European MNCs and what is also empirically more feasible (since it is hard to find cases of outsourcing relationships from Western Europe to Eastern Europe), it seems more promising to concentrate on captive offshoring.

- Since we intend to analyze not only headquarters but also subsidiaries and to talk to representatives from both sides, it is in principle easier to get access to subsidiaries once headquarters agree. This is not necessarily true of external providers who might still be hesitant to talk to researchers even if their customers have agreed to discuss the relationship. Thus, focus on captive offshoring units will help us to gain a complete picture of the relationship.

- The differences between in-house offshoring and offshore outsourcing might be too large to be captured in a single empirical study. It the scope of this work were too broad, the quality of results would be jeopardized. In addition, the pure differentiation between in-house execution and outsourcing is a topic that has long been researched by publications in the context of transaction cost economics.

---

[122] Poppo/Zenger (1998), p. 853. This consideration is confirmed by other authors who define outsourcing as limited to "non-strategic activities" Espino-Rodríguez/Padrón-Robaina (2006), p. 52.
[123] For this discussion, see also Poppo/Zenger (1998), p. 872.

2 – Theoretical Foundations

2.2.4.2 DIFFERENTIATION OF MANUFACTURING AND SERVICE OFFSHORING

The relocation of economic activity to another country is not new. The offshoring of manufacturing activities has been discussed for some considerable time in international business literature.[124] Many MNCs have gone through phases of moving manufacturing facilities to another country.[125] This phenomenon, which is commonly known as manufacturing offshoring, has gained ground for several reasons. According to research on this topic, the main motives were lower labor costs and easier access to new markets and technologies.[126] For example, car manufacturers could avoid high tariffs on their products by producing cars abroad and selling them locally.

It is important to analyze if – and if so, how – the phenomenon under consideration – service offshoring – differs from manufacturing offshoring. In doing so, we need to first describe manufacturing offshoring and then compare it to the offshoring of services. We will base our analysis on contributions from both fields.

The international division of labor has been most intensely discussed with regard to the maquiladora industry in Northern Mexico. "Maquiladoras are Mexican assembly plants located on the Mexican side of the United States-Mexico border. A maquiladora plant is a labor-intensive plant in which the labor assembly work is performed in Mexico, whereas the technical, marketing and engineering functions are kept in the United States."[127] These firms export "virtually all of their production."[128] This industry has been promoted by the U.S. government to allow industry access to cheap labor and by the Mexican government to develop the region economically.[129] One important characteristic of this movement was that production had already reached a phase in which it no longer required highly skilled labor because research and development had already been concluded in the home market.[130] Thus, the movement of manufacturing processes is typically an expression of "home-base exploiting" FDI.[131] The low cost of low-skilled labor seems the main motives for moving production.[132] Firms generally do not see the

---

[124] See, for instance, Blakley et al. (1987), Kotabe (1990), Kotabe/Swan (1994), Sweeney (1994), Ritter/Sternfels (2004), Dowlatshahi (2005).
[125] Kotabe/Swan (1994), pp. 115-116, Colquhoun et al. (2004), p. 9, Ge et al. (2004), p. 2.
[126] Kotabe/Swan (1994), p. 134, Kuemmerle (1997), p. 63.
[127] Feinberg et al. (2003), p. 209.
[128] Biles (2004), p. 520.
[129] Hansen (1981), p. 1.
[130] Hansen (1981), p. 2.
[131] Kuemmerle (1999), pp. 3-4.
[132] Anderson (1983), p. 30, Brouthers et al. (1999), p. 42. Still, Kotabe/Swan (1994), p. 134 suggest that other reasons such as unavailability in the home market, might also play a role.

need to upgrade their employees' skill profile because their chief interest is in low labor cost.[133] The movement of manufacturing activity was often also dependent on the host country's government offering duty exemption on raw materials and preferential tariffs.[134] Over time, it has grown and extended beyond the U.S.-Mexico border region.[135] Not only has Mexico attracted investment from countries other than the U.S.,[136] but other developing countries, too, have tried to set up a similar industry to benefit from its positive effects.[137] By now, manufacturing offshoring has reached a more global level.[138] The primary host countries of the first wave of manufacturing offshoring were Spain, Portugal, Greece, Yugoslavia, Brazil, Mexico, Hong Kong, Korea, Taiwan, and Singapore – also called newly industrialized countries (NICs).[139] Today, China plays an important role as destination of manufacturing offshoring. Manufacturing offshoring programs were often specifically designed to fit taxation and tariff schemes. U.S. companies, for instance, were allowed to import goods tax-free from their Mexican subsidiaries if they had also sent them the raw materials.[140] Physical proximity too was important for manufacturing offshoring, not only because of lower transportation costs for goods but also because expatriate managers of the subsidiaries could still live at home.[141] In a study of the factors for manufacturing offshoring, Clark et al. (1993) found transportation costs to be significantly and negatively correlated to the likelihood of moving manufacturing work abroad.[142] Other studies (for instance, Hansen (1981)) point to the fact that the maquiladora program leaves the employees in the same unskilled category, with few chances of advancing to better-paid positions. Manufacturing offshoring has been a source of concern with regard to job stability and has caused fears of massive layoffs in the originating countries.[143] Consequently, there have been several

---

[133] Brouthers et al. (1999), p. 42.
[134] Hansen (1981), p. 3, Brouthers et al. (1999), p. 38.
[135] Biles (2004), p. 521.
[136] See Paik/Sohn (1998) for Korean investment in the Mexican maquiladora industry and Paik/Teagarden (1995) for a comparison of different management styles of Japanese, Korean and US firms toward their maquiladora operations in Mexico.
[137] See DeVault (1997) for the example of offshore assembly in the Dominican Republic.
[138] For the movement of production on a global level, see Kotabe/Swan (1994) and Alguire et al. (1994).
[139] Hansen (1981), p. 3.
[140] Hansen (1981), p. 5, see also Clark et al. (1993), p. 775.
[141] Hansen (1981), p. 5.
[142] Clark et al. (1993), pp. 778-779.
[143] Hansen (1981), p. 7.

evaluations of the benefits and shortcomings of manufacturing offshoring, particularly the effects on employment, that come to equivocal results.[144]

What now are the differences between manufacturing and service offshoring? These can be considered on several dimensions:

- *Type of firm:* Whereas Clark et al. (1993) found that capital-intensive industries are less prone to manufacturing offshoring,[145] Abramovsky/Griffith (2005) postulated that the opposite is true of service offshoring: more capital-intensive firms are more likely to offshore services.[146]

- *Coordination requirements:* Management also seems to require different skills: In a comparison of maquiladoras and service companies, Feinberg et al. (2003) found significant differences between the beneficial aspects of an ISO 9000 quality program for the two types of firms.[147]

- *Skill type required:* Where service offshoring centers typically employ university graduates, manufacturing offshoring units rely on lower-skilled employees.

- *Reasons for offshoring:* As discussed above, service offshoring often aims not only for cost reduction, but also for increases in flexibility and access to high-talent labor pools. Manufacturing offshoring is often undertaken to achieve cost reduction together with tariff evasion and access to the local sales market.

- *Transport cost and time:* The cost and duration of transport do not play a role in service offshoring, whereas they are important factors for manufacturing offshoring.

- *Fragmentation:* Because of the negligible effect of transport cost and time, service processes can be much more fragmented than manufacturing production processes.

---

[144] For the effects on employment in the manufacturing offshoring industry, see Arndt (1997), Coronado et al. (2004). For a general ethical reflection on manufacturing offshoring, see Gordon (1998), Brouthers et al. (1999), p. 41.
[145] Clark et al. (1993), pp. 777-779.
[146] Abramovsky/Griffith (2005), p. 11.
[147] Feinberg et al. (2003), pp. 213-214. His findings are confirmed by research that compares the coordination of "blue-collar" and "white-collar" workers (Davis (1991), pp. 55-56).

- *Flexibility:* Whereas service offshoring often does not require more than an office and university graduates to set up a new location, manufacturing offshoring typically requires higher investment in infrastructure and equipment. As a rule this equipment is rather specialized and can be used only for a specific product. The equipment for service offshoring – offices and computers – can in principle be used for many different services and a change might require only the installation of new software programs.

- *Investment:* Based on the reasoning above, there are also differences in the magnitude of investments. These are typically rather low for service offshoring and rather high for manufacturing offshoring.

- *Risk:* A lower investment also brings a lower risk of losing assets for service offshoring in comparison with manufacturing offshoring.

Table 2-4 summarizes the differences between the two phenomena.

Table 2-4: Differences between service and manufacturing offshoring (Source: Own table, partially based on UNCTAD (2004b), pp. 152-153)

Criteria	Service Offshoring	Manufacturing Offshoring
Type of firms	Typically more technology-intensive firms	Typically more labor-intensive firms
Skill type required	High skills required, typically university graduates	Low skills required, often unskilled workers are employed
Reasons	Mainly cost reasons but also quality, higher speed and flexibility	Primarily cost reasons but also tariff evasion
Transport cost and time	Not relevant	High relevance, important factor in location decision
Fragmentation	Services can be very fragmented and the value chain split over several locations	As products need to be transported the potential for fragmentation is limited

2 – Theoretical Foundations

Criteria	Service Offshoring	Manufacturing Offshoring
Flexibility	High, since configuration of network can be easily changed, as most flows between different units of the network take place in digital form and can be routed differently, stopped or added to easily. Also, service offshoring centers often provide the infrastructure that can potentially be used for many different types of "digitizable" services	Low, as configuration of network is often subject to contractual conditions with local partners and long lead periods are needed to change factory setup. Also, manufacturing offshoring centers are typically designed for the production of a specific set of products
Investment	Low, as service offshoring centers for simple processes often do not require more than office space and access to the MNC's global IT network. However, more complex processes, e.g., R&D, can require larger investments	Medium to high, as manufacturing offshoring typically requires investment in a plant with specific machinery. Cost depends on the tasks to be carried out
Risk	Limited, as service offshoring centers often do not cater for the most critical processes. Besides, there is low involvement with local environment	High, as manufacturing locations are often integrated in local networks and can be adversely affected by political risks in their local environment

Is there a clear answer to the question whether manufacturing and service offshoring are different? It depends to a high degree on the specific context. For our specific question – the coordination of service offshoring subsidiaries – there are several reasons to treat the two phenomena as related but to analyze service offshoring individually. There seems to be a different type of firm that leans toward service offshoring and there can very well be strong implications on coordination because the people in service offshoring centers belong to a very different skill category than that in manufacturing offshoring. In addition, with near-zero transportation costs, an increased dispersion of tasks can take place that calls for higher levels of coordination. Partially building upon the factors above, we will now describe a model that has been mentioned from time to time[148] but that has not yet made its way into the academic discussion. It has been called the "24-hour knowledge factory"[149] or "follow the sun"[150] principle and a few examples have been established. Our example will serve to show how service offshoring differs in practice from manufacturing offshoring.

Service offshoring can function as follows: An MNC sets up at least three centers that work continuously on a project. At the end of the working day in one center, the job is forwarded to another location where the job is continued until it is forwarded to yet another center. These centers can have different capabilities[151] but there may also be a situation where all necessary capabilities have to be available in all locations. Consider, for instance, an IT helpline where an employee of the MNC posts a request in one center just before the end of the working day. If the employee has an additional question related to that request just an hour later, his call would be routed to another center that would need to be prepared to fully service his request. This is distinctive from manufacturing companies in which activities can be spread over several countries, but often with a clear sequence.[152] For instance, carmaker Audi produces automotive engines in Hungary and then transports them to Germany to be incorporated in cars.[153] Even though there is a division of labor, it is characterized by a distribution of capabilities and an inherent inflexibility since an engine cannot be shipped to three different locations around the world three times a day.

Thus, we conclude that the coordination of service offshoring is a new phenomenon for MNCs and there is reason to believe that firms will have to develop unique coordination strategies to deal with it. This is the topic upon which this work will focus.

2.2.4.3 DIFFERENTIATION OF SHARED SERVICES CENTERS AND SERVICE OFFSHORING

Shared services centers are organizational units that carry out services for more than one other unit in the firm.[154] While there were some initial ideas around the concept of shared services as early as the 1970s,[155] companies engaged in this practice increasingly

---

[148] Bottino (2004), Inside Market Data (2004).
[149] Gupta/Seshasai (2004), p. 2.
[150] Kranz (2005).
[151] Gupta/Seshasai (2004), p. 3.
[152] See on basic options of interdependencies Baliga/Jaeger (1984), pp. 32-33 and Thompson (1967), pp. 54-55.
[153] Schmid/Machulik (2004).
[154] Berry (2006), p. 89.
[155] Friedman (1975).

in the 1990s.[156] Such a center is an entity in its own right – organizationally or even legally separated – that is established for the execution of internal service tasks.[157] These services cover areas such as "finance, law, information systems, human resources, real estate, and security"[158] and they are typically considered support services of less strategic importance that help their customers focus on their core processes.[159] A shared services center typically results from the combination or consolidation of services from within a firm.[160] Some authors describe shared services centers that start their offerings with services for internal customers but eventually also sell their services to external parties.[161] The reasons for the growth in shared services were the need for companies to reduce costs, the possibilities that information technologies offered for a centralized execution of services, and firms' desire to concentrate more on core processes.[162] In addition, by establishing these centers, firms aim at reducing risks by introducing standardized processes that are consistent with standards of risk management. They also want to reduce cycle times and increase employee motivation by offering a better environment for support process execution.[163]

These centers are often set up to strike a balance between the complete centralization of similar tasks (for instance, in a functional organization) and the complete decentralization of similar tasks in different business units. In this way, businesses still have flexibility with regard to their most important tasks but they can rely on the efficient execution of non-core services in a shared services center.[164] However, this only gives the firm an advantage if the additional cost and time for coordination are more than offset by the gains through standardization and economies of scale that the firm can achieve if it concentrates all similar tasks in one center.[165]

In comparing shared services centers and service offshoring, there are several differences around common themes: The primary motivation for shared services centers is to

---

[156] Quinn et al. (2000), Forst (2001), p. 13.
[157] Zimmermann (1992), p. 55, Kreisel (1995), pp. 121-122, Connell (1996), p. 55, Campenhausen/Rudolf (2001), p. 82.
[158] Ulrich (1995), p. 14. For a concrete example of a human resources shared services center, see Donnely (2005).
[159] Kagelmann (2001), p. 45.
[160] Ulrich (1995), p. 14.
[161] Connell (1996), pp. 56-57, Quinn et al. (2000).
[162] Ulrich (1995), Campenhausen/Rudolf (2001), Westerhoff (2006), pp. 62-63
[163] Kagelmann (2001), pp. 75-77.
[164] Karsatos (1988), p. 36.
[165] Kreisel (1995), pp. 180-181, Campenhausen/Rudolf (2001), p. 83.

consolidate and centralize services. This is not necessarily the case in service offshoring, although it can be.[166] The services are of less strategic relevance; they are often described as "support processes".[167] With both concepts a separate entity carries out services primarily for internal customers, and they both focus on specific activities.[168] However, a shared services center will always have (far) more than one customer. A service offshoring subsidiary can serve one customer or more. The most important difference, however, is the *international* transfer in service offshoring. Whereas the concept of shared services centers is focused mainly on the consolidation of services and the centers are often located domestically, service offshoring always has an international component. Therefore, it seems justified to analyze it as a new phenomenon.

The differences we have just discussed are summarized in Table 2-5.

Table 2-5: Differences between shared service centers and service offshoring subsidiaries

Dimension	Shared service centers	Service offshoring subsidiaries
Centralization of activities	Constitutive characteristic	Possible but not constitutive
Strategic importance of service provided	Typically low	From low to high
Number of customers	More than one (> 1)	One or more (≥ 1)
International service delivery	Possible but not constitutive	Constitutive characteristic

2.2.5 Our Service Offshoring Definition

Having reviewed existing service offshoring definitions and discussed the differences between our topic and related topics we can now present our own definition. We have developed it based on the evaluation of existing contributions and with the purpose of our work in mind. The definition is as follows:

---

[166] Berry (2006), p. 92.
[167] Kagelmann (2001), p. 42.
[168] Schulman (1999), p. 10.

Service offshoring is the practice of firms to internationally distribute activities with immaterial results that are sent back to the originating location(s) via computer and telephony networks.

We illustrate our understanding and thereby our definition of service offshoring in Figure 2-4. A given process within an MNC in a given country (here referred to as "home country") is split up and one part of that process is carried out in another location (here referred to as "offshore location"). The result of the preceding step is transmitted to the offshore location and the result of the step that is carried out there is ultimately sent back to the home country. This distribution can happen between one originating country (unit) and the offshore location or between several originating countries (units) and the offshore location. In the latter case, there would be an additional concentration of activities in the service offshoring center.

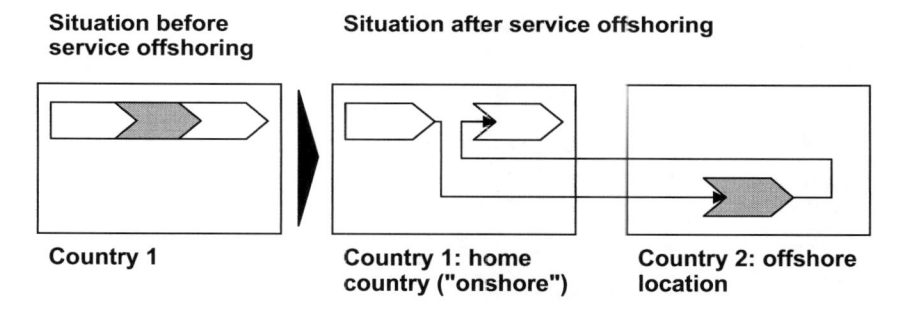

Figure 2-4: Illustration of the definition of service offshoring

To provide a better overview of the current status service offshoring, the next section will give a more complete description of the phenomenon.

2.2.6 Description of Service Offshoring

2.2.6.1 History

The emergence of service offshoring is attributed to the outsourcing boom in the 1980s. One often-cited instance was Kodak's decision to hand over its entire IT function to IBM. The next logical step was the international movement of services. It was mainly U.S. and UK corporations that started to relocate activities to India which had originally been carried out in their country of residence. General Electric was one of the first companies to establish a service offshoring center in India that initially carried out only internal services, then also offered its services to external customers and finally was sold by General Electric and is today operating as an independent company under the name Genpact.[169] Other market-making deals were those of American Express and Eastman Kodak which were the first of many companies to transfer increasingly complex services abroad.[170] More and more companies followed, including MNCs from Continental Europe that moved some services to India but in parallel opted for offshoring to Eastern Europe. Offshoring was a much discussed topic during the U.S. presidential elections in 2004 when there was much anxiety about job losses. Since then, some regulations have been put in place that partially prohibit firms from using offshore resources when participating in a governmental tender. Still, the breadth and depth of the services that are shifted to offshore locations have been growing steadily and the topic still seems to be on the agenda of corporate decision makers who are concerned about the global distribution of their activities.

2.2.6.2 REASONS FOR SERVICE OFFSHORING

In the initial assessment of the phenomenon, some authors focus mainly on the rationales behind service offshoring.[171] One frequently cited argument is cost reduction and consequently, some contributions discuss how to maximize monetary benefits from service offshoring and to gain *cost benefits* by moving labor-intensive processes to countries with lower cost of labor. Cost savings are often the most important aspect as they can reach dimensions of 20 to 40 per cent, in optimistic cases even in excess of 50 per cent. This is achieved by cheaper labor, by exploiting economies of scale and by redesigning and standardizing processes.[172] However, gains can derive from more areas:

- Offshoring can also bring a substantial *quality increase,* as the skill level of people who carry out services in developing countries is typically higher than in the developed world. This is the case because the labor cost difference is so large, e.g., between the U.S. and India, that Indian companies can hire university graduates for jobs that are typically carried out by part-time labor in the U.S.[173]

- A further benefit can be *improved transparency* that can come with the explicit definition of interfaces between originating unit and offshore location, bringing

---

[169] Baily/Lawrence (2004), p. 230, Bhambal (2005).
[170] Clott (2004), p. 157.
[171] See, for instance, Colquhoun et al. (2004), p. 9.
[172] Roland Berger/UNCTAD (2004), p. 2; Robinson/Kalakota (2004), p. 1; Agrawal et al. (2003), p. 24.
[173] Agrawal et al. (2003), p. 27.

2 – Theoretical Foundations   47

an end to convoluted and often complex processes within the same location. Thus, offshoring can lead to better monitoring compared to the traditional in-house execution.[174]

- *Higher speed of operation* can be an additional benefit, especially in the case of processes that can be carried out around the clock once they are moved to an offshore location where three shifts a day are often typical.[175]

- Besides, a company achieves *more flexibility* if it has the opportunity to use an offshore service center to handle peaks in demand. In this way, it can deal much more easily with additional demand without being subject to strict labor laws, especially in Continental Europe, that prohibit the hiring of personnel only for periods of high-peak demand.[176] Less regulation can also be expected in other areas in which developing countries often create financial and non-financial incentives to promote foreign direct investment, such as tax exemptions and help in setting up legal entities.

- Offshoring can moreover allow managers to better *focus on their core tasks* by reducing the amount of time they spend with operating services instead of on activities that add value to the company. Along that line of argument, offshoring can help the company *focus on its core competencies* and potentially lead to a *decrease in complexity* by freeing the organization from non-core activities.[177] While this reason is often specifically mentioned with regard to outsourcing, it can also apply in offshoring, when the relocation of activities forces companies to better define interfaces and streamline processes.

Of course, there are also potential disadvantages to service offshoring. These will be discussed in the next section.

---

[174] Dittrich/Braun (2004), pp. 63-64.
[175] By contrast, manufacturing offshoring does not usually result in higher speed of operations if long shipment periods have to be included in the manufacturing process.
[176] Burgmaier et al. (2004), p. 24.
[177] Berggren/Bengtsson (2004), p. 211, Ramachandran/Voleti (2004).

2.2.6.3 BARRIERS TO SERVICE OFFSHORING

Although there are strong arguments in favor of service offshoring, there is an array of reasons to discourage MNCs.[178] These can be categorized in the following domains:

- Offshoring – for both manufacturing and service – is often perceived negatively. Thus, companies might fear *image losses* or union actions and decide not to embark on service offshoring.[179]

- Companies may shy away from the *high coordination requirements*. Processes that require intensive supervision might not be considered for offshoring because the cost of supervision might increase if it is carried out on an international level. For instance, the increase in travel costs might be higher than the savings that stem from labor cost arbitrage.[180]

- In some circumstances, offshoring might *not be economically attractive*. Companies that have a very high degree of automation in their internal processes might not benefit from offshoring as much as companies with only few automated processes. The latter can benefit much more from lower labor costs in offshoring locations.

- Companies might *lack clearly defined processes*. To engage in service offshoring, firms need to create interfaces between the headquarters, international subsidiaries and the service offshoring center. If a company is unwilling or unable to clearly define these processes and divide them between countries, it can hardly enter an offshoring arrangement.[181]

- *Insufficient capabilities of information technology* can hinder the use of service offshoring since the relocation of services typically requires extensive IT support. In settings where sufficient IT capabilities are not available companies might choose to refrain from offshoring.[182]

---

[178] Recent survey results of perceived risk of service offshoring can be found in Lewin/Peeters (2006).
[179] Farrell et al. (2005), p. 50.
[180] McCarthy (2003), p. 3.
[181] Farrell et al. (2005), p. 46.
[182] Farrell et al. (2005), pp. 50-51.

- Companies might decide not to offshore as it can represent a *loss of control*. The remote execution of services can decrease the level of direct management control.

- Companies may fear *privacy issues and data leakages* when processing their data in a location with less strict privacy laws than in their home countries.[183]

- Companies might fear the *loss of crucial capabilities* if they move them abroad.[184] This is even more likely for offshore outsourcing, but captive offshoring too could lead to a disturbance of formal and informal communication channels that might have adverse affects on other units of the firm.

- Offshoring can also be hindered by *regulatory hurdles*. Companies may in fact be prohibited outright from moving jobs offshore. Even though Western European countries can hardly be inhibited from moving work to another place within the growing European Union, there are restrictions that prevent companies from moving work abroad.[185] Moreover, in countries with highly regulated labor markets, such as Germany and France, companies might choose not to offshore because potential cost savings cannot be achieved on account of labor market regulations inhibiting the layoff of personnel. Also, in some countries, companies such as banks are not allowed to transfer data outside the originating country and are therefore prohibited from offshoring.[186]

In spite of the potential disadvantages, the potential benefits seem to make service offshoring attractive enough for many MNCs to consider it.

2.2.6.4 CURRENT SIZE AND EXPECTED GROWTH OF SERVICE OFFSHORING

To measure the current size and the expected growth of service offshoring is not an easy task. There have been two major approaches:

(1) Some analysts have based their estimate of growth on firm surveys that have evaluated how many companies have already offshored part of their services and how many

---

[183] Swartz (2004).
[184] Reppesgaard (2004).
[185] For instance, radiology services in the US require registration in the state where the service is carried out and therefore there are several regulatory hurdles to be overcome before radiology service offshoring is possible (Stack et al. (2007), p. 47).
[186] Farrell et al. (2005), pp. 51-52.

are planning to do so in the future. Service offshoring has been increasing in volume and scope recently and is predicted to grow exponentially in the next years.[187] An indication of the growth can be given by estimating the number of jobs that are moved to a location abroad. The technology consultancy Forrester anticipates that by 2015 around 2.3 per cent to 2.5 per cent of all jobs in the UK and the U.S. will have shifted offshore (see Figure 2-5). In Continental Europe, jobs moved abroad due to service offshoring could account for around 0.3 per cent of the total labor force. Another analysis predicts a 22 per cent average growth rate in offshore service employment from 2003 to 2008, or in absolute numbers from 1.6 million to 4.1 million employees worldwide.[188]

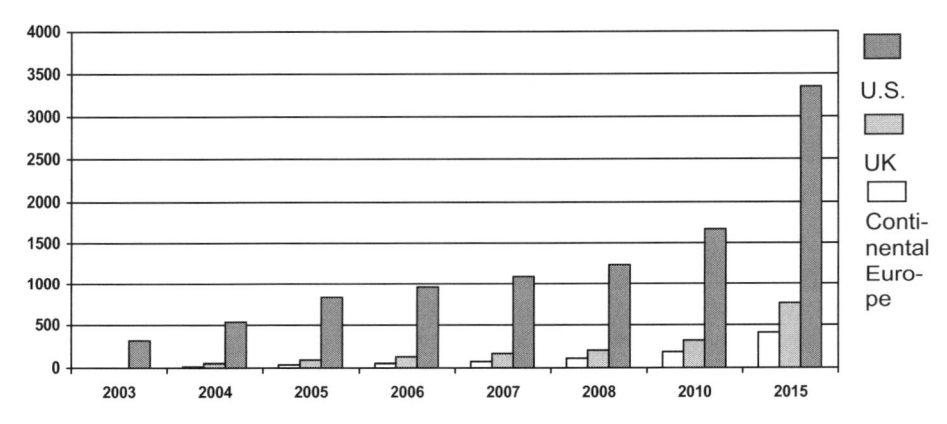

Figure 2-5: Cumulative number of service jobs (in thousands) moved offshore per region (Source: McCarthy (2003); Parker (2004))[189]

Besides, there are estimates that indicate how much different types of captive and outsource offshoring will grow over time. Figure 2-6 shows an estimate for market sizes for captive and outsource offshoring as well as for domestic outsourcing. As domestic outsourcing has already been a common business practice for several years, its market volume is much larger. However, the main development in terms of growth rates and new business models is in the area of offshoring, which is expected to grow by 30 per

---

[187] Estimates of development are of different magnitudes, but the same underlying tendency is confirmed by Deloitte (2004), McCarthy (2004), Parker (2004).
[188] Farrell et al. (2005), p. 41.
[189] Numbers are based on McCarthy (2004), p. app. 41302/sect. "Summary", Parker (2004), p. app. 43818/sect. "Output". In our work, we refer to Continental Europe as Western Europe excluding the UK. The data for job movements includes Germany, France, Netherlands, Italy, Sweden, Belgium, Switzerland, Denmark, Spain, Austria, Finland, Ireland, Portugal, Greece, Luxembourg. See also Schmid/Daub (2005), p. 2.

2 – Theoretical Foundations   51

cent annually over the next five years while single-digit growth is anticipated in other areas.[190]

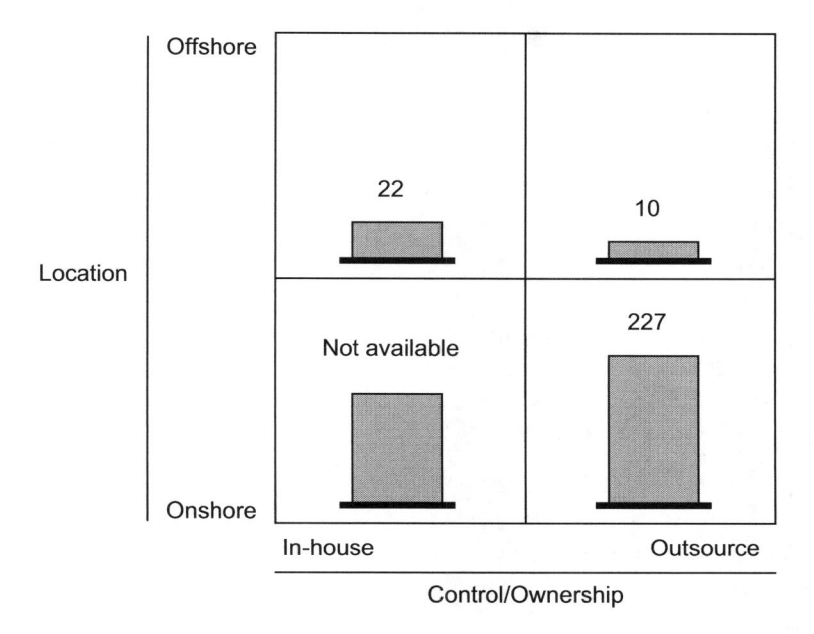

```
            Offshore
              ┌─────────────┬─────────────┐
              │     22      │     10      │
              │    ▄▄▄      │    ▄▄       │
              │             │             │
 Location     ├─────────────┼─────────────┤
              │             │    227      │
              │Not available│   ████      │
              │             │   ████      │
              │             │   ████      │
            Onshore────────────────────────
              In-house         Outsource
                  Control/Ownership
```

Figure 2-6: Market sizes 2001 in billion USD for offshoring and outsourcing (Source: Slightly adapted from Farrell et al. (2005), p. 15)

(2) Other estimates for the growth of service offshoring derive from the overall growth of international trade in services. One indicator for the increasing significance of services is the development of FDI activity in the tertiary sector. In the early 1970s, the service sector accounted for only one quarter of FDI stock. In 2002, this value reached about 60 per cent. During the same time, the share of the manufacturing sector fell from 42 per cent to 34 per cent and that of the primary sector from 9 per cent to 6 per cent.[191] Even though these figures do not directly relate to service offshoring, they give proof of the increasing importance of services FDI.

---

[190] Farrell et al. (2005), pp. 18-19. The significant growth rates and impact on global distribution of work are confirmed by later research (Dossani/Kenney (2006), Farrell et al. (2006)).
[191] UNCTAD (2004b), p. xx.

Still, only 10 per cent of these services enter international trade (compared to about 50 per cent of manufactured goods).[192] Even though many services are not tradable (as they have to be consumed where they are produced), advancements in information and communication technologies have made a larger variety of services tradable. Thus, a large increase in the trade of services can be expected.[193]

Looking at offshoring, both sides – the importing and the exporting country – have to be considered: In the U.S., as primary originator for service offshoring, the import of services such as computer and data processing saw annual growth rates of 31 per cent between 1992 and 2002.[194] Those countries that export services also show a strong growth in service offshoring. India alone, one of the largest markets for IT and service offshoring, is expected to grow from a market volume of USD 12 billion in 2004 to USD 38 billion in 2008.[195]

2.2.6.5 INDUSTRIES AND FUNCTIONS

Service offshoring is not restricted to a specific industry or specific function. One categorization distinguishes three main areas in which service offshoring can be used: (1) front-office activities such as call centers, (2) back-office activities such as finance and accounting, IT services, and human resources, and (3) industry-specific activities such as airline ticket accounting. Most projects that are already operational and are in the back-office area and within that area specifically in IT services.[196] The relocation of IT activities seems a logical step. As discussed above, a prerequisite is computer readability, which is per definition given in the area of IT. Thus, companies have started to move software application development and software application maintenance abroad. The offshoring of other back-office processes such as bookkeeping is often labeled "BPO" which stands for business process outsourcing/offshoring.[197]

While there are industry-specific evaluations of service offshoring,[198] there has been no attempt to identify different types of service offshoring centers in the service offshoring literature. Some authors concentrate on the question which services lend themselves to

---

[192] UNCTAD (2004b), p. xxiv.
[193] UNCTAD (2005), p. 31.
[194] UNCTAD (2004b), p. 151.
[195] Schaaf (2004), p. 1.
[196] Roland Berger/UNCTAD (2004), p. 6.
[197] Ramachandran/Voleti (2004), p. 49.
[198] See for the financial services industry for instance Deloitte (2004). For venture capital, see Angelos (2004). For investment bank research, see Grote/Täube (2007).

offshoring[199] but in general it is expected that service offshoring might extend to increasingly more services over time.[200]

2.2.6.6 CHARACTERISTICS OF SERVICE OFFSHORING CENTERS

The next topic to be discussed is the organizational setting in which service offshoring is performed. One major question is the decision whether services should be performed by a foreign subsidiary or by a foreign service provider.[201]

As this work focuses on captive centers, we will consider a typical setup for service offshoring, these being service centers. A service center is an organizational unit that focuses exclusively on the execution of one or more services. Common examples of services that are moved to a service center are accounting services which were previously carried out in the MNC's headquarters. Once established, the service offshoring center often takes over responsibility for a specific service not only for the MNC's headquarters but also for other (international) subsidiaries.

Even though a complete list of characteristics is hard to draw up, a few common characteristics can be distinguished:

- Service offshoring centers are often in a location that offers *lower labor cost* relative to the headquarters location.[202] This is because many MNCs are looking for ways to increase their operational efficiency. However, it is not necessarily a defining feature of service offshoring as companies could also opt for a service offshoring center in a location that has a high availability of required skills even if those skills are costly to hire.

- *Service centers focus on a limited number of tasks:* They are not set up to be a national representative of an MNC and thus do not have many external relations (except for recruiting). Nor do they have a wide variety of activities that other international subsidiaries might have whose responsibilities have grown over time. They often do not carry out tasks that are of high strategic importance for the MNC. Their focus is typically more on the repeated, efficient execution of standardized tasks. However, service centers can be of overall strategic impor-

---

[199] See for instance Robinson/Kalakota (2004), p. 4.
[200] Maskell et al. (2007), p. 255.
[201] See for instance Ge et al. (2004), pp. 6-7.
[202] Drechsler (2006).

tance as they can help the MNC to gain a better competitive position through higher efficiency.[203]

- Their main *focus is often on efficiency* by the exploitation of economies of scope by constantly improving the processes they carry out and on economies of scale by taking over the same tasks for as many units as possible (and feasible).

- They *serve one or more international units of the MNC*. They can serve the headquarters only, one or more international subsidiaries only, or both the headquarters and international subsidiaries. Thus, they can become the service center for only one country but also for a continent or even for the whole world.

- They have only *limited relations to the local environment*. They have to rely on the local talent pool but they do not need many local suppliers. Moreover, they do not have local customers and are therefore not subject to local competition. They also do not necessarily have a very specific relationship to an existing local subsidiary of the MNC that caters to the local market. Thus, in Bartlett/Ghoshal's framework of the international subsidiary they are characterized by a very low degree of "strategic importance of the local environment"[204].

2.2.6.7 EXAMPLES OF SERVICE OFFSHORING

A number of service offshoring centers have recently been given some coverage in the press. Here we will present three examples:

- *Lufthansa* has a service center that is part of the finance and administration function in Poland. The center is focused on efficient execution and standardized processes.[205] It serves all European subsidiaries and is part of a global network of three centers (in Mexico, Thailand and Poland). The main reasons for the establishment of these centers are the lower labor and factor cost.

- *Deutsche Bank* was an early proponent of service offshoring and founded a service offshoring subsidiary as early as 1992. This unit was responsible for the development of financial software. Since then, several activities from the area of

---

[203] Of course, the breadth of services can grow over time but new centers typically start with a limited set of tasks.
[204] Bartlett/Ghoshal (1986), p. 90. This is true even if they are located in an important sales market of the MNC since the service offshoring subsidiary focuses on internal tasks. Thus, the sales responsibility for that market would typically not be carried by the service offshoring subsidiary.
[205] Anonymous (2003).

IT but also services such as investment analysis have been moved to offshore locations in Russia and India. By the end of 2007, the bank plans to have one-half its 4000 employees in the trade area and 500 of its 1000 investment analysts in offshore locations.[206] For some services, Deutsche Bank has used external partners such as IBM or Accenture.[207]

- *Commerzbank* has only recently started to move service activities abroad. It has set up a center with about 60 employees in Prague, Czech Republic, to process money transfers.[208] More activities might be delegated to Commerzbank's Polish subsidiary.[209]

2.3 TYPOLOGIES OF INTERNATIONAL SUBSIDIARIES

One purpose of our research is to distinguish types of service offshoring subsidiaries. Research in the social sciences has long used typologies for such differentiation, and – following this tradition – international business research has developed typologies of the international subsidiary. In this section, we will explain what typologies are, what they are good for, and in which areas they have been applied (section 2.3.1). We will then proceed to give an overview of typologies of the international subsidiary in international business research where typologies were first used when the network view of the MNC started to evolve. From that time on it was important not only to look at the headquarters but also to take into consideration the subsidiary (section 2.3.2). This apart, we will discuss what relevance typologies generally can have for service offshoring (section 2.3.3) and examine existing typologies and their (in-) appropriateness for service offshoring (section 2.3.4).

2.3.1 TYPOLOGIES IN BUSINESS RESEARCH

Typologies are "*theoretical conceptual classification schemes* [emphasis in original]"[210]. They are used to break down a large number of items into a smaller number of categories by identifying commonalities between them. The underlying notion can be

---

[206] Anonymous (2006).
[207] Burgmaier et al. (2004), p. 22.
[208] Anonymous (2006).
[209] Burgmaier et al. (2004), p. 22.
[210] Dess et al. (1993), p. 776.

expressed as: "*Phenomena of interest do not occur in infinite combinations, at least not with equal likelihood.* [emphasis in original]"[211]

Generally speaking, typologies consist of two components: the individual types and the typology that combines these individual types. All the types need to be described according to the same dimensions to form *one* typology. All items that fall into one type should be as similar as possible (internal homogeneity) and should be as different as possible from the other types in the typology (external heterogeneity).[212] Typologies are often used in the social sciences where items very often cannot be as unequivocally classified as in the natural sciences. The natural sciences therefore typically rely on classifications that match new items to existing classes by evaluating whether or not all necessary criteria are fulfilled.[213] By contrast, types in the social sciences tend to be more "blurred" since they distinguish items by order of degree of a given criterion. As a result, the types are not as clear and there can be both intermediate types and overlaps between types.[214]

There are two ways to make a typology: Authors typically distinguish between empirically derived taxonomies and theoretically developed typologies.[215] We will also work with this differentiation. Thus, a cluster analysis of an existing data set can be thought of as creating a taxonomy. By contrast, the theoretical derivation of different dimensions and types that we employ in our research is considered typology development. An evaluation of the differences between typological and taxonomical approaches is displayed in Table 2-6.

The ways to create typologies and taxonomies are different, although the motive is often similar and is one of their advantages: Researchers have tried to find ways to reduce complexity and identify similarities among a group of items. To that end, it is essential to find dimensions that can be used to differentiate objects. These dimensions can be derived either empirically (for taxonomies) or theoretically (for typologies). Once a typology or a taxonomy is established it can help not only to pare down the "vast array of

---

[211] Hambrick (1983), p. 214, for similar statements see also Miller (1981), Meyer et al. (1993), pp. 1175-1176.
[212] Kluge (1999), pp. 26-27.
[213] Amshoff (1993), pp. 90-92.
[214] Kluge (1999), pp. 31-34.
[215] Hambrick (1984), p. 28, Meyer et al. (1993), p. 1182. See, however, McKelvey (1975), p. 509 who discusses contradicting definitions of the terms. While the different labels are not important, the underlying differentiation is considered crucial (Carper/Snizek (1980), p. 65).

combinations a researcher must consider"[216], reduce complexity,[217] and separate a few types[218] but also to infer from a few variables to a complete type and thus make predictions on other items by simply analyzing the relevant dimensions.[219] In addition, typologies and taxonomies can be "a basis of theory development and hypothesis testing"[220].

Table 2-6: Typologies versus taxonomies (Source: Slightly adapted from Bensaou/Venkatraman (1995), p. 1472)

Distinctive characteristics	Testing typologies	Uncovering taxonomies
Major advantages	Theory-driven and hence results can be assessed against a priori specifications	Naturally occurring patterns may be uncovered that might shed on the limits of extant theories
Disadvantages	Empirical results that refute the theoretical specification may not be powerful to highlight any inherent weaknesses in the integrity of the typology	No underlying theory or conceptual model to guide the selection of variables
Theoretical assumptions	Positivist; typology is mutually exclusive and collectively exhaustive	Interpretive; taxonomies are casually interpreted in light of a conveniently available set of theories
Methodological assumptions	Methodology is assumed to be in line with the theoretical typology (for instance, discriminant analysis would discriminate across the different types)	Stability of the configurations; configurations are not an artifact of the chosen analytical method

---

[216] Hambrick (1983), p. 214.
[217] Tsikriktsis (2004), p. 44.
[218] Carper/Snizek (1980), p. 73.
[219] Carper/Snizek (1980), p. 73, Hambrick (1984), p. 27. Typological research is however not restricted to research on organizations. It has also been used in other social sciences, for instance, in linguistic research to develop typologies of languages (Palek (1997), Whaley (1997)).
[220] Rich (1992), p. 758.

Typologies and taxonomies have been applied extensively in the research on organizations, for instance, to classify organizations,[221] strategies,[222] and environments.[223] A well-known example in international business is the Bartlett/Ghoshal typology of the multinational corporation.[224] Some of the more prominent typologies such as the Miles-Snow typology of strategic orientations or the Bartlett/Ghoshal typology have been put to test by other authors.[225] Ketchen Jr. et al. (1997) carried out a meta-analysis of 40 studies and concluded that typologies can serve to differentiate the performance of organizations. Research was originally enthusiastic about the possibility of developing an overarching hierarchy of organizational taxonomies and typologies that would contain all relevant organizational configurations.[226] Even though this optimism seems to have faded, typologies and taxonomies can still be considered valuable methods in organizational research.

2.3.2 OVERVIEW OF SUBSIDIARY TYPOLOGIES

MNCs have long been researched in international business, though mainly from a headquarters perspective.[227] International subsidiaries were only relevant as one form of internationalization. Even where the research subject was the international subsidiary, the focus was very often on the headquarters perspective and important developments in the relative importance of international subsidiaries were not taken into account:[228]

- International subsidiaries have grown in size. As MNCs have entered more international markets and often have not expanded their business in their home country, to the same degree, international activities have increased their share in the business portfolio. While this is true of all MNCs, it applies particularly to MNCs with relatively small home markets, such as the Swiss company Nestlé.[229]

---

[221] Blau/Scott (1963), Etzioni (1975).
[222] Miller/Friesen (1977), Miles/Snow (1978), Miller/Friesen (1978), Miller/Friesen (1980), Hambrick (1984).
[223] Hambrick (1983). For an overview of taxonomies and typologies, see Carper/Snizek (1980).
[224] Bartlett/Ghoshal (1989).
[225] See Zahra/Pearce II (1990) for an evaluation of the Miles-Snow typology, see Leong/Tan (1993), Harzing (2000) for an analysis of the Bartlett-Ghoshal typology, and Harzing/Noorderhaven (2006) for a test of the Gupta-Govindarajan typology.
[226] Carper/Snizek (1980), pp. 73-74, Hambrick (1984), p. 31.
[227] Nohria/Ghoshal (1997), pp. 7-8.
[228] Schmid et al. (1998), pp. 2-3.
[229] Kutschker et al. (2001), p. 1.

2 – Theoretical Foundations 59

- In addition, subsidiaries have taken on increasingly important activities for the MNC. This development culminates in the establishment of centers of excellence that can have more competence for a given topic than any other unit in the MNC, including headquarters.[230]

This has led to the replacement of a purely hierarchical model of MNC organization and coordination with a model that has more than one center.[231] Eventually, the importance of the subsidiary has been recognized in international business research. During the last twenty years, scholars from this discipline have increasingly acknowledged that MNC subsidiaries can take on various roles. Once international subsidiaries became more significant – e.g., measured by their profit or revenue share – research started to evaluate parts of the MNC that lie outside the original country of residence.[232] Consequently, one stream within international business research emerged that has made extensive use of typologies to differentiate and describe international subsidiaries.[233]

Among the first publications to develop a subsidiary typology are those by White/Poynter (1984) that were inspired by the question whether the increase of foreign subsidiaries in Canada was beneficial to the economy as they brought investment and employment, or would they rather create a too strong dependency on the foreign investor. Later classifications took a firm perspective, analyzing which different subsidiaries exist and how they need to be coordinated. Not only were many new dimensions introduced over time but the typologies also became more specialized, such as typologies specifically developed for R&D subsidiaries.[234]

While each of the contributions in this research stream has its own findings, we propose to organize these around the following notions: (1) Typologies focus on the subsidiary as an independent company that can take on a specific role. (2) The roles that subsidiaries have can impact their relationships to headquarters, to other subsidiaries, and to external partners. (3) Subsidiaries can develop over time and change their roles. (4) The

---

[230] Moore (2001), p. 276.
[231] Schmid et al. (1998), p. 4.
[232] Schmid (2004), p. 237.
[233] For an overview of subsidiary roles, see Schmid/Kutschker (2003). Also within international business research, typologies have been used for several purposes. For instance, Calori et al. (2000) develop a taxonomy of innovative international strategies. As discussed above, there is a distinction between a theoretically derived typology and an empirically developed taxonomy. In this work, the term "typology" will be used, as is common in MNC research, to refer to "subsidiary typologies".
[234] For instance, Kuemmerle (1999).

entire MNC needs to adapt to the demands that are placed on it globally and locally. These four levels of findings are detailed below and are illustrated in Figure 2-7.[235]

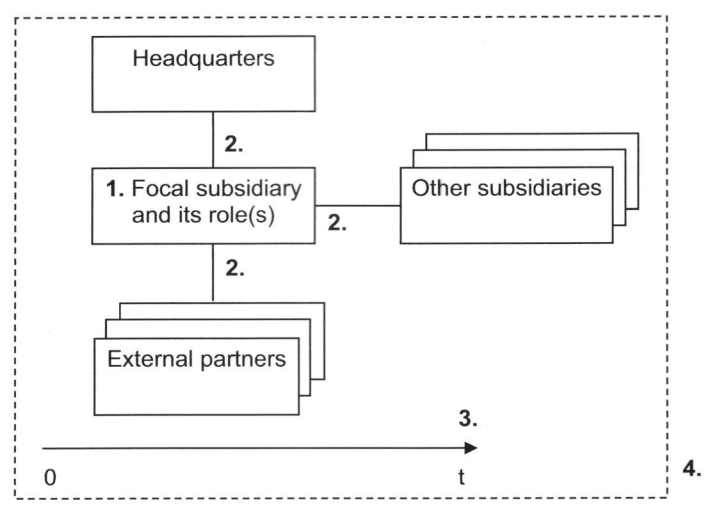

Figure 2-7: Differentiating levels of findings on the international subsidiary

1. *Focus on the international subsidiary as independent company:* The description of activities of an international subsidiary serves as basic information to differentiate between various types of subsidiaries. This differentiation has been helpful in deriving approaches for typologies of international subsidiaries that describe and categorize subsidiaries according to different criteria. The typologies distinguish the different roles that subsidiaries can have.[236] This detailed look at parts other than the headquarters allows the MNC to recognize whether or not a subsidiary is well positioned to exploit specific local advantages such as lower factor cost or specific knowledge that is available only in one location. Many authors have developed typologies of MNC subsidiaries which cluster subsidiaries according to one or more criteria and propose different, distinguishable types.[237] Some typologies describe the roles that a subsidiary has for the MNC by differentiating them by criteria such as the subsidiary's product scope[238] or

---

[235] It has to be noted that the different topics have often been researched in parallel and that the proposed structure does not necessarily represent a chronological order.
[236] It has been noted that a subsidiary has not only one role but plays different roles depending on the partner with which it is interacting (Schurig (2002), pp. 112-113).
[237] Birkinshaw/Morrison (1995), p. 732.
[238] White/Poynter (1984), D'Cruz (1986).

they combine strategic and organizational measurements to derive different types.[239] Examples of dimensions include the strategic relevance of the local market, the strategic relevance of the subsidiary's competences, or the amount of strategic planning within a subsidiary. Well-known approaches stem from White/Poynter (1984), from Bartlett/Ghoshal (1986), from Gupta/Govindarajan (1991), or from Ferdows (1997).[240] Some of these approaches are based on empirical studies, others are conceptual. Once these different roles have been recognized, MNCs view their subsidiaries not as a group of homogeneous units but rather as a set of distinctive entities with specific tasks, capabilities and resources.[241] The different roles that subsidiaries have are important not only for the description of the MNC, but they also imply specific questions how the MNC has to deal with the different roles. However, many typologies fail to derive specific (management) implications.[242]

2. *Focus on the relationships of an international subsidiary:* Researchers have also looked into the relationships between the subsidiary and the parent company, other subsidiaries (intra-organizational relations), local partners (local relations), and external partners (inter-organizational relations). This approach helped to gain a better understanding of the network of which MNCs consist and within which they act.[243] Different roles are reflected in specific characteristics of the relationships between headquarters and subsidiaries. For instance, different roles will require different models of coordination.[244] Thus, the subsidiary role impacts on the headquarters-subsidiary relationship. Several subsidiary typologies have established not only different types but also derived implications for management. Bartlett/Ghoshal (1986) distinguish types and provide specific management recommendations how to develop and/or use each type. Birkinshaw/Morrison (1995) link different types from existing typologies and performance and propose a "fit" model. Gupta/Govindarajan (1991) evaluate in more detail the relationships between headquarters and subsidiary and their potential implications, such as different coordination mechanisms. The

---

[239] Bartlett/Ghoshal (1986), Ferdows (1997).
[240] For a short overview of typologies, see Schmid/Kutschker (2003) or Schmid (2004), pp. 240-241. For a more detailed description, see Schmid et al. (1998).
[241] Schmid (2004), p. 237.
[242] Some exceptions are Gupta/Govindarajan (1991) and Nobel/Birkinshaw (1998).
[243] Schmid et al. (2002), pp. 45-47.
[244] See, for instance, Edwards et al. (2002), pp. 185-186.

same approach is taken by Jarillo/Martinez (1990) and Martinez/Jarillo (1991) who first develop a typology and then link each type to a specific set of coordination mechanisms.

3. *Focus on the development of an international subsidiary:* In addition to the static description of a subsidiary and its role, some authors have focused on the development of subsidiaries over time, taking a process view. This viewpoint helps to understand how subsidiaries come into existence and how they change.[245] Birkinshaw (1996), for instance, evaluates how a subsidiary gains or loses a specific mandate and thereby stresses that subsidiaries are not to be considered static units but that they develop in the course of time. Birkinshaw (1998) discusses how subsidiary initiative can impact the development of the MNC, and Schmid/Schurig (2003) analyze how foreign subsidiaries acquire capabilities that are important for the entire corporation. Uhlenbruck (2004) researches how subsidiaries recently acquired by MNCs develop over time.

4. *MNCs as networks:* Subsidiaries are not only part of the MNC but they can be considered firms themselves. The recognition of the subsidiaries' relevance was an important step for the "paradigm" shift from a homogeneous and hierarchical organization to a "differentiated network"[245] Several subsidiaries of large MNCs are amongst the biggest corporations in their host countries. They often have a substantial amount of autonomy which they use to find optimal solutions for the local environment in which they are located. These solutions, however, might not be optimal from a global or corporate-wide point of view. Finding a way to deal with the demands of the headquarters while at the same time coping with those of the local environment is a struggle that many researchers have addressed and that is often described as the competing demands of global integration and local differentiation.[247] How the MNC responds to these demands depends on the individual situation of each subsidiary and might be different for each subsidiary. The notion of the MNC as a network warrants more extended

---

[245] Andersson (2003), p. 427, Schmid (2004), p. 239.
[246] Nohria/Ghoshal (1997), p. 4.
[247] See, for instance, Ghoshal/Nohria (1989), Nohria/Ghoshal (1997). This general integration-differentiation framework has been applied in several industries. For a specific application in the consulting industry, see Kriegmeier (2003).

discussion on its own, and we will return to the topic later in the section on underlying organization theory where we again consider network approaches.[248]

Our research is in the first two areas. We will develop a typology to differentiate types of service offshoring subsidiaries and discuss implications for the relationships of the different subsidiary types to the headquarters and – where applicable – to other subsidiaries. We will, however, not consider relationships to external partners. We stress that very often the situation in the local goods market plays a very important role for describing the subsidiary and that the relationships to local actors such as suppliers, customers, and government have often been neglected by research on the international subsidiary (see for exceptions, however, Forsgren/Pedersen (1997), who focus on the relations within the MNC's and the subsidiary's external network). Service offshoring centers are somewhat different, as their role in the MNC is not defined by their position in a local goods market and, consequently, they do not depend as much on the local environment as other subsidiaries, even though they also have local relationships – but mainly for recruitment. Their government relationships are typically somewhat less important than for other subsidiaries as they are not affected by as many local regulations as, for instance, a unit that is directly involved in the goods market. In addition, they might not attract as much interest from host country governments because they often do not come with the multi-million dollar investment that manufacturing offshoring units can bring to a country when they invest in expensive factories and equipment.

We will very briefly touch upon the third point, the development of subsidiaries over time but this is not our main focus. And however interesting the question of how an MNC deals with different subsidiaries to reach a balance of integration and differentiation may be, we have to exclude this discussion and refer it to later research efforts.

2.3.3 TYPOLOGIES AND SERVICE OFFSHORING

Typologies seem ideal for differentiating between the various roles that international subsidiaries can have. Of course, typologies have not gone uncriticized but for our purpose it still seems appropriate to use this methodology. Since many of the shortcomings of other subsidiary typologies are grounded not in the principle of typologies but rather

---

[248] See section 3.3.2.

in the ways that existing examples have been developed, we have decided to discuss the criticism when we describe how we develop our own typology.[249]

To put it very simply, typologies of international subsidiaries are appropriate for dealing with offshoring, as an international subsidiary is needed to do captive offshoring. Since the research questions aim particularly at the different forms of service offshoring subsidiaries, a typology is a logical component of the answer. A subsidiary typology can help explain which types of offshoring centers can exist and how they might differ from each other. Captive service offshoring centers are one form of the international subsidiary and a highly specialized one. However, this specialization is frequently observed within subsidiary research since the process of viewing subsidiaries as an important part of an MNC's network has not yet concluded and is resulting in an ever-increasing differentiation of subsidiary types of which the service offshoring center could be considered one of the most recent forms.

The discussion from above shows how our research is connected to existing research on subsidiaries. However, there is one question that still needs to be answered: Why should we develop a new typology instead of using one of the existing typologies? To discuss this question, we shall now show several criteria that are relevant for our typology:

1. *Coordination as a dependent variable:* As we have already discussed, we want to develop a typology that provides a basis for management implications particularly relating to coordination mechanisms. Thus, we need to exclude typologies that either do not indicate any management implication at all or that use coordination mechanisms as an independent variable.

2. *Theoretical foundation:* To develop sound propositions we need a typology that is firmly based on organizational theory. This has the advantage of making the typology easier to connect to the existing body of knowledge and free it from the criticism that typologies result from "armchair reasoning".

3. *General scope of typology:* Some typologies have their focus on a specific function. Unless there was a typology for service offshoring, these would not be appropriate for our research. We could however, use a more general typology and adapt it to our purpose.

---

[249] See section 4.1.2.

2.3.4 EVALUATION OF EXISTING TYPOLOGIES

We have evaluated a range of subsidiary typologies to determine whether they are appropriate for our research. We base our analysis on the comprehensive review of Schmid et al. (1998) and apply the criteria we established above. The results of our analysis are shown in Table 2-7. The first column indicates the typology under consideration. In the second column we show whether or not the typology uses coordination mechanisms as a dependent variable and mark relevant typologies with a tick ("✓"). In the next column we identify whether the typology derives its dimensions and causalities from an underlying organizational theory (again we mark those which do with a tick ("✓"). Finally, we mark those typologies that claim to be adequate for any type of subsidiary and not, for instance, restricted to a specific function.

Table 2-7: Evaluation of subsidiary typologies for service offshoring (Source: Partially based on Kutschker/Schmid (2005), p. 335)

Typology	Coordination as dependent variable	Grounding in organizational theory	General scope, e.g., not function-specific
White/Poynter (1984)	Emphasis of importance of world product mandates for local economy, but no reference to coordination	Not explicitly mentioned	✓
D'Cruz (1986), p. 77	"Formal and informal strategic plans" is one dimension	Not explicitly mentioned	✓
D'Cruz (1986), p. 77[250]	"Decision-making autonomy" is one dimension	Not explicitly mentioned	✓

---

[250] As Schmid et al. (1998) point out, Surlemont presents two typologies in one publication that we here also present separately (Schmid et al. (1998), p. 25).

Typology	Coordination as dependent variable	Grounding in organizational theory	General scope, e.g., not function-specific
Bartlett/Ghoshal (1986)	✓	Not explicitly mentioned	✓
Ferdows (1997)[251]		Not explicitly mentioned	(Focused on manufacturing units)
Jarillo/Martinez (1990)	✓	Not explicitly mentioned	✓
Taggart (1997)[252]		Not explicitly mentioned	✓
Gupta/Govindarajan (1991)	✓	Not explicitly mentioned	(Focused on knowledge flows)
Birkinshaw/Morrison (1995)		Not explicitly mentioned	
Forsgren/Pedersen (1997)		Not explicitly mentioned	✓
Surlemont (1996)		Not explicitly mentioned	
Nobel/Birkinshaw (1998)*	✓	Not explicitly mentioned	(Focused on R&D units)
Kuemmerle (1999)*		Not explicitly mentioned	(Focused on R&D units)

---

[251] Ferdows has presented his typology already in an earlier publication (Ferdows (1989)).
[252] In one of his articles Taggart also evaluates the typology by Jarillo/Martinez and extends it by one type (Schmid et al. (1998), pp. 58-59). Since this is not a new and independent typology, we have not evaluated it separately.

Typology	Coordination as dependent variable	Grounding in organizational theory	General scope, e.g., not function-specific
Jones/Davis (2000)*		Not explicitly mentioned	(Focused on R&D units)

✓ – criterion is fulfilled

Note: * These subsidiary typologies were published only after the evaluation by Schmid et al. (1998).

This overview of existing typologies shows that some of them fulfill some of the criteria that are relevant to our research; however, none fulfills all criteria:

- Most typologies do not specify which coordination mechanisms are to be used with a specific type. Those typologies that do are not applicable for our research because of their narrow scope (such as, for instance, Gupta/Govindarajan (1991)) or because they are not based on organizational theories (such as, for instance, Bartlett/Ghoshal (1986)).

- None of the publications on typologies explicitly explains the foundation in organizational theory that we need to derive propositions on coordination mechanisms. This implies that our table cannot serve as a distinguisher between typologies on that dimension any more. We still decided to leave it in to demonstrate the lack of (explicit) theoretical foundation. We admit there is room for discussion on this point since many of the authors have probably been guided by theoretical considerations; however, none makes these considerations explicit. Still, it is argued that many typologies assume a contingency approach.[253]

- With regard to our last criterion – general scope of the typology – most typologies are not geared towards a specific kind of subsidiary but rather claim to be

---

[253] Kutschker/Schmid (2005), p. 354. For the relationship between typologies and the contingency approach, see section 4.1.2.

applicable to the entire spectrum – with the exception of a series of recent additions that focus on the R&D function.[254]

While we cannot review the entire spectrum of subsidiary typologies listed above, we want to present one typology (Ferdows (1997)) that is used to differentiate between different manufacturing subsidiaries. We do this for two reasons: First, it shall serve to illustrate how a typology works. Second, we selected this particular example to demonstrate the different aspects that Ferdows emphasizes for manufacturing offshoring subsidiaries versus those that we want to analyze with regard to service offshoring.

Ferdows argues that managers need to be aware of the differences between subsidiaries and have high expectations from each of the sub-units.[255] He distinguishes between six types of subsidiaries and proposes ways in which subsidiaries can migrate from a low value-adding position to one that adds more value.[256] There is one subsidiary type that could potentially be used to describe the low-cost end of the service offshoring phenomenon: For low-value, mostly administrative activities Ferdows' "offshore" type can be a good approach. He explains that "an offshore factory is established to produce specific items at a low cost"[257], adding that such a factory is not intended to be innovative but rather to execute the instructions handed down to it.[258] However, in Ferdows' opinion, MNCs should seek to upgrade their existing subsidiaries. Even though he admits that it can make sense to leave them in their current position he claims that there are huge benefits to be gained from upgrading them.[259] This recommendation can be considered a management implication, although there is no reference to the coordination mechanisms in which we are interested. Also, Ferdows does not explicitly refer to organizational theory, and it is not entirely clear how he developed his typology.[260] Interestingly, service offshoring centers are typically set up with a very narrow scope and without (at least the planned) intention to be upgraded in the foreseeable future. Also, not all service offshoring centers do not correspond to the statement that "the subsidiaries of a multinational organization develop unique, differentiated sets of competencies and capabilities due to the different international environments in which they oper-

---

[254] Ferdows (1989), Ferdows (1997), Nobel/Birkinshaw (1998), Kuemmerle (1999), Jones/Davis (2000).
[255] Ferdows (1997), p. 74.
[256] Ferdows (1997), p. 79.
[257] Ferdows (1997), p. 76.
[258] Ferdows (1997), p. 77.
[259] Ferdows (1997), p. 79.
[260] Schmid et al. (1998), p. 41.

ate"[261]. Service offshoring centers serve only internal customers and thus do not have direct contact with competitors. Consequently, they will not be able to learn from local competition. Equally, they do not have many local suppliers.[262] As they focus on only one or a few services they do not acquire pre-products from local suppliers. Thus, their competencies are very much focused on the efficiency that they gain by using cheaper local labor and by optimally designing their processes.

As a consequence of our evaluation, it seems appropriate to develop a new typology which takes into account the specific characteristics of service offshoring and which is the basis for delineating coordination requirements. Our typology should be capable of describing several scenarios in which MNC pursue offshoring. However, before we begin developing the typology, we will discuss its second element, namely coordination.

2.4 COORDINATION MECHANISMS

This section will introduce coordination and define it for the use in this study. We will briefly outline different dimensions of coordination and then focus more on the most relevant topic for our further research: coordination mechanisms. We will provide an overview of coordination mechanisms in the subsequent section, evaluate them and show their relevance for the current research. The operationalization for the empirical part of our research will not be addressed here but will be provided in chapter 5 together with the description of the methodology.

2.4.1 OVERVIEW OF COORDINATION

Mintzberg called coordination one of the two main principles of management.[263] The first one is differentiation which relates to the division of a system into several components that then have to be coordinated to work as a whole.[264] The discussion of coordination has deep roots in the history of management, and this is not the place for a complete review. In any case, the core of the concept is relatively stable – even if there is an ongoing discussion surrounding the relationship of coordination and control. We will comment on that discussion later but will first provide our definition of coordination. While coordination can generally be thought of as the process of aligning several dis-

---

[261] O'Donnell (2000), p. 530.
[262] Not having local competitors and/or local suppliers is very different from what is considered typical for an international subsidiary (e.g., O'Donnell (2000), p. 530).
[263] Mintzberg (1989), p. 112.
[264] Khandwalla (1973b), pp. 481-482.

persed activities for a common goal, we want to be more specific and use a definition that is tuned to the dispersed activities of an MNC.

Within an MNC, coordination can be understood as "the process of integrating activities that remain dispersed across subsidiaries"[265]. Coordination itself has several facets. It is carried out by (1) actors that use (2) different coordination mechanisms to cope with situations with (3) different coordination requirements. Moreover, coordination can (4) change over time and it is (5) interdependent with organizational structure:

1. It is typically thought that coordination is actively carried out or at least influenced by *actors*. Actors can be individuals or organizations. They can have different levels of involvement in coordination and can be responsible for the design of coordination or for the continuous execution of coordination. They can also be described in terms of their hierarchical level and with regard to their involvement in the specific coordination situation under consideration (for instance, is a specific coordination job the main task of the actor or is it just one of his/her many tasks?).

2. Coordination is achieved by means of *coordination mechanisms*.[266] Thus, coordination mechanisms serve to integrate the dispersed activities of an MNC and, in our case, the activities of service offshoring centers. Different coordination mechanisms can be understood as alternative ways to achieve a common goal – that of coordination. However, not every coordination mechanism might be appropriate in every setting.

3. MNCs have high *coordination requirements* as they are characterized by a high degree of dispersion of activities across different countries. Although there are many different possible configurations of an MNC there will always be at least a minimal requirement for coordination due to this division of activities and the resulting interdependencies and interfaces.[267] Even within MNCs there can be different levels of coordination requirements as some situations might call for very intense coordination whereas others do not.

---

[265] Martinez/Jarillo (1991), p. 431. For different definitions of coordination see Van De Ven et al. (1976), Wolf (1994), pp. 25-28, Reger (1997), pp. 36-37. However, none of these differ greatly from the one proposed here.
[266] Wolf (1994), p. 27.
[267] Kutschker/Schmid (2005), pp. 991-996.

2 – Theoretical Foundations 71

4. Coordination can change *over time*. When a coordination system is initially designed or emerges, this can be analytically distinguished from the phase in which the coordination is operating in a "steady state". However, coordination is not a "one-off effort". Rather, it can be considered a continuous process whose individual steps are carried out repeatedly.[268]

5. Coordination is interdependent with *organizational structure* (which we understand as the division of labor in different departments and hierarchies). A decision on organizational structure will almost inevitably influence coordination.[269] And vice versa, decisions on coordination can also alter the structure of an organization even if coordination is seen as more flexible and adaptable. However, it is important to regard coordination in conjunction with a given organizational structure.[270]

In the current research, the focus will be on *coordination mechanisms* and their specific adaptation to the characteristics of an MNC subsidiary and the MNC network. We will also consider the intensity of coordination, as expressed in overall *coordination requirements*. The coordinating actors will of course play an important role, but not as a contingency in our research. We will consider the relationships between organizations (in our case headquarters and subsidiaries) and not the role played by an individual in that constellation. We will only evaluate the coordination that affects the organization as a whole and not the individual perceptions of the managers in charge. In addition, the focus here is on an operating system and not one that is still in the design phase. Since this is very hard to distinguish (especially in younger organizations), we cannot exclude cases in which coordination mechanisms are in a constant state of adaptation. However, we exclude cases that have not progressed beyond the conceptual stage and where no operations are in place. With regard to organizational structure, we will concentrate on the coordination mechanisms that are in use *between* the different units of an MNC and not *within* one unit. Moreover, we will not question the MNC's decision to offshore a given activity but will ask what coordination mechanisms are applied after the structural decision has been taken.

---

[268] Wolf (1994), p. 27.
[269] Pugh et al. (1969), Child (1972), Ouchi (1977).
[270] Wolf (1994), p. 117.

Performing research on coordination almost always leads inevitably to the question how coordination and control are linked. Coordination and control are often discussed together and are seen as methods of integrating the dispersed activities of the MNC.[271] Cray is potentially the one author who has made the most prominent differentiation in international business research: In his contribution, coordination represents a looser form of organizing, especially when it comes to a larger number of entities and their functions that need to be organized.[272] On the other hand, the "purpose of *control* [emphasis added] is to minimize idiosyncratic behavior and to hold individuals or groups to enunciated policy, thus making performance predictable"[273]. Other authors, however, use the two terms synonymously.[274] Yet others refer only to control and include coordination implicitly.[275] We have not found arguments that would make a specific differentiation necessary for the purpose of this work and will thus work with *coordination* as the overarching term.[276]

We have discussed how we understand coordination but have not yet considered in more detail what coordination is good for. We therefore want to look at the extreme of (1) an imaginary MNC without any coordination between headquarters and subsidiaries and (2) at the specific needs for coordination in service offshoring situations:

(1) In an imaginary MNC without coordination the different subunits could very easily carry out redundant or even incompatible activities. It would also most likely lead to non-compliance with financial regulations, as companies are required to report financial data on their international subsidiaries – something that is not possible without coordination between them. Coordination is not only necessary for the MNC to create economies of scale and prevent redundancy.[277] Some organizational forms will not be possible without sufficient coordination. For instance, some MNCs have concentrated the entire responsibility for one process in their value chain at a single location. If there is

---

[271] Cray (1984), pp. 85-87.
[272] Cray (1984), p. 87. For a critique of (t)his differentiation, see Roth/Nigh (1992), Wolf (1994), p. 115.
[273] Cray (1984), p. 86.
[274] Ouchi speaks mainly of "control" but also uses both terms coordination and control together, without further differentiation (Ouchi (1977), p. 96). Mascarenhas (1984) and Marcati (1989), pp. 42-44 use the terms interchangeably. Roth/Nigh (1992), pp. 281-283 distinguish between coordination and control; however, they use "coordination" for more informal coordination mechanisms and "control" for bureaucratic/technocratic coordination mechanisms.
[275] Egelhoff (1984).
[276] We will actually introduce output control later as one coordination mechanism and in this case refer to "control" since the term "output control" is established in the literature.
[277] Reger (1997), p. 5.

no coordination between this location and the other units, the whole firm might be negatively affected. Thus, coordination is needed in the first place to secure alignment of the parts that have been distributed in an international division of labor – such as in the case of service offshoring.

(2) Service offshoring creates a new form of division of labor since it increases the degree of specialization in the different units. Thus, there are new interfaces to be coordinated. Not only can the number of interfaces increase, but also the coordination mechanisms can possibly change. Take for instance an MNC that bundles accounting departments located in several foreign subsidiaries into a single service offshoring center. For headquarters and many MNC units, this new center will be geographically more distant than the previous accounting departments so that personal, face-to-face coordination might no longer be effective. In addition, the center will also have to supply services to a number of internal clients whereas previously each of the accounting departments had just one client which was the respective subsidiary.

Therefore, it is necessary to create an appropriate configuration of activities and to decide upon the coordination mechanisms to be used. International business research has found that there is a link between the activities and the role a subsidiary has and the level and kind of coordination that is required.[278] Based on different types of service offshoring subsidiaries to be identified within this study, we will ask which coordination mechanisms companies are using. The next section will discuss different coordination mechanisms in more detail and show how they can be categorized.

2.4.2 EVALUATION OF COORDINATION MECHANISMS

Research on coordination has a long tradition. Scholars have analyzed the types and determinants of coordination mechanisms[279] and have then connected the different MNC types to different coordination mechanisms in order to answer questions like: "Which coordination mechanism is most likely to occur in a transnational/multinational/ international firm?" In time, the focus of research turned toward an individual analysis of the subsidiary. Each subsidiary can be considered with its specific environment and characteristics that need to be taken into account.[280] The present research can be seen in this

---

[278] Bartlett/Ghoshal (1986), pp. 92-94, Martinez/Jarillo (1991), p. 441.
[279] Hage/Aiken (1967), Van De Ven et al. (1976).
[280] O'Donnell (2000), p. 530.

tradition as it tries to find coordination mechanisms that are consistent with the characteristics of the subsidiary.

The identification of different coordination mechanisms was an initial step in coordination research. It led to the question which factors determine the choice of coordination mechanisms. Early studies pinpointed factors such as size, interdependence, uncertainty and heterogeneity/complexity.[281]

International business research has identified a large variety of coordination mechanisms[282] which have been classified in various ways. A very early classification is that of Leavitt (1964). He sees organizations as an interplay of structure, technology and actors that work together to accomplish the tasks of the organization. For the management of the organization, he distinguishes between structural, technical and human approaches.

- *Structural approaches* work through the decision for an organizational structure, through the establishment of corporate centers or project organizations, and through the centralization of decision making (which reduces autonomy on the lower levels of the hierarchy).

- *Technical (or technocratic) approaches* work through the prescribing of behavior that is often done by standardizing of tasks through, e.g., rules and programs, plans, budget. Often, standardization leads to formalization, with standard processes documented in practice manuals.

- *Human (or personal) approaches* directly guide behavior through personal interaction that can take place by direct personal coordination, visits, transfers and cultural coordination that is a more implicit coordination mechanism.

Leavitt's classification has been widely used by other authors[283] and will be used for our study as well.

---

[281] Harzing (1999), p. 82. Some of the early studies include Lawrence/Lorsch (1967), Thompson (1967), Pugh et al. (1969), Khandwalla (1977).

[282] Ouchi (1977), Ouchi (1979), Baliga/Jaeger (1984), Egelhoff (1984), Martinez/Jarillo (1989), Roth/Nigh (1992).

[283] For existing applications, see Lundberg (1972), Nielsen (1984), Martin (2003), Kutschker/Schmid (2005), p. 1005. Leavitt's classification can also be found in Khandwalla (1973a), p. 285.

Later classification schemes added another dimension. It was mainly Ouchi's work to differentiate coordination mechanisms by the object to which they refer. He distinguishes mechanisms that directly guide the behavior of actors (behavior control) and those that establish the goal (output control).[284] The approaches we have mentioned above – structural, technocratic, and personal – fall into the category that primarily affect the behavior of the actors in an organization. Ouchi's second category focuses on coordination through the control of the result of that behavior. We add his dimension to our threefold classification and distinguish between structural, technocratic, personal and output-based mechanisms of coordination. An overview of our categorization and the difference between behavioral coordination and output control can be found in Figure 2-8.

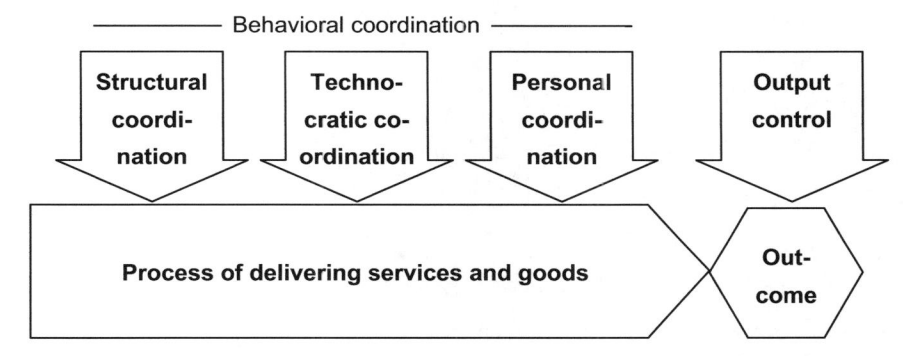

Figure 2-8: Differentiation between behavioral coordination and output control

Our four-fold approach is in line with several of the existing classification schemes:

- The approaches by Ouchi (1977), p. 97 and Baliga/Jaeger (1984), p. 26 add the important differentiation between output-based and behavior-based coordination mechanisms that we will adopt for our research.

- Martinez and Jarillo's classification is commonly cited in international business research.[285] They distinguish coordination mechanisms based on the degree of subtleness and determine the two classes "structural and formal mechanisms"

---

[284] Ouchi/Maguire (1975), Ouchi (1977). This differentiation was adopted in later coordination research (see, for instance, Gençtürk/Aulakh (1995), p. 757, Cardinal et al. (2004), p. 414, Baldauf et al. (2005), p. 8, Brown et al. (2005), p. 157, Turner/Makhija (2006), p. 203).

[285] Martinez/Jarillo (1989).

and "more informal and subtle mechanisms". Our categories can be matched to their approach as well.

- Harzing (1999) compares different classification schemes for coordination mechanisms and establishes a new scheme that distinguishes personal centralized control, bureaucratic formalized control, control by socialization and networks, and output control. While Harzing combines structural and personal approaches in what she calls "personal centralized control" we consider it more appropriate to follow the majority of scholars who distinguish between the two approaches. On the other hand, we include her type "control by socialization and networks" into our category "personal approaches".

- Kutschker/Schmid (2005) provide an extensive overview of coordination mechanisms and apply Leavitt's original categorization. However, they also mention other mechanisms that are closer to market approaches.[286]

- Other prominent examples include Wolf (1994), p. 117 and Kenter (1985), p. 81 from the German academic community. They also refer to Leavitt's original contribution but use it in an adapted form.

Thus, the classification we apply is consistent with many of the existing approaches.[287] But even if there can never be one categorization that suits all of the possible diverse applications, we believe that our qualitative research design allows us to derive findings on the level not only of the category of mechanisms but also on the individual mechanism. In addition, on the level of the individual instruments it seems that research has identified a fairly complete and consistent list of entries.[288] However, these coordination mechanisms have been applied only rarely to subsidiary types (with few exceptions such as Gupta/Govindarajan (1991) and Nobel/Birkinshaw (1998)). Some previous studies that adopted a network perspective on the MNC have analyzed only price, au-

---

[286] Kutschker/Schmid (2005), pp. 1023-1032.
[287] For another example, see Kim et al. (2003), pp. 329-330. There are, however, also classification schemes that do not readily fit the mainstream categories and that do not seem free of overlaps or omissions (see, for example, Mascarenhas (1984), p. 95 who distinguishes impersonal methods, system-sensitivity, compensation system, and personal communication). We also do not consider another, less frequently mentioned coordination mechanism, namely input control. In this case, coordination takes place through the control of the membership of the organization (Jaeger/Baliga (1985), p. 118).
[288] At least the lists of coordination mechanisms to be found in Harzing (1999), pp. 18-19 and Wolf (1994), p. 116 show many repeating entries for differently labeled categories.

thority and trust as coordination mechanisms.[289] We feel that this categorization is too broad and have therefore developed a more fine-grained approach.

Even though we consider the classification that we will describe in more detail below adequate for our research, we want to emphasize that coordination mechanisms are often not easy to single out and identify. Also, they are typically used in parallel and "occur in various combinations"[290]. Accordingly, there will almost always be an overlap of different, often competing mechanisms.[291] Thus, questions on the use of coordination mechanisms will probably focus more on "how much" rather than on "if at all".

2.4.3 RESULT OF EVALUATION AND CONSEQUENCES FOR THIS STUDY

Since no contributions in international business research have hitherto investigated coordination mechanisms for service offshoring subsidiaries, we will try to fill this gap and apply the findings from research on coordination mechanisms to research on service offshoring.

In doing so, we will adopt the classification of structural, technocratic, output-based and personal coordination. Within each of these four categories, we chose to concentrate on specific coordination mechanisms which will be outlined below:

1. *Structural instruments*: Within the category of structural instruments, we will concentrate on the degree of *autonomy in decision making*. Service offshoring centers can vary in terms of how much decision making power is centralized at a higher hierarchical (most often headquarters) level and how much decision making power is transferred to them.[292] Thus, we will look at the degree of autonomy a service offshoring subsidiary has when making decisions.[293] Other structural instruments, such as the overall organizational structure or the division of a unit into separate departments, are not of relevance for our study. This is because we focus on the inter-unit coordination with a given service offshoring constellation and not on the coordination that take place within one unit.

---

[289] Håkansson/Snehota (1995), pp. 361-362.
[290] Ouchi (1979), p. 834.
[291] Nobel/Birkinshaw (1996), p. 166.
[292] Martinez/Jarillo (1989), p. 491, Kutschker/Schmid (2005), p. 1011.
[293] We consider autonomy to be the opposite of centralization of decision making. Thus, an increase in centralization of decision making reduces autonomy and vice versa.

2. *Technocratic mechanisms*: Within the category of technocratic mechanisms we will consider the degree of *standardization* of the relationship. We define *standardization* as the degree to which procedures and roles within and across relationships are established in rules and plans and maintained independently of the time or the interacting parties.[294] In addition, we will ask how *formalized* the relationships are. A relationship can be formalized, for instance, by documenting rules and plans which render procedures explicit and make knowledge available in documents.[295]

3. *Output-based coordination:* When the focus of coordination on the results instead of the process and the behavior, one speaks of output-based coordination.[296] Output control is used to "regulate results or outcomes."[297] We define output-based coordination as the up-front definition of results and the eventual evaluation of results.

4. Coordination based on *personal approaches:*[298] Within the category of personal approaches, we focus on *direct personal coordination* (the coordination of activities through – in our case remote – interaction of two or more people), *visits* and *employee transfers* between the offshoring subsidiary and other MNC units as well as on *culture-based coordination*.[299] By culture-based coordination we mean normative integration; we assume that culture can be the glue that holds various MNC units together.[300]

An overview of the coordination mechanisms together with their definitions can be found in Table 2-8. In addition to these categories, we will consider the extent of *coordination requirements* that points to the amount of coordination mechanisms needed for

---

[294] Pugh et al. (1968), p. 74. In their extensive overview, Kutschker/Schmid (2005), pp. 1012-1017 differentiate methods for standardization even further into rules, programs, plans, budgets, and reporting systems. However, most of these can be considered special cases of rules and plans to which we refer here. Formalization is the degree to which all of these mechanisms are fixed in documents.
[295] Pugh et al. (1968), p. 75, Harzing (1999), p. 21, Kutschker/Schmid (2005), pp. 1017-1018.
[296] Ouchi/Maguire (1975), pp. 559-560, Ouchi (1978), p. 174, Gençtürk/Aulakh (1995), p. 757.
[297] Cardinal et al. (2004), p. 414.
[298] Here again we build on the classification by Kutschker/Schmid (2005), p. 1007. However, we do not include self alignment (Kutschker/Schmid (2005), p. 1020), which comes very close to our understanding of autonomy. Also we do not consider the standardization of roles a personal coordination mechanism (Kutschker/Schmid (2005), p. 1022) since we do not evaluate the level of the individual actor. We treat standardization in the category of technocratic mechanisms.
[299] Kutschker/Schmid (2005), pp. 1019-1023.
[300] See Ouchi (1980), Hedlund (1986), Hedlund/Rolander (1990).

the coordination of the service offshoring center (for instance, the time and resources that are needed for coordination).

Table 2-8: Coordination mechanisms in use for this study

Category of coordination	Mechanisms	Definition
(Overarching)	Coordination requirements	Resources needed for the coordination of the service offshoring subsidiary
Structural coordination	Autonomy	Level of hierarchy where a decision is taken
Technocratic coordination	Standardization	Establishment of procedures and roles in rules and plans that are independent of time and actors
	Formalization	Documentation of activities on paper or in systems
Output-based coordination	Output control	Up-front establishment of goals and control of results
Personal coordination	Direct personal coordination	Personal (remote) instructions by another person
	Visits	Short-term trip to subsidiary by headquarters employee or vice versa
	Transfers	Long-term assignment of headquarters employee to subsidiary or vice versa
	Cultural coordination	Normative integration, shared values across units

Now we have defined the framework that we will use to discuss coordination in service offshoring settings.[301] However, before we proceed, we still need to answer one last question: does the research deal with the coordination of the service offshoring subsidiary or with the coordination of the service delivery out of a service offshoring subsidiary? The assumption that we make is that the two will be very closely aligned, if not entirely identical. There are several reasons for this approach:

- The first reason is related to the research area. Service offshoring subsidiaries are – at least compared to the MNCs they belong to – typically rather small units without large overheads. Their only purpose is to deliver the services they were designed for. As a consequence, much of the decision making authority is located in units other than the service offshoring subsidiary. If this is the case, then the only coordination requirement that arises is that of the service delivery. This can be very different for a large international subsidiary of an MNC. Take, for instance, Siemens USA where coordination not only occurs between many different business units (such as for the distribution of a product that is developed in Germany and sold in the U.S.) but also for the entire country (such as for the consolidation of financial statements). In such a case, coordination obviously takes place on many different levels. In the case of a service offshoring center with a limited service portfolio and with a very flat hierarchy there is just one activity – the execution of services – to be coordinated. Besides the limited size and complexity, the service offshoring subsidiary does not usually have responsibility for a local market.

- An additional reason to look at the coordination of the service as being identical with the coordination of the center is that only activities can be coordinated.[302] Coordination always refers – as discussed above – to activities and not to structures. Structures cannot be coordinated, thus, when authors refer to the coordination of subsidiaries, they typically refer to the coordination of the activities of the subsidiary. When there are many different activities, there needs to be additional differentiation. When there is just one activity, i.e. the execution of the service, the coordination of the service delivery becomes the coordination of the subsidiary. For instance, a typical budgeting process with several interactions between headquarters and the subsidiary is something that might be very com-

---

[301] This result corresponds to the findings in section 2.4 in Schmid/Daub (2005).
[302] Baliga/Jaeger (1984), p. 25.

mon for a sales subsidiary but not for a service offshoring subsidiary.[303] That is why we consider it appropriate to take these two levels of coordination as one.

- Finally, coordination research frequently addresses the activities that a subsidiary carries out when researching the coordination of the entire unit. For instance, Cray (1984) asks for the functions the subsidiary provides. Martinez/Jarillo (1991) specifically research the coordination of the R&D, marketing, purchasing, and manufacturing functions. Björkman et al. (2004) consider the activity "transfer of knowledge". Thus, for our research, it seems reasonable to concentrate on the activity "service delivery".

---

[303] For instance, in one interview it was mentioned that there was not a separate budgeting process but that the subsidiary would be regularly reimbursed for the costs that it had incurred.

3 Research Model and Propositions – Deriving Typology Dimensions from Organizational Theories

"There is nothing so practical as a good theory"

Kurt Levin

Summary

We have shown how typologies can be used to distinguish types of international subsidiaries and which set of coordination mechanisms is relevant for our research. This chapter develops a) dimensions to characterize service offshoring subsidiaries and – based on these dimensions – b) propositions on the application of coordination mechanisms in these centers. For our first dimension, we take the resource-based view to differentiate service offshoring centers with different strategic relevance. Our second dimension results from an evaluation of network approaches. We use network embeddedness as a concept to distinguish between centers with different degrees of relatedness to their network. For both dimensions, we provide an operationalization that not only helps characterize service offshoring centers in our research but also furthers the methods available to researchers in the traditions of the resource-based view and network approaches.

3.1 SELECTION OF ORGANIZATIONAL THEORY

Any research in the social sciences will be faced with the question of the theory upon which the work should be based. While theories do not necessarily and always make research better, they help to guide it. In addition, without a guiding theory the results of the research are hard to connect to the existing body of research. Ideally, an organizational theory has "proved useful in understanding, explaining, and predicting the functioning of organizations or the behavior of people in them"[304]. For this research, we will use organizational theories to provide a solid basis on which to develop our typology. A common criticism of typologies of international subsidiaries is that they do not provide clear arguments as to how the dimensions are derived and what theories the propositions are based upon.[305] We will base our dimensions on established contributions from the extant knowledge on organizational theories and not only connect our typology to these theories but also further the body of knowledge in this field, especially with regard to empirical applications of the resource-based view and network approaches.

An organizational theory is a statement that explains the relationship between a cause and an effect. It is termed "organizational" because it refers to the ways in which organizations operate. Thus, an organizational theory explains the underlying causes of effects that can be observed in organizations or, alternatively, it shows which effects might be caused by certain circumstances in an organization. This also includes explanations for the existence of organizations. Over time, research has developed a wide variety of organizational theories and it is hard to distinguish what an organizational theory should contain and what excludes a statement from being an "organizational theory".[306]

Obviously, organizational theories are also relevant for the MNC as a special form of organization. However, not all of the wide range of organizational theories have been employed in MNC research.[307] In their discussion of organizational theory in MNC research Ghoshal/Westney distinguish three major perspectives: the organization in its

---

[304] Miner (1984), p. 297.
[305] Schmid et al. (1998), pp. 95-96.
[306] Hatch (1997), pp. 3-9.
[307] Ghoshal/Westney (1993), p. 16.

interactions with the environment, the organizational structure and governance, and organizational culture and norms.[308]

Despite several efforts to summarize and classify them, there is still a huge variety of, in some case highly complex, organizational theories,[309] and it is close to impossible to evaluate every single one for a research project. We therefore opted for a two-pronged approach: First, we will discuss several mainstream theories and show why we decided not to make them the basis of our research. We will then present the organizational theories selected for this research and explain the reasons for our selection. Theories can be evaluated based on their appropriateness for the research project under question. The selection of the appropriate approach is based on three main considerations:[310]

- The opportunities for advancing knowledge on the given topic,
- the practicability and implementability of the approach, and
- the individual position of the researcher regarding ontological, epistemological, anthropological and methodological questions.

As the individual position of the researcher is independent of the organizational theory under consideration, we want to start by briefly explaining our standpoint. From an epistemological perspective, we take a positivist stance. We consider the world as an objective reality that can be observed and described as an independent object. With regard to methodology, we are more inclined to qualitative approaches that are generally considered more interpretative. We do not see this as conflicting with a "realist" standpoint but rather as an expression of the view of the world as complex and multi-facetted (though not exclusively socially constructed).[311] In addition, our view is non-deterministic. We do not believe that companies have only one choice in any given situation but that there are often several equally valuable solutions to their problems (equifinality). However, it is our belief that a solution once implemented depends more

---

[308] Ghoshal/Westney (1993), pp. 10-20. In the second edition of the book, the authors combine the last two perspectives in one category (Ghoshal/Westney (2005), pp. 7-17).
[309] See for an overview Hatch (1997), Jones (2001). For overviews from the German academic community, see Türk (2000), Weik/Lang (2001), Kieser (2002), Weik/Lang (2003). In his reviews of organizational theories, Miner (1984), Miner (2003) empirically evaluates the importance of 24 and 73 theories, respectively.
[310] Schmid (1994), p. 39. Scherer differentiates between the (similar) criteria research interest, ontology and methodology (Scherer (2002), p. 5).
[311] For more on the reasons of our methodological choices, see chapter 5.

on a thorough design of the roles than on the people that fill these roles. Even though the establishment of service offshoring centers is typically a concern for top management and is also dependent on the personalities of managers, the day-to-day coordination of these centers is done on levels below top management. We argue that these levels have less freedom for decisions than top management has. Therefore, an approach that focuses more on formal positions and roles than on individuals should deliver valid results that are more easily transferable to other companies and/or situations (because they depend less on the individual character of the persons involved than on the structural circumstances that can be more easily replicated).[312]

For our evaluation of organizational theories we focus on those that have been frequently used in contributions on outsourcing.[313] We are aware that outsourcing and offshoring are different phenomena.[314] However, the two are similar in that they both involve a relatively new form of division of labor. Thus, we also assume a similarity of the underlying theories and will discuss them with regard to the two other criteria indicated above – knowledge advancement and applicability.

- The organizational theory most prevalently used to analyze outsourcing and offshoring is *transaction cost theory*. For instance, eight out of 21 papers on outsourcing that were examined by Klein (2002) had a transaction cost focus.[315] Transaction cost theory can be very useful in providing answers to why firms use external versus internal partners. We do not see, however, any benefit in using it to describe or explain various types of service offshoring subsidiaries and the resulting coordination mechanisms, since subsidiaries are always hierarchical solutions and we do not consider the decision between a market and a hierarchical solution that precedes the establishment of a captive offshoring center. Also, a perspective that includes not only the dyadic perspective between buyer and provider but also the network that both actors are involved in, has so far not

---

[312] Thus, our approach is rather a modern perspective as opposed to classical, symbolic-interpretative, or postmodern perspectives and the organization is rather considered an organism than a machine (classical view), a culture (symbolic-interpretative view) or a collage (postmodern view) (Hatch (1997), pp. 52-54). In Burrell and Morgan's framework, our stance is most appropriately characterized as "functionalist" (Burrell/Morgan (1979), p. 22.

[313] See for an overview of theoretical foundations for the analysis of outsourcing De Looff (1995), Klein (2002).

[314] This is what we aimed to demonstrate in section 2.2.4.1.

[315] Klein (2002), p. 26; see for some examples from this edition Schott (1997), Aubert et al. (2004). For other contributions see, for instance, Ngwenyama/Bryson (1999), Logan (2000).

been integrated in the transaction cost theory.[316] Williamson acknowledges that "network relations are given short shrift"[317]. Thus, it seems that transaction cost theory does not advance knowledge on our topic nor does it seem very applicable for our purposes.

- In addition, there have been contributions based on *behavioral decision making theory*.[318] Decision making theory analyzes decision processes since it is assumed that "[d]ecision-making processes hold the key to the understanding of organizational phenomena"[319]. This theory takes into account the individual human being who takes decision for and within organizations without actually being the organization (and thus pursuing other interests as well) and with only limited information (bounded rationality).[320] In our case, such a theory can help to better structure an offshoring decision situation, but mostly does not relate to the coordination of the resulting outcome. Thus, it would not be helpful for our purposes either in respect of knowledge advancement or applicability since decision making theory works on the level of the individual and does not take a firm perspective.

- *Resource-dependence approaches* can be applied to both outsourcing and offshoring;[321] however, while they can explain the dependence of an organization on resources from the outside,[322] they do not provide the internal view that we want to take in regard to service offshoring, which takes place in the intra-organizational network of the MNC. While the resource-dependence approach helps to explain why there are relationships between units,[323] it has little explanatory power for our research questions. Thus, while it might have potential for both knowledge advancement and applicability to other aspects of the offshoring topic, we see limited use for our purposes.

---

[316] Jones et al. (1997), p. 912.
[317] Williamson (1994), p. 85.
[318] See, for instance, Nagengast (1997). See also Lee/Kim (2005) who compare three different theoretical perspectives on outsourcing and find that the behavioral model is the most appropriate to explain outsourcing success.
[319] Simon (1997), p. XL.
[320] Berger/Bernhard (2002), p. 133.
[321] Cheon et al. (1995).
[322] Hatch (1997), pp. 78-81.
[323] Auster (1994), p. 6.

3 – Research Model and Propositions

- *Contingency approaches* were popular starting in the 1950s as a means of determining the organizational structure based on external influences. These approaches are also called "situative" since they do no longer assume the single best organizational structure but try to determine the most appropriate structure as a function of specific factors. Examples of research under this paradigm are Woodward (1965); Lawrence/Lorsch (1967); Kubicek/Welter (1985); Schreyögg (1995). While contingency approaches have been credited for taking into account external influences and for refuting the existence of a single best way of organizing, they have also been criticized for putting too much emphasis on organizational structure as the only influencer of organizational action and organizational efficiency. With regard to outsourcing, contingency approaches have been used to identify success factors.[324] While we do not take a contingency stance, our research is nevertheless influenced by contingency approaches in the sense that we do not consider one solution the best way to organize. However, we do not share the view that organizational structure is purely determined by external forces and that it, in turn, is the only factor that determines organizational efficiency. Rather, we consider a given organizational structure (a service offshoring subsidiary with one or more internal customers, one of them being the MNC's headquarters) and ask which coordination mechanisms are appropriate in view of the service that is provided and the setup of the organizational network. We therefore do not deem contingency approaches to be applicable since we do not differentiate between organizational structures but evaluate other influencing factors on coordination mechanisms. Our typological approach therefore seems more adequate to the task at hand.[325]

We have shown why four mainstream theories are not appropriate for the scope of our research. We will now turn to those theories that we have selected. Our typology will be grounded in the *resource-based view* and *network approaches*. The reasons for this se-

---

[324] See, for instance, Cheon et al. (1995), Gilley/Rasheed (2000), Mol et al. (2004).
[325] In addition, it was found that typologies can help to explain outsourcing success better than contingency approaches (Lee et al. (2004)). This confirms our approach to developing a typology. On the relationship between contingency approaches and typologies, see also section 4.1.2.

lection will be outlined in the following sections. Furthermore, we will elaborate on operationalizations and derive propositions.[326]

3.2 THE RESOURCE-BASED VIEW OF THE FIRM

In the following sections we will present an overview of the resource-based view of the firm. We will start out with a definition and a discussion of the main principles (section 3.2.1) before turning our attention to the question how can the resource-based view – with its initially domestic perspective on the firm – be used from an international angle as well (section 3.2.2). In what regard the resource-based view can be of avail for the analysis of service offshoring, will be considered in section 3.2.3.[327] We will then introduce the main concept – strategic relevance of the service that a service offshoring subsidiary provides – that we will use later on for the construction of our typology (section 3.2.4). Based on these theoretical considerations, we will show how we operationalize the concept (section 3.2.5) for subsequent use in case studies and derive propositions on coordination mechanisms (section 3.2.6).[328]

3.2.1 INTRODUCTION TO THE RESOURCE-BASED VIEW

Despite some recent discussions about her contributions[329] many authors give credit to Penrose (1959) for laying the foundation for the resource-based view.[330] Later on, the landmark publications of Wernerfelt and Barney refined and extended the concept.[331] It

---

[326] One could ask why we have not selected theories from the core of international business research. As we discussed in section 2.1, many theories from international business research touch upon different aspects of service offshoring. We in fact draw from that body of knowledge for the coordination mechanisms that we include in our typology. However, for the dimensions of the typology, we find the resource-based view and network approaches more appropriate. We actually use the network view of the MNC for our research, which has been explicitly applied for research of the MNC.

[327] Following our above line of argument: Several authors have successfully analyzed outsourcing from the perspective of the resource-based view. See Espino-Rodríguez/Padrón-Robaina (2006) for a review.

[328] This chapter builds on an earlier discussion of the resource-based view in chapter 4.3 of the working paper Schmid/Daub (2005).

[329] Dunning (2003), Anonymous (2004a), Kor/Mahoney (2004), Lockett/Thompson (2004), Rugman/Verbeke (2004).

[330] For the impact of Penrose (1959) on the resource-based view see Barney/Arikan (2001), pp. 129-130.

[331] Wernerfelt (1984), Barney (1991). However, the resource-based view has been developed by many authors. Amongst commonly cited contributions are Rumelt (1984), Dierickx/Cool (1989), Reed/DeFillippi (1990), Collis (1991), Collis/Montgomery (1995), Wernerfelt (1995), Barney (2001a), Barney (2001b), Barney et al. (2001). Even if many authors have participated in the development of the resource-based view and there are sometimes confusing and unanimous usages of terms (Peteraf (1993), p. 185, Collis (1994), pp. 144-145), the resource-based view can still be considered a relatively homogeneous theory.

views "the firm as a bundle of human and non-human resources"[332] and takes the standpoint that each firm can have a unique set of resources. Wernerfelt understands resources as "anything which could be thought of as a strength or weakness of a given firm. More formally, a firm's resources at a given time could be defined as those (tangible and intangible) assets which are tied semipermanently to the firm"[333]. These resources can be of different kinds; a distinction is commonly made between physical assets such as machines and plants, intangible assets such as patents and goodwill, and financial resources.[334] In addition, organizational capabilities such as a fast product development cycle are mentioned.[335] Some authors define organizational capabilities as meta-resources as they are concerned with the management of the other resources.[336] For the purpose of our analysis, we do not need to further distinguish between different categories of resources but will follow Barney's original broad definition.[337]

Not everything is considered a resource in the resource-based view, though. It is argued that there is a distinction between resources as understood by the resource-based view and other input factors from neoclassical theory.[338] An important element for the differentiation between any input factor and resources is that resources can be used on markets to convert the benefits that they bring into economic returns.[339] According to Barney's original considerations (which are still deemed valid today), resources can be differentiated by four characteristics: they need to be a) valuable, b) rare, c) imperfectly imitable, and d) they cannot be substituted by other resources.[340]

Resources are "*valuable* when they enable a firm to conceive of or implement strategies that improve its efficiency and effectiveness."[341] Resources are *rare* if they are exclu-

---

[332] Pitelis (2004), p. 525. See also Wernerfelt (1984), Barney (1991), Wernerfelt (1995), Barney (2001a), Barney et al. (2001), Peng (2001).
[333] Wernerfelt (1984), p. 172.
[334] Barney (1991), pp. 101-102, Chatterjee/Wernerfelt (1991), pp. 35-36, Mahoney/Pandian (1992), p. 364, Bamberger/Wrona (1996), p. 132.
[335] Some authors count organizational capabilities as intangible assets (such as Collis (1991), p. 50).
[336] Eschen (2002), p. 136, Morash/Lynch (2002), p. 28.
[337] See also Barney/Arikan (2001), pp. 139-140 who argue that a finer distinction between resource categories can be helpful for specific purposes, but the authors call it "counterproductive" (Barney/Arikan (2001), p. 140) to compete for the right label of the theory and the right categorization of resources. Since we do not deal with a specific class of resources, we will stick to the original broad terms.
[338] Freiling (2001).
[339] Freiling (2001), p. 34.
[340] Barney (1991), pp. 105-112. See also Freiling (2001), pp. 14-19 for a discussion on the right definition of resources.
[341] Barney (1991), p. 105.

sively owned by one or very few firms in one industry.[342] Resources are *imperfectly imitable* if the firm that holds them has obtained them through unique historical conditions, if the link between the resources and the resulting competitive advantage is causally ambiguous, or if the resource is socially complex.[343] Finally, resources are *not substitutable or hard to substitute*, if there is no other resource that could replace it. If other firms can deploy a similar resource or if other firms can deploy other resources that serve the same purposes, then a resource is substitutable.[344]

All four above characteristics lead to resource heterogeneity. This is one of the main assumptions of the resource-based view and means that each firm has a different set of resources and can use its resources differently.[345] This is a major deviation from the previously dominating market-based view that argued on an industry level and considered all firms in one industry or in one strategic group to be in the same situation.[346] The resource-based view takes the firm rather than the industry as the unit of analysis[347] and proposes that firms can – by effective combination of their resources – gain a competitive advantage. If the firm manages to create an advantage in the market of a kind that other firms cannot easily emulate or acquire, one speaks of sustainable competitive advantage.[348]

Still, even if all these conditions are fulfilled resources do not automatically lead to a competitive advantage, but should rather be seen as potential sources of competitive ad-

---

[342] Barney (1991), pp. 106-107.
[343] Barney (1991), pp. 107-111.
[344] Barney (1991), pp. 111-112. Moreover, there are three additional, more technical assumptions that must be fulfilled in order for resources to result in competitive advantages. These are a) ex post limits to competition that help the firm with an advantage to prevent other firms from copying or substituting its valuable resources, b) imperfect resource mobility, which prevents the resources from being easily transferable to other firms, and c) ex ante limits to competition that would destroy potential gains from resources by increasing their prices so much that they would offset returns (Peteraf (1993)).
[345] Peteraf (1993).
[346] One of the main proponents of the market-based view is Michael Porter. His view suggests that an industry's profitability depends on factors such as the competition within the industry, the entry barriers for new entrants, the power that suppliers and customers have and the threat of substitutability by other products. This perspective does not put the unit of analysis on the firm level, but on the industry level. For this so-called industry economics perspective, see Porter (1980), Porter (1985). The initial presentation of the resource-based view as an antipode to the market-based view has since been reneged on by several authors; instead the two perspectives are now seen as complementary (Mahoney/Pandian (1992), p. 374, Eschen (2002), pp. 127-128).
[347] Madhok/Phene (2001).
[348] Peteraf (1993). Competitive advantage is, however, not a concept that is used only within the resource-based view. It has been employed before, for instance, by Coyne (1986) and Aaker (1989) who define it in a similar way.

3 – Research Model and Propositions 91

vantage.³⁴⁹ Even valuable resources need to be exploited and combined with other resources so that they can realize competitive advantage.³⁵⁰ Thus, an imaginative firm without resources will never have a competitive advantage, but neither will a firm endowed with many resources achieve a sustainable competitive advantage unless it uses those resources in an effective way.³⁵¹ Often the capability to combine resources is called a competency or organizational capability in itself.³⁵²

The relationships between factors, resources, competencies, and competitive advantages that were discussed above are expressed graphically in Figure 3-1. On the left hand side, the figure shows a set of boxes that stand for any kind of resources. It seems reasonable to assume that there is no dichotomous distinction between unimportant factors and resources but that there is difference in degree.³⁵³ These resources are combined with the help of the competencies the firm has at its disposal. As a result, a firm can achieve a competitive advantage.

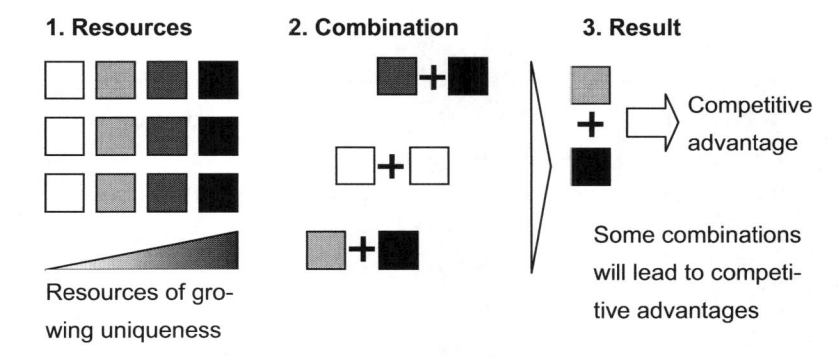

Figure 3-1: Relationship between resources, combination of resources and competitive advantage

---

[349] Popović (2004).
[350] Ray et al. (2004), p. 26.
[351] Amit/Schoemaker (1993), Dutta et al. (2005), p. 278. Collis names the coordination of activities one of the top priorities for the development of a global strategy (Collis (1991), p. 49).
[352] Freiling (2001), pp. 19-27. As with many theories, these concepts have been named differently, for instance, valuable resources have been named "strategic resources" by Warren (2002), p. 44. However, the major lines of distinction between resources, capabilities and competitive advantages are shared by many authors (Freiling (2001), Morecroft et al. (2002), Warren (2002). Alternatively, authors speak of assets and skills as being equivalent to resources and competences, respectively (Aaker (1989), pp. 91-92). This is also sustained by the research stream that focuses on the application of the resource-based view to dynamic markets and uses the concept of dynamic capabilities (Teece et al. (1997), Eisenhardt/Martin (2000)).
[353] This view is supported in Schmid/Gouthier (1999), p. 19, Makadok (2001), p. 397.

Before we can use the resource-based view to differentiate service offshoring centers and derive propositions with regard to coordination mechanisms, we need to clarify some open questions and reply to criticism that has been leveled at the resource-based view:

1. Schmid criticizes that neither international business research nor resource-based view research considers how subsidiaries develop resources.[354] For our research it is important to evaluate, however, how a subsidiary can acquire or develop resources. It has also been called into question if – and if so, how – the resource-based view can be applied in international settings as it was not developed with an international focus. This question is relevant to our research and we will accordingly evaluate the connection between the resource-based view and MNCs in the next section.

2. Some authors criticize that the importance of the coordination of resources has not been sufficiently emphasized. Researchers have identified the problem that resources do not generate the expected competitive advantages unless they are managed appropriately.[355] Once a firm has acquired resources, it has to use them to build up a competitive advantage. It is argued that a firm with valuable resources will not be able to gain a competitive advantage if it does not use them in the right way. Thus, research so far has focused more on the final consequences of the resources than on the initial step. In that sense, we want to take a step backwards to focus on the coordination of resources which is not only relevant to our study. It also creates a methodological advancement for the resource-based view as "understanding the relationship between a firm's resources and the effectiveness of its activities, routines, or business processes is particularly fruitful ground for analyzing the empirical implications of resource-based theory."[356] We will discuss this in more detail in the section that deals with the relationship between offshoring and the resource-based view.

3. The resource-based view has been criticized for being hard to operationalize and evaluate empirically.[357] To address this point we propose one possible operationalization to differentiate resources by their degree of strategic relevance

---

[354] Schmid/Schurig (2003), p. 757.
[355] Freiling (2001), p. 27.
[356] Ray et al. (2004), p. 35.
[357] Williamson (1999).

and show in the empirical section of our research how this can be applied in case studies.

Thus, we want to work on these three "loose ends" and propose possible solutions. Of course, the resource-based view has been confronted with more criticism, but this is not the place to discuss all other possible shortcomings of this concept. However, we want to briefly describe how we deal with two additional common critiques:

- Some authors accuse the resource-based view of being tautological by defining valuable resources as those that bring value to a firm.[358] Our research is not directly affected by this critique as our discussion focuses primarily on the coordination of resources and not on the effect they have on competitiveness.[359] We simply argue that resources of different importance need to be coordinated differently.

- The resource-based view puts a firm-internal focus on resources.[360] Some authors consider this a too strong internal focus that could lead to a neglect of the market side.[361] For an analysis of internal service centers this critique does not apply.

The three points outlined above will be addressed in the subsequent sections.

3.2.2 RESOURCE-BASED VIEW AND INTERNATIONAL BUSINESS RESEARCH

Before we discuss the specific application of the resource-based view for our research, we need to focus on the relationship between the resource-based view and international business research. Our research is clearly situated in one of the main domains of international business research – relationships between headquarters and subsidiaries – and we want to apply the resource-based view to explain and evaluate phenomena in this domain. However, we need to ask if such an approach is valid after all, given the fact that the resource-based view was originally not conceived with an international scope.[362] Of course, its authors do not explicitly exclude its application in an interna-

---

[358] See for this discussion Barney (2001a), Priem/Butler (2001), Eschen (2002), pp. 176-177.
[359] Besides, there is a way in which this tautology can be avoided (see Eisenhardt/Martin (2000), p. 1108).
[360] For instance, Dierickx/Cool (1989), pp. 1505-1506 show that some resources can only be accumulated internally, but not acquired from external markets.
[361] Eschen (2002), pp. 177-179.
[362] Fladmoe-Lindquist/Tallman (1994), p. 56.

tional context, but we still want to analyze if our approach is in line with the basic assumptions of the concept. Therefore, we want to first evaluate the current status of the application of the resource-based view in international business research before discussing the acquisition of resources by the subsidiary. It was originally assumed in international business research that only the headquarters had resources in the sense of the resource-based view.[363] Our proposition, however, is that the subsidiary can also have resources. We therefore need to consider in more detail how a subsidiary can acquire resources.

Publications from international business research have applied the resource-based view explicitly. In an evaluation of major international business and strategic management journals, Peng (2001) found 61 contributions from 1991 to 2000 that cite Wernerfelt (1984) and/or Barney (1991). He also noted a growing importance of the resource-based perspective in international business research over time.[364] He concludes that the resource-based view has made substantial inroads into international business and can be considered a "theoretical innovation"[365]. Peng further subdivides these contributions according to their content in the categories MNC management, strategic alliances, international entrepreneurship, and emerging markets. Within the category relevant to our research – MNC management – Peng distinguishes the topics global strategies, subsidiary capability development, and human resource management.[366] Thus, there seems to be a wide array of applications of the resource-based view for international business research, and the resource-based view can be considered an established approach within the realm of international business.

In an analysis of Penrose's contribution to international business research, Pitelis (2004) argues that her original principles for the resource-based view are still important today and can also be applied to the MNC. Whereas Penrose's early writings did not account specifically for the MNC, this changed over time to explicitly consider the circumstances that MNCs face.[367] More recent contributions from international business show the continued application of the resource-based view: Kotha et al. (2001) evaluate the

---

[363] Bartlett/Ghoshal (1986), p. 87.
[364] Peng (2001), p. 806. For the role of the resource-based view in international business, see also Barney (2001b), pp. 629-630. Barney/Arikan (2001) review contributions that make use of the resource-based view and cite – among many others – 16 publications from international business research which show that the resource-based view can be applied fruitfully in an international setting.
[365] Peng (2001), p. 803.
[366] Peng (2001), pp. 810-812.
[367] Pitelis (2004), p. 528.

effects of owning intangible resources on internationalization for internet firms. Trevino/Grosse (2002) explicitly point to the value that the resource-based view can bring to international business research: "Extending resource-based thinking to the international arena, the RBV may be able to offer partial insight into the rationale behind the deployment of firm-specific assets in foreign markets."[368] Hansen/Nohria (2004) discuss how global collaboration can become a valuable resource for an MNC. Wan (2005) uses the resource-based view to analyze how host country characteristics shape firms' capabilities when diversifying into emerging markets.

Thus, there is now an established tradition of applying the resource-based view in an international setting. However, we need to specifically evaluate how an MNC can actually gain control over a resource in a subsidiary. In strategic management literature, two ways of gaining control over resources are suggested: a) they can be transferred from other units of the same firm or acquired from another firm (picking of existing resources) or b) they can be created (new resources, capability-building).[369] Additionally, in order to have a resource in a subsidiary, we can differentiate from an international business perspective a) situations in which resources originally stem from the headquarters country (resource crosses borders) and b) cases in which the resource stems from the subsidiary country (local resource). These two dimensions with two possibilities each can be combined in a two-by-two matrix as displayed in Figure 3-2.

The resulting possibilities are the following:

(A) The subsidiary can receive resources from the headquarters.[370] Resources are transferred within the MNC network. This is the most relevant case for our study, especially if the service offshoring subsidiary is a newly-founded entity within the MNC network with the purpose of delivering services. Due to its importance for our work, we will discuss this case in more detail below.

---

[368] Trevino/Grosse (2002), p. 433.
[369] For the differentiation between these alternatives and the circumstances in which they can be used, see Makadok (2001), Espino-Rodríguez/Padrón-Robaina (2006), p. 53. A third possibility to gain control over resources is engaging in alliances in which resources are shared with other firms (Bowman/Collier (2006), p. 199; another example could also be the use of external resources by an outsourcing contract (Espino-Rodríguez/Padrón-Robaina (2006), p. 52)). Since our research takes an MNC-internal perspective, we do not include this possibility here.
[370] See, for instance, Uhlenbruck (2004) for an evaluation of the transfer of knowledge to newly acquired subsidiaries.

	Headquarters country	(A) Headquarter transfers existing resource into subsidiary	(B) Headquarters creates a new resource
Original resource location		HQ → SUB	HQ💥 SUB
	Subsidiary country	(C) Headquarter acquires existing company with resources	(D) Subsidiary creates new resource
		HQ ← SUB	HQ SUB💥
		Transfer/acquisition of an existing resource	Creation of a new resource
		Mode of gaining control of resource	

■ Resource
💥 Resource creation

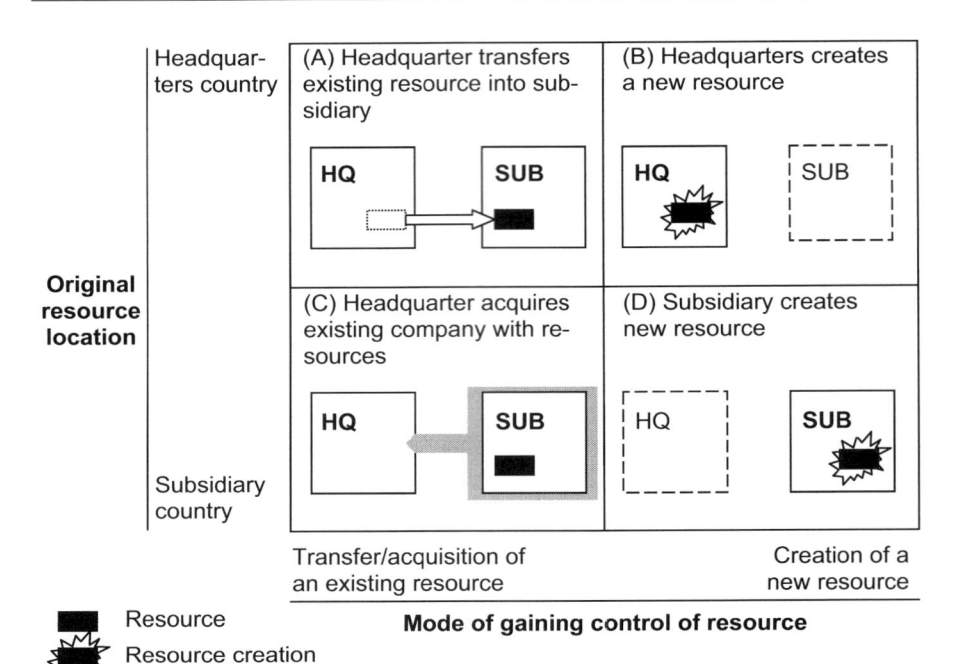

Figure 3-2: Possibilities for the combination of resource location and mode of gaining control of resource

(B) The headquarters can create new resources. This case is not relevant to our study since it leaves the subsidiary untouched. Resources that are created by the headquarters can of course be transferred to the subsidiary eventually, but this situation is already covered by possibility (A). Thus, we will consider possibility (B) no further.

(C) Resources are incorporated into the MNC from the outside. This is subject to intensive discussion[371] since especially valuable resources can often not be fully described and are hard to acquire on markets. Consequently, the acquisition of resources typically occurs through the acquisition of entire companies.[372] Thus, we here especially consider cases in which the headquarters acquires an existing company with a resource and includes it in its network of subsidiaries and can then access and use that resource. When a service offshoring subsidiary is not set up as a new entity but through the acquisition of an existing company in another country, the MNC can gain control over resources

---

[371] Chi (1994).
[372] Luo (2000), p. 363, Mathews (2002), p. 33, Bowman/Collier (2006), p. 198.

that this company holds. This might occur in cases where the resources are of importance to the MNC and could point to a high strategic relevance.[373]

(D) Alternatively, the unit can build new resources internally. This aspect has been somewhat neglected in international research, but there are some contributions that explicitly evaluate resource development within the subsidiary.[374] For our research, the internal development of resources does not play an important role since the development of resources take time and we are looking at service offshoring subsidiaries that are relatively young and most likely have not developed new resources themselves. If their role as internal service provider changes over time, they might also create unique resources but this would be more relevant in a longitudinal study covering the development of service offshoring subsidiaries. Thus, we concentrate here on cases (A) and (C).

Our focus is on the transfer of resources that takes place when an MNC initially sets up a service offshoring center, since the MNC then needs to transfer at least a minimum set of resources to the center.[375] We therefore need to analyze this process. Approaches from international business research have long been concerned with the transfer of resources, even before the resource-based view gained popularity. Hymer (1976) proposes that MNCs create a monopolistic advantage in their home location and subsequently move it to other countries to further exploit it.[376] Also Dunning's OLI paradigm deals with the exploitation of MNC advantages in foreign markets that could be well considered resources within the resource-based view.[377] Besides these more traditional approaches from market power and transaction cost perspectives, the resource-based view has also started to be considered in international business research, for instance, in explaining entry mode choices.[378] Tallman (1991) discusses ways in which the resource-

---

[373] In the empirical part of this research, we cover both cases in which subsidiaries are acquired or build up as new units.
[374] See for the influence of the subsidiary's network on the development of its critical capabilities, Schmid/Schurig (2003). Birkinshaw (1996) explains how subsidiaries grow, depending on the capabilities that they build up.
[375] This is also the case for the establishment of a subsidiary by acquisition. For its use as a service offshoring center, the MNC will very likely have to transfer resources into that subsidiary; however, complementing those resources that the acquired firm already held.
[376] For a critique of the importance of Hymer's work for international business research, see Dunning/Rugman (1985).
[377] Dunning first presented his theory to explain MNC internationalization in the 1970s and has since extended it (Dunning (1973), Dunning (1979), Dunning (1988), Dunning (1989), Dunning (1995), Dunning/Narula (1995), Dunning (2000)). Madhok/Phene (2001) support our argumentation by showing how the resource-based view and the OLI paradigm can be combined.
[378] Tallman (1991).

based view can be used in international settings. He finds that it can be applied to explain how an MNC develops a specific strategy for each market it enters based on the resources it has at its disposal in its home market and the use of these resources abroad. After market entry, however, the MNC can also develop new resources in the host country. The new market then becomes a part of the firm's resource structure.[379]

To our knowledge, there is no research stream that deals explicitly with the transfer of resources in the sense of the resource-based view across borders.[380] However, many authors discuss the acquisition of resources from abroad[381] and the access of resources in international joint ventures[382] or in international collaborations.[383] Other authors focus more on the transfer of knowledge,[384] technology,[385] management practices,[386] innovations,[387] or organizational culture,[388] without explicit reference to the resource-based view.

Nothing within the resource-based view seems to directly contradict the possibility of transferring resources.[389] However, as resources are idiosyncratic, their transfer can be difficult. The one area that has probably received the most attention and that has the closest affinity to our analysis, is the transfer of knowledge. One frequently quoted contribution is that of Gupta/Govindarajan who analyze different types of subsidiaries based on the knowledge outflow into and inflow from the MNC network.[390] Knowledge transfer is commonly understood as a process by which a sender initiates and transfers knowledge and the receiver gains knowledge and implements it.[391] Also, research has identified several factors that can hinder knowledge transfer such as knowledge ambiguity, negative prior experience with knowledge transfer, lack of communication, low de-

---

[379] Tallman (1991), pp. 70-72.
[380] See, however, Scott-Kennel/Enderwick (2004), on the transfer of knowledge and resources from subsidiaries to local network partners.
[381] Trevino/Grosse (2002), Poon/MacPherson (2005).
[382] Glaister (2004), Jolly (2005).
[383] Perks (2004).
[384] Foss/Pedersen (2002), Minbaeva et al. (2003), Minbaeva (2005).
[385] Jeannet/Liander (1978), Tsurumi (1979).
[386] Beechler/Yang (1994), Dedoussis (1995).
[387] Özsomer/Gençtürk (2003), pp. 6-7.
[388] Jaeger (1983).
[389] On the contrary, Uhlenbruck points out that the resource and capability perspective already acknowledges potential problems of knowledge transfer between separate firms (Uhlenbruck (2004), p. 110).
[390] Gupta/Govindarajan (2000). Other examples include Hansen (1999), Holm/Pedersen (2000), Tsai (2001), Andersson (2003), Monteiro et al. (2004).
[391] Minbaeva et al. (2003), p. 587.

gree of richness of transmission channels, and lack of absorptive capacity.[392] Building on these findings, authors have evaluated how knowledge transfer is impacted by different headquarters control mechanisms.[393] However, we have not found arguments that would rule out the possibility of knowledge transfers between international units of the firm. Rather, authors have suggested that some resources cannot be transferred easily or in a single person but require the transfer of complete routines[394] and will therefore necessitate the transfer of a larger group of personnel.[395] Thus, we conclude that knowledge transfer is difficult but in principal possible.[396] In addition, we believe that knowledge as an ambiguous resource can be a good example of the range of resources that we want to consider in our research.[397]

As an alternative, resources can also be exchanged between organizations using mergers and/or acquisitions.[398] In this case, resources are transferred in an embedded way, that is, they are not sold or purchased separately but embedded in the organization that contains them. For our research, this is relevant if the MNC acquires an existing company and sets it up as a service offshoring subsidiary.

We still need to explicitly address some reasons why the resource-based view may not work on an international level. Those include the following:

- The coordination of resources across language, culture and country borders is more challenging than in a domestic setting. Because this is directly related to our research question, we will still be able to evaluate the appropriateness of the resource-based view for international business research.

- On an international level the definition of valuable resources could be more difficult. It might be that resources are rare in one country but that they are plentiful if considered internationally. However, this case would not impact the logic of

---

[392] Ghoshal/Bartlett (1988), Szulanski (1996), Gupta/Govindarajan (2000), Minbaeva et al. (2003).
[393] Björkman et al. (2004).
[394] Nelson/Winter (1982), pp. 76-78.
[395] Teece (1981), p. 86.
[396] Szulanski (1996).
[397] Moreover, the current research design that focuses on transfer to subsidiaries rather than to external partners seems especially appropriate in the light of the findings of Kogut/Zander (1993) who recognized that MNCs prefer internal governance models (i.e. subsidiaries) for knowledge-intensive work over external partners (Kogut/Zander (1993), pp. 639-640). For a discussion of the importance of these findings for international business research, see also Kogut/Zander (2003), Tallman (2003).
[398] Friedrich von den Eichen (2002), p. 242.

the resource-based view, even if it could have enormous effects on the firm that has to deal with a situation where its resources are less valuable. Conversely, a firm that acts internationally has the opportunity to acquire and develop resources in a more diverse environment.[399] Again, this can change the setting in which the individual firm finds itself, but it does not affect the reasoning of the resource-based view.

In conclusion, it seems safe to assume that the resource-based view will work on an international level. Thus, we will deploy it in the current work and add to the growing body of international business literature that has used this approach already. With our analysis we are in line with Fladmoe-Lindquist/Tallman (1994) who discuss the appropriateness of the resource-based view for the analysis of internationalization activities and who conclude that it "provides a theoretical framework which can be used to integrate the previous work on MNE strategy and structure"[400]. The only addition that they propose is to include financial and political resources that might be different on an international level. For instance, the political relationships between a host country and the home country of the MNC can be considered a political resource that needs to be included in the analysis. While per se a very important observation, the authors do not deem this to be a potential barrier to applying the resource-based view but rather see it as an enhancement of the theory. This argument does not directly affect our research because we focus more on intra-organizational relationships and not on political and financial resources.

3.2.3 RELEVANCE OF THE RESOURCE-BASED VIEW FOR SERVICE OFFSHORING

When offshoring parts of its activities, a firm changes its resource configuration. As discussed before, MNCs can offshore resources with different degrees of strategic relevance. Once these resources are moved offshore, they are used to provide services to the rest of the MNC. Here, we want to demonstrate that the resource-based view has explanatory value for service offshoring because it can help to better understand how resources of different value can be coordinated.

---

[399] As discussed above, some resources might not be acquired externally. However, with access to more (international) markets, there is an increasing likelihood of finding resources on external markets that are unavailable in the MNC's home market.
[400] Fladmoe-Lindquist/Tallman (1994), p. 69.

We argue that an MNC has several resources in a service offshoring subsidiary that might be of strategic relevance.[401] But in order to use them to their maximum benefit, the MNC needs to coordinate them appropriately.[402] The ownership of valuable resources is not sufficient for a firm to create sustainable competitive advantages: "economic value can only be realised when they are *coordinated* [emphasis in original] in a given use."[403] So far, the resource-based view has produced only few results on how resources are organized and managed. Specifically, there has been little discussion on the services that resources deliver.[404] Our analysis starts at the level of resources. We argue that unless resources are coordinated, they cannot bring value to the firm. And only if they are valuable can they eventually lead to sustainable competitive advantages. However, not all resources are of the same importance to the firm. We want to evaluate the effect of the differing degree of importance that a resource has for the firm on the coordination that is needed to manage that resource appropriately. Actually, we will not discuss the coordination of the resources themselves, because the concept of resources is still somewhat "fuzzy" and does not lend itself easily to empirical analysis. Rather, we will address the services that are provided based on these resources.[405] To that end, we assume that a strategically relevant resource also delivers a strategically important service, whereas a strategically less relevant resource delivers a less important service.

An excellent ability to coordinate service offshoring subsidiaries can eventually become a valuable organizational skill.[406] Consequently, the capability to execute service offshoring can become a competitive advantage in itself[407] and would fall into Dunning's "Ot advantages" category that represent the better usage of "existing assets"[408]. Thus, in our case, besides gaining new resources, the firm can use its existing resources more efficiently and effectively. Dunning calls this strategy the leverage of resources.[409] Our discussion of service offshoring refers to the leverage of existing resources. When offshoring, the firm utilizes existing resources in new ways with the goal of becoming

---

[401] See section 3.2.2 above for how the resources have been transferred there.
[402] Collis/Montgomery (1995), p. 124. This view goes back to Penrose (1959), p. 54 who argued that firms cannot only gain a competitive advantage by having better resources but also by using them better.
[403] Sanchez (2000), p. 102.
[404] Foss/Robertson (2000), p. 2.
[405] It is common to think of resources as the originators of services and products (see, for instance, Penrose (1959), p. 75, Mahoney/Pandian (1992), p. 364, Markides/Williamson (1994), p. 152).
[406] Fladmoe-Lindquist/Tallman (1994), p. 48.
[407] Madhok/Phene (2001), p. 253.
[408] Dunning (2003), p. 7.
[409] Dunning (2003). A similar argumentation can be found in Tallman/Fladmoe-Lindquist (2002).

more efficient and/or more effective. Eventually this can lead to a competitive advantage. However, the concept of the resource-based view can also be applied to the services that are actually moved to a service center. In this case we use the resource-based view to describe the kind of activity that is relocated and to evaluate the extent to which it represents a valuable resource for the firm. The next section will deal explicitly with the differentiation of resources and the corresponding coordination requirements.

There is another reason why the resource-based view is relevant for service offshoring: On the level of a nation's economic development there have been many discussions about the transfer of low-value adding activities (that were typically associated with manufacturing offshoring) and the transfer of high-value adding activities (that were traditionally considered the stronghold of developed countries).[410] This can be understood as a shift of resources of different degrees of value. That the resource-based view is an appropriate concept with which to analyze service offshoring is also confirmed by authors who discuss offshoring and who implicitly take this perspective in arguing that firms have to find "ways to perform higher level IT activities that are better than those offered by vendors, are difficult to imitate, and cannot be readily duplicated outside the firm."[411]

Finally, we want to highlight again that our point of departure is a center that is already in place. We do not discuss the process by which resources are transferred (the transfer of resources such as best practices, knowledge, procedures has been discussed in the literature[412]) and neither do we reflect upon the decisions in favor of one service versus another or of one location versus another. At least in regard to location choices we believe that the literature already provides a rich background.[413]

---

[410] Burgmaier et al. (2004), p. 21.
[411] King (2005), p. 80.
[412] See also above.
[413] For an overview, see Kutschker/Schmid (2005), pp. 434-439.

Several authors claim that resources can be clustered into categories: For instance, Hamel/Prahalad (1994) distinguish market access capabilities, integrity-related competencies, and functionality-related competencies. There are other classifications of competencies and resources, but all have in common the underlying reasoning that resources can belong to different categories.[414] Moreover, the authors agree that there is a hierarchy in resources. For instance, FedEx's topmost competency could be considered logistics, but that is built up on underlying competencies such as package tracking or the operations of an airport hub.[415] Thus, resources not only need to be combined but they also build on other resources to form top-level competencies. While a company is typically associated with very few competencies (such as FedEx with logistics, Honda with engine development, Toyota with product development[416], etc.), every company needs a set of lower-level resources that in their aggregation deliver the top-level competency. This system is actually not limited to two levels but can be thought of as a hierarchy of resources. These can be understood as in Figure 3-3.

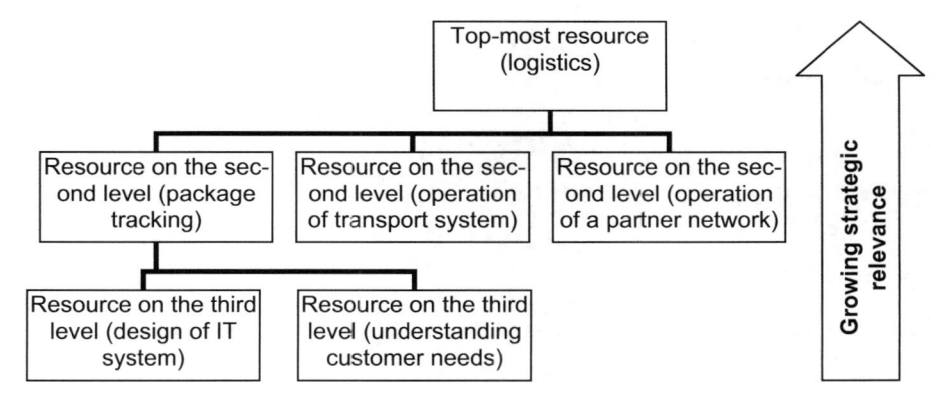

Figure 3-3: Hierarchy of resources (with the example of resources for a logistics company)

The top-most resource is the resource for which the company is well-known and which determines its competitiveness. This resource – which is sometimes referred to as "meta-competence" – is a compound of several other resources, in our case of package tracking, operation of a transport system, and the operation of a partner network on the second level. The second-level resources again are a compound of underlying resources

---

[414] Henderson/Cockburn (1994), p. 65, Marino (1996), p. 40, Mascarenhas et al. (1998), pp. 118-123.
[415] Srivastava (2005), p. 52.
[416] Eisenhardt/Martin (2000), p. 1107.

on the third level, such as in the package tracking example that could be built up on the resource to design the necessary IT system as well as the specific resource to understand customer needs. More levels could be added to describe resources in greater detail. Generally, the strategic relevance declines along the hierarchy, i.e., the top-most resource is the most important for the firm, resources on lower levels play a less important role.[417]

The resources are not identical with the organization of the company and there are very likely overlaps between different firms and between different business units[418] but at least in functional organization the above-mentioned classification by Hamel/Prahalad (1994) might also be found in an organization chart, for instance, the market access capabilities might be typically found in a marketing department. In any case, different organizational units contribute to different resources. Following this logic, service offshoring subsidiaries can also contribute to the overall resource set of a corporation. A service offshoring subsidiary with high strategic relevance might directly support one of the top-level competencies of the firm. For instance, a service offshoring subsidiary that is responsible for the product development of a software company clearly contributes to the functionality-related competencies. In that case, it seems likely that this resource is strategically relevant. A service offshoring center that provides internal support services, such as an internal IT helpdesk, might provide only a very indirect benefit to the top-level competencies of the firm. Thus, the strategic relevance of a resource could also be expressed by its position in the company's hierarchy of resources.

3.2.4 STRATEGIC RELEVANCE AS DIMENSION OF SERVICE OFFSHORING

As discussed above, resources are hard to discern. Therefore, we equate the outcome of resources with the resources.[419] Specifically, we assume that the service provided by a service offshoring center reflects the characteristics of the resource. This approach seems to us the only feasible way to differentiate between resources, even though we cannot preclude that a firm uses a very important resource to provide very unimportant services. However, as the value of a resource depends not only on some intrinsic characteristics of that resource but also on its coordination and usage, our assumption seems to be valid.

---

[417] We will discuss the concept of "strategic relevance" in more detail in the next section.
[418] Mathews (2002), pp. 45-46.
[419] Doing so, we follow the example of other studies, for instance, Merchant (2005), p. 194.

3 – Research Model and Propositions   105

As already discussed, it appears reasonable to suppose that there is a continuum of value that resources can contribute toward the final goal of achieving a competitive advantage for the firm.[420] At the one end of the spectrum there can be resources which are indisputably very valuable and which every competitor would willingly pay for. At the other end of the spectrum there can be resources which are far less important and valuable, but there will also be something in between. The traditional division between valuable resources and non-valuable factors seems arbitrary. In our research we want to distinguish resources (and services) by their degree of importance for the firm which we refer to as strategic relevance and define it as the degree of value, rareness, inimitability and non-substitutability of a resource in line with Barney's original definition of resources. He viewed these four characteristics as essentially necessary for a valuable resource. Since the main body of research on the resource-based view is still relatively homogeneous,[421] we find it appropriate to use Barney's original concept.[422] A strategically relevant resource can translate into a competitive advantage when it is managed with a competency of the firm.

We believe that the different degree of strategic relevance is a good way to distinguish not only between resources but also between different kinds of services that a subsidiary can provide, as these services are based on the center's resources and reflect the strategic relevance of these resources. We will refer to this as the "strategic relevance of the service for the MNC" or – more succinctly – "strategic relevance". At one extreme, the resources at a center's disposal do not directly have strategic relevance, or only to a limited extent. Consequently, such a center would carry out a service with a very low degree of strategic relevance for the MNC. At the other extreme, a center that is endowed with strategically highly relevant resources could execute services of a high degree of strategic relevance. If strategically relevant resources of the firm such as, for instance, product development services, are moved overseas, the resulting degree of strategic relevance is high.[423] Strategic relevance can shift from resources to the services and might eventually also extend to the subsidiary as a whole. Accordingly, subsidiaries

---

[420] It is common to differentiate resources of different value, either in two categories (for instance, Henderson/Cockburn (1994) distinguish component and architectural capabilities) or in more categories (for instance, Markides/Williamson (1994), pp. 157-158, Ray et al. (2004). A difference in degree is emphasized by Barney/Arikan (2001), p. 149.
[421] Schmid/Gouthier (1999), p. 13.
[422] This is a difference to our second dimension – network embeddedness – for which we will review the associated stream of research to derive a common definition and operationalization (see section 3.3).
[423] Kotabe/Murray (2004), p. 616.

providing strategically relevant services become strategically relevant themselves. For the purpose of our analysis it is sufficient to analyze at the resource and service level.

We believe that the possible differences in resource endowment create the need for different coordination of these centers. This is confirmed by existing research that postulates different coordination mechanisms[424] and different overall coordination requirements[425] for resources of different strategic relevance.

Firm resources	Strategic relevance	Coordination mechanisms	Result
Firm resource heterogeneity Firm resource immobility	Value Rareness Inimitability Non-substi-tutibility	Structural Technocratic Output-based Personal	Sustainable competitive advantage

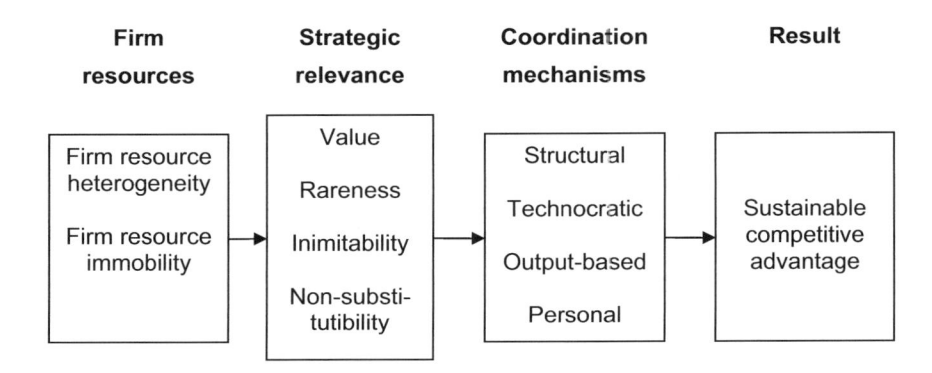

Figure 3-4: Relationship between firm resources, strategic relevance, coordination mechanisms and sustained competitive advantage (Source: Based on Barney (1991), p. 112)

Our concept is visualized in Figure 3-4. The strategic relevance of firm resources is determined by their value, rareness, inimitability and non-substitutability. Based on these characteristics, appropriate coordination mechanisms have to be found. If these are applied, the firm can obtain a sustainable competitive advantage.[426]

3.2.5 OPERATIONALIZATION OF THE RESOURCE-BASED VIEW

The resource-based view has been criticized for failing to differentiate valuable from non-valuable resources.[427] Several authors report on difficulties in operationalizing the value of resources.[428] For instance, some contributions discuss the strategic relevance of

---

[424] Argyres (1996), pp. 395-396.
[425] Argyres (1996), p. 408.
[426] As discussed above, we focus on the evaluation of coordination mechanisms and do not include sustainable competitive advantage.
[427] Morecroft (2002), p. 20.
[428] Kotha et al. (2001), p. 772, Merchant (2005), p. 194.

resources but stop short of developing an operationalization.[429] Existing operationalizations are often very specific to a study.[430] Some authors focus on only one specific resource such as reputation that has been considered valuable in the literature.[431] Rouse/Daellenbach propose to identify valuable resources by analyzing the differences between high and low performing firms in detailed qualitative research.[432] Christensen differentiates innovative from complementary, generic from firm-specific and domain-specific from integrative resources.[433] While we agree that it is very important to analyze resources in more detail, we find it more appropriate – not only for empirical research – to develop a continuous measure for the strategic relevance of a resource. In order to determine the differences in the strategic relevance of resources, one measure is to test for "value, scarcity and imperfect imitability"[434]. This is what we intend with our operationalization.

In following, therefore, we will discuss the four variables value, rareness, inimitability and non-substitutability:

1. The *value* of resources generally needs to be evaluated by models of the competitive environment of the firm.[435] Resources are only considered valuable if they eventually lead to value creation for the firm in the form of lower costs or higher net revenues.[436] The value of services can thus be operationalized by the degree to which the services allow the firm to become more efficient and/or effective.[437] Consequently, the primary reason for the establishment of the service center could be an indicator for the strategic relevance of the underlying resources. As we mentioned in the introduction, lower cost is probably the main

---

[429] Eschen (2002), Friedrich von den Eichen (2002).
[430] For instance, Merchant operationalizes valuable resources as the magnitude of competitive pressure encountered by an international joint venture parent in its core business (Merchant (2005), p. 194).
[431] Kotha et al. (2001), p. 772. Other resources that have been identified as valuable include employee know-how (Hall (1993)), the comprehension of a management team working on the development of a competence (McGrath/MacMillan (2000)), property-based resources such as long-term exclusive contracts (Miller/Shamsie (1996)), and unique project management techniques (Moingeon et al. (1998)).
[432] Rouse/Daellenbach (1999), pp. 488-489.
[433] Christensen (2000), pp. 124-126. Other examples are the differentiation in "(1) production/maintenance resources (the lowest level), (2) administrative resources, (3) organizational learning resources, and (4) strategic vision resources." (Brumagim (1994), p. 89) or the industry-specific perspective taken by Aaker (Aaker (1989), p. 92).
[434] Powell (1995), p. 15.
[435] Barney (2001a), p. 42.
[436] Barney/Arikan (2001), p. 143
[437] Barney (1991), p. 106.

driver for the setup of most offshoring centers. However, there might be other drivers such as, for instance, accessing an offshore talent pool. We believe that there is a connection between the strategic relevance and the main motive for setting up the unit. Where its strategic relevance is low, the main focus will be (only) on cost/efficiency, whereas centers with strategically highly relevant resources will (also) aim for other goals. The example that we want to use of other goals is quality/effectiveness. Other operationalizations for the value of a resources are given by Henderson/Cockburn (1994) who measure the value of resources by estimating their impact on the firm's research productivity. Makadok (1999) considers a firm's level of economies of scale as value and analyzes the resulting impact on the firm's market share.[438]

2. A service's *rareness* is considered in terms of its availability in other firms or on external markets.[439] For instance, Barney (1986) names the relative number of firms in which a resource exists.[440] One contribution evaluates the distribution of economies of scale across different firms and uses this as a measure of rareness.[441]

3. With regard to *inimitability*, one could measure the degree of complexity of the service.[442] Complexity will hinder the imitation of resources by other firms. Makadok (1999) proposes to measure inimitability by the gap in market shares between firms over time.[443] He argues that large market share gaps speak for inimitable resources whereas a narrowing of those gaps results from firms' replication of resources. Another potential operationalization for inimitability is competitors' knowledge on how to develop the same resource.[444]

4. Lastly, the *non-substitutability* of a resource means that there "must be no strategically equivalent value resources that are themselves either not rare or imitable."[445] Thus, the non-substitutability of services can be measured by the ex-

---

[438] Makadok (1999), pp. 937-938.
[439] Barney (2001a), pp. 43-44.
[440] Barney (1986), p. 660.
[441] Makadok (1999), pp. 937-938.
[442] Dierickx/Cool (1989).
[443] Makadok (1999), p. 938.
[444] Miller/Shamsie (1996), p. 521
[445] Barney (1991), p. 111.

tent to which other firms are in a position to achieve the same result with similar or different services.

This operationalization goes beyond the typical differentiation between strategically relevant and non-relevant resources. These have sometimes been defined only within the context of a given industry but without strictly examining all the four criteria established by Barney.[446] Our operationalization by contrast helps to distinguish resources of different strategic relevance.[447]

Before using this operationalization in the empirical part of our study, we need to touch upon another topic that is not only of methodological relevance. We have argued that we want to distinguish resources of different levels of strategic relevance. At the same time, we have shown that resources within firms are not only "bundles" as they are often called but that they rather form hierarchies. This leads to the ambiguous situation that the strategic relevance of resources can depend not only on their intrinsic value, rareness, inimitability, and non-substitutability but also on the relative level of measurement. For instance, on the top-most resource level of the corporation, there might be only one or two resources that are of high strategic relevance. If instead we look a few resource levels below, we find several resources that are of high strategic relevance for the next higher resource but do not play a major role for the top-most resources. For this reason we have to use some kind of "absolute" measure for the strategic relevance of resources and have found that measure on the level of the entire MNC and with a market perspective.[448] Thus, only those resources that are strategically relevant to the entire MNC and that "make a difference" on the market, will meet our criterion of strategic relevance. This was considered in our interviews where we discussed the strategic relevance of resources in the context of the entire MNC. Specifically, we have asked for the importance of services to the MNC's customers to ensure that we have overall comparable results.

---

[446] See, for instance, Combs/Ketchen Jr. (1999) who state that managerial talent and brand reputation are important for the restaurant industry whereas slack capital is not (Combs/Ketchen Jr. (1999), p. 872). Other authors give industry-specific examples of the college book publishing industry or machine tools industry (Day/Wensley (1988), p. 6).
[447] For an overview of the measures that we use, see section 5.2.3.4.
[448] Barney/Arikan (2001), p. 143, Espino-Rodríguez/Padrón-Robaina (2006), p. 53.

3.2.6 PROPOSITIONS DERIVED FROM THE RESOURCE-BASED VIEW

Based on the discussions above we will derive propositions that relate to the degree of strategic relevance and coordination mechanisms.

We want now to consider the relation between the variety of coordination mechanisms that are used and the kind of service that is provided by a service offshoring subsidiary. According to findings from the literature, the more important a service is, the harder it is to describe it in full.[449] Building on this relation, we conclude that more coordination mechanisms will be needed to coordinate a more strategically relevant service. Other authors have found that the more complex and uncertain a service is, the higher the potential involvement of the receiver of the service will be.[450] This again translates into higher coordination requirements. A resource that caters directly to the core competencies of the firm will probably need a higher degree of overall coordination. Moreover, there are findings reported that the more important the service is for the receiving unit, the more effort it will put into coordination.[451] Based on these considerations, we conclude:

P1: The more strategically relevant a service is, the greater the coordination requirements.

In the discussion on centralization and autonomy, a large body of research has identified that subsidiaries with high resource endowment, with specialized skills and tasks are more effective when they have a high level of decentralization and decision making authority and thus more freedom to innovate.[452] We associate these service characteristics with higher strategic relevance and therefore conclude:

P2: The more strategically relevant a service is, the higher the degree of autonomy that is given to the subsidiary.

The less strategically relevant a service is the fewer are the options and the necessity for the subsidiary to develop creative and new solutions. Research has found that where the

---

[449] Polanyi (1962), pp. 62-63, Winter (1987), Fahy (1996), p. 27. Grant (1996).
[450] Poppo (2003), p. 420.
[451] Cheng/Miller (1985), p. 25, Gittell (2000), p. 114.
[452] Perrow (1967), Hage/Aiken (1969), Schoonhoven (1981), Garnier (1982), p. 897, Ghoshal/Nohria (1989), p. 326, Nohria/Ghoshal (1997), p. 3, Edwards et al. (2002), pp. 185-189, Özsomer/Gençtürk (2003), p. 16. Garnier also notes that autonomy might depend on the overall importance of foreign operations for the MNC (Garnier (1982), p. 894); however, this characteristic will not help to explain differences between subsidiaries of the same MNC.

focus is more on exploiting existing procedures than on the development of new knowledge, formalization seems to be more appropriate.[453] Other findings point out that repeated tasks that are carried out without variation or interruption are best coordinated by formalization.[454] We associate exploitation of existing procedures and the repetition of tasks with lower strategic relevance. Moreover, formalization can be a hindrance to creativity and motivation[455] that can be prerequisites for the execution of strategically relevant services. Taken together, we conclude:

P3: The more strategically relevant a service is, the lower the degree of formalization.

A higher degree of strategic relevance will most likely lead to results from the service offshoring subsidiary that are harder to describe from the outset. Thus, output cannot be exactly specified upfront. In this case, the use of output control does not seem to be very appropriate.[456] If, on the other hand, results can be clearly described and measured, output control is more often applied.[457] Consequently, we postulate:

P4: The more strategically relevant a service is, the lower the degree of output control.

We suggest a relationship between the strategic relevance of a service and the use of personal coordination mechanisms. More strategically relevant services might not be fully codified or transferred in procedures, difficult to plan completely upfront,[458] and harder to quantify.[459] In addition, the underlying resources cannot be easily moved and explicitly described.[460] In these situations, personal coordination mechanisms seem more appropriate. Higher task uncertainty – that typically comes with increased strategic relevance – has been found to increase the degree of personal coordination.[461] Also, changes might have to be made frequently. Therefore, greater flexibility is required that can be better achieved through personal coordination mechanisms than through technocratic or structural instruments. For instance, the relocation of personnel can help trans-

---

[453] Bensaou/Venkatraman (1995), Özsomer/Gençtürk (2003), p. 17.
[454] Hansen et al. (1999), p. 109, Gençtürk/Aulakh (2007), p. 101.
[455] Walsh/Dewar (1987), p. 228, Agarwal (1993), p. 735, Meilich (2005), p. 161.
[456] Ouchi/Maguire (1975), pp. 559-560, Ouchi (1977), pp. 97-98, Ouchi (1978), p. 175.
[457] Snell (1992), p. 296, Brown et al. (2005), p. 160, Turner/Makhija (2006), p. 204.
[458] Ouchi/Maguire (1975), Ouchi (1977), pp. 836-837, Ouchi (1979), Eisenhardt (1985), Gupta/Govindarajan (1991), p. 782, Andersson et al. (2001), pp. 188-189, Kim et al. (2003), p. 330.
[459] Maleri (1997), pp. 118-119.
[460] Wernerfelt (1984), p. 172, Barney (1991), p. 107, Fahy (1996), p. 26.
[461] Van De Ven et al. (1976), p. 72.

fer knowledge to other parts of an organization where an explicit transmission through documents etc. is difficult. Thus:

P5: The more strategically relevant a service is, the higher the degree of personal coordination with its elements direct personal coordination, transfers, visits and culture-based coordination.

3.3 THE VIEW OF THE MNC AS A NETWORK

This section will set out the ways in which network approaches will be used for our work. We will start with a brief overview of network approaches in general (section 3.3.1) and the view of the MNC as a network in particular (section 3.3.2) before we discuss the relevance of network approaches for service offshoring in section 3.3.3. We will then introduce network embeddedness as the main concept that we will use later for the construction of our typology (section 3.3.4). Based on these theoretical discussions we then consider how we operationalize the concept (section 3.3.5) and derive propositions relating to coordination (section 3.3.6).[462]

3.3.1 INTRODUCTION TO NETWORK APPROACHES

Network approaches were developed in disciplines other than management research. They were first discussed in sociology and anthropology.[463] Despite the wide variety of applications of network approaches, there are some understandings that are widely shared: Networks are thought to be made up of ties that connect different nodes. Nodes can be anything from individuals to departments or firms. Ties stand for the interactions between these nodes.[464] A network is "any collection of actors (N ≥ 2) that pursue repeated, enduring exchange relations with one another"[465]. The exchange relationships that take place between different units can have different content. The content is often

---

[462] This chapter extends some earlier findings that were discussed in chapter 4.2. in Schmid/Daub (2005). Specifically, the contents on network embeddedness and its operationalization have been partially developed in Schmid/Daub (2007). The concepts in both previous studies are in the same line of argument that is expressed here. Additionally, we now analyze in detail the use of embeddedness in international business research and develop a multi-faceted operationalization for network embeddedness.

[463] See Renz (1998), pp. 110-112 for an introduction to the history of network theory. See also Tichy et al. (1979), p. 508 for its use in different disciplines.

[464] Mahon et al. (2004), p. 174.

[465] Podolny/Page (1998), p. 59. We do not go along with the authors' exclusion of authority in a network as intra-organizational networks have hierarchy as their distinctive characteristic (Böttcher (1996), p. 131).

3 – Research Model and Propositions 113

categorized as "expressive (affect), cognitive (information), instrumental (power), and objective (goods)"[466].

Network approaches do not form a single, homogeneous theory that establishes clear relationships between cause and effect. Thus, there is not one *network theory*. Moreover, network approaches do not have a single level of analysis (compared to the resource-based view that relates predominantly to the firm level) but rather they represent a perspective that can be applied to a large variety of existing research topics. For instance, with the view of the MNC as a network, a firm is no longer considered a homogeneous hierarchical organization but rather a network of differentiated actors. Within the disciplines that have used the network perspective, individual approaches have developed more fine-grained methods, causal relationships and specific operationalizations and measures. This is not the place to review them all and therefore we will limit this introduction to a short presentation of the different levels at which networks can be analyzed before we describe in more detail the particular network approach that we apply for our research: the view of the MNC as a network.

Network research can typically take place on three levels: "nodal (i.e., a focus on the behavior of individual units), dyadic (i.e., a focus on the joint behavior of unit pairs), and systemic (i.e., a focus on the behavior of the entire network)"[467]. Many research projects in international business research have focused on the first level of analysis.[468] We want to go one step further and carry out analysis on the second level, too. Thus, we will look at the relationship between units and in limited areas try to gain a more systemic picture by including not only the relationship between headquarters and service offshoring subsidiary, but also that between the service offshoring subsidiary and other international subsidiaries. The reason for such a design is that "the payoffs ... are likely to be high"[469] when a better understanding of the network design and behavior is gained.

Often network approaches are divided into a social network level that analyzes relationships between humans and an inter-organizational network level that addresses the relationships between organizations.[470] We will see in the next section that a further separa-

---

[466] Feinberg/Gupta (2004), p. 1, see also Tichy et al. (1979).
[467] Gupta/Govindarajan (2000), p. 474.
[468] See, for instance, Forsgren et al. (1999), Gupta/Govindarajan (2000).
[469] Gupta/Govindarajan (2000), p. 491.
[470] See Tichy et al. (1979), p. 507.

tion into three different organizational levels can be helpful for our analysis of the MNC.

3.3.2 NETWORK APPROACHES OF THE MNC

As mentioned above, MNCs can be considered networks instead of homogeneous units. Bartlett/Ghoshal propose to view the MNC "as an interorganizational grouping rather than as a unitary *organization* [emphasis in original]"[471].

Other contributions emphasize the point that not only units of the MNC should be regarded as network but that its external relationships to customers, suppliers, and authorities should also be included in the network analysis.[472] As indicated above, three levels of networks are differentiated in international business research:

- First, there are relationships within the firm, i.e. relationships between the various units of an MNC (*intra-organizational networks*). In particular, we refer to relationships between headquarters and subsidiaries and to the relationships subsidiaries have with each other.

- Second, there are relationships between different organizations, which constitute the so-called *inter-organizational network*. These inter-organizational relationships are, for instance, the result of joint ventures, strategic alliances, and license and franchise agreements.

- Third, each unit, whether headquarters or subsidiary, has links to *local networks* such as, for instance, to customers, suppliers, shareholders or research institutions. The local network perspective takes into account that MNC units are embedded in their stakeholder web.[473]

Figure 3-5 illustrates these three levels of networks which can be separated for analytical reasons.

---

[471] Ghoshal/Bartlett (1990), p. 604.
[472] See, for instance, Renz (1998), Kreikebaum et al. (2002), pp. 147-156, Kreikebaum/Gilbert (2003), p. 141.
[473] Schmid (2005), pp. 239-241.

3 – Research Model and Propositions 115

Figure 3-5: Differentiating network levels (Source: Translated from Schmid (2005), p. 240)

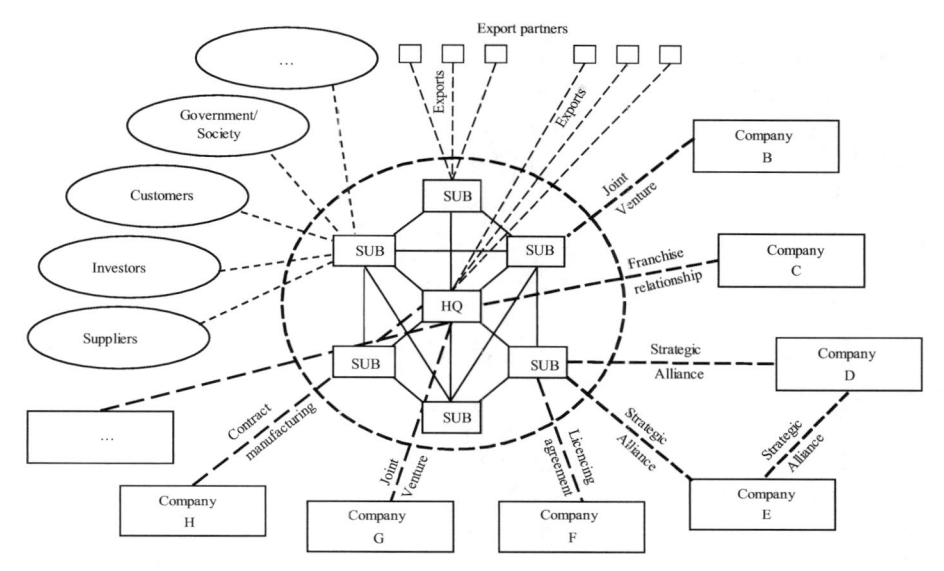

The focus of this study is on the intra-organizational network, as these relationships are the most important for a service offshoring center.[474] We can therefore build on a series of prominent international business research publications since the 1980s that view the MNC as an intra-organizational network.[475] Potentially the most prominent approach is the "transnational company" by Bartlett/Ghoshal who conceptualize the relationships in an MNC as a network that is characterized by complex coordination and control as well

---

[474] Of course we acknowledge that it is in general very important to consider the inter-organizational relationships of the MNC as well as the subsidiary's local network (Renz (1998), pp. 76-77). One can even argue whether it is necessary to create a new research stream on intra-organizational (versus inter-organizational) networks, e.g. networks between dependent organizations or whether many of the findings from the existing research on networks apply equally. Böttcher (1996) argues for a separate stream, whereas many other authors – including ourselves – see the MNC network perspective as compatible to existing network research and base their work on this research (White/Poynter (1989), Ghoshal/Bartlett (1990), Doz/Prahalad (1991), Brass et al. (2004), p. 800). In any case, it seems that the network perspective is very valuable for the analysis of subsidiaries (Malnight (1996), pp. 59-60).

[475] O'Donnell (2000), p. 526.

as intense exchange of goods, capital, technology, values, norms and capabilities.[476] An alternative approach is Hedlund's "heterarchy" that sees the MNC as an agglomeration of several (international) centers. Not only headquarters but also international subsidiaries are centers which have different competencies and which fulfill different positions.[477] There are many more approaches that view the MNC as a network, albeit less explicitly.[478] Several of these publications have also pointed out that the MNC is characterized as having many inter-organizational relationships. For instance, Hedlund stressed that the heterarchical MNC is open for coalitions with other firms.[479] Other authors implicitly put the emphasis on inter-organizational network relationships in which the MNC is embedded. A prominent area is the research on strategic alliances or joint ventures of MNCs.[480]

Based on these findings, another research stream emerged which has focused on subsidiaries. This strand of research was devoted to analyzing their responsibilities, tasks and roles as well as their development.[481] Many authors shifted their perspective from MNC headquarters to MNC subsidiaries, paying more attention to subsidiaries, the web of relationships between headquarters and subsidiaries and between two or more subsidiaries, and to the relationships of company units with external units. This research has come up with fruitful ideas such as the existence of centers of excellence and centers of competence,[482] their web of relationships, and their position within MNC networks and within local networks.[483] For instance, this stream of research has shown that the relationship between headquarters and the center of excellence or the center of competence subsidiary is not only affected by the position of that center. It has also found that relationships to headquarters, to other subsidiaries and to local partners directly or indirectly influence this position to a great extent. Thus, not only the dyadic relationship between headquarters and subsidiaries has an impact on the behavior of subsidiaries and

---

[476] Bartlett/Ghoshal (1988), Bartlett/Ghoshal (1989).
[477] Hedlund (1986).
[478] Perlmutter (1969), White/Poynter (1989), Doz/Prahalad (1991), Nonaka/Takeuchi (1995), see for an overview Schmid et al. (2002).
[479] Hedlund (1986), p. 26.
[480] Luo (1997), Child/Faulkner (1998), Doz/Hamel (1998), Rondinelli/Black (2000), Contractor/Lorange (2002).
[481] See Bartlett/Ghoshal (1986), D'Cruz (1986), Gupta/Govindarajan (1991), Birkinshaw (1996), Ferdows (1997), Birkinshaw (1998), Randoy/Li (1998).
[482] Centers of excellence do not necessarily need to be international subsidiaries. See Kreikebaum (2004) who uses the term to describe a domestic center.
[483] Forsgren/Pedersen (1997), Moore/Birkinshaw (1998), Andersson/Forsgren (2000), Holm/Pedersen (2000), Schmid (2000), Moore (2001), Frost et al. (2002), Schmid/Schurig (2003).

headquarters; rather, the whole network in which units are embedded has to be considered.[484]

While many authors have implicitly assumed that the MNC is a network, Bartlett/Ghoshal have explicitly modeled the MNC as an inter-organizational network.[485] These authors have gone beyond a pure description of the MNC as a network and have analyzed several characteristics in the MNC network and proposed specific behavior patterns. For instance, they argue that density (which they define as the number of actual versus potential ties in a network) has a strong impact on the autonomy of a subsidiary.[486] That way, they developed initial steps toward an MNC network theory. The notion that the structure of a network affects the involved actors' behavior is however not new. Bartlett/Ghoshal refer to Granovetter (1985) and build some of their considerations on the concept of *embeddedness*. We will introduce the embeddedness concept – that is virtually inseparable from the view of the MNC as a network – in the next section when we evaluate what network approaches can contribute to our analysis of service offshoring.

3.3.3 Relevance of Network Approaches for Service Offshoring

The MNC network approach provides an interesting basis for analysis of service offshoring. When an MNC sets up a service offshoring center, it changes the shape of its network. Service offshoring leads to a greater dispersal of resources as existing tasks are moved to a different, often new, location. Besides, it can lead to a higher centralization of resources if a service center is responsible only for a very limited range of activities (increased specialization of activities and increased division of labor). Following Bartlett/Ghoshal's line of argument, a change in the network structure will have an effect on the coordination mechanisms in place. Thus, network approaches can help to establish a relationship between the network structure and coordination mechanisms.

However, there is not just one possible network structure for service offshoring. Our understanding is that different constellations in the network will lead to different behavior in a broader sense and to different use of coordination mechanisms in particular. For instance, a unit that is only loosely connected to another unit will potentially be coordi-

---

[484] For more on subsidiaries and their specific roles, see section 2.3.2.
[485] Ghoshal/Bartlett (1990). This contribution has since appeared in an edited book on organization theories for MNCs (Ghoshal/Westney (1993)). Its unchanged re-publication in the second edition of the book (Ghoshal/Westney (2005)) indicates that the original concept is still relevant today.
[486] Ghoshal/Westney (2005), p. 84.

nated differently from a service offshoring subsidiary that has close relationships to many other international subsidiaries. In addition, there can be changes to the structure: In one scenario the relationships might change over time when new units are connected to the service offshoring subsidiary. At the other extreme, relationships might be very stable and not subject to changes. In short, the question of how strongly the subsidiary is embedded in the MNC network is a question of degree.

In network approaches, it is understood that the behavior of actors in a network is in some way influenced (constrained, enhanced, modified) by the network. Authors rooted in network research often stress the fact that the "whole truth" in regard to behavior cannot be uncovered unless an actor's relationships are considered in economic analysis.[487] This notion is exactly what is captured in the embeddedness concept. Hence, we very often find a link between embeddedness and network approaches.[488] Authors who apply a network perspective focus not only on actors, but on the overall set of relationships which actors have with other actors.

What exactly is embeddedness and how can it be used for our research? The embeddedness concept dates back to a seminal publication of Granovetter in which he states: "the behavior and institutions to be analyzed are so constrained by ongoing social relations that to construe them as independent is a grievous misunderstanding"[489]. The original definition coined by Granovetter was that embeddedness describes how "behavior and institutions are affected by social relations"[490]. While this definition has been adapted and slightly changed by different authors, its core has remained the same over time.[491] Granovetter's (1985) emphasis on an actor's relationships is primarily a statement against neoclassical economic analysis where the actor is considered a homo oeconomicus who always behaves in a rational way and independently of other actors. Granovetter argues that it is important to consider the social structure of the actors' net-

---

[487] See also Andersson/Forsgren (2000), p. 335.
[488] Andersson et al. (2005), Echols/Tsai (2005).
[489] Granovetter (1985), p. 482.
[490] Granovetter (1985), p. 481.
[491] Dacin et al. (1999), p. 320.

works which includes their history and their previous experiences. Neoclassical theories fail to do this.[492]

The importance of embeddedness has been confirmed by its application in many disciplines, including sociology, economics, and business.[493] Granovetter's article has sparked off a deep interest in the concept of embeddedness within academic research, and many authors have built on his contribution to further analyze how the relationships of an economic actor affect his behavior.[494] Embeddedness has since been developed further and deployed in different research scenarios.[495] Dacin et al. (1999), however, having carried out a thorough evaluation of embeddedness research,[496] concluded that new research should move beyond the level of the individual to an organizational or industry level[497] and that more effort is needed to better measure embeddedness.[498] We want to build on their findings and provide an embeddedness concept that is both better measurable and that works on the organizational level and not on the level of the individual actor.

In international business research, Granovetter's original contribution has been used by several authors whose perspective on the MNC has shifted away from the traditional view that MNCs are strictly hierarchical institutions.[499] As discussed above, many authors in the international business field prefer to consider the MNC as a network of heterogeneous units connected to each other in a "tangle" of relationships[500] that affect the behavior of the network actors. For instance, Andersson/Forsgren (1996) emphasize the

---

[492] We concentrate here on Granovetter's initial publication (Granovetter (1985)). There have been several important contributions on embeddedness. For instance, Zukin/DiMaggio (1990) add to the social structure that Granovetter introduced the three dimensions cognitive, cultural, and political embeddedness which can help to better explain situations neoclassical theory was unable to analyze (Zukin/DiMaggio (1990), pp. 14-23). Roughly a decade later, Dacin et al. (1999) present an exhaustive review of the embeddedness concept in organization research. They give an overview of the history of research on embeddedness, describe sources for embeddedness and discuss mechanisms by which embeddedness affects organizational structures and activity. They conclude that embeddedness has proven to be helpful for the analysis of complex environments, and that embeddedness has been successfully used in a large variety of studies (Dacin et al. (1999), p. 343).
[493] Dacin et al. (1999), pp. 317-318.
[494] See, for instance, Kostova (1999), Moran (2005), p. 309.
[495] See, for instance, for the financial service industry, Fischer/Pollock (2004), for emerging economies Choi et al. (1999), for behavioral studies Noordegraaf/Stewart (2000).
[496] For an alternative review see also Halinen/Törnroos (1997).
[497] Dacin et al. (1999), p. 347.
[498] Dacin et al. (1999), p. 343.
[499] Andersson et al. (2001), pp. 1015-1016, Birkinshaw et al. (2002), pp. 276-277.
[500] Hedlund (1986), Bartlett/Ghoshal (1989), Forsgren/Holm (1990), Böttcher (1996), Pahlberg (2001), Schmid (2004).

influence of corporate embeddedness – which is similar to our understanding of network embeddedness – on coordination.[501] Wildemann (1997) describes the dependence of coordination mechanisms on the type of relationships between network partners.[502] Cray (1984) proposes a relation between the number of connections of a unit and the unit's flexibility.[503] Grandori (1997) also interprets different coordination mechanisms as a function of the relationship between partners. She distinguishes pooled, intensive, sequential and reciprocal interdependences and combines them with coordination mechanisms.[504]

With regard to our analysis of service offshoring subsidiaries, the embeddedness approach is very helpful in establishing a relationship between the setup of the network and the resulting impact on the coordination of the service offshoring unit. However, whereas the embeddedness approach is very popular, it nevertheless remains somewhat vague. And a brief look at the literature reveals that the term network embeddedness can have many different meanings.[505] It is the main objective of this section to find out how embeddedness – as one of the pillars of the network view – has been used in international business research and to develop an appropriate operationalization for our purposes. Therefore, in the next sections we will systematically review how embeddedness has been applied and operationalized in recent contributions before we present our own operationalization.

3.3.4 NETWORK EMBEDDEDNESS AS DIMENSION OF SERVICE OFFSHORING

The research on embeddedness falls into two main areas:[506] first, research which concentrates on the structural aspects of relationships and second, research which focuses on the contents of relationships.[507]

Research on *structural* embeddedness refers to the factual characteristics that relationships and an actor's network can have.[508] Indicators can include, for instance, the number of relationships an actor has, the position of an actor in a network of relationships, or the likelihood of adding new relationships to existing ones. The other main stream of

---

[501] Andersson/Forsgren (1996), pp. 493-494.
[502] Wildemann (1997), p. 428.
[503] Cray (1984), p. 87.
[504] Grandori (1997), pp. 901-904.
[505] Halinen/Törnroos (1997), pp. 188-189.
[506] This sub-section corresponds to chapter 3 of the working paper Schmid/Daub (2007).
[507] This distinction is widely used, see Gulati (1998), p. 296, Gnyawali/Madhavan (2001), p. 432, Andersson et al. (2002), p. 980, Moran (2005), p. 1130.
[508] Newburry (2001), p. 499, Karamanos (2003), p. 1872.

embeddedness research deals with *relational* embeddedness and emphasizes the content of the exchanges that take place between two or more actors, for instance, the exchange of information, goods, services, trust or power.[509] While the content of relationships can also be considered an important research topic,[510] we will focus here on structural embeddedness.

The purpose of our analysis is to evaluate how structural embeddedness has been defined and operationalized in international business literature so far. Accordingly, we have selected publications that deal with relationships within the MNC network (intra-organizational network) and publications that address the relationships of MNC actors with external actors (inter-organizational and local network).[511] We have reviewed articles from the major international business journals (Journal of International Business Studies (JIBS), International Business Review (IBR), Management International Review (MIR)) and from major general management journals (Strategic Management Journal (SMJ), Journal of Management Studies (JMS), Academy of Management Review (AOMR), and Academy of Management Journal (AOMJ)).[512] We analyzed all volumes between January 1970 and December 2005,[513] and we searched for all articles that refer to embeddedness in their title, abstract, or keywords. We then excluded all articles ("not relevant") that focus on other than structural embeddedness (for instance, Dhanaraj et al. (2004) who work with relational embeddedness), those articles that do not take an organizational network perspective (for instance, Regnér (2003) who focuses on the individual actor), those articles that use embeddedness in a very different context (for instance Lee/Mitchell et al. (2004) who define and work with *job* embeddedness) and those that mention embeddedness only as a side topic (for instance, Jacobson et al. (1993)). The results of our search are presented in Table 3-1.

---

[509] Rowley et al. (2000), p. 369, Moran (2005), p. 1130.
[510] See, for instance, Dhanaraj et al. (2004), Rutten (2004).
[511] The focus of our study is on intra-organizational networks. We have nonetheless included publications that deal with inter-organizational networks since there are only few contributions that take an exclusively intra-organizational perspective. In addition, the inter-organizational and local network perspectives are closely related to the intra-organizational perspective and can thus add to our findings.
[512] The selection of journals is based on an almost identical selection for international business research in Peng (2001) and on the journal evaluation in Tahai/Meyer (1999). In comparison to Peng (2001) we, however, added Management International Review as a genuine international business journal and did not include Organization Science and the Journal of Management.
[513] With the exception of IBR and SMJ which were first published in 1993 and 1980, respectively.

Table 3-1: Journal contributions on embeddedness

Journal	No. of contributions	Not relevant	Relevant
JIBS[514]	4	Dyer/Chu (2000); Dhanaraj et al. (2004); London/Hart (2004)	Newburry (2001)
IBR	8	D'Cruz/Rugman (1994); Leeds (1998); Araujo/Rezende (2003)	Andersson/Forsgren (1996); Andersson/Forsgren/Pedersen (2001); Schmid/Schurig (2003); Young/Tavares (2004); Andersson et al. (2005)
MIR	3	Choi et al. (1999)	Andersson/Forsgren (2000); Håkanson/Nobel (2001)
SMJ	8	Uzzi/Gillespie (2002); Moran (2005); Villalonga/McGahan (2005)	Gulati (1998); (1999); Rowley et al. (2000); Andersson et al. (2002); Echols/Tsai (2005)
JMS	6	Jacobson et al. (1993); Noordegraaf/Stewart (2000); Levy/Egan (2003); Regnér (2003)	Hardy et al. (2003); Karamanos (2003)
AOMJ	6	Whiteman/Cooper (2000); Mitchell et al. (2001); Gimeno (2004); Lee/Mitchell et al. (2004)	Fischer/Pollock (2004); Venkatraman/Chi-Hyon (2004)
AOMR	6	Brass et al. (1998); Kostova (1999); Scott/Lane (2000); Seo/Creed (2002)	Jones et al. (1997); Gnyawali/Madhavan (2001)

The results of our analysis are presented in a table in the appendix.[515] The most important results of our literature review refer to (1) the timeliness of the concept, (2) the dif-

---

[514] One reference to a dissertation abstract from this journal has not been included.
[515] See appendix, Table: Definitions and uses of embeddedness in a network context. We did not include the table in the text section due to its size.

ferent network levels, (3) the neglect of the intra-organizational perspective, and (4) the breadth of existing operationalizations.

1. The term "embeddedness" is used in a similar way by nearly all authors. There have not been major deviations from Granovetter's (1985) original definition, although there have been some rewordings. Thus, embeddedness today still refers to the fact that the behavior of actors is influenced by their relationships.

2. In the literature on MNCs, embeddedness has been analyzed at several network levels – the intra-organizational, the inter-organizational and the local network level. However, as our results reveal, studies covering all network levels simultaneously do not exist. This shows that most international business authors focus only on specific aspects of international business reality. While we admit that taking into account all three network levels is complex, a concentration on only one or two levels nevertheless remains problematic because some research questions require parallel consideration.[516]

3. It is particularly striking that the intra-organizational network level has not been addressed to a high degree. Thus, despite the prominence of concepts such as Bartlett/Ghoshal's (1989) Transnational Firm, Hedlund's (1986) Heterarchy, White/Poynter's (1989) Horizontal Firm or Doz/Prahalad's (1991) DMNC, there are only very few that refer conceptually or empirically to intra-organizational embeddedness.

4. As far as operationalization is concerned, none of the conceptual publications explicitly dealt with the wide range of potential operationalizations. Not surprisingly, empirical publications contain some information on the operationalization of embeddedness. However, most of the empirical contributions refer to one dimension only. Only a few contributions look at two dimensions, and the only contribution to come up with three dimensions to capture embeddedness is an exploratory study that identifies embeddedness as an important factor (Hardy et al. (2003)). Even those publications which operationalize embeddedness are weak on indicating appropriate measures.

---

[516] For instance, take the example of an MNC that gets important resources from the local network of one of its subsidiaries or the example of how an MNC influences various network units.

We derive two findings from this: The fact that several empirical contributions contained no detailed information on the measures they used seems to underline our initial assumption that embeddedness is very hard indeed to measure. Nevertheless, embeddedness still seems to be a relevant topic worth the "struggle" to capture it in a conceptual and empirical setting, as attested to by the sheer number of contributions which highlight diverse aspects of the concept and take different methodological approaches. However, the broadness of embeddedness is not reflected in the low number of dimensions that the publications listed have used to operationalize it. We thus believe that our attempt to find a more complete operationalization is necessary. The conclusions drawn by other authors have been on similar lines. For instance, after carrying out an empirical study on the impact of structural embeddedness on firm performance, Rowley proposed to look at more dimensions of embeddedness in future studies.[517]

3.3.5 OPERATIONALIZATION OF THE MNC NETWORK APPROACH

We have now discussed how network embeddedness can serve to differentiate service offshoring subsidiaries. However, we still need to develop an operationalization that we can apply in our empirical research. For this purpose we used the framework that was suggested by Schmid (2005) and that can be found in Figure 3-6.

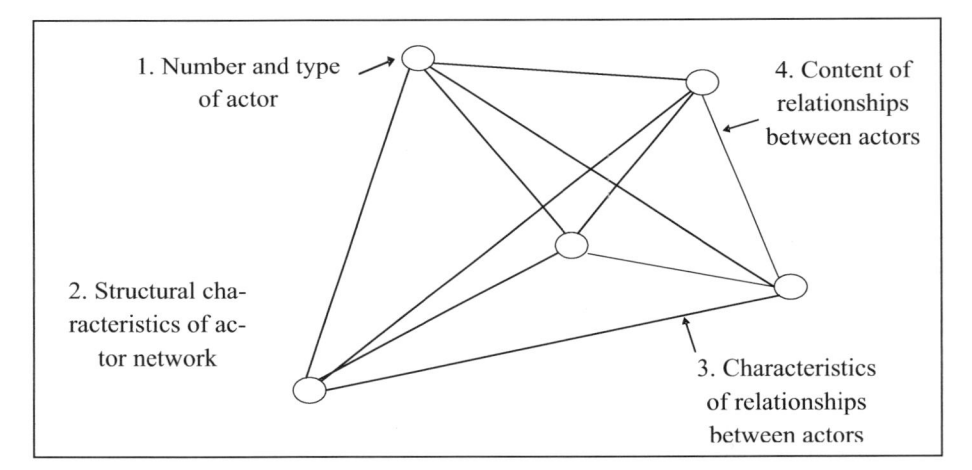

Figure 3-6: Levels of network analysis (Source: Translated from Schmid (2005), p. 243)[518]

1. Number and type of actor
2. Structural characteristics of actor network
3. Characteristics of relationships between actors
4. Content of relationships between actors

---

[517] Rowley et al. (2000), pp. 385-386.
[518] While Schmid uses this figure to discuss different interaction theories, we consider his framework equally helpful to structure operationalizations for embeddedness.

3 – Research Model and Propositions 125

The basic unit of a network is the actor (1). The actor can be an individual, a group or an organization and has often been the unit of analysis in (international) business research – however, without taking into account the aspects of the network that the actors are placed in. Structural characteristics of the network (2) and the characteristics of relationships between actors (3) are dimensions that relate closely to structural embeddedness. Finally, the content of relationships between actors is what relational embeddedness is built upon (4).[519] We will discuss the dimensions (2) and (3) in more detail by going through the different operationalizations that we have analyzed:

Structural characteristics: These characteristics describe the dimension and the configuration of the network. We have encountered several operationalizations in our analysis that fall into this category. Interestingly, they have the commonality that they are often more quantitatively oriented. The basic form is the number of partners that an actor has. For instance, Hardy et al. (2003) base their structural analysis on how many other actors a partner is linked to. Fischer/Pollock (2004) describe how concentrated a network is and how frequently the network changes. Echols/Tsai (2005) use redundancy to describe a similar constellation. Venkatraman/Chi-Hyon (2004) call it "pattern of distribution" but also point out how dense a network around an actor is. Gulati (1998); (1999) uses centrality and density as well as changes in the network structure (frequency and likelihood of adding new ties). The structural characteristics can be easily expressed graphically, as is shown in Figure 3-7. In the left-hand graph which stands for a low degree of embeddedness, there are very few relationships not only between the focal actor (in black) and other actors, but also between other actors. In the right-hand graph which signifies a high degree of embeddedness, every actor (including the focal actor) is connected to many other actors (in this case, to all others, giving the highest possible degree of embeddedness).

The one basic measure that all these operationalizations have in common is the number of relationships the focal actor has. Some authors take into consideration only the number of relationships, others focus more on the proportion of actual to potential number of relationships. But in any case, the number of relationships is a common denominator for all operationalizations. A second notion is added by those operationalizations that include the change in relationships over time.[520] Thus, our first operationalization is the *number of relationships of the focal actor and changes in these relationships over time.*

---

[519] As discussed above, we will not consider relational embeddedness further.
[520] Gulati (1998), Fischer/Pollock (2004).

We assume higher embeddedness for a growing number of relationships and for a higher frequency of change (since a higher frequency of change implies more relationships in a given period of time).[521]

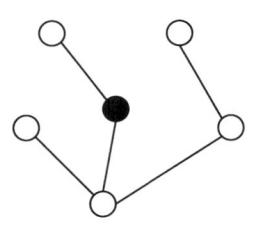

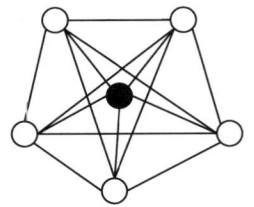

Low embeddedness   High embeddedness

Figure 3-7: Examples for low and high degrees of embeddedness (Source: Inspired by Echols/Tsai (2005), p. 222)

Characteristics of relationships between actors: We now turn our focus to those operationalizations that describe the characteristics of relationships. A group of authors around Andersson and Forsgren has introduced adaptation between partners as an important characteristic of structural embeddedness.[522] Adaptation describes how much actors had to change because of the relationship. With high embeddedness, adaptation is high and vice versa. The "degree of influence" that Schmid/Schurig (2003) use, expresses a similar notion, as does "strength" by Newburry (2001). Hardy et al. (2003) add the dimensions "representative network structure" and "multi-directional flow of information" that can be understood as finer aspects of the same aspect. The first of these describes how well partners feel represented by their counterparts (which increases with mutual adaptation/closeness) and the second considers whether information flows in both directions (which is typically the case with high adaptation/closeness). Finally, the dimension "importance of relationship" by Andersson/Forsgren/Pedersen (2001) is also a characteristic of the relationship. The authors do not specify exactly why they include this dimension but they use it in close association with adaptation. Thus, it seems reasonable to include it in an aggregate operationalization comprising all the dimensions that refer to characteristics of the relationships. We name this operationalization *close-*

---

[521] For instance, we would consider a unit that has has two relationships at any point in time but changed these four times a year to have a higher embeddedness than one that has the same two relationships for the entire year.
[522] See Andersson/Forsgren (1996), Andersson/Forsgren (2000), Andersson et al. (2001), Andersson et al. (2002), Andersson et al. (2005).

ness of relationships. We assume that increasing structural embeddedness is expressed through increased closeness of relationships.

Based on the discussion above, we propose a more complete operationalization of structural embeddedness as *the number of relationships of the focal actor and changes in these relationships over time as well as the closeness of relationships.*

We consider this proposal an advancement compared to existing contributions. We do not think of it as contradictory to the body or embeddedness research, but rather a step towards a more concrete concept and a better operationalization. The major advancements are presented in Table 3-2.

Table 3-2: Differentiating existing embeddedness research from our contribution

Criteria	Existing research	Our proposal
Embeddedness definition	Many existing contributions are based on Granovetter's understanding that embeddedness describes how behavior and institutions are affected by social relations	No difference to existing contributions
Embeddedness concept	Embeddedness is considered the phenomenon that relationships affect behavior	Embeddedness is considered the phenomenon that relationships affect behavior (no change to existing understanding). In addition, the degree of embeddedness can be measured and depending on the degree of embeddedness, different behavior can be expected from the embedded actors
Embeddedness operationalization	Despite its many facets, embeddedness is often operationalized as a one-dimensional construct	Building on existing research, a three-dimensional operationalization for embeddedness has been developed

3.3.6 PROPOSITIONS DERIVED FROM NETWORK APPROACHES

Based on network approaches, we can formulate some propositions on service offshoring subsidiaries and coordination mechanisms.

There are many reports of a negative relationship between the network embeddedness of a unit and its degree of autonomy.[523] The more relationships an entity has, the less it can decide freely about how to behave. Also, when the achievement of scale effects is important, the subsidiary's autonomy will potentially decrease.[524] Scale effects seem to be associated with a higher number of relationships and, thus, higher embeddedness. The more relations a unit has, the closer and the more frequent these relationships are, the fewer options it will have for individual freedom.[525] Thus, we conclude:

P6: The higher the network embeddedness of a service offshoring center, the lower the subsidiary's autonomy and the higher the degree of centralization.[526]

Secondly, we propose a positive relationship between network embeddedness, specifically in form of the number of internal customers that a service offshoring subsidiary serves and the degree of standardization.[527] The higher the number of units to be coordinated is the more important standardization.[528] More customers also mean more interfaces and potentially higher complexity. A way to reduce this complexity would be through standardization.[529] Finally, economies of scale become more relevant for a unit that distributes to a large customer base. Thereby, the importance of standardization also increases.[530] Based on these findings, we can state:

P7: The higher the network embeddedness of a service offshoring center, the higher the level of standardization.

---

[523] Hedlund (1981), Garnier (1982), Andersson/Forsgren (1995), p. 80, Birkinshaw/Morrison (1995), Andersson/Forsgren (1996), Renz (1998), p. 76, Håkansson/Johanson (2001), p. 4, Edwards et al. (2002), p. 185, Young/Tavares (2004), pp. 217-220.
[524] Kim et al. (2003), p. 330.
[525] Cray (1984), p. 87.
[526] We are aware that there can be subsidiaries that are highly integrated into the MNC network and still have a high degree of autonomy, such as – for instance – centers of excellence (see Kutschker et al. (2001)). However, we follow here the general tendencies from traditional literature that point to a decrease of autonomy with increasing integration (see also Young/Tavares (2004), p. 217).
[527] Grant (1996), p. 379, Renz (1998), p. 119.
[528] Van De Ven et al. (1976), p. 331.
[529] Pugh et al. (1968), p. 74, Doz/Prahalad (1984), pp. 59-60.
[530] Quelch/Hoff (1986), p. 62.

Thirdly, we identified reports of a positive relationship between the network embeddedness of a unit and the degree of formalization that is applied.[531] In a situation with many customers and much change in customers it seems likely that formalization will be applied to reduce errors and facilitate the establishment of relationships between new customers and a service offshoring center. Other findings report that higher levels of integration between different units can be reached by higher degrees of formalization to clarify the different roles.[532] Similarly, other authors find that the interaction of many teams and close collaborations occur together with higher degrees of formalization.[533] It is also argued that formalization increases with higher interdependence (which is similar to our closeness facet of network embeddedness).[534] This leads to the following proposition:

P8: The higher the network embeddedness of a service offshoring center, the higher the level of formalization.

When an organization becomes larger and more globally distributed, the role of output-based coordination grows because behavior-based coordination takes more resources and attention. Therefore, for a service offshoring center with organization-wide relationships, output-based coordination is more appropriate.[535] Sales management research reports that groups of sellers with many relationships and close linkages are unlikely to accept formal coordination measures but need performance orientation through output control.[536] When there are frequent changes in the way and the constellation in which a service is provided (which we associate with higher network embeddedness) output control is more recommendable.[537] Also, the higher the within-density in a network of units, the greater the need for the up-front establishment of clear result expectations in order to create a situation in which all the clients of the service offshoring unit receive services of the desired quality. With low within-density, there is much more leeway for follow-up feedback and direct control.[538] Therefore, we conclude:

---

[531] Grandori/Soda (1995), p. 203, Grant (1996), p. 379.
[532] Ayers et al. (2001), p. 142.
[533] Homburg et al. (2002), p. 50.
[534] Ghoshal/Nohria (1989), p. 326.
[535] Ouchi (1978), p. 175.
[536] Brown et al. (2005), p. 158.
[537] Turner/Makhija (2006), p. 204.
[538] Ghoshal/Bartlett (1990), pp. 615-616.

P9: The higher the network embeddedness of a service offshoring center, the higher the level of output-based control.

We summarize our propositions in an overview in Figure 3-8. Not all independent variables influence all dependent variables since the literature did not provide background to establish well-grounded propositions for all possible relationships. It also shows that the influences are partially conflicting. Below, we will discuss the effects of these influences for each individual case.

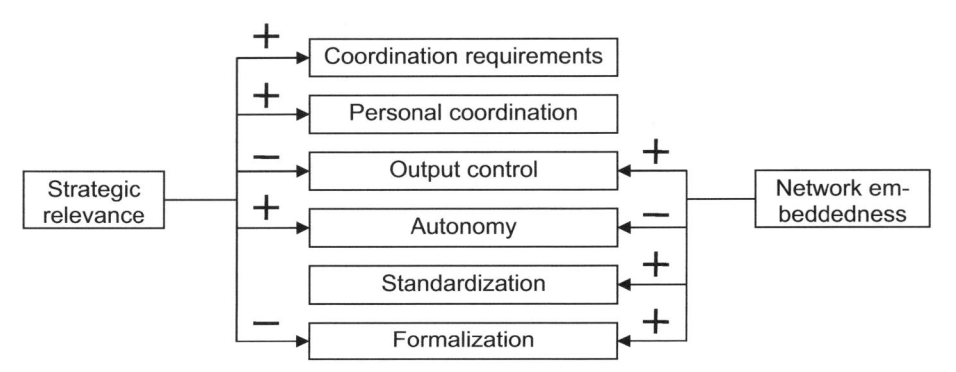

Figure 3-8: Overview of propositions

3.4 RELATIONSHIP BETWEEN RESOURCE-BASED VIEW AND NETWORK APPROACHES

We need to briefly discuss how the two approaches taken in this work relate to one another. We will first discuss similarities of the approaches and then show how they have been combined in prior research.

Both approaches can be seen in a tradition of approaches that take a more "embedded" view, i.e. they consider economic action to be dependent on the historical, cultural, and cognitive links that actors have. These links can be the relationships between actors as the network approaches emphasize and which enhance and constrain an actor's behavior. However, the "embeddedness" idea can also be found in resource-based approaches that see the firm as embedded in its resources.[539] In addition, resources are idiosyncratic and need to be analyzed in their historical circumstances. This embeddedness of re-

---

[539] Baum/Dutton (1996), p. 4.

sources is recognized in the literature on the resource-based view and is regarded, for instance, as making a relocation of resources complicated.[540]

Our two approaches share another similarity: They both consider the individual (organizational) actor. Whereas the resource-based view clearly takes a firm-level perspective, this is not necessarily the case for network approaches. These can be applied on a variety of levels, such as the individual (organizational) actors, network groups or the entire network. As shown above, we take the service offshoring subsidiary as our unit of analysis and therefore use the network approaches on the level of the individual actor. Thus, we have the same level of analysis for both approaches.

As several examples have shown, the two approaches can be meaningfully combined. Dagnino (2004) combines the two approaches in a theoretical contribution and introduces network resources as "resources that emerge from firms' participation in interfirm networks."[541] Zaheer/Zaheer (1997) demonstrate how firms that make use of network resources can gain competitive advantages over their competitors that do not access resources in their network. Other contributions show conceptually and empirically how resources can be accessed in a network of strategic alliances.[542] Jarvenpaa/Leidner (1998) propose an enhancement to the resource-based view to explain how firms in developing countries can interact in their local networks.[543]

To conclude, there are both theoretical alignments between the approaches and sufficient examples of a fruitful combination of the approaches to justify our perspective.

---

[540] Chi (1994). On the embeddedness of resources, see also Karnøe (1995), Lee et al. (2005).
[541] Dagnino (2004), p. 63. As confirmation of that thought, Madhok/Tallman (1998), pp. 336-337 directly relate the value of an alliance to the embeddedness in intra- and inter-organizational relationships.
[542] Eisenhardt/Schoonhoven (1996), Das/Bing-Sheng (2000).
[543] There are more examples that might however not always draw explicitly on both theories. For instance, Combs/Ketchen Jr. (1999) use the resource-based view to discuss interfirm collaboration but do not explicitly refer to network theories.

4 A Typology of Service Offshoring Subsidiary – Combining Building Blocks and Dimensions

"An Ancient Chinese Classification of Animals:

Animals are divided into (a) those that belong to the Emperor, (b) embalmed ones, (c) those that are trained, (d) suckling pigs, (e) mermaids, (f) fabulous ones, (g) stray dogs, (h) those that are included in this classification, (i) those that tremble as if they were mad, (j) innumerable ones, (k) those drawn with a very fine camel's hair brush, (l) other, (m) those that have just broken a flower vase, and (n) those that resemble flies from a distance."

Jorge Luis Borges

Summary

This chapter combines the propositions that we have derived from the resource-based view and from the MNC network approach to a typology that enables us to differentiate between service offshoring subsidiaries and to make propositions on the coordination mechanisms in place. We show how we can overcome certain shortcomings of typology development by our research design. We then describe four extreme types – the service factory, the internal competence center, the support center, and the specialized contributor – for high and low values of strategic relevance and network embeddedness. Finally, we argue along the lines of proponents of middle-range theories that an extension of our typology is in principle possible but not necessary for our research.

4.1 METHODOLOGY OF TYPOLOGY DEVELOPMENT

4.1.1 APPLICATION IN CURRENT RESEARCH

While we have already presented an overview of typologies in general and of subsidiary typologies in international business research in particular, we have so far dealt with existing typologies. However, as we indicated above, we have not found an existing typology that we could readily apply to service offshoring and have therefore decided to develop one that is aligned with our purpose. We will now turn our focus to this task.[544]

Our typology must fulfill three major goals in accordance with our research questions:

1. It shall serve to differentiate types of service offshoring centers. Differentiation will be oriented towards the dimensions that we developed above in the context of the resource-based view and network approaches.

2. In addition, the typology shall be used to combine the propositions we derived above with regard to coordination mechanisms for each of the ideal types of service offshoring subsidiaries.

3. Finally, the typology shall provide the basis for an empirical assessment of service offshoring subsidiaries in MNCs.

To reach the first goal, it is necessary to discuss how the dimensions are used in the development of the typology. This question has been assessed by Dess et al. (1993) in a publication that deals with the evolvement of typologies. The authors define the number of dimensions and the resulting types as one of the major questions to be answered. While the number of dimensions increases arithmetically, the number of resulting types increases geometrically. This leads to a higher degree of differentiation that comes most likely at the expense of rich description of the individual type.[545] Our typology will be based on two major dimensions – network embeddedness of the subsidiary and strategic relevance of the service provided by the offshoring subsidiary. The reasons for the choice of these dimensions were discussed in chapter 3 of this work. However, why do we use two dimensions instead of one or more than two? Firstly, we settled for no fewer than two dimensions because we wanted to go beyond traditional single-domain studies.

---

[544] A first version of the service offshoring subsidiary typology was already presented in chapter 5 of Schmid/Daub (2005). In this broader discussion here we discussed the methodology for typology development in more depth and address typical criticism that is leveled at subsidiary typologies.

[545] Dess et al. (1993), pp. 777-778.

Secondly, we opted for two dimensions (and not more) because the field of study is already narrowed down to a specific type of international subsidiary. A more fine-grained approach could lead to theoretical differentiation but not necessarily to more substance. Thirdly, we need to control complexity. More dimensions would mean many more types that are harder to understand and to differentiate. Fourthly and finally, we decided for this (necessary) simplification in comparison to multiple domain studies because of the time and budget constraints that are especially relevant in our research design, which involves much international travel. Rather, we collected a substantial amount of information per case to provide rich descriptions.

To reach the second goal we will analyze how the dimensions as independent variables relate to the control mechanisms as dependent variables. Dess et al. (1993) point out that independent variables need to be outside the control of dependent variables and need to be fixed over time.[546] With regard to our dimensions, this condition seems to be fulfilled. As outlined above, our typology is not an end in itself; rather, the two dimensions and the subsidiary types (as independent variables) are the basis for delineating the coordination requirements for these subsidiaries (as dependent variables). In management practice, most MNCs first establish subsidiaries and then install the appropriate coordination mechanisms. We admit, however, that subsidiaries, once established, might take over different tasks or have their organizational setup changed based on past cooperation and specifically based on past coordination experiences. Furthermore, some MNCs may even consider questions of coordination before and when making their decision on creating or developing their service offshoring subsidiaries. Nevertheless, we can assume that, in many cases, coordination mechanisms are a function of organizational setup and kind of service (and not vice versa).

With regard to this second goal, we need to point to the possibility of conflicting propositions on coordination mechanisms deriving from the different dimensions. While some propositions from the dimensions seem to complement one another, others might not be consistent or even turn out to be conflicting. We decided to describe these conflicts as part of our typology as we considered this a more appropriate approach than to conceal them. In the empirical part of our research, we will specifically evaluate those constellations with conflicting propositions.

---

[546] Dess et al. (1993), p. 780.

We will discuss how we intend to reach the third goal in the subsequent sections on the case study method. Having discussed the basic principles of our typology, we will follow the step-wise approach for typology creation that was proposed by Doty/Glick (1994) and was successfully used in earlier research.[547] According to the authors, typology development should encompass the following steps:[548]

1. *Statement of grand theoretical assertion(s)*: The underlying assumptions should be made explicit. They can refer to the effectiveness of the different types and to the relationship between the independent and the dependent variables. From the outset, all of our types are equally effective and we do not include an effectiveness measure in our typology. With regard to the second point, we assume that the coordination mechanisms depend on the choice of organizational setup (as expressed by the dimension "network embeddedness") as well as on the kind of service offshored (as expressed by the dimension "strategic relevance").

2. *Complete definition of the set of ideal types*: The definition of types has two aspects. On the one hand, researchers should develop ideal types within their typology. On the other hand, they should explain what kind of hybridization between ideal types is possible to increase the "likelihood that their typology meets the criterion of falsifiability"[549]. Ideal types can be developed either theoretically by defining the ideal types as the endpoints on a continuum or empirically by selecting ideal cases from a set of data. The theoretical approach is more appropriate since ideal cases might not be found in the available data set.[550] Thus, we will derive the ideal types based on the theory. After defining them, we will present possibilities for hybridization together with the typology below.

3. *Complete description of each ideal type with the same set of dimensions*: Researchers should describe resulting types according to the same dimensions. In our case, all types of service offshoring subsidiaries will be depicted using the two dimensions of the typology and the same set of coordination mechanisms.

---

[547] See, for instance, Potter et al. (2004), who explicitly refer to Doty/Glick (1994) in their development of a typology for capability assessment.
[548] Doty/Glick (1994), pp. 245-247.
[549] Doty/Glick (1994), p. 246.
[550] Doty/Glick (1994), pp. 238-239.

4. *Explicit statement of importance of each construct*: Researchers are encouraged to explicitly describe the different constructs in their typologies and explain their relative importance. We will satisfy this requirement by describing the constructs and discussing the importance of each of them. With regard to the relative importance of the dimensions, we have no reason to assume anything other than an equal importance of network embeddedness and strategic relevance.

5. *Test with conceptual and analytical methods that are consistent with the theory*: We will evaluate the theory – which is our typology – by carrying out case studies for the extreme cases of our typology. We prefer to speak of "evaluation" instead of "testing" which is generally associated with large-scale quantitative studies. We consider this evaluation to be a method that is consistent with the theory since our propositions are grounded in organizational theory; however, we want to leave room and flexibility for enhancing the typology and therefore opted for a qualitative research design.[551]

The present research will follow these steps in the proposed order.

4.1.2 CRITICISM OF TYPOLOGY RESEARCH AND POSSIBLE ANSWERS

Typology development faces a range of criticism. We focus here on the specific criticisms that have been leveled at subsidiary typologies. Typological research has several shortcomings which Schmid et al. (1998) describe in their comprehensive overview of subsidiary typologies. We have listed these shortcomings in the first column of Table 4-1 and indicated in the second column how we shall address them.

---

[551] See section 5.2 for a detailed discussion of the choice for a qualitative research approach.

Table 4-1: Typical shortcomings of subsidiary typologies and possible solutions (Source: Shortcomings are taken from Schmid et al. (1998), pp. 95-99)

Typical shortcoming	Possible solution
Dimensions are not theoretically grounded	We consider the resource-based view and network approaches to be relevant theoretical groundings for our research question and base our typology on them. Admittedly, we have no possibility to explain for each alternative theory why it has not been selected. However, this is not a specific problem of typological research but a question that any research has to deal with.
Typologies simplify too much which can lead to inaccurate results if normative prescriptions are derived from oversimplified types	Of course, complexity reduction is a feature of typologies that we want to make use of in our research. However, we want to make it explicit that our research aims not only at the development of discrete types but also at the description of ranges and causal relationships that allow for intermediate types. In addition, we want to position our typology as a relevant one but by no means as the only possible to describe and evaluate service offshoring subsidiaries. Furthermore, since we do not intend to develop normative results from our study, this criticism does not directly apply.
Typologies are deterministic as they define a specific role based on a few dimensions (closeness to contingency approaches)	Even though some authors explicitly differentiate typologies/configurational approaches from contingency approaches,[552] several other researchers see typologies close to contingency approaches.[553] We also see clear links between the two and cannot refute this argument in its entirety. We believe, however, that our approach to explain causal relations but not to claim them as the only possible ones is a working solution for this issue – even though there is no final resolution since every typology is a reduction to a few dimensions.

---

[552] Miller (1981), p. 2, Meyer et al. (1993), and Colbert (2004), pp. 344-345.
[553] Pinder/Moore (1979), p. 100, Gresov (1989), p. 431.

Typical shortcoming	Possible solution
Many subsidiary typologies see the headquarters at the center of attention defining subsidiary roles top-down	We agree that several subsidiary typologies have this shortcoming and often do not attach enough attention on the subsidiary as an individual firm. However, in our research with relatively "young" service offshoring subsidiaries that are established by the headquarters, we think this approach is adequate. In addition, our unit of analysis is the subsidiary itself.
Sampling from different companies disregards the relationships within one MNC	Our approach considers only those subsidiaries where we can also include the headquarters in our sample, thus allowing better analysis of the relationships within one MNC.
Overrepresentation of empirically derived taxonomies versus theoretically derived typologies	We have decided to develop a theoretically derived typology that helps to overcome this imbalance. According to Ketchen Jr. et al. (1993), theoretically derived typologies also give better predictive results compared to empirically derived taxonomies.[554]

To conclude, we can counter the typical criticism with regard to lack of theoretical grounding, sampling from different companies, and overrepresentation of taxonomies through our research design. We have also provided answers to the other points of criticism – simplification, closeness to contingency approaches, too much attention on headquarters – although we are not able to refute them completely since they are very closely linked to the very concept of typological research which we still consider an invaluable research stream for a better understanding of the international subsidiary. Accordingly, we deploy it in our own study.

4.2 PRESENTATION OF TYPOLOGY

As outlined above, our differentiation of offshoring subsidiaries is based on a two-dimensional matrix: Whereas the horizontal dimension relates to the kind of service that the service offshoring subsidiary carries out, the vertical dimension describes the organ-

---

[554] Ketchen Jr. et al. (1993), p. 1308.

4 – A Typology of Service Offshoring Subsidiary

izational setup in which it operates. The kind of service builds on the resource-based view and distinguishes services by their strategic relevance for the MNC. The organizational setup builds on network approaches and captures the embeddedness of the service offshoring subsidiary in the MNC network.[555] In combining these two dimensions, we derive the typology that is presented in Figure 4-1.

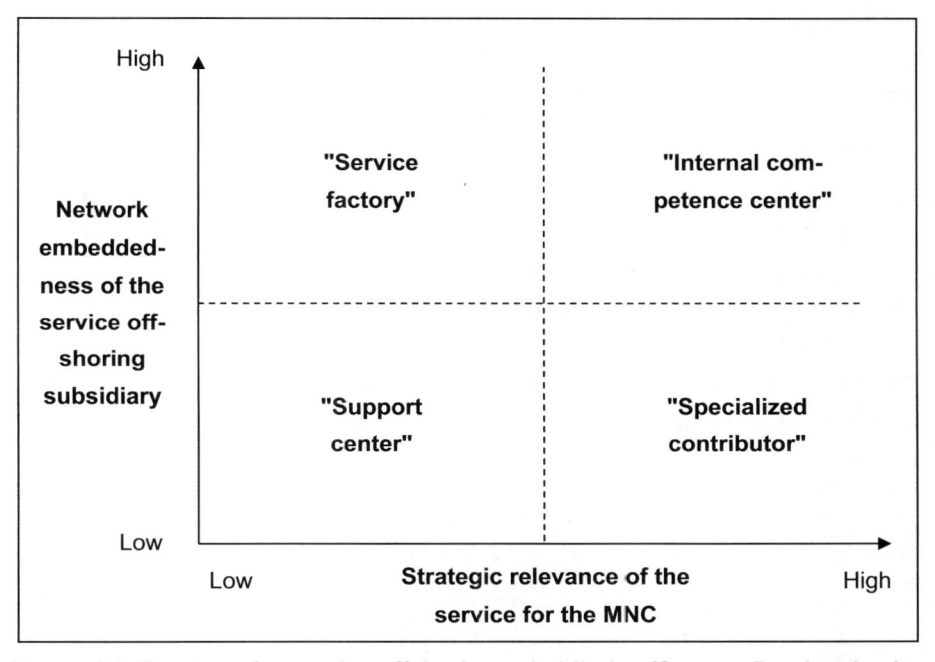

[Figure: 2x2 matrix. Y-axis: "Network embeddedness of the service offshoring subsidiary" (Low to High). X-axis: "Strategic relevance of the service for the MNC" (Low to High). Quadrants: High embeddedness/Low relevance = "Service factory"; High embeddedness/High relevance = "Internal competence center"; Low embeddedness/Low relevance = "Support center"; Low embeddedness/High relevance = "Specialized contributor".]

Figure 4-1: Typology for service offshoring subsidiaries (Source: Previously also in Schmid/Daub (2005), p. 17).

4.3 DISCUSSION OF RESULTING TYPES

We will now proceed to describe the resulting types. We will refer to the dimensions introduced above and relate the coordination mechanisms to the subsidiary types. To be able to differentiate types, we chose to describe the extremes of our dimensions. In reality, however, a center could be of a given type even if not all the elements are present. Having said this, it is important to note that the typology does not represent a categorization of just four types. Rather, since we have developed each dimension as a contin-

---

[555] We will from now on refer to the dimensions succinctly as "strategic relevance" and "network embeddedness".

uum, we believe hybrids between the extremes are possible as well.[556] We expect this to be reflected in the choice of coordination mechanisms. For instance, we assume that strategic relevance and network embeddedness can vary in degree. In cases of medium values, we imagine a center that is endowed with resources of medium strategic relevance and that serves several other units within the MNC but does not have very many relations. In this case, the coordination mechanisms could also be adapted. Standardization and formalization would still need to be applied but potentially to a different degree than in extreme cases. The same would hold true for other coordination mechanisms.

4.3.1 SERVICE FACTORY

The service factory is a unit that is very highly embedded in the MNC's network. We chose to call this type of subsidiary a service factory as it has characteristics reminiscent of a factory that produces a standardized set of products for a large number of customers. It has links not only to MNC headquarters but also to a high percentage of other international subsidiaries in the MNC's network. Its relationships to other units within the MNC are close and there is a high frequency of changes to the relationships with its MNC network partners, such as additions of new relationships.

The resources it holds are not of high strategic relevance for the firm and the services it provides based on these resources are typically not very valuable in a sense that they would meet a key need of its customers. The services will be also available in other firms or even on external markets. They are not very complex, which facilitates their imitation; they could in fact be considered a commodity. Also, they could be substituted by other or similar services. The primary motive for the establishment of the center is cost and efficiency.

The interaction between the service factory and the other units will be driven by the need to carry out the interaction as efficiently as possible, while maintaining the desired levels of quality. As there are a large number of customers to be dealt with, there is probably a tendency to centralize decisions regarding service execution (implying a low degree of autonomy). It seems likely that headquarters will define the main principles of interaction between the service factory and its clients in a top-down fashion. This leads to formalization and standardization of the resulting relationship. Methods employed could be IT-based order-tracking systems that make personal involvement in coordina-

---

[556] Other typologies specify propositions for each type and do not allow for hybrids (see for an example Adam Jr. (1983)). Moore finds hybrid type for the Miles-Snow typology (Moore (2005), p. 702).

tion less necessary. Also, output-based coordination seems very appropriate to deal with many similar relationships and is expected to be at a high level. Lastly, the overall extent of coordination required is only low to medium.

This type of center could be of interest for an MNC that wants to standardize and rationalize services which are needed in many parts of the corporation. The main focus will be on economies of scale.

4.3.2 Internal Competence Center

The term "internal competence center" used here to denote one type of service offshoring center is very close to "competence center" that has been used frequently in international business literature. We stick to the definition put forward by Schmid (2000), but omit the (external) market responsibility, since this is not a necessary characteristic for the *internal* service offshoring subsidiary. Thus, the internal competence center is highly regarded within the MNC's network for its competence on a specific topic.[557] An internal competence center shows a high degree of network embeddedness in the MNC's network. It has relationships not only to the headquarters but it is linked to many other units in the MNC network, as the resources it has are rare and required by many other units. These relationships are close as they show a high degree of adaptation between the partners. Furthermore, there are frequent changes to the structure of the relationships.

With regard to its strategic relevance, the internal competence center provides services that are of high value for the MNC and that meet important needs of its customers. It provides a broad range of services. These services are not available elsewhere and they cannot be imitated easily as they are very complex. Also, there is no substitute for these services available. The primary motive for the establishment of the center is quality and effectiveness.

In this case, there is a trade-off between standardizing and individualizing service delivery between the internal competence center and the other units. This conflict is displayed in the competing demands for autonomy and integration that we have derived above.[558] On the one hand, there are many other units to be dealt with. In order not to increase complexity too much, it will be necessary to streamline communication and

---

[557] See also Schmid (1999), pp. 5-6.
[558] For a similar case, see Schmid et al. (1998), p. 82.

coordination. On the other hand, the complexity and relevance of the service carried out by this center are so high that it is hard to coordinate in a standardized fashion. The MNC has to implement flexible measures that allow it to reach a tailored result for all the individual requirements while dealing with many internal customers. Thus, there will be medium to high autonomy to allow the internal competence center to remain flexible. One possible solution to this conflict of interests could be to clearly separate those areas in which the subsidiary is allowed to make its own decisions and those areas where the headquarters retains decision making power.[559] Also, standardization and formalization will only be at a medium level as they have to reflect the competing demands for economies of scale and individual requirements. Output control will be at low to medium levels since the complexity of the services does not allow an exact specification which might be considered desirable to better deal with many relationships. Personal coordination on the other hand seems to be necessary for this type of service offshoring center. Equally, there could be a high number of personnel transfers to ensure smooth operations and transfer of knowledge. Given the complexity of the service, it seems likely that the extent of coordination required will be medium to high.

This type of center can be used by MNCs that want to build a strong unit for a strategically relevant service for many or all MNC units. One example could be the execution and delivery of research and development services for an entire corporation.

4.3.3 SUPPORT CENTER

The support center is in the lower left corner of the typology. We call it support center because its main role is to support other units of the firm. It is characterized by low network embeddedness, as it serves only one or very few other units in the MNC network and is not closely connected to other units. Also, there will be only infrequent changes to the number and structure of relationships with its partners in the MNC network.

Moreover, the services it provides are of low strategic relevance. They are not very valuable, as they do not help the firm improve its performance neither are they rare, as they could also be bought from outside sources. Not being complex, the services could be imitated by other firms. Finally, the services could be substituted by other services. As with the service factory, the main focus of the support center will be cost and efficiency.

---

[559] Herbert (1984), p. 265.

Due to the limited scope in both number of internal clients and degree of strategic relevance of this type of service offshoring center, coordination will most likely be less formal and without a high degree of standardization but at the same time it will not allow for high flexibility. Thus, there will be a low level of autonomy. Output control can play some role for coordination as it can be an efficient means that avoids more costly personal interaction.

Personal coordination might be required only to a lesser extent as the services are of relatively low complexity. For instance, there will only be few transfers. Finally, the extent of coordination required will be low.

This type of center could best be used as a unit that takes over excess capacity of the service that is carried out. An example could be a center that carries out low-value services for a given function, for instance, services for a function that executes more complex services in the headquarters.

4.3.4 SPECIALIZED CONTRIBUTOR

The specialized contributor is a unit that executes services only for one or few units of the corporation. Because of this specialization on a few units and on strategically highly relevant services that it contributes to the MNC, we decided to use the term "specialized contributor". It does not have very close relationships to other units, and changes to the structure and number of relationships are infrequent.

However, its services are carried out on the basis of resources that belong to the strategically highly relevant resource-set of the corporation. The services it carries out help the firm become more effective. In addition, these services are rare and cannot be purchased from the outside. Also, they are rather complex which prevents their imitation. Finally, they cannot be substituted by other services as the desired results can only be achieved with the given services. The primary motive for the establishment of the specialized contributor is quality and effectiveness. It can exploit low labor costs and tap the local talent pool but does not aim for economies of scale.

Consequently, while individualized interaction and coordination are necessary, there is not such a strong need to standardize coordination. This is because the specialized contributor deals only with very few other units; however, some level of technocratic mechanisms might be needed to provide guidelines for dealing with the complex services. Thus, levels of standardization and formalization will be rather low to medium, as the complexity of the service requires more personal coordination and higher autonomy for the subsidiary, which means less centralization of decisions. Output control seems unlikely to be important since the results are too complex to allow for pre-specification. To ensure knowledge transfer, personal coordination will probably play an important role; for instance, there will be regular visits to the center from other units of the MNC. The overall extent of coordination required will be high.

This type of center could best be used by an MNC that is still very much focused on its headquarters but wants to make use of service offshoring as well. It could move parts of its service operations to an offshore location without changing the entire organizational structure. An example could be a software company that moves parts of its product development division to an offshore location. While it is not necessary that the specialized contributor deals with many units in the MNC network, coordination has to be flexible to allow it to carry out the complex tasks.

4.3.5 Summary of Characteristics of Service Offshoring Subsidiaries

Based on the propositions and the descriptions above we have summarized the characteristics of the service offshoring subsidiaries in Table 4-2. We display all coordination mechanisms (in the rows) for all types (in the columns) and represent the expected values low (L), medium (M), or high (H) by squares of different sizes.

Table 4-2: Overview of characteristics of service offshoring subsidiaries

Coordination mechanism	Service Factory	Internal Competence Center	Support Center	Specialized Contributor
Overarching				
Extent of coordination requirements	■-■ (L-M)	■-■ (M-H)	■ (L)	■-■ (M-H)
Structural coordination				
Degree of autonomy	■ (L). Low strategic relevance does not need high degree of autonomy	■-■ (M-H). High strategic relevance in the center requires more autonomy	■ (L). Services are ordered from the customer on a case-by-case basis; decisions are taken by customers	■ (H). As services are of high relevance; decisions are delegated to where the knowledge is

4 – A Typology of Service Offshoring Subsidiary

Coordination mechanism	Service Factory	Internal Competence Center	Support Center	Specialized Contributor
Technocratic coordination				
Degree of standardization	■ (H). As many customers need to be served, aiming for economies of scale	■ (M). High strategic relevance will require flexibility but trade-off because of high number of customers that will require standardization for complexity reasons	▪ (L). As support center is used on a case-by-case basis, standardization is not necessary/possible	▪-■ (L-M). High strategic relevance will require flexibility
Degree of formalization	■ (H). Many standardized cases make formalization appropriate	■ (M). High number of clients require formalization but individual solutions cause trade-off	▪ (L). Few standardized cases do not require formalization	▪-■ (L-M). Individual cases and high competences will need flexibility
Output control				
Degree of output control	■ (H). Many network partners require pre-specification of results	▪-■ (L-M). Diversified and complex requirements prevent pre-specification of results; however, partially offset by need to deal with many network partners	■ (M). Low strategic relevance does not justify resource-intense behavior control	▪ (L). Behavior control more appropriate for high strategic relevance

Coordination mechanism	Service Factory	Internal Competence Center	Support Center	Specialized Contributor
Personal approaches				
Degree of personal direct coordination	■ (L). Execution of standardized, less complex services needs little direct interaction	■-■ (M-H). Strategic relevance makes personal interaction necessary	■-■ (L-M). Execution of strategically less relevant services needs little direct interaction	■-■ (M-H). Strategic relevance makes personal interaction necessary
Number of visits	■ (M). Medium number of visits, medium duration per visit	■ (H). High number of visits, long duration per visit	■ (L). Low number of visits, short duration per visit	■ (H). High number of visits, long duration per visit
Number of transfers	■ (M). Medium number of transfers; potentially mainly management, locals in line positions	■ (H). High number of transfers; potentially in management and line positions	■ (L). Low number of transfers; potentially only management	■ (H). High number of transfers; potentially in management and line positions
Importance of culture-based coordination	■ (M). Medium level of normative integration	■ (H). High level of normative integration	■ (L). Low level of normative integration	■ (H). High level of normative integration

4.4 EXTENSION OF SERVICE OFFSHORING TYPOLOGY TO OTHER SUBSIDIARIES

One could ask if the typology that is developed in this work would not lend itself for use with any type of subsidiary. There is no easy response to this question. Before discussing an answer, there should be some reflection on the background of the question which is natural as research obviously tends to aim for generalizable results. Thus, the question expresses the interest in obtaining results which have implications that go beyond service offshoring subsidiaries. It would indeed be useful to have a general theory of how to coordinate subsidiaries of all kinds, and the initial tendency might be to make the typology applicable to any type of subsidiary. However, there are also some pitfalls to

4 – A Typology of Service Offshoring Subsidiary

consider when seeking an answer some of which are methodological in nature, others refer more to potential contradictions in content.

With regard to methodology, it has to be questioned whether or not generalizable theories are always desirable. Many scholars have called upon researchers to develop more middle range theories which would be more helpful for concrete managerial problems.[560] Many findings from business research have been discredited in the management world as being too general and of little benefit to managers in improving the management of their companies and thus, not applicable.[561] Theories that intentionally limit their scope to allow for more precise results might be of more value to practitioners. Moreover, our research question has a narrow and specific focus and we have found a methodology that is consistent with our purpose. A generalizable typology can hardly be evaluated with the approach that we have opted for.

When it comes to the actual content of the typology, it is important to analyze the two dimensions in more depth in order to find out whether or not they are specific to service offshoring. Of course, any kind of subsidiary can be described in regard to the two chosen dimensions. But service offshoring centers could be unique as we shall demonstrate separately for each of the dimensions:

Service offshoring has the potential to reach a higher degree of *network embeddedness* than has been possible before. Manufacturing offshoring is always limited by the speed at which physical goods can be moved and by the cost of these movements. With transportation costs and transportation time almost zero, service offshoring can lead to a situation where a firm's value chain is split into many more elements than would be feasible in manufacturing offshoring. Thus, there will be higher coordination requirements (as the coordination effort will most likely increase with the number of units to coordinate). As a result, the network embeddedness that expresses the degree to which a unit is linked to other units will be different – probably higher – in service than in manufacturing offshoring. For example: A service offshoring center can easily connect to several hundred other units in the MNC network and change these relationships very frequently. If it works in a "follow-the-sun" mode, the relationships can even change on a daily basis. This seems hard to imagine for a car manufacturer that could potentially deliver cars from one factory to many international subsidiaries but could not switch re-

---

[560] Weick (1974), p. 357, Pinder/Moore (1979), p. 100, Sanchez (1993), pp. 73-74.
[561] Priem/Rosenstein (2000).

sponsibility for car production between different centers several times a day since the product itself cannot be moved so quickly between locations.[562]

Service offshoring also has the potential to affect the second dimension of the typology. Of course, every subsidiary can be judged based on its *strategic relevance*. Still, service offshoring provides a unique setting in that it potentially allows for very high levels of strategic relevance. Whereas manufacturing offshoring is typically concerned with the devolvement of low-complexity jobs,[563] service offshoring can include a wide variety of services, from very standardized to highly complex ones that are at the core of the corporation. In this respect, there can be a vast difference between service and manufacturing offshoring subsidiaries.

We have now argued why we limit our typology to service offshoring versus manufacturing. However, there is another important argument why we limit it to service offshoring as compared to any other subsidiary. The reason is simply that there needs to be some level of constant coordination between the provider and the receiver of a service. This is not necessarily the case with other subsidiaries. For instance, subsidiaries in a financial holding company might have interaction with the headquarters only once a year when they need to report some financial data. Only a permanent (service) delivery agreement makes ongoing coordination necessary and therefore makes this research different. Besides, a service offshoring center has limited or no relationships to the local market, which might also impact the coordination mechanisms between them and other units of the firm.[564]

Thus, a subsequent extension of the typology might be possible but does not seem adequate or necessary for the scope of our research.

---

[562] See also the description of the "follow-the-sun" principle in section 2.2.4.2.
[563] See also discussion in section 2.2.2.2.
[564] Andersson (2003), p. 438.

5 Methodology – Preparing and Conducting Qualitative Research

"Method goes far to prevent trouble in business:
for it makes the task easy, hinders confusion,
saves abundance of time, and instructs those that have business depending,
both what to do and what to hope."

William Penn

Summary

This chapter shows how we execute the empirical part of our study. We have decided to use case studies to explore and explain the new phenomenon service offshoring. They have been selected from German MNCs and their Eastern European service offshoring subsidiaries to exclude influences of different home countries on coordination and to further the knowledge on service offshoring to Eastern Europe. Our functional focus is on subsidiaries that carry out information technology services. During site visits, we interviewed 24 managers in headquarters, service offshoring subsidiaries, and other international subsidiaries. The interviews were transcribed and then subjected to content analysis. Based on the assignment of codes to the transcripts, we evaluated the appropriateness of the propositions from our typology. In accordance with the literature on qualitative research, we took several measures to ensure the quality of our findings.

5.1 OVERVIEW OF CHOICES

This chapter introduces the methodological choices that we had to make in the framework of the present empirical research. Choices had to be made in three areas:

1. *Illustration and evaluation of typology:* The research entails an empirical component for illustration and evaluation of our typology. The first major decision then was between a qualitative and a quantitative research design.[565] We opted for the former. Within qualitative research, there are again many different methods,[566] of which we selected case studies. In the section on case study methodology (section 5.2), we will present the reasons for our choice and discuss the consequences. We will also present further methodological choices we had to make such as, for instance, interview design.

2. *Regional focus of empirical research:* While our research topic is not primarily related to a specific geographic region, it was necessary to focus on a specific region in order to make our cases more comparable. We decided to carry out case studies with German MNCs that have service offshoring centers in Eastern Europe. We describe the motive for this choice in section 5.3.

3. *Functional focus of empirical research:* Along the same lines of reasoning that we followed for regional focus, we argue that it was necessary to limit our empirical research to a single company function. We opted to concentrate on the IT function. Why we take this stance, is discussed in section 5.4.

In the following sections, we discuss each of these choices in more detail. We do not limit ourselves to "textbook"-like accounts of the available options, but rather, describe in depth the solutions that we deploy in the current research.

---

[565] We understand research design as "the overall structure and orientation of an investigation. This structure provides a framework within which data are collected and analyzed" (Bryman (1989), p. 28).

[566] "*Research methods* [emphasis in original] ... refer to operational techniques of data collection. They are less the overall strategy of investigation than the actual means to seek empirical data and information." (Yeung (1995), p. 316).

5.2 Typology Illustration and Evaluation

5.2.1 Description of the Case Study Method

5.2.1.1 Overview of Qualitative Research and the Case Study Method

Our research is an explanatory study into the new phenomenon of service offshoring. To support our research empirically, the use of case studies as research methodology seems to be the most appropriate. Case studies typically fall within the category of qualitative research approaches. This section will briefly describe qualitative research approaches and define and discuss the case study method, before the next sections present reasons why it was given preference for this research, and finally explain in more detail the way it has been used in the present work.

Qualitative research methods are typically seen as being more adaptable to the subject under study. Qualitative research is not unequivocally defined,[567] but there are some basic principles that can usually be encountered. According to Mayring (2002), these are the following:[568]

1. Qualitative research relates to research subjects in their *everyday lives*. Unlike quantitative approaches that typically try to control external influences, qualitative research emphasizes the natural setting. In addition, it is stressed that all the facets of a phenomenon need to be considered in their relationships to one another and its entirety.[569] Qualitative research also takes into account the historical circumstances, and, lastly, it is supposed to deal with concrete problems and to offer possible solutions.[570]

2. The basis for analysis is a *detailed description* of the research area. It is important to have descriptions on the level of individual cases to ensure that the methods and results are adequate for each case under consideration. Besides, qualitative research needs to be open to changes and innovations of content and methods in order to deal with the research subject as effectively as possible.[571]

---

[567] Mason (2002), p. 3.
[568] We here refer to Mayring (2002), however, similar elaborations can be found in Lamnek (1995), pp. 21-30 or Flick et al. (2003), p. 24.
[569] Flick (2002), p. 17.
[570] Mayring (2002), pp. 33-35.
[571] Mason (2002), pp. 3-4.

However, to prevent this openness from affecting the reliability of the research, there should be regular control and documentation.[572]

3. The research subject is never entirely evident, but knowledge has to be generated by *interpretation* rather than by statistical analysis.[573] Since interpretation is also dependent on the researcher's knowledge, this knowledge and its evolution have to be made explicit in the research process.[574]

4. Results from qualitative research cannot be "automatically" generalized by specific statistical methods.[575] Rather, *generalization* has to be discussed for the individual research approach. Therefore, the researcher needs to show which results can be generalized and which cannot. In addition, induction is an important principle in qualitative research. It is thought that repeated observation can lead to insight. However, qualitative research very rarely leads to the creation of law-like statements but rather to rules that are context-bound. And even though they do not depend on statistical analysis, qualitative research methods do not preclude them and can also form the basis for later quantitative studies.[576]

There is little doubt that qualitative research can help bring to light new topics and develop new theories.[577] Where there is no previous theory, the use of quantitative testing approaches is precluded from the outset. Once a theory is created, it can be tested with the help of statistical methods. However, even if it is not generally accepted, qualitative research can also be helpful in testing a theory, especially when it comes to complex research subjects, for which qualitative methods can be adapted more flexibly to the specific circumstances.[578] And while qualitative methods do not allow for statistical representativeness – and do not even aim for it – it is possible to apply inferences from the analysis of a few cases to other cases. However, the results from qualitative research will initially remain middle-range theories that are context-bound and that do not claim the nomothetic results of quantitative analysis.[579]

---

[572] Mayring (2002), pp. 25-29.
[573] This point is also confirmed by Mason (2002), pp. 3-4.
[574] Mayring (2002), pp. 29-32.
[575] Cassell/Symon (1994), p. 4, Mason (2002), pp. 3-4.
[576] Mayring (2002), pp. 35-38.
[577] Lee (1999), p. 38, Yin (2003), Wrona (2005), p. 3.
[578] Mayring (2002), pp. 1-2.
[579] Wrona (2005), pp. 11-12.

5 – Methodology

Case studies are only one of the many possible research methodologies within qualitative research. It is even argued that a case study does not imply any specific methodology but that it can be used and has been used with "a variety of different epistemological positions, from positivist to phenomenological"[580] as well as with different methods of data collection.[581] Before discussing the reasons for using case studies, we want to present the case study definition from Yin which we consider adequate for our study. He defines that "*a case study is an empirical inquiry that* [emphasis in original] investigates a contemporary phenomenon within its real-life context, especially when the boundaries between phenomenon and context are not clearly evident."[582]

Even though there is an overall trend toward quantitative studies,[583] there are also calls such as Mintzberg's for better and more in-depth description: "There has been a tendency to prescribe prematurely in Management Policy – to tell how it should be done without studying how it is done and why ... Prescription become useful only when it is grounded in sophisticated description."[584] The increased need for description might be one of the factors that has led to the more frequent use of case studies as research methodology in recent times, even though its critics claim that the results provided by case studies are too weak.[585] However, they serve to create a more in-depth picture.[586] Like other qualitative research methods, case studies were long believed to be appropriate only for investigative research as a predecessor to descriptive and explanatory phases.[587] Today, however, they are used for a variety of purposes – exploration, description and explanation.[588]

There is a growing literature on case studies that documents the wider and more elaborated use of this research strategy.[589] It is recommended in the relevant literature that case studies always require both a clearly defined research question and an identifiable

---

[580] Ghauri (2004), p. 109, see also Cassell/Symon (1994), Hartley (1994), p. 208.
[581] See also section 5.2.3.
[582] Yin (2003), p. 13.
[583] Venkatraman/Grant (1986), p. 72. This trend is also confirmed by Rouse/Daellenbach (1999), p. 489.
[584] Mintzberg (1977), p. 91.
[585] Yin (2003), p. xiii.
[586] Hartley (1994), p. 212.
[587] In many instances case studies have been used "only" as an explorative study (Marquardt (2003)) or to demonstrate how a conceptual model could be implemented (Wiedenhofer (2003)).
[588] Lee (1999), Yin (2003), p. 3.
[589] McClintock et al. (1979), Yin (1981), Eisenhardt (1989), Rose (1991), Yin (1993), Hartley (1994), Kelle/Kluge (1999), Gummesson (2000), Yin (2003).

unit of analysis as well as a theoretical framework[590] to generate not only "fascinating details about life in a particular organization"[591] but also results that can be generalized. In the current case, the theoretical framework is the typology that was developed above.

5.2.1.2 REASONS FOR THE USE OF CASE STUDIES IN THIS STUDY

There are several situations in which the use of a case study research design is recommended.[592] In our research, the following arguments led to the decision for this approach:

- *Topic:* The topic and our specific research questions have a bearing on the empirical part of the research. There are two points that place certain demands on the research design:

    - *Research questions:* The type of questions that we ask lend themselves to a qualitative research design. Answers to research questions that ask "how" and "why" are typically derived from qualitative research. When the focus is on contemporary events (as in our case) and when there is no need to control behavior (as in our case) case studies are especially appropriate.[593]

    - *Newness of phenomenon:* Captive offshoring centers are a relatively new phenomenon, and case studies can be effectively used to better grasp and describe it before proceeding to quantitative studies to refine and test theories.[594] Thus, our study needs "local grounding"[595] in the sense that it requires more context information than could be captured in a quantitative analysis. In such a situation where richness and holism are required, the use of case studies is more appropriate.

- *Theoretical background:* Our theoretical considerations also suggest the use of case studies for two reasons. One is based in the organizational theory that we have selected, the other in the propositions that we have developed:

---

[590] Lee (1999), pp. 58-59.
[591] Hartley (1994), p. 210.
[592] Lee (1999), pp. 38-41.
[593] Yin (2003), p. 5.
[594] Mintzberg (1977), p. 91.
[595] Lee (1999), p. 38.

- *Organizational theory:* Several authors propose qualitative approaches when applying the resource-based view in organizational analysis.[596] Case studies especially are considered useful in analyzing the effects of resources in organizations.[597] They argue that the effect of valuable resources and firm heterogeneity cannot be measured in large-scale random samples since they are not easy to perceive. Our chosen approach helps to better identify and measure the value of resources. Also researchers who have evaluated MNC network suggest more detailed qualitative analysis.[598]

- *Certainty of propositions:* Finally, we do not assume that our theoretical groundings cover all the potential variables that influence coordination mechanisms. Thus, we also aim to discover new variables which is more possible with qualitative research. As a result, we chose case studies that "are likely to be better able to adapt to and probe areas of original but also emergent theory."[599]

- *Methodological considerations:* In addition to the reasons that relate to the content of our study, there is also evidence to suggest that a case study design is appropriate because of methodological considerations:

    - *Identification of research subjects:* Captive service offshoring centers are international subsidiaries. However, they cannot be easily identified as they typically do not have many external relationships and thus, the direct contact to a few offshoring centers for individual case studies is more promising than sending out a mail survey to a large population of MNCS that might not even have a service offshoring subsidiary. MNCs often do not disclose the establishment of such centers, since they focus on internal services. Moreover, offshoring is sometimes considered as potentially negatively impacting the reputation of the firm. In addition,

---

[596] Rouse/Daellenbach (1999), p. 489, Barney et al. (2001), p. 636, Eschen (2002), p. 183. The research of Rose gives an example of the evaluation of resources and shows that the results are very firm-specific and hard to generalize (Rose (2000), pp. 182-206).
[597] Rouse/Daellenbach (1999), p. 492.
[598] Schmid et al. (2002), p. 68.
[599] Hartley (1994), p. 210.

the newness of the phenomenon makes the number of cases very small anyway.

- *Population frame:* Qualitative research approaches are often criticized because they do not allow for a statistical generalization. Even though we admit that this feature is indeed desirable, we regard the argument as rather weak in our case because our research falls within an area where a population frame is not available.[600] Since a business directory of service offshoring centers does not exist, a case study approach with a few known examples can prove very helpful as a first approach toward the topic. In addition, as we will show below, there are very few potential cases that would not be sufficient for statistical representativeness anyway.

- *International setting:* Case studies can also be especially suitable for research in international business where different languages can make survey research rather difficult or less reliable.[601]

Of course, the case study approach has its limitations, too. While we do not pretend to overcome all these limitations, we want to discuss how they affect our research and what measures we can take to attenuate these effects:

- Qualitative research is often criticized because it is considered not reliable and not rigorous.[602] The inappropriate application of methods and the weakness of documentation may have resulted in some "bad press" for case studies.[603] Contributions might not always have adhered to high methodological standards.[604] However, several of these standards have only been developed in the last few years and they might not even be applicable and/or necessary in every kind of setting. Applied correctly, these guidelines can help to make case study research more reliable: For instance, the direct interview in case study settings gives the researcher much more control over the data collection process and helps to avoid

---

[600] Yeung (1995), p. 330.
[601] Ghauri (2004), p. 111.
[602] Yin (2003), p. 10.
[603] Lee (1999), pp. 16-17.
[604] For instance, in his dissertation, Reger (1997) works with case studies without giving explicit reasons for this methodology and without describing how cases were selected and how interviews were conducted and analyzed.

problems such as the questionnaire being completed by an inappropriate respondent or the interviewee not understanding the questions in a mail or online survey.[605] The "interviewer's effect" that can skew results and that occurs when several people carry out interviews[606] is avoided in our research design by having only one researcher conducting all the interviews.

- It is harder to derive representative results from a case study. Case studies do not allow for "statistical generalization"[607] which is the generalization procedure in quantitative studies. Still, the use of case studies allows for "analytical generalization"[608] which does not argue based on the statistical significance of the results. Rather, the generalization refers not to the population but to the theoretical propositions.

- Case studies require more detailed immersion in the subject and more resources; moreover, the amounts of resulting data might lead to high complexity.[609] Having established a theoretical framework in the form of our typology and by rigorously aggregating data, the present approach should still allow for "parsimony"[610]. The development of case studies is also typically thought to be very "labour-intensive"[611]. This criticism is probably true, but not a real shortcoming of the case study method. And while experience from the current research project attests to this notion, we still consider the execution of case studies a worthwhile endeavor.

Based on these considerations, we argue that case studies are the most appropriate research method for our purposes.

5.2.1.3 Types of Case Studies

Not all case studies are the same, but rather there is a wide variety of different models that are used for different purposes. Case studies can be differentiated based (1) on their objective and (2) by the number of cases.

---

[605] Yeung (1995), p. 330.
[606] Yeung (1995), p. 331.
[607] Yin (2003), p. 32.
[608] Yin (2003), p. 32.
[609] Eisenhardt (1989), p. 547.
[610] Eisenhardt (1989), p. 547.
[611] Hartley (1994), p. 212.

(1) Objectives typically fall into three major categories:[612]

- *Exploratory* case studies serve as an initial step towards defining a new phenomenon. An exploratory study can help to better define relevant constructs and develop theory that can then be tested in further case studies or in surveys. This is often thought of as the predominant area in which case studies are used.[613]

- *Descriptive* case studies describe in great detail a current phenomenon and identify multivariate constructs that help to capture complexity in more than one dimension.

- *Explanatory* case studies look for causal relationships and describe reasons for a specific configuration.

The present research works with explanatory case studies that evaluate the propositions from our typology and expand the existing body of knowledge on service offshoring. This is appropriate in our case in which the "researchers may have some clear propositions to explore"[614]. Of course, the basis for this is also a detailed description of the phenomenon. Thus, our cases are descriptive and explanatory, serving both to illustrate and to evaluate the typology.

(2) With regard to the number of cases, we can distinguish between a single case study design and a multiple case study design. Single cases are preferably used for unusual, rare or revelatory cases.[615] Multiple cases are considered to be more robust[616] but they require more resources.[617] To conduct a multiple case study it has to be decided whether the cases will be used to replicate the initial findings (literal replication) or to give empirical evidence to contrasting examples (theoretical replication).[618] Yin strongly argues for a study with more than one case to be able to extend and test empirical findings.[619]

---

[612] Kelle/Kluge (1999), pp. 38-53.
[613] Hartley (1994), p. 213.
[614] Hartley (1994), p. 210.
[615] Ghauri (2004), p. 114. For more details on single-case studies, see Kratochwill/Levin (1992).
[616] Hartley (1994), p. 226.
[617] Yin (2003), pp. 46-47.
[618] Yin (2003), p. 53.
[619] Yin (2003), see also Hartley (1994), p. 214.

5 – Methodology

The current research design is a multiple case study, capable of considering different fields in the typology.[620]

There still remains the important question of how many case studies should be conducted. This strongly depends on the way the case studies are selected. Below, we will first discuss options for case study selection and then derive the number of necessary cases.

5.2.2 CASE SELECTION

5.2.2.1 ALTERNATIVES FOR CASE SELECTION

With regard to the selection of case studies, methodologists point to the difference between random sampling (e.g., for a survey) and the purposeful selection of case studies. Case studies do not purport to achieve a result that is as representative as those from large surveys. As a rule, they are selected specifically, using one of the following approaches:

1. *Counter examples* can help to present contrasting cases and can be used to test theory (and potentially confute it).[621] In this case, there is the need for at least two cases. This iterative method is typically used when the researcher already has a theoretical foundation and hypotheses.[622]

2. *Theoretical sampling* means to search for examples that have significant differences ("maximization" strategy) or that are very similar ("minimization" strategy). By minimizing differences, the researcher confirms his proposed theory. Conversely, by maximizing differences, the researcher can cover the complete extent of the phenomenon under consideration. As with counter examples, this approach works in an iterative fashion.[623]

3. When using *selective sampling* (also called *qualitative sampling plan*), the researcher considers first the salient features of the cases and defines what values these features should take before establishing the number of cases in order to cover the complete variety of a phenomenon.[624] This approach can be taken

---

[620] Yin further differentiates between case studies with a single unit of analysis ("holistic") and multiple units of analysis ("embedded") (Yin (2003), pp. 39-45). In that sense, our case studies are "holistic".
[621] Kelle/Kluge (1999), pp. 40-44.
[622] Kelle/Kluge (1999), p. 44.
[623] Kelle/Kluge (1999), pp. 44-46, Wrona (2005).
[624] Kelle/Kluge (1999), pp. 46-49, Wrona (2005).

when a set of knowledge and working hypotheses on the subject already exist allowing the researcher to define the number of cases upfront. It is thus a non-iterative approach.

In the current research, selective sampling is applied, as the salient features and their possible values are derived from the typology, i.e. low and high values on the two dimensions network embeddedness and strategic relevance. Thus, in order to populate the typology we need four cases to fill all the relevant sections. Of course, one could carry out eight or twelve case studies to have more than one case for each of the sections. However, the gain from additional information is potentially low relative to the resources and time required to multiply the number of cases. Instead, it seems more worthwhile to elaborate in greater detail on the selected cases by including more interviews. Three important perspectives have to be taken into account: the service offshoring subsidiary on the one hand and its customers, i.e., the MNC headquarters and other international subsidiaries on the other. It makes sense to include all three perspectives in the research. This requires at least three interviews for the cases with high network embeddedness and at least two interviews for the cases where network embeddedness is low. In the latter cases, there are few relationships beyond the relationship between the headquarters and the service offshoring subsidiary. Therefore, for low network embeddedness two perspectives seem to be sufficient. In total, this leads to a minimum requirement of ten interviews. However, we actually carried out 20 interviews with 24 senior managers (some of the interviews were with groups) in order to get a better perspective and more rounded information. The interviews were carried out between November 2005 and April 2006 and lasted between one hour and two and a half hours. In addition, we conducted one discussion per case upfront with senior managers of the respective firms to gain a better understanding of the appropriateness of the case.[625] The extension of the interviews depended on both the need for additional information and the openness of the participating firms to provide more contacts.[626]

---

[625] Even though some of these discussions lasted for up to two hours we do not include them here, since they were on a more general level and it was inappropriate to record them. Still, they provided valuable background information and helped to understand the larger setting in which the specific offshoring relations are placed.

[626] An overview of the interviews can be found in the appendix.

5.2.2.2 Selection Criteria for Cases

A list of possible cases has to be compiled before the actual cases can be selected.[627] As there is no official information available about offshoring service centers, the list was put together using press information and personal contacts in industry and academia. These contacts were consequently used not only to glean some first criteria for case selection but also, in a later stage, to obtain an overview of the firms on our list.[628]

Cases are selected based on a set of criteria.[629] In the present research, the following criteria were applied:

1. We limited our research to service offshoring centers that are mainly owned by an MNC. Thus, we required a capital stake of at least 50 per cent for the center to be considered a captive offshoring center as opposed to an outsourcing agreement. This was done to exclude situations in which there is a strong external influence on coordination mechanisms. Also, it is unlikely that services of high strategic relevance are outsourced. Had we included outsourcing service providers, we would potentially have created disturbing effects. Therefore, we focus on captive centers.

2. In addition, we established criteria for size: Only MNCs were considered that employ more than 250 people and generate revenues of at least EUR 50 million. This restriction was introduced as size can have an influence on coordination mechanisms.[630]

3. Centers that we included in our population list had to be operational, i.e., they already carry out services. Thus, we did not consider centers that were in the planning phase only. We did not, however, exclude centers that were changing and potentially taking over other services as this is a) hard to perceive from the outside and b) a natural setting for businesses so that it would have meant an needless narrowing down of our population.

---

[627] Hartley (1994), p. 216.
[628] Hartley (1994), p. 218.
[629] Hartley (1994), Yin (2003), p. 78.
[630] Child (1972), p. 166. 250 employees and 50 million EUR sales are common size criteria (Tu et al. (2004), p. 166) that we apply here as well.

4. We consider only MNCs from Germany and their service offshoring subsidiaries in Eastern Europe. The reasons for these choices are explained in section 5.3.

5. Offshoring centers were chosen that serve only one set of company functions, e.g., an IT function or a finance function. This was done to reduce agglomeration effects that can occur if several departments or units are in the same place.[631] We chose the IT function and will discuss this choice in more detail in section 5.4.

5.2.2.3 SELECTION PROCESS AND OUTCOME

Once we had defined these criteria for our population, we put together a list of potential cases. Initial information was obtained on the type of center that a case would fit. We did this rough estimate of the type based on information from press articles and personal contacts and based the judgment on the two dimensions strategic relevance and network embeddedness. Since detailed information on these dimensions is typically not freely available, we obtained a first estimate by approximating the number of relations that a center is seen to have and by the type of activity it carries out. Table 5-1 gives an overview of the population of cases that we were able to identify from press searches and personal contacts.[632] Since we have promised the selected cases anonymity, we also keep this table anonymous.

Table 5-1: Overview of case population (Source: Press research)

No.	Name	Country	Service	Relationships
1	Alpha*	(Eastern European country)	IT Infrastructure	Worldwide
2	Beta*	Russia	Application development	Worldwide
3	Delta*	Bulgaria	Application development	Germany
4	Gamma*	Hungary	Application development	Germany

---

[631] Schmid et al. (1998), p. 26.
[632] This list is as of autumn 2005.

5 – Methodology

No.	Name	Country	Service	Relationships
5	Software firm	Turkey	Call center	Worldwide
6	Software firm	Poland	Application development	Germany
7	Bank	Russia	IT Infrastructure	Worldwide
8	IT company	Czech Republic	Application development	Germany
9	Car manufacturer	Czech Republic	n/a	n/a
10	IT company	Poland	Application Development	Germany
* – selected case n/a – not available				

There are not very many companies that fit our criteria. However, based on forecasts,[633] a great deal more will follow. As there was no possibility to gain an overview of the total population, we cannot guarantee that there are not more cases. Still, having asked for additional contacts and new cases in all of our interviews, we believe that there are at least not many cases that we might have overlooked. Moreover, our research design does not depend on a complete population frame.

From this initial list we contacted companies based on how well they seemed to fit to the extreme cases that we were aiming for. Even though we cannot expect a center to exactly fit one ideal type,[634] we tried to find cases at the extremes of both dimensions. This approach has the advantage of showing which centers can possibly exist and thus be inspiring for business practice.[635] However, we had to adapt our selection process to the realities of the cases that we could actually identify. Thus, even though we selected cases purposefully, they still might "only approximate ideal types because organizations

---

[633] See for growth estimates section 2.2.6.4.
[634] Kabanoff et al. (1995), p. 1084.
[635] Schmid et al. (1998), p. 99.

are subject to various contaminating influences or are in transition, moving from one type to another."[636]

In the initial discussion with a senior executive from the headquarters of the firm, we established whether the company would fit the present research approach based on its strategic relevance and network embeddedness.[637] In that first discussion, we focused on the type of service the service offshoring subsidiary provides and on the way the service offshoring subsidiary is integrated into the MNC network. Besides, we asked questions on the size and age of the subsidiary and its number of employees.

If the initial case information was evaluated positively and there was continued interest from the MNC, personal interviews were then set up at the headquarters.[638] These interviews were either with the same person from the phone interview or with somebody to whom we had been referred on that occasion. Once the meetings at the headquarters were successfully completed, we were given further contacts at the service offshoring subsidiary and set up personal interviews. Whenever possible we decided to visit the location of the headquarters and the service offshoring subsidiary personally instead of carrying out a phone interview. All of our cases accepted personal visits. In both locations – headquarters and service offshoring subsidiary – we evaluated the possibility of conducting additional interviews at other subsidiaries of the MNC. As it turned out in cases with low network embeddedness, this was not necessary since there were very limited or no relationships beyond the dyadic relationship between headquarters and the service offshoring subsidiary. In the two cases with high network embeddedness, we obtained additional contacts and carried out more interviews with other members of the respective MNC networks.

5.2.3 DATA COLLECTION

5.2.3.1 DATA COLLECTION METHODS

As already indicated, we made extensive use of personal interviews. However, there are more data collection methods that can be used in case study research. From the outset six major different methods of data collection lend themselves to case study research: document analysis, archival records, interviews, direct observation, participant observa-

---

[636] Kabanoff et al. (1995), p. 1084.
[637] For this discussioin we used an "evaluation guide" that can be found in the appendix.
[638] In one of our cases (Alpha) we had contacts in both the headquarters and the service offshoring subsidiary and started our interviews in the subsidiary. For all other cases we started with the headquarters.

5 – Methodology 165

tion and physical artifacts.[639] It is always advisable to rely not only on one data source to ensure or increase reliability, to thoroughly document all the findings and to clearly structure the findings and arguments underlying them.[640]

In the present setting the use of interviews, document analysis, and – partially – direct observation were selected as being most appropriate.

- The main data source for this study are *interviews*. In general, interviews can be more open-ended or more structured, depending on the time available and the information accessible to the researcher before the interview. As an introduction to a completely new topic an open-ended interview might serve the best, whereas a structured interview can be valuable for confirming information already obtained.[641] In our case, the interviews were semi-structured interviews. Thus, they were not completely open but focused around the themes that had been deduced from our theoretical framework. At the same time, they were not completely determined by a questionnaire but allowed for open-ended questions and discursive discussions.[642] Such expert interviews are frequently used in social science research.[643] The advantage of an expert interview is that it can be easier to motivate people to participate in research than when asking them to fill out a survey questionnaire. Moreover, interviews can be very helpful in setting up additional contacts and they can benefit from the direct interaction between interviewer and interviewee.[644] Interviews are typically conducted on the basis of a written interview guide.[645] The interview guide and the basis for it will be discussed in the next section.

- *Document analysis* is the evaluation of any kind of documentation, often available only in an unstructured form or proprietary structure.[646] Documents include external sources such as newspaper and magazine articles that were accessed by extensive press search as well as a firm's internal documents that were obtained

---

[639] Yin (2003), p. 86.
[640] Yin (2003), p. 83.
[641] Yin (2003), pp. 90-91.
[642] Lee (1999), pp. 61-63.
[643] Bogner/Menz (2002), p. 7.
[644] Bogner/Menz (2002), pp. 8-9.
[645] Bogner/Menz (2002), p. 17.
[646] Yin (2003), pp. 85-86.

during our visits at the firms. Such documents include product brochures or process descriptions.

- *Direct observation* is used to examine the building and setup of the operations in order to gain additional information on the topic.[647] Where possible, we asked to be guided through the buildings so that we could gain additional information through observation.

A short discussion on the relative importance of the data collection methods in our study: Interviews are the most important and most reliable data source. Interviewees were selected with great care to make sure that the most suitable person is asked. In all service offshoring centers we interviewed the person with the highest position in the hierarchy, typically the general managers who oversee the entire operations and who then referred us to colleagues with specialized knowledge. In every case, we made sure that we obtained an organization chart and understood the organizational structure so as not to overlook important discussion partners.[648] We also asked for the names of their counterparts in headquarters and other MNC units. In our discussion with the MNC's headquarters we selected the person who had overseen the build-up of the center and the person responsible for the interaction with the center. Through repeated interaction, through additional referrals and organizational charts we ensured that we talked to the most appropriate and most knowledgeable people.

Document analysis was used to prepare the company profiles up-front and to test data gained from the interviews. Relevant examples include annual reports or company presentations. Wherever appropriate we also collected documents that gave specific details about coordination. However, because we very often found that the topics we discussed were not covered in documents, we had to collect the information in interviews. Moreover, to provide an in-depth analysis of the way standardized reports are actually used (and not that they simply exist), a researcher needs to spend a substantial amount of time on the evaluation of just one report. Personal coordination mechanisms are typically not documented at all. In addition, documents from the different cases are very hard to compare. Finally and most importantly, companies were very hesitant to provide exhaustive access to company documents and reports.

---

[647] Yin (2003), pp. 92-93.
[648] See also the representation of the company's organization charts in chapter 6.

Direct observation again was used in every case to add data to the descriptions and gain a better understanding of how a specific organization works. However, the limited access to organizations and the high number of organizational units visited made it impossible for us to apply a more advanced model of direct observation in our case studies.

The other methods – *analysis of archival records, participant observation* and the analysis of *physical artifacts* – were either not possible or not appropriate in the corporate setting in which our research took place.[649]

5.2.3.2 INTERVIEW PROCESS

This research follows the process that is proposed in the exhaustive documentation on interviews by Kvale (1996). He proposes a seven-step process that is outlined in Table 5-2. Kvale's approach, however, not only covers the interview phase of research in a narrow sense but shows which role interviews play in the entire research process, from the original research question to the evaluation of results. We have decided to show all the steps proposed by the author and then explain overlaps with our own approach.

The initial stage of our research – the typology development – can count as thematizing (step 1). It is there where we explain the "why?", "what?", and "how?" of this study. In Kvale's terminology, this research is designed to "*test hypotheses* [emphasis in original]"[650] To make the distinction from quantitative research design easier, we prefer to refer to the *evaluation* of propositions since our approach cannot yield a statistical analysis of hypotheses. This chapter on methodology has already set out the reasons for the use of a qualitative research design and more specifically, for the use of interviews (step 2). The remainder of this chapter will cover the design and setup of the interviews (step 3). Transcription and analysis (steps 4 and 5) will be covered in section 5.2.4, verification will be a topic in 5.2.5, and the results (step 7) will be presented in sections 6 and 7.

To obtain a complete picture of the offshoring service subsidiary, interviews were held for each case with the head of the service offshoring subsidiary, with the responsible manager at the MNC's headquarters and potentially an additional interview with a responsible manager in another international subsidiary. Interview recording depended on the interviewees' agreement; in 19 out of 20 interviews our respondents agreed to the

---

[649] See also Yin (2003), p. 96.
[650] Kvale (1996), p. 97.

conversation being recorded. An overview of the interviews can be found in the appendix. The number of interviews we carried out – 20 – is well within the number of 15 +/- 10 interviews typically recorded in studies.[651]

Table 5-2: Steps for interview investigation (Source: Based on Kvale (1996), pp. 88-92)

Step	Name	Description
1	Thematizing	Description of research topic
		Definition of research question(s) and research motivation
2	Designing	Planning of research method
		Preparation of interview guide
3	Interviewing	Data gathering through interviews
4	Transcribing	Transferring the oral speech to written text
5	Analyzing	Decision on method for text analysis
		Execution of text analysis
6	Verifying	Probing data for reliability (consistency of results)
		Probing data for validity (appropriateness of results for question under consideration)
7	Reporting	Compilation of results

Of course, our approach had both advantages and disadvantages. An important prerequisite for the design of successful interviews is the expertise of the interviewer.[652] Also, ideally all interviews are conducted by the same person or the same group of persons to ensure consistency. Both criteria were fulfilled in the present research: The interviewer

---

[651] Kvale (1996), p. 102.
[652] Kvale (1996), pp. 103-104.

had interview expertise from earlier research projects and from work experience in a management consultancy where interviewing is a regular part of the work. However, reliance on one group of employees is a limitation: As the interviews were carried out with managers, the results reflect their perceptions and can suffer from a range of deficiencies.[653]

5.2.3.3 INTERVIEW DESIGN

The interviews were structured in four main phases:

1. *Introduction:* The interviews began by explaining the topic and the main assumptions. As suggested in the literature, the interviewer first described the purpose of the study and the background of both the study and of himself. Only at the end of the introduction did the researcher ask if the interviewee[654] felt comfortable about having the interview recorded. If the interviewee answered in the affirmative, the interviewer then switched on the recorder.[655]

2. *Opening:* The opening was used to ask the interviewee for his experience with the offshoring situation and to provide a "broader picture" of it. This had two major motives: Firstly, it allowed the interviewer to gain a better overview and allow him to adapt his questions to the specific situation, for instance, by directly referring to other organizations or persons by their correct names. Secondly, a more open start is a better way of "breaking the ice" than starting directly with questions that the interviewee might consider threatening.[656]

3. *Questions:* Having completed the rather open-ended introductory phase, the interviews then focused more on specific questions. These were asked in the order displayed in the interview guide. In some cases, additional questions were asked to gain an even deeper understanding of some issues. Sometimes it was necessary to skip questions. This was the case when the interviewee had already talked about a specific topic before the actual question was raised. At the end of

---

[653] See Downey/Ireland (1979) for a review.
[654] Since most of our interviews were with a single respondent, we here refer to the singular form "interviewee". For the few cases with more than one interviewee our elaborations refer to the group of interviewees.
[655] Kvale (1996), pp. 127-128.
[656] The specific content of the opening phase can be found in the appendix in the representation of the interview guide.

the questions phase, interviewees were asked to bring up any additional topics they might consider relevant. Only after this part was the recording stopped.

4. After the interview, there was a short debriefing of the discussion: Interviewees were asked if they could share documents that would be helpful to illustrate the discussion during the interviews. This was especially important when interviewees had referred to a specific documentation. To better assess quality, the researcher asked for a brief feedback after the interview.[657] Interviewees mainly reacted positively to the open atmosphere during interviews and often offered their help with additional contacts inside or outside their firm and the provision of follow-up information. Also, every interviewee showed interest in receiving the results of the study.

After completion of the visit, we sent the interviewees a brief thank-you note.

5.2.3.4 INTERVIEW GUIDE AND MEASURES

The interview guide was developed based on the theoretical concepts presented above. The document served to guide the discussion between the researcher and the interviewees. It was used in discussions with interviewees at the service offshoring subsidiary, at the MNC's headquarters and at other international subsidiaries. We used the same interview guide for all interviews since our purpose was to carry out additional interviews to receive richer information and to confirm the results of previous interviews. The individual items had been operationalized before by researching the relevant literature. Whenever possible, we tried to use established measures from the literature and used the same scales. However, it turned out that very often it was difficult for interviewees to exactly determine the position of their organization on a given scale. Where not available from previous studies, we developed our own measures. There were three cases in which we had to establish new measures:

---

[657] Lee proposes to assess the interview quality by the following questions (Lee (1999), p. 85):"
  1. Was the conversation spontaneous, rich, and specific?
  2. Were the answers relevant to the questions asked?
  3. Were the interviewer's questions short and the subject's responses long?
  4. Did the interviewer follow up or clarify the meanings of the interviewee's answers throughout the interview?
  5. Did the interviewer interpret interviewee responses throughout the interview?
  6. Did the interviewer corroborate interpretations during the course of the interview?
  7. Did the interview itself appear self-communicating?"

5 – Methodology

- Some measures were developed after the first test interviews. Our interviewees asked for clarification on specific topics and sometimes even used expressions (such as "commodity" to refer to a standardized service of little strategic relevance) that we introduced in our interview guide to make it easier to understand for our interviewees.[658]

- A few measures are very specific to our study and we could not expect to find measures in the existing literature. The only example of this is the location of the units to which the service center delivers its services. We introduced this in order to better understand the geographic reach of the service offshoring subsidiary's network.

- Finally, some measures are specific to our research model. We were, however, unable to find appropriate measures in the existing body of research and had therefore to develop new measures.[659] In some cases, this came as a surprise as we had expected to find measures for such topics as overall coordination requirements.[660]

A first version of the interview guide was discussed with two researchers from international business research and two researchers from strategic management research. In addition, it was tested in an interview with the general manager of a service offshoring

---

[658] We have added the following measures for clarification purposes: effect of a sudden loss of the service offshoring center for the MNC, degree to which service is considered a "commodity", final decision making in case of conflict, presence of team spirit across locations.

[659] These new measures have worked well in our study. However, for a quantitative study they would need to tested for their validity and reliability. We have developed the following new measures:
 - "Planned number of relationships of the service offshoring subsidiary": This measure was introduced to better measure the frequency of change.
 - "Resources (time, finances) needed for coordination and "number of employees needed for coordination": These measures were introduced to have a more concrete way of determining the requirements that the coordination of a service offshoring subsidiary create.
 - "Frequency and duration of interaction and number of participants": This measure helps us to better assess the breadth and depth of personal coordination and is in line with the similar measures for visits and transfers.
 - "Duration of transfers from other units to service offshoring unit": We consider not only the number of transfers to be important but also their duration (also to differentiate from short-term visits).

[660] However, out of 51 measures only five fall into this category. These are "planned number of relationships of the service offshoring subsidiary", "resources (time, finances) needed for coordination", "number of employees needed for coordination", "final decision making in case of conflict", "frequency and duration of interaction and number of participants", "duration of transfers from other units to service offshoring unit". All the other measures either serve for better clarification or were taken from existing research (many with repeated usage in several studies).

center. Recommendations for improvements and changes were incorporated in the final version. For instance, it was suggested to ask for the impact of language differences on coordination. The complete interview guide can be found in the appendix. Here, we give an overview of the questions and the measures used. We start with the independent variables (strategic relevance and network embeddedness) for which we derived the constructs in our discussion above. We then proceed with coordination mechanisms.[661] For both independent and dependent variables, we distinguish between low, medium, and high values.

Strategic Relevance

Some authors define the *value* of a resource by its ability to meet a key buyer need.[662] Even though a service offshoring subsidiary has no external customers, there are still internal customers. Other authors confirm the customer aspect and in addition introduce the relative importance of a resource in comparison with that of competitors' resources.[663] The value can also be assessed by asking interviewees about the consequences of a potential loss of the service offshoring center. The value itself can have different attributes for each situation,[664] but might be attributed to one of the categories monetary, quality or flexibility advantages.

The second criteria to determine the relevance of a resource is its *rareness*. Rareness can be measured by the degree to which there is perfect competition for the resource and if the resource is available in other firms.[665] Another measure of rareness is the extent to which the services are custom-tailored to the firm.[666]

---

[661] An exhaustive overview of measures for coordination mechanisms can also be found in a publication from the Aston study; see Pugh et al. (1968). However, many of these measures work at a very detailed level and were found inappropriate for use in our study.
[662] This view stems from Coyne (1986), Aaker (1989). These authors are not directly associated with the resource-based view. Contributions from within the "inner circle" of the resource-based view, such as Collis (1991), Collis (1994), however, confirm this view.
[663] Day/Wensley (1988), p. 9.
[664] Makadok/Walker (2000), p. 856 gives the example of superior forecasting ability in the financial services industry that can lead to increased profits for the firm.
[665] Barney (2001a), p. 43.
[666] See, for instance, Peteraf (1993). Poppo/Zenger (1998), p. 866 suggest asking: "To what degree must individuals acquire company-specific or division-specific information to adequately perform the IS [information systems] function?", "To what degree is your approach to this function (or set of applications) custom-tailored to the company?", "How costly in terms of time and resources would it be to switch to outsourcing this function?".

With regard to *inimitability*, authors propose to measure the inimitability of a resource by the capability of other firms to copy it in the course of time and the time that it might take to copy it.[667] The main source of inimitability in our case, which concerns organizational capabilities, is causal ambiguity, i.e. the impossibility to clearly recognize the resource which again inhibits its imitation.[668] This results in tacit knowledge that is potentially not available on markets.

When it comes to *non-substitutability*, the measurement typically proposed is the possibility of exchanging one resource with another.[669]

Network Embeddedness

Many authors call the *number of relationships* or composed measures such as density an important influence factor on embeddedness.[670] Thus, the basic measure is the number of relationships a service offshoring center has. Here, we considered only those relationships with regular interaction. To better understand the network structure, we also asked for the location of the network partners. Typically we also drew the network structure on paper together with the interviewee to receive more reliable information.

The second indicator we consider is the frequency with which new relationships are added to the network.[671] Here, we asked for the number of additions per year and the number of units to which the service offshoring center will eventually be connected. We also evaluated the number of changes to existing relationships.

Another important indicator of network embeddedness is the *closeness* of the relationship. One possible measure is the breadth of resource exchange, e.g., in the form of (mutual) investments, another is the mutual adaptation of the partners in the relation-

---

[667] Henderson/Cockburn (1994), pp. 7-8, Barney (2001a), p. 45.
[668] Collis/Montgomery (1995), p. 122. The authors – like many others (see also Fladmoe-Lindquist/Tallman (1994), p. 48) – distinguish as sources for inimitability physical uniqueness, path dependency, economic deterrence.
[669] Collis/Montgomery (1995), p. 123, Barney (2001a), p. 47.
[670] Ghoshal/Bartlett (1990), pp. 609-610, Brass/Burkhardt (1992), pp. 194-195, Rowley et al. (2000), p. 378, Hadjikhani/Thilenius (2005), p. 27.
[671] Gulati (1998), p. 301, Newburry (2001), p. 501, Hadjikhani/Thilenius (2005), p. 27.

ship.[672] The complexity of the exchange can be another measure for the closeness,[673] as can be the degree to which a relationship is a "special relationship"[674].

We have summarized the variables, the measures, and the sources from the literature in Table 5-3. We want to point out that we often have redundant measures for a given variable in our interview guide. The interview guide was designed specially in that way to give flexibility in questioning in case one measure does not apply to a specific situation and to make information more reliable.

Table 5-3: Overview of measures for independent variables

Dimension	Variable	Measure	Supporting literature
Strategic relevance	Value	Degree to which service meets a key need of the customer	Coyne (1986); Aaker (1989); Collis (1991); (1994)
		Effect of a sudden loss of the service offshoring center for the MNC	(own measure)
		Value for competitor to access service offshoring center	Day/Wensley (1988), p. 9
		Motivation for setting up service offshoring center: monetary, quality or flexibility advantages	(own measure, based on Makadok/Walker (2000), p. 856)
	Rareness	Availability of service on markets	Barney (2001a), p. 43
		Degree to which service is considered a "commodity"	(own measure)
		Degree to which services are tailored to specific firm	Peteraf (1993); Poppo/Zenger (1998), p. 866

---

[672] Hadjikhani/Thilenius (2005), pp. 23-24.
[673] Hadjikhani/Thilenius (2005), p. 27.
[674] Uzzi (1996), Uzzi (1997).

Dimension	Variable	Measure	Supporting literature
		Availability of services in other firms	Barney (2001a), p. 43
	Inimitability	Difficulty for other firms to imitate service	Henderson/Cockburn (1994), pp. 7-8; Barney (2001a), p. 45
		Time required for other firms to imitate service	Henderson/Cockburn (1994), pp. 7-8; Barney (2001a), p. 45
		Market availability of knowledge to imitate	Fladmoe-Lindquist/Tallman (1994), p. 48; Collis/Montgomery (1995), p. 122
		Tacitness of knowledge to imitate	Fladmoe-Lindquist/Tallman (1994), p. 48; Collis/Montgomery (1995), p. 122
	Non-substitutability	Existence of alternatives to internal service delivery	Collis/Montgomery (1995), p. 123; Barney (2001a), p. 47
		Existence of general alternatives to service	Collis/Montgomery (1995), p. 123; Barney (2001a), p. 47
Network embeddedness	Network structure	Current number of relationships of the service offshoring subsidiary (only relationships with regular interaction)	Ghoshal/Bartlett (1990), pp. 609-610; Brass/Burkhardt (1992), pp. 194-195; Rowley et al. (2000), p. 378; Hadjikhani/Thilenius (2005), p. 27
		Location of units to which the service offshoring subsidiary is connected	(own measure)

Dimension	Variable	Measure	Supporting literature
	Change to network structure	Frequency with which new relationships are added	Gulati (1998), p. 301; Newburry (2001), p. 501; Hadjikhani/Thilenius (2005), p. 27
		Planned number of relationships of the service offshoring subsidiary	(own measure)
		Frequency of changes to existing relationships	Gulati (1998), p. 301; Newburry (2001), p. 501; Hadjikhani/Thilenius (2005), p. 27
	Closeness	Degree of resource exchange between service offshoring center and other units of the firm, e.g., in the form of (mutual) investments	Andersson et al. (2005), p. 528; Hadjikhani/Thilenius (2005), pp. 23-24
		Degree of adaptation of partners to the new situation	Andersson/Forsgren (2000), p. 339; Hadjikhani/Thilenius (2005), pp. 23-24
		Degree to which a relationship is a complex relationship versus a market relationship	Hadjikhani/Thilenius (2005), p. 27
		Degree to which one of the relationships is special in comparison to all other relationships the service offshoring unit has	Uzzi (1996); (1997)

Coordination mechanisms

The *coordination requirements* can be measured by the resources (time, finances, employees) that are needed for coordination. In addition, another measurement for the di-

5 – Methodology 177

versity and breadth of coordination can be obtained by asking for the coordination needs in ten functional areas.[675]

Cray (1984) proposes to measure the autonomy of a unit by asking for the location of decision making.[676] This is in line with the proposal of Gates/Egelhoff (1986) who ask for the locus of a decision for 22 individual decisions from the areas of marketing, manufacturing and finance.[677] Fischer/Behrman (1979) distinguish absolute centralization, participative centralization, supervised freedom, and total freedom to measure the degree of autonomy.[678] A very similar approach is put forward by Ghoshal/Nohria (1989) who ask for "levels of autonomy for deciding their own strategies and policies"[679]. Ouchi (1978) adds the element of creativity by asking "how often are you given a chance to try out your own ideas on your job?"[680]

Mascarenhas (1984) proposes to identify *technocratic mechanisms* by the use of formal policies and procedures and the use of work plans and schedules on a 7-point scale from "never" to "very often"[681]. Van De Ven et al. (1976) ask for the degree of "formally or informally understood policies and procedures"[682]. Cavusgil et al. (1993) measure standardization by the degree to which products are adapted by the subsidiary.[683] Griffith et al. (2000) add the degree to which relationships differ and the standardization of addition of new relationships.[684] Nobel/Birkinshaw (1996) measure formalization by asking for the existence of standardized reports and the use of technical standards for the specific tasks within a subsidiary.[685] Ghoshal/Nohria (1989) evaluate "instruments such as manuals, standing orders, standard operating procedures"[686]. Formalization can also occur through automation of processes in electronic tools.[687]

---

[675] Cray (1984), p. 90.
[676] Cray (1984), p. 90.
[677] Gates/Egelhoff (1986), p. 74.
[678] Fischer/Behrman (1979), p. 30.
[679] Ghoshal/Nohria (1989), p. 335.
[680] Ouchi (1978), p. 179.
[681] Mascarenhas (1984), p. 104.
[682] Van De Ven et al. (1976), p. 327. For a similar measure, see Harzing (1999), p. 187.
[683] Cavusgil et al. (1993), p. 492.
[684] Griffith et al. (2000), p. 631.
[685] Nobel/Birkinshaw (1996), p. 167. For a similar measure, see Zeffane (1989), Harzing (1999), p. 187.
[686] Ghoshal/Nohria (1989), p. 335.
[687] Zeffane (1989), p. 631.

Ouchi (1978) operationalizes *output-based coordination* as the degree to which employee evaluation is based on their output records on a 7-point scale (from "output records are not considered at all in the decision" to "decision is entirely based on output records").[688] Harzing (1999) refers to the degree of "continuous evaluation of the results of subsidiaries"[689] and the degree of "detailed planning, goals setting and budgeting system"[690]. Another aspect is the degree to which performance is measured based on pre-specification of results.[691]

Harzing defines *personal coordination* as the degree of direct personal surveillance.[692] Van De Ven et al. (1976) used a similar measure by asking for coordination through a supervisor or assistant supervisor.[693]

For *visits*, Trent/Monczka (2002) identify their number and frequency.[694] Barner-Rasmussen/Björkman (2005) also propose to measure the duration of visits.[695]

For *transfers*, Björkman et al. (2004) measure the number of expatriate managers in a given subsidiary.[696] This is also referred to as the assignment of employees from the headquarters to the subsidiary.[697]

Ouchi (1979) suggests that cultural coordination is reflected in shared values, common goals, teamwork.[698] Ghoshal/Nohria (1989) measure it by shared values by asking for different levels of being "in tune with the overall goals and management values of the parent company"[699]. Birkinshaw/Morrison (1995) ask how far "managers share a common mission/set of goals"[700]. Harzing (1999) measures the degree of "international (as opposed to purely national) management training programmes"[701], Barner-Rasmussen/Björkman (2005) the opportunity for the development of personal relation-

---

[688] Ouchi (1978), p. 177.
[689] Harzing (1999), p. 187.
[690] Harzing (1999), p. 187.
[691] Gençtürk/Aulakh (1995), p. 769.
[692] Harzing (1999), p. 187.
[693] Van De Ven et al. (1976), p. 327.
[694] Trent/Monczka (2002), p. 72. See also Barner-Rasmussen/Björkman (2005), p. 35.
[695] Barner-Rasmussen/Björkman (2005), p. 36. See also Trent/Monczka (2002), p. 72.
[696] Björkman et al. (2004), p. 449.
[697] Harzing (1999), pp. 188-189, Delios/Björkman (2000), p. 284, Harzing (2001), p. 371.
[698] Ouchi (1979), pp. 836-837. For a similar measure, see Harzing (1999), p. 188.
[699] Ghoshal/Nohria (1989), p. 335.
[700] Birkinshaw/Morrison (1995), p. 743.
[701] Harzing (1999), p. 189.

ships.[702] Björkman et al. (2004) determine if trainings are held with participants from different locations.[703] While not strictly related to cultural coordination, we here also ask for the impact of language differences on coordination.[704]

Again, we have compiled an overview of the variables and measures in Table 5-4.

Table 5-4: Overview of measures for dependent variables

Category	Variable	Measure	Supporting literature
(Overarching)	Coordination requirements	Resources (time, finances) needed for coordination	(own measure)
		Number of employees needed for coordination	(own measure)
		Functional areas that need to be coordinated	Cray (1984), p. 90
Structural coordination	Autonomy	Freedom of decision making in specific functional areas	Fischer/Behrman (1979), p. 30; Cray (1984), p. 90; Gates/Egelhoff (1986), p. 74; Ghoshal/Nohria (1989), p. 335
		Final decision making in case of conflict	(own measure)
		Possibility of bringing new ideas to service delivery	Ouchi (1978), p. 179

---

[702] Barner-Rasmussen/Björkman (2005), p. 32.
[703] Björkman et al. (2004), p. 449.
[704] Barner-Rasmussen/Björkman (2005), p. 34, Welch et al. (2005), pp. 23-24

Category	Variable	Measure	Supporting literature
Techno-cratic co-ordination	Stan-dardiza-tion	Degree to which policies and procedures are used	Van De Ven et al. (1976), p. 327; Masca-renhas (1984), p. 104; Cavusgil et al. (1993), p. 492; Harzing (1999), p. 187.
		Degree to which the relationships between various partners of the service off-shoring subsidiary differ	Griffith et al. (2000), p. 304
		Availability of standardized process for addition of new relationships to the service offshoring unit	Griffith et al. (2000), p. 304
	Formal-ization	Degree of process documentation	Zeffane (1989), p. 631; Nobel/Birkinshaw (1996), p. 167
		Degree of automation of processes in electronic tools	Zeffane (1989), p. 631
		Frequency of application of formal work plans, schedules, manuals, and standing orders	Ghoshal/Nohria (1989), p. 335; Harzing (1999), p. 187
Output-based co-ordination	Output control	Degree of pre-specification of results	Ouchi (1978), p. 177; Harzing (1999), p. 187
		Degree to which performance is measured based on pre-specification of results	Gençtürk/Aulakh (1995), p. 769
Personal coordina-tion	Direct personal coordi-	Degree of personal supervision between other units and the service offshoring unit	Van De Ven et al. (1976), p. 327; Harzing (1999), p. 187

Category	Variable	Measure	Supporting literature
	nation	Degree of personal relationships between other units and the service offshoring unit	Van De Ven et al. (1976), p. 327; Harzing (1999), p. 187
		Frequency and duration of interaction and number of participants	(own measure)
	Visits	Number and frequency of visits from other units to service offshoring unit	Trent/Monczka (2002), p. 72; Barner-Rasmussen/Björkman (2005), p. 35
		Duration of visits from other units to service offshoring unit	Trent/Monczka (2002), p. 72; Barner-Rasmussen/Björkman (2005), p. 36
	Transfers	Number of transfers from other units to service offshoring unit	Harzing (1999), pp. 188-189; Delios/Björkman (2000); Harzing (2001); Björkman et al. (2004), p. 449
		Duration of transfers from other units to service offshoring unit	(own measure)
	Cultural coordination	Importance of (possible) language differences	Barner-Rasmussen/Björkman (2005), p. 34; Welch et al. (2005), pp. 23-24
		Presence of team spirit across locations	(own measure)

Category	Variable	Measure	Supporting literature
		Presence of shared values and goals across locations	Ouchi (1979), pp. 836-837; Ghoshal/Nohria (1989), p. 335; Birkinshaw/Morrison (1995), p. 743
		Opportunity for the development of personal relationships in cross-location meetings	Barner-Rasmussen/Björkman (2005), p. 32
		Availability of cross-location trainings	Harzing (1999), pp. 188-189; Björkman et al. (2004), p. 449

5.2.4 DATA INTERPRETATION

5.2.4.1 EPISTEMOLOGICAL UNDERPINNINGS OF DATA INTERPRETATION

Data interpretation depends on the data collection method. Information from documents and from direct observation was added to the case descriptions and evaluations, but since data obtained across methods and across cases was very different, systematic analysis was not possible. Interview recordings on the other hand were transcribed and used for systematic content analysis.

There are three ways to interpret data from an interview: statements can be taken literally, i.e. as the objective representation of reality. Alternatively, data can be taken interpretatively, meaning that the researcher has to "read between the lines" and deduce the actual meaning of what has been said. Finally, interview data can be taken reflexively, which implies that the researcher has to evaluate not only the statements but also the context and its influence on the interview setting.[705] In the current research, data was taken literally, as the discussion was more about structures and relations which had been established upfront and which the interviewee might have a certain opinion on but which do not necessarily change according to that opinion. Questions were typically

---

[705] Lee (1999), pp. 33-35.

5.2.4.2 TRANSCRIPTION OF INTERVIEWS

asked in a way that respondents could answer by primarily giving facts and only secondarily giving opinions/evaluations.

Interviews can be analyzed by four different methods with a decreasing degree of richness: Direct analysis of videotapes, direct analysis of audiotapes, analysis of transcribed voice, or analysis of notes taken during the interviews. Whereas videotaping provides the richest basis for later analysis, we deliberately decided not to use this method: Not only do interviewees find it obtrusive, it is also costly to carry out and analyze. Most importantly, however, it does not yield any better results than direct analysis of audiotapes or analysis of transcribed voice.[706] Actually, Kacmar/Hochwarter (1996) found no differences in the results obtained from direct analysis of videotapes, direct analysis of audiotapes, and analysis of transcripts. Since we recorded interviews whenever we obtained permission from the interviewee, we developed a large database for later analysis. In the one case where recording was not allowed, we took extensive notes during the interview and did a detailed write-up within a few days of the interview. The recorded interviews were transcribed within about a week of the interview, and data was then interpreted based on the transcripts. This method was chosen since it provides the possibility of analyzing the text in more detail, while providing the same quality of results as a direct analysis of audiotapes. However, it has to be kept in mind that "[t]ranscripts are decontextualized conversations"[707]. To make up for that effect, every transcript included regular timestamps that facilitated repeated listening to the recorded interview in case of ambiguity. In addition to text analysis, each interview was listened to at least once in its entirety by the researcher.

Transcription was carried out by experienced transcribers – one person for English interviews and another person for German interviews. Since we took the data literally, the transcripts were denaturalized, i.e. accents and involuntary vocalization were not shown, so that the focus was on the "substance of the interview, that is, the meanings and perceptions created and shared during a conversation."[708] However, all transcriptions show the original word order and grammar. Thus, it is still easy to recognize that many of the English interviews were with non-native English speakers. All transcriptions were evaluated by the researcher at least once and were added to and corrected, if necessary.

---

[706] Kacmar/Hochwarter (1996), p. 473.
[707] Kvale (1996), p. 167.
[708] Oliver et al. (2005), p. 1277.

In addition, the researcher transcribed part of the interviews and compared the results with the transcriptions made by the external transcribers.[709] Data was found to be very reliable, and apart from some different ways of spelling there were very few omissions or other differences.

5.2.4.3 CODING OF INTERVIEWS

Once the transcripts were completed and corrected, the analytical work began.[710] To this end, we made use of the software program ATLAS.ti which allows the user to assign codes to text and thereby to differentiate and combine the retrieved data.[711] Coding is the assignment of categories to the content of a certain piece of information, in our case the interview transcripts. An important item for coding is the coding scheme which contains a series of relevant codes and which also shows how individual codes relate to each other.[712] When coding, the researcher makes a choice about which meaning to interpret from the text.[713] A recommended technique to make coding more reliable is to develop a set of codes from the theoretical framework at the beginning and then apply these to the data rather than to develop codes only when analyzing the data.[714] Therefore, an expected pattern was established in the typology and was then compared with the data found in the case studies.[715] Obviously, there can be various approaches to coding a given text depending on the research question, for instance, a researcher interested in language use might code completely different statements in the text and assign other categories. Thus, the research question and the coding scheme serve to guide the coding process and make the interpretation more reliable by "concentrate[ing] on the substantive research topic"[716].

---

[709] This approach is also recommended by Kvale (1996), pp. 168-170.
[710] In line with the recommendation by Miles/Huberman (1994), p. 65 we started coding early on in the study: The transcript was created within a few days of the interview, and again coding was started once the transcript was finished. We thus allowed for "a reshaping of your perspective and of your instrumentation for the next pass" Miles/Huberman (1994), p. 65.
[711] Smith/Short (2001), Gilbert (2002). For examples of the application of this type of software in different disciplines, see Widener/Selto (1999), pp. 63-65, Akintoye et al. (2003), p. 464, Sullivan (2004), p. 58.
[712] Weston et al. (2001), p. 384.
[713] Miles/Huberman (1994), pp. 56-57.
[714] Miles/Huberman (1994), p. 58. This approach is different from the grounded-theory approach developed by Glaser/Strauss (1980) that builds codes only after the data has been collected. That approach, however, is more appropriate for theory generation than for theory explanation and enhancement (Hartley (1994), p. 210). In addition, its complexity should not be underestimated and the approach should be selected with caution (Lee (1999), p. 50).
[715] Lee (1999), p. 76.
[716] Manwar et al. (1994), p. 287.

5 – Methodology 185

As we had an extensive theoretical framework to start from, we were able to generate an exhaustive list of codes that are presented in Table 5-5 together with their description that helps for more exact assignment of codes. We have categorized the codes and indicated whether they are part of our typology ("typ") or serve to better describe the case ("info"). In the course of the text analysis, we established several additional codes which are also included in our list as a separate category ("new").[717] Some codes serve as aggregated code (such as "strategic relevance" or "network embeddedness") that were introduced to build a complete hierarchy of codes but that were typically not directly assigned to text because of being to unspecific.[718]

Table 5-5: Codes used for transcript analysis

Code	Description	Category
Autonomy	Degree of freedom of decision making of the service offshoring subsidiary	Typ
Closeness	Degree of closeness of relationship, influenced by mutual adaptation and mutual investment	Typ
Commitment	Headquarters' commitment for making the service offshoring subsidiary successful	New
Company size	Number of employees in the different units and the entire MNC	Info
Coordination need	Need for coordination which is influenced by strategic relevance and network embeddedness (aggregated code)	Typ
Coordination requirements	Resources needed for coordination (people, finances, time)	Typ

---

[717] We present and discuss the new codes in section 7.2.5.
[718] See Figure 5-1.

Code	Description	Category
Cultural coordination	Coordination by normative integration, for instance, through team spirit, shared values and norms, cross-locational trainings	Typ
Direct coordination	Direct personal coordination (also remote) through supervision from another unit	Typ
Entry mode	Influence of entry mode on coordination	New
Formalization	Degree of formalization of the relationship, degree of documentation	Typ
Frequency	Frequency of change and additions to the structure of the relationship	Typ
Future plans	Plans to change the service portfolio or the network structure of the service offshoring subsidiary	Info
Inimitability	Degree of inimitability of the service(s); ease of replication of the existing service by a competitor	Typ
Language skills	Effect of language differences on coordination	New
Local network	Description of the service offshoring subsidiary's local network; potential effects on coordination	New
Motivation	Primary motivation for setting up the service offshoring subsidiary (sub-code of value)	Typ
Network embeddedness	Degree of network embeddedness of the service offshoring center (aggregated code)	Typ
Network structure	Description of the network structure, especially number of relationships	Typ
Non-substitutability	Degree of non-substitutability of the service(s), ease of substituting the existing service by another service	Typ

5 – Methodology

Code	Description	Category
Output control	Degree of output control, possibility to exactly pre-specify results and eventual comparison to initially established expectations	Typ
Personal coordination	All personal coordination mechanisms (aggregated code)	Typ
Physical distance	Influence of physical distance on coordination	New
Service offshoring problems	Specific (coordination) problems that occur in a service offshoring relationship	New
Rareness	Degree of rareness of the service(s), availability of service on (external) markets	Typ
Service description	Description of the service(s) that the service offshoring subsidiary delivers	Info
Standardization	Degree of standardization of the relationship, degree of policies and procedures	Typ
Strategic relevance	Degree of strategic relevance of the service(s) delivered by the service offshoring center (aggregated code)	Typ
Structure	General reference to company structure	Info
Technocratic coordination	All technocratic coordination mechanisms (aggregated code)	Typ
Transfers	Number of transfers (and their duration) between service offshoring center and other units	Typ
Value	Degree of value of the service(s), degree of importance for the customers of the service offshoring unit	Typ
Visits	Number of visits (and their duration) between service offshoring center and other units	Typ

Coding then took place in several steps: (1) Each section of the interview documentation consisting of a question and answer in the transcript was read several times to ensure a complete understanding. (2) The answer was divided into logical units containing one statement each. For instance, when an interviewee referred to several coordination mechanisms, several statements – one for each coordination mechanism – were created. A statement can contain a few words up to a few sentences that explain a specific circumstance. (3) Each statement relevant to the study[719] was then coded with one or more codes from the code list. Generally, the statement was compared to the list of codes (and their descriptions) to check which codes would apply. Appropriate codes that the statement referred to, were then assigned to the statement.

The choice of the "right" code was also facilitated by the fact that our questions were designed in a way that they referred to one code only. Thus, in principle it was possible to assign the answer the code to which respective question referred. Of course, interviewees sometimes expanded on a question or mentioned other side topics when discussing a specific aspect and thus, some answers were assigned several codes. (4) During the coding process, the correct coding was tested in iterations to ensure that codes were always used for similar circumstances and that all circumstances were considered in coding. (5) As a final check, parts of the transcripts were re-coded to ensure that the coding process was as transparent and reliable as possible.[720]

Data was thus interpreted by condensing the meaning from the interviews and categorizing it.[721] After developing the initial codes as described above, we started to establish links between them based on our typology. These links are expressed visually in Figure 5-1. Here we display only the original codes ("typ"). Those codes that serve only informational purposes are evaluated for case description.[722] We will discuss new codes in our cross-case analysis.[723]

---

[719] Statements were considered to be not relevant when the interview diverted to other topics – for instance, the weather in the offshore country.
[720] Kvale (1996), pp. 196-199. For different coding techniques, see also Flick (2002), pp. 257-286.
[721] Lee (1999), p. 89.
[722] See chapter 6.
[723] See chapter 7.

5 – Methodology

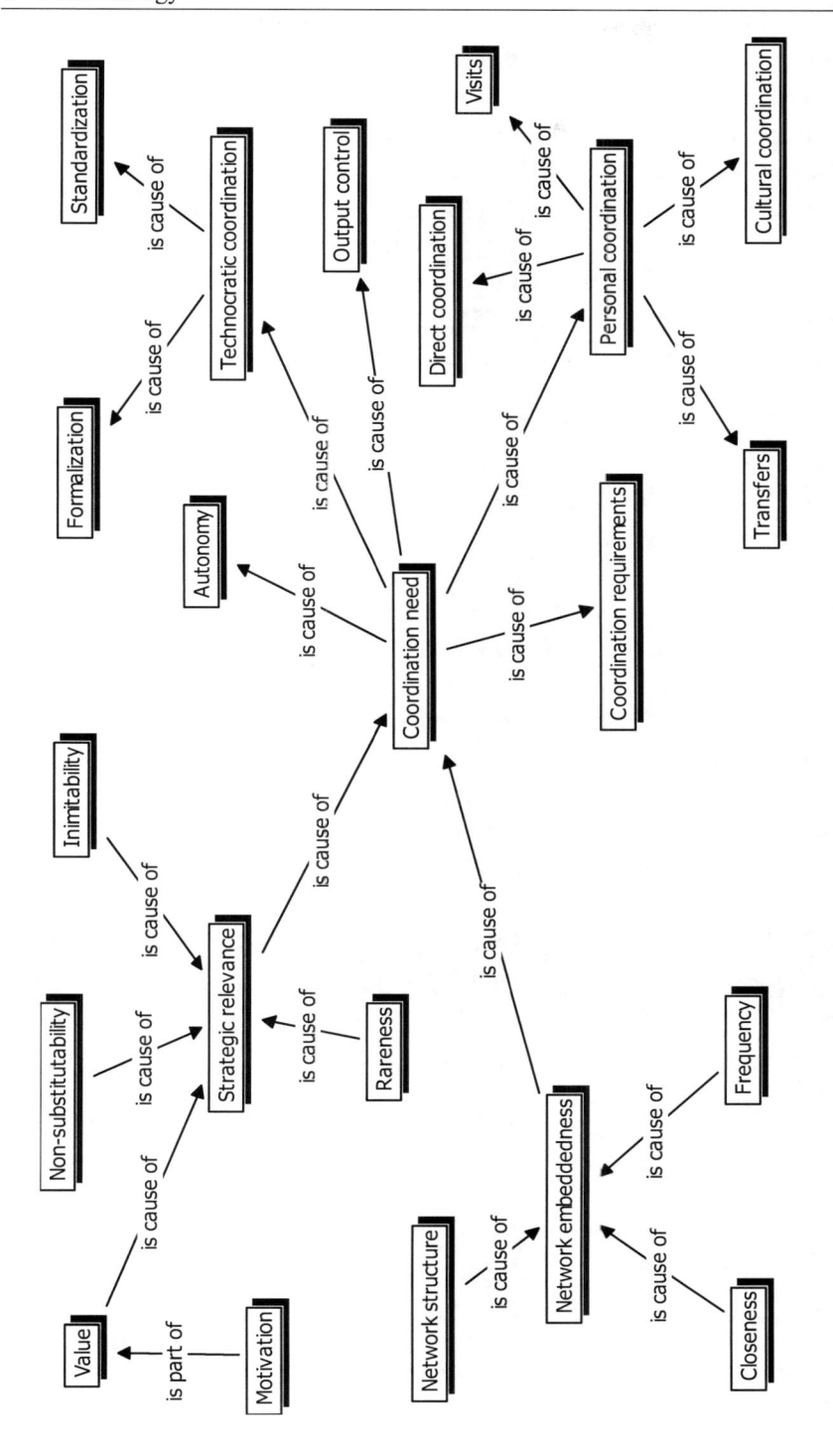

Figure 5-1: Initial relationships between codes

The figure displays the relationships between codes as developed in our typology. On the left-hand side of the figure the two dimensions – strategic relevance and network embeddedness – are displayed. They are surrounded by their respective variables (value and the associated code motivation (for setting up the service offshoring subsidiary), non-substitutability, inimitability, and rareness for strategic relevance and network structure, frequency, and closeness for network embeddedness). These two values determine the coordination need which is displayed in the center of the figure. The overall coordination need then results in the different coordination categories with their individual mechanisms. Coordination need also causes overall coordination requirements.

5.2.4.4 CASE DISPLAY

Based on a first review of the data, we started to do a write-up of each case. For this purpose, a generic structure had been developed beforehand that was subsequently used to fill in case information. This structure can be seen in Table 5-6. The data was then analyzed a second time and the case description was broadened and deepened. Whereas the first analysis cycle mainly helped to assign existing codes to the data, the second cycles helped to uncover more details, new codes and causal relationships between data chunks. We also categorized quotations that we collected under one coding according to the different facts to which the interviewees referred. For instance, if several interviewees refer to the frequency, the occasions and the duration of visits, we presented these sub-topics in our case display.[724] In this way, we followed the approach that is proposed by Miles/Huberman (1994) for case studies with pre-structured theory.[725]

Table 5-6: Structure for case display

Category	Content
Company overview	Presentation of MNC and the business unit under consideration
	Description of history and motivation of offshoring situation
	Description of services provided by service offshoring subsidiary

---

[724] This also explains why the case display discusses different sub-topics for each case. For instance, in some cases interviewees pointed to the use of electronic tools with regard to technocratic coordination. In cases without these tools they are obviously not referenced.
[725] Miles/Huberman (1994), p. 85.

5 – Methodology

Category	Content
Type of service offshoring subsidiary	Analysis of strategic relevance of services provided by the service offshoring subsidiary Analysis of network embeddedness of service offshoring subsidiary Result of evaluation of subsidiary type
Coordination mechanisms	Individual analysis of structural, technocratic, output-based and personal mechanisms of coordination Comparative analysis of coordination mechanisms
Results of case	Evaluation of appropriateness of propositions for individual case Presentation of additional information gained from the individual case

When starting to write a new case, we extracted all the statements pertaining to one code from our interview database. The ATLAS.ti software facilitated this process with a query system that allows one to create lists of interview statements that stem from a selected interview and that refer to one or more selected code(s). With these lists of statements, the transcripts of the interviews were evaluated again to check for ambiguous codings and potential sources of misunderstanding. We then had to decide whether to incorporate all codings in the main text or to select only some codes. Since the latter approach is subject to additional subjectivity and difficult to comprehend for the reader, we introduced all codings for the main variables to the final case display. That way, we ensured the presentation of a complete picture. Therefore, many direct quotations are added to the case display. We indicate for each quotation the number of the interview and the paragraph number from which the quotations stem.[726] Only after discussing all information regarding the respective independent or dependent variable, we conclude with our estimate of low, medium, or high value.[727] We thereby assign a low value to those cases where (almost) all indicators point to the lower end of the respective meas-

---

[726] All interviews are numbered with a complete list available in the appendix. Transcripts and other documents are not added to the appendix due to their large size but can be reviewed upon request.
[727] Bryman (1989), pp. 50-51.

ure. A high value is consequently assigned when (almost) all indicators point in that direction. Where we find a balance between ambiguous arguments, we assume a medium value.[728]

To protect confidential information, some words are substituted by placeholders. This is indicated by the use of '[]'. In some cases it is necessary for a better understanding of a quote to supply additional comments that explain what was happening in the course of the interview, for instance, interviewees pointing out of the window or at a document. We have added these comments in parentheses and introduce them by '#'.

Our interviews were carried out in English or German, depending on the preference of the interviewee. We had the choice of translating German quotations into English before data display, which would have resulted in a loss of data quality and richness.[729] Given the importance of language in interview research[730] and in order to display results as correctly as possible, we have chosen to leave German quotations in their original form. However, we do not use them as direct citations but rather explain their content and only then present the original German statement in parentheses to allow readers – of whom several are from the German-speaking community – to develop their own impression. Therefore we also decided against "relegating" the German quotations to footnotes or the appendix which would have implicitly devalued them. In doing so, we are in line with the recommendations of other international business researchers who argue for the use of multi-lingual data collection and display.[731] Every alternative would have reduced the richness of data that was the original motivation for the data collection method applied in this study and we therefore decided to go the more elaborate way of providing the translation of the meaning together with the original German version.

In most cases, the information obtained from headquarters, service offshoring centers and other international subsidiaries does not show any contradictory data or perception gaps. Thus, we decided not to explicitly distinguish these levels in case display. However, where we find differences, we discuss them separately.[732]

---

[728] For a similar approach see Cavusgil et al. (1993), p. 491.
[729] Macdonald/Hellgren (2004), p. 272.
[730] Kirkman-Liff/Mondragón (1991), McCormack (2004), pp. 225-226.
[731] Marschan-Piekkari/Reis (2004).
[732] See, for instance, section 6.3.3 for differences in the judgment of coordination mechanisms in case 3 "support center").

When we display the results of an individual case, we will compare the predictions from our typology with the empirical findings. Besides congruencies that we count as a first step of confirmation, there will most likely be divergences to the propositions and additional topics/ideas that were raised during the fieldwork. For those cases where there seem to be divergences, we will further evaluate the topic within the individual case. Additional ideas will be considered in cross-case analysis. Cross-case analysis will abstract from the individual case results and see if the tendencies that we have proposed in our typology were found in the empirical study.

5.2.4.5 GENERALIZATION OF RESULTS

A major question in any qualitative research project is the generalization of results. While our case studies can at least illustrate our topic, it has to be discussed how relevant the findings are for a larger set of data. The challenge that faces any kind of qualitative research is that there is no standard repertoire of procedures to make results generally applicable. With quantitative data, this challenge can be dealt with more easily by applying statistical methods to find representativeness in the data. However, even these methods do not guarantee the possibility of generalization. For every research project it has to be analyzed how results from a small group of cases can be applied to a larger group of cases in a population – not only for qualitative but also for quantitative studies. Simply because there is statistical representativeness does not imply that it is possible to generalize: "generalizing from case studies can be difficult", however, "*the same is true for quantitative studies* [emphasis in original]"[733].

Even though case studies do not satisfy the criteria for statistical representation, it is still possible to come to more general results. In-depth knowledge enables the researcher to better specify the conditions in which the results can be expected.[734] By then analyzing the processes in detail, the researcher can judge whether a specific process is general or peculiar to the organization under consideration. It is important to note that the generalization does not relate to a population but rather to the theoretical propositions.[735] Thus, we will not be able to infer from the four cases we are targeting to the entire population of service offshoring centers, but we can suggest that the use of a specific coordination mechanism in a service offshoring center depends on a set of factors that we have evaluated. Thereby we show the logic behind the decision for a given coordination

---

[733] Hartley (1994), p. 225.
[734] Hartley (1994), p. 225.
[735] Hartley (1994), p. 225.

mechanism.[736] In addition, by choosing a multi-case design, there is already some possibility to increase reliability by comparing cases with one another.[737]

5.2.5 QUALITY CRITERIA FOR CASE STUDIES

Some authors argue that quality measures are intertwined with the ontological premises of the research. These can lead to different quality criteria for qualitative research than those that are known from quantitative research.[738] In our approach, which is more positivist, we think that – as in any other empirical research – the quality of case studies can be judged on four measures: (1) construct validity, (2) internal validity, (3) external validity, and (4) reliability.

(1) Construct validity means that the researcher selects the right operational constructs to measure the concepts under study.[739] As discussed above, we based our operationalization on established measures from the literature. Construct validity can be improved by using multiple sources of evidence,[740] by clearly structuring the case study incorporating all pieces of evidence and linking them to the question under consideration,[741] and by having the key informants review the draft of the case study report.[742] We used different methods of data collection, involved several interviewees per case, and related all the findings to the structure from our typology. In addition, we held follow-up discussions with the executives to discuss open and unclear points. Due to the time constraints of the senior managers we interviewed, it was not possible to have them completely review the case display. However, we presented and discussed individual findings with our interviewees.

(2) Internal validity signifies a valid causal relationship which ensures that no other variable explains the obtained results. This measurement is only necessary in explanatory case studies, but not in descriptive or exploratory studies.[743] While we obviously did not have the opportunity to evaluate all possible influence factors on coordination mechanisms, we tried to increase the validity of our findings by reformulating questions in the course of an interview. We addressed the dimensions network embeddedness and

---

[736] Hillebrand et al. (2001), pp. 653-654.
[737] We show the different possibilities for evaluation in section 7.1.
[738] Cassell/Symon (1994), Symon/Cassell (1998), p. 6, Flick (2004), pp. 47-48.
[739] Yin (2003), p. 34.
[740] Yin (2003), p. 35.
[741] Yin (2003), pp. 105-106.
[742] Yin (2003), p. 36.
[743] Yin (2003), p. 36.

strategic relevance at the beginning of the interview and then proceeded to ask about the use of coordination mechanisms. While discussing coordination mechanisms, we repeatedly asked why a specific coordination mechanism was chosen to see if interviewees would list the same factors that we were considering based on our theoretical considerations. It was confirmed in the interviews (as we will show in individual case display) that the factors we identified indeed determine coordination.

(3) External validity is achieved when the results from a case study can be applied to a setting beyond the single case. In traditional measures of statistical generalizations, a single case study cannot satisfy this criterion. However, if results are replicated in a second and a third setting, support for generalization becomes increasingly strong.[744] Also, as discussed above, we analyze which of our findings can be generalized and which cannot. Finally, we repeat that our generalization relates to theoretical propositions rather than to a population.[745]

(4) Reliability means that another investigation would come to the same results. This requires first and foremost good documentation.[746] In the current case, reliability was analyzed by having a second transcription made from the audiotape of an interview and then comparing the two results. The two transcriptions were virtually identical, which points to a high degree of reliability. In order to increase reliability further, a sample of interviews was recoded after a few weeks and intra-coder agreement was measured. The value obtained here was between 82 per cent and 85 per cent accuracy (measured by number of correct code assignments divided by all code assignments) which is considered a good value.[747] Unclear cases were evaluated again until remaining ambiguities were remedied.

5.3 REGIONAL FOCUS OF EMPIRICAL RESEARCH

The empirical study includes MNCs from Germany that offshore to centers in Eastern Europe. The reasons for this regional focus are the outlined below:

1. Eastern Europe is becoming increasingly important as an offshoring location.[748] Service offshoring has long been the domain of Anglo-Saxon countries but is

---

[744] Yin (2003), p. 37.
[745] Hartley (1994), p. 225.
[746] Yin (2003), pp. 37-38.
[747] Miles/Huberman (1994), p. 64. Other studies report only 80 per cent of final inter-coder reliability (Cavusgil et al. (1993)).
[748] Wildemann (2005), pp. 7-9.

now quickly extending into Continental Europe as well.[749] The major destination for offshoring has been and still is India. It has a large labor pool that is proficient in English allowing it to cater especially to U.S. and UK companies that desire to offshore activities. American companies started to outsource to India as early as the 1980s. Now, Eastern Europe is attracting more offshore contracts. This comes as companies from Continental Europe increasingly consider offshoring as a way to increase their competitiveness. Some factors, however, can make Eastern Europe more attractive to them than India.[750] While wage levels are typically higher, cultural differences and language barriers are usually far lower. In addition, transport and communication costs are in favor of Eastern Europe.[751] However, while there is abundant literature on offshoring to India,[752] Eastern Europe has been less covered.[753] In sum, there are still many degrees of freedom in the development of this region as a destination for service offshoring that are worthy of evaluation.

2. Offshoring to Eastern Europe differs in several respects from the offshoring that took off in the U.S. (and the UK) many years ago. In Eastern Europe, there is no single target market such as, for instance, India, with a high proficiency of the home market's language, but there is a large variety of languages, skills and cultures in the region, which could make it more attractive for specialized offshoring than for pure cost-cutting efforts. For instance, the cultural proximity of several Eastern European countries, including many historical linkages, can make service offshoring to this region especially attractive for MNCs from Continental Europe which need specific language skills.[754]

3. Our focus on captive offshoring situations is also related to the specifics in Eastern Europe. International subsidiaries that carry out offshoring are especially relevant for MNCs from Continental Europe wishing to offshore to Eastern Europe but unable to find – unlike MNCs that go to India – a large and ma-

---

[749] Reinhardt (2004).
[750] Lewin/Peeters (2006), pp. 230-231.
[751] Reinhardt (2004).
[752] Kapur/Ramamurti (2001), Dossani/Kenney (2003), Kumra/Sinha (2003), Davies (2004), Farrell/Zainulbhai (2004), Nair/Prasad (2004).
[753] See, however, Zatolyuk/Allgood (2004), Marin (2006).
[754] Reed (2006).

ture provider market that could take over specific services in the framework of an outsourcing agreement.[755]

4. Researchers have found that coordination can be influenced by the country in which the company is located.[756] We wanted to exclude this factor and thus focus on companies from Germany that offshore to Eastern Europe. Previous research indicates that it is appropriate to combine countries in Eastern Europe in a research sample since they are "fairly homogeneous with respect to many relevant country factors"[757].

5.4 FUNCTIONAL FOCUS OF EMPIRICAL RESEARCH

Earlier research has found differences between functional areas with regard to coordination. For instance, the finance function in subsidiaries has been quoted as having little autonomy.[758] We therefore decided to highlight one functional area – namely information technology[759] – that has, first, not received much attention in international business research and that, second, allows us to better control for functional influences. The reasons for this decision were the following:

1. Information technology seems to be the primary function that is offshored.[760] This is because it lends itself to relocation since its processes and results are digitalized and do not require many changes before being moved to an offshore location. In addition, many receiving countries (especially those in Eastern Europe) have established a reputation for a good educational standard in the fields of computer science, engineering and the like. Thus, employees can probably be more easily found for the IT function than for other functions that require more management knowledge. This is typically scarce in former socialist countries that do not have a long history of a market economy.[761] Thus, information technology seems to be of special relevance for MNCs.

2. Information technology comprises a large variety of services that do not limit what we want to capture in our typology. For instance, information technology

---

[755] Kobayashi-Hillary (2004), p. 79.
[756] Young/Tavares (2004), p. 217.
[757] Uhlenbruck (2004), p. 114.
[758] Young/Tavares (2004), p. 217.
[759] For a definition of IT, see Section 1.3.
[760] Berry (2006), p. 23.
[761] Hoskisson et al. (2000), p. 257, Uhlenbruck/De Castro (2000), p. 382.

services can be of high strategic relevance where a subsidiary has the responsibility for product development. With the human resources function, for instance, this seems harder to imagine. On the other hand, subsidiaries that provide IT services can also be highly embedded in the MNC network since IT services can in principle be standardized for use internationally and do not depend on local specifics that would apply, for instance, in the case of legal services which are bound to one country's legislation. Thus, services within the realm of information technology seem to be a good example with which to illustrate and evaluate our typology.

3. Finally, and potentially due to the first reason, service offshoring subsidiaries from the IT function were among the first to provide offshore services in the MNC network and more centers have been established for the IT function than for any other service. Thus, it seems more likely that we shall find appropriate cases here for our research.

6 Results – Presenting Four Case Studies of Service Offshoring Subsidiaries in Eastern Europe

> *"In theory, there is no difference between theory and practice.*
> *But, in practice, there is."*
>
> Jan L.A. van de Snepscheut

Summary

In this chapter, we present our findings for the individual cases. We start with an illustration of the firm and the services under consideration. We then assess for each case the strategic relevance and the network embeddedness. We proceed to describe how coordination works and evaluate each coordination mechanism in detail. A comparative analysis of the coordination mechanisms shows how they relate to one another. Finally, we discuss each case and consider how the results are in alignment with our expectations. Where they are not, we give potential explanations. Besides, we report on new insights we gained during the data collection and analysis.

6.1 CASE 1: SERVICE FACTORY ALPHA

6.1.1 COMPANY OVERVIEW

Presentation of MNC and the business unit under consideration

Alpha operates in the logistics industry. It has several 100,000 employees in more than 200 countries worldwide. Its revenues totaled some 40 billion EUR for the fiscal year 2005. The firm is organized in business units (BU), each of which focuses on a different aspect of logistics services. Every business unit has its own international subsidiaries that are often grouped by regions with regional headquarters. Alpha has acquired several other companies from the logistics industry worldwide in recent years.[762] In the course of the integrating of these independent companies, Alpha has introduced two main principles for support services. On the one hand, services such as finance, human resources, and IT (on which we will focus here) have been consolidated in shared service centers that provide services across business units and across country borders. On the other hand, the company has also introduced internal markets for these services by segregating the demand side (in the business units) and the supply side (in newly-established service centers).[763] These shared services centers formally belong to Alpha's Corporate Functions unit that is on the same hierarchical level as the other business units. Each international subsidiary can be considered a customer of these service centers, even though sometimes a region's demand is bundled in a regional headquarters first and then purchased from the service centers. An overview of this constellation can be seen in Figure 6-1.

Description of history and motivation of offshoring situation

The demand-supply split mentioned above was also introduced in the area of IT. In a first step, the internal IT function that had previously been carried out in many countries was centralized in four major centers. These centers were pooled in one organization – AlphaIT – Alpha's new internal IT provider. AlphaIT's centers are located in North America (NA), Western Europe (WE), Eastern Europe (EE), and Asia-Pacific (AP). The centers in North America and Western Europe were existing IT centers within the pre-

---

[762] The financial data is taken from the corporation's annual report for the fiscal year 2005. In addition, information from Alpha's web site and internal information brochures from Alpha center were evaluated for this overview.

[763] For a discussion of how to set up internal services like market services see Vandermerwe/Gilbert (1989).

6 – Results 201

vious organizational structure; the centers in Eastern Europe and Asia were built as new centers.

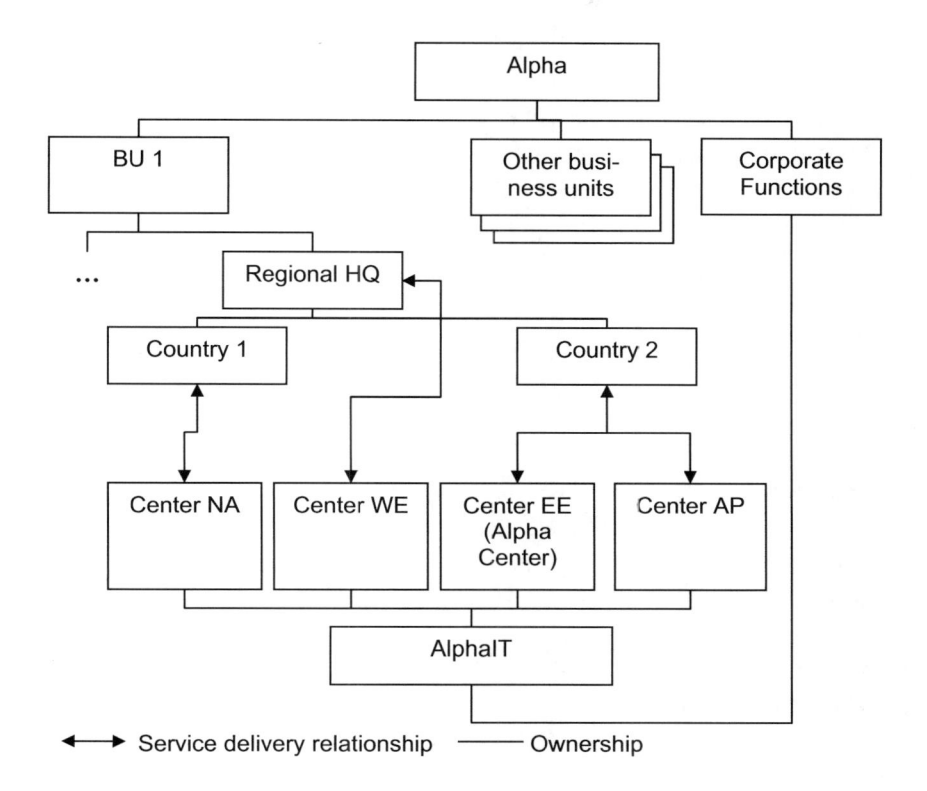

```
                        ┌─────────┐
                        │  Alpha  │
                        └────┬────┘
        ┌────────────────────┼────────────────────┐
   ┌────┴────┐         ┌─────┴─────┐         ┌────┴─────┐
   │  BU 1   │         │Other busi-│         │ Corporate│
   │         │         │ness units │         │ Functions│
   └────┬────┘         └───────────┘         └──────────┘
        │
   ┌────┴──────┐
   │Regional HQ│◄─────
   └────┬──────┘
   ┌────┴────────────┐
┌──┴───┐         ┌───┴───┐
│Country 1│       │Country 2│
└──┬───┘         └───┬───┘
```

Figure 6-1: Service delivery within Alpha's network

Centers: Center NA, Center WE, Center EE (Alpha Center), Center AP — all connected to AlphaIT.

◄──► Service delivery relationship   ──── Ownership

After having set up these centers, Alpha started to move IT services from individual countries to the respective regional center. Thus, services for Germany are now primarily provided by the center in Eastern Europe. However, the centers are not independent of one another. Rather, there are plans to run about 20 per cent of all software programs as so-called *"global applications"*[764]. These applications are needed for all countries in which Alpha operates. They are designed in a way that they can run without interruption even if one of the centers should need to shut down because of technical or other problems. Thus, the centers serve as a so-called "fall-back" solution. In addition, there are

---

[764] Currently, about 10 per cent of all applications run as "global" applications.

also areas for which the centers work in a *"follow-the-sun"*[765] fashion. The operation of the global telecom network, for instance, shifts from Asia through Eastern Europe to North America in the course of 24 hours. That way, it is not necessary to have employees working on expensive night shifts in all locations. In addition, the center organization can channel larger projects to individual centers even if their customers are not from that specific region. For instance, an application development project for a customer from Europe could be carried out in the North American center as well, even if as a rule the center in the respective region takes care of requests.

For our further considerations, we will focus on the center in Eastern Europe (Alpha Center) that mainly provides services to customers in Europe, Africa and the Middle East.

Description of services provided by service offshoring subsidiary

The center in Western Europe provides only software development services. The other centers provide both software development services (so-called "build"-services) and infrastructure services such as the hosting of applications, the support of applications, and the provision of email and telephony services (so-called "run"-services). These services are categorized in a "service catalog", the structure of which is represented in Table 6-1.

We here focus only on the run services because this area is the biggest in Alpha Center (roughly two-thirds of the 1200 employees work in this area). Alpha Center provides these run services to approximately 500 customers. However, Alpha Center does not execute all tasks in-house, but also cooperates with external providers. That way, it bundles services from external partners with internal services before it provides them to internal customers. The internal customers are not obliged to purchase their IT services from Alpha Center. Rather, the demand-supply split introduced a market model in which the customers can select other providers as well. Thus, both customers in the business units as well as Alpha Center have the freedom to contract with one another and external providers. This design of relationships was introduced by a unit in Alpha's global headquarters that still monitors and sets broad guidelines. An overview of these relationships is displayed in Figure 6-2.

---

[765] Interview 15:45.

Table 6-1: Structure of AlphaIT's service catalog (Source: Alpha internal document)

Type	Category	Example for service
Build	Software Development	Development of a new software application
Build	Consulting & Project	Evaluation of existing application
Run	Maintenance & Support	Telecommunication support
Run	Service Desk	Information request
Run	Desktop Computing	Email account
Run	Hosting	Windows or Linux server
Run	Telecom	Network access

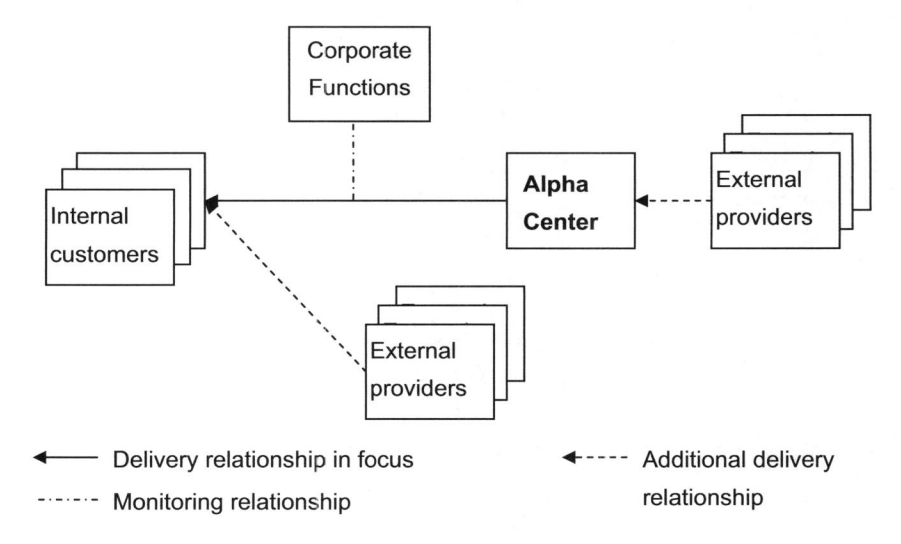

Figure 6-2: Alpha Center's service delivery relationships

6.1.2 Type of Service Offshoring Subsidiary

6.1.2.1 Analysis of Strategic Relevance

To discuss the strategic relevance of services provided by Alpha Center to its customers we will analyze the (A) value, (B) rareness, (C) inimitability, and (D) non-substitutability of the services.[766]

(A) We first consider the *value* of the services with regard to (1) the importance of IT in comparison to that of other functions within Alpha, (2) the range of services that Alpha Center provides, and (3) Alpha's motivation for setting up Alpha Center:

1. The *importance of the IT function* in comparison to other activities is expressed in one statement by a representative of Alpha Center who shows that IT is not the core business of Alpha: *"If it's a good business proposition, if it's a good business project, then the fact that they will run a non-standard version of Informix which someone has to be specifically trained on and costs 150,000 Euros, it is irrelevant. ... You have to look at the big picture. You can't get IT on its own, you have to see how it fits into the business."*[767] Another interviewee compared the fire in a shipment facility with that of an IT failure and concluded that IT is less critical to the business (*"Als eine Verladefabrik mal abgebrannt war, was da passiert ist, wenn Engpässe plötzlich kommen, wie es dann weiter geht, ja. Ich meine, das sind Dinge, die kann man nicht so von heute auf morgen kompensieren. Aber so ein Thema kann man eher organisieren."*[768]). However, it is also acknowledged that in the future IT will become a more important production factor which might eventually lead to competitive advantage (*"Weil IT immer mehr zu einem wichtigen Produktionsfaktor wird. Und ich denke, das ist auch ein Wettbewerbsvorteil."*).[769]

2. The *range of services* that Alpha Center provides is broad and it seems that there are differences in value. There are services that add only low value for the customer of the service (*"hosting and outsourcing type of arrangement that we could take what we do here and plug it over to another company overnight and they run it the same way"*[770]; *"Und der Mehrwert besteht nicht darin, dass er in der Lage ist, einen*

---

[766] As discussed above, we concentrate on the "run" services.
[767] Interview 15:29.
[768] Interview 19:65.
[769] Interview 19:63.
[770] Interview 18:42.

Data Center zu betreiben, Kisten hinzustellen usw."[771]). On the other hand, it was noted that *"the IT people here [in Alpha Center] have probably the most knowledge about the IT systems and businesses processes behind it than anybody."*[772] The difference in value is also recognized by Alpha Center and affects the way that services are offered. One representative indicated that he *"can measure the value to the customer, the value to ourselves, and the complexity. ... And then there are some areas where really we should reconsider whether I can sell that to my customer."*[773]

3. There were several statements with regard to Alpha's *motivation for setting up Alpha center*. The motivation for centralizing IT in few locations is explained in the statement: *"... you consolidate all these topics to make it more efficient."*[774] Other interviewees frequently referred to efficiency as motivation and important measure: *"... we are way ahead of our original financial projection for the savings we've had on moving here."*[775] To increase efficiency and put more pressure on the internal supplier was also the motivation for setting up a market-like structure (*"Das ist ja auch das Ziel. Man möchte gerne auch vor allen Dingen die Effizienz steigern, indem man die Kollegen auch ein bisschen unter Druck bringt."*[776]). Alpha intends to increase efficiency through a clearer allocation of cost to the unit that has ordered a service (*"Dass eine klare Allokation stattfindet. Dass man die Bestimmung der Kosten, die Allokation zu den Business-Units und 'Make-Own-Charging' stattfindet im Grunde nach dem Verursacherprinzip."*[777]). One interviewee also mentioned flexibility as a motivation for setting up the current structure: *"As an organization overall, the centralization works allows [Alpha] to be far more flexible because they can make changes around the globe much quicker in the future."*[778]

---

[771] Interview 19:43.
[772] Interview 18:42; confirmed by Interview 16:48. The wide variety of value is also confirmed by interview 20:14.
[773] Interview 17:54; confirmed by interviews 17:10 and 17:58.
[774] Interview 15:1.
[775] Interview 16:7; focus on efficiency also confirmed by interviews 15:1; 18:4; 18:16; 18:22; and 18:42.
[776] Interview 20:105.
[777] Interview 19:45.
[778] Interview 18:44. In addition, one interviewee mentioned that the change in structure was also intended not only to ensure cost savings but that IT works more stably: "[U]nd man muss wissen, dass das Thema nicht nur darin besteht, Kosten zu senken, falls überhaupt, sondern dass diese Dinge laufen." (Interview 19:41).

The first point as well as the last point suggests a rather low value of the services that Alpha Center provides. However, it would not be appropriate to classify the value all of Alpha Center's services as low. As some statements indicated (see point 2), there are also services with higher value. Due to the large variety, we need to focus on a specific set of services, namely those run services that are on the lower end of the value continuum (as already discussed above). We can thus treat the services considered here as being of low value.[779]

(B) Our focus now is on the *rareness* of the services provided by Alpha Center. Here, we will evaluate whether the services that Alpha Center provides are freely available on external markets. The general notion was that other firms also offer the services that Alpha Center provides: *"There are capable providers global."*[780] One interviewee in Alpha Center stated that their services *"... are complex, but there are always people who can do that."*[781] That services are not rare can also be seen by the fact that several international subsidiaries are already using external providers to purchase services that they could also purchase from Alpha Center: *"The reality is that my customer is already using six external vendors and external suppliers so we're in a competitive market place, plus they can do work locally, so they have a set of suppliers in each of those individual countries providing IT services and they do it."*[782] Actually, the entire setup of an internal market place had the objective of making services less rare. This allowed units from within Alpha to compare the services provided by Alpha Center to those from external vendors as if Alpha Center was an external vendor (*"Aber wie gesagt, das Entscheidende ist, dass der Interne gebenchmarked wird irgendwann auch, und dass er Preise, Prozesse und Leistungen erbringt, als ob er im Markt wäre, dass er im Grund wettbewerbsfähig ist."*[783]). The possibility to purchase from external vendors is used and can lead to a loss of business for Alpha Center when units within Alpha compare services from Alpha Center to those that they can source externally (*"Und dann haben wir [Alpha Center] mit [name of external vendor] gebenchmarked, die Preise sind bekannt aus den Verträgen. Und Tatsache war, [name of external vendor] war günstiger, muss man feststellen. War eben so. Und dann haben wir das bei [name of external ven-*

---

[779] We will later discuss how we can deal with service offshoring subsidiaries that provide services with a variety of strategic relevance.
[780] Interview 15:55.
[781] Interview 15:57.
[782] Interview 17:12.
[783] Interview 19:45; confirmed by interview 20:10.

6 – Results 207

dor] machen lassen. Wie gesagt, in diesem Einzelfall damals haben wir das schon gemacht, und das werden wir in Zukunft sicherlich häufiger machen."[784]).

Based on these considerations we conclude that the services provided by Alpha Center are of low rareness. We here again focus only on the "run" services as discussed above.[785]

(C) The next indicator we consider is the *inimitability* of the services. We will examine whether another firm could imitate the services by building up a similar center. We will evaluate (1) the possibility of setting up a similar service center in the location of Alpha Center and (2) the complexity of services that influence the duration of training for the services and therefore the time it would take to build up a similar center.

1. Interviewees judged the *possibility to build new service centers* as high. For instance, they mentioned that many firms have set up service centers in the city where Alpha Center is located and that there are more new centers in the pipeline: *"I think that how many similar projects [name of the city] could take would be an interesting question. How many more, because there are some big. All this park was built in the last two years [# interviewee points out of the window to neighboring buildings]. Accenture is this building, this is the CA, Sun has set shop over there, HP, IBM is here with hundreds of people. So it's all technological park, all competing on the same market right now."*[786] Hiring technical employees was not a problem for Alpha Center; however, the availability of management skills is still rather low which can affect the inimitability of the services: *"As far as getting technical people, it was far more successful than I thought it would be. ... They don't have those management capabilities. Before, management was a different business under communism, right? So, it's completely changed and so finding those people is sometimes challenging. People familiar with industry best practices and IT processes, things like that, you don't really find a lot here."*[787]

2. The *specific knowledge* that is needed to provide services is not judged as very complex; rather, the average learning time was estimated at four months: *"I had*

---

[784] Interview 20:107.
[785] In the broad spectrum of services, there are also services that are not freely available on external markets (20:14). However, they are not in the range of services that we consider here.
[786] Interview 15:87.
[787] Interview 18:14.

anticipated a long training curve to bring people over from London and our average knowledge transfer time ... was four months."[788] Besides the actual provision of services, there is another set of knowledge that relates to integrating new customers to the service center: *"We are in the integration business. We are integrating the many many many companies in Europe and in the U.S. That's very specific when you need to have the knowledge and basic knowleage from the business background. So you may look inside the IT portfolio, as we do regularly and what we do internally and what we outsource as we have outsourced the coding and big development pieces already, we outsource a lot of telecom activities too."*[789]

Based on these considerations, we argue that the services provided by Alpha Center are of rather low inimitability. However, the coordination of the process to take over services from other locations seems to be more difficult to imitate. As we focus on the coordination of service delivery only, we conclude that inimitability is low.

(D) As the last indicator of strategic relevance, we consider the *non-substitutability* of the services provided by Alpha Center. The indicators that we look at include (1) the possibility and (2) the actual practice of substituting services provided by Alpha Center by other services, such as from external vendors. In addition, we also discuss (3) the possibility for a complete substitution of Alpha Center.

1. The *possibility of substituting services* provided by Alpha Center is given through the design of the relationships as internal market. This design allows for competition and the substitution of services. Interviewees from Alpha Center even expressed the view that Alpha Center does not want to be in a monopoly position: *"So you have a semi-monopoly which is always unhealthy. We don't have it."*[790]; *"You don't want to be in a monopoly business really."*[791] The entire setup does not differ greatly from the purchase of services from an external market, for instance, the provider management is similar for both internal and external purchases (*"Und letztlich gibt es auch ein Provider-Management für den internen Supplier. Also, wie ich eben schon sagte, das unterscheidet sich auch nicht im Endeffekt."*[792]; *"Und im Grunde, solche Prozesse hat man normalerweise intern nicht aufge-*

---

[788] Interview 18:14.
[789] Interview 15:51.
[790] Interview 15:23.
[791] Interview 18:32.
[792] Interview 19:49.

setzt, wenn man einen internen Supplier hat."[793]). In addition, the people delivering the services are also easy to substitute and replace (*"da sind die Leute ... im Grunde sag ich mal, bis auf Sprachthemen vielleicht, austauschbar."*[794]). However, interviewees also noted differences to an outsourcing relationship such as the lack of a formal contract (*"Deshalb ist das auch in Richtung Policy und nicht in Richtung Vertragentwicklung, das ist aber eine Guidance, die sich das Unternehmen gegeben hat, bestimmte Dinge gibt es dann halt in dieser Zusammenarbeit nicht, die man intern, die man ein bisschen anders macht, als mit einem externen Supplier."*[795]). An interviewee from Alpha Center also gave better quality as one reason for the preference of Alpha Center over external suppliers: *"I think if you want to have people that care about the process, care about the quality and things, you build it like we've done, you have people that learn the business and that. If you go for the absolute lowest price, you can put it any place."*[796]

2. The current practice of substituting services from Alpha Center by other services (such as from external vendors) is still somewhat limited because of *"a policy statement from [Alpha] saying that during 2006 they would purchase all what we call build services from us ... So the policy statement which says in 2006 they have to and in 2007 they have choice. ... I think that's just not reality. The reality is that my customer is already using six external vendors and external suppliers so we're in a competitive market place"*[797] Many units within Alpha already purchase IT services locally: *"they have an IT budget of their own, and they'll spend locally mostly."*[798]

3. There were also statements that left room for *complete substitution of Alpha Center* through an external provider: *"We may be looking into it later, in Germany we have outsourced run [services] to [name of external provider], so that's happened."*[799]; *"[interviewer:] ... couldn't [Alpha] still decide to outsource the infrastructure part? – [interviewee:] Absolutely."*[800]

---

[793] Interview 19:19.
[794] Interview 19:21.
[795] Interview 19:4; confirmed by interview 19:6.
[796] Interview 18:42.
[797] Interview 17:12; confirmed by interviews 18:32 and 20:107.
[798] Interview 17:4. In addition, Alpha Center itself purchases from external providers to substitute services that it could otherwise provide internally as well (Interview 18:30).
[799] Interview 15:51.
[800] Interview 16:31-32; confirmed by interviews 19:21; 19:41 and 20:4.

Thus, services from Alpha Center can be substituted and are in fact already substituted by other services. In addition, there are considerations for a complete substitution of Alpha Center by an external vendor. We therefore argue that the non-substitutability of the services is low. Overall, therefore, with all four indicators showing low values, the strategic relevance of the services that Alpha Center provides is low.

6.1.2.2 ANALYSIS OF NETWORK EMBEDDEDNESS

We discuss the network embeddedness of Alpha Center with regard to (A) the number of relationships, (B) the changes to the relationships, and (C) the closeness of the relationships.

(A) We start with the *number of relationships*. Since Alpha Center delivers services to all international subsidiaries of Alpha (though primarily in Europe[801]) it has relationships to about *"four, five hundred"*[802] other units within Alpha. Eventually, *"probably 70 to 80 per cent of IT will be centralized and the management of it centralized."*[803] Thus, the number of relationships has almost reached its potential maximum and we consider it high.

(B) We now analyze the *frequency of change* to the relationships. These changes occur often as centralization is still ongoing and Alpha Center regularly adds new relationships: *"We'll be addressing country IT organizations for the next couple of years, bringing them in here, bringing parts of it in."*[804] In addition, Alpha has in recent years acquired a series of firms that are integrated into Alpha's network and that also become customers of Alpha Center: *"The only reason it works here is that change pressure is always on. So we just moved, we bought a company called [company name] in the U.K., and we just moved all their computing resources here over the last three weekends. This is a very normal process for us. We move something in here every weekend from all over the place. It's a constant state of change."*[805] We thus conclude that the frequency of change to the relationships is high.

(C) To judge the degree of *closeness* of the relationships we evaluate (1) the adaptation that the network partners have gone through and (2) the investment in time and resources that they have made to the relationship.

---

[801] Interview 20:17.
[802] Interview 16:23.
[803] Interview 18:30.
[804] Interview 18:16.
[805] Interview 16:72; confirmed by interviews 15:33; 19:69 and 20:4.

1. What was initially one IT organization with local service provision in all the locations where Alpha operates has been transformed into a centralized form of IT service delivery with a split between the demand and supply side. This required substantial *adaptation by the network partners* and is still supported by projects that are carried out together by headquarters, supply and demand organizations to develop and introduce standard procedures for interaction (*"Ja, das ist das, was auf der Supply-Seite in großen Programmen aufgelegt ist. Und sagen wir mal die Prozesse an sich, die Einführung, läuft so, dass Prozessverantwortliche in jeder Business-Unit definiert werden müssen, die natürlich diese Leadership übernehmen, wobei natürlich auch jede Business-Unit für sich selbst diese Dinge einführen muss."*[806]). Thus, the adaptation of network partners is on a high level.[807]

2. The *investment of the partners in the relationships* can be seen in the process that has been elaborated to transfer existing services to Alpha Center: *"We have a formal take-on process and that covers all the infrastructure requirements, all of the application descriptions and functions, so we go and document because invariably when we move something here or take on something here, it's badly documented. So go in, document it and then we have a process of moving it in, both from the infrastructure standpoint and the knowledge management standpoint. So we have a knowledge management data base that has all of the documentation and everything else inside it."*[808] Alpha Center also invests financially in a relationship at the beginning. Its general manager explained: *"So sometimes you can say - you know what? I can migrate it for free because I have capabilities to do that for you and I won't charge you for the migration."*[809] The investment does not stop at financial investments, though. Time has also be invested: *"So when you are making this transitional migrations, to maintain good relationship is so critical, so important to invest time with the stakeholders and to help you in the journey."*[810]

With the partners adapting greatly to one another and constantly investing in one another, we conclude that the closeness of the relationships is high. With high values for all three indicators of network embeddedness, we consider the level of network em-

---

[806] Interview 19:4.
[807] This is also confirmed by an internal publication that describes the new IT vision for Alpha. The CEO introduces the new concept and asks all Alpha employees for their support in the transition.
[808] Interview 16:58; confirmed by interviews 16:66 and 16:68.
[809] Interview 15:29.
[810] Interview 15:25.

beddedness to be high overall. Combined with the low value for strategic relevance, we therefore regard Alpha Center as a service factory.

6.1.3 COORDINATION MECHANISMS

6.1.3.1 OVERVIEW OF COORDINATION

We have equated the coordination of the service offshoring subsidiary with the coordination of the delivery of the service itself. While this is appropriate for many smaller service offshoring centers, we needed to slightly adapt our approach for the analysis of Alpha Center. As shown above, Alpha Center is a part of an internal IT service provider with several locations. As such, it is not directly governed by headquarters but rather acts as a semi-independent firm that belongs to Alpha. In this case, coordination takes place on several levels. On the one hand, there is the coordination of the delivery of services and on the other hand, the coordination of AlphaIT as a large subunit within Alpha with over 3,000 employees. We focus here – as for all the other cases – on the coordination of service delivery. We do so to have a better basis for comparison with other cases where the coordination of the service offshoring subsidiary and the coordination of the service delivery from the service offshoring subsidiary can be considered the same.

The coordination of service delivery in Alpha takes place between a person responsible for a service on the provider side and one person on the receiver side. Both are responsible for a specific service that can have very high volumes. For instance, a group of only three people is responsible for services worth 10 million Euro.[811] Overall, the rate of employees responsible for coordination compared to those that deliver service is five per cent.[812] This is a rather low value.[813] However, the regular evaluation of outputs necessitates a certain level of coordination (*"[M]an muss auch verarbeiten können, das man da nicht Datenfriedhöfe schafft. Also in Deutschland haben wir sehr viele Prozesse in place, da sind welche die sind nützlich, gewichtig und schwierig. ... Und das sind auch Folgekosten, die da kommen."*[814]). Thus, coordination requirements appear to be on a medium level.

6.1.3.2 STRUCTURAL COORDINATION MECHANISMS

Autonomy can be considered with regard to several dimensions. We discuss (1) the role of headquarters, (2) the relationship between Alpha Center and other units of the firm,

---

[811] Interview 20:83.
[812] Personal follow-up communication with interviewee from interview 20.
[813] This judgment results from the comparison to other cases. In the other cases, the values range from 5 per cent to 10 per cent (see below).
[814] Interview 19:19; confirmed by interview 20:41.

(3) the coordination of several suppliers, and (4) autonomy in new network constellations.

1. The *role of the headquarters* is to set the guidelines for the relationships between demand and supply (*"Also wir hier vom Corporate IT-Office haben letztlich die Hoheit, sag ich mal, über die Change-Prozesse"*[815]; *"Sie ... dokumentieren am Ende über die Einführung von [project name], das die Beziehung zwischen Demand und Supply regeln soll."*[816]). In addition, headquarters also uses its autonomy in case of conflicts between the service offshoring subsidiary and its customers (*"Wenn man sich nicht einig ist... da brauchen wir natürlich wieder einen Eingriff von oben"*[817]; *"Der Vorteil an der ganzen Sache ist, dass ja das ganze Thema im Konzern spielen, Demand-Supply, und dass die steuernden Kräfte im Konzern - also die Governance-Schiene, die wir haben, durch den Vorstand, den Herrn Dr. [person's name] und den Herrn [person's name]."*[818]). In cases of conflict, the partners can use escalation mechanisms through the "IT-board" committee that was set up to govern the relationships and that is chaired by the demand side (*"Es gibt das IT-Outsourcing-Board. Es gibt ein IT-Board intern. Also in dem Fall jetzt bei uns gibt es eine IT-Board, das ist das oberste Gremium. ... Da sind halt jeweils die Business-Units vertreten und auch Supply. Und in der Regel liegt der Chair derzeit auf der Business-IT-Seite, auf der Demand-Seite, ja. Weil die neue IT schon sehr stark eine Demand-IT ist, ja. Wir machen das, um das Business zu stärken."*)[819]

2. In the *relationship between the service offshoring subsidiary and other international units* of Alpha, the split between demand and supply has an effect on Alpha Center's autonomy. The former hierarchical model was given up in favor of a pricing-based model. The new model would in principle reduce the decision making power that the customer has with regard to direct intervention in the service delivery process and would give Alpha Center more autonomy. Price would in that case be an additional coordination mechanism. However, Alpha currently does not have a complete price model for the services that are delivered from Alpha Center but rather the entire IT costs are allocated to the business units according to a negotiated distribution that does not directly depend on

---

[815] Interview 19:6.
[816] Interview 19:4.
[817] Interview 20:17.
[818] Interview 20:10.
[819] Interview 19:111; confirmed by interview 19:4.

individual consumption. Thus, price negotiations are currently not possible and cannot be applied to the relationship (*"Bei IT-Services kann ich nicht gut über Preise verhandeln, weil wir sind noch nicht in dem Modus. Da arbeiten wir ja noch dran sozusagen dahinzukommen, dass wir wirklich preisbasiert, marktorientiert zusammenarbeiten, das haben wir noch nicht. Wir haben halt so einen großen Kostenblock, der halt dahingestellt wurde erst mal, so. Und der wird sagen wir mal mehr oder weniger sinnvoll, verursachergerecht, konzernfair irgendwie aufgeteilt. Und kriege ich einfach mein Päckchen übergebraten. Da habe ich auch keinen Verhandlungsspielraum."*[820]). Thus, the model implies less centralization of decision making as compared to a traditional model with a clear hierarchy. However, it has not yet reached a stage where it can be considered a market model. In any case, it seems to result in an increase in autonomy for Alpha Center.

3. When the receiver of services splits the demand between *different suppliers*, the coordination between these suppliers can in principle be left to them or taken on by the receiver of the service. In Alpha, the customers of Alpha Center decided to keep rather than to relinquish that responsibility (*"Hab's gleich so gemacht, wie ich jetzt anfangs erläutert hab, um die Kontrolle einfach auch zu behalten."*[821]). Strictly speaking, this is not exactly centralization of decision making since different hierarchical layers are not necessarily involved but the outcome of this coordination mechanism is similar to that of centralization of decision making, in that it reduces Alpha Center's autonomy.

4. Centralization of decision making seems to play a role in *new network constellations*. It has growing importance for the relationship between the service offshoring subsidiary and other international units of the firm. Recently, several international subsidiaries that demand the same service from Alpha Center have set up the concept of a "lead" customer. This customer bundles the demand of the group of customers and represents the group in discussions with the supplier. Even though there is no explicit hierarchy involved, this bundling of demand leads to more influence for the customers in negotiations with Alpha Center and can also be counted as lowering its autonomy.[822]

---

[820] Interview 20:87.
[821] Interview 20:39.
[822] Interview 20:15.

Based on these considerations, we find that there is still a high degree of centralization of decision making at headquarters and other units of the firm and therefore only little autonomy at Alpha Center. In addition, new elements are being introduced into the relationship which have similar effects to centralization. However, Alpha Center seems to have gained autonomy through the split between supply and demand. We would therefore argue that Alpha Center's autonomy is at a medium level.

6.1.3.3 TECHNOCRATIC COORDINATION MECHANISMS

The degree to which the relationship relies on (A) standardization and (B) formalization will be our next topic.

(A) We discuss *standardization* with regard to (1) the interaction between Alpha Center and its customers, (2) a standardized service catalog, (3) the use of industry standards, (4) the relationship between Alpha Center and the other IT service centers, (5) the relationships to external partners, (6) other processes within Alpha, and (7) the relevance for internal management of Alpha Center.[823]

1. Alpha tries to make the *interaction between Alpha Center and all its customers* the same. For that purpose, it has developed and implemented specific roles and processes that govern the interaction (*"Die Prozesse zwischen Demand und Supply haben wir im Unternehmen ... durch eine Provision-Policy [gesteuert], letztlich wo wir die Relationship dokumentieren."*[824]). They are the same for all units, even though reports might be adapted to the specific requirements of an individual unit (*"Die sind gleich. Weil wir sagen eigentlich müssen Prozesse gleich sein. Wenn was standardsiert ist, dann die Prozesse. Das macht eigentlich wenig Sinn, Prozesse unterschiedlich zu gestalten. Was am Ende etwas unterschiedlich sein kann, sind Reportings, die erstellt werden. Das ist von Business-Unit zu Business-Unit ein bisschen anders, keine Frage. Aber die Prozesse sind gleich."*[825]). Despite these efforts, not all standards that are being implemented are always identical across units which requires some flexibility and adaptations: *"[W]e are using ... a pretty much defined toolset, defined processes and we try to sell them to the customer. But if the customer*

---

[823] In addition to these topics, there are some mentions that point to the benefit of standardization such as increased "visibility" (interview 18:24), complexity reduction (interview 20:55), control over remote locations (interviews 19:19; 20:29), a uniform perspective on situations independent of location (interview 20:29) and the possibility to get to a market-based mode of collaboration (interviews 18:38; 18:44; 20:105).

[824] Interview 19:4.

[825] Interview 19:6; confirmed by interviews 17:6; 19:51; 20:4 and 20:49.

has a different project methodology ... you have to respect that. So you can't enforce what you have always. You try to do that because it reduces your cost and it takes risk out and improves quality but if the customer wants to do it differently, you either take the business or not, if you take the business, we have to respond to the requirements."[826]

2. Alpha has developed a *service catalog* that serves as a basis for all its offerings. Even though the implementation is not complete yet,[827] it comprises several service categories that can be combined and enhanced to meet the specific needs of the individual customer: *"We have a set of standards, so we try to adhere to a set of software standards and a set of hardware standards and infrastructure standards. But that doesn't stop us getting outside of the standards. The difference is the price."*[828] This standardized set of services needs regular updates to reflect ongoing changes in technology: *"The strategy is to standardize services as much as possible. Use standard tools. But, of course, technical environments change and it makes it hard."*[829] Even though a standardization of the service offering is not directly related to the standardization of relationships, it can enable standardization as a coordination mechanism.

3. Alpha relies to a substantial part on *industry standards* for the processes that guide the interaction between supplier and provider of services. For instance, it makes use of the standard framework ITIL[830] (*"Die Prozesse, die wir definiert haben, ..., sind die ganzen ITIL Prozesse."*[831]), and even though that framework had to be adapted, it is still considered helpful to have a common understanding of the processes (*"Also, jeder definiert seine eigenen Standards bei outsourcing, offshor-*

---

[826] Interview 15:27; confirmed by interviews 20:23 and 20:25.
[827] As of April 2006.
[828] Interview 16:21; confirmed by interviews 17:8; 18:40 and 18:42.
[829] Interview 17:22; confirmed by interviews 19:75; 19:79 and 19:103.
[830] ITIL stands for Information Technology Infrastructure Library. It is considered a "set of best practices" (Eckhaus (2005), p. 43) of standardized process descriptions that can serve as guideline for all activities and roles around the setup and running of an IT infrastructure such as a data center. It includes processes such as incident and problem management (for the collection and resolution of problems) and capacity management (for the planning of capacity to support current and future demand). It was initially developed by the British government and is now widely used in corporations (McLaughlin (2005)). For more details on the framework and its application, see also Bigio et al. (2004), Beachboard/Beard (2005), Dubie (2005), Thibodeau (2005).
[831] Interview 19:9; confirmed by interviews 19:33 and 20:47.

ing, bin ich mir sicher. Aber es ist eine sehr gute Basis, wo man sich, und das ist wichtig, in diesen Dingen weltweit versteht."[832]).

4. The standardization of relationships comprises not only Alpha Center and its direct customer relationships but also the *relationships to the other IT service centers*. The standards are the same for all centers which makes interaction easier (*"Wenn Sie nach [location of Asian center] gehen, sollten Sie am Ende die selben Dinge erleben, wie in [location of Eastern European center] auch. Und die Reports sollten auch nicht so viel anders aussehen. Das ist eigentlich auch der Vorteil, wenn man das mal so durchstandardisiert und das ist der Grund, warum wir das letztendlich auch gemacht haben"*[833]). Moreover, it allows the centers to take over tasks from one another: *"The first step is to get the help desk harmonized and how to handle things with the knowledge that's available to the agents. The next layer is who to call and which support groups are certified and the global owner is responsible for making sure that we certify people in each region to provide support and that they are skilled and ready to do it. After all that happens then we can talk about how to transition calls from one to the other."*[834]

5. Alpha has also standardized *relationships across its internal and external units*. With regard to an external vendor, it was mentioned that the relationship is based on the same standard as the internal relationships (*"Aber das ist mit [external vendor] ähnlich, ich meine, es gibt auch mal die eine oder andere unterschiedliche Ausgestaltung in den Business-Units, aber in der großen Linie ist da alles gleich."*[835]).

6. *Standardization of processes* is a topic that has a wider relevance for Alpha. For instance, when integrating different acquired companies, it is necessary for all units to *"harmonize their business processes"*[836]. One interviewee expressed this necessity as follows: *"We do [our business] in dozens of different ways with different systems all across the globe. ... It doesn't make a lot of sense but you can understand how we got there, through acquisitions ... Then all of a sudden you say - I want to change pricing on a service offering that we have. And you can't do it. It takes eight*

---

[832] Interview 19:21; confirmed by interview 19:41.
[833] Interview 19:21.
[834] Interview 18:104.
[835] Interview 19:79; confirmed by interviews 20:4; 20:10 and 20:129.
[836] Interview 18:26.

> *months to change pricing because you have to touch each system."*[837]; *"Centralization and standardization is the way to go. The countries are getting that message. They are working towards that now. They are starting to harmonize processes, product lines and things like that."*[838]

7. Standardization is also seen as an important mechanism for *internal management* within Alpha Center and to overcome differences in national backgrounds: *"We have 53 nationalities here in the building, it's 53, something like that and most people are Czech, but these guys don't need telling what to do. You provide a framework in which they work. That's it."*[839]

Standardization is thus not only relevant for the coordination of services but also for a wide variety of topics in Alpha Center's relationships and beyond. We therefore consider the degree of standardization of the relationships to be high.

(B) We will now analyze the degree of *formalization* with regard to (1) the use of documentation, (2) the use of electronic tools, and (3) implications of a formalized service offering.

1. There is a general tendency to give relationships a stronger structure and formalize them (*"Und wir versuchen das eben stärker zu strukturieren und durchaus auch zu formalisieren"*[840]). The *use of documentation* is indicated, for instance, by a standard handbook that describes the interaction between the international partners. This document is *"binding"*[841] for the partners and describes a formal interface (*"Aber das ist eine sehr formalisierte Schnittstelle. Das ganze ist dokumentiert in einem sogenannten [name of project]-Handbuch. Das muss dann entsprechend auch wieder angepasst, komplettiert werden."*[842]). Extensive documentation is available both on paper and online in Alpha's intranet (*"Also erstmal die Dokumentation, Online und Papier, wie man will."*[843]). This documentation is developed in a way that it can be used for both internal as well as external suppliers (*"Mit [external vendor]*

---

[837] Interview 18:26.
[838] Interview 18:44.
[839] Interview 16:66.
[840] Interview 20:4.
[841] Interview 19:21.
[842] Interview 19:6; confirmed by interviews 19:33 and 20:49.
[843] Interview 19:39; confirmed by interview 19:21.

haben wir das sogar an den Schnittstellen vertraglich vereinbart, wie das funktioniert, und das ist 100 Prozent passend, convergent."[844]).

2. Several processes of interaction between the partners are formalized in *electronic workflow tools* that follow a pre-specified logic without requiring personal interaction. Currently, two major processes (from the underlying ITIL framework) are supported by electronic tools (*"Tool-unterstützt sind im wesentlichen Config-Management und Order-Management. Das sind die, die durchgängig organisiert werden müssen."*[845]). There are other processes that are partially supported or that are planned to be supported by electronic tools (*"andere Sachen, ... da würde ich mir zum jetzigen Zeitpunkt ... eine Tool-Unterstützung wünschen"*[846]). The implementation of tools helps not only to automize processes but also to create a common understanding of things, such as when a given situation has to be judged as critical (*"Das hilft auch in der Zusammenarbeit, muss man schon sagen. Nicht weil das automatisch geht dann, sondern weil man wirklich auch die gleiche Sichtweise auf die Dinge hat. Grad im Incident-Management, das ist ja nun wirklich daily business und daily operations, ist das entscheidend, dass das, was für den einen ein kritischer Fall ist, dass es auch für den anderen kritisch ist. Und das ist ganz einfach, wenn man das in einem Tool dazwischen spielt, weil dann gibt es ja keine Differenzen, das ist ja dann klar, sortiert."*[847]). However, the implementation of electronic tools is both difficult and expensive (*"und insbesondere wo Tools drin stecken, das ist wahnsinnig kompliziert und man muss sich natürlich auch auf bestimmte Reporting-Strukturen einigen. Man kann alles bekommen, aber dann kostet es auch Geld."*[848]). Therefore, the decision to implement such tools for more processes is stretched over a period of time and will only happen after an analysis of where they are actually meaningful (*"Und die Entscheidung über Tools und so weiter werden wir später treffen. Weil das eine kostenintensive Entscheidung ist ... Und da werden wir noch mal einen Review machen, Ende des Jahres und sehen, wo brauchen wir Tool-Unterstützung, und wo hat's halt keinen Sinn."*[849]).

---

[844] Interview 20:49.
[845] Interview 19:4.
[846] Interview 20:57.
[847] Interview 20:29.
[848] Interview 19:19.
[849] Interview 19:11; confirmed by interview 20:57.

3. The services that are provided by Alpha Center are *formalized in a service catalog*.[850] *"[T]he basic service catalog we have is 2000 to 3000 pages"*[851] and describes in detail the different offerings. As with standardization, this does not have a direct bearing on the coordination mechanisms of service delivery, but it can be considered a factor in formalizing those relationships.

Based on these indications, we argue that the degree of formalization is high.

6.1.3.4 OUTPUT-BASED COORDINATION MECHANISMS

The next coordination mechanism is *output control* for which we will discuss (1) the importance of output control for offshoring, (2) the measurement and reporting of output, (3) the consequences of output control, and (4) the current use of output control.

1. Interviewees considered *output control an important mechanism* for the coordination of remote operations: *"[Y]ou also need to have people who understand the difference between output driven management and input driven management. Most senior managers drive by giving input. Do this, do that. ... You can't do that when somebody's five thousand miles from here. So what you can do is output management. You have to describe to them the output and actually rely on them to derive the inputs and process them to get outputs."*[852] One interviewee explained that output control is the preferred mechanism for coordination: *"The last thing you want is a guy come to you and says 'I want a HP UX Server, it's a 4340, it needs to be in a blue box and it's got to do this.' What you want a guy to do is come along and say 'I've got a business problem and my business problem is this, I have this idea of how to solve it and you tell me how to do that.' That's what my job is."*[853] It is considered possible to accurately describe the expected outcome at the start: *"It always is. The really difficult thing is to get people to sit down and think about that. ... So getting somebody to sit down and intellectualize what the world will be like is far harder than what the world is now."*[854]

2. *Evaluations of output* are regularly used to coordinate service delivery. Alpha has defined a system of reports that works on several levels and allows a de-

---

[850] For an overview of the service catalog, see section 6.1.1.
[851] Interview 17:52.
[852] Interview 16:7; confirmed by interview 16:19.
[853] Interview 16:13.
[854] Interview 16:15.

tailed analysis of key performance indicators (KPIs): *"There are some measures such as service quality, turn-around time is important, ... [# interviewee points at the report overview] Here are the different reporting areas, stacks of reports, incidents, summary of the last 13 weeks, you can open incident analysis, we do a lot of reporting, problem management, top ten problems."*[855] KPIs are *"typical of the [Alpha] culture. Particularly now that we have this amalgamated [Alpha]. Very focused on hard measures."*[856] There are not only pre-defined reports but users can also define new reports: *"Most of it being in our data base and you can cube and look at reporting."*[857] The most important KPIs are arranged in templates that allow for a structured overview of the current status (*"Das ist dann auch in viele Templates verpackt, wo man im wesentlichen die Kerninformation zusammenhält, die da notwendig ist, um letztlich das in eine Struktur zu bringen."*[858]). These reports as well as the overall interaction are regularly evaluated by the responsible people on both sides (*"Man muss die Pärchen definieren, die miteinander reden, die ganz konkret bezogen auf Applikationen dann Reportings auswerten zu SLAs usw."*[859]) and are even discussed on board level.[860] To evaluate relationships with its customers, Alpha has introduced a vendor score card that is regularly reviewed. This score card measures the following four dimensions:[861]

- Agreement: Existence of written agreements for all services delivered by Alpha Center to the respective customer,

- Monitor: Monitoring and reporting on key applications against the goals established in the agreements,

- Perception: Customers in all countries complete a monthly "Perception Survey", rating service delivered and detailing any issues that occur,

- Reviews: Regular monthly reviews to discuss issues raised in perception reporting and any failures highlighted in monitoring.

---

[855] Interview 17:93; confirmed by interview 19:39.
[856] Interview 17:91; confirmed by interview 19:13.
[857] Interview 17:95.
[858] Interview 19:15.
[859] Interview 19:4; confirmed by interviews 17:28; 17:30; 17:89; and 19:15.
[860] Interview 19:21.
[861] Information taken from an Alpha-internal document.

3. The results from output control have several *consequences for decisions* within Alpha: *"Our annual appraisals are based predominantly by hard drivers, but we all try to add an influence on this softer side. I will always try to make sure the team appraisals are based on those measures that really acknowledge the softer side"*[862]; *"Management bonuses are based on these things."*[863] Also, the charging model is currently changing from an input-based to an output-based model: *"We are charging them on a man-day rate, and that's probably an interim step that we're working on, going to transaction based costing models."*[864] In addition, many management decisions are based on cost, performance and quality indicators (*"Und die Business-IT managed alles in Richtung Kosten, Performance usw. und alles, was dazu gehört, ja, Quality."*[865]).

4. Alpha is *introducing increasingly more measures* to implement output control. However, in some areas, this process is not completed and output control cannot be used because relevant KPIs have not been defined or are not measured (*"Das ist dieses Thema fehlender Service-Level-Management. Also, es fehlen uns ja noch die Basisdaten, die Hard-Facts, auf die man aufsetzt, bevor man dann wirklich drauf geht: 'Was ist jetzt eigentlich Erfolg für uns?' Ein Stück Hard-Facts natürlich, ein Stück auch andere Dinge dann letztlich. So weit sind wir noch nicht, muss man zugeben."*[866]).

Despite the last point, the importance of which will most likely decline over time, we argue that the other points indicate a high level of output control.

6.1.3.5 PERSONAL COORDINATION MECHANISMS

As the last coordination mechanism, we evaluate *personal coordination mechanisms*. We start with (A) direct personal coordination, and then discuss (B) visits and (C) transfers before analyzing (D) cultural coordination.

(A) We discuss *direct personal coordination* with regard to (1) the structure and intensity of the coordination and (2) the medium of the interaction.

---

[862] Interview 17:91.
[863] Interview 18:94.
[864] Interview 18:4; confirmed by interview 18:36.
[865] Interview 19:55.
[866] Interview 20:115.

1. We first consider the *structure and intensity* of the coordination. In Alpha, direct personal coordination takes place in a pairwise relationship between the receiver and the provider of a service. The interface is typically defined by one person who is responsible for the evaluation of reports and discussion of recent results and developments and a person from the supplier side (*"Und dann hat man Service-Owner auf der Demand-Seite und Service-Manager auf der Supply-Seite. Und umgekehrt, je nachdem, wie man die Begriffe definiert. Man muss die Pärchen definieren, die miteinander reden, die ganz konkret bezogen auf Applikationen dann Reportings auswerten zu SLAs usw."*[867]). These relationships between two persons are the most frequent. From time to time, however, there are also interactions between larger groups when it is important to coordinate between more than one unit (*"Es ist so, dass es oft nur wenig Leute sind. ... Dann sind das zwei Leute aus [Alpha Center location] und einer aus Deutschland ... Das ist sicherlich ein häufiger Fall. Aber dadurch, dass es auf beiden Seiten einen hohen Verteilungsgrad von Aufgaben gibt auf Organisationseinheiten und damit auf Menschen, ist es oft auch so, wo es auch mal durchaus auch eine Telefonkonferenz mit 20 Leuten gibt. Weil da jeder was dazu zu sagen hat. ... Also, es gibt eine hohe Bandbreite von Teilnehmerzahlen an solchen Meetings und dann eben auch an Videokonferenzen je nachdem."*[868]). Direct personal coordination is also needed in case of conflicts when members of the management team *"serve as an escalation point ..., so we are actively managing the relationship in different ways. But yeah, an escalation point, really when it comes to when there is a friction or when there needs to be something smoothed, something like this or a tough decision needs to be made."*[869] Besides the routine interaction, there are also projects that require personal interaction to coordinate different units (*"Also, wie man es macht, ist, indem man einfach Projekte aufsetzt, die cross-divisional besetzt sind. Ganz klar, indem man auch versucht, Spezialisten dort rein zu bringen, und indem man halt 'ne Menge Überzeugungsarbeit leistet, damit es denn so ist, ja. Weil die Stände unterschiedlich sind, die die Leute mit rein bringen."*[870]).

2. Telephone conferences seem to be the preferred *medium for interaction* (*"Ja, TelKos sind das beliebteste Instrument. Das muss man schon feststellen, es gibt Leute hier, die sind von morgens bis abends nur in TelKos, von einer TelKo in die andere so-*

---

[867] Interview 19:4; confirmed by interview 20:29.
[868] Interview 20:77.
[869] Interview 17:48.
[870] Interview 19:79.

zusagen."[871]). Telephone conferences are preferred over video conferences or other remote forms of communication despite the fact that there are *"a lot of tools at our disposal to meet distance, ... so every meeting room in this building has a video conferencing unit"*[872]. One interviewee indicated that it might be a part of Alpha's culture to have telephone conferences instead of video conferences (*"Video wird kaum benutzt. Zu meinem persönlichen Bedauern, weil ich das gerne mache eigentlich. Wenn man sich schon nicht persönlich treffen kann, dann sollte man sich irgendwie sehen und technisch ist das ja auch gar kein Problem. Eigentlich ist es egal. ... Da hat jeder ein Kärtchen, wo man spontan eine TelKo anmelden kann in so einem System. Das Kärtchen habe ich auch gekriegt. Kriegt ja jeder bei der [Alpha]. Das ist glaube ich ein Stück Kultur. Und das passiert auch ständig. Dass man ständig irgendwelche TelKos kriegt, wo man hinsoll. Aber keine Videokonferenz. Aber es funktioniert, sagen wir mal so. Ich will mich nicht beschweren. Ich wundere mich nur so ein bisschen. Aber es geht auch."*[873]).

Based on these arguments, we conclude that direct personal coordination is still an important coordination mechanism for Alpha, though, mostly in the event of changes to the existing relationship and less for the coordination of everyday cooperation. We thus conclude that the level of direct personal coordination is medium.

(B) *Visits* are used by Alpha as well and we will discuss (1) the reasons and the different types of visits as well as (2) the frequency of visits.

1. There are several *reasons for and types of visits*: Customers visit Alpha Center because they want to get a personal impression of the place where they have moved their services *"The other thing is people like coming here to see what we've done. ... Plus this is a very much state of the art technology center. It's pretty impressive to look around it. It's a good thing to let them go back and they can sell their bosses on the benefits of consolidation."*[874] A reason for outbound travel from Alpha Center is that it is an important aspect of an attractive job with an MNC: *"... travel is another attraction for retaining employees here as well, the salaries in [country in Eastern Europe] don't allow locals to travel very easily, so when we send them away*

---

[871] Interview 20:67; confirmed by interview 17:46.
[872] Interview 17:34.
[873] Interview 20:69; confirmed by interview 20:71.
[874] Interview 16:54.

on a business trip, it's a big deal to them."[875] However, inbound travel also happens for similar reasons: "... number of reasons for that. One is [Alpha Center location] is a nice place to come to."[876] Another reason for visits are international workshops that are held to disseminate knowledge and introduce changes or new elements to the daily coordination ("Also global auch, wir haben jetzt Workshops, Handover-Workshops in die Business-Units, was ganz wichtig ist."[877]). Internal conferences are organized for "the rapport building relationship that you need to have"[878]. Besides, visits are seen as the most intense form of interaction and are considered necessary to keep or establish good working relationships ("Wenn man ein gemeinsames Meeting machen will, und sollte man hin und wieder durchaus schon mal tun, abseits von E-Mail, Telefon und Videokonferenz muss ich einfach mal gegenüber sitzen können."[879]).

2. The visits occur with differing *frequency*. A representative from Alpha Center reported: "we travel occasionally when it's necessary"[880]; "Sometimes the client groups come here. This year I've been lucky. I've only had to travel once or twice, whereas they have arranged half a dozen conferences here. I've been lucky."[881] Visits typically last about one day ("nach [Alpha Center location] kommt man ja relativ leicht, da kann man sogar eine Eintagesreise machen, abends ist man dann wieder da"[882]). One interviewee from a customer reported that about one person from his department vists Alpha Center each week to increase visibility in the big supplier organization and to enhance mutual understanding and communication ("Sagen wir mal jede Woche ist einer aus meinem Team in [Alpha Center location]. Das ist so, ich habe aber auch so ein großes Team. ... das ist auch wichtig, damit die auch wissen, dass wir ja für sie wichtig sind, dass es wichtig ist, für uns Services zu erbringen. Man muss auch präsent sein. Sonst geht das unter in so einem großen Laden, das ist dann sicherlich auch so. Und es sorgt einfach auch für die menschliche Komponente. Dass die Leute sich auch dann gut verstehen, wenn man über Tools miteinander kommunizieren muss, weil man weiß, am anderen Ende sitzt der Kollege so

---

[875] Interview 18:80.
[876] Interview 16:52.
[877] Interview 19:39; confirmed by interview 20:37.
[878] Interview 17:36.
[879] Interview 20:17.
[880] Interview 17:34.
[881] Interview 17:42 (refers to the period January to April 2006).
[882] Interview 20:19.

> *und so, mit dem ich letzte Woche in [Alpha Center location] noch ein Bier getrunken habe."*[883]).

Thus, visits occur relatively frequently, even though they mostly seem to involve individuals rather than entire groups. However, several of the reasons for visits are not directly related to the delivery of services but can be attributed more to the ongoing change of the organizational structure within Alpha. Thus, we conclude that the level of visits is medium.

(C) Alpha does not use *transfers* as a coordination mechanism between Alpha Center and other units of the firm. However, eight to nine per cent of the employees in Alpha Center are expatriates who were hired from other units of Alpha or externally because their skills were needed for building the service offshoring subsidiary: *"There are some skills that we need to get from the outside, they aren't fully developed here in this market space."*[884] One interviewee also stated that transfers might not be helpful for coordination since the demand and supply organization had been deliberately split recently and should not intermix so soon again (*"Ehemals alle aus einer Truppe, Global IS letztlich, da gab es eine Teilung, die einen sind jetzt Supply und die anderen Demand, jetzt auszutauschen wäre meiner Meinung unglücklich, weil beide müssen sich erst mal in ihre Rolle bewegen, und dann kann man irgendwann mal wieder anfangen irgendwas auszutauschen."*[885]).

(D) Finally, we evaluate the role of *cultural coordination*. We look at (1) shared goals, (2) the impact of different national cultures, (3) the impact of organizational structure, and (4) the establishment of a common corporate culture.

1. Currently, the degree of *shared goals* across international units of Alpha seems rather low since one section of employees within Alpha might lose their jobs if Alpha Center is successful: *"the local IT people who, if we're successful, they will lose their jobs, so that's the dilemma."*[886] There are efforts to align the different goals. One approach is to direct the organization away from internal fights and towards a common goal by appealing to competitive threat: *"My thing is, I keep this on my desk because this is about [competitor] [# interviewee shows press article about competitor]. When you go in the hallways, you hear people talk about this or-*

---

[883] Interview 20:33.
[884] Interview 18:12; confirmed by interview 18:80.
[885] Interview 20:113.
[886] Interview 18:36.

ganization and [Alpha] is bad. These guys, we beat them, we are competing with ourselves, so I think this is who our competition is."[887] One interviewee compared working internally to working with an external supplier and explained that appealing to commonalities is used to bring a project to a successful end ("*Das ist eben nicht das knallharte Dienstleister-Verhältnis, was man da anstrebt oder hat, sondern es sind ja alle in der [Alpha] letztlich, und haben auch alle, zumindest ganz groß am Horizont, ein gleiches Ziel. Das ist sicherlich auch eine Hilfe, letztlich kann man sich sicherlich darauf zurückziehen in der Diskussion. Wenn es ein bisschen härter rangeht, dann versuchen wir zu überlegen, was sind denn die gemeinsamen Ziele, die wir eigentlich haben. Wenn man die voranstellt, dann kommt man schon ein gutes Stück voran.*"[888]). However, this opinion was not unanimously shared. Another interviewee contradicted: "*[T]he internal customers are the worst ones. Because normal customers who want to do business with you they are much better, they are much more polite, much better relationship. Internal customers, many times, are just the most difficult ones. Most difficult ones. In many cases they are forced to use you.*"[889]

2. Cultural coordination is impacted by *different national cultures*. Alpha Center deals with customers from many different backgrounds and tries to adapt to possible differences: "*We also have decision making matrices, so I am able to take all my clients and the key clients and the roles they play and define what kind of culture they come from, whether they come from an Egalitarian context like I would, Anglo-Saxon, or whether they come from an Egalitarian machine, very Germanic, or Czech, or whether they come from a hierarchical structure*"[890]). The differences between "*53 nationalities*"[891], which one of the interviewees called "a motley crow" ("*zusammengewürfelter Haufen*"[892]), and the fact that the leadership style in Alpha Center is oriented towards an "American" management style lead to various kinds of friction ("*Weil der Aufbau dieses Rechenzentrums ist ja unter amerikanischer Leitung erfolgt. ..., wie die Vorstellung aus den USA eben war. Jetzt haben wir, ..., ein U.S.-amerikanisch geprägtes Rechenzentrum mit einer bunten Mischung von Menschen*

---

[887] Interview 18:56; confirmed by interview 18:58.
[888] Interview 20:10; confirmed by interviews 19:43; 20:39; 20:87 and 20:93.
[889] Interview 15:23.
[890] Interview 17:76; confirmed by interview 17:80.
[891] Interview 16:66.
[892] Interview 20:4.

aus verschiedenen Ländern mitten in Europa. Und das führt jetzt zu verschiedenen Friktionen."[893]).

3. Changes in *organizational structure* have also impacted cultural coordination. Acquisitions led to different value systems within Alpha. Being asked if there is common team spirit across the units, one interviewee stated: *"Oh, not a bit. It's we and they. There is a lot of competition going on, but that's more a function of, well, any time you have an acquisition, you have that. It's built in because we still have people saying I am from [acquired firm 1], right, with [Alpha] or [acquired firm 2] now, so every company out there they have that culture. The [acquired firm 1] people felt that they had some very good things and some things are broken now and eventually they recognize that some things are better as well, but those are cultural differences."*[894]. In addition, the organizational split between supply and demand meant a substantial change in the way that coordination takes place (*"Und dann wurde sozusagen umgeschwenkt auf das Demand-Supply-Modell. Und das war sowohl für die Demand schwierig, die jetzt plötzlich sagt, wir sind jetzt Demand, wir sollen nichts mehr selber machen, sondern sollen die Anforderungen beim Kunden, also den eigentlichen Business identifizieren, da auch mithelfen, die auch zu strukturieren, geeignete Supplier finden und sicherstellen, dass die Anforderungen auch erfüllt werden."*[895]; *"Ach, das ist aus der ehemaligen gemeinsamen Organisation heraus, das ist einfach so. Die, die heute Demand sind, waren gestern noch Supply, nur hieß das damals noch nicht Supply, sondern Global IS. Es gibt halt viele persönliche Beziehungen, zum Teil sind sie durchaus auch mit Problemen behaftet."*[896]). On the other side, personal relationships from the "old" organization also help people to work together more easily (*"Auch dadurch, dass die Leute sich schon kannten vorher. Das ist natürlich bei jedem Projekt so, wenn die Leute sich kennen, dann geht es besser oder schneller."*[897]).

4. Within Alpha, the need to *establish a shared culture* across its diverse units was recognized (*"Das muss man etablieren, das ist halt auch ein Prozess. Das Mindset dazu muss man ändern. Eine Kultur muss es auch geben. Also ich meine, wir sind sehr unterschiedlich, je nachdem, ob wir in Asien, Amerika oder in Europa sind. Am

---

[893] Interview 20:6; confirmed by interview 20:8.
[894] Interview 18:52.
[895] Interview 20:10; confirmed by interview 19:85.
[896] Interview 20:103.
[897] Interview 20:39; confirmed by interview 20:131.

Ende muss es aber trotzdem dazu führen, dass man sehr stark harmonisiert. Sonst funktioniert das nicht."[898]). Alpha has recently introduced a set of values that are to be shared by all its units. They seem to be having an effect but only slowly: *"Yeah, and people are starting to feel more a part of [Alpha] and feel that culture as well. But those things do take time."*[899] One interviewee, however, was skeptical that the values would really impact behavior (*"Nicht, dass sie überall hängen, sondern, dass sie auch gelebt werden. Und das ist individuell sehr unterschiedlich, sagen wir mal so."*[900]) and added that they would anyway not affect the coordination between Alpha Center and the customers (*"In der Zusammenarbeit mit IT-Services spielt das überhaupt keine Rolle, ehrlich gesagt. Da geht es wirklich mehr drum, professionellen IT-Service zu machen. Teile dieser Welt sind die Qualität, also finden sich da im Praktischen wieder, das ist klar. Aber mit und ohne diese Werte würde man die Qualität schon im Fokus sehen, das ist schon klar. Also es gibt kaum Berührungspunkte zu dem Thema."*[901]). Other initiatives address *"cultural awareness, business language skills"*[902] to avoid situations as described by one interviewee: *"It's things like when we have system outages we send bulletins out via text message to the subscribers. It's a simple thing that having a conversation face to face, you would have no problem at all with that communication. A guy, for an example, we're experiencing problems on a system with this thing we expect it to be an hour. They will say 'system all screwed up', and it goes out to the business. Or 'data base screwed up'. In a casual conversation that would be perfectly fine, right? That's what they would say in the hallways."*[903] Trainings with participants from different units that are sometimes seen a mechanism to increase cultural coordination, are currently not used by Alpha. One interviewee considered them a possibility, however, with limited applicability since the roles of demand and supply are very different (*"Aber das ist durchaus möglich. Kann ich mir schon vorstellen."*[904]; *"Wenn man jetzt hingeht und sagt, gemeinsame Trainings, dann muss man sich die Themen dafür natürlich gut überlegen, weil die Rollen ja sehr verschieden sind."*[905]).

---

[898] Interview 19:87; confirmed by interview 19:73.
[899] Interview 18:54; confirmed by interview 19:91.
[900] Interview 20:97.
[901] Interview 20:97.
[902] Interview 18:48.
[903] Interview 18:46.
[904] Interview 20:101.
[905] Interview 20:99.

There is no homogeneous picture with regard to cultural coordination. On the one hand, it is recognized as an area that needs closer attention. On the other hand, there are only sporadic signs of cultural coordination that seem to result mainly from older personal ties between members of the different organizational units. Since the efforts to increase cultural coordination do not appear to be effective so far, we consider the level of cultural coordination to be medium.

6.1.3.6 COMPARATIVE ANALYSIS OF COORDINATION MECHANISMS

We have now evaluated the coordination mechanisms individually. It seems that technocratic mechanisms of coordination (standardization and formalization) play the most important role within Alpha together with output control. Autonomy is also of considerable importance. Personal approaches to coordination are not very important within Alpha.

Several statements from the interviewees also addressed the relative importance of technocratic and personal coordination mechanisms. One person explained that the ideal situation for a process is when personal interaction is no longer needed since it disturbs the efficient execution of a standardized and automized process. However, whenever automation does not work, personal interaction is needed (*"Das Ziel ist es natürlich, ... dass wir über das Tool arbeiten und zwar möglichst ausschließlich. Weil das sorgt ja dafür, dass man gewisse Freiheitsgrade dann am anderen Ende hat. Es ist mir egal, wer das Ticket bearbeitet sozusagen, es ist technisch sichergestellt, workflow-artig, dass es bearbeitet wird, und dass ich eine Rückmeldung kriege und so weiter. Wenn ich anfange, jemanden anzurufen auf der anderen Seite, zerstöre ich letztendlich diesen Freiheitsgrad, indem ich dann einfach jemand binde, der vielleicht gar nichts damit zu tun hat."*[906]; *"Immer dann, wenn das gut läuft mit dem toolbasierten Prozess, dann gibt es praktisch keine direkte Interaktion. Wenn das nicht gut läuft ... dann greift natürlich nach kurzer Zeit wieder der menschliche Prozess und dann wird doch einer angerufen, im Zweifelsfall. Wir sind natürlich bestrebt, wo man dann am Prozess oder am Tool vorbeiarbeiten muss, zu minimieren, weil das ja Aufwand auf beiden Seiten erzeugt letztlich. ... Ziel an dieser Stelle ist, sagen wir mal zu 100 Prozent automatisch zu haben."*[907]). Asked about the relative positioning of personal mechanisms of coordination

---

[906] Interview 20:61.
[907] Interview 20:63.

and output control one interviewee answered: *"You shouldn't need it, personal interaction. If you can describe to an individual what it is you want ..."*[908]

6.1.4 DISCUSSION OF CASE

Evaluation of appropriateness of propositions for individual case

We compare the results of the case to the original propositions in Table 6-2. We display the original proposition, the empirical result and indicate whether or not we find agreement with the proposition. The original proposition stems from the description of our typology, the empirical result from the discussion of the case. We represent the values low (L), medium (M), or high (H) by squares of different sizes.

Table 6-2: Evaluation of suitability of propositions for service factory

Coordination mechanism	Original proposition	Empirical result	Agreement with proposition	Remark
Extent of coordination requirements	▪-■ (L-M)	■ (M); only few people involved in the coordination of service delivery	Proposition initially supported	--
Degree of autonomy	▪ (L); low strategic relevance does not need high degree of autonomy	■ (M); organizational split in demand and supply sides gives Alpha Center more autonomy	Proposition not supported	E1: Autonomy can be influenced by organizational structure

---

[908] Interview 16:50.

Coordination mechanism	Original proposition	Empirical result	Agreement with proposition	Remark
Degree of standardization	■ (H); as many customers need to be served, aiming for economies of scale	■ (H); high degree of standardization across customers and over time	Proposition initially supported	--
Degree of formalization	■ (H); many standardized cases make formalization appropriate	■ (H); high degree of formalization (documentation and use of electronic tools)	Proposition initially supported	--
Degree of output control	■ (H); many network partners require pre-specification of results	■ (H); it is intended to describe all results exactly upfront	Proposition initially supported	I1: Output control is interdependent with direct personal coordination
Degree of personal direct coordination	■ (L); execution of standardized, less complex services needs little direct interaction	■ (M); direct personal coordination plays a role in supporting other mechanisms	Proposition not supported	E2: Direct personal coordination seems to be necessary in all settings to complement other mechanisms
Number of visits	■ (M); medium number of visits, medium duration per visit	■ (M); medium number of visits, short duration per visit	Proposition initially supported	I2: Duration of visits not only impacted by coordination needs but also by ease of travel

6 – Results   233

Coordination mechanism	Original proposition	Empirical result	Agreement with proposition	Remark
Number of transfers	■ (M); medium number of transfers; potentially mainly management, locals in line positions	■ (L); no transfers	Proposition not supported	E3: Organizations are deliberately split, transfers would have undesired effects; number could increase later
Importance of culture-based coordination	■ (M); medium level of normative integration	■ (M); medium level of normative integration	Proposition initially supported	I3: Cultural coordination might not be desired in all cases
E: Possible explanation for difference; I: Idea, new thought; -- no additional comment				

The table shows that most propositions are supported by the case. However, there are some areas that need further discussion:

- E1: Alpha is currently in transition away from a completely internal model of IT service provision that was governed by hierarchical decision making. The change to a demand-supply split has already led to a structure that is like an internal market. However, an important coordination mechanism on markets – competitively established prices – has not yet been completely implemented. On the other hand, hierarchical measures are no longer fully in place.[909] Therefore, the autonomy of Alpha Center is higher than expected.

- E2: The degree of direct personal coordination is higher than expected. As already indicated in the comparative analysis of coordination mechanisms, it seems that direct personal coordination is often a complement to other coordination mechanisms. Thus, even an organization that relies to a great extent on technocratic and output-based coordination will need personal coordination

---

[909] Interview 20:89.

mechanisms to review outputs, decide on new targets, and the like. Besides that, whenever other coordination mechanisms fail, organizations seem to "fall back" on direct personal coordination.

- E3: Alpha in fact uses no transfers, whereas we had expected some, albeit low, transfer activity. As discussed above, this can be explained by the fact that the recent organizational split between demand and supply has led to the establishment of different roles. Transfers might hinder the process of creating distance between the organizational units.

Presentation of additional information gained from the individual case

We have derived several new ideas from this case:

- I1: It was made explicit by our interviewees that different coordination mechanisms are interdependent. For instance, the results from output control are shared in personal interactions in which all results and improvement potentials are discussed (*"Also, beispielsweise zum Thema Service-Level-Management haben wir monatlich ... ein Service-Review-Management-Board ..., wo wir ganz differenziert durch die ganzen Service-Level, durch Reports, durch Maßnahmen und Verbesserungspotentiale durchgehen"*[910]). This observation underlines the fact that none of the coordination mechanisms is sufficient in itself for coordination but that an interplay of different mechanisms is needed.

- I2: The number of visits is as we expected, however, the duration is shorter. This can probably be explained by the fact that Alpha Center is located in a city with good air and rail links which makes short trips more feasible.

- I3: Cultural coordination is typically seen as positive since it helps to align employees across different organizational units. It can be expressed in shared goals and vision. In the Alpha case, however, we have observed the implementation of a slightly adverse constellation in which the supply side is supposed to be under price pressure from the demand side that has the freedom to purchase services from external providers. Interviewees expressed that the split between the organizational units has led to competing goals that are considered necessary for an

---

[910] Interview 20:65.

efficient delivery of services. Thus, cultural coordination might not always be desired (at least not in the sense of shared goals).

6.2 CASE 2: INTERNAL COMPETENCE CENTER BETA

6.2.1 COMPANY OVERVIEW

Presentation of MNC and the business unit under consideration

Beta is a wholly-owned business unit of the German corporation BetaCorp that operates in the high-technology industry. The corporation employs several 100,000 people worldwide and has annual revenues of more than 70 billion EUR. The holding company has a large variety of subunits with different activities, among them is the information technology provider Beta.[911] Beta itself also qualifies as a multinational corporation with around 15,000 employees in Germany and around 25,000 employees in 40 countries outside Germany. Annual sales exceed 4.5 billion EUR, with more than 50 per cent of revenues from outside the home market. Beta originated as the internal IT service provider for the entire corporation. It was set up as a separate entity in 1995 and now more than 70 per cent of its revenues stems from business with customers outside the corporation. Beta's business can be categorized in the following two segments:

1. *Customized IT solutions*: Beta develops and implements software that helps its customers to run processes more effectively and efficiently. These solutions are provided for supply chain management, enterprise resource planning, customer relationships management, systems integration, business information management, and software application management.

2. *Outsourcing*: Beta offers to take over customers' IT functions, either as a whole or selectively and to develop and service them. In addition to the administration of data centers, Beta also provides help desk and other services such as the installation of new computers at the customer's site. Apart from IT, Beta takes on business processes (for instance, accounting processes) for its customers.[912]

---

[911] Unlike AlphaIT from the first case, Beta also offers its services to external customers.
[912] All the financial data is taken from the corporation's annual report for the fiscal year 2004. In addition, Beta's image brochure and web site were evaluated for this overview.

Beta has decided to set up service offshoring subsidiaries in several countries to be able to offer more competitive prices. However, Beta uses service offshoring not only in the captive offshoring mode[913] but in three different scenarios:

1. Beta has set up its own captive centers that are specifically used to provide services to the parent company. These will be the focus of this analysis.

2. In addition, Beta can rely on the international network of BetaCorp. BetaCorp itself has several other units that also provide IT services. For instance, one business unit within BetaCorp started already in the 1990s to establish a network of software development centers in Eastern Europe. These centers provide services not only for that business unit but also serve as internal IT provider to other units. Thus, Beta can use these services as well.[914]

3. Besides the internal partners, Beta works with external providers from typical offshore locations. For instance, a software development company from Belarus carries out several projects as an external partner.[915]

These three different configurations are shown in Figure 6-3.

Thus, Beta as part of BetaCorp works with different suppliers on the "production" side and delivers its services to both internal and external customers. Only the offshore centers (marked with "1") are actually owned by Beta, the internal providers ("2") are owned by other units in BetaCorp. In addition, Beta also acquires services from external providers ("3") and makes these services part of its own service portfolio to internal and external customers. Besides these focal service delivery relationships, there are additional relationships we want to briefly mention without further evaluating them: Other internal providers ("2") within BetaCorp also provide services to those internal customers that Beta serves. Moreover, the centers that Beta owns have started to offer their services directly to other internal customers, albeit only gradually and to a limited extent. Still, the centers might eventually be in a position to provide services to external customers themselves.

---

[913] See section 2.2.4.1.
[914] Interview 5:11.
[915] Interview 5:11.

6 – Results

BetaCorp diagram showing:
- External customers
- 1. Offshore centers
- Beta
- Internal customers
- 2. Internal providers
- 3. External providers

← Delivery relationship in focus   ←---- Additional delivery relationship

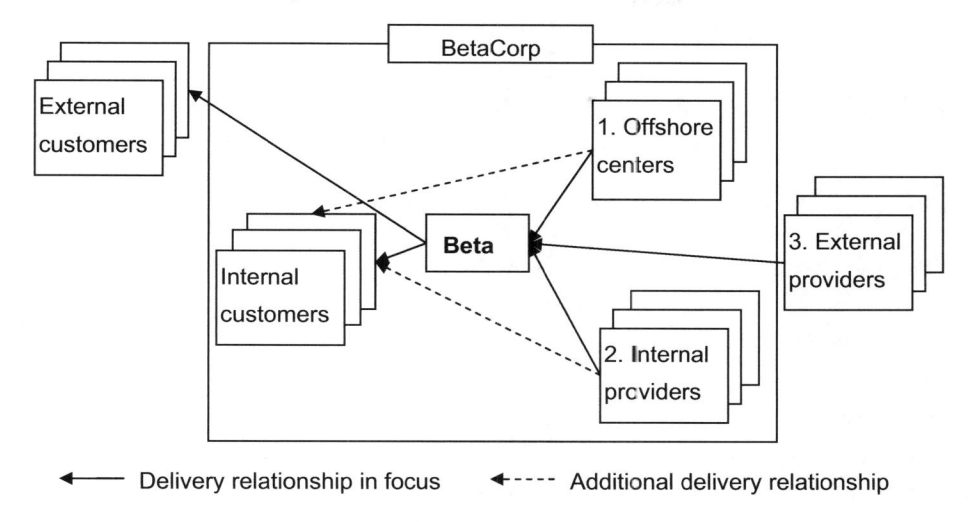

Figure 6-3: Different configurations of IT service delivery within BetaCorp

As a consequence, Beta has a large network of partners of different types that can be involved in the delivery of services. Beta's current international network is represented in Figure 6-4.

Data centers ■   Call centers ▨   Development centers ●

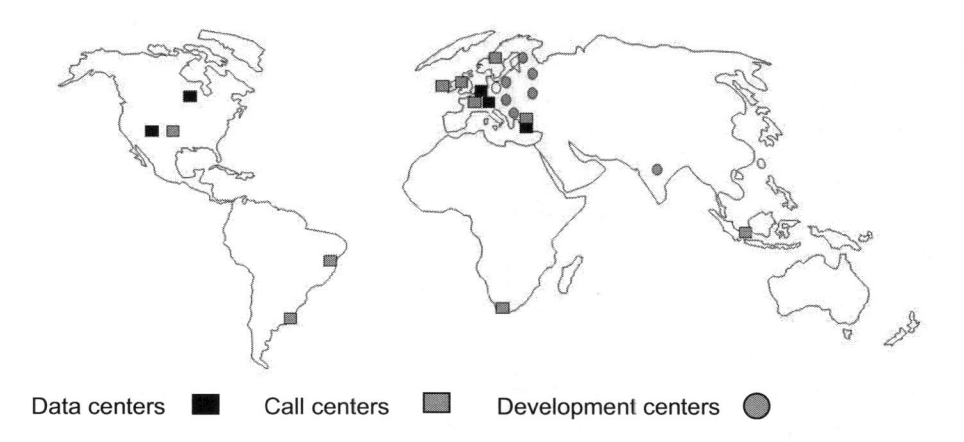

Figure 6-4: Beta's international delivery network (Source: Based on information from Beta's web site)

Beta uses data centers, development centers and call centers to provide different services to a range of customers. Data centers are used to host and run IT applications and to store data. Development centers are home to IT services that range from the development of new applications to the maintenance of existing applications. Call centers are deployed to provide customer support services. On the one hand, Beta provides call services for the products that Beta's parent produces, e.g., help for the customers of technical devices. On the other hand, Beta offers call services also as an independent customer offering. For instance, Beta provides technology companies with call center facilities to offer customer service for the technical devices that these companies sell.

Description of history and motivation of offshoring situation

The focus in the current case is on those IT services that are provided out of a center that Beta opened in 2003 in a mid-size Russian city. Beta recognized that it was losing competitive advantage in the field of IT services because it could not match the cost advantages that several of its competitors had achieved by offshoring parts of their business. Therefore, Beta carried out a location analysis to find suitable locations for its own service portfolio. Locations were judged in three steps: In a first step, the labor market, the infrastructure, the time difference to home location and the social environment were evaluated. In a second step, a more fine-grained analysis was carried out that also considered several country factors, detailed factor costs, and the possibility to develop new businesses for Beta. The eventual decision was taken based on the quantity and quality of German and European language speakers, the labor costs, the potential to standardize services across Beta's parent company, and the possibility for a fast ramp-up.[916]

Parallel to the location analysis, Beta conducted internal "offshoreability" workshops for each of its business units to determine which services could be moved to an offshore location. For business units with an offshore potential of more than 30 per cent of all services a detailed analysis was carried out and a final decision was made with the heads of each business unit. There had been a clear top management commitment to send as many services abroad as possible despite much resistance from the individual business units.

As a result of the location analysis and with the input from the offshoreability analysis, five locations were finally selected: Turkey, Ireland and Canada as locations for call centers, Turkey and Canada for data centers, and India and Russia for development centers. The call centers and data centers are part of the outsourcing business division, whereas the Russian development center belongs to the customized IT solutions division. Unlike other centers, the Indian center was not set up as a captive center of Beta, but Beta rather decided to acquire services from an existing IT center that the Indian

---

[916] Based on information from internal Beta documents.

subsidiary of BetaCorp had already established in India. This center mainly serves English-speaking countries, whereas the center in Russia serves both German and English-speaking countries. Currently, Beta has around 6 per cent of its development resources in offshore centers and is aiming eventually for a total of 20 per cent. Some of Beta's competitors from the Western hemisphere have already achieved an offshore capacity of over 20 per cent of its employees and Beta wants to increase its own share substantially in the future to become more competitive.

The center in Russia – here called Beta Center – opened in 2003 and had 350 employees as of December 2005. There are plans to increase the number of employees to 500-600 by the end of 2006. Unlike outsource service providers, these employees are part of the international network of Beta's parent and have to adhere to the same international standards and procedures. However, the flexibility in Russian labor law allows the center to operate in a "24*7" mode and carry out services in several shifts. Since Beta Center is the first major Western employer in the city, it has the advantage of being very sought after by university graduates. In addition, Beta Center was able to establish an exclusive contract with a local university to include topics in the curricula that are important for it (such as German language courses and specialized software programming classes).

Beta Center operates as a cost center. It offers its customers rates that are as low as 20 per cent of a typical Western rate. By including services from the Russian center in its calculation, Beta is then able to achieve a mixed calculation and offer prices that are more competitive. Beta Center provides services in two main categories. First, it offers IT services that are subdivided into SAP services, software development, and IT help desk services. SAP project support consists of development and enhancement of applications for SAP projects. Software development is the design and coding of software programs. IT help desk services comprise technical advice and consultation on the use of IT devices and programs. Second, Beta Center offers back-office services such as document indexing and slide design.

Beta Center supplies only Beta-internal customers and customers from BetaCorp; it does not have any contact to external customers.[917] Beta Center organizationally belongs to Beta Russia, Beta's Russian subsidiary. However, its customers are acquired initially through a German unit that was set up to promote Beta Center. Actually, it mainly works for Beta in Germany and is also managed by that German unit. The rela-

---

[917] Interview 5:35.

tionships can be thought of as depicted in Figure 6-5. The dashed line between Beta Germany and Beta Center stands for the actual management through Germany.

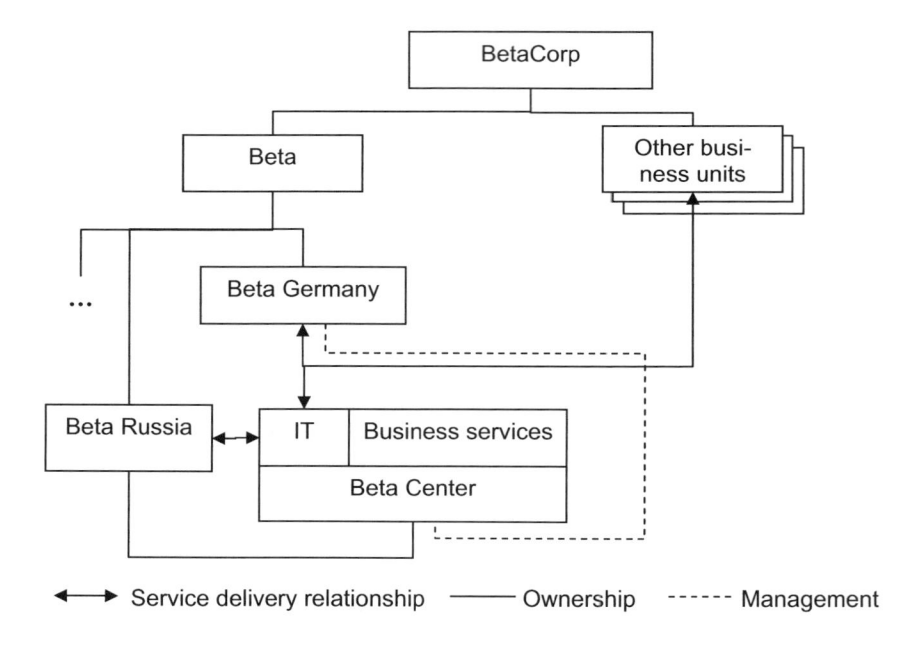

Figure 6-5: Service delivery within Beta's network

IT services are supplied for Beta Germany, but also for other business units within BetaCorp. One of the main customers is located in the USA, many others are in Germany.

Description of services provided by service offshoring subsidiary

Beta Center is organized as shown in Figure 6-6. Every service offering is organized in its own department, each of which is led by one manager. Each manager has several groups that work for the different projects. Each of the departments has about 50 to 80 employees. The center management coordinates all the departments and provides the necessary infrastructure such as office space, hardware, and software.

```
                    ┌─────────────────┐
                    │ Center man-     │
                    │   agement       │
                    └─────────────────┘
              ┌──────────┴──────────┐
        ┌───────────┐         ┌──────────────┐
        │ Human re- │         │  Finance &   │
        │  sources  │         │Administration│
        └───────────┘         └──────────────┘
```

SAP services	Software development	Help desk services	Back-office services
1. SAP Consulting	5. Banking Software	8. Mobile phone support	11. Document indexing
2. ERP development	6. Human Resource SW	9. IT Infrastructure	12. Invoice management
3. Application Management	7. Document Management	10. Software support	13. Invoice checking
4. Enterprise Portal			14. Design Services

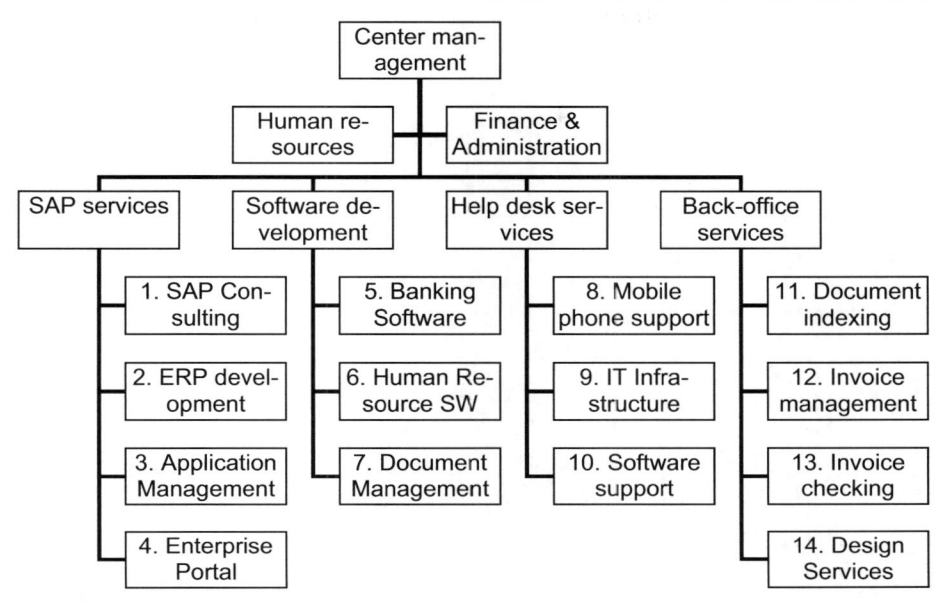

Figure 6-6: Organization chart Beta Center

Each of the departments has its own set of customers that potentially might be overlapping but are currently not. For instance, back-office services are provided to several customers that require design services. In this case, the same service is offered to more then one customer. In other instances, a service is carried out only for one customer. An overview of the service delivery to Beta center's customer is shown in Figure 6-7. To simplify, Beta Germany is not included in the picture, even though it was the unit that initially set up the contact and is still called upon in the event of problems. It is, however, not involved in the everyday service delivery. The upper part of the figure shows the different departments within Beta Center. In the lower part, one box stands for one customer. The numbers in the box refers to the service that the customer purchases from Beta Center (for the numbers see Figure 6-6).

The *SAP services* department serves four partners within the network of BetaCorp. These are all located in Beta Germany and all of them receive different services. The *software development* department provides its offering for three different customers and the *IT help desk* services are also provided for three distinct customers within the network of BetaCorp. The area of business processes – that is not considered further here – provides its offerings to about six customers. It is noteworthy that three of the customers receive the same service, in this case indexing. Thus, the business processes department has entered delivery agreements where one kind of service is delivered to several customers. This is different from the three other departments we are evaluating in more detail.

```
                              Center management
                                      |
        ┌─────────────────┬──────────────────┬─────────────────┐
   SAP services    Software devel-    IT help desk ser-   Back-office ser-
                     opment                vices              vices
```

- 1. Consulting
- 2. ERP
- 3. AMS
- 4. Portal
- 5. Bank
- 6. HRM
- 7. Doc
- 8. Phone
- 9. IT Infrastructure
- 10. SW
- 11. Index
- 12. Invoice
- 13. Check
- 14. Design
- 14. Design
- 14. Design

⟷ Service delivery relationship

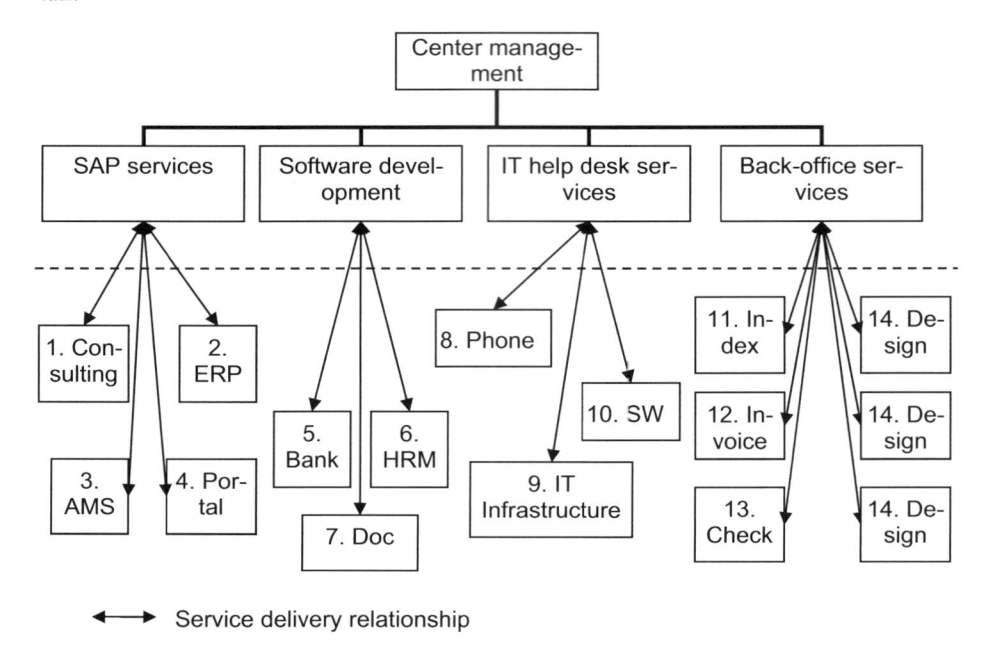

Figure 6-7: Beta Center's service delivery relationships

6.2.2 TYPE OF SERVICE OFFSHORING SUBSIDIARY

6.2.2.1 ANALYSIS OF STRATEGIC RELEVANCE

We first evaluate the strategic relevance of the services that are provided by Beta Center to the rest of the corporation. Since Beta Center is a rather large center, it not only provides one very focused service but rather a portfolio of services that are centered around IT.[918] Thus, the evaluation will need to differentiate according to the services. For that purpose we have separated them in two categories. On the one hand, we evaluate the software development services that are provided by the SAP services and software development departments. On the other hand, we analyze the IT help desk services. To combine the first two departments (and the services they provide) seems justified since their activities are rather similar and so is their strategic relevance. We now appraise (A)

---

[918] The department providing business services will not be considered here since it is not in the area of information technology. This approach is chosen to ensure better comparability with the other cases and justified since there is no interference with the IT departments.

the value, (B) the rareness, (C) the inimitability, and (D) the non-substitutability of the service.

(A) We will assess the *value* of the services with regard to (1) the motivation for setting up Beta Center, (2) the adherence to international standards, (3) the value of the services to Beta Center's customers, and (4) potential differences between services.

1. Beta Center was set up to supply *services that are directly fed* into products and services for the customers of the entire BetaCorp. Not only are the services as such important for Beta. They also represent a very important factor in regaining and maintaining Beta's competitiveness since they permit Beta to lower its prices in competitive bids with IT providers that already have more operations in locations with lower labor costs. Beta is well aware of the potential benefits it gains through Beta Center. Therefore, it is not willing to share information about the center with potential competitors since it does not want to encourage more MNCs to set up shop in the same city (*"Wir wollen gar nicht, dass die etwas davon erfahren. [Competitor's name] hat schon angefragt, was wir denn da machen. Und wir sagen: Ach, nichts... Wir wollen nicht, dass noch jemand dorthin kommt."*[919]). Beta also sees itself as being in an advanced position vis-à-vis its competitors from India. One interviewee compared IT providers from India with electronics manufacturers that carry out a prespecified task very efficiently but that do not offer self-contained products such as Beta does (*"Die konnten perfekt fertigen. Aber sie hatten keine eigenen Produkte, die irgendwo den Kunden interessiert hätten. Und ich vergleiche das so ein bisschen."*[920]).

2. The value that Beta Center has for Beta can also be deduced from the fact that Beta had the center certified by *international standards* immediately after opening (*"Das Zentrum ist nach ISO 9001, BS 7799, BS 15000 zertifiziert"*[921]) even though this had not been necessary for legal or regulatory reasons. However, Beta wanted to adhere to the stricter German norms abroad in order to represent a high common standard for its customers (*"Alle Offshore-Sites haben wir zertifiziert. Die sind nach Qualitäts- und Umwelt-Audits haben die entsprechend ihre deutschen Einheiten die gleichen Zertifikate bekommen und die gleichen Approvements*

---

[919] Interview 4:20.
[920] Interview 5:15.
[921] Interview 4:7.

durchlaufen. ... Ist auch wichtig für die Kunden, also wir wollen da keine zwei Klassen aufbauen."[922]). The high investment and the commitment to the location is also confirmed by the personal impression from our visit to Russia: Every piece of equipment – from desks to computer hardware and security standards – was of the the same or even higher quality than in the German headquarters that we had visited before.

3. The services Beta Center provides play a very important role for its customers. A potential loss of the service offshoring subsidiary would result in problems that the internal customers would not be able to cope with. These problems would translate into quality of service loss for external customers as well (*"D.h. hier, wenn ich das jetzt wegbrechen würde, dann habe ich Business-Cases erstellt, Was-wäre-wenn-Szenarien, Flugzeug landet hier auf dem Gebäude, da hätte in der Tat die Delivery in Deutschland ein Problem beziehungsweise es gibt gar keine Zweitdelivery mehr in Deutschland."*[923]). An interviewee at the headquarters stated that the center is very important since the services delivered from Russia directly enter the end customer offering (*"Ja, das Zentrum ist absolut wichtig für uns, da diese Leistungen sofort in Kundenprojekte einfliessen."*[924]). A loss of the center would result in a "catastrophe" since Beta would be faced with a backlash in its cost position and would again have to offer based on the German cost position (*"Das wäre eine riesige Katastrophe für uns. Wir wären nicht mehr in der Lage, eine günstige Mischkalkulation anzubieten, sondern müssten wie früher deutsche Preise anbieten. Damit wären wir absolut nicht mehr wettbewerbsfähig."*[925]).

4. We argue that both software development and IT help desk services are of high value for the respective customers. This might seem surprising at the outset since help desk services are typically not thought of as something very valuable, but the complex problems that are resolved in some of the help desk calls show that the value provided here is rather high: *"We're not expected to do resolution within one minute, two minutes. It's good for our statistics if we can resolve within fifteen minutes. Lots of fifteen minute resolution looks very nice on our statistics. But it's not always possible, sometimes we have to investigate problems, check in the sys-*

---

[922] Interview 5:75.
[923] Interview 8:30.
[924] Interview 4:16.
[925] Interview 4:18.

tems."[926] A potential loss of the help desk services would be *"very upsetting."*[927] The value of the help desk services is also reflected in the fact that Beta Center's customers have given the same service portfolio to the Russian location that they have in their traditional, Western European locations.[928] In addition, the services that their customers have offshored to Beta Center are considered part of their own core offering,[929] which again indicates a high value of the services. The value of the software development services is also high since they are directly used for Beta's products for external customers[930] and contribute to important product developments (*"They develop web interface for [proprietary name] system. So each user can access this system using just simple browser like Internet Explorer and so on."*[931]) and directly participate in the development of new creative solutions (*"...sometimes our developers have good ideas."*[932]). This is also confirmed by the steady growth of the group that started from six developers (*"... we started [name of project] only with six persons, only with web interface team"*[933]) and now has around 40 members.

Based on these considerations, we conclude that the value of the services provided by Beta Center is high.

(B) We now analyze the services' *rareness* by discussing (1) their specificity, (2) Beta Center's location and local network, and (3) the availability of knowledge for the service provision.

1. *Specificity of the services:* They do not have commodity character, but are rather carried out to specific orders (*"Vieles wird für den Kunden spezifisch angefertigt."*[934]) and many of them are only required by one customer and not by a larger market (*"Teilweise schon, nicht alle, aber einige sind schon sehr spezialisiert."*[935]). With specific regard to the Russian location, there is a high degree of rareness since there is no other provider in the region of Beta Center. This leads to a

---

[926] Interview 6:40.
[927] Interview 6:66.
[928] Interview 9:20-22.
[929] Interview 9:60.
[930] Interview 7:1.
[931] Interview 7:11.
[932] Interview 7:51.
[933] Interview 7:193.
[934] Interview 4:26.
[935] Interview 4:28.

significant cost advantage (*"Übrigens, [Beta Center] ist aus dem Grund entstanden, weil wir dort bisher keinen westlichen Mitbewerb gesehen haben. Und damit das Preisniveau noch stimmt."*[936]). The rareness of the help desk services (especially the mobile phone support) is however lower than that of the other services from Beta Center. This is due to the fact that *"... in tne area of mobile phones support there's a limit to the amount of innovation you can do"*[937] and *"[b]ecause of the customer base, because of the skill base required for the agents, because of the product, there has to be at least some commonality in how we do things."*[938]

2. *Location and local network:* As the only Western employer in the city, Beta Center has advantages in attracting qualified personnel compared to cities in which employers compete for competent employees. Besides, Beta Center maintains good relationships to universities and local government (*"Jeder Wettbewerber hat ähnliche Zentren; für die ist unser Zentrum interessant, weil es einen außergewöhnlichen Standort hat und wir so gute Beziehungen zu Unis und dem Vizegouverneur der Gegend haben."*[939]). This advantage arises from the fact that the Center is located in a city that is not a major offshoring location for Western companies. This has the benefit of lower labor costs, however, there are no established providers that help set up an offshoring center within several weeks as in Budapest or Prague (*"Das geht nicht so schnell. Das ist ja nicht so wie in Budapest oder Prag, wo sie ein fertiges Zentrum kaufen können. In [Beta Center location] waren wir die ersten und jeder, der jetzt kommt, würde es genauso schwierig haben."*[940]).

3. *Knowledge:* In addition, Beta transfers increasingly more knowledge to the Russian center and is currently also building up a small consulting unit. The consulting unit will not work in the traditional offshoring model but will rather employ consultants for a lower local wage but then send them on international assignments (*"Es sammelt sich dort ja immer mehr Wissen an; zum einen kommt immer mehr Prozesswissen zu bestimmten Themen dort hin. Außerdem bauen wir jetzt die Consulting Einheit dort auf. Der langfristige Weg geht dahin, mehr dort aufzubauen."*[941]). Moreover, Beta Center had to build up some knowledge that is not

---

[936] Interview 5:17.
[937] Interview 6:68.
[938] Interview 6:78.
[939] Interview 4:32.
[940] Interview 4:34; confirmed in interview 8:26.
[941] Interview 4:36.

readily available in offshore locations and that makes the services provided by Beta Center very rare (*"Of course it was not so easy to find Cobol developers here in [Beta Center location]."*[942]). In addition, Beta Center together with its customers had to invest in training to deliver the services (*"And so for Cobol, we have four-week trainings here. So training plan from the beginning was the following: First we hired people from job market, we give them German language education because it's not very easy to find IT specialists in [Beta Center location] with German language, mostly its only English. So but [the customer], it's a very special client because they develop this software a long time. Some project managements are very old, they don't know English language. And doesn't want to learn, and the German was really necessary to communicate with [the customer]. So we educate these people eight weeks, eight hours per day, for German after they train in Cobol four weeks and send to [the customer] approximately two months. And then [the customer] at first, it was lectures about [the customer], about the systems, the technologies, and after that some kind of training on the job."*[943]).

Generally speaking, the high specificity, the unique setting, and the knowledge requirements seem to make the services rare. The specificity of the help desk services seems slightly lower, which however, does not change the overall assessment of the services' rareness.

(C) We now discuss the *inimitability* of the services by reviewing (1) the time to build up the center, (2) the time to understand the local culture, and (3) the complexity of the services.

1. *Time to build up center:* One indicator for the inimitability of services is how long it takes to build up the providing unit from the start. Estimates vary among the interviewees but it is generally thought that it takes at least two years, with some areas ready for a faster ramp-up (*"Ich glaube, die Anstrengung, die wir hier wirklich unternommen haben vor drei Jahren, und dann proaktiv und hier in Russland wahrscheinlich weit vor der Zeit, das war damals gute Entscheidungen, auch aus der Sicht von heute, ich glaube der Weg ist schwierig. Denn er war jetzt auch lange. Wir haben jetzt gemerkt, was wir investiert haben und gebraucht haben an Zeit, um Leute zu entwickeln, auch wenn wir kulturell näher liegen als Indien wahrscheinlich und auch*

---

[942] Interview 7:97.
[943] Interview 7:123.

die deutsche Sprache vermittelbar ist und das alles viel näher liegt, braucht es seine Zeit, die Personen zu entwickeln. Nicht nur Sprache, sondern auch ein bisschen zu vermitteln, um was geht das Mindset, was ist Geschäft. Also, das ganze aufzubauen und rein produktiv in der Breite mit der Wertschöpfung. Würde die Zeit sicher auch in Anspruch nehmen. Von daher bestimmt alles machbar, aber ein bisschen schwierig."[944]).

2. *Time to understand local culture:* Interviewees expressed that it would take about 18 months for the projects to pay off. This is because to understand the local culture and mentality needs more time than in other countries (*"Wir rechnen mit einer Payback-Dauer von etwa 18 Monaten, das geht in anderen Ländern auch schneller, aber man braucht diese Zeit, um die russische Kultur und Mentalität zu berücksichtigen."*[945]).

3. *Complexity of the services:* The software development services are rather hard to imitate since they require much accumulated knowledge and experience (*"Da kann ich nicht sagen, ich baue jetzt mal AMS-Second-Level-Support gegenüber auf. Keine Chance."*[946]). The help desk services are much less complex and can be imitated more easily (*"And they're, it's very simple work compared say, for example, IT help desk in that they have a good knowledge base system and you know when it's a mobile phone and you know somebody says "I can't do this.", and its like click click click, oh yeah, this is how you do it. So the skill set for this team is a little bit lower."*[947]). However, not all help desk services are that easy to perform. With regard to IT infrastructure support, the interviewee explained: *"And unlike some help desks, the solutions for these can be a bit more involved, not so quick."*[948]

Thus, the inimitability of the services provided by Beta Center is high for the software development services and low to medium for the help desk services.

---

[944] Interview 8:40, confirmed by interviews 7:191 and 6:80. Help desk services of low complexity could also be built up faster (see interviews 6:82 and 6:88).
[945] Interview 4:13.
[946] Interview 8:36.
[947] Interview 6:14; confirmed in interview 8:34. The ease of imitating the help desk services is also similarly judged by a customer of that service. He stated that other units within BetaCorp could have carried out the service as well (interview 9:29-30); however, even for this service it was acknowledged that the build-up of a new center would be difficult ("Selber was aufbauen ist schwierig, weil Sie dann wirklich von Grund auf alles machen müssen." interview 9:28).
[948] Interview 6:40.

6 – Results

(D) To evaluate the *non-substitutability* of the services we talked with the interviewees about (1) the possibility of acquiring substitute services from an external provider (2) and the possibility of substituting the services through other internal sources.

1. *Possibility of acquiring substitute services from an external provider:* The services purchased from Beta Center could potentially be provided by other firms as well, though, not in the way that Beta requires them. In addition, they would be more expensive and thus not serve Beta's interests (*"Ja, vielleicht, aber nicht in der Ausprägung, wie wir es jetzt haben. Außerdem ist es ja Teil von unserem ureigenen Geschäft, das wir natürlich selber machen wollen und an dem - wie schon gesagt - wir auch etwas verdienen wollen und nicht alles einem Partner abgeben müssen."*[949]). Thus, Beta decided not to acquire the services from external sources; other solutions were not available (*"Wir haben uns ja früh gegen einen externen Partner entschieden. Andere Alternativen gab es keine, wir mussten billiger werden."*[950]).

2. *Possibility of substituting the services by other internal sources:* Several of the services that are provided by Beta Center are exclusively provided from this center; thus, there is no other unit that could easily deliver the service (*"Wir haben in der Tat Themen, da sind wir von heute auf morgen unersetzbar. ... Gerade im Thema Enterprise Portal, den Herr [person's name] kurz erwähnt hat, direkten Kundenkontakt, da gibt es wirklich keine weitere Option mehr, da ist es wirklich kritisch."*[951]).

Based on these considerations, we deem the non-substitutability to be high. In conclusion, the value and the rareness of the services from Beta Center are high, as is the non-

---

[949] Interview 4:24.

[950] Interview 4:38; confirmed in interview 4:40. There was, however, one mention of a possible closer cooporation with external partners ("Es gibt durchaus Sichten, unser Einkauf vertritt das sehr stark, warum fahrt ihr mit diesen zweitklassigen Providern, geht doch mal zu den ganz Großen. Geht doch mal in die indische Champions-League, da gibt es eine Tata, eine Info-Sys, das sind Firmen die 15.000 Leute beschäftigen und durch die ganze Welt in Projekte bringen. Und natürlich auch solche Services, wie wir sie offshore erledigen, also Application-Management oder Call-Service-Desks anbieten. Haben wir bisher nicht gemacht. Müssen wir uns auch anschauen, ob wir das nicht vielleicht tun." (interview 5:13)). However, for this view other confirmations were not found and it also referred more to low-complexity services (see interview 5:15); thus it is not considered a real contradiction.

[951] Interview 8:30; confirmed by interviews 8:32 and 8:34. Some services could be more easily replaced since there are similar resources in other parts of the corporation (see for the help desk services 6:33; 6:36; 6:65 and 6:76; for some of the software development services see interviews 7:45; 7:47-49, and 7:103).

substitutability. The inimitability is high for most of the services Beta Center provides, with the exception of some of the help desk services (which represent only about one third of the services we consider). Thus, the strategic relevance of Beta Center is high.

6.2.2.2 ANALYSIS OF NETWORK EMBEDDEDNESS

We now turn to the network embeddedness and evaluate (A) the number of relationships to other units, (B) the frequency of change to the relationships and (C) the closeness to other units.

(A) For the *number of relationships* we consider again only the three IT departments and not the business processes department.[952] Beta Center currently has six relationships to units within Beta Germany,[953] three relationships to Beta Russia, and one relationship to an Austrian unit within BetaCorp.

(B) With regard to the changes to the network structure, there are currently ten relationships for service delivery that are very likely to increase further as the Center grows to its current target of around 600 employees. For instance, the IT infrastructure support could be offered to more Beta units, with Japan being the first within the next few months (*"The idea is it will be rolled out, and the solution is already used in other countries. There are countries which are interested. Japan for example, is currently in roll-out phase. They are, they make for them, like on the system within a couple of months. And we are hoping that we will also take calls from them because all the engineers speak English."*[954]). In total, there could be four more relationships from the IT help desk services area alone, which would increase the number of relationships by 40 per cent: *"it's possible within a year I will have four more projects"*[955] The other areas were also trying to add new relationships, however, could not yet estimate the exact number of additions. We consider this a high *frequency of change*.

(C) With regard to *closeness*, we review (1) the investments that the headquarters has made, (2) the investments of Beta Center's customers, (3) the partners' mutual adaptation, and the (4) flow of information.

---

[952] See also Figure 6-7.
[953] The services for these relationships can eventually be delivered even outside Germany (such as in the case of one help desk service that is delivered to a BetaCorp unit in the U.S.), however, they are contracted by Beta Germany.
[954] Interview 6:48.
[955] Interview 6:157.

1. The partners have made substantial *investments* in the relationships. Beta Germany has established a fund that was used to cover the investments needed to launch a given service but that no single customer was prepared to pay for. For instance, some customers were not willing to pay for the training of new employees and for the equipment that they would need. They wanted to pay only a transaction fee or a daily rate but not the full investment that would also benefit other customers. Thus, Beta Germany set up the fund that helped to promote the activities of Beta Center (*"Wir haben die Anschubfinanzierung geleistet. Offiziell gehört das Zentrum dort der [Beta Russia], aber wir haben es ja aufgemacht und auch fast exklusiv genutzt."*[956]). In addition, a unit in Beta Germany was set up to promote service offshoring to Beta Center and to guide the buildup of the center and also to work as a transition manager between the units that were interested in offshoring and Beta Center (*"Das ganze internationale Geschäft läuft über uns. Dann ist das Management aus Deutschland, wir suchen weiterhin Leute, die dorthin gehen."*[957]).

2. The notion of close relationships is confirmed by the view of a customer who had been *willing to invest* in the setup cost for the relationship (*"Wo es nach einer bestimmten Call-Anzahl es sich gerechnet hat, dass ich hier diese Setup-Kosten übernehme."*[958]) and in the ongoing management (*"Also, das würde kaum funktionieren, dass Sie einfach sagen, ok hier habt ihr das SLA, das sind die Präsentationsunterlagen und ich möchte, dass es in einer Woche funktioniert. Also, das geht nicht. Sie müssen schon selbst die Steuerung haben, ... Also, sind wir hier, wir machen die SLAs, wir machen Monitorings, wir machen die Qualitätsprüfungen usw."*[959]). Many customers contributed substantially to the relationships by inviting employees from Beta Center for purposes of training and ongoing support. For the help desk services, the customers "... *provide training at the start to get the project started. ... it's written in the contract that Germany is responsible for providing any additional training that is required.*"[960] In addition, the customers "... *give us good support from their end as well. It's quite good to work with these guys as customers.*"[961] The customers from the software development units also "... *invest some money*

---

[956] Interview 4:46.
[957] Interview 4:46.
[958] Interview 9:24.
[959] Interview 9:26.
[960] Interview 6:119.
[961] Interview 6:70.

to education. And educate our developers for another technology. We have people from the market without any Cobol knowledge. [The customer] sent here to [Beta Center location] a trainer. We train people, after that we send these people to [the customer] for some time to receive know how and it works."[962]

3. The *adaptation* of both the provider and the receiver of the service is rather high, which again is indicative of a high closeness. This is expressed in a comment by the leader of the offshoring initiative who explained that some considerable pressure had to be put on the receiving parties to send their work abroad (*"Das ist schon etwas anderes, wenn sie so über die Entfernung arbeiten im Vergleich zu früher, wo man Tür an Tür arbeitete. Die Arbeit in virtuellen Teams ist eine große Herausforderung für uns. Daher mussten wir am Anfang auch viel Druck aufwenden, um die Leute überhaupt dazu zu bringen, mit [Beta Center location] zusammen zu arbeiten - und das trotz des hohen Kostendrucks."*[963]). Only for one unit within the software development department was the adaptation somewhat easier, since they had worked with other offshoring partners before (*"No, not new situation because before [Beta Center location], they worked with Minsk, one team from Minsk."*[964]).

4. Other indicators of closeness are a constant *flow of information* (*"Zudem gibt es auch einen großen Informationsfluss hin und her."*[965]) and mutual access to computer systems.[966]

Due to the high investments, the high level of mutual adaptation, and the other indicators we consider the closeness to be high. As a result of our evaluation, we conclude that the network embeddedness – measured by the number or relationships, the frequency of change in relationships and the closeness of these relationships – is high. This is also confirmed by the fact that the close relationships between the organizational units on the service delivery side have also led to the development of better personal relationships, *"real friendship"*[967]. The outcome of our analysis is that Beta Center can be characterized

---

[962] Interview 7:79.
[963] Interview 4:48; confirmed by interview 6:125.
[964] Interview 7:99.
[965] Interview 4:46.
[966] See, for instance, for the help desk, interview 6:117 and for software development: "Of course we have remote access to their systems." (interview 7:121).
[967] Interview 6:121.

as an internal competence center. It shows high values on both dimensions, network embeddedness as well as strategic relevance.

6.2.3 COORDINATION MECHANISMS

6.2.3.1 OVERVIEW OF COORDINATION

The coordination for Beta Center takes place on several levels. The initial contact between Beta Center and a potential internal customer is handled by a unit within Beta Germany. Beta Germany set up this unit with 10 employees to help the ramp-up phase of Beta Center and to facilitate investment in Beta Center. Once a contact has been established between Beta Center and the customer, there is a direct interaction between the customer and Beta Center. However, the coordination unit within Beta Germany is still involved for conflict resolution.

Within Beta Center, coordination is channeled through the general manager and the department heads and – if necessary – also his subordinates who interact with their customers.

Based on the number of people involved in coordination, the overall *coordination requirements* seem rather high. There are around 20 people involved within Beta Germany and Beta Center. In addition, there are a varying number of people involved in coordination within customer units. This results in a ratio of people responsible for coordination compared to people who deliver services of around ten per cent.[968]

6.2.3.2 STRUCTURAL COORDINATION MECHANISMS

The *autonomy* of Beta Center is considered in the following section. We addressed the following points during our discussions with managers from Beta: (1) the responsibility of the customer, (2) Beta Center's freedom in the service delivery, (3) resolution in cases of conflict, (4) the development of an independent market offering, and (5) the general attitude between the partners.

1. The customer who orders a service has the *main responsibility* for it.[969] Beta Center does not have an independent offering of products that it creates based on its own judgment and then sells. Rather, it carries out projects for its customers. Thus, it is still restricted in its autonomy by its customers' orders *("Die Au-*

---

[968] Which is rather high compared to the other cases.
[969] In disciplinary terms the Center reports to Beta Russia. However, the work instructions come from the customer (interview 5:27).

tonomie ist in der eigentlichen Projektausführung nicht so hoch, da soll gemacht werden, was der Unternehmer, der ja das Risiko trägt und der meist in Deutschland sitzt, anfordert."[970]). However, Beta Center has much freedom with regard to hiring and also has increasingly more autonomy with regard to its budget ("Daneben ist das Zentrum bei Einstellungsfragen frei, natürlich nur in den Mengen, die für beide Seiten Sinn machen. Auch budgettechnisch haben sie inzwischen mehr und mehr Spielraum."[971]). Most of the decisions regarding human resources are taken together by the different units ("Generally across the board, we need to get agreement."[972]).

2. Beta Center is *free to recommend improvements* in the service delivery process. However, the final decision over which improvements to implement lies with the customers ("And if you have some ideas, we can describe these ideas to project management and they will decide is it suitable for their needs or not. Sometimes it happens, but not so often."[973]).

3. In *cases of conflict*, the final decision will still be taken by the customer who generally is from Germany ("Der Auftraggeber, der ja meist in Deutschland sitzt."[974]). However, in many cases, decisions are already taken locally and the decision autonomy is shifting from Germany to Russia ("im Prinzip entscheiden wir 90 Prozent schon hier, weil wir von Anfang an Teil der russischen Organisation waren, was in der Matrix auch für Probleme gesorgt hat. Offshore-Zentrum für Deutschland, aber Teil der russischen Organisation. Und jetzt sind wir dann immer weiter mit dem Selbständiger-Werden, und auch dort angekommen zu sein, aber wir sind in der russischen Organisation und deshalb machen wir auch hier die lokalen Entscheidungen."[975]).

4. The strongest sign of Beta Center's autonomy is probably the aspiration to develop a *separate market offering* for external customers. The offshoring subsidiary is making first attempts to establish relationships with external customers ("One exception to this, we are next two months, going to London for a conference entitled 'Outsourcing to Russia' and we're hoping to draw up some business

---

[970] Interview 4:75.
[971] Interview 4:75; confirmed by interview 9:48.
[972] Interview 6:169; confirmed by interview 7:147.
[973] Interview 7:145; confirmed by interview 6:14 and 6:199.
[974] Interview 4:77.
[975] Interview 8:46.

there."⁹⁷⁶). One manager in the Center said: *"I want to be the master of my own destiny."*⁹⁷⁷ This shift is also confirmed by the fact that the mitigating organization in Germany is about to lose this role and Beta Center will have more direct contacts with its customers (*"Und damit war das jetzt eine gewollte, naturgemäße Auflösung des Implementierungsteams. Und bewusst keine Nachfolger, weil jetzt sollen die Direktkontakte zwischen Kunde oder Zwischenunternehmer und Offshore Shared-Service-Zentrum direkt stattfinden."*⁹⁷⁸).

5. The *general attitude* of the subsidiary towards the headquarters is more that of an evolving partnership than that of a hierarchy: *"No, we are not slaves to Germany. ... Germany acts as a partner, they guide us, they have some ownership of us."*⁹⁷⁹

We conclude that the level of autonomy can be considered medium. There is a wide range of activities where Beta Center can act autonomously; however, there are certain limits to these.

6.2.3.3 TECHNOCRATIC COORDINATION MECHANISMS

We now turn our attention to *technocratic coordination mechanisms* by assessing (A) the degree of standardization and (B) the degree of formalization.

(A) We start with the degree of *standardization* with regard to (1) a standardized customer approach, (2) the goal of standardization, and (3) the extent of standardization.

1. To introduce a *standardized approach across different customers* of Beta Center is a wish that was expressed more than once by interviewees (*"Jede Beziehung ist individualisiert. Man versucht natürlich, Sachen gemeinsam zu machen, aber man muss sich da den Kunden schon anpassen."*⁹⁸⁰).

2. This wish is inspired by the general *need to gain economies of scale* and reduce complexity; but currently the level of complexity does not seem to be too high and the savings that are achieved through labor arbitrage seem to be sufficient. However, over time as more customers have relationships with Beta Center, the

---

[976] Interview 6:181.
[977] Interview 6:183.
[978] Interview 8:2; confirmed by interview 8:42.
[979] Interview 6:183.
[980] Interview 4:81; confirmed by interview 6:129.

need to standardize will most likely grow further ("*For the moment we are using one system, we may use two in the near future, which is acceptable to some degree. But if it starts going to three, four then, you have to say ok, this is too much. You know, we need to standardize.*"[981]).

3. At present, *standardization is rather limited*. As a general tendency, standardization is intended but the need to adapt to the customers' wishes overrides this ("*Man versucht natürlich, Sachen gemeinsam zu machen, aber man muss sich da den Kunden schon anpassen.*"[982]; "*So each group has different types of communications.*"[983]). Still, there are several approaches to standardardizing relationships within one department and across departments but they are not very far-reaching. For instance, the process of relocating activities from abroad into Beta Center had been standardized to a certain degree to make it easier and more predictable how other Beta units can move activities into the center ("*Da gab es Standardabläufe. Wie stelle ich unten ein? Wie starte ich eine Ausbildung? Was muss ich in Deutschland vorbereiten, wenn ich Leute von Russland hierher zur Ausbildung hole? Das ist hier niedergeschrieben gewesen. Das war ja der sogenannte Implementation-Prozess. Und den hat jeder Unternehmer gleicherweise genutzt.*"[984]). Moreover, in the IT help desk area, the repeated delivery of a service within one project is similar over time, even if it differs between projects.[985] Several interviewees claimed that the complexity and the value of the services and the differences between services[986] inhibited a stronger standardization even though they would like to implement it. The interview partners compared the IT area with the business process area that is of lower strategic relevance and much more prone to standardization ("*Das ist im BPO-Bereich auch wieder anders. Hier wird einmal ein Standardprozess definiert und den müssen dann alle nutzen.*"[987]).

Overall, standardization is used but not in all cases and not as the most important coordination mechanism. Thus, we consider it to be of medium importance.

---

[981] Interview 6:58; confirmed by interview 6:54.
[982] Interview 4:81; confirmed by interviews 4:29 and 6:52.
[983] Interview 7:9.
[984] Interview 5:61; also confirmed by an internal document that exactly describes all the necessary steps.
[985] Interview 6:70.
[986] Interviews 6:129; 6:159.
[987] Interview 4:81; confirmed by interview 5:53.

6 – Results   257

(B) As the second aspect of technocratic coordination mechanisms, the degree of *formalization* is analyzed based on the discussions we had with interviewees. We refer here to (1) the degree of documentation and (2) the importance of formalization for Beta Center's customers:

1. It became evident in our interviews that there is a rather low *degree of documentation* overall and even if there is documentation, it does not play an important role (*"Die Dokumentation ist nicht so ausgeprägt, vieles beruht auf persönlicher Zusammenarbeit."*[988]). Besides that, formalization is rarely used (*"Selten"*[989]). Many areas have some kind of documentation that helps to guide the process, but it is not seen as the most important coordination mechanism[990] and it is not standardized across projects (*"No, no, no. [Name of form] is a special [project name] form"*[991]). In the help desk area, formalization has some significance. This is reflected less in extensive documentation or procedures than in the computer systems that the call agents work with, and that often have specific procedures incorporated (*"press one for this, two for this and it routes to the appropriate agent."*[992]).

2. Formalization is *important for the customers* of Beta Center as well;[993] however, it is acknowledged that the definition of rules and plans alone is not sufficient but their implementation needs to be controlled (*"Sie können das natürlich als Regelung weitergeben, aber ob die Regelungen dann genau in dieser Art und Weise eingehalten werden oder nicht, oder ob sie anders interpretiert werden."*[994]).

In conclusion, formalization plays a role, but as with standardization, not the most important one. Thus, the use of formalization is at a medium level.

6.2.3.4 OUTPUT-BASED COORDINATION MECHANISMS

Output control is used to some extent for the coordination of the help desk department, but is generally of less importance. It was explained by the interviewees that the expected results are hard to describe upfront but that there is an iterative approach required that needs personal interaction (*"Das lässt sich nicht 100-prozentig beschreiben, da muss

---

[988] Interview 4:85.
[989] Interview 4:89.
[990] Interview 4:69; confirmed by interviews 7:29; 7:31.
[991] Interview 7:83; confirmed by interview 7:26.
[992] Interview 6:129.
[993] Interview 9:6; confirmed by interview 9:58.
[994] Interview 9:16.

man im Laufe der Zeit miteinander sprechen."[995]). For the help desk department, output control is based on the evaluation of statistics and customer feedback (*"Statistics and obviously which is tied to service levels, feedback from customers"*[996]). A customer of the help desk services welcomed the possibility to evaluate the results from the offshore location remotely (*"Und wir haben Online-Zugriff auf die Daten der Telefonanlage. ... wir sehen, so und so viele Leute sind eingeloggt, die Bearbeitungszeiten, das Servicelevel HCR, also handled call rate ... Wir bekommen dann auch statische Auswertungen über die vergangenen Tage."*[997]). However, he also admitted that output control was not enough but needed to be complemented by personal coordination mechanisms.[998] As this view is shared by representatives of both the IT help desk (*"[C]ustomer looks at statistics, the partner looks at statistics, but realistically, it's up to me and the team leader to guide the team and the other teams"*[999]) and the software development department (*"Yes, it is not so easy [to clearly define outcomes], first establishments come from client side, after that we think about it and give our information to client"*[1000]), we come to the conclusion that output control plays a medium role in the coordination of Beta Center.

6.2.3.5 PERSONAL COORDINATION MECHANISMS

Personal coordination plays an important role within the range of coordination mechanisms. We discuss it with regard to (A) direct personal coordination, (B) visits, (C) transfers, and (D) cultural coordination.

(A) We start with *direct personal coordination* and consider (1) its importance as a coordination mechanism, (2) the actors responsible for coordination, and (3) the variety of interaction modes.

1. Direct personal coordination is an *important means of coordination*. It was explained that there is a certain degree of technocratic coordination but that the focus is on direct personal coordination (*"Bei Softwareentwicklung ist das natürlich anders [als bei business processes]. Hier gibt es auch einige Vorgaben, wie man miteinander umgeht, Standarddokumente, etc. Aber auch die persönliche Koordination*

---

[995] Interview 4:91; confirmed by interview 4:79.
[996] Interview 6:196; confirmed by interview 6:194.
[997] Interviews 9:2; 9:54.
[998] Interview 9:16.
[999] Interview 6:198; confirmed by interviews 6:188; 6:190; 6:192.
[1000] Interview 7:149; confirmed by interviews 7:155 and 7:157.

spielt eine Rolle."[1001]; "Einen automatisierten Prozess gibt es nur beim BPO, bei IT ist vieles personalisiert."[1002]).

2. The responsibility for coordination in Beta Center is *bundled at the department heads*. One important part of their tasks is the personal interaction with their designated counterparts (called channel or partner managers) at the customers to coordinate the work from the subsidiary (*"Ja, die Anweisungen werden direkt aus Deutschland erteilt. Außerdem sind die jeweiligen Abteilungsleiter in [Beta Center location] oft Deutsche, die dann die Übersetzungsarbeit für die russischen Kollegen leisten."*[1003]). The customers have set up a key contact person as well who interacts with his counterpart in Beta Center (*"Also bezüglich dieser Koordination hatten wir gesagt, es ist letztens der Unternehmer, der meistens jemanden abstellt, und sagt 'Du bist mein - ja wir wissen immer noch nicht wie wir ihn nennen - sagen wir mal Partnermanager, Channel-Manager. Du bist jedenfalls die Schnittstelle zum Standort.' Und über den läuft dann alles."*[1004]). Despite these general responsibilities, the interaction occurs on several levels and involves headquarters and customers (*"There's a whole variety of cross communication, yeah different people talking to different people coming together. I support this kind of communication, ... There needs to be good communication ... the information has to flow."*)[1005].

3. Personal coordination occurs through a *wide variety of interaction modes* such as phone, email, instant messaging over the internet, and video conferences (*"Phone, ICQ, Mail and so on and so on, all kind of communications."*[1006]). There is typically daily communication by all these means on the working level; the more important issues are discussed between the offshore coordinators (*"They communicate directly only on usual daily moments, daily tasks. 'Please clarify this sentence, please clarify this questions, and so on.' So and but overall, coordination which project will happen next month or so, it is mostly task for offshore coordinator."*[1007]).

[1001] Interview 4:69.
[1002] Interview 4:87.
[1003] Interview 4:93.
[1004] Interview 5:55; confirmed by interviews 7:139 and 9:46.
[1005] Interview 6:153; confirmed by interview 6:155.
[1006] Interview 7:25; confirmed by interviews 6:151 and 7:81. ICQ is the name of an instant messaging program that allows exchanging text messages over the internet in real time.
[1007] Interview 7:63; confirmed by interviews 4:54-58, 6:137, and 9:34.

With interviewees unanimously pointing to the importance of direct personal coordination, we consider the degree of direct personal coordination to be high.

(B) However, the amount of information that can be transported by remote direct coordination is limited and that makes *visits* between the locations necessary. We will consider (1) the general motivation for visits and (2) the frequency and intensity of visits.

1. The *motivation* for personal coordination by face-to-face interaction was emphasized by a customer of Beta Center who compared remote discussions and visits and argued that some facts can be only uncovered in visits (*"Das können Sie dann rausfinden, indem Sie persönlich mit den Leuten unterwegs sind."*[1008]). He argued that personal contact is very important and should be facilitated – as far as possible – through modern means of communication such as video conferences; however, visits will remain important for coordination (*"Das zweite ist sicherlich der persönliche Kontakt, der natürlich notwendig ist. Sie können das ein bisschen eindämmen, indem Sie statt einer Telefonkonferenz z.B. ein Net-Meeting mit Video verwenden. Also, das Gegenüber sehen und das Gesicht sehen, ist schon mal eine wichtige Sache. Das ist etwas, was wir jetzt noch intensivieren wollen."*[1009]).

2. Visits are *frequently* used by all departments in Beta Center and all its customers. One interviewee said – only half joking – that a recently introduced weekly direct flight between the German headquarters location and the location of Beta Center is fully booked with Beta employees on business visits, thus, emphasizing the practice of frequent personal visits (*"Es gibt jetzt eine direkte Flugverbindung [German headquarters location]-[Beta Center location] einmal die Woche. Und wenn das mit unseren Besuchen so weitergeht, fliegen die bald nur noch für uns. Zum einen bin ich mit meinen Leuten öfter dort, aber auch die Kunden senden Leute hin. Es geht viel über den persönlichen Besuch."*[1010]). There is no regular schedule for visits, rather they are handled on a case-by-case basis.[1011] For instance, the help desk department has around ten international business visits to customers mainly in Germany and Austria and around 30 visits to customers in Moscow per year.[1012] The trips abroad last for about a week, while the domestic trips are

---

[1008] Interview 9:16.
[1009] Interview 9:6.
[1010] Interview 4:99.
[1011] Interview 6:137.
[1012] Interview 6:216.

typically day trips: *"There is kind of the inverse ratio depending on distance and the frequency. Generally, the less frequent it is, the longer the visit is for. Perhaps even if there is no real business reason for the visit to be long, I think people stretch it and you know why, I go for Germany for some training, across three days, we say let's make it a week anyway, you might as well spend some time, meet the people plus some extra time with them. It doesn't hurt too much, we've already spent but not much on the flight and everything. To Moscow, it's generally like one day, if you could do it in half a day, better."*[1013] The software development department on the other hand has fewer trips but generally with longer durations: *"For this situation here, I could say, at least six people stay abroad maybe from three, four months."*[1014] These employees spend half their time at Beta Center and the other half at the customers' sites.[1015] In addition, the two employees from Beta Center who are on a business transfer to other countries (see below) also come back twice a year for a week or two.[1016] In addition to the trips that originate from Russia, there are frequent visits to the help desk department from its customers, about two to three people every quarter for half a week, accounting for about 10 additional visits per year.[1017] Visits to the software development department also take place frequently and from all of the project partners.[1018] On top of these regular visits, there are irregular visits to and from all departments for training purposes and the like.[1019]

Based on these considerations, we conclude that the importance of visits is high.

(C) As another coordination mechanism from the category of personal coordination mechanisms, we analyze the use of *transfers*. We discuss (1) transfers from headquarters and (2) transfers from Beta Center to other international units of the firm.

[1013] Interview 6:141.
[1014] Interview 7:77; confirmed by interview 7:79.
[1015] Interviews 7:57; 7:59.
[1016] Interview 7:37.
[1017] Interview 9:6; confirmed by interview 7:137.
[1018] Interview 5:55.
[1019] Interview 9:32; confirmed by interviews 6:2 and 7:71.

1. The two general managers of Beta Center are *permanent transfers from the German headquarters*. One of the department heads is also on transfer from Germany.[1020]

2. The software development unit has *two Russian employees* from Beta Center who spend one to two years at the customer's site in Germany. They are so-called "bridge heads" through which all communication is channeled.[1021] The *"main task for 'Brückenkopf' [is] to clarify all questions, to communicate this to all persons in [customer] and after that provide answers back to [Beta Center]."*[1022] Bridge heads are used for large, complex software development projects. In other areas that work mainly with many small projects, coordination works in different ways: *"And 'Brückenkopf' model will not, doesn't work in such case. 'Brückenkopf' cannot know what special things for each sub-project."*[1023] The other departments have not sent employees on long-term assignments abroad.[1024]

Thus, Beta uses transfers as a coordination mechanism in several instances, from top management to line positions. We thus consider the degree of transfers to be at a high level.

(D) As last coordination mechanism we want to consider *cultural coordination* with regard to (1) sharing of standards and norms, (2) the enforcement of norms, (3) tensions from different corporate cultures, (4) relevance for relationship with customers, (5) the influence of national cultures, (6) the use of trainings, and (7) differences in career perspectives between units.

1. *Sharing the same standards across units* is frequently mentioned by interviewees. This refers to stricter, technical standards such as the international certificates that were obtained for Beta Center, to the very similar type of building, architecture and furniture as well as to shared values and norms: *"Well, you know the kind of corporate image: One [Beta]."*[1025] To display a common image towards the customer, Beta invests time and resources in the alignment of the different units: *"And it's one of the issues when we go to this conference, we need to make*

[1020] Interviews 4:97; 5:65.
[1021] Interviews 7:13; 7:15.
[1022] Interview 7:23.
[1023] Interview 7:75.
[1024] Interviews 9:61-62; 6:207.
[1025] Interview 6:218.

sure we're presenting the same image, these presentations that we do, so we will get together in a week's time and compare our presentations you know, do they look the same? You know as simple as that, do they look the same format, template reviews, you know, do we have the same common focus, strategy. Content's of course different, but you know it's the strategy that you know we're giving our message to potential customers."[1026]

2. Interviewees take the *enforcement of this set of norms* seriously: *"It's up to management, top to bottom, giving the same message. You know, we are world leaders. We do, we are innovators. We do this, we're high performers. And it's for us to make sure that this message comes down. So [the Beta Center CEO] needs to remind me every now and then, we're innovators, and I will go to my staff, we're innovators."*[1027]

3. Despite the fact that the Beta Center's customers belong to BetaCorp as well, there can be some *tensions* from time to time because of the wide variety of sizes of the different units within BetaCorp. In Beta Center, this becomes obvious by the fact that people from one group in the help desk department work for an Austrian customer (a small unit of around 200 employees within BetaCorp) that has a slightly different culture because of size differences and that wants the employees in Beta Center to adapt to that culture (*"Aber es ist einfach von der Größe her ein Unterschied."*[1028]). On the other hand, the leader of the help desk department needs to find the right balance to integrate this group of people into his team and make sure they still feel like Beta Center employees (*"It just means that I need to try and convince them: 'Yes, you are [Beta] employees.'"*[1029]).

4. Cultural coordination helps in the *relationship with customers* as the following example demonstrates: *"For example, you know on one project, [name of project], we're not meeting service levels all of the time. Because when they were defined, nobody knew what was required when the project started, they were just defined. But we can show time and time again we're giving good service, the customers are happy and we're working to resolve the issues they have. So the help desk is running well, but not meeting service levels. And within [Beta] is good about this and they understand this,*

[1026] Interview 6:218.
[1027] Interview 6:222. These norms were also supported by the introduction of a bonus system for employee recommendations for innovations (see interview 6:205).
[1028] Interview 9:66.
[1029] Interview 6:202; confirmed by interviews 9:54; 9:64.

and they're helping us with this. And nobody wants to go away, reads the contract, says this was wrong, this was right."[1030]

5. Cultural coordination is *influenced by country culture*. It is generally reported by interviewees that they do not see the differences between the Russian and the customers' cultures (mainly German) as problematic. However, some business customs first had to be established between the counterparts since the Russian employees (who in most cases had never before worked for a Western MNC) had to become acquainted to the Western style of doing business (*"Auf russischer Seite sehe ich das Problem vor allem darin, dass von allererster Stunde an ein deutscher Partner vor Ort sein muss. D.h. sie können sie nicht einer 100-prozentig russischen Organisation, alle sind Russen, überlassen, in einem deutschen Unternehmen, mit den deutschen Gegebenheiten, mit der deutschen Kultur zu arbeiten. Das fängt bei ganz einfachen Dingen an, wie E-Mail-Verkehr. Was tue ich, was lasse ich, was ist Muss, was sollte man auf keinen Fall? Da brauchen Sie jemanden, der Sie da ein bisschen sozusagen an der Hand nimmt. Das ist die Rolle auch dieses deutschen Coaches. Und wenn Sie das dann haben, das geht ganz schnell, dass persönlich sehr gute Beziehungen aufgebaut sind, die Russen sind auch sehr warm und kontaktfreudig, neugierig auch, dann läuft das eigentlich ganz gut. Aber die Regeln der westlichen oder von mir aus deutschen Geschäftsprozesse, die hat man nicht erfunden, das ist völlig fremd teilweise."*[1031]). These differences have led to some conflict situations such as new Russian employees not respecting certain security standards[1032] or not being very sensitive to expenses on their first business trips abroad;[1033] however, these have never seriously endangered the relationships.

6. The shared values and norms can be partly learnt in *trainings* that are set up to provide employees not only with technical skills, but also with *"soft skills"*[1034]. There is a designated person responsible for trainings in Beta Center who also adapts trainings to local needs.[1035] Cultural coordination is also fostered by the high investment in language courses that are already offered at the city's univer-

---

[1030] Interview 6:192.
[1031] Interview 5:77.
[1032] Interview 4:103.
[1033] Interview 5:81.
[1034] Interview 7:46.
[1035] Interviews 9:70; 9:72.

sity to a selected group of students and that are ongoing and take place on a regular basis in the Beta Center site.[1036]

7. Cultural coordination is, however, *negatively affected* by the fears of job losses that occur in Germany as the size of Beta Center is increased. Therefore employees of Beta Germany start to view employees in Beta Center as competitors for the same amount of available work *("Das ist hier schon so, das war am Anfang nicht, es ist heute so, dass die deutschen Kollegen die russischen Kollegen als Konkurrenz ansehen. Das wird leider immer noch mächtig gepflegt durch die Betriebsräte. 'Was macht der hier? Warum sollte der ausgebildet werden? Wir widersprechen dem.' ... Also, diese Arbeitsplatzangst hat natürlich auch zu einem bestimmten Verhalten geführt, gar keine Frage."*[1037]).

Despite the last point, cultural coordination plays a central role in the coordination of service delivery and we regard its importance as high. To conclude, the general attitude towards cultural coordination is well expressed in this quotation: *"Mostly, we feel like one big team. Mostly, mostly each person involved in this project is interested in the final results. And they are friendly."*[1038]

6.2.3.6 COMPARATIVE ANALYSIS OF COORDINATION MECHANISMS

Our analysis above indicates that personal coordination mechanisms are the most important instruments for coordination. All instruments – direct coordination, visits, transfers, and cultural coordination – are used and each seems to have an important role. Technocratic and output-based coordination mechanisms are of less importance; however, there are attempts to increase standardization and formalization. At the same time, the use of centralized decision making is on the decrease so that the autonomy of Beta Center seems set to grow in the future.

6.2.4 DISCUSSION OF CASE

Evaluation of appropriateness of propositions for individual case

A detailed evaluation of the suitability of our propositions can be found in Table 6-3. We display the original proposition, the empirical result and indicate whether or not we find agreement with the proposition. The original proposition stems from the description

---

[1036] Interviews 4:109; 7:187.
[1037] Interviews 5:77.
[1038] Interviews 7:181.

of our typology, the empirical result from the discussion of the case. We represent the values low (L), medium (M), or high (H) by squares of different sizes.

Table 6-3: Evaluation of suitability of propositions for internal competence center

Coordination mechanism	Original proposition	Empirical result	Agreement with proposition	Remark
Extent of coordination requirements	■-■ (M-H)	■ (H); many people involved in coordination, requiring substantial financial and time resources	Proposition initially supported	--
Degree of autonomy	■-■ (M-H); high strategic relevance in the center requires more autonomy	■ (M); autonomy is medium and growing to higher levels over time	Proposition initially supported	I1: Autonomy develops over time and is growing as Beta Center builds up
Degree of standardization	■ (M); high strategic relevance will require flexibility but trade-off because of high number of customers that will require standardization for complexity reasons	■ (M); Beta intends to introduce more standardization but predicted trade-off could be found empirically; standardization at medium level	Proposition initially supported	--
Degree of formalization	■ (M); high number of clients require formalization but individual solutions cause trade-off	■ (M); Formalization is available and in use; however, not in all projects; thus, only medium level	Proposition initially supported	--

6 – Results

Coordination mechanism	Original proposition	Empirical result	Agreement with proposition	Remark
Degree of output control	■-■ (L-M); many network partners require pre-specification of results; however, partially offset by need to coordinate behavior	■ (M); Beta tries to use output control even though some results are hard to prescribe up-front	Proposition initially supported	--
Degree of personal direct coordination	■-■ (M-H); strategic relevance makes personal interaction necessary	■ (H); importance of direct personal coordination is emphasized by every interviewee	Proposition initially supported	--
Number of visits	■ (H); high number of visits, long duration per visit	■ (H); high number of visits, long duration per visit	Proposition initially supported	--
Number of transfers	■ (H); high number of transfers; potentially in management and line positions	■ (H); high number of transfers, in management and line positions	Proposition initially supported	I2: Beta Center would like to employ more transfers but high number of visits seems to make more transfers unnecessary
Importance of culture-based coordination	■ (H); high level of normative integration	■ (H); high level of normative integration	Proposition initially supported	--
E: Possible explanation for difference; I: Idea, new thought; -- no additional comment				

Presentation of additional information gained from the individual case

The table above shows that all propositions are initially supported by the case. Besides the results that we compared with propositions from the typology, we want to further elaborate on two aspects that touch upon areas that we had not covered in our theoretical considerations:

- I1: The autonomy of the service offshoring subsidiary is growing over time as the subsidiary builds up more competences that it wants to use for external customers. One motivation for this is that Beta Center wants to decrease its dependence on internal customers. These are very reliable on the one hand; however, their willingness to use offshoring hinges always on the general offshoring decisions taken by Beta on the other hand. Orders from external customers could therefore be an attractive possibility for additional business and growing importance as a more independent provider of services in Beta's network. Additional customers and the build-up of additional competences are likely to change Beta Center's position in the typology slightly by increasing the values for both network embeddedness and strategic relevance. Thus, we have an indication for a movement in the typology.

- I2: While there is already a substantial number of transfers, we were told that Beta Center would like to hire even more transfers. However, this seems difficult since the location of Beta Center is not a very attractive destination for expatriates.[1039] In addition, it might simply not be necessary to have more transfers when there are frequent visits.

6.3 CASE 3: SUPPORT CENTER GAMMA

6.3.1 COMPANY OVERVIEW

Presentation of MNC and the business unit under consideration

Gamma is part of a holding company. The holding company is a mid-size family-owned firm that employs about 32,000 people worldwide and that has annual revenues of ca. 4.5 billion EUR.[1040] As a conglomerate, the holding company has a large variety of business units that are active in as different business fields as information technology

---

[1039] One interviewee said that it is hard to find people willing to go there.
[1040] All the financial data is taken from the holding company's annual report 2004.

services and household cleaning products. One of these business units is Gamma. Gamma was set up in 1995 as a separate entity and all IT activities of the holding company were concentrated in it. Thus, Gamma became the main IT provider of the holding company. Initially, all holding companies had to contract with Gamma and Gamma had to accept all orders from holding companies. After a while, these obligations to contract were abandoned and holding companies could acquire IT services from external providers just as Gamma could offer its services to external customers. As of 2005, the holding company buys about 50 per cent of all its IT services (measured in revenues) from Gamma and out of Gamma's revenues, around 50 per cent stem from business with holding companies. Today, Gamma employs around 350 people and has annual revenues of 50 million EUR.

Gamma provides services in the following areas:

1. *Hosting*: Gamma runs customers' IT programs on its own servers in three computing centers worldwide. By bundling demand, Gamma can achieve economies of scale and therefore offer its customers advantages compared to internal hosting. As the hosting unit does not interact with the service offshoring subsidiary, this part of the business will not be considered in detail here.

2. *Configuration and installation of enterprise resource planning (ERP) software (consulting):* ERP programs support processes from a company's entire value chain in a software product. They are typically very complex and need additional configuration to be adapted to each customer's need. Gamma offers its customers this kind of customization. Gamma's consultants evaluate the customers' business needs and then define which product is suitable and which configurations need to be carried out. This activity is bundled in Gamma's consulting unit. Out of these activities, a range of niche software products has been developed, for instance, products for the management of sport events. These products are sold as additions to existing ERP installations.

3. *Production system (software):* In 2000, Gamma acquired the previously independent software development company Gamma A. Gamma A had developed a program that can be used to automate the production process of industrial companies. The software is a so-called Manufacturing Execution System (MES). It monitors and executes the entire production process of a physical good from order creation to delivery to the customer. It can handle stock levels and can program machinery in a production facility to allow for an almost complete automation of the production process. The program consists of several modules that

can also be purchased and installed individually. In many cases it is necessary to make changes to the program to fit the customer's production process. Some of these changes are made only once for one customer. Other changes are initially done for a single customer but then become part of the standard version of the software because they are seen as enhancements of the software for other customers as well. Thus, there are always individual configurations of the software but also an ever-progressing standard version into which innovations are fed.

The organizational structure of Gamma is by business unit and by geography. In addition to the three business units hosting, consulting, and software as described above, there are three geographical areas that are represented in one department each: Hungary, U.S., and China. These international departments have only one location each and represent Gamma's entire service offering in the respective region. In Germany, Gamma has more than one location. The hosting arm is represented in Germany only at the headquarters location. Besides its four domestic locations, the consulting department also has a location in Spain. The software area has one German location. An overview of the German locations can be seen in Figure 6-8.[1041]

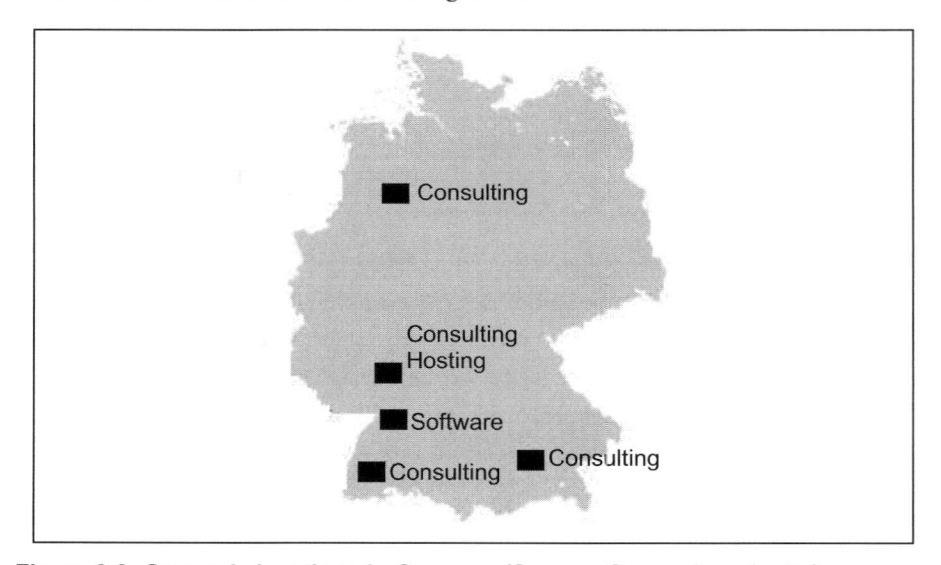

Figure 6-8: Gamma's locations in Germany (Source: Gamma's web site)

[1041] For reasons of anonymity, the names of the locations have been deleted.

Gamma's customers are mainly mid-size production companies that buy IT services from Gamma. Gamma provides most of the *consulting* and *software services* out of its headquarters and a second location near Frankfurt, Germany. However, the *hosting services* are provided out of three centers worldwide. One is located in Germany, one in China and the third in the U.S.

Gamma's current service and product portfolio for external customers comprises these three categories. Internally, the organization is additionally subdivided into the customer-facing organizations (hosting, consulting, software) and the "back-office" software development organization. Software development was originally carried out in the consulting and the software unit. However, now, much of the programming work has already been shifted to the offshore location. The software unit still has a German development center, though the tendency is towards moving software development tasks to Hungary. The split of work across different locations can be seen in Table 6-4.

Table 6-4: Gamma's split of activities across locations

Activity	Western Europe	Eastern Europe	China	USA
Consulting	X	X	X	X
Software product distribution	X	(X)	(X)	(X)
Hosting	X		X	X
Software development	(X)	X		
X – Activity is carried out in this location				
(X) – Activity is partially carried out in this location				

Description of history and motivation of offshoring situation

Gamma has several subsidiaries in Germany and a few international subsidiaries. These are located in the USA, China, Spain and Hungary. The location in Budapest, Hungary was added to Gamma's subsidiaries through the acquisition of Gamma A. Gamma A had a long-standing freelance programmer – Mr. R. – of Hungarian nationality who initially worked for Gamma A in Germany and then helped to set up a subsidiary in Hungary in which he personally held a 50 per cent stake while the other 50 per cent were in Gamma A's ownership. This happened in 1996 when Gamma A had around 20 employees all of whom know Mr. R. personally. The main reasons for shifting work to Budapest were the lower cost of that location and the availability of potential employees in this 2-million people city compared to the small German city in which Gamma A is located. Mr. R. consequently managed the development of one part of the MES program from the new location in Hungary. The new location employed no more than eight employees who were all directly managed by Mr. R. When Gamma A was acquired by Gamma, the Budapest location was initially kept as a 50:50 joint venture between Gamma A and Mr. R. In 2005, however, Gamma purchased Mr. R.'s stake and converted the Hungarian subsidiary into a wholly-owned subsidiary (Gamma Center). Now, Gamma Center works as a profit center that charges the other units within Gamma a daily rate for its services.

Description of services provided by service offshoring subsidiary

Gamma Center originally provided only the development services for one module of the MES program for the software unit. Parallel to the transformation into a wholly-owned subsidiary, Gamma decided to move more activities to Gamma Center. The main reason for this decision was the lower cost of Hungarian software developers. This cost advantage translates into cheaper prices: For a Hungarian software developer, Gamma Center charges a daily rate of 360 EUR as compared to 640 EUR in Germany. Gamma is still in the process of moving activities to Gamma Center. Initially, the location in Hungary was used as an "extended work bench" for the German development center. In the extended work bench model, Gamma Center took over work for which the German location did not have enough capacity or – as one interviewee explained – which was not very attractive to the German unit. This model also meant that the Hungarian location did not have responsibility for the product that it was helping to develop. Rather, individual people from Budapest were managed by the German headquarters as an extension to the departments in Germany.

Now, Gamma Center's tasks are more precisely defined, even though more tasks have been added to its portfolio and Gamma Center is also continuing to hire more people to take over more work for Gamma. Gamma Center has no external customers but works only for Gamma. However, with the conversion of Gamma Center into a profit center there are plans to use Gamma Center as a Hungarian sales subsidiary that will eventually cover the Eastern European market.

Currently, as of December 2005, Gamma Center works for (1) Gamma's consulting and (2) software business. The hosting division does not purchase services from the Hungarian location.

1. The *consulting business* decided to acquire services from Hungary when in summer 2004 it was faced with the decision to close down a small subsidiary in Eastern Germany that had previously developed software tools which the consulting business sells as add-on software to ERP software. It had to find a new solution to have these software tools updated and further developed. The alternatives were to find an external partner or to give these tasks to Gamma Center. The consulting business decided to give the tasks to Hungary because Gamma's board had pushed towards moving programming work to the new location. In autumn 2004, there was the need to do some programming on a second product. The consulting unit discussed the matter with Gamma Center and agreed on an extension of the collaboration.

2. Gamma Center also carries out work for the *software business*. It had started with the initial move of Mr. R. from Germany to Hungary and has since then extended. The driving force behind the move was Gamma's establishment of a policy stating that development work has to be carried out in Hungary if Gamma Center is to be able to make a good offer. Therefore, Gamma's software business decided to move all programming work on the standard platform to Budapest. Customization of the program to meet specific customer requirements will be carried out in Germany but the maintenance of the program's standard version will be taken care of in Budapest. For some modules – especially the one under Mr. R.'s responsibility – this goal has already been achieved, a second module has just completed its move and the other modules will follow one by one. As the modules are moved, the German programmers are retrained to do more consulting and customization work.

An overview of the resulting relationships can be found in Figure 6-9.

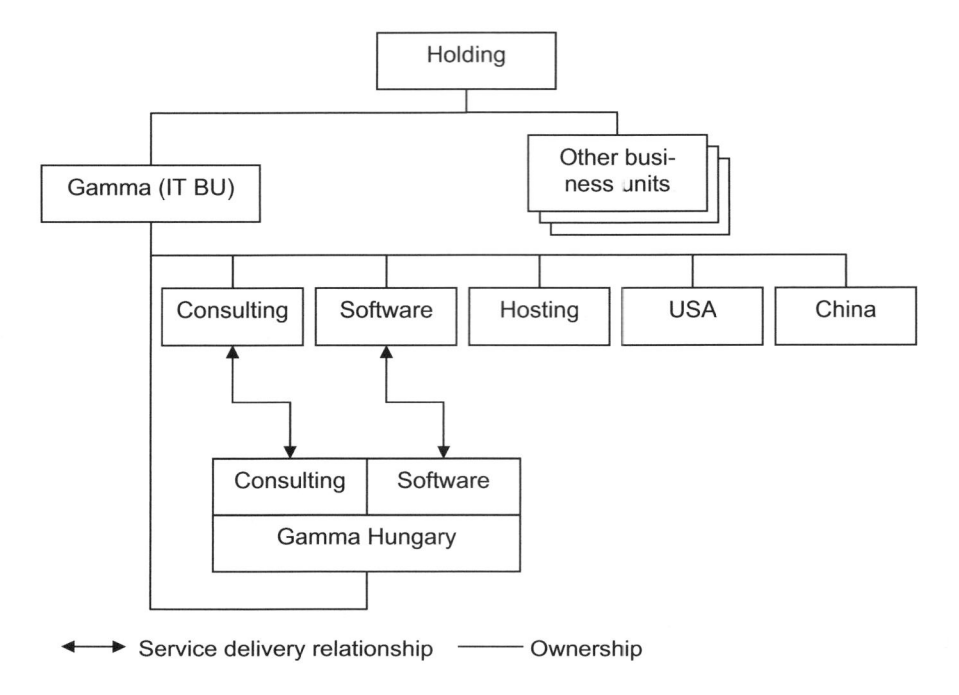

Figure 6-9: Service delivery within Gamma's network

6.3.2 TYPE OF SERVICE OFFSHORING SUBSIDIARY

6.3.2.1 ANALYSIS OF STRATEGIC RELEVANCE

We now consider the strategic relevance of the services that Gamma Center carries out for Gamma by evaluating (A) their value, (B) their rareness, (C) their inimitability and (D) their non-substitutability.

(A) With regard to the *value* of the services we discuss (1) the role of the services for Gamma Center's customers and (2) the motivation to set up the center.

1. The services from Gamma Center currently play only a *minor role* for its customers. One interviewee explained that the center carries out *"more the side topics"*[1042] In addition, he stated that the services provided by Gamma Center are needed to regularly update a product but that the product is not really Gamma's core offering: *"They need to have a release each year but we are not in the market*

[1042] Interview 1:12.

6 – Results

focus with this product, we are too small."[1043] An interviewee from the service offshoring subsidiary mentioned that the center has received several smaller projects that do not require much special knowledge ("*Aber wir haben auch von anderen Produkten kleine Tätigkeiten bekommen, aber es ist eigentlich eine Fleißarbeit, besonders viel Know-How brauchen wir dafür nicht.*"[1044]). A potential loss of the center would not result in a "catastrophe" for Gamma since most of knowledge is still located in the headquarters ("*Aber das Know How wäre ja noch da. Das Wissen, wie man programmiert, wäre ja noch da. ... Da würde, so gesehen, nichts anbrennen. Das wäre in dem Maße kein Risiko.*"[1045]). Such a situation would of course mean that Gamma needs to look for "*a new developer*"[1046].

2. The primary *motivation* for setting up Gamma Center was that the Hungarian location is "*cheaper*"[1047]. Thus, the focus is on efficiency. However, it was also mentioned that Gamma Center in the future could serve as an entry point in the local market as Gamma is trying to extend its business in Eastern Europe and Asia ("*Alle Wettbewerber streben nach Osten, nach Nahosten oder Osteuropa oder nach Fernost. Alle gehen nach Ungarn, alle gehen nach China.*"[1048]).

With low value for the customers and the focus on efficiency gains, we conclude that the value of the services is low. Once the plan to develop the Hungarian subsidiary into a sales subsidiary with responsibility for the entire Eastern European region is realized, this will potentially change.

(B) With regard to *rareness*, we look at (1) the specificity of the services, (2) the availability of necessary skills in other firms and (3) freedom to acquire services from the market.

1. The *services are not very specific* as the knowledge necessary to provide them is not very specialized and could be provided in another location with other people equally well ("*[interviewer] War auch das Wissen so speziell, dass das niemand anders hätte machen können? – [interviewee 1] Ich denke nicht. Ich denke, wenn man jemanden hingebracht hätte nach [location in Germany], dann hätte er das*

[1043] Interview 1:149.
[1044] Interview 3:48.
[1045] Interview 2:157.
[1046] Interview 1:18.
[1047] Interview 1:20.
[1048] Interview 2:159; confirmed by interview 2:161.

nach zwei Jahren machen können. - [interviewee 2] Auch nach einem Jahr schon. – [interviewee 1] Ja, auch nach einem Jahr schon. Das ist auch der Unterschied zu meinem früheren Arbeitgeber. Dort wären das fünf-sechs Jahre gewesen und deswegen war die Hemmschwelle so groß."[1049]).

2. In addition, the *necessary skills* are available in every market and that can help to build up a similar center ("*Und es war relativ schnell, wie die SAP-Gruppe dann aufgebaut werden konnte, weil SAP-Spezialisten kann man eigentlich in jedem Land finden, es ist nicht zu speziell [Gamma A]- oder [Gamma]-Spezifika, und dann kann man halt jemanden finden.*"[1050]).

3. Gamma Center's customers can easily *acquire services from the external market* (which they could not if the services were rare) whereby the price is the major argument: *"If I would want to buy something from outside? If it were cheaper than in Hungary, then I would do it."*[1051]; *"This was the other idea we had. If Hungary wouldn't work, we had to look for another one."*[1052]

Based on these considerations, we consider the rareness of the services from Gamma Center to be low.

(C) When it comes to *inimitability*, respondents pointed to (1) the complexity of services and to (2) the time it takes to build up a similar center.

1. The *complexity of the services* that are provided by the center seems low as they account for only a small part of the entire software product that Gamma offers: *"You have to see that the software is not that big. The price for the software licence is 20.000 EURO and hardware and so on. The whole projects are between 50 and 100 thousand EURO normally ... it'ss not as big as an SAP solution or something else."*[1053] Despite the planned changes of having more local autonomy, Gamma Center is still an extended workbench that has little responsibility for an entire product ("*Wir müssen jetzt von dieser Auftragsentwicklung zur Produktverantwortung überge-*

[1049] Interview 3:61-64.
[1050] Interview 3:64. This is a difference to Gamma Center that had to send its Russian employees to trainings in Germany and bring German trainers to Russia to teach a very specialized programming language.
[1051] Interview 1:75.
[1052] Interview 1:28.
[1053] Interview 1:42; confirmed by interview 1:38.

hen."[1054]; "Und wir waren bis heute oder Mitte dieses Jahre eine verlängerte Werkbank."[1055]). One of the the interviewees from the service offshoring subsidiary called the kind of people that do the work within Gamma Center "coding slaves" ("Kodiersklave"[1056]). Gamma Center deals mainly with maintaining and extending the standard version of the software ("Also, dieses sehr kundennahe wird momentan ... nicht in Ungarn gemacht. Ungarn hat zunächst einmal die Aufgabe, die Basis oder den Standard zu betreuen und weiterzuentwickeln"[1057]), while the innovation and product management are carried out in the headquarters ("Die Produkthoheit sozusagen, das Produktmanagement liegt noch in der [Gamma A], ja."[1058]).

2. Another indicator of low inimitability seems to be the fact that another center of the same kind could be established in a *short time period*, between three and six months: "So, for the developers down there to understand the source code it was around quarter of a year. To establish the relationship on the soft facts it was about half a year."[1059] The responsibility for development could also be transferred to other units and imitated there: "The knowledge is still there. The source code is with comments, with notes. And what we have to do, we have to transfer again, we would take the source code and then the programmer has to go through the source code and then we, especially the two product managers would explain the functionality, would explain also that they understand a bit the source code and then they have to start from scratch."[1060] Asked if the knowledge was so special that nobody else could learn it, the answer was simply: "No, no, no, no..."[1061].

With low complexity of services and a relatively short time needed to imitate the existing center, we conclude that inimitability is low.[1062]

[1054] Interview 3:43.
[1055] Interview 3:81.
[1056] Interview 3:56.
[1057] Interview 2:25.
[1058] Interview 2:33; confirmed by interview 3:48.
[1059] Interview 1:40; confirmed by interview 3:64. However, it might be two years until the relationship is running smoothly (interview 3:73).
[1060] Interview 1:59; confirmed by interview 2:157.
[1061] Interview 1:34.
[1062] This seems to be justified for both consulting and software services even if one interviewee suggested that the consulting services are somewhat less complex ("Vielleicht besser überschaubar und nicht so breit gestreut von der Thematik her." (interview 2:19)).

(D) Finally, we evaluate *non-substitutability* with regard to the possibility of substituting services from Gamma Center with other services. The discussions with interviewees show that outsourcing is a possibility: *"If Hungary wouldn't work this would be the solution."*[1063] In case of problems with Gamma Center *"[w]e have to look immediately for a new developer. Somewhere in Germany or somewhere else but we definitely have to."*[1064] Even a forced closure of the center which required a fast substitution of the services would not be dramatic for Gamma (*"Da würde, so gesehen, nichts anbrennen."*[1065]). It was, however, pointed out that the knowledge transfer to an outsourcing partner would need time and resources (*"dann müssen Sie natürlich mit der Ausbildung beginnen, mit Know-How-Transfer bei Null anfangen"*[1066]).

With the consulting business having explicitly considered another alternative – namely outsourcing – and the software business judging it possible, we consider the non-substitutability of the services from Gamma Center to be low. In conclusion, with all indicators having low values, the strategic relevance of the center seems low.

6.3.2.2 ANALYSIS OF NETWORK EMBEDDEDNESS

To evaluate the network embeddedness of Gamma Center we consider (A) the number of relationships and (B) the frequency of changes to these relationships and discuss (C) the closeness of the relationships.

(A) As shown in Figure 6-9, Gamma Center maintains *relationships to only two other units* in the firm network. The subsidiary has only connections to the German headquarters and one additional German subsidiary. The remaining four international and three domestic subsidiaries do not interact with the Hungarian subsidiary.

(B) In addition, there have been no relationships added, and there are no plans to add more units to the service offshoring center. Thus, the *frequency of change* to the relationships is low.

[1063] Interview 1:32.
[1064] Interview 1:18. One interviewee, however, recalled a bad experience with an outsourcing partner that Gamma had a few years ago and warned against loss of control ("Sie hatten mit einer fremden Firma angefangen, etwas aufzubauen, aber es ist irgendwie schief gegangen. Und deswegen haben sie gesagt, eine fremde Firma, wo kein Einfluss, keine langjährigen Erfahrungen und so weiter vorhanden ist, das ist viel gefährlicher als eine Firma, die schon mehr oder weniger zu dieser Gruppe gehört, und durch langjährige Zusammenarbeit sehen wir, dass es funktioniert." (interview 3:60)).
[1065] Interview 2:157.
[1066] Interview 2:169; confirmed by interview 2:167.

(C) We analyze the *closeness* of the relationships with regard to (1) the adaptation of the partners and (2) the investment in one another.

1. The partners did *not adapt very much* to one another. For the consulting unit the relationship had always been a relationship over a long distance, and the level of adaptation was rather low: *"No, we always try to get in a direct contact, which was the same as Dresden."*[1067] For the software unit, adaptation was on about the same level; however, the interviewee noted an increased need for formalization of the relationship (*"Die Organisation hat sich geändert und es muss halt ein bisschen formaler werden, als es in der Vergangenheit war, wobei das jetzt aber nicht an der Organisation liegt und an den verschiedenen Gesellschaften, sondern daran, dass das in der Vergangenheit zu wenig formal gehandelt wurde."*[1068]). For the service offshoring subsidiary itself, adaptation was somewhat more intense because of the additional responsibilities that the management of a firm entails (*"Das war eine ziemlich neue Situation für mich. Weil ich als Geschäftsführer tätig wurde und weil ich allein die Entscheidungen treffen sollte."*[1069]) and because of the distance to the customers (*"... lernen, wie man über eine größere Entfernung zusammenarbeitet."*[1070]).

2. The only *investment* that was made was the invitation of few Hungarian programmers to Germany to allow them to get to know the headquarters better. However, there was no investment with regard to other financial or human resources: *"Yes, because we were inviting people here and also we were going down to work together, to write together the new specifications. This is the investment, but we are not doing investment in the sense that we will pay them a special ABAP or C++ training."*[1071]

Based on these indicators, we consider the closeness of the relationships to be low. Combined with a low number of relationships and a low frequency of change to the relationships, we also deem the network embeddedness low. Thus, the values of both strategic relevance and network embeddedness are located at their lower extremes. Therefore, we conclude that Gamma Center is a support center.

[1067] Interview 1:91.
[1068] Interview 1:147; confirmed by interview 1:149.
[1069] Interview 3:87.
[1070] Interview 3:87.
[1071] Interview 1:81.

6.3.3 COORDINATION MECHANISMS

6.3.3.1 OVERVIEW OF COORDINATION

Coordination for the consulting unit is mainly channeled through two product mangers at Gamma who work with the individual programmers at Gamma Center. In case of problems, they also involve the programmers' manager in Budapest, Mr. S. Within the software unit, there is an offshore coordinator – Mr. B. – who collects all the tasks that are to be carried out in Hungary and then hands them over to Mr. R. in Budapest. Thus, for both units, coordination is typically concentrated on these three people. Gamma considered installing a parallel position to Mr. B on the consulting side; however, that had not taken place when the interviews were conducted. The overall constellation is depicted in Figure 6-10 (with the position yet to be filled indicated by "NN").

The overall *coordination requirements* seem rather low. Interaction is irregular, *"there is no jour fixe"*[1072] but on an as-needed basis. For the software unit, meetings occur approximately every month.[1073] For both units, there are daily phone calls and email exchanges.[1074] The interactions typically do not involve many people but rather are restricted to one person from each side.[1075] The frequency of interaction between the units is rather low. For the consulting unit, there is one meeting per quarter involving one person from both sides.[1076] One interviewee indicated that coordination accounts for only about *"[o]ne or two per cent"*[1077] of the working time of the interaction managers. In total, the interaction between Gamma Germany and Gamma Center that affects around 60 people is coordinated by three managers who also have additional tasks, which results in a ratio of less than five per cent. Thus, coordination requirements can be considered rather low.

[1072] Interview 1:29.
[1073] Interview 3:103.
[1074] Interviews 2:153, 3:95.
[1075] Interviews 1:101, 2:151, 3:102.
[1076] Interview 1:97.
[1077] Interview 1:121.

6 – Results   281

```
                    ┌─────────┐
                    │  Gamma  │
                    └────┬────┘
              ┌──────────┴──────────┐
        ┌─────┴─────┐         ┌─────┴─────┐
        │ Consulting│         │ Software  │
        └─────▲─────┘         └─────▲─────┘
              │                     │
           ┌──┴──┐               ┌──┴──┐
           │ NN  │               │Mr. B│
           └──┬──┘               └──┬──┘
              │                     │
              └──────┐     ┌────────┘
                  ┌──┴──┐ ┌┴────┐
                  │Mr.S.│ │Mr.R.│
                  └──┬──┘ └──┬──┘
                     ▼       ▼
              ┌──────────┬──────────┐
              │Consulting│ Software │
              ├──────────┴──────────┤
              │    Gamma Center     │
              └─────────────────────┘
```

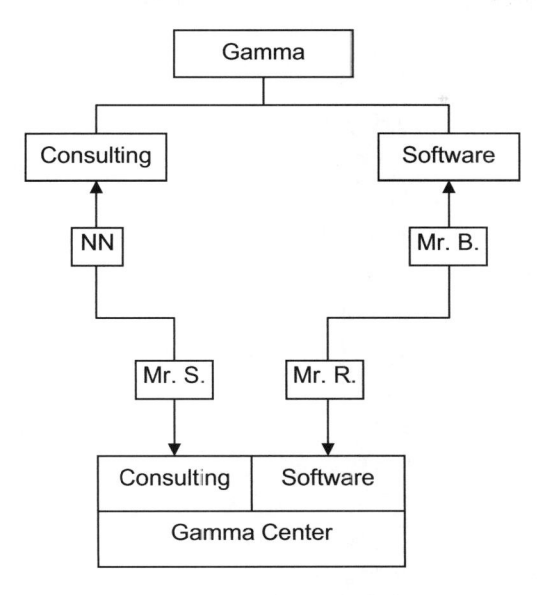

Figure 6-10: Coordination between Gamma and Gamma Center

6.3.3.2 STRUCTURAL COORDINATION MECHANISMS

We evaluate the *autonomy* of the Hungarian subunit with reference to (1) the consulting unit, (2) the software business, and (3) the differences of judgment between headquarters and the service offshoring subsidiary.

1. For the *consulting unit*, an interviewee at the headquarters stated: *"We give them [Gamma Center] the tasks."*[1078] Gamma Center is *"... not very free, they are free in how to develop the programmes, how to make the coding, but the results are defined from the product, the definitions are given by the product managers definitely."*[1079] Sometimes the Hungarian subsidiary makes suggestions for improvement of the services it delivers. However, these proposals have to be decided upon by the German product managers: *"They are sometimes doing their own ideas of new developments, so they make some suggestions on how we can develop our new products, but this is all!"*[1080]; *"[W]hen there is a suggestion for the development we say 'O.K. how expensive is it?' and 'Can we do this?', 'Do we have enough resources?' and*

[1078] Interview 1:8.
[1079] Interview 1:135.
[1080] Interview 1:135.

then we say 'O.K., yes or no' ... And if we say 'No', that's O.K. too."[1081] Conflicts appear to be rare, as the split of responsibilities seems to be clear.

2. The level of autonomy is similar for the *software unit* where the product management responsibility is in Germany and Gamma Center has only a consulting role (*"Die Produkthoheit sozusagen, das Produktmanagement liegt noch in der [Gamma A], ja. Also die [Gamma Center], und das wird auch so bleiben müssen, entscheidet jetzt nicht, was kommt in den Standard oder nicht. Natürlich müssen die beratend mitwirken"*[1082]). It was even mentioned that the less autonomy Gamma Center has, the better it is for the interaction since expectations are clearer (*"Die Freiheiten liegen ... nicht auf der produktinhaltlichen Ebene, die wird ja vorgegeben. Das und das muss rein. Und je knallharter das vorgegeben ist, umso besser ist es."*[1083]). With regard to the delivery of the service (i.e. the programming of the software product) there is no autonomy whatsoever with regard to the software tools used by Gamma Center (*"Alles, was das Produkt betrifft, da sind sie abhängig. Das kriegen sie vorgegeben. Die Technik, die Technologie, die Tools, die Entwicklungsumgebung, die Programmiersprachen, alles, was technisch ist, das kriegen sie vorgegeben."*[1084]).

3. There are some *differences between the perspectives* of the headquarters and the subsidiary. The service offshoring subsidiary sees its autonomy as limited, especially at the beginning (*"Am Anfang haben wir ziemlich wenig Freiheit gehabt und ziemlich wenig Verantwortung."*[1085]). Also, for the subsidiary the situation was not as clear and, more importantly, not as satisfying as for the headquarters. Respondents expressed discontent with the split of responsibilities in the initial phase (*"Die Verantwortlichkeiten waren nicht ganz gut verteilt. Es war nicht eindeutig, wer wofür verantwortlich ist. Deswegen war dieses Projekt nicht so gut, wie wir das geplant haben."*[1086]). The low degree of autonomy can also lead to technical problems when the headquarters impose a certain standard on the subsidiary that might not be fully compatible with the subsidiary's standards (*"Und dann hatte ich plötzlich ein McAfee [# software program] gekriegt, wo ich der einzige war,*

[1081] Interview 1:137.
[1082] Interview 2:33.
[1083] Interview 2:83.
[1084] Interview 2:95.
[1085] Interview 3:4.
[1086] Interview 3:48.

der ein McAfee gekriegt hat. Das sind so Sachen, wo Entscheidungen getroffen wurden, die sich woanders ganz komisch anhören."[1087]). In addition, the service offshoring subsidiary expects its own autonomy to be higher in the future – which seems to conflict with the view that was expressed by interviewees at the headquarters (*"Und wir sind gerade bei der Umstellung, also an der Schnittstelle hier. Das bedeutet, dass wir nicht nur die Programmierung, sondern dass wir eine größere Verantwortlichkeit, eine Produktverantwortlichkeit übernehmen."*[1088]; *"... des Produkts, [für] das wir jetzt die Verantwortung kriegen"*[1089]). The subsidiary has learned where to take the initiative and where to act autonomously (*"Lernen, wann soll ich das Telefon abnehmen, wann soll ich eine E-Mail schicken, wann soll ich nicht stören und allein die Entscheidungen treffen. Das war nicht immer ideal. Manchmal habe ich falsche Entscheidungen getroffen."*[1090]). However, its freedom is restricted by financial limitations (*"Eine Entscheidung zu treffen, das tun und machen wir gern, kein Problem. Wir haben es gelernt in den letzten Jahren. Bloß, wenn diese Entscheidungen finanzielle Auswirkungen haben, haben wir auch gelernt, dass wir solche Entscheidungen vorsichtig treffen müssen."*[1091]). Still today, the subsidiary needs to adjust towards a situation where there might be more autonomy and is currently struggling to implement this new way of thinking. For instance, a new employee explained that he sometimes discusses with his older colleagues about the adaptation and how the current mindset still needs to change to be ready to take over more responsibility (*"Etwas Anekdotenhaftes. Immer wieder habe ich in den letzten zwei Monaten hier Situationen erlebt, dass ich gefragt habe, warum ist das so und wie kann man das ändern, und in welche Richtung könnte man das jetzt weiterentwickeln. Ja, wir wissen, dass das ganz schlimm ist, aber die in [location of Gamma A] wollten das so. Oder anders 'Ja, wir könnten es auch anders machen, aber wir müssten sie überzeugen, dass sie das bestellen. Ja, die werden das sowieso nicht bestellen.' und so was. Dann sage ich: 'Halt. Neu denken. Wir werden die Produktverantwortung haben.' Dann kommt ein bisschen so ein Licht auf: 'Ach ja, dann können wir das auch noch so machen. Das da könnten wir noch einbauen.' und dann sage ich 'Ok, ok, was kostet das?' 50 Manntage. Darüber reden wir schon lange. Das geht*

[1087] Interview 3:107.
[1088] Interview 3:54.
[1089] Interview 3:43.
[1090] Interview 3:87.
[1091] Interview 3:108.

doch. Und dieses Umdenken ja wir können eigentlich selbst über 50 Manntage entscheiden und dann wird es besser, das müssen wir lernen."[1092]).

We see the autonomy of the service offshoring subsidiary as relatively low, but in light of the plans for the future, it seems set to grow. For the current situation, we still consider it to be low.

6.3.3.3 TECHNOCRATIC COORDINATION MECHANISMS

Within the category of *technocratic coordination mechanisms*, we consider the level of (A) standardization and (B) formalization.[1093]

(A) We discuss the degree of *standardization* with regard to the use of standardized processes or standard schedules. Currently, there are *no standardized processes* or standard schedules by which services are delivered to headquarters: *"We decide when we want to have a new release, there's no standard process."*[1094]; and the schedule of delivery *"is always individual standard."*[1095] Also the relationships between different departments is not standardized: *"We have no general structure between Germany and Hungary. This is...each department is doing this on its own."*[1096] We thus conclude that the degree of standardization is low.

(B) We now turn to the evaluation of *formalization*. There are development guidelines in Gamma that also apply to the Hungarian subsidiary. In addition, there are programming handbooks that are published by the manufacturer of the ERP program; however, these do not describe the coordination of the interfaces between the headquarters and the subsidiary: *"We have a development guideline in the [Gamma] and the topic is that there are special SAP guidelines to develop SAP products and this is familiar to every developer in the SAP area and if there is a new developer, the Hungarian colleagues take care of that they know these guidelines, so we don't bother about these guidelines."*[1097] Thus, the degree of formalization is also low.

[1092] Interview 3:169.
[1093] This section is structured slightly differently from the descriptions of technocratic mechanisms in other cases. This is because in the Gamma case we found perception gaps between the headquarters and the service offshoring subsidiary and therefore report individually on these.
[1094] Interview 1:147; confirmed by interview 1:145.
[1095] Interview 1:151.
[1096] Interview 1:71, confirmed in interviews 1:73 and 3:85.
[1097] Interview 1:141.

For future use, Gamma is currently implementing a standardized and formalized process for the relationship between Gamma Center and the German headquarters. This process will be based on a folder per project that has a standard structure and in which all information relating to the project shall be stored.[1098] This documentation is intended to completely describe the volume and the expected outcome of the project and is developed in discussions between the provider and the customer of a specific service.[1099] Only when the complete scope of the project is agreed upon, will work start. This is very different from the current, more iterative process that is not documented in detail but relies more on personal interaction.[1100] The structure of the templates that describe the standardized process steps can be seen in Table 6-5.

Table 6-5: Template for project folder in Gamma (Source: Delta internal document (translated))

Main step	Sub-steps
Request for development	Product idea
	Service idea
	Presentation
	Release
Feasibility study	Description
	Team members
	Result
	Release

[1098] Interviews 2:55; 2:65.
[1099] Interview 2:65.
[1100] Interview 2:79.

Main step	Sub-steps
Development plan	Book of requirements
	Sub-tasks
	Project plans
Development	Acceptance
Reports	Internal reports
	Controlling
Release for sales	Presentation
	Release
Quality management	Project progress indicators
	Project reviews
Internal release	Training plan
	Training documentation
Appendices	(no sub-steps)

One interviewee from the headquarters stressed the importance of moving towards more standardization and formalization. He pointed to the advantages that Gamma has from a recently finalized process of gaining an ISO certificate for the quality and reliability of its processes.[1101] The interviewee also stressed that standards and formalization can and should be used independent of the type and size of the project[1102] and that official guidelines for software development can enhance the quality of the results;[1103] however he acknowledged that Gamma is still in the process of implementing the new processes and

---

[1101] Interview 2:51.
[1102] Interviews 2:53; 2:61; 2:63.
[1103] Interview 2:99.

that not everything is working as it should since the employees are slow to abandon old habits of personal coordination (*"Da passiert jetzt noch vieles per Telefon, oder per E-Mail, informal. Das ist noch nicht alles so dokumentiert, wie es sein sollte, auch von [Gamma A]-Seite."*[1104]).

Subsidiary representatives were sceptical of the *benefits* of the current standardization project because standards are not always clearly defined (*"Die Prozesse standardisieren, das ist wichtig. Aber wenn diese Standards nicht gut definiert sind, dann kann das mehr vom Nachteil als vom Vorteil sein. Deswegen lieber noch ohne Standard arbeiten, und wir müssen noch solche Standards finden, die uns helfen können, aber die müssen alle gut sein. Wenn wir einen guten gefunden haben, dann einbinden und dann ergänzen."*[1105]). They recognized the general benefits of standardization and the definition of well-defined interfaces (*"hier und hier sind solche Schnitte, wo ziemlich wenig Komplikationen oder gut definierte Schnittstellen zwischen Gruppe existieren."*[1106]). They suggested observing which practices work best and then introducing them as standards (*"Wir müssen beachten, was wirklich gute Praxis ist. Und das dann zum Standard machen."*[1107]; *"Wir versuchen herauszufinden, wo klemmt es am besten und dort müssen wir uns etwas ausdenken, um das ein bisschen besser zu organisieren. Und dann, wenn das gut läuft, konzentrieren wir uns auf andere Bereiche, wo es nicht ganz gut funktioniert. So, dass ich an meinem Schreibtisch sitze und versuche, verschiedene Standards herauszuarbeiten und dann zwangsmäßig verwenden, also das funktioniert nicht."*[1108]).

Interviewees from Gamma Center also complained about incomplete formalization (*"Leider ist es mehr oder weniger eine Formalität. Weil es gibt 12 Punkte und nur zwei werden ausgefüllt und die anderen bleiben leer ... oder Copy und Paste."*[1109]). In addition, an existing template is often used in very different forms (*"Es gibt ein Template. Dieses Template ist mehr oder weniger veraltet. Manchmal überhaupt nicht. Wir kriegen manchmal eine pdf-Form, also nicht in einem Word-Dokument, sondern Microsoft Visio, in dieser Frage müssen wir uns noch besser einigen, also in welcher Form die kommen müssen und welche Punkte drin sein müssen. Wir können natürlich auch mit unterschiedlichen Formen arbeiten, aber es wäre besser, wenn wir eine einheitliche Form hätten."*[1110]). Subsidiary representatives were more

---

[1104] Interview 2:57; confirmed by interview 2:59.
[1105] Interview 3:186.
[1106] Interview 3:54; confirmed by interview 3:28.
[1107] Interview 3:188.
[1108] Interview 3:189.
[1109] Interview 3:154-155, confirmed in interview 3:149 and interview 3:159.
[1110] Interview 3:159.

open to the idea of developing standards incrementally and not for the purpose of fulfilling ISO norms.[1111]

We thus conclude that standardization and formalization are still on a low level. They seem set to increase in the future, but at this stage it is not possible to see the extent to which the ongoing standardization project will be successfully implemented.

6.3.3.4 Output-based Coordination Mechanisms

We now consider the degree of *output control*. Output control is done on the basis of requirement specifications (*"Pflichtenhefte"*[1112]) that are exchanged before a new project starts. In some cases, these specifications even make personal interaction completely unnecessary (*"Manchmal kriegen wir eine Pflichtenheft, bei der wir nichts fragen müssen, da wissen wir sofort, was wir machen müssen. Alles hängt davon ab, wie tief wir uns in einem bestimmten Bereich schon eingearbeitet haben. Dort wo wir schon Kenntnisse haben, genügt ein halber Satz."*[1113]). However, one interviewee from the subsidiary argued that the specifications are often too vague and of varying quality (*"Die Qualität ist sehr, sehr variabel"*[1114]). The evaluation of results does not follow a specific scheme but is rather based on the judgment of the departments in the headquarters (*"Thumb up or down"*[1115]). Based on these considerations we argue that the level of output control is medium.

6.3.3.5 Personal Coordination Mechanisms

With regard to *personal coordination mechanisms,* we analyze (A) direct personal coordination, (B) visits, (C) transfers, and (D) cultural coordination.

We evaluate *direct personal coordination* based on the (1) reasons for using it and (2) the media in use.

1. Direct personal coordination is driven by the fact that the founder of Gamma Center has *good personal relationships* to people within Gamma Germany and he personally brought the relevant knowledge to the subsidiary (*"das liegt jetzt an der Person des einen Mitarbeiters in Ungarn, der Herr [name of person], das war dieser freie Mitarbeiter der [Gamma A], der die [Gamma A] schon länger kennt, und der

---

[1111] Interviews 3:157; 3:188-189.
[1112] Interview 3:167.
[1113] Interview 3:149; confirmed by interviews 1:152-153; 1:156-157.
[1114] Interview 3:148; also confirmed in interviews 3:147 and 1:149.
[1115] Interview 1:165; also confirmed in interviews 2:101 and 2:103.

> *wesentlich bei einem der Hauptprodukte der [Gamma A], diesen Fertigungsleitstand mit entwickelt hat und programmiert hat. Und dort die Basislogik, die Standardlogik kennt von diesem Produkt."*[1116]).

2. Both sides agreed that the *most important medium* for direct personal coordination are phone calls and e-mails. In addition, Gamma Center recently acquired video conferencing facilities.[1117] Still, phone calls and e-mails are the two communication channels that are mainly used for direct coordination (*"Da passiert jetzt noch vieles per Telefon, oder per E-Mail, informal."*[1118]).

Direct personal coordination is used frequently to guide the relationship between headquarters and the service offshoring subsidiary. However, it involves only few, designated people. Thus, we conclude that it is of medium importance.

(B) We now turn to visits and consider (1) the frequency and length of visits, (2) reasons for visits, and (3) the perception of visits by headquarters and the subsidiary.

1. Visits occur approximately every three to four weeks,[1119] involve generally one to two persons, and last between one and three to four days (*"Myself, more a day, [names of project managers] sometimes up to three or four days, but this is always less than a week."*[1120]).

2. The most important *reason* for visits is the coordination of project work and the need for more intense collaboration on specific projects. There are regular coordination meetings (*"Jour-Fix, die wir jeden Monat ein Mal machen"*[1121]), and there are ad-hoc meetings for the resolution of problems or the initiation or closure of a project.[1122] One interviewee explained that *"only video and telephone conference are not enough."*[1123] In addition, some new employees in Hungary visit the German headquarters for several weeks as an introduction (*"dass neue Mitarbeiter, die dann für die [Gamma A] gearbeitet haben, erst mal einige Wochen in [location of*

[1116] Interview 2:29; confirmed by interview 2:31.
[1117] Interview 3:81.
[1118] Interview 2:57; confirmed by interviews 2:65; 2:75; 2:153; 3:95.
[1119] Interviews 3:99; 3:100.
[1120] Interview 1:169; confirmed by interviews 2:113, 2:115, and 3:93. It was also added that visits have been made feasible recently by the emergence of low-cost airlines (interview 3:81).
[1121] Interview 3:103.
[1122] Interviews 2:115; 2:119; 3:160.
[1123] Interview 1:6; confirmed by interview 2:119.

Gamma in Germany] waren und ausgebildet wurden und dann zurück sind"[1124]). In total, around 15 people from Germany have so far visited the Hungarian subsidiary.[1125]

3. Visits are *judged somewhat differently* by the headquarters and the subsidiary: An interviewee from the headquarters said that there should be a shift to more formal procedures to replace travel (*"Aus meiner Sicht, noch, Stand heute, zu viel [visits]. Wir sind natürlich in der Anfangsphase, liegt sicherlich auch daran, aber es ist sicherlich ein Zustand, der so nicht bleiben kann."*[1126]). An interviewee at the subsidiary expressed the wish to have even more personal contact (*"Es wäre sehr wichtig, dass wir weiterhin viel reisen, viel miteinander zu tun haben, und vielleicht auch mal für Monate einen Austausch machen, in beide Richtungen."*[1127]).

Thus, on the one hand, there is a low frequency of visits and only few people involved in travel. On the other hand, there are some few visits for training purposes that are substantially longer (several weeks). While these visits can help in the longer term by building personal relationships and increasing cultural coordination, they do not directly serve the coordination of service delivery. Therefore, we consider the degree of visits to be low.

(C) There are no *transfers* except for the general manager of the subsidiary.[1128] We thus consider the role of transfers to be of low significance.

(D) With regard to *cultural coordination*, we discuss (1) the development of a "team spirit" across units, (2) how cultural coordination helps in daily interaction, and (3) how tensions adversely affect coordination.

1. Interviewees expressed that it is important for them to have a common set of norms and values and to have a "team spirit" that crosses locations. Some people were willing to invest in relationships to gain a better understanding and appreciation of the other side: *"And then just to try to set up a kind of a friendly environment we went out with them to have a glass of beer and then to show them that you are interested in Hungarian culture. For example, the first time when [name of project*

[1124] Interview 2:110; confirmed by interviews 3:4; 3:89.
[1125] Interview 3:182.
[1126] Interview 2:113; confirmed by interview 2:115.
[1127] Interview 3:137.
[1128] Interviews 1:166-167; 1:189; 2:109.

manager] and I spent in Hungary we said 'O.K. it's 17:00 o'clock or 18:00 o'clock, we want to go to a supermarket our plane will leave in three hours, we want to buy some Hungarian food and some Hungarian drinks and then they went with us and said we can recommend this ... and this is very good...and this is very good ... And I think that this helped them that we are interested in how they live and so on ... I think this is extremely important. Not that you say 'O.K. You are the cheap developers, we are the big Germans to explain to you how to do it', so this...together we have to do this and this helps ..."[1129] Subsidiary representatives also pointed to the commonalities between German and Hungarian national culture (*"Ja, Ungarn hat mehr oder weniger eine gemeinsame Geschichte mit Österreich, also die Österreich-Ungarische Monarchie. Deshalb sind die Unterschiede wohl nicht so gravierend groß"*[1130]) and the desire to invest in the relationships (*"In einem Raum, in einem Zimmer sitzen, zusammen essen gehen oder Bier trinken, das finde ich sehr, sehr wichtig"*[1131]). Due to the fact that the founder of Gamma Center had worked for Gamma in Germany, he knew many employees personally and considered this an important factor in establishing good relationships between the locations (*"Als ich weggekommen bin, waren 20 Mitarbeiter bei [Gamma A] und mit allen diesen Mitarbeitern hatte ich ein sehr gutes Verhältnis."*[1132]).

2. How better understanding can *help in the coordination of daily interaction* was expressed in a statement by one interviewee from the headquarters. He explained that better understanding of his colleagues in Hungary helped him to react more adequately in his interaction with them (*"I think you have to be down there, you have to see how they work. ... then you will understand them a bit better."*[1133]). Another interviewee from the headquarters also acknowledged the importance of mutual acceptance; however, he judged adherence to agreed upon processes to be more significant (*"Unabhängig von dem, wie sich die Menschen untereinander verstehen. Die müssen einfach den Prozess umsetzen. ... Die Ungarn bleiben Ungarn und die Deutschen bleiben Deutsche. Sie brauchen so gemeinsame Regeln, an die sich beide halten"*[1134]).

[1129] Interview 1:171.
[1130] Interview 3:131.
[1131] Interview 3:145.
[1132] Interview 3:19; confirmed by interview 3:70.
[1133] Interview 1:171; confirmed by interview 3:19.
[1134] Interview 2:133.

3. Interviewees from both headquarters and the subsidiary admitted that there are still *tensions* and that they have to deal with misunderstandings (*"Worte, Mimik, Gestik, Augendrehen, Augenraunen."*[1135]) which also affect behavior and lead to problems with coordination (*"Ja, ja, und so, wir sind wieder schuld, und hat uns ja keiner gesagt."*[1136]). In addition, the feeling of belonging to the same team is not yet fully developed (*"Sehr oft kommt der 'die-da-Gedanke' hoch. Aber viel weniger, als es für mich natürlich wäre."*[1137]). Interviewees from Gamma Center felt that German customers were demanding a higher quality than they were able to deliver themselves and than what was actually needed (*"Und die versuchen also überflüssig solche hohe Qualität von uns anzufordern, damit die beweisen können, na siehst du, die Ungarn können das nicht schaffen. Das, was die geliefert haben, ist nicht so gut, wie wir das erwarten. Und das ärgert uns, weil unsere Mitarbeiter gesehen haben, wie die Leute in [Gamma A German location] eigentlich arbeiten. Sie haben ein bestimmtes Niveau, aber sie erfordern von uns ein so hohes Niveau und wir fragen uns, wieso plötzlich."*[1138]). This might have been driven by the fear in Germany of losing programmer jobs to Hungary (*"[interviewee 1] Es gibt schon Spannungen, wir spüren es, das ist ganz natürlich, wir verstehen uns auch, die Tatsache, dass hier in Ungarn ein Entwicklungs-Zentrum aufgebaut ist, macht Angst, viele Entwickler in Deutschland, die sehen ihre eigene Zukunft nicht so klar. [interviewee 2] In einem Jahr werden sie keine Entwickler mehr sein."*[1139]). Subsidiary representatives also acknowledged that they might need to give up some established customs when they grow further; e.g. meeting with all employees for lunch.[1140] However, they also recognized that this was not affecting their relationships with Gamma but that it was more a natural phenomenon for a growing firm.[1141]

Thus, it seems that there are individual efforts to build personal relationships and increase normative integration and that employees in both the headquarters and the subsidiary have recognized potential payoffs. However, there are still many tensions that prevent cultural coordination from reaching higher levels. Moreover, there are no planned efforts such as trainings or the establishment of common corporate values that

---

[1135] Interview 2:131.
[1136] Interview 2:131.
[1137] Interview 3:137.
[1138] Interview 3:142.
[1139] Interview 3:138-139.
[1140] Interview 3:132-134.
[1141] Interview 3:135

could help in increasing cultural coordination. We therefore consider cultural coordination to be at medium level.

6.3.3.6 COMPARATIVE ANALYSIS OF COORDINATION MECHANISMS

Personal coordination mechanisms play a significant role in the coordination of the service offshoring subsidiary. Direct personal coordination, visits and cultural coordination seem to be the main principles that are used to coordinate the subsidiary. According to interviewees these personal coordination mechanisms play an important role in every project (*"Meiner Meinung nach hat jedes Projekt kritische Teile. Dann ist der persönliche Kontakt viel wichtiger als die Formalisierung."*[1142]). Technocratic mechanisms do not play an important role, although there are some changes planned that might lead to a different picture within the next years: In addition to the coordination mechanisms that are currently in use, there are plans to introduce more formal coordination. Currently, most coordination processes do not rely on formalization. However, ongoing projects have already determined a standardized approach that lays out the necessary steps for all projects.

6.3.4 DISCUSSION OF CASE

Evaluation of appropriateness of propositions for individual case

The results of the case are compared to the propositions in Table 6-6. We display the original proposition, the empirical result and indicate whether or not we find agreement with the proposition. The original proposition stems from the description of our typology, the empirical result from the discussion of the case. We represent the values low (L), medium (M), or high (H) by squares of different sizes.

Table 6-6: Evaluation of suitability of propositions for support center

Coordination mechanism	Original proposition	Empirical result	Agreement with proposition	Remark
Extent of coordination requirements	▪ (L)	▪ (L); only few people involved in coordination	Proposition initially supported	--

---

[1142] Interview 3:162; confirmed by interview 3:163.

Coordination mechanism	Original proposition	Empirical result	Agreement with proposition	Remark
Degree of autonomy	■-■ (L-M); services are ordered from the customer on a case-by-case basis	■ (L); HQ sees autonomy as low; subsidiary claims more autonomy for future	Proposition initially supported	I1: Subsidiary desires to have more autonomy in the future
Degree of standardization	■ (L); as support center is used on a case-by-case basis	■ (L). Currently low, almost non-existing: however, implementation of formalized measures also brings standardization	Proposition initially supported	I2: Shows how service offshoring subsidiary is changing coordination mechanisms
Degree of formalization	■ (L); few standardized cases do not require formalization	■ (L). Currently low, almost non-existing; however, implementation of more formal approaches planned	Proposition initially supported	I3: Shows how service offshoring subsidiary is changing coordination mechanisms
Degree of output control	■ (M); low strategic relevance does not justify resource-intense behavior control	■ (M); output control is regularly used; however, not to the full extent	Proposition initially supported	I4: Output control and personal coordination work complementarily

6 – Results

Coordination mechanism	Original proposition	Empirical result	Agreement with proposition	Remark
Degree of personal direct coordination	■-■ (L-M); execution of strategically less relevant services needs little direct interaction	■ (M); somewhat higher than expected	Proposition initially supported	E1: Some form of coordination will always be needed and direct personal coordination seems the fallback solution in any case
Number of visits	■ (L); low number of visits, short duration per visit	■ (L); low number of visits, short duration per visit	Proposition initially supported	--
Number of transfers	■ (L); low number of transfers; potentially only management	■ (L); only one transfer, only management from abroad	Proposition initially supported	--
Importance of culture-based coordination	■ (L); low level of normative integration	■ (M); medium level; based on personal relationships	Proposition not supported	E2: Cultural coordination higher than expected because of personal efforts to make relationship work (not supported through corporate measures)
E: Possible explanation for difference; I: Idea, new thought; -- no additional comment				

There were some deviations from our propositions which we want to discuss here:

- E1: The degree of direct personal coordination is slightly higher than we had expected. One explanation for this difference can be that some form of coordination will always be needed to cover coordination needs. Direct personal coordination is the coordination mechanism that requires the lowest effort to implement and can also work as a fallback solution in the event that other coordination mechanisms do not work as intended. For instance, if an exception to a prescribed, standardized behavior occurs, it will most likely be resolved through direct personal coordination. Thus, it seems justified that its level is higher than expected.

- E2: We also found the level of cultural coordination to be higher than expected. There are two conflicting tendencies in this area: On the one hand, there are very few efforts to create shared values and goals across the locations. Thus, our initial expectation was supported with regard to the dimension of a planned cultural coordination. However, we underestimated the influence of personal efforts to make relationships work (unplanned cultural coordination). These efforts lead to personal investments in time and the wish to get to know people from the other location beyond the pure working level. Besides, the fact that the current relationship manager within Gamma Center worked for a long time in Germany has led to many personal relationships that are maintained to the present day and that facilitate everyday interaction. Thus, cultural coordination in this case is more a function of personal initiative and historical circumstances than of a planned and conscious effort for normative integration.

Presentation of additional information gained from the individual case

We have found some additional information that we consider worth discussing:

- I1: In the future, Gamma wants to use its Hungarian location as a springboard to sell Gamma's products and services on the local market. Local market here refers not only to Hungary, but rather the entire Eastern European region, which is why the new CEO was hired. However, currently, there are only two people hired in the subsidiary who could work as consultants with local clients. Currently, the local sales level is still very low, the main task of the subsidiary being the execution of the offshored services. As Gamma Center slowly becomes more focused on the local market, the local network will be more important. Therefore, it has some autonomy with regard to acquiring new local contracts and extending the local business ("*Die Freiheiten liegen auf der Geschäftsebene*"[1143]; "*Da dürfen sie alles machen, was ihren Gewinn optimiert und das Geschäft ausbaut.*"[1144]).

- I2/I3: A change of coordination mechanisms is planned. Gamma Center plans to introduce more standardization and formalization following the introduction of an ISO standard that requires the documentation of a firm's processes. However, these standards are typically not introduced for their own sake. Rather, we can assume that Gamma intends to achieve better cooperation between its different units by introducing a standardized process.[1145] However, as the project is just starting to be implemented, we can only see the first reactions that range from very positive to more hesitant opinions on the introduction of more technocratic coordination mechanisms.[1146] For now, we just take this as an indication that coordination mechanisms can change over time. We will discuss these changes in more depth in our cross-case analysis.

- I4: The case shows how coordination mechanisms work complementarily. While there is reliance on output control, interviewees explained that they will switch to personal coordination and set up a visit to solve problems ("*... so this is why we are flying down to Hungary because we have to do it together and normally we have what we want and then we have to do the specifications, sometimes together and then they develop.*"[1147]).

6.4 CASE 4: SPECIALIZED CONTRIBUTOR DELTA

6.4.1 COMPANY OVERVIEW

Presentation of MNC and the business unit under consideration

Delta is a large German software development company. It offers business software that helps its customers to administer business processes electronically. This kind of software is typically labeled enterprise resource planning system. Delta currently employs about 35,000 people in more than 50 countries worldwide and has annual revenues of some 8 billion EUR, of which around 70 per cent are from the sales and maintenance of

---

[1143] Interview 2:83.
[1144] Interview 2:97.
[1145] Of course, there can be many reasons for the implementation of such a standard such as pressure from customers that require their suppliers to be certified. However, the underlying belief is that certification leads to better quality of processes.
[1146] See discussion of technocratic measures in section 6.3.3.3.
[1147] Interview 1:159.

software products, the rest from services such as consulting and training.[1148] The company has a functional organization that is split into the areas research, product development, sales, service, finance, and human resources. Our focus is on the development department that is responsible for the definition of the requirements for new products, the definition of the software architecture and the subsequent coding. The development department carries out most of the development tasks itself, but it also employs some domestic and international external providers. In addition, Delta has several partnerships with software and hardware providers to ensure that its products are compatible with its partners' products, to benefit from references from its partners, and to be able to offer a more complex product offering together with its partners. These partnerships are extremely common in the IT industry, as very often firms are highly specialized and the needs of a customer can only be covered by the bundled offering from several providers.

Description of history and motivation of offshoring situation

Delta was originally very much focused on Germany as development location. The export of software was not restricted by tariffs, and transport costs were insignificant compared to the value of the software. Thus, Delta initially saw no need to set up foreign subsidiaries with the exception of local sales offices that were responsible for sales and service in foreign markets. However, with steady growth of the firm and the market offering, Delta had to increasingly integrate new knowledge into its products. For several reasons it was necessary to increase the international distribution of software development activities:

1. Delta wanted to set up development centers in the biggest, most important markets in Europe and the U.S. This was done to be closer to the local markets and to find out earlier about important trends and changes in customer requirements.

2. Also, Delta acquired some other German and non-German companies with products complementary to its own portfolio. The locations of these companies had subsequently to be integrated into Delta's network of national and international subsidiaries.

[1148] All financial information is taken from Delta's annual report for the fiscal year 2005. Additional information stems from Delta's company presentation (available online).

3. Finally, Delta was interested in hiring well-trained programmers to cope with increasing demand for its products. The focus was not only on Germany, but increasingly on typical "offshore" locations such as Eastern Europe, India, and China. An important argument was also to reduce labor cost which is the most significant share of all the cost types for a software company.

Delta has bundled its development activities in development centers that are named according to the country in which they are located. In total, Delta has seven development centers that are located in the U.S., India, China, Canada, Israel, Hungary, and Bulgaria. The subsidiary in focus here, the Center Bulgaria, is located in Sofia, the capital of Bulgaria, a country of roughly eight million inhabitants in South-East Europe. During socialist times in which responsibility for industries was split over the entire sphere of Soviet influence, Bulgaria was – together with neighbouring Romania – responsible for the development of information technology systems. The knowledge that was acquired during that period still carries forward until today and explains the strong status of information technology in the local education systems.

A group of students at the IT faculty of Sofia University founded the software company ForDelta in 1998 and started to develop software that attracted Delta's attention when it was looking for a potential acquisition target to add that specific knowledge to its portfolio. The local company had developed an application server which is a software program that serves to run other programs. Thus, the software does not perform business tasks itself but facilitates running other programs. It also helps to distribute applications over a computer network, so that people in different places can use one program together. Delta entered the Bulgarian market in 2000 by acquiring that part of ForDelta with its about 60 employees that was developing the software product. The other part of ForDelta remained with its local owners and still works as an independent company. Initially, Delta kept the Bulgarian subsidiary as an independent company that continued to promote its software product as a self-contained market offering. From 2001 to 2002, the subsidiary was more closely integrated into Delta and while still offering its rebranded product to external customers, it increasingly adapted the software to internal requirements. However, the application server was still an independent product and the requirements for future developments were primarily determined by external customers' needs and by the technical standard that was developed by an international standard setting organization for this type of software product. Therefore, Delta's internal requirements were often not considered in their totality so that the software had to be adapted at the end of the development cycle. This was not only more costly but also could cause delays. Thus, in 2003, the subsidiary was integrated in Delta's network of development centers and the product was no longer sold to external customers but tightly integrated into Delta's product offering.

Description of services provided by service offshoring subsidiary

Today, the center – which we will call Delta Center – still maintains the development of the application server. Besides, it has taken over responsibility for other services that surround software development. Today, Delta Center has around 300 employees and is one of the largest software companies in Bulgaria. The location Sofia was not specifically selected but was added to Delta's network because of the acquisition. The services that Delta Center provides are carried out together with Delta's headquarters in Germany. Besides this relationship, Delta Center maintains an infrequent relationship with the Center Israel (Delta IL) for cooperation on some projects. Both Delta Center and Delta IL belong to the group of development centers mentioned above. Organizationally, they belong to the human resources department, but their direct supervisors are the different subunits within the software development unit. This constellation can be characterized as in Figure 6-11.

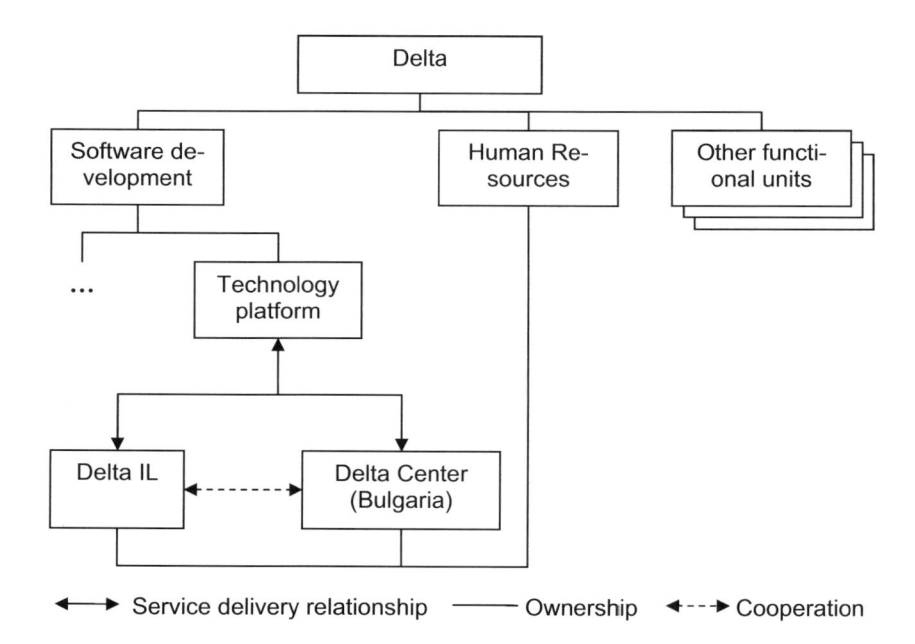

Figure 6-11: Service delivery within Delta's network

The focus of our considerations is on the software development unit within Delta. The software development unit is located in Germany, but makes extensive use of the development centers we discussed above. The technology platform unit is responsible for the development of a platform that is the used as a basis for other products in Delta and it has assigned the main responsibility for this development to the center in Bulgaria. Delta Center works together with the technology platform unit in Delta Germany as one integrated department. Thus, projects are staffed across locations depending on the availability and specific knowledge of the people available in both places. In some instances, the development center in Bulgaria cooperates with its counterpart in Israel (which also works for the development department in Germany).

Delta Center is organized as shown in Figure 6-12. Every service offering is organized in its own department, each of which is led by one manager in Germany and one manager in Bulgaria. The departments are the following:

- *Application development:* This group develops the core product. It receives the new requirements from other units in Delta through the technology platform unit in Germany and then converts them into new product development plans that are eventually build into the next version of the software.

- *Lifecycle management:* This group develops all the surrounding procedures and technologies that are necessary to integrate all the different components into the final product, and to enable it to run in the customer setting.

- *Abstraction layer:* Based on the application server, this department develops an interface that allows for easy and automated access to the functionalities of the application server. That way, development of applications that use the server, is facilitated.

- *Workflow automation:* For the repeated execution of standardized tasks, the workflow automation group develops tools such as templates and forms that allow users to design collaborative business processes on the basis of the application server.

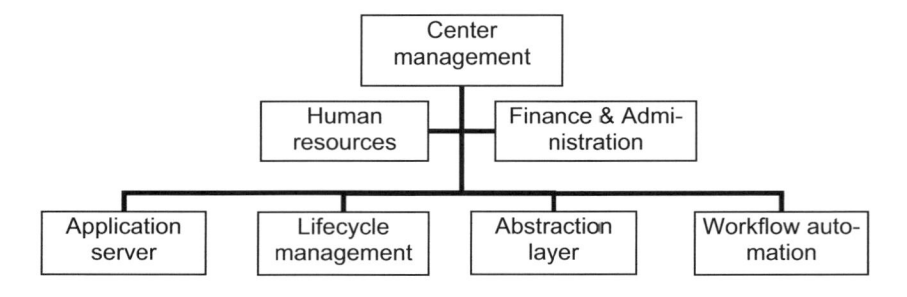

```
                    Center
                  management
                      │
        ┌─────────────┼─────────────┐
        │             │             │
     Human                    Finance & Admi-
    resources                   nistration
        │
   ┌────────┬─────────┬─────────┬──────────┐
Application  Lifecycle  Abstraction  Workflow auto-
  server    management    layer        mation
```

Figure 6-12: Organization chart Delta Center

6.4.2 TYPE OF SERVICE OFFSHORING SUBSIDIARY

6.4.2.1 ANALYSIS OF STRATEGIC RELEVANCE

We will now analyze the strategic relevance of the services by (A) their value, (B) their rareness, (C) their inimitability, and (D) their non-substitutability. Despite its size, Delta Center provides a focused and homogeneous set of software development services and surrounding services such as testing that are needed to support the core development service. Thus, all services can be considered together.

(A) We discuss the *value* of the service with regard to (1) the importance for the headquarters, (2) their role for the entire corporation, (3) the competitors' perspective on Delta Center, and (4) a potential loss of the center.

1. The center's *importance* is expressed in attributes such as "mission-critical" or "decisive" that interviewees gave the center. They emphasized that it is not just an "extended workbench" but produces a critical technology component (*"Also in dem Sinne absolut mission-critical, nicht verlängerte Werkbank, nicht Auslagern von Test und Support"*[1149]; *"Das war das erste Mal in dem Sinne, dass wir wirklich eine entscheidende, damals aber nicht völlig akzeptierte Technologie-Grundlage woanders gemacht haben."*[1150]). Even in comparison to other development centers, for instance, the center in India, the center in Bulgaria was of critical importance for Delta since it had the responsibility for an entire part of Delta's product (*"Indien hatte damals nicht so einen hochkritischen Impact. D.h. da wurden Sachen gemacht, die man halt ausgelagert hat, die aber nicht so im Herzen des Produkts waren."*[1151];

[1149] Interview 10:2.
[1150] Interview 11:1.
[1151] Interview 10:4.

"Bulgarien war da halt sehr, sehr anders, weil hier wirklich das Gesamtprodukt da war."[1152]). This importance stems mainly from the fact that the services Delta Center provides are the basis for an entire range of products that Delta offers its customers (*"Also im Prinzip die Basis für alle Java-Produkte [von Delta]"*[1153]). An indicator of the high value of Delta Center's services is the potential that these services give Delta for offering integrated solutions. While the software product that Delta Center develops could in principle also be purchased from another vendor,[1154] it is the internal development that allows for the integration of Delta Center's software product with Delta's other products (*"But there is a lot of value that comes from the platform; from the other side, there is nothing we are behind, let's say, to the competitors. It's actually, we are in many things, we try to innovate"*[1155]). Besides the services actually provided, the employees of Delta Center were also very valuable to Delta (*"Aber inhaltlich waren die Leute einfach top. Unglaublich gut. ... Preisgefüge gut. Die Fluktuation extrem gering. Also, eigentlich ideale Zustände."*[1156]).

2. The value of the services that Delta Center delivers is reflected by the fact that solutions that were initially developed in the Bulgarian center are now used in the *entire corporation* and that they are crucial for the release of new versions of Delta's products (*"[The solution] is company wide. Everybody will benefit from it. It is one of the release criterias of [Delta's product]"*[1157]). Delta Center thus developed and maintained its own set of software products (*"It was developed here, the [name of product] suite. It was developed here initially and still maintained here. The ownership shifted from within the Java Server technology to another group and right now the responsible manager is in [the headquarters], for example, but he has a bigger group that takes care about everything, all the tools."*[1158]).

3. When we asked interviewees if *competitors* could be inclined to build up a similar center in Sofia, it was was suggested that this might actually happen to weaken Delta. However, Delta Center is not considered so critical to Delta that

---

[1152] Interview 11:1.
[1153] Interview 10:16; confirmed in interview 10:18.
[1154] We discuss this below with regard to non-substitutability.
[1155] Interview 12:8.
[1156] Interview 10:6.
[1157] Interview 13:162.
[1158] Interview 13:164.

it could not compensate a competitor's attack on the center (*"Außer die wollen [Delta] da schwächen, aber dafür ist es auch nicht entscheidend genug."*[1159]).

4. A *potential loss of the center* and its services would lead to serious problems (*"Das wäre schon ein mächtiges Problem. Das ist schon kritischer Bestandteil."*[1160]). Not only would these problems be felt internally, but they would also create difficulties in customer service and would lead to a loss of about a year and a half in new development (*"Das wäre ein Problem. Das wäre definitiv ein Problem. Ich glaube, wir könnten es abfedern. Aber man würde es merken, man würde es auch nach außen merken. Zwei Punkte: Wir würden vom Support her, ich würde mal schätzen, für ein halbes Jahr deutlich Schwierigkeiten haben. Dieses halbe Jahr würde uns komplett für irgendwelche Weiterentwicklung oder sonst was fehlen. Dann ein Team aufzubauen, das die Entwicklung noch mal allein bringt, würde uns sicher noch ein Jahr kosten."*[1161]).

Based on these discussions, we consider the value of the services to be high.[1162]

(B) We now evaluate the *rareness* of the services based on (1) the location of Delta Center and (2) the availability of services on the market.

1. There are *few other countries* in the world that have such high and specialized IT know-how at a comparable cost level. This is due to the specialization during the country's socialist history (*"Bulgarien war schon das IT-Land, sage ich mal"*[1163]).

2. Besides, there are only *very few firms* that have a software comparable to that developed by Delta Center (*"Das wäre wahrscheinlich äußerst mühselig gewesen. Es gab nicht viele Alternativen, also echte Alternativen."*[1164]). In addition, a few

---

[1159] Interview 11:13.
[1160] Interview 10:36.
[1161] Interview 11:39. In another statement (interview 11:41) it is confirmed that smaller subunits can be shifted from one location to another but the loss of an entire unit would create a difficult problem for Delta.
[1162] During our visit to Delta Center, we were guided through the building and shown an office that was occupied by two lawyers specializing in intellectual property protection. They were responsible for registering patents (in Bulgaria and internationally) of new developments that Delta Center makes. This also speaks for a high value of the services.
[1163] Interview 10:6; confirmed by interview 14:3. This is also indicated by recent announcements of technology firms Microsoft and Google to open development centers in Bulgaria (Heise Online News (2006)).
[1164] Interview 10:14.

companies might provide similar software but none of them fulfills Delta's needs exactly (*"Der [application server] stellt eigentlich eine Standardfunktion zur Verfügung. [name of international standard] ist ein offener Standard, er implementiert auch diese Funktion und stellt sie zur Verfügung, er stellt aber auch andere Dinge zur Verfügung, die sehr wichtig sind und die nicht standardisiert sind."*[1165]; *"This is not something that is available in the specifications, for example. So there was a lot of, in the run time part of the [product name], there was a lot of investment in components that are basic components. They are somehow part of the lowest layer in the stack but they are not needed, let's say by the [name of international standard] implementation, but just by the different components built in [Delta's products]."*[1166]).

With no real alternatives to the services that are provided by Delta Center, we deem the rareness of the services high.

(C) We now consider the *inimitability* of the services and evaluate how easy it would be for a competitor to replicate the services that Delta Center provides. We therefore look at (1) how advanced Delta Center is in comparison to its competitors and (2) the actual possibility of building up a similar center.

1. Firstly, comments were made on a more general level with regard to Delta's overall division of labor that was seen as *advanced*. An advanced center is potentially one that is harder to imitate. Competitors would be interested in building up a similar structure with important services delivered from units other than the headquarters (*"Ich glaube, [Delta] ist da relativ innovativ, weil... Gut, [Competitor 1] hat auch viele Leute in Indien, [Competitor 2] hat auch Leute in anderen Erdteilen. Aber 90 Prozent der kritischen Dinge werden dann doch an einem Ort gemacht, in der Zentrale. Also, [Delta] ist da ziemlich innovativ. Es gibt natürlich eine Menge Start-ups, die das auch machen. Die alle möglichen Erdteile nutzen, um Entwicklung zu machen. Aber sagen wir mal für die großen Firmen ist [Delta] schon ziemlich weit."*[1167]).

2. Competitors' potential *possibilities* for setting up a similar service offshoring center as Delta Center were seen with considerable scepticism. On the one hand, the market for specialized talent is rather small – as discussed already

---

[1165] Interview 11:45.
[1166] Interview 12:10.
[1167] Interview 10:40.

with regard to rareness *("Das ist die Frage, was jetzt einen echten Competitor dazu treiben würde, dahin zu gehen und welche Möglichkeiten er hat. Meine Einschätzung ist, der Markt ist im Endeffekt zu klein, als dass es sich rentieren würde."*[1168]*)*. Besides, the process of building up a similar center is complex and hard to imitate. The purchase of an existing company might be an easier way to go; however, as discussed above, there are few companies with such specialized knowledge *("Vom Scratch so was aufzubauen, halte ich für sehr schwer, muss ich zugeben. Also, man müsste sich schon irgendwo eine Keimzelle kaufen, glaube ich schon auch, nach meinen Gesprächen mit den Geschäftsführern drüben über seine Historie und wie es läuft und wie das alles so gelaufen ist. Also, entweder man kennt das Land gut oder man muss sich irgendwo eine Keimzelle kaufen. Jetzt zu sagen, ich gehe dahin und mach, ohne dass ich groß was weiß und kenne, da anzufangen ist, glaube ich, sehr, sehr schwer."*[1169]; *"I think the market is really one of the biggest problems. Because it's not a big market. It's not possible to get fifty guys and build a center. You either end up with not so good guys or you need to pick up guys from another company and things like this. I think building a team itself, a good enough team, is one of the biggest challenges."*[1170]*)*.

Since it seems rather difficult to set up a similar center and replicate the services that Delta Center provides, we judge the inimitability to be high.

(D) The *non-substitutability* of the services is the next indicator which we evaluate with regard to (1) the possibility of substituting the services from Delta Center by purchasing services from external providers and (2) the benefits that Delta would give up by substituting the services from Delta Center.

1. The purchase of these services *from an external partner* (as the main possibility of substitution) is judged as inappropriate because the services are too "close to the heart" of Delta. It was compared to the automotive manufacturer BMW outsourcing its engine development – one of the areas which is typically considered BMW's core competence *("Weil das ist zu kritisch, als dass man das irgendjemandem gibt, der dann über Nacht nicht mehr da ist. Das ist, wie wenn BMW die komplette Motorenentwicklung outsourced."*[1171]; *"Aber mein Fazit nach vier Jahren

---

[1168] Interview 11:13.
[1169] Interview 11:57.
[1170] Interview 12:150.
[1171] Interview 10:48.

[product name] ... ist, es ist auf jeden Fall extrem schwierig, und den richtigen zu finden noch schwieriger. Bisher, glaube ich, fahren wir mit dem eigenen wirklich am besten."[1172]). In addition, the knowledge that has been accumulated in Delta Center makes a substitution of the Delta Center services hard ("Ja, aber das sind 300 Leute, die wirklich das Wissen haben. Wenn die weg wären, wäre das schon ein Problem, das kann man nicht so einfach transferieren."[1173]).

2. Besides the complexity of a transfer and the inappropriateness of other software products for Delta, there are also a range of *advantages* that Delta would give up by purchasing the services from an external partner, such as the higher internal speed of turn-around and the low risk of confidentiality breaches ("First of all, if we buy it from another company, this means that we need to license it for each and every installation that we do. Another thing is that if we go that way it means that we would need to expose all our internal infrastructure like integration with [internal programming language] to some external company."[1174]; "And we also need to, any kind of request that we need to do to take a very long round-trip to the company, we first need to request something, then they need to include it into the release cycle, which in some point in time needs to come back to us, and so on. So the turn-around time would be really high. That was, I think the main reason in the past for [Delta] we decide to buy [ForDelta]. ... In order to be able to develop what's needed for its platform."[1175]; "It's a constant evolution and the APIs in the very beginning like the early J2E versions for example, they were not enough. ...we will get only drawbacks from the outsourcing that you mentioned. So all the quality, the communication channels, ... So you get all the drawbacks."[1176]). As the product that Delta Center develops is directly incorporated into the services that Delta offers its customers, Delta also needs to support these products, which in the software industry can often mean support for several decades. It was mentioned that this support is very difficult to guarantee if the knowledge is not available within the boundaries of the firm ("Another important point to put here is that the time for which [Delta] supports their product is basically unlimited, that means there is a standard mainstream support, so to say, for six or seven years, then there is extended maintenance for another ten years and af-

---

[1172] Interview 11:45.
[1173] Interview 10:38.
[1174] Interview 13:87.
[1175] Interview 13:89.
[1176] Interview 13:91.

terwards it's for customer maintenance. So, this means that the company cannot afford to ship something on the market and then to lose the knowledge, because there will be people that will use it and they will have a support contract."[1177]).

Thus, it is not only difficult to substitute services from Delta Center but a substitution would also lead to several disadvantages. We therefore consider the non-substitutibiliy of the services to be high. With all four indicators of strategic relevance being high, we can conclude that the overall strategic relevance is also high.

6.4.2.2 ANALYSIS OF NETWORK EMBEDDEDNESS

In our discussion of network embeddedness, we analyze (A) the number of relationships, (B) the frequency of change to these relationships, (C) and the closeness of these relationships.

(A) We first judge the *number of relationships* that the service offshoring subsidiary has. As discussed in the company presentation, there is one main relationship between Delta's headquarters and the Bulgarian center.[1178] In addition, there is one relationship with some contact from time to time to the Israel center. All the other relationships are very sporadic and would not satisfy our criterion of regular interaction.

(B) The relationships once established are very stable and there are only very few changes over time. Thus, the *frequency of change* to the network structure is low. This also means that there is no standard process for integrating new units into the existing structure since acquisitions happen only very rarely (*"Dafür gibt es nicht genug Akquisen, dass es hochstandardisiert wäre."*[1179]). In addition, existing relationships do not change very often. Instead, they remain the same over years (*"Ja. Ach, die sind über Jahre stabil. ... Es ist kein Projektgeschäft, es ist ein Produktgeschäft. Es ist schon eine langfristige Angelegenheit."*[1180]). In recent years, there has been only one major change when the responsibility for one service shifted from a center in France to the center in Bulgaria (*"Such big changes happen very rarely. Less than once a year. Transferring responsibilities between locations, this is something very rarely happening. It's usually an exception that is behind some bigger thing, but I know about this that happens from France and it was part of trying to focus

---

[1177] Interview 13:110.
[1178] We count the relationship to the headquarters as a single relationship since it involves only one unit in Germany. This is different for the relationships in the other cases where different international units or different business units of the firm are involved and which we therefore count separately.
[1179] Interview 10:110.
[1180] Interview 10:152-154.

the labs, or a transfer or responsibility, I don't know the details, however. But this is not something that happens often."[1181]). New relationships are also established very infrequently. During the last five years there has been only one new team added in Sofia (*"Diese Teile sind der klassische Java-Server auch, alle arbeiten im Endeffekt am gleichen Produkt. Es gibt noch einen zweiten Bereich ... Dieses Team ist komplett neu entstanden, vor zwei Jahren, drei Jahren."*[1182]).

The *closeness* of relationship between the service offshoring subsidiary and the headquarters is high. Both partners adapted substantially to the relationship. For the German headquarters it was one of the first times that work was distributed internationally. In the first phase, while Delta Center was still kept as a rather independent company, there were no major adaptations: *"Once the company was bought by [Delta], I think it was acquired, but it was not integrated as a [development center]. The difference is that you still keep almost everything local. You don't have access, for example, to confidential information within [Delta]. This is technically like defined by the users you have, so, basically the people in Sofia they have the same access right for any partner company or any external company, so they had no access, for example, to confidential information. Also, the complete infrastructure it was local for the labs or the network, for example, it was not integrated with the [Delta] network. It was almost impossible to transfer data between the two networks, so there was a special way of delivery. So, the complete technical infrastructure was separated. The complete organization was separated, in Sofia it was more or less structured like there was a technical director in there who was keeping communication to the development manager here at [Delta's headquarters]"*[1183]

In the second phase, when Delta Center started to interact more with Delta it meant some change in the communication patterns, but the rate of adaptation was still low (*"So in the beginning it was like nothing changed for most of the people. Then slowly as [colleague] said, team-leads started communicating with [name of headquarters location] more and more."*[1184]).

Finally, the Bulgarian company was integrated into Delta which also meant a substantial financial investment in infrastructure such as adequate office space and information systems (*"Die ganze Infrastruktur wurde an westliche Standards angepasst, das Gebäude..., Infra-*

[1181] Interview 12:94.
[1182] Interview 11:29; confirmed by interview 12:94.
[1183] Interview 12:4.
[1184] Interview 13:17.

struktur, IT, Kantine, all diese Dinger halt."[1185]). Today, the organization has teams that are split across locations and these team cooperate very closely (*"Jetzt spielen die Themen so zusammen, dass die Teams sehr eng zusammenarbeiten müssen."*[1186]; *"These are, they work together, so basically, if you develop here something and break something, then the guy on the other side can see that you broke something."*[1187]).

In Delta Center's second relationship – to Delta IL – the closeness is far less. There is less frequent interaction and little adaptation. There have not been shared trainings or financial or other investments in each other (*"Basically the interaction is on a need basis, so the people they, here the people in Sofia they know a lot of people in Israel for example, because of the joint projects they did. If you have some integration activity or something like this, it brings people together, like a workshop in Israel or a workshop in Sofia. So it happened several times so far that people from Israel they travel to Sofia and people from Sofia they travel to Israel and people from [name of headquarters location] to Israel and so on. The teams they know each other on management level because of common events and common meetings and so on. From the other side, the developers they also know each other because of the interaction and the work together. It's not that all developers know all developers or all developers know some developers, things like this but on a team per team basis"*[1188]).

We conclude that there is a low number of relationships and very little change in the structure of relationships. The closeness of the relationship between Delta Center and Delta Germany is high, while it is low for the relationship between Delta Center and Delta IL.[1189] We therefore consider the network embeddedness to be also on a low level, though not on the absolute low extreme. With this kind of network embeddedness and high strategic relevance, we consider Delta Center to be a specialized contributor.

[1185] Interview 10:90.
[1186] Interview 11:7.
[1187] Interview 12:46.
[1188] Interview 12:71.
[1189] For the first time in our cases, we here encounter a situation with indicators of opposite values. We had some variance in the strategic relevance of Beta but not so such an extent. We understand our indicators as causes for the dimensions, that is, their values influence the value of the dimension (formative indicators). Thus, they are not just representing the effect of the underlying concept. In our formative case, not all indicators need to be on the same level, they do not need to be (positively) correlated in all cases (Bollen (1984), pp. 378-381; for a discussion of the different type of indicators see also Diamantopoulos/Winklhofer (2001)).

6.4.3 COORDINATION MECHANISMS

6.4.3.1 OVERVIEW OF COORDINATION

The coordination of Delta Center is implemented through a parallel hierarchical structure. Every department has one location in Sofia and one in the German headquarters. In each of these locations, every department has one manager. Both managers report to a vice president who is typically located in Germany. Only the largest department in Sofia has its own vice president.

These managers and vice presidents do not work exclusively on coordination; rather it is only one part of their tasks. Coordination is generally not only the responsibility of management. Many employees are involved in the interaction between Delta Center and Delta Germany. Therefore, interviewees found it hard to estimate the degree of overall *coordination requirements* ("*I can say that there is no explicit time spent on communication. ... it's part of the normal work.*"[1190]). However, they indicated that coordination accounts of ten per cent of all working time[1191] or several man-days per day ("*Also es sind mehrere Stunden oder Manntage pro Tag*"[1192]). Since it requires a substantial amount of working time and involves many employees it seems that coordination requirements are rather high.

6.4.3.2 STRUCTURAL COORDINATION MECHANISMS

We analyze the degree of *autonomy* based on the examination of (1) the areas in which headquarters takes decisions, (2) the areas in which Delta Center has freedom to decide, and (3) shifts in autonomy.

1. The main management decisions are *taken at headquarters*. Thus, Delta Center has no entrepreneurial responsibility in a sense that there is ownership of a separate business. Therefore, the general manager of the center is responsible for assuring a smooth operation of the human resources processes and the necessary infrastructure but has no influence on the product that is developed in Delta Center ("*Nein, nicht unternehmerisch. Dem kann höchstens vorgeworfen werden, du stellst nicht genug Leute ein. Die Retention ist schlecht, weil die Leute unzufrieden sind, also mehr diese logistischen, HR-ischen Themen, dafür ist er verantwort-*

[1190] Interview 12:96.
[1191] Interview 10:176.
[1192] Interview 10:120. Man-day is a typical measurement in the IT industry to measure the quantity of work. One man-day stands for the amount of work that one employee can accomplish in one day.

lich. Aber nicht dafür, dass ein Produkt nicht hinhaut. Außer es hat massive personalpolitische Gründe, weil er irgendwie ein Diktator ist oder so was. Aber ansonsten hat er keinen Einfluss aufs Produkt."[1193]). In case of conflict, managers at the headquarters take critical decisions. Interestingly, however, the board member responsible for the development of the technology platform is not located at the Germany headquarters any more but in the U.S. ("[interviewer:] Aber es ist klar, dass die finale Entscheidungsgewalt hier [in the headquarters] ist? – [interviewee:] Ja. Aber die finale Entscheidungsgewalt für mich sitzt in [Delta Center U.S.]"[1194]). This was confirmed by another interviewee, however, it was also argued that autonomy is not very important once a good working mode had been found ("Basically there is some kind of control in [name of headquarters location]. Before that was more explicit like the manager in [name of headquarters location] - there was no VP in Sofia - of the team was reporting to the manager in Sofia and the manager in Sofia was reporting to the manager in [name of headquarters location] for the run-time. That was on a more fine granularity per manager, and now it's just the VP's, the Sofia one reports to the [name of headquarters location] one. Before it was more to make aware the people in [name of headquarters location] that they really need to do the common organization and they really need to care for what's going on in there and so on. This motivation somehow disappeared with time because when it started to really work in a good way then this was no longer needed."[1195]).

2. However, there are several areas in which the center is *free to decide*. Firstly, with regard to recruiting, Delta Center – like any other unit within Delta – has to get top management approval for opening new positions ("First about hiring the new people, if you want a headcount at the end or an opening, you don't have freedom here even on the vice president level in [headquarters]. It's not possible that a vice president here he can invent like an opening. He has to get it from senior or executive levels. From the executive level it can come like we have five openings and we can hire five guys. Usually topics to hire in Sofia or in [headquarters] are taken centrally on a really high level."[1196]). After that, Delta Center decides autonomously whom to hire, even though it often involves German managers in the hiring process to test the candidates' skills in dealing with foreigners ("About the filling the position

---

[1193] Interview 10:184.
[1194] Interview 11:84-85.
[1195] Interview 12:98.
[1196] Interview 12:100.

themselves so once you have the headcount then to hire the people itself there is a local HR in Sofia which is common for the whole lab. This is something established for the lab."[1197]; "So, for some people it was extremely important, because the guy just show himself perfectly on the interview, which is usually in Bulgarian, we talked on English, just to estimate how the person talks in English, the same person will interview with the German colleagues he just passed completely, like black-out, like cannot talk, he doesn't understand what he is asked, so it is important."[1198]). Besides recruiting, the center is also free to define its own new projects and has the same right to propose them for the company-wide project approval process ("Some of the projects we decide, we define them ourselves here. Of course all the projects within our development cycle they need to go through a review process in the beginning of each development cycle. Like of some of them are defined in [headquarters], some of them are defined here, for example, [name of colleague] is in the architectural area, we have another architect which is in my particular area, so most of the ideas and the feedback and so on is collected from the developers, from the support organizations and stepping on top of that, we define the projects that we work on. So, at the end all of them should be approved, like by committee ..."[1199]).

3. In addition, autonomy does not seem to be something that is in place per se in the relationship between headquarters and the subsidiary. Rather, it *shifts on a per-project basis*. For instance, responsibility for the maintenance of older versions of the software had been assigned to a manager in Bulgaria who then also had autonomy over people at headquarters for this particular area ("Es ist so autonom wie ein Team dieser Größe, wie ein Management-Team von 30 Leuten autonom agieren kann. D.h. die internen Ressourcen, wie man das macht... wir hatten z.B. auch die Verantwortung für die releasten Versionen, die habe ich irgendwann delegiert an einen Manager in Bulgarien, wo er dann die Freiheit hatte und dann auch eine gewisse Weisung hier auch nach [name of headquarters location] hatte. Also, ich würde sagen, für mich war es kein Unterschied. Ob ich jetzt ein Team hier habe von 30 Leuten oder dort, und die gleiche Autonomie. Teilweise in Bulgarien nochmal größer, weil es eben diese Cross-Identität hatte. Ich habe also dem [manager name] in Bulga-

---

[1197] Interview 12:100; confirmed by interviews 10:172 and 13:279.
[1198] Interview 13:279; confirmed by interview 12:102.
[1199] Interview 13:271; confirmed by interviews 13:78 and 13:80.

rien gesagt 'Hier, Java-Server hat ein Problem, fix mir das.' Dann hat er da die Autonomie. Aber das würde ich [at the headquarters] genauso machen."[1200]).

To conclude, the major decisions are taken at headquarters. However, there are several areas in which Delta Center can operate freely and has the same rights as any other unit within the firm. We therefore deem the level of autonomy medium.

6.4.3.3 TECHNOCRATIC COORDINATION MECHANISMS

To establish the level of *technocratic coordination*, we now evaluate the application of (A) standardization and (B) formalization of the relationship.

(A) For *standardization*, we check (1) how standardization is applied to the relationships between the different units and (2) the goal of standardization within Delta.

1. The standardization of relationships occurs through a *set of processes* that govern the entire software development process: *"There is this [proprietary name] process established over in [Delta]. Product innovation lifecycle, everybody knows it as [proprietary name]. It has a define phase, then design, develop, test, maintenance and so on. Usually before every new release there is a define phase. Which is a big portfolio around that involves there are also tools to support this"*[1201]. These processes have been put to the test of international standard committees to implement a standardized process (*"Wir haben da auch so eine ISO-Zertifizierung gemacht, und all diese ganzen Standards bezüglich Projektmanagement und was man einfach alles machen muss, um einen hochqualitativen Prozess zu haben. Der TÜV hat die ISO-Zertifizierung durchgeführt."*[1202]). The overall process serves to set up the main phases of a software development project. These often include a phase to define the requirements before the overall design and the coding of the software follows. Software coding is different from organization to organization and there are several different methodologies available[1203] which are often used in parallel in one organization. There are *"... several different development methodologies in [Delta] itself. It's like [the product] global, I would say. So we have the [abbreviation of*

[1200] Interview 11:83.
[1201] Interview 12:106.
[1202] Interview 10:126.
[1203] There are several different methodologies for software development that differ with regard to such dimensions as number of iterations or number of phases. For an introduction to some modern methodologies and how to select the appropriate methodology, see Glass (2004), Lindstrom/Jeffries (2004).

6 – Results   315

> *the standardized process], we are so used to the abbreviations. I just forgot the translation. That's a kind of comprehensive approach, like step-by-step, like design review implementation, q-gates between the things, and so forth. That was their process, and now we are trying with two different Agile methodologies, one is Six Sigma. In the lab, we already have a black belt trained to Six Sigma, several green belts, yellow belts, and we have currently three to four Six Sigma projects that they are running here. They have also some of them have cross-staffing. And also one additional is SCRUM. SCRUM Methodology."*[1204]).

2. The objective of standardized processes is to *align several hundred developers* across many different units of the firm toward a common delivery deadline of new software (*"Also ways of communicating in such a big company, there are big processes. It's a huge company so if you need to get at the end a common delivery like [product name], which should be released at one date and there are like 1500 people working in different organizations, you need a really stable process, you need people to follow them and there is a lot of understanding that you need to do this"*[1205]). This process is not only independent of the time when it is carried out, but also independent of location: *"It's an integrated process that runs independent of location and independent of organization. You have no chance to do it otherwise because the software it grew too much. It's beyond any, it's really gigabytes of [name of file type] files that we have developed technically. The process is set up in a way that it's really independent from location and independent from organization because these are usually the two challenges. To integrate on the location side and to integrate on the organization side."*[1206]

To conclude our analysis of standardization, there are many instances where a standardized process is used (*"Es gibt eine Menge standardisierter Prozessschritte"*[1207]). However, the relative importance of standardization is low compared to personal coordination.[1208] We therefore consider the degree of standardization to be medium.

[1204] Interview 13:283.
[1205] Interview 12:34.
[1206] Interview 12:50; confirmed by interviews 10:200; 10:166; 10:168 and 12:108.
[1207] Interview 11:91.
[1208] We discuss the relative importance of the coordination mechanisms in section 6.4.3.6.

(B) Standardization can be a prerequisite for *formalization* which we evaluate next. We discuss the role of electronic tools in (1) software development and (2) supporting processes.

1. The main element in Delta's formalization is a *system of software programs* that support the standardized processes. Thus, many of the plans and rules are not necessarily documented in handbooks but they form the basis of the software programs that govern the relationship. This software integrates all the parts that are developed in all the locations worldwide. It then combines these parts and creates a so-called "daily built" which is the most recent version of the software that is then subjected to a series of tests to evaluate its quality (*"Da gibt es eine große technische Maschinerie, die das integriert, jede Nacht die ganze Software zusammenschmeißt, das ist eine Welt für sich. Und da ist Bulgarien genauso gleichberechtigt wie alle anderen Standorte. Das ist eine rein technische Lösung."*[1209]). The results of the work are captured in reports that show the level of progress (*"So you can see aggregated traffic light for each project"*[1210]) and which parts of the software work as supposed and which not (*"Also sehr viele wöchentliche und wir haben jetzt im Development-Prozess tägliche Status-Reports, wir haben sehr klar gesagt, welche Tests laufen müssen, welche Reportings über unsere Problemmeldungsstatistiken, was sehr hilfreich ist. Da greifen wir teilweise auch auf Standard zu. Grad bei den Kundenmeldungen gibt es Standards, die wir ganz gut nutzen können."*[1211]).

2. These software tools also help in the *structuring of everyday work and interaction* (*"There is a formal way to collect requirements. There is a formal way to respond to requirements. And a formal way to structure your work. Like these are our four investment areas, like [name of area], run-time, tools, whatever. Then you can assign work packages, and to work packages you can assign people."*[1212]; *"There is this central and formalized define state which also defines the tools, C-ARC and so on, after that point the development organization is involved also in the define phase of course. But here it takes completely control. So it's just a matter of transparency, they have the tools, one is C-ARC for the requirements and C-PRO so both are for project management and work packages and so on."*[1213]). The reportings that are created from this

---

[1209] Interview 10:160.
[1210] Interview 12:108.
[1211] Interview 11:93.
[1212] Interview 12:106.
[1213] Interview 12:108.

6 – Results

supporting software sometimes also form part of the compensation of management so they are considered important *("Ich kann sagen, auf Basis dieses Reportings ist teilweise der Bonus meines Nachfolgers letztes Jahr bestimmt worden. Das haben wir vorher reingeschrieben, das ist das, was ich erwarte an Deliveries oder Qualität. Und das hat er sich schon zu Herzen genommen. Ich mache es nicht immer so formal, aber für mich ist das ein ganz klares Kriterium."*[1214]).

Thus, there are a range of tools to formalize relationships. However, the relative importance of these tools – especially in comparison to personal coordination mechanisms – was judged to be low.[1215] Based on these considerations, we conclude that the level of formalization is medium.

6.4.3.4 OUTPUT-BASED COORDINATION MECHANISMS

We discuss the level of *output-based coordination* with regard to (1) the complexity of the output, (2) the costs of output-based control, and (3) alternative mechanisms to output control.

1. Interviewees argued that the development of *software is too complex* to make it possible to exactly specify the outcome upfront *("Habe ich noch nie erlebt, dass das in der Softwareentwicklung funktioniert."*[1216]; *"Nicht immer, definitiv. Das ist oft schwierig bei unserem Job, von vorn herein zu sagen, was ist die Leistung, wie will ich sie denn messen Ich bin schon der Meinung, dass bei dem, was wir machen, schon sehr viel Judgment dabei ist. Es gibt Leute, die sagen, alles muss faktenbasiert sein. Ich glaub da nicht dran. Aber ich habe Meinungen, jeder hat Meinungen. Und das ist auch richtig so. Aber diese Meinung muss man hinterfragen können und dafür brauche ich Fakten. Aber ich sehe die Fakten eigentlich immer nur vor einer, ich denke eigentlich so sollte es sein, sonst weiß ich gar nicht, wie man auf die Fakten kommt."*[1217]). Therefore, interviewees are aware that the expected outcome cannot be and is not described exactly but rather there is room for interpretation *("Usually we try to get it very well defined but during the development phase overall [product name] it*

[1214] Interview 11:95.
[1215] We discuss the relative importance of the coordination mechanisms in section 6.4.3.6.
[1216] Interview 11:101; confirmed by interview 12:112.
[1217] Interview 11:97; confirmed by interview 10:198.

happens that a lot of things change and the end result is not very often the same as the initial design."[1218]).

2. Output control is not seen as something negative per se; however, the exact specification of the outcome is not seen as something that is *economically feasible*. In addition, it limits flexibility: *"It always depending on how much time you are willing to spend on that. There is some bounds that you need to follow, so of course it's very good if everything is specified from the beginning and you have all the requirements there and you know everything up front, but in reality this doesn't really work. Especially for the projects that need a lot of consolidation it never works. So we need be agile enough to handle that."*[1219]).

3. The software development service can be described as an *iterative process* that has target setting at every stage; however, the subunits such as Delta Center participate in this definition of targets. Thus, it is less typical output control, but rather a participative process (*"Das ist wieder Teil des Gesamtentwicklungsprozesses. Es hat eigentlich mit der Standortfrage nichts zu tun. Es geht darum, Requirements umzusetzen in detaillierte Funktionsbeschreibungen umzusetzen und dann umzusetzen in detaillierte Architekturpläne. Und da waren die genauso beteiligt, wie alle anderen halt auch."*[1220]; *"For example, that here, we started very strong with consolidation, and we'll see how it continues. Actually now, for example, we have all the planning for the next four months, which is our current development cycle. And we also have some plans for longer term projects which clearly cannot get within that time frame. So on the next product definition phase, we will review them again, and we'll see."*[1221]).

We therefore conclude that the level of *output control* is low.

6.4.3.5 PERSONAL COORDINATION MECHANISMS

We finally evaluate *personal coordination* mechanisms. Specifically, we look at the degree of (A) direct personal coordination, (B) visits, (C) transfers and (D) cultural coordination.

[1218] Interview 12:110; confirmed by interviews 10:172 and 12:112.
[1219] Interview 13:306.
[1220] Interview 10:194.
[1221] Interview 13:309.

6 – Results

(A) We evaluate *direct personal coordination* in the form of remote personal communication with regard to (1) the modes that are used for it, (2) the occasions for using it, (3) the intensity of interaction, and (4) the role of common teams across locations.

1. This form of coordination takes place in *several ways*. There are phone discussions (*"The setup is really like that and if two developers from both locations discuss something, they just pick up the phone."*[1222]), email exchanges, phone conferences and video conferences that take place every day (*"Viele Videokonferenzen, jeden Tag. Ich hab glaube ich jeden Tag Videokonferenzen gehabt."*[1223]).

2. These interactions are either planned or spontaneous: *"So there is a daily meeting to see what's going on, problems, customer escalations, new features in the old release and so on."*[1224]; *"These are always video conferences. And there are a lot of meetings on demand. When there is a specific topic to discuss then a meeting is done."*[1225] Many of the planned interactions have a weekly rhythm, in addition to that are daily, more spontaneous interactions, especially on the working level or lower management levels (*"Wenn ich mal auf den Java-Server zurückgreife, die Historie, da war es so, ich würde sagen auf der Development-Manager-Ebene war es ein täglicher Austausch. Auf meiner Ebene VP war es ein wöchentlicher Austausch. Auf jeden Fall regelmäßig, ein Mal die Woche gab's ein Coordination-Meeting mindestens."*[1226]).

3. With regard to the *intensity of interactions*, there are one-on-one phone and email exchanges but also phone or video conferences that comprise entire teams from up to three locations (*"Das sind Gruppen, also diese Coordination. One-by-one das geht telefonisch, spontan. Aber wir haben z.B. im Java-Server ein wöchentliches Coordination-Meeting. Da treffen sich alle Manager und Architekten. Das sind 15-20 Leute. Das ist eine Videokonferenz. Zwischenzeitlich hatten wir mal eine französische Gruppe dabei, da hatten wir eine Drei-Wege-Videokonferenz. Da wurde es ein bisschen kompliziert, aber haben wir auch gemacht. Und das ist ganz etabliert, 1 Mal die Woche, zwei Stunden: Wo stehen wir?"*[1227]). Direct personal coordination goes so

---

[1222] Interview 13:47.
[1223] Interview 10:100; confirmed by interviews 12:80-82 and 13:53 and 13:196-199.
[1224] Interview 12:25.
[1225] Interview 12:26.
[1226] Interview 11:73; confirmed by interview 12:46.
[1227] Interview 11:79.

far that one interviewee told us that the actual software programming is done more on email programs than in program languages: *"Sometimes people are joking, that they are coding not on Java but on Outlook, the whole day they are doing email exchange."*[1228]

4. Direct coordination is both motivated and fostered by the fact that the units in Sofia and at headquarters form *common teams*. Thus, employees work together in teams independent of their location. This working mode has made physical distance almost negligible: *"The next one is not only the travel time, is the video conference and the telephone calls, the audio conferences that they're having. They are working around the same product and they are working like one and the same team. Now it is not a logistic problem, not only for your personal travel but to export and to work with one and the same tools on one and the same problems, internet is the way to go. That is why I don't think that they find any problem on the fact that they have to work remote and they have to see each other very rarely."*[1229] This structure is explicitly determined by senior managers who consider managers at headquarters and at the Sofia location as peers, a fact that requires good personal relationships between them (*"Ich habe ihnen eigentlich immer gesagt, 'Ich sehe euch immer als Paare. Und der Deutsche ist halt näher, den erreiche ich schneller, ja, er ist 'primus inter pares', aber im Endeffekt ihr seid ein Paar und der bulgarische Manager hat immer die Möglichkeit, mich zu erreichen.' ... Es funktioniert nur, wenn die beiden Manager sich verstehen und sich als Paar empfinden. Wenn das nicht der Fall ist, funktioniert das nicht."*[1230]). Management encouraged links between Delta Center and Delta Germany at all levels of hierarchy to create a network of relationships (*"Ich habe gewisse Bedenken, ob das so formalistisch gut ist. Weil ich halt sag, ein anderes Prinzip, was ich immer gesagt hab, wir brauchen ein Netzwerk. Wir können nicht diese Single-Connects..., sondern auf allen Ebenen muss es die Verbindung geben."*[1231]). An additional element to support direct personal coordination is the technical infrastructure which allows for an easy setup of video conferences, for instance: *"The infrastructure is basically also quite synchronized in here so it's you can book a room with the video conference to Sofia and via the system and you make sure*

[1228] Interview 13:231.
[1229] Interview 14:19.
[1230] Interview 11:23.
[1231] Interview 11:23; confirmed by interview 11:25.

6 – Results 321

that nobody else has booked this room and so on. There is an infrastructure support really."[1232]

We conclude that direct personal coordination plays a very important role for the coordination of Delta Center and consider it to be on a high level.

(B) *Visits* are the next coordination mechanism we address. We discuss (1) the frequency of visits, (2) occasions for visits, and (3) the intensity of visits.

1. There are around *400 visits per year* between the headquarters and Delta Center (*"Wir haben 400 Trips gehabt im Jahr. Also mehr oder weniger 1,5 Trips pro Person vor Ort. D.h. 400 Mal ist jemand hin und her geflogen. Ob das 400 Mal der gleiche war oder ob das 400 unterschiedliche Leute sind, das weiß ich jetzt nicht. Aber das war ein aktiver Austausch mit Deutschland, auch physisch."*[1233]). Travel on management level occurs typically every four to six weeks and lasts for half a week.[1234] On the level of team leaders, visits occur more frequently[1235] and last about a week.[1236] Therefore, there is a constant flux of visitors and *"[i]t's not unusual to have even ten [visitors]. And it's the same probably, traffic from the lab to [name of headquarters location], so we are joking that Lufthansa can close the flights but they still need to keep one: Sofia."*[1237]

2. There are several *occasions* for meetings: a meeting is typically held at the beginning of each project that involves all the developers, in order to create alignment across the locations: *"But basically all the people gather at the same place, so we know the discussions, like what are the priorities for the particular development cycle or what we want to achieve at the end."*[1238] These meetings are then repeated to plan for the next project cycle: *"[I]f we have some major stuff in one or two months, we can get again, meet in one place and discuss important problems and normally we have regular meetings like video conference to discuss important issues, so this is how it works."*[1239] Besides, there are regular information sessions and

---

[1232] Interview 12:56.
[1233] Interview 10:88; confirmed by interview 12:60. In the time after the acquisition, visits between locations were more rare (interviews 12:32 and 13:14).
[1234] Interview 11:73; confirmed by interview 11:77.
[1235] Interview 11:73.
[1236] Interview 13:242-244.
[1237] Interview 13:238; confirmed by interviews 10:124; 12:32 and 13:38.
[1238] Interview 13:43; confirmed by interview 13:65.
[1239] Interview 13:46; confirmed by interview 13:53.

joint workshops *"like there is strategic [product name] business 'One' meeting, which is also performed at each location where all the senior management team like [manager's name] and so on, they visit every location and they are like sessions, asking questions, so on. There are a lot of channels to transfer information and the whole infrastructure is somehow integrated."*[1240] A particularly intensive form of visit is the "war room" that is set up in critical project phases. Employees from the two locations meet in one location and work together on the solution of a specific, urgent problem: *"It was the work which we call war room and so the people that are sitting together with a colleague got together all the guys in one room here, the location was Sofia."*[1241] However, managers especially travel not only in the event of urgent project problems but also to keep the information flow going (*"Die Developer und Team-Leads mehr on request, wenn's wirklich was zu tun gibt. Die Manager und Architekten auch, die Manager definitiv einfach um zu reisen. Ich hab nur, um zu reisen bin ich gereist. Aber die letzten Jahre habe ich eigentlich nur gesagt, so und so, ich muss mal wieder hin. Ich hatte nie das Gefühl, jetzt völlig weg zu sein, aber diese Sichtbarkeit, das Lab zu sehen und sich sehen zu lassen, halte ich für sehr, sehr wichtig. Das ist so eine Erfahrung, was ich mit allen Labs erlebe, das ist extrem wichtig, dass insbesondere die Leute aus der Zentrale zu den Labs kommen."*[1242]).

3. The *intensity of visits* has led to a situation where employees in both locations do not consider the physical distance between Bulgaria and Germany to be an inhibitor to effective cooperation (*"Basically, really you can think about the location here, this is what we are trying to achieve, that the location here is no different than any other location. We have a lab in Berlin, so Berlin - [name of headquarters location] I think is even far away from Sofia - [name of headquarters location]. Transport-wise, because with a car you have four hours to Berlin, four and a half depending on the traffic, and from Sofia to [name of headquarters location], you need three hours. And then we have a very early plane in the morning recently, in [name of headquarters location] the guys just joked that he went in his office with a plane because the flight is very early in the morning, like 7 o'clock and you go to [name of headquarters location] about 9 o'clock and we are right on time for working."*[1243]; *"Wenn das schafft, wenn man den*

[1240] Interview 12:48; confirmed by interviews 12:52 and 12:58.
[1241] Interview 13:53.
[1242] Interview 11:75.
[1243] Interview 13:57; confirmed by interview 14:19. This was anecdotally confirmed by a (not recorded) staircase conversation where a Bulgarian manager mentioned that he visits headquarters more often than his grandmother who lives a two-hours' drive away from Sofia.

> *Austausch von allen Mitteln nutzt, von Mail, Telefon, Videokonferenzen, Reisen, alles ist wichtig, in der richtigen Balance. Wenn man das schafft, sehe ich überhaupt kein Problem, gerade bei diesem Near-Shoring, gleiche Zeitzone, wo man eben diese Medien nutzen kann jederzeit. Für mich ist es kein großer Unterschied, ob jemand in Bulgarien sitzt oder hier sitzt."*[1244]).

Thus, visits between headquarters and Sofia occur very often and involve all levels of hierarchy. We therefore consider them a very important mechanism for coordination.[1245]

(C) While there are no *transfers* in Delta Center or in Delta for the coordination of the service delivery, there are some related topics we want to point to. We discuss (1) the current situation regarding transfers, (2) the general policy of Delta regarding transfers, and (3) moves between locations.

1. Currently, there are no *transfers either from headquarters to the Sofia location or from Delta Center to the headquarters*. There was one such case when a developer wanted to move to Sofia for a six-month assignment (*"We have, for example, a project for which there was one lady from [name of headquarters location] for half a year for the project. But then she moved back."*[1246]). Interviewees did not consider it necessary to have transfers between headquarters and the Sofia location (*"... und da es dann doch wirklich in die Richtung geht, wir müssen jemanden dahinschicken, der das aufbaut. Das war in Bulgarien meiner Meinung nach nicht notwendig. Wir haben jemanden mal hingeschickt, eine Entwicklerin ein halbes Jahr, das war ihr eigener Wunsch gewesen, und haben hinterher festgestellt, das hat eigentlich nicht viel gebracht. Das war einfach auch nicht notwendig."*[1247]). In addition, it is also considered cheaper to fill positions locally than to send expensive expatriates.[1248]

[1244] Interview 11:7.
[1245] Visits between Sofia and locations other than headquarters were not mentioned by the interviewees and are not considered here. Visits to or from Israel were mentioned once: "For Israel and Sofia travels are not so often, so I can say, like average is one person per month or maybe rarely. If it happens that there is a kind of task force or workshop then it may happen that two or three guys from Israel they come to Sofia or vice versa. But it's mostly, it's not something frequent. Once per month and even less, let's say." (interview 12:80).
[1246] Interview 13:195. Right after the acquisition of Delta Center, there was another example of a transfer when a manager from Delta was sent to Sofia: "There was a guy in [headquarters], who is so to say serving as a communication point and also roll-out point for any information from Sofia to [headquarters] on this particular topic" (interview 13:19).
[1247] Interview 11:3.
[1248] Interview 10:188.

2. However, this does not reflect a *general policy of Delta* not to have transfers, but rather it is seen as an advantage for the Bulgarian location that interactions run smoothly even without transfers. As a comparison, in the interaction with the development center in India, it is considered absolutely necessary to have transfers from headquarters (*"... das ist anders, ich habe jetzt gerade weit mehr Gruppen in Indien übernommen, und da ist z.B. einer der Mitarbeiter ein Deutscher, der jetzt zwei Jahre in Indien war. Das ist eine ganz andere Situation, dort war es, nach dem, was ich mitbekomme, sehr viel notwendig. Großer Vorteil für einen Standort wie Bulgarien, dass das eigentlich nicht notwendig ist."*[1249]).

3. Instead of a formalized transfer, however, Delta offers its employees the opportunity to *move to another location* (in this case, to move from Bulgaria to Germany or even to locations in the U.S. or Canada) if they want to or if Delta is in danger of losing a good employee otherwise (*"Das ist dann immer so ein Abwägen. Bevor man so jemanden verliert, bietet man ihm einen Job in Deutschland an. Das waren so die Ideen, bevor er geht, soll er lieber in Deutschland arbeiten."*[1250]; *"But for us it's also the case that there, initially there are about ten or fifteen people that moved already from Sofia and now they switched positions within [Delta] so now within Java Server there are maybe four or five left out of these, so the rest they moved to another organization that has nothing to do any longer with the lab in Sofia. But still, there are several people like me that are within the organization and they work with Sofia occasionally."*[1251]).

We therefore consider the significance of transfers to be low. However, the moves between locations can effect cultural coordination which we will evaluate next.

(D) We now focus on *cultural coordination* and discuss (1) the team spirit across locations, (2) the effect of moves between locations, (3) the impact of country cultures, (4) the planning of cultural coordination, (5) the tolerance for differences and (6) results of cultural coordination.

1. Several interviewees referred to the *strong team spirit* (*"Ja, sehr stark"*[1252]) that crosses locations. It is so strong that Bulgaria is not considered a distant entity

---

[1249] Interview 11:3.
[1250] Interview 10:243.
[1251] Interview 12:126.
[1252] Interview 10:236.

but rather an integrated part of the entire organization ("... *genau noch mehr in Richtung 'Na, da gibt halt Leute in Bulgarien.' Aber nicht negativ gemeint.*"[1253]; "*Bulgarien nicht, ne. Mit anderen Standorten gibt es das, aber Bulgarien. Ja, es gibt immer solche Reibereien. Aber die waren jetzt nicht überproportional stark ausgeprägt.*"[1254]). The team spirit across locations is sometimes even stronger than the team spirit within one location: "*That worked and with time, people just get used to it and it turned out to be a kind of team spirit. It worked out nice. Right now, there also from time to time kind of struggles but these are really individual things. At the present moment, for example, I can say that sometimes I see more clashes or arguments between the teams in Sofia because they report to a different line organization and different VP areas so sometimes there are more arguments and more battles, not blames or finger pointing, but really a little bit explosive environment. Like in a meeting or something, a disagreement and so on, I see more clashes between the different line organizations rather than clashes between based on like Sofia or [name of headquarters location]. Not that these are too many, but still they are more than the clashes on the occasion.*"[1255]

2. As discussed above, transfers are not very frequent within Delta, but the *frequent moves between locations* in general and from Delta Center to headquarters in particular have led to personal relationships across locations and facilitated information exchange as well as conflict resolution. One interviewee at headquarters explained: "*It's a good idea because it helps. It's hard to explain why exactly, but that is what happens often without a reason. I speak, for example, to a manager in Sofia for two hours on the phone and we just discuss overall items or overall topics. It's not driven by a need. It just happens and it helps for additional kind of roll-out of information and synchronization of what's going on. ... it helps to some extent to address like if there is an issue with a German colleague ... then it's easier for a guy in Sofia to first complain to somebody else in [name of headquarters location] and then get an opinion, discuss it a little bit and then decide if the problem is on his side, or if he can then escalate it to somebody in [name of headquarters location]. It's not a*

[1253] Interview 10:225.
[1254] Interview 10:228.
[1255] Interview 12:90; confirmed by Interview 13:326.

big deal in the end, but in some small situation from time to time, it helps in this respect."[1256]

3. The team spirit and shared values are supported by relatively *small cultural differences* between German and Bulgarian national cultures (*"Es ist eine Frage des Egos und der Persönlichkeit und der Mentalität. Die Bulgaren sind nicht so Ego-stark, hoppla, jetzt komme ich. Daher hat das die Sache ein bisschen vereinfacht."*[1257]). Interviewees considered the culture rather a facilitator of good interaction than a hindrance, even though the Bulgarian employees were generally seen as very strong on technical skills but somewhat weaker on communication skills: *"A lot of technical people and not so many people that are able to communicate in such a way."*[1258] This is expressed in an anecdote which was shared with us. One German manager visiting Delta Center had tried unsuccessfully to start a discussion with a group of local employees. He had to leave the room at one point but rejoined the meeting after just a few seconds to hear the Bulgarians discussing openly among themselves. He asked them to discuss with him in the same manner (*"Er hat erzählt, also in Bulgarien, ach, typische Situation, er wäre da im Team gesessen und alle haben zugehört, und er hätte ihnen erzählt, was er machen will und so, und alle hätten ihn angeschwiegen. Und da hätte er aufs Klo gemusst, ist rausgegangen, und da hat er kurz inne gehalten, 10 Sekunden gewartet, den Kopf wieder reingesteckt, alle haben geredet, was er genau erwartet hat, und er hat gemeint, so möchte er auch diskutieren. Er hat's geknackt im Endeffekt."*[1259]).

4. Is was mentioned on several occasions that the team spirit that links the locations was the *result of planning and work*. For instance, managers reported that the culture of Delta Center had to be changed purposefully from that of a small, independent firm to that of a part of a much larger entity (*"Dadurch, dass es ein Firmenkauf war, musste man erst mal die Idee einer eigenständigen Firma abbauen und die Idee, dass man ein integrierter Teil eines viel, viel größeren Gesamtprodukts ist, muss man erst mal aufbauen"*[1260]). In addition, managers are actively involved in fighting tendencies to split teams: *"That is extremely important and even the slightest notion of splitting us and them is killed very, very early. It needs to be 'us'. It's*

[1256] Interview 12:130.
[1257] Interview 10:230.
[1258] Interview 12:10; confirmed by interviews 10:94 and 11:19.
[1259] Interview 11:21.
[1260] Interview 10:88; confirmed by interviews 11:1; 12:34 and 12:138.

important. Otherwise, we will not benefit from the synergy, we will just get into in-fights and things like that. Sometimes it happens, I try to resolve it. It's one of the main tasks that the managers have."[1261] This commitment was considered necessary to overcome several differences such as teams that were not aligned and skeptical of one another at the beginning,[1262] problems with cultural differences (*"Die hatten irgendwann ein interkulturelles Training bekommen, was ihnen all ihre Vorurteile bestätigt hat. Das war wirklich, seitdem habe ich meine Zweifel, was interkulturelle Trainings angeht."*[1263]), and differences in communication styles.[1264] Moreover, both at the headquarters and in Sofia new people were hired and employees from other units moved to facilitate the cultural change (*"... ich habe sowohl Leute von ganz extern geholt als auch Leute aus der Organisation hier in [name of headquarters location] dann dazugeholt, die ich kannte, und das war sehr fruchtbar, muss ich sagen. ... Und wenn man dann Leute von draußen reinkriegt, ist es einfacher zu vermitteln. Dann habe ich da sehr stark auf Leute geachtet, die auf der Kommunikationsseite stark und offen sind. Also Offenheit war eigentlich das Kriterium. Und das hat sehr viel gebracht."*[1265]). Another element of the investment in a common corporate culture are trainings that are offered centrally by headquarters and to which Bulgarian employees have the same access as all other Delta employees (*"Es gab Standard-Produkt-Trainings. Trainings wurden aber auch teilweise übergreifend gemacht. Bei [Delta] gibt es ein sehr stark ausgeprägtes zentrales Training. Genauso wie alle anderen Mitarbeiter sind sie auch nach [name of headquarters location] gekommen und da haben sie spezifisches Training bekommen. Nicht nach dem Motto, dass die Bulgaren anders behandelt wurden als alle anderen, sondern die wurden genauso behandelt."*[1266]).

5. One element of cultural coordination seems to be *tolerance for differences* in personal working styles: *"Right now I can say that this is not something really visible because also here in [name of headquarters location], it's the working environment it's very individual, so you can see people they come at nine o'clock in the morning precisely and they leave at six o'clock precisely. So, if he writes a mail, and it's six o'clock, he will shut down his monitor and go home in the middle of the email. And for the other*

[1261] Interview 13:319.
[1262] Interview 11:7; confirmed by interviews 11:1 and 11:9.
[1263] Interview 11:7.
[1264] Interview 11:7.
[1265] Interview 11:7.
[1266] Interview 10:242; confirmed by interviews 12:140 and 13:337.

side, there are guys that are really passionate and they can stay until eleven o'clock here. So, it's really a mixed environment here in [name of headquarters location]. But also this changed during the year and for example, in the beginning, it was not so usual for the people in Sofia to see really like this strict working time. Also a lot of the people in Sofia, they were coming from the Universities, so they were more or less students, they have kind of a different life-style and they don't, almost none of them has a family, so he cannot understand that somebody can go home with the kids and stuff like this. So, also there were such kind of differences even not coming from like cultural differences, like Germany or Bulgaria, but they were more like a lifestyle differences and also differences associated with the company."[1267]

6. Eventually, common values and experiences have led to *personal friendships* that extend over and above work (*"Persönliche Bekanntschaften, Freundschaften entstehen. Wir haben auch sehr stark, am Standort, weil das auch von der Größe machbar war, sehr viele gemeinsame Incentive-Veranstaltungen gemacht. Und das hat auch dazu geführt, dass viele persönliche Kontakte entstanden sind."*[1268]). These personal contacts lead to personal help on topics unrelated to work: *"From one of the developers in Israel, her parents are now here on summer vacation in Borovitz, so I looked at some hotels last week to send them back to her, so it's normal."*[1269] One statement from an interviewee can be seen as summing it up: He expressed the desire to build personal relationships and to focus on human beings instead of remote resources (*"Und wir müssen davon weg bei Offshoring da hinten irgendwelche User-IDs oder Telefonnummern sehen oder sonst was und nicht den Menschen. Da habe ich z.B., als ich Bulgarien übernommen habe, dafür gesorgt, das war eine der ersten Sachen, dass allen ein Foto ins Adressbuch getan wird. Weil ich das früher selber erlebt hab in Palo Alto, da hatte ich mehr Kontakt, das waren immer nur Nummern im Endeffekt. Man guckt ins Adressbuch, da war kein Raum gepflegt, kein Foto drin, wenn für uns interpretierbare Telefonnummern drin waren, da hatten wir schon Glück. Das wirkt seltsam. Und diese Kleinigkeiten, im Endeffekt sind die, glaube ich, extrem wichtig. Man hat so wenig Möglichkeiten beim Offshoring, den Menschen zu sehen. Da sind auch die Kleinigkeiten so wichtig."*[1270]).

[1267] Interview 12:34.
[1268] Interview 10:238.
[1269] Interview 13:313; confirmed by interview 12:116.
[1270] Interview 11:7.

Therefore, the role that cultural coordination plays seems high.

6.4.3.6 COMPARATIVE ANALYSIS OF COORDINATION MECHANISMS

While structural instruments and output control play only a minor role, the relative importance of technocratic and personal coordination mechanisms still needs closer evaluation. Several statements during the interviews suggest that the latter actually play the most important role. One interviewee said that personal coordination on its own (without technocratic coordination mechanisms) would in itself result in good relationships whereas exclusive focus on technocratic mechanisms would not help at all *("Mit reiner Kommunikation habe ich schon eine ganze Menge erreicht. Mit reinem Messen erreiche ich nichts."*[1271]). In addition, he explained that formalized measures help only if they are supervised and personally controlled by management (*"Die Status-Reportings, wo stehen wir, da habe ich mir beibringen müssen und auch selber lernen müssen, dass wenn ich etwas haben will, im Endeffekt es erhalte, wenn ich selber hinterher bin. Wenn ich sage, ich möchte, dass die Fehlerrate runtergeht, muss ich jede Woche draufgucken. Wenn ich das tu, geht sie runter."*[1272]). In addition, an interviewee explained that formalized reports cover only the standard performance and that good performance goes beyond what can be captured in formalized reports (*"Auf der anderen Seite, ich sag mal so, das was man in ein Reporting packt, ist für mich bei vielen Dingen nicht bei allen selbstverständlich. Die wirkliche Leistung steckt darin, was darüber hinaus geht."*[1273]). Besides, even within a standardized and formalized project approach there are many instances where personal coordination is necessary for project success: *"The general part is standardized. There is of course the initial kick-off, the project charter, I mean, following the books basically. But the projects in general differ to the type, so ... one group of the projects, they just focus on providing certain functionality which means that you need to specify it in the beginning, then the implementation and testing, do the qualification, then provide it. ... most of the other projects, they involve heavy consolidation. That means you provide something but part of the project is for the upper layers to adapt to it. Which means that you need to go there, present it, program them, try to coach them, provide information, just in case they are needed. So the, yes some of the projects are just pure development, and some of the projects, they involve heavy communication."*[1274]). To conclude, both technocratic and personal coordination mechanisms play a role, with personal mechanisms clearly being the most important ones.

[1271] Interview 11:89.
[1272] Interview 11:87.
[1273] Interview 11:95.
[1274] Interview 13:282; confirmed by interview 13:60.

6.4.4 DISCUSSION OF CASE

Evaluation of appropriateness of propositions for individual case

We compare the results of the case to the original propositions in Table 6-7. We display the original proposition, the empirical result and indicate whether or not we find agreement with the proposition. The original proposition stems from the description of our typology, the empirical result from the discussion of the case. We represent the values low (L), medium (M), or high (H) by squares of different sizes.

Table 6-7: Evaluation of suitability of propositions for specialized contributor

Coordination mechanism	Original proposition	Empirical result	Agreement with proposition	Remark
Extent of co-ordination requirements	■-■ (M-H)	■ (H); high number of people involved in coordination	Proposition initially supported	--
Degree of autonomy	■ (H); as services are of high relevance; decisions are delegated	■ (M); subsidiary has same rights as other units of the firm but critical decisions are taken at headquarters	Proposition not supported	E1: Higher levels of autonomy might not be achieved without sales responsibility for important local market I1: Interviewees do not consider higher autonomy necessary
Degree of standardization	■-■ (L-M); high strategic relevance will require flexibility	■ (M)	Proposition initially supported	--

Coordination mechanism	Original proposition	Empirical result	Agreement with proposition	Remark
Degree of formalization	■-■ (L-M); individual cases and high competences will need flexibility	■ (M)	Proposition initially supported	--
Degree of output control	■ (L); behavior control more appropriate for high strategic relevance	■ (L); very limited possibility to describe desired outcomes	Proposition initially supported	--
Degree of personal direct coordination	■-■ (M-H); strategic relevance makes personal interaction necessary	■ (H); high degree of direct personal coordination	Proposition initially supported	I2: Personal coordination mechanisms are complementary
Number of visits	■ (H); high number of visits, long duration per visit	■ (H); high number of visits, long duration per visit	Proposition initially supported	--
Number of transfers	■ (H); high number of transfers; potentially in management and line positions	■ (L); no transfers	Proposition not supported	E2: Personal coordination is already achieved by high degree of direct personal coordination and high number of visits

Coordination mechanism	Original proposition	Empirical result	Agreement with proposition	Remark
Importance of culture-based coordination	■ (H); high level of normative integration	■ (H); high level of normative integration	Proposition initially supported	I3: Cultural coordination is explicitly encouraged by management
E: Possible explanation for difference; I: Idea, new thought; -- no additional comment				

While most of propositions are supported by the findings for Delta, there are some areas that need further explication:

- E1: The degree of autonomy that Delta Center has is lower than predicted. It seems that a service offshoring subsidiary might not in principle reach higher levels of autonomy. High levels of autonomy might only be found in subsidiaries that have complete responsibility for a specific product or that serve an important local customer market.

- E2: We had expected a high degree of personal coordination and accordingly a high number of transfers. We have, however, found no transfers at all between the units. We therefore will need to discuss the role that transfers play in service offshoring subsidiaries.[1275]

Presentation of additional information gained from the individual case

In addition to the findings that relate to our propositions we have found other aspects that we want to briefly discuss:

- I1: While it is sometimes assumed that subsidiaries should work towards establishing higer levels of autonomy for themselves,[1276] this was not confirmed in the current case. Rather, interviewees in the service offshoring subsidiary appreciated working in a team that is split across locations. This gives them easier access to new developments in the headquarters even if it means having less local

---

[1275] See below chapter 7.
[1276] Edwards et al. (2002), pp. 183-184.

autonomy ("*From one point it is a key value that we have our group in [name of headquarters location] like Dobromir said he's VP for the [name of department] for Bulgaria and there is another group in [name of headquarters location] which is basically working in the same area. So, from one perspective, could he have been an opportunity to have the component in Sofia, but then it would have been a loss for us. Because currently there are always people there that can answer questions, can talk to people, can communicate there locally and so on and so on. One thing is to have some formal meeting with people through phone or video, it doesn't matter. It's another thing to go to have lunch with the guys. From an effectiveness point of view, it's very much better for us.*"[1277]).

- I2: It was made explicit that all the different instruments available for personal coordination are complementary: "*[interviewee1] The other side of this set-up meetings in the beginning of each project are to meet the people face-to-face, to know each other, so it's easy to talk on the phone with them. – [interviewee2] – It's one thing if talk to a man that you found in Outlook, it's another thing if you know them. – [interviewee 1] – But we have reached something like that point between everybody, important people, so they can it do it like on the phone now. Just any new people to meet with them. So everybody knows each other.*"[1278]

- I3: The commitment by which the management of Delta decided to integrate Delta Center and go through a phase of difficult changes in the acquired unit ultimately had a very positive effect on coordination, especially on cultural coordination. Cultural coordination is now so strong that it covers much of the coordination requirements resulting from the physical distance. Moreover, the strong desire not to treat the developers in Bulgaria as "cheap resources" has created a working atmosphere that is characterized by a high degree of mutual respect.

[1277] Interview 13:24.
[1278] Interview 13:65-67.

7 Discussion – Findings from Cross-Case Analysis and Beyond

*"It doesn't matter how beautiful your theory is,
it doesn't matter how smart you are.
If it doesn't agree with experiment, it's wrong"*

Richard Feynman

Summary

We find initial support for most of our propositions. However, we need to adapt those propositions that assume a relationship between network embeddedness and technocratic coordination. Based on our empirical results, there is no support for the proposition that assumes a positive relationship between strategic relevance and autonomy. With regard to specific coordination mechanisms, we find that autonomy generally does not seem to play a very important role. Transfers are hardly used, most likely because of their high cost, which is especially relevant in cost-sensitive service offshoring situations. Personal coordination is found not only to play an important role for coordination itself but also to be a complement to other mechanisms. Despite minor adaptations, we consider our typology initially supported by our findings.

7 – Discussion

7.1 OVERVIEW OF FINDINGS

In this chapter, we present the findings we generated from the comparison of the cases. They are categorized in four sections. (1) In the first section, we describe those findings that pertain to the use of coordination mechanisms in our cases and draw conclusions for our typology (section 7.2). We also present additional variables that we identified in our research and that can influence coordination mechanisms. (2) We then discuss the results on a more abstract level with regard to the use of our typology (section 7.3). (3) Next, we present what we have learned about the future of service offshoring (section 7.4). (4) Finally, we report some observations with regard to methodology (section 7.5).

7.2 FINDINGS REGARDING COORDINATION MECHANISMS IN SERVICE OFFSHORING CENTERS

While we have described and discussed findings for individual cases, we now compare results across cases and evaluate in more detail the coordination mechanisms that we found in our cases. In doing so, we take a five-step approach:

1. First, we discuss each of our propositions. We can "test" each proposition using two data points. For instance, the impact of a change in strategic relevance on autonomy can be seen by a comparison between the upper left case and the upper right case of the typology as well as by a comparison of the lower left case and the lower right case. If in both cases we find an increase in autonomy, we will count that as initial support for our proposition. Otherwise, we will discuss alternative explications and changes to our theoretical framework.

2. We then consider the relevance of each coordination mechanism for service offshoring. To do this, we compare the results that we obtained for one coordination mechanism across all cases. This could lead to the re-evaluation of coordination mechanisms that we have over- or underestimated.

3. We use the limited possibilities for quantitative analysis that qualitative text analysis offers in order to generate findings that can help to underline the relative importance of each coordination mechanism. We show both our findings and the limitations of this approach.

4. Based on the findings relating to the individual propositions and coordination mechanisms, we discuss the overall results per case. We can then determine how adequate our initial descriptions of types were and/or where they need to be changed.

5. Finally, we discuss new variables that we found through our case studies and explain what influence they have on coordination in service offshoring and how they might affect our findings.

We will discuss each of these findings in one of the subsequent sections.

7.2.1 FINDINGS FOR EACH PROPOSITION

Table 7-1 presents the evaluation of our propositions with the number of the proposition in the first column. The second column shows the relationship that is stated in the respective proposition. We then give the independent and the dependent variable, and indicate in parentheses whether a positive (+) or negative (-) relation is assumed.[1279] While the first five rows deal with strategic relevance, the next four relate to network embeddedness. The third column displays the results that we obtained for low values of the independent variables (strategic relevance and network embeddedness, respectively). We indicate the name of the case, and the result for the coordination mechanism (dependent variable) under consideration. The value of the dependent variable (low (L), medium (M), and high (H)) is represented by squares of different sizes. The same is valid for the fourth column, only here we show the results of the dependent variable for high values of the independent variable. The last column represents the results of the evaluation. We indicate whether the proposition is initially supported (✓), not supported (✗) or whether there are ambiguous results that need further discussion (?).

Table 7-1: Evaluation of propositions

No.	Relationship	Result for low value of independent variable	Result for high value of independent variable	Support for proposition
P1	Strategic relevance ⇒ Coordination requirements (+)	Alpha: ■ (M) Gamma: ■ (M)	Beta: ■ (H) Delta: ■ (H)	✓ ✓
P2	Strategic relevance ⇒ Autonomy (+)	Alpha: ■ (M) Gamma: ▪ (L)	Beta: ■ (M) Delta: ■ (M)	? ✓

[1279] For a discussion and complete version of the propositions, see sections 3.2.6 and 3.3.6.

7 – Discussion 337

No.	Relationship	Result for low value of independent variable	Result for high value of independent variable	Support for proposition
P3	Strategic relevance ⇒ Formalization (-)	Alpha: ■ (H) Gamma: ▪ (L)	Beta: ■ (M) Delta: ■ (M)	✓ ✗
P4	Strategic relevance ⇒ Output control (-)	Alpha: ■ (H) Gamma: ■ (M)	Beta: ■ (M) Delta: ▪ (L)	✓ ✓
P5*	Strategic relevance ⇒ Personal coordination (+)	Alpha: ■ (M) Gamma: ■ (M)	Beta: ■ (H) Delta: ■ (H)	✓ ✓
P6	Network embeddedness ⇒ Autonomy (-)	Gamma: ▪ (L) Delta: ■ (M)	Alpha: ■ (M) Beta: ■ (M)	✗ ?
P7	Network embeddedness ⇒ Standardization (+)	Gamma: ▪ (L) Delta: ■ (M)	Alpha: ■ (H) Beta: ■ (M)	✓ ?
P8	Network embeddedness ⇒ Formalization (+)	Gamma: ▪ (L) Delta: ■ (M)	Alpha: ■ (H) Beta: ■ (M)	✓ ?
P9	Network embeddedness ⇒ Output control (+)	Gamma: ■ (M) Delta: ▪ (L)	Alpha: ■ (H) Beta: ■ (M)	✓ ✓
* The results reported refer to the mechanisms direct personal coordination, visits, and cultural coordination. Transfers are not included since they play almost no role.[1280]				

Propositions 1, 4, 5, and 9 show the expected results for both data points and we therefore consider them initially supported. We now want to discuss the remaining propositions. We found no support for Proposition 3 and Proposition 6 for the following reasons:

- Proposition 3: This proposition assumed a negative relation between the strategic relevance and the degree of formalization. While the comparison between

---

[1280] See the next section for a discussion on the role of transfers in service offshoring.

the service factory Alpha and the internal competence center Beta supports this assumption, the relationship shows inverse results for the comparison between the support center Gamma and the specialized contributor Delta. None of our interviewees specifically commented on this relationship. We had originally assumed that strategically less relevant services will be coordinated with more formalization since they are easier to codify. However, it could be that it is just not necessary to use formalization to coordinate such services. Taking these considerations, the empirical results together with the rather weak support that this relationship has in the literature,[1281] we conclude that we have not found support for this proposition.

- Proposition 6: We assumed a negative relation between network embeddedness and a subsidiary's autonomy. We were aware that there had been conflicting findings in previous contributions but still considered the support in the literature for this proposition sufficient.[1282] However, our empirical results show the opposite effect in the comparison between support center Gamma and service factory Alpha and ambiguous results for the comparison between specialized contributor Delta and internal competence center Beta. We therefore have found no support for this proposition. This could be taken as an indication that the internal competence center has more characteristics of a "center of excellence" which has a high level of network embeddedness but can still work autonomously.[1283]

The remaining Propositions 2, 7, and 8 are not fully supported by our findings, but they cannot be rejected outright. We therefore want to evaluate them individually:

- Proposition 2: We assumed a positive relationship between strategic relevance and a subsidiary's autonomy. While the comparison between support center Gamma and specialized contributor Delta supports this relationship, both the service factory Alpha and the internal competence center Beta show the same values for autonomy. We can offer two explanations for this: On the one hand, it

---

[1281] See for the discussion of this proposition section 3.2.6.
[1282] See for the discussion of this proposition section 3.3.6. For an explicit discussion of the relation between embeddedness and autonomy see Young/Tavares (2004), pp. 217-220.
[1283] Kutschker et al. (2001), Schurig (2002). This result questions findings such as those of Garnier (1982), p. 899 who finds a positive relationship between "workflow integration" (which is similar to our network embeddedness) and autonomy.

seems that autonomy in Alpha is somewhat higher than expected due to the setup of Alpha Center as a market-like provider.[1284] On the other hand – as we will show in the next section – several values for autonomy that we found in other cases are lower than expected. We came to the conclusion that autonomy in service offshoring constellations is generally not very high and this again prevents a relatively autonomous center such as Beta Center from being even more autonomous. We still regard the underlying positive relationship between strategic relevance and autonomy as appropriate and, thus, consider Proposition 2 to be initially supported. However, every analysis of autonomy needs to involve a thorough evaluation of other influencing factors (which we will address below).

- Propositions 7 and 8: We discuss the Propositions 7 and 8 together since both show the same values across cases and findings apply to both. Here, we have assumed a positive relationship between network embeddedness and standardization and formalization, respectively. This is supported by the comparison between support center Gamma and service factory Alpha. However, the values for standardization and formalization are the same for specialized contributor Delta (with low network embeddedness) and internal competence center Beta (with high network embeddedness) even though we expected them to be lower for the specialized contributor. Our comparative analysis of coordination mechanisms for Delta shows that standardization and formalization are not the most important coordination mechanisms. Rather, Delta relies primarily on personal coordination to guide the relationship.[1285] However, due to the complexity of the software that it develops involving participation from many locations within Delta, the firm has introduced a more standardized and formal approach. Since this system is rolled out internationally it is also used in the relationship between Delta and Delta Center. However, it might not per se be needed for the specific dyadic relationship we considered. Therefore, lower levels of standardization and formalization might be found in other service offshoring constellations that have the same strategic relevance and network embeddedness but that lack the distribution of work that we found in Delta. We therefore still consider propositions 7 and 8 appropriate. However, we emphasize the need to identify other influencing factors on technocratic mechanisms such as those we found in Delta.

[1284] See also the discussion of the Alpha case in section 6.1.4.
[1285] See the discussion of the Delta case in section 6.4.4.

In conclusion, we find initial support for Propositions 1, 4, 5, and 9 and – with some qualifying adaptations – also for Propositions 2, 7, and 8, but find no support for Propositions 3 and 6.

7.2.2 Findings for Each Coordination Mechanism

Table 7-2 gives an overview of the coordination mechanisms for each case. We present both the proposed value ("Prop.") and the empirically observed result ("Res.") for each coordination mechanism (in the rows) and for each case (in the columns), representing the values low (L), medium (M), and high (H) by squares of different sizes.

For *coordination requirements*, technocratic mechanisms (*formalization* and *standardization*), for *output control*, and *visits* we find a high degree of initial support for our original assumptions. We therefore consider them appropriate and will now turn to the coordination mechanisms that show somewhat differentiated results.

We have ambiguous findings for *autonomy*: Overall, our proposition was appropriate in only two cases. Autonomy in Alpha is higher than expected (for the reasons discussed above), while it is lower than expected in Delta and at the lower end of what we expected in Beta. There is no occurrence of high autonomy in any of our cases. We consider Alpha an exception for the reasons already stated. Thus, autonomy generally tends to be lower than expected. We therefore argue that autonomy as coordination mechanism does not play an important role in the context of service offshoring. After all, it is in most cases "just" an internal service process. In none of our cases there is a responsibility for an important local market which seems the main element to drive autonomy.[1286]

This could potentially be true of many service offshoring centers in Eastern Europe that are located in one of the smaller countries that individually do not have the same importance as markets such as China or India. This is backed by the view of one interviewee from Delta who explained that Delta Center in Bulgaria – despite delivering a service of high strategic relevance – might not have the same strategic relevance as a similar center in a major customer market (*"[I]ch glaube das bulgarische Lab wird nicht strategisch werden. Das indische Lab ist strategisch. Dass wir in China ein Lab aufbauen, ist auch strategisch, das ist einfach ein großes Land. Bulgarien hat diesen großen Markt nicht. Und daher ist das Lab eine reine Development-Execution-Einheit und nicht eine 'ich brauch den Kontakt in diesen*

[1286] Garnier (1982), p. 901.

Markt rein.' Und das ist das, was das Lab in Bulgarien strategisch immer schwächt. Und dem muss man sich stellen."[1287]).

Table 7-2: Overview of coordination mechanisms

Coordination mechanism	Service Factory Alpha		Internal Competence Center Beta		Support Center Gamma		Specialized Contributor Delta	
	Prop.	Res.	Prop.	Res.	Prop.	Res.	Prop.	Res.
Extent of coordination requirements	(L-M)	(M)	(M-H)	(H)	(L)	(L)	(M-H)	(H)
Degree of autonomy	(L)	(M)	(M-H)	(M)	(L)	(L)	(H)	(M)
Degree of formalization	(H)	(H)	(M)	(M)	(L)	(L)	(L-M)	(M)
Degree of standardization	(H)	(H)	(M)	(M)	(L)	(L)	(L-M)	(M)
Degree of output control	(H)	(H)	(L-M)	(M)	(M)	(M)	(L)	(L)
Degree of direct personal coordination	(L)	(M)	(M-H)	(H)	(L-M)	(M)	(M-H)	(H)
Number of visits	(M)	(M)	(H)	(H)	(L)	(L)	(H)	(H)
Number of transfers	(M)	(L)	(H)	(H)	(L)	(L)	(H)	(L)
Importance of culture-based coordination	(M)	(M)	(H)	(H)	(L)	(M)	(H)	(H)

[1287] Interview 11:47.

Direct personal coordination seems to play a more important role than anticipated. In one case, its value was higher than expected, in three other cases the values were at the upper end of what we had expected. We can derive two findings from this: Direct personal coordination seems to be the one mechanism of relevance for many kinds of service offshoring relationships. Its importance varies but it is always on a high level, which is exactly the opposite finding of what we have learned with regard to autonomy. In addition, it is also needed to change or to complement other coordination mechanisms, such as, for instance, personal discussions to evaluate the results from output control. Thus, direct personal coordination can be considered a) in itself an important coordination mechanism in service offshoring and b) an important complement to other coordination mechanisms.

Contrary to expectations, we found almost no *transfers* between providers and receivers of services. We can offer a number of explanations for this phenomenon: As discussed in the introduction, an attractive characteristic of service offshoring is the low labor cost that the destination countries offer. This advantage, however, is reduced by expensive transfers. One interviewee explained that a single expatriate could cost as much as 25 local employees (*"So jemand kostet so viel wie 25 Mitarbeiter. Mit Haus und Auto und pi-pa-po und Riesengehalt und Expatriate. Der kostet dann noch mehr als er in Deutschland kostet. Es ist nicht so, dass es weniger wird, weil er in Bulgarien ist. Und deswegen lohnt sich das überhaupt nicht.*"[1288]) In addition, the short distances between Western Europe and Eastern Europe make frequent visits feasible which in turn limits the need for transfers. This is supported by the fact that the only transfers we found in our research were in the case of Beta Center, which is located in a Russian city with few flights to Western Europe. Finally, with a small cultural distance – as between Western and Eastern Europe – MNCs are less likely to use transfers.[1289] We therefore conclude that transfers do not play an important role in service offshoring, at least not when the service is provided from relatively near locations.

Finally, the degree of *culture-based coordination* is in one case higher than expected and in the other three as assumed. While this result is close to our expectations, the one deviation towards a higher value could point to a similar finding as in the case of direct personal coordination. Cultural coordination is considered important in many circum-

---

[1288] Interview 10:188.
[1289] Gong (2003).

stances (even in cases such as Gamma where it is not explicitly promoted by top management).[1290]

Besides these specific findings relating to the coordination mechanisms, we have collected several indications that point to some specific coordination problems in service offshoring situations. We discuss them here since they underline the necessity for our research once more. Our interviewees pointed to three specific problems:

(1) A new service offshoring unit in an MNC can be seen as a threat to the job security of the employees in the original location. This can lead to situations in which there are exaggerated demands from the service offshoring unit,[1291] or to prejudices such as described by a manager of Delta Center who explained that at the beginning of the collaboration he was confronted with statements from his German colleagues that he should lay off 90 per cent of the staff in the Bulgarian subsidiary without affecting the results *("Und da war schon sehr viel gegeneinander, so als Zitat. Jemand sagte: 'Von den 100 Bulgaren kannst du 90 rauswerfen, das gleiche wird dabei rauskommen'"*[1292]*)*. This might increase especially the need for cultural coordination to achieve alignment of goals.

(2) The explicit move of tasks and responsibilities to another location also makes the need for a clear interface between the units become very evident. Each party needs to know exactly what its tasks are, since the physical distance often makes ad-hoc coordination much more difficult than before. *("All the problems like the overhead of the management, overhead of the communication, the ownership of the main, the headquarters is missing, things like that, so it's not working. ... so if we here as location are not well integrated it's not going to work."*[1293]*)*. And despite the physical separation there is a need to identify the right measures to make the "chemistry work" between the sub-units; one interviewee explained that interpersonal relationships are necessary for offshoring success but cannot be established through electronic exchange alone *("Die Chemie kann elektronisch nicht stimmen."*[1294]*)*.

(3) Finally, the offshoring of tasks that nobody at the headquarters wants to bother doing, will most likely not result in a success. The "offshoring of problems" might gain

---

[1290] In addition, we found another influencing factor on cultural coordination that we will discuss in section 7.3.2.
[1291] Such as in the case of Gamma (see section 6.3 for the case description).
[1292] Interview 11:7. These problems, however, have now been overcome (interview 11:15).
[1293] Interview 13:59; confirmed by interviews 3:81, 5:5, and 20:10.
[1294] Interview 3:12.

some time by delegating a problem to an offshore unit but the underlying problem is unlikely to be resolved. One interviewee from Delta explained that it is a difficult situation when the person taking a decision (he referred to headquarters) does not directly suffer any consequences (at least in the short term) (*"Es ist ein Problem, wenn die Entscheidungsträger nicht direkt Notleidende sind bei einem Problem."*[1295]).

To sum up, we have overestimated the role that autonomy and transfers play for service offshoring and underestimated the importance of direct personal coordination and, to a very slight degree, that of cultural coordination. For the other coordination mechanisms (formalization, standardization, output control, visits) and overall coordination requirements, our expectations were appropriate. While we have not identified additional coordination mechanisms, we have found several indicators for specific coordination needs in service offshoring situations.

7.2.3 COMPARATIVE ANALYSIS OF COORDINATION MECHANISMS

While we think that the analysis of interview content is the most important and most reliable source of information, we also have the (limited) possibility of quantitative analysis by counting codings per category. The underlying assumption is that the more often a specific code occurs per case, the more important that code is for the case. Obviously, one can easily create counter-arguments and therefore, we need to be cautious in the quantitative part of our analysis. However, we believe that there are some interesting indications to be gained from this sort of analysis. Therefore, we calculated how often each coordination mechanism was discussed per case. We counted the codings per coordination mechanism and divided them by the number of all quotations that relate to coordination mechanisms, of which we found 528 in total. The distribution over the different coordination mechanisms can be seen in Table 7-3. We have highlighted in bold figures the highest value for each coordination mechanism that we obtained.[1296]

The highest value for *structural mechanisms* is in Beta, though this is only very slightly higher than Gamma's value, making it hard to derive more robust findings. Overall, however, the low values for structural mechanisms can be seen to support our above finding that structural mechanisms do not play the most important role in service offshoring constellations.

[1295] Interview 3:105.
[1296] In addition, we carried out a Chi-Square analysis that tests for significant differences between the distribution of quotes across our cases. We found highly significant results for Alpha and Delta (p < 0,001).

7 – Discussion

Table 7-3: Distribution of quotations over coordination mechanisms

Case	Structural mechanisms	Technocratic mechanisms	Output-based mechanisms	Personal mechanisms	Total codes
Alpha	1.7%	**11.2%**	**5.1%**	11.6%	156
Beta	**3.0%**	4.7%	3.0%	11.6%	118
Gamma	2.8%	6.8%	1.7%	10.8%	117
Delta	2.5%	3.8%	1.9%	**17.8%**	137
Sum	10.0%	26.5%	11.7%	51.7%	528

With regard to *technocratic mechanisms*, we found the highest value in the case of Alpha. This is supportive of our earlier findings which showed that Alpha relies to a great extent on technocratic mechanisms such as standardization and formalization. For the other cases, the values are again rather similar which makes it hard to derive additional findings. In the case of Gamma, however, it shows the effect of the extended discussion we had with interviewees about the usefulness of implementing technocratic measures.

Output-based coordination is most often cited in Alpha. This again is in line with the findings of our interviews' content analysis which show that output control is an important mechanism for the service factory. The close proximity of the figures for the other cases again makes further differentiation hard.

Delta shows the highest value for *personal coordination mechanisms*. This reflects what we derived earlier from our content analysis. However, in our content analysis we found the same importance of personal coordination mechanisms in the case of Beta. This is not reflected in the numbers in the table, which is testimony to the limitations of the quantitative approach. However, we still consider it relevant for another reason: In our last column, we show the number of total codes per case that relate to coordination mechanisms. It shows that we have roughly the same number of codes per case which is a good basis for comparison. In addition, it shows that each of our findings is based on a large number of individual indications. This makes our findings more robust. Used in this way, quantitative analysis can serve as a "sanity check" for the findings of qualitative research and can thereby increase its reliability and credibility.

7.2.4 IMPLICATIONS OF FINDINGS FOR TYPES OF SERVICE OFFSHORING SUBSIDIARY

We now focus on the implications of our findings for each of the types we have derived theoretically. We exclude transfers from our further considerations, as these do not seem to play an important role for service offshoring.

- Our original description of the *service factory* seems appropriate, as a high degree of initial supported propositions attests. However, autonomy was higher than expected. We have explained this in the case of Alpha by the organizational split in a supply and a demand organization that display market-like behavior. Still, for a service factory like Alpha, which strongly resembles a profit center, a higher level of autonomy is supported in the literature.[1297] Thus, we think for further applications of our typology one should distinguish between cases where a service factory is designed as a profit center like Alpha (with somewhat higher autonomy) or as a traditional cost center (with low autonomy). In addition, we underestimated the degree of direct personal coordination that is required to coordinate a service factory. Despite the reliance on technocratic measures and the findings that support our assumed focus on efficiency, direct personal coordination still plays an important role for a service factory.

- When we initially described the *internal competence center*, we assumed a conflict between the demands for autonomy and technocratic measures. It seems that the degree of autonomy is only medium for the internal competence center for the reasons we discussed above. Indeed, this type of center relies primarily on personal coordination as the most important mechanism and complements it with some elements of standardization, formalization, and output control to make coordination more efficient. However, in cases of conflict, the individual adaptation of services and personalized coordination (in the form of personal coordination mechanisms) will be more important than increasing efficiency. Thus, autonomy does not play such an important role. The assumed focus on quality and effectiveness was initially supported by our findings.

- For the *support center* we found the levels of direct personal coordination and cultural coordination to be higher than expected. As discussed above, direct per-

---

[1297] See Ronen/MacKiney III (1970), pp. 99-101, Colling/Ferner (1992), pp. 209-211, Dorestani (2004), p. 1905.

sonal coordination serves as a default coordination mechanism and consequently plays this role for the support center as well. The same argument holds true for cultural coordination.

- Finally, the initial description of the *specialized contributor* still seems appropriate. We found autonomy to be less than expected and argue that this is due to the fact that the role of autonomy is overall limited for service offshoring (as we have argued above). In addition, we found technocratic mechanisms to be at the upper end of the expected values. We tend to think that this is due to the complexity of Delta's product and can be ascribed to the individual case rather than to the specialized contributor as general type.

Overall, we were able to empirically identify the types we had derived theoretically. We not only found clear differences in the independent variables but also many agreements with regard to coordination mechanisms. We therefore regard our typology as initially supported. The only changes we propose to the original types are a higher level of direct personal coordination, exclusion of transfers, and reduction of autonomy. Accordingly, we arrive at the new overview of types as displayed in Table 7-4.

Table 7-4: Overview of adapted characteristics of service offshoring subsidiaries

Coordination mechanism	Service Factory	Internal Competence Center	Support Center	Specialized Contributor
Extent of coordination requirements	▪-■ (L-M)	■-■ (M-H)	▪ (L)	■-■ (M-H)
Degree of autonomy	▪ (L). Low strategic relevance does not need high degree of autonomy	■ (M). High strategic relevance in the center requires more autonomy but limited due to focus on internal services	▪ (L). Services are ordered from the customer on a case-by-case basis; decisions are taken by customers	■ (M). High strategic relevance in the center requires more autonomy but limited due to focus on internal services

Coordination mechanism	Service Factory	Internal Competence Center	Support Center	Specialized Contributor
Degree of standardization	■ (H). As many customers need to be served, aiming for economies of scale	■ (M). High strategic relevance will require flexibility but trade-off because of high number of customers that will require standardization for complexity reasons	■ (L). As support center is used on a case-by-case basis, standardization is not necessary/possible	■-■ (L-M). High strategic relevance will require flexibility
Degree of formalization	■ (H). Many standardized cases make formalization appropriate	■ (M). High number of clients require formalization but individual solutions cause trade-off	■ (L). Few standardized cases do not require formalization	■-■ (L-M). Individual cases and high competences will need flexibility
Degree of output control	■ (H). Many network partners require pre-specification of results	■-■ (L-M). Diversified and complex requirements prevent pre-specification of results; however, partially offset by need to deal with many network partners	■ (M). Low strategic relevance does not justify resource-intense behavior control	■ (L). Behavior control more appropriate for high strategic relevance

Coordination mechanism	Service Factory	Internal Competence Center	Support Center	Specialized Contributor
Degree of personal direct coordination	■ (M). Execution of standardized services needs little direct interaction; however, needed as complement to other mechanisms	■ (H). Strategic relevance makes personal interaction necessary	■ (M). Execution of strategically less relevant services needs little direct interaction; however, needed as the standard coordination mechanism	■ (H). Strategic relevance makes personal interaction necessary
Number of visits	■ (M). Medium number of visits, medium duration per visit	■ (H). High number of visits, long duration per visit	▪ (L). Low number of visits, short duration per visit	■ (H). High number of visits, long duration per visit
Importance of culture-based coordination	■ (M). Medium level of normative integration	■ (H). High level of normative integration	▪ (L). Low level of normative integration	■ (H). High level of normative integration

7.2.5 NEWLY IDENTIFIED FACTORS INFLUENCING COORDINATION

During the case study research and the interview data analysis we identified several variables that seem to influence coordination in service offshoring situations. Our categorization of coordination mechanisms worked well and we found no additional mechanisms. But service offshoring seems to have some specifics that can impact on the use of coordination mechanisms.

However, before we report on these findings, we discuss how they influence our initial model. We identified additional factors that have an impact on the use of coordination mechanisms. However, they do not per se create coordination need (that is in our research influenced by strategic relevance and network embeddedness). Rather, they have an influence of how the need for coordination translates in coordination mechanisms. We had originally assumed that the coordination need directly causes the use of different coordination mechanisms. Now, we introduce the new factor coordination use that stands for the mix of coordination mechanisms actually applied. The coordination need determines the use of coordination mechanisms (as expressed in coordination use). However, from our empirical findings we learned that a series of factors can impact upon the relationship between coordination need and coordination use. Thus, we introduce these factors as moderating variables. The change of our model is represented in Figure 7-1.

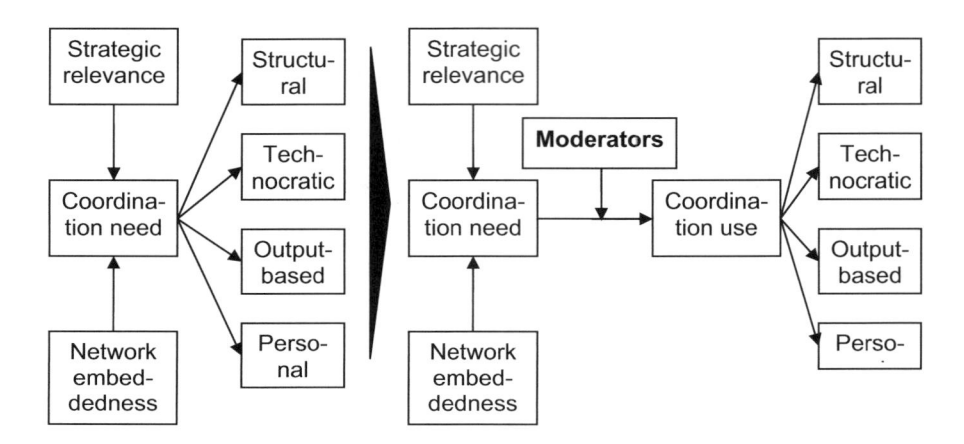

Figure 7-1: Change in factor model

Our initial understanding is represented on the left-hand side of the figure. The coordination need directly influences the use of coordination mechanisms. We have identified several moderating variables that can influence the actual use of coordination mechanisms and have therefore introduced the new factor "coordination use". All of the new factors work as moderators and all but one directly influence the relationship between coordination need and coordination use. We will now discuss in detail each of the additional factors (1) language skills, (2) technological infrastructure, (3) top management commitment, and (4) physical distance.

(1) The influence of *language skills* on coordination is a topic that almost all of our interviewees addressed. There were several concerns about language barriers that prevent efficient interaction and that result in errors and duplication of effort (*"Und ich glaube, das ist ein Thema, das viele noch unterschätzen, dass es da eine grundsätzliche Sprachbarriere gibt."*[1298]). In addition, translations between languages are costly, take time and might

---

[1298] Interview 2:1; confirmed by interview 2:3.

7 – Discussion   351

lead to information losses (*"Ein Problem ist, dass wir die Pflichtenhefte ... auf Deutsch bekommen. Das müssen wir übersetzen. Ich übersetze es am besten, denn wenn wir es mit einem Übersetzungsbüro machen, dann geht die Information leider verloren."*[1299]; *"Wenn wir ein Angebot ausgeben, ... dann schreibe ich fünf Tage, davon drei Tage Übersetzung."*[1300]). It might also be difficult to agree on a common language for interaction especially if German companies need to opt for either German or English in their interactions with Eastern European service offshoring subsidiaries. Although English is the language that is more used in Gamma, employees speak better German than English both at the German headquarters and in the Hungarian subsidiary (*"[Gamma] muss ein internationales Team sein und das bedeutet, dass wir eine Sprache wählen müssen, die die offizielle Sprache sein wird und das ist Englisch. ... Ich denke Englisch ist eine Scheinlösung. Weil keiner von den Deutschen wirklich gut Englisch spricht und wir müssen zugeben, eigentlich auch keiner von uns."*[1301]). However, other interviewees reported that even basic language skills are sufficient if both parties are willing to work together and develop their "own" mix of languages (*"... and they talked together in a kind of mix of English, German and Hungarian, but it works perfectly."*[1302]; *"If you see the e-mail ... the English is very funny, but they understand each other and this is the important thing. It does not have to be Oxford English."*[1303]). However, it was stressed that theoretical language skills alone are not sufficient (*"It's interesting because you can have people that pass language tests and they get certified at a level of competency and then you still have language issues."*[1304]). Rather, it seems important to have employees who have broad general communication skills; therefore, in one case the management offered not only language training but also general communication training courses (*"Und überhaupt Kommunikationsfragen. Wir haben allen Englischkurse verordnet im Endeffekt und wir haben auch Kommunikations- und Präsentationskurse gemacht."*[1305]). In conclusion, testable language skills are important but need to be complemented by general communication skills to make coordination work and avoid misunderstandings. Even though they might especially facilitate personal coordination mechanisms, they support all categories of coordination mechanisms. We thus propose a moderating role of language skills (including general communication skills) on the relationship between coordination need and coordination use.

[1299] Interview 3:118; confirmed by interview 3:126.
[1300] Interview 3:122.
[1301] Interview 3:122-123.
[1302] Interview 1:6.
[1303] Interview 1:193; confirmed by interviews 4:101, 7:177, 10:92, and 19:93.
[1304] Interview 18:44; confirmed by interviews 12:30 and 12:132.
[1305] Interview 11:19.

(2) The *technology infrastructure* was addressed in some cases by interviewees, especially in subsidiaries that had been acquired and not set up as new units of an MNC. The technology infrastructure consists mainly of access to phones, email/internet, video conferencing facilities, and the MNC IT network. The acquired subsidiaries in our sample (Gamma Center and Delta Center) started with very few phones, without internet and email access for all employees, and with only restricted access to the MNC IT network (*"there were four phones in the building, ... one phone number for the development team, and the development team is basically seven or eight guys"*[1306]; *"That's really the key with the connectivity. Because before ... we were not seeing each other and everything was transferred through Hotmail ... This was not so secure to send it."*[1307]). After the acquisition, they were either raised to modern standards shortly after the takeover (in the case of Delta Center) or they were slowly upgraded over time (Gamma Center).[1308] The lack of access to phones and email leads to coordination occurring only at the level of management (*"... a lot of people in Sofia they are not exposed. They are developers and they need to speak to other developers, but very often the communication was via other people."*[1309]; *"... only the managers and team leaders were communicating directly with headquarters in Germany."*[1310]). On the other hand, the broad availability of video conferencing facilities, which has now been introduced, helps to include many employees from all levels of hierarchy in the coordination of service delivery (*"Four tele-conference rooms which we use like all the time."*[1311]). Eventually, Delta Center was upgraded to a technological status that makes the distance between the service offshoring subsidiary and the headquarters hardly matter (*"Citrix terminal which he can use for the mail and office and everything ... or if we go to the separate location many people export their machines with Win-C or with NetMeeting share, so it doesn't matter. The location doesn't matter."*[1312]). In the case of Alpha Center, the technology in the center is so advanced that it has surpassed that of other units of the firm. Thus, there is no technological hurdle for coordination but rather a motivation for other units to learn from Alpha Center (*"Plus this is a very much state of the art technology center. It's pretty impressive to look around it."*[1313]). To sum up, the level of technological infrastructure can influence coordination and either facilitate or hinder the use of coordina-

---

[1306] Interview 12:32.
[1307] Interview 13:249-250.
[1308] Interview 3:91.
[1309] Interview 12:32.
[1310] Interview 13:14.
[1311] Interview 13:40.
[1312] Interview 13:246. Citrix is a software product that allows remote access to applications.
[1313] Interview 16:54; confirmed by interview 18:36.

tion mechanisms. Therefore, we propose a moderating influence of the level of technological infrastructure on the relationship between coordination need and coordination use.

(3) Another factor is the *commitment* that the management of the MNC makes to the service offshoring subsidiary.[1314] In the case of Delta Center, one interviewee explained that he – as the former managing director of the center – had invested a lot in the infrastructure of the center to enhance the quality of the services and to convince the employees that Delta was in there for the long term. This paid off over time since employees were more motivated and Delta was taken very seriously as an important and attractive employer in the country (*"Was ich denke, dass wichtig ist, ist, dass man die Standards richtig setzt. Also viele gehen in diese Länder und machen erst mal so Minimalinvest. ... Und wenn man sich so aufstellt, dass man mehr oder weniger über Nacht alles in einen Koffer packen kann und abreisen kann, dann hat man auch die entsprechende Mentalität. Und das habe ich sehr schnell sehr stark geändert. ... Das ist zwar ein initialer Invest, der teuer ist. Aber das zahlt sich schon langfristig aus, weil die Leute merken, wow, die meinen es echt ernst. Das ist nicht irgendwie eine Spielwiese, die wir dann schnell schließen, wenn es nicht tut, sondern es ist ernst gemeint. ... Es ist wichtig, dass die Leute erkennen, aha, da kommt einer rein, der meint es wirklich ernst, der hat langfristig Interesse am Land. Das geht vom Mitarbeiter bis hin zur Regierung."*[1315]). Commitment is not limited to financial investment. It can also have the effect of overcoming internal resistance to service offshoring and giving the center more credibility (*"... ich hab die Bulgaren im Endeffekt auch darüber gewonnen, dass sie gemerkt haben, ich stehe vor ihnen. ... nach außen eigentlich von Anfang an mich vor sie gestellt und gesagt, diese ganzen Vorurteile "bunch of students", ... das kann nicht die Arbeitsgrundlage sein. ... Und das habe ich auf allen Ebenen gemacht und das haben sie gesehen und sehr honoriert."*[1316]). Thus, commitment seems to be positively related to the creation of shared goals and team spirit. We therefore consider it a factor that is associated with cultural coordination. While it can be relevant in any kind of international distribution of labor, we think it seems to be of special importance for service offshoring where there might be an increased risk of the service offshoring center and its employees being considered "a cheap resource". We therefore propose a moderating role of commitment on the relationship between personal coordination and cultural coordination.

[1314] Management commitment is also counted as a key success factor for offshoring by other authors (see, for instance, Williams (2003), p. 19, Reichert (2005), pp. 91-93).
[1315] Interview 10:254; confirmed by interviews 3:30, 10:90 and 11:3.
[1316] Interview 11:7; confirmed by interviews 1:187 and 5:1.

(4) Finally, we evaluate the influence on coordination of the *physical distance* from the service offshoring subsidiary to other units. Several interviewees reported that the moving of services away from the original location changes coordination mechanisms and makes coordination more difficult (*"Die Erfahrung, die wir damit gemacht haben, ist, dass es schwierig ist, auf so einer großen Distanz gut zu steuern."*[1317]; *"Sie können nirgendwo reinschauen, und das ist schon ein Problem, mit dem man umgehen muss"*[1318]). In addition, new information needs to be explicitly made available to the offshore location (*"Die Schwierigkeit ist immer, also das Geschäft entwickelt sich ja immer weiter in [headquarters]. ... Und diese Neuigkeiten müssen erst einmal transportiert werden."*[1319]). The larger the distance between units, the more difficult coordination becomes. Therefore, several interviewees reported on their preference to move services from Continental Europe to Eastern Europe rather than to a more remote location such as India (*"However, I think what is a trend that's starting ... is that many offshore companies, ... I am referring to India, China or Asia in general, are looking to the Central Europe and around to establish themselves also in Europe. They are responding to the desire of some of the decision makers in European context who are not so adventurous to go and establish themselves or invite a partner from India. It's a hassle to fly there, it's long and expensive and there is a big culture difference, ... If they had this opportunity nearshore, which would be Central Europe and around, they would probably be less reluctant to go that direction. So what we see is the Tata, Infosys and other companies building up their bases in Hungary, Poland, Slovakia, Czech Republic and so on and offering pretty much the same prices as their counterparts in India."*[1320]). In addition, it seems that companies find ways to alleviate the initial difficulties that come with the physical distance. This can be done by increased visits, by the development of a common team spirit and by the development of personal relationships between units (*"It is the mainly the people, that if you are working in two offices. One is here and one is in the other part of the city and you have to go from here to the other part of the city and it will take you one hour or two hours, it's not a big difference if you have to take the plane and go to [location of headquarters]. ... That's why I think that even for a small country like Bulgaria to the way of thinking that you have to travel several hours and sit with people to work after that for several days, it's considered the absolutely normal. ... The developers here know very well that for the projects we develop we need far more people, so with the 300 developers, that's not enough to create such important product. ... So having in mind that they have to make it really very regular, it is a part

---

[1317] Interview 9:2; confirmed by interview 9:4.
[1318] Interview 9:6.
[1319] Interview 9:16; confirmed by interviews 20:17 and 20:19.
[1320] Interview 15:1; confirmed by interviews 11:5 and 16:1.

7 – Discussion 355

of the working time."[1321]). Thus, physical distance generally seems to lead to an increased need for coordination to which MNCs need to react by adapting their use of coordination mechanisms.[1322] Over time, the perceived coordination need might decrease slightly as people get used to working at a distance. However, the different collaboration modes in service offshoring in comparison to local collaboration persist. To conclude, we propose a moderating role for physical distance on the relation between coordination need and coordination use.

The newly identified factors do not make changes to our typology necessary since they impact all types in the same way. Rather, they can be considered context factors that need to be analyzed in future studies on the coordination of service offshoring subsidiaries. We have, therefore, incorporated them in our factor model that we introduced in its original form above.[1323] We now present and discuss this enhanced version. Figure 7-2 shows the original model where we introduced "coordination use" as just explained. Other changes were not necessary change since our main propositions were initially supported. We have added the factors identified above. Most of these work as moderators on the relation between coordination need and coordination use. The factors language skills, technology infrastructure, and physical distance impact upon this relation. Commitment works as moderating variable on the use of cultural coordination.

[1321] Interview 14:19; confirmed by interviews 11:3 and 20:39.
[1322] We have also observed that the physical distance is also negatively related to the duration of visits (see section 6.1.4).
[1323] For the description of the original model see section 5.2.4.3.

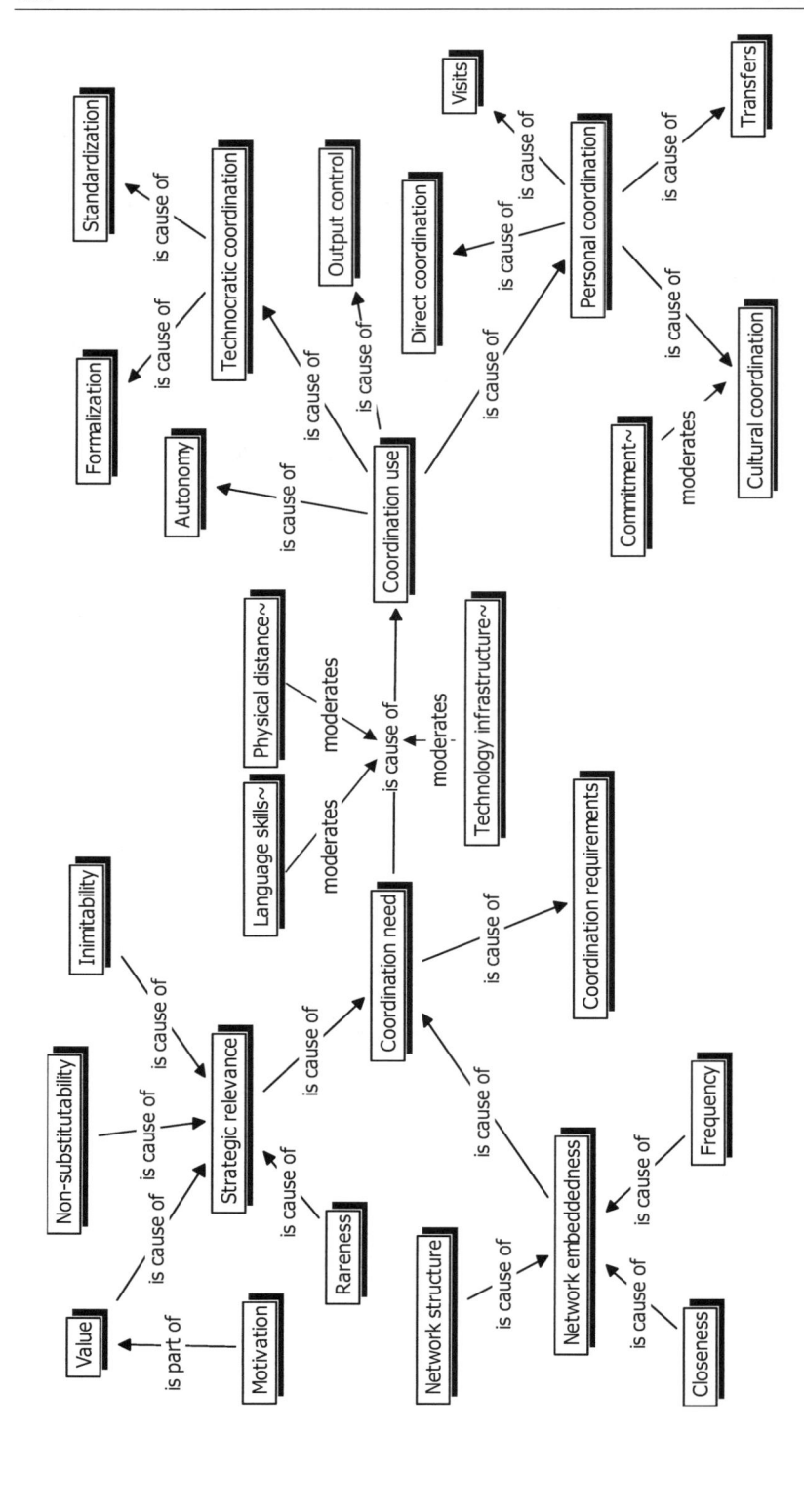

Figure 7-2: Enhanced factor model

7.3 ADDITIONAL FINDINGS RELATING TO TYPOLOGY

We have now discussed all our findings relating to the core topic of our study – coordination mechanisms. However, we have also derived several other findings that relate to our typology.

7.3.1 APPLICATION OF THE TYPOLOGY TO DIFFERENT LEVELS OF ANALYSIS

In our first case study (service factory Alpha Center) we had to limit our analysis to a part of the services that Alpha Center provides.[1324] This is due to the fact that Alpha Center is a very large service offshoring subsidiary with over 1,000 employees. However, smaller subsidiaries can also provide a variety of services. We found services with different levels of strategic relevance within Alpha Center and therefore focused on those services that are at the lower end of strategic relevance. Some comments in interviews allude to the fact that those services within Alpha that are of higher strategic relevance also require different coordination mechanisms. This argument is supportive of our typology. However, it also shows that the typology can be applied at the level of an individual department if the service offshoring center is rather large and diverse. Our typology would support an analysis of a lower level such as, for instance, a department instead of the entire subsidiary.

However, it might also prove interesting to analyze service offshoring at a higher level. Again, we refer to our experiences from Alpha Center. Alpha Center is only one in a group of four international centers that provide IT services to Alpha. Our analysis focused on one service offshoring subsidiary and its service delivery relationships to other units of the firm. The Alpha Center case shows how service offshoring can be used to distribute work around the world in a rotating system and gives initial confirmation to the "follow-the-sun" model that we described above and that is one of the differences between service and manufacturing offshoring.[1325] Since our unit of analysis is the service offshoring subsidiary, our findings do not directly relate to the coordination of a worldwide distributed system. We think that the typology can still be used to explain the coordination of a single center but it would be more difficult to apply it to the coordination of several – potentially different – centers within one MNC.

[1324] The same was true of Beta Center, though for Beta we only had to exclude one department.
[1325] For that discussion, see section 2.2.4.2.

7.3.2 IMPACT OF ENTRY MODE DECISION ON COORDINATION

One question within international business research is the setup of an international subsidiary as a new center or by an acquisition. The service center Alpha Center and the internal competence center Beta Center were both set up as new centers, while the support center Gamma Center and the specialized contributor Delta Center were built from the acquisition of existing companies. However, the influence of the original company is no longer felt in Delta Center. The former managing director explained that it has disappeared ("... *der ist verschwunden*"[1326]). Another interviewee added: "*... everybody more or less now likes being part of the bigger company. Nobody really wants to or likes having this independent company.*"[1327] That Gamma Center was an independent company, however, still plays a role in Gamma (*"Und das sind so Sachen, wo die eingefleischte Kultur in [name of old company] langsam nachgeben muss, damit es in eine etwas steifere [Gamma]-Kultur eingliedern kann."*[1328]) even though both companies are roughly of the same age. The new centers on the other hand, again differ from one another: In Alpha Center it seems more difficult to build up a single corporate culture since many expatriates were hired from other units within Alpha. Beta Center, however, has only employees who are new to the firm together with a few transfers. Thus, it has been able to develop its own corporate culture. Consequently, there seem to be several important factors that can emphasize or smooth the effects of the original entry mode decision.

7.3.3 RELEVANCE OF THE SERVICE OFFSHORING SUBSIDIARY'S LOCAL NETWORK

We focused our analysis on the intra-organizational network. This approach was appropriate as the intra-organizational network seems the most important for the subsidiaries that do not have many local relationships. We found one indication of this in the case of Delta: Even though Delta Center is located in the same office building as the local sales organization that distributes Delta's product in Bulgaria, there are almost no relationships between the two organizations (*"We share only the network."*[1329]). This confirms the minor importance of the local sales market for the service offshoring subsidiary Delta Center. Interestingly, however, it was also Delta Center where we found that the local network can still be of some significance for other areas. Delta Center had long attracted many programmers because it is not only one of the largest software firms in Bulgaria but also the only one that develops a complex product and has therefore more challeng-

---

[1326] Interview 10:240.
[1327] Interview 12:152; confirmed by interview 12:154.
[1328] Interview 3:134; confirmed by interview 3:132.
[1329] Interview 13:339; confirmed by interviews 10:65-66, 10:68, and 14:3.

ing work to offer than the typical Bulgarian software firm which carries out mainly short-term projects without much product responsibility (*"Und wir sind die einzige Firma, die ein Produkt in Bulgarien entwickelt. Dadurch sind wir immer sehr attraktiv für potenzielle Bewerber."*[1330]). However, given the relatively small market for software engineers in Bulgaria, Delta Center realized after a while that it would destroy the local recruiting market if it attracted too many of the best employees. Therefore, it started a program to develop and increase the size of the entire market so that it would also eventually benefit from easier access to future qualified employees. Interviewees referred Delta Center's intention of wanting to protect and develop the local *"eco system"*[1331] of education in computer science, employment opportunities, and a network of other software development firms. Delta Center consequently started to purchase software services from eight local providers. As a result, it not only released itself from the pressure to hire more employees, but it also gained access to some specialized knowledge that it needed only from time to time and therefore was too costly to build up internally. By now, almost all major software companies in Bulgaria are Delta Center's partners and Delta Center has introduced these partners in the list of Delta's worldwide network of contractors (*"Almost all big companies in Bulgaria that we have are our partners. Recently we had something like an audit and we created the list of preferable clients and they will be published [Delta]-wide"*[1332]). We have here an example of how a service offshoring center actively develops capabilities in its external partners to improve its service offering to internal customers.[1333] Moreover, and potentially the most important argument, it trained employees from other firms by working with them according to Delta-internal standards (*"... we started the same principles that we have with [name of headquarters location]. So regular meetings, regular calls, regular workshops, we have a kind of good training facility here and the people gather together in big rooms and they discuss the projects and everything, so, it's more or less the same principle."*[1334]). That way, it will be much easier to recruit people with the right skills in the future (*"This is the source of new experienced people that we potentially can have."*[1335]).

[1330] Interview 11:9; confirmed by interview 10:80 and 11:11.
[1331] Interview 13:146; the wish to grow the local market is confirmed by interviews 14:5, 14:8, and 14:9.
[1332] Interview 13:139.
[1333] See Schmid/Schurig (2003) for the development of capabilities in subsidiaries.
[1334] Interview 13:157; confirmed by interviews 13:124 and 13:128.
[1335] Interview 13:170. There are of course contractual obligations that Delta Center cannot immediately hire away contractors from other companies (interview 13:168).

In Beta Center, an important element in the local network was the cooperation with local universities that helped Beta Center – together with its attractiveness to students as the only foreign employer in the city – to train potential future employees with those skills that the center needs for the execution of its services (*"We cooperate with University. In [city name] University we have sixty students. They each train according to our training plans in addition to their main academic training plans."*[1336]). This has led to a situation where Beta can very easily hire the graduates it needs for further growth and thus potentially build a competitive advantage over competitors with centers in more "crowded" cities (*"But there is definite potential for growth across the board ... the state university here churns out thousands of degree students every year so we have the potential, and that's not the only university."*[1337]). Thus, the local network can be used in different ways by service offshoring subsidiaries to improve their effectiveness and efficiency.[1338] It also confirms existing research that sees a positive relationship between the strategic relevance and the likeliness of creating local networks.[1339]

7.3.4 PERCEPTION GAPS BETWEEN HEADQUARTERS AND SERVICE OFFSHORING SUBSIDIARY

Our research design took into consideration the potentially different perspectives between headquarters, subsidiaries and service offshoring centers. We would have observed these by asking all parties the same set of questions and comparing their answers. In most cases, however, we actually did not encounter any major divergences, though in the case of Gamma, some perception gaps were identified. While headquarters considered itself to make most of the decisions (high centralization of decision making), some interviewees from the service offshoring subsidiary argued that they had more autonomy. Similarly, a project from headquarters aiming at a higher degree of standardization and formalization was not unanimously viewed as necessary and positive by all interviewees. There are a number of possible reasons for these differences: On the one hand, there could be genuine differences. A potential remedy could be a higher degree of cultural coordination that could help to better align goals and create a shared vision across the units. Alternatively, the difference could also stem from the fact that Gamma Center is slowly increasing the strategic relevance of its services. By doing

---

[1336] Interview 7:165.
[1337] Interview 6:94; confirmed by interview 4:7.
[1338] Recent research has shown that scientific institutions in the local network of an international subsidiary can have positive influence on subsidiary R&D activity (Davis/Meyer (2004)).
[1339] Chen et al. (2004), pp. 328-329.

7 – Discussion

so, coordination mechanisms will most likely change over time. This process might lead to different perspectives on the appropriate use of these mechanisms. Thus, perception gaps might be only temporary. However, if they persist, the can severely impede coordination.

7.3.5 CHANGES OF TYPES OVER TIME

An interesting aspect is the development of the service offshoring subsidiaries over time. In almost all of the cases, we witnessed a planned or ongoing organizational change. These changes can be discussed along the dimensions of our typology and also had some effects on coordination mechanisms. We will discuss the changes for (1) Alpha, (2) Beta, and (3) Gamma.[1340]

1. *Alpha* is undergoing a large-scale transformation in which it has centralized several support functions in shared services centers (some of them offshore as in the case of Alpha Center). At the same time, it has established some market-like principles between the provider and receiver of services. While these new principles had been decided upon already, implementation is still ongoing. In our case study, we found that the centralization of IT services was still in progress, with increasingly more services being moved into Alpha Center. In parallel, the former IT function that had formed one organizational unit, had been split up into a demand and a supply organization. The demand side is working with the business units to define their IT requirements. The supply side is now centralized in four centers around the world and is in charge of responding to demands from the business units. While this principle has been clearly established, implementation is still ongoing. It is supported by projects that define the interfaces between the two sides and establish principles of coordination. Thus, the current movement can be seen as an increase in network embeddedness that should, in accordance with the propositions from our typology, also lead to higher levels of standardization and formalization. We were actually able to observe this in our empirical findings as well. Interviewees frequently referred to the changes and the need to standardize and formalize in order to make the interaction and the delivery of services more efficient. Thus, the Alpha case is an indicator that the typology can also be used to analyze the movement between different types.

[1340] In the case of Delta, the only ongoing change was the development of a local network of suppliers. We have already discussed this point above.

2. *Beta* Center is currently taking on more projects from other international subsidiaries of Beta. It is establishing closer collaboration and thus, increasing the level of network embeddedness. While strategic relevance is already on a high level, it is aiming to offer its customers even more value-added services and to take over services that are even more valuable, rare, inimitable and non-substitutable. That way, it is also increasing its strategic relevance. An increase in both dimensions should theoretically lead to an increase in autonomy (a decrease in centralization of decision making) and a higher degree of technocratic coordination mechanisms. We were in fact able to observe both tendencies. On the one hand, Beta Center was gaining more autonomy which is probably best expressed through its desire to acquire its own local customers. On the other hand, it had recognized the need to standardize relationships to be able to deal with the increase in complexity that comes with the addition of new relationships. Thus, Beta Center is another example of how our typology can be used to handle changes in the type of service offshoring subsidiary.

3. As already discussed, *Gamma* is in the process of introducing more technocratic coordination to obtain an ISO certificate. We want to discuss this change with regard to our typology: It shows us in a very basic case how a subsidiary can develop over time and eventually change its coordination mechanisms.[1341] Besides, it demonstrates that there can be different factors that influence coordination mechanisms apart from the two dimensions that we have included in our typology. However, we still want to evaluate another ongoing change. In addition to the development towards greater standardization and formalization, Gamma Center also seems to be gaining strategic relevance (at least from the perspective of the service offshoring subsidiary itself).[1342] But if we look at our propositions, we find that an increase in strategic relevance is not expected to lead to a higher degree of technocratic measures. Our propositions rather suggest that such a move is caused by an increase in network embeddedness. During our interviews, however, we did not find any indication of a transition towards a higher level of network embeddedness. There could be two possible explanations for this: One could argue that these are two independent situations with the implementation of the ISO standard (and the increase in technocratic

---

[1341] See also our discussion of hybridization in section 4.3.
[1342] See the description and discussion of the case in section 6.3.

7 – Discussion

coordination) being caused by an event that is not related to the expected increase in strategic relevance.[1343] However, it is also possible that Gamma reacts to the anticipated higher strategic relevance with the implementation of technocratic coordination. This would challenge both our propositions and our typology. However, we have seen in other cases that an increase in standardization and formalization is caused by an increase in network embeddedness (and not in strategic relevance). Thus, we could also argue that the firm might not act consistently with the current development, which could be the reason for the skepticism that we have encountered with regard to the introduction of technocratic coordination.[1344]

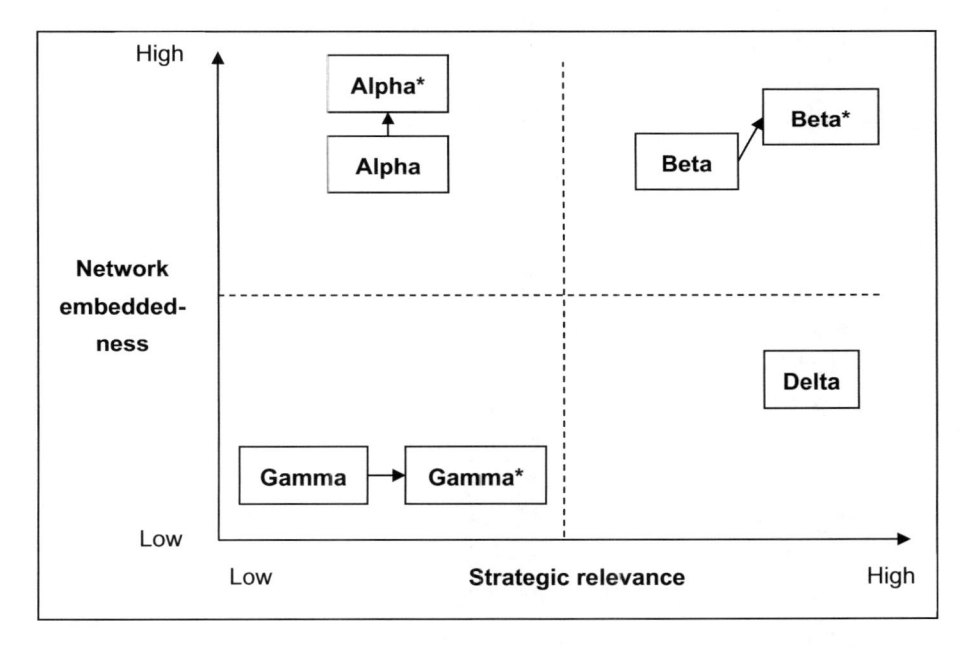

Figure 7-3: Current positions and expected movements of cases in typology[1345]

[1343] This increase in formalization could also be casued by the growth of the service offshoring subsidiary (see Hedlund (1984), p. 122 for a similar discussion).
[1344] We have discussed this finding in an informal setting with members of the organization; however, without reaching a conclusion. We are therefore not in a position to make a final judgment.
[1345] The box with the name of the firm indicates the current position, the name with a star ("*") indicates the future position. The figure is meant to be only conceptual, i.e. the distances of moves do not represent the magnitude of expected changes.

As a result of this discussion, we have found that the cases Alpha and Beta are supportive of the propositions upon which our typology is based. The third case, Gamma, does not contradict the findings directly, nor is it fully supportive of the propositions either. We therefore conclude that the typology can serve as a good starting point to analyze the development of service offshoring subsidiaries over time. We display the dynamic development along the dimensions in Figure 7-3.

7.4 FINDINGS REGARDING TRENDS IN SERVICE OFFSHORING

Our research represents one of the first studies of service offshoring on the level of the MNC. We have shown by our general description of the phenomenon but particularly by our case studies how service offshoring is used in corporate settings. Based on the discussions with our interviewees, it seems reasonable to assume that the offshoring trend is likely to continue. While our research design does not permit us to forecast the quantitative growth of service offshoring, we have found some indications of trends:

- *Ongoing cost pressure*: Some companies that have already offshored part of their services continue to seek ways of further reducing the cost that is associated with the execution of those services. In our study, these were those companies that focus on strategically less relevant services. Alpha was itself outsourcing some services to external providers and Gamma was considering moving some less complex services to a location that offers even lower factor costs than Budapest. This focus on cost is especially relevant for Alpha and Gamma which are located in the Czech Republic and Hungary – both countries that show some signs of "overheating" in the sense of increased prices for labor and infrastructure due to the large demand from companies building service offshoring centers. Beta and Delta, on the other hand, have their centers in a remote town in Russia and in Sofia, both locations that are faced with little competition for offshored services. Besides, the two companies focus more on strategically relevant services that are generally less prone to cost pressure.

- *Diversification of models*: Our typology is a first step towards showing which kind of models can be feasible for service offshoring subsidiaries. We believe that we have found good cases in the sense that we cover the opposite extremes of our typology. However, once established and running, service offshoring centers might further affect the distribution of labor within the MNC. The first signs can be seen in the few services that Alpha Center runs – together with its partner centers – in a "follow-the-sun" mode.[1346] Today, MNCs seem to have the technological capabilities and the organizational skills to provide services in this globally distributed mode. Thus, we can expect more companies to emulate Alpha Center's model in the future. This might require them eventually to reconsider the way in which the distribution of labor should take place. For instance, should every business unit define its own offshoring strategy or will there be one global process architecture that assigns all relevant processes to the right location? Our research cannot answer this question but we have received several indications that the models currently deployed might further diversify. Also, our research shows that offshoring cannot be considered a pure cost-cutting effort.[1347]

- *Changes of the service offshoring subsidiary over time*: In all of our cases, we found several indications that the service offshoring center is changing over time. This is true even with the regard to relatively young service offshoring subsidiaries – those that we evaluated were not older than four years. Thus, it could be important to consider the potential development of the subsidiary right from the start. The prevailing perspective with regard to service offshoring is that the service offshoring subsidiaries are set up in a "top-down" approach by the headquarters. Our research has shown that this is correct at least for the cases we considered: All of "our" service offshoring centers were set up by headquarters and had relatively little autonomy. Given the recent tendency in international business research to view the international subsidiary as an independent creator of capabilities,[1348] this perspective seems to be rather anachronistic. It remains to be seen if service offshoring subsidiaries really represent a special form of the international subsidiary or if they will turn into "regular" subsidiaries over time. In our data set, this could be true for Beta Center and Gamma Center. Both intend to offer their services to the local market in which they are placed. However, both Alpha Center and Delta Center clearly focus on their international, MNC-internal customers and do not intend to build up sales capabilities. Thus, at least for the time being it seems to be appropriate to treat service offshoring subsidiaries as a special form of the international subsidiary.

[1346] See section 6.1.1 for the description of the "follow-the-sun" in Alpha.
[1347] This is confirmed also by Hagel/Brown (2005), p. 35.
[1348] Kutschker et al. (2002), p. 6.

- *Importance of local network*: As discussed above, there are situations in which a service offshoring subsidiary's local network can become an important factor in determining its performance. While the local network is per se less important for service offshoring centers than for subsidiaries that sell to the local market, it should not be neglected altogether but rather specifically evaluated in which ways service offshoring centers can use their local network to increase their effectiveness and efficiency.

- *Effects of location choices:* We have not specifically evaluated the location choices that the companies in our case studies have made. However, we can distinguish between two strategies: Alpha and Gamma have located their centers in popular locations in major cities in Eastern Europe. Beta and Delta on the other hand have selected cities that are less known as offshoring destinations; in the case of Beta they are hardly known as destination for any foreign investment. The careful decision making process through which Beta went with regard to location selection helps the service offshoring subsidiary to overcome other problems it might face. Through this decision, Beta is able to maintain a very attractive cost position that will further improve its position within and beyond Beta's network. More popular locations might lose their potential for factor cost arbitrage if more companies set up service centers and thus increase demand for limited factors such as employees and office space and eventually drive prices up. This could make the locations less attractive and prompt more companies to seek less-known cities.

7.5 FINDINGS REGARDING METHODOLOGY

We finally want to shed some light on findings relating to our methodology. Specifically, we address the topics (1) measurement of the dimensions strategic relevance and network embeddedness and (2) the use of case studies.

(1) With regard to the dimension "strategic relevance" we found non-substitutability to be relatively hard to measure. As recommended in the literature and introduced in the section that describes our measures,[1349] we asked about alternative resources that could deliver the same services. One of the alternatives that interviewees evaluated is the external acquisition of the same service, which represents one possible form of substitution. However, this also touches upon the inimitability of the resource. In addition to

---

[1349] See section 5.2.3.4.

this difficulty, "[s]atisfactory substitutes and alternatives to superior technologies and managerial talents are often not available."[1350] Thus, interviewees found it hard to name and evaluate possible alternatives for the substitution of existing resources. While our findings regarding strategic relevance still seem valid (especially given the fact that in most cases all four indicators had the same value), there is one remaining question: Are the two indicators inimitability and non-substitutability really independent? Theoretically, there is good reason to distinguish these indicators: Inimitability means that a resource (or in our case a service) cannot be imitated (easily) by a competitor. Non-substitutability means that a competitor cannot substitute a resource (or a service) through another resource (or service). However, it is not entirely clear how to treat the substitution of a previously internally executed service through an externally acquired service if the external service is very similar and thus can also be considered to be an imitation. Still, if a service can be substituted by an external service, that means that the knowledge is available in other firms or that it can be transferred to other firms. In both cases, the knowledge is not inimitable and there is no causal ambiguity (that is generally associated with inimitability). Thus, both indicators are aligned in the present case but do not contradict each other. It would be interesting to see if there is a case in which inimitability is low and non-substitutability is high. This means that the service can be imitated. However, if it can be imitated, then it can also be substituted by that imitated service. To construe non-substitutability as referring only to a very different substitute seems difficult. However, assuming this understanding, we do not see the indicators as conflicting. Thus, theoretically the indicators of the resource-based view still seem appropriate. However, we encourage future empirical research to pay attention to the potential overlap between inimitability and non-substitutability.

(2) The reasons for a qualitative research design and the use of case studies have been discussed extensively[1351] and overall the research design has proven suitable for our questions. There are still a few additional lessons that we have learned during the interviews and data analysis that we want to point to:

- The framework and the questions have worked well. Feedback and participation from the interviewees showed that questions were relevant and interesting.

[1350] Das/Bing-Sheng (2000), p. 42.
[1351] See section 5.2.1.2.

- The decision for a qualitative research design seems to be appropriate. Participants talked openly about their experiences and provided several interesting additional hints: For instance, one interviewee offered to arrange a contact for the researcher at another company that is also engaged in offshoring. In addition, the researcher was invited to join a lunch where several people from the company expressed the feeling that the coordination of a remotely located unit is difficult and cannot be managed very easily.

- The questions were generally appropriate, though they could not always be followed in the intended sequence and some had to be skipped altogether because they had already been answered in previous responses by the interviewee or it had become obvious that the question did not apply to the current case. For instance, it did not make sense to ask the interviewee to draw a map of the relationships that the service offshoring unit has after he had mentioned that the unit cooperates only with the headquarters.

- Allowing some time before and after the interviews was helpful to talk to additional people if the opportunity and the need occurred. Establishing good working relationships can also be helpful. Interviewees were open to share documents and offered their help should questions occur in later stages of the research.

8 Conclusions – What we have learned, What We Have Not learned, and What Might Come Next

8.1 Major Contributions

This study of the coordination of service offshoring subsidiaries intended to differentiate types of service offshoring subsidiaries and to evaluate which coordination mechanisms are appropriate for each type. We have therefore used existing contributions from the field of subsidiary typologies and coordination mechanisms and combined them with the specific requirements of a service offshoring subsidiary to develop a new typology.

Our typology distinguishes types of service offshoring subsidiaries and the coordination mechanisms in use. In doing so, we have answered both our research questions. First, we found initial support for our typology by identifying clearly distinguishable types. The cases that we have described show that there can be different types of service offshoring subsidiaries. Second, we established congruence between the coordination mechanisms we have proposed and those that we found in our case studies. Thus, we have given an answer to our second research question: Not only are different types coordinated differently but they also seem to behave according to our propositions.[1352]

We want to briefly highlight the major contributions that relate to (1) service offshoring, (2) coordination mechanisms, (3) research on headquarters-subsidiary relationships, (4) organizational theories, and (5) methodology.

(1) Our study discusses questions of coordination that result from changes in organizational design. In our specific case, the change is determined by the *service offshoring* decisions of MNCs. On the one hand, our research represents an answer to the call for more service studies. On the other hand, we have described and discussed this recent phenomenon and provided one of the first evaluations on firm level. Our findings show that service offshoring has moved beyond the initial cost focus and that it can be used in a variety of scenarios. Our cases provide detailed descriptions of service offshoring and its application in MNCs. Accordingly, our empirical research not only points to more advanced deployments of service offshoring in individual MNCs but also shows directions for the future development of the phenomenon.

[1352] For a detailed discussion of the appropriateness of the propositions see chapter 7.

(2) Our detailed findings on individual coordination mechanisms have been presented above. We have worked with a broad set of coordination mechanisms and gone beyond the set of mechanisms that is typically evaluated in comparable studies.[1353] The set of mechanisms that we have evaluated was a relevant and appropriate classification of coordination mechanisms. Overall, most of the propositions were initially supported by our empirical findings. We found, however, that autonomy and transfers do not appear to play important roles in service offshoring settings. Direct personal coordination, by contrast, seems to be relevant in many settings and to be the basic coordination mechanism for the coordination of remote service offshoring subsidiaries. Beyond this, we have singled out additional factors – language skills, physical distance, technological infrastructure, and commitment – and explained how they impact upon the use of coordination mechanisms in service offshoring.

(3) The findings that relate to our typology extend the research on relationships between headquarters and subsidiaries. We have not just created another typology. Rather, we have introduced an innovative research design by including not only headquarters and subsidiaries in our sample but also other international units of the firm (albeit to a lesser extent). Our typology adds to the diversity of existing typologies of the international subsidiary. Our empirical results corroborate recent findings that call for an individual management approach for international subsidiaries[1354] and have shown how this can be achieved for service offshoring subsidiaries.

(4) Our theoretical model also provides some enhancements to the underlying organizational theories. Not only have we used them as the basis for our typology, but we have also shown how the resource-based view and network approaches – both approaches that are typically considered hard to operationalize – can be used in empirical research. We achieved this by operationalizing two important concepts that can help future research to better distinguish between resources of different degrees of strategic relevance and different degrees of embeddedness. Existing contributions have often treated them as "digital" variables – being either given or not. In addition, many previous contributions have come up with simple, one-dimensional operationalizations. Our considerations help to make differentiations of degree and with regard to many dimensions.

[1353] Gates/Egelhoff (1986), Martinez/Jarillo (1991), Björkman et al (2004).
[1354] Schmid/Schurig (2003), p. 774.

(5) Our contribution shows how a typology can be derived with a grounding in organizational theories and subsequently subjected to empirical evaluation. We thus provide one of the few examples where a typology is both theoretically developed and empirically evaluated by its authors and thereby overcome several typical shortcomings of existing subsidiary typologies. In the empirical evaluation, we have also shown how the typology can be applied on a departmental level instead of a subsidiary level. In addition, we have provided an example of the use of advanced software technologies for the evaluation of interviews. In existing research, they have often not been applied to their full potential even though they can help to enhance the validity of the data[1355] and increase the amount of data that can be processed. Our approach can thus help to advance the use of qualitative research (not only) in international business studies.

8.2 Implications for Management and Policy Makers

Our research has some far-reaching consequences for practitioners. We first consider those on firm level:

Our findings show that the realities of service offshoring have left the perception of "labor arbitrage" far behind. The most advanced companies have moved activities abroad that form part of their core competence and play an important role in the entire MNC, as the new service offshoring centers are highly regarded by other units and form an indispensable part of a company's value chain. This trend indicates that we might see ever more advanced services being moved abroad, allowing those MNCs that make use of service offshoring to increase their competitiveness and leaving behind those that do not. The trend will not go away but rather represents a challenge for companies to reconsider the distribution of their activities worldwide. There is a constant need to evaluate the best possible location for each activity which translates into increased levels of organizational flexibility. Moreover, there is a strong requirement to put in place the mechanisms that can provide such increased coordination. This might have implications for HR-related topics such as recruiting, training, and compensation but also for overall organizational design that might include coordination units for worldwide-distributed service offshoring centers. Information technology systems need to be adapted so that they can be accessed remotely and deliver the required data anywhere in the world.

Specific offshoring projects within MNCs might also benefit from our results: We show several, clearly distinguishable, types of service offshoring subsidiaries. We hope that

---

[1355] Grunenberg (2004), p. 79.

especially the presentation of cases will capture the interest of practitioners because they demonstrate that service offshoring has moved beyond a focus on cost and that there is a need to identify the appropriate model for each company. Our detailed case descriptions can be a first step towards the development of a specific service offshoring strategy. The findings regarding coordination mechanisms can serve as indications for the establishment of an appropriate governance model (even though we have not provided performance implications). The very limited use of autonomy and transfers can be indications for the design of new centers and their coordination mechanisms. Moreover, the importance of personal direct coordination seems important in any kind of setting and should not be underestimated. This needs to be reflected in investment and cost estimates where often the cost of travel for service offshoring is underestimated. This "personal touch" is not to be neglected even when cooperating across large distances.

In addition, our cases might be helpful as they reveal in which directions service offshoring subsidiaries can develop. Additional influencers of relevance for service offshoring might also guide discussions and decision making in MNCs. For instance, the effective use of a service offshoring subsidiary's local network might be one way to improve performance. Finally, we discussed the importance of perception gaps and their specific importance for service offshoring.

It is true that we do not provide performance implications. However, we would argue with Ketchen: "It is essential that researchers develop valid, parsimonious, theory-based configurations at the industry, organization, and even top management level of analysis ... before making attempts to relate configurations to outcome variable such as performance."[1356] Judging by the interest that we have received from our interviewees, we tend to see the motivation of our research confirmed by Hambrick's statement: "[W]hen an academic field has as its charge the thoughtful preparation and guidance of practitioner professionals, and when an academic field deals in a domain that vitally affects societal well-being, then that academic field must enter the world of practical affairs. Without being co-opted, it must strive for influence and impact. That is our challenge. We should matter. We must matter."[1357] The invitations to follow-up discussions that we have received and the request from all interviewees to receive the results of the study show some impact that the current study has already had.

[1356] Ketchen Jr. et al. (1993), p. 1306.
[1357] Hambrick (1994), p. 16.

We believe that the outcome of our analysis can also be important from a macro-level perspective. The case studies show that service offshoring is not limited to tasks of low complexity but support the notion that increasingly complex services are being moved abroad. This poses again the question what activities will eventually remain in high-cost locations such as, for instance, Germany. Our research clearly cannot give a final answer. However, with the enlarged European Union there are many destinations that fall within one common legal framework with freedom of locating businesses. This will make any legislation trying to ban offshoring almost impossible to implement unless the basic principles of the EU are substantially altered. Still, there is also good news for the job market in the established locations: The higher need for overall coordination that we have found with increasing strategic relevance shows that the coordination of service offshoring centers is an important task that could become an important resource for the MNCs and their home countries. Still, to judge the effect on the labor market is beyond our scope and our empirical findings. Thus, we can also conclude that the study of international trade of services – that has received less attention than trade in manufactures[1358] – still provides many interesting avenues for further research efforts.

8.3 Limitations of Study and Avenues for Future Research

The previous section showed how we reached the research goals presented in our introduction and how we have contributed to the existing body of knowledge. In the design and in the course of the study, however, we also encountered several limitations on which we wish to report. These can be turned into avenues for future research.

- *Limited generalization*: Due to our case study design we have no possibility to make statements with regard to the population of service offshoring subsidiaries in Eastern Europe. While we have argued and shown that theoretical generalization of our propositions is feasible, there are some questions we cannot answer based on our data. For instance, it would be very interesting to find out about the distribution of the types from our typology in the entire population of service offshoring subsidiaries. Of course, our findings also lack statistical significance. Thus, further research could produce quantitative data from a survey of a large number of companies. This scope would allow for results that are easier to generalize and statistically significant. Such a study could use our findings on coor-

---

[1358] Pain/Van Welsum (2004), p. 68.

dination to derive an enhanced set of measures and then test for further empirical support for our typology.

- *Neglect of coordination beyond coordination mechanisms:* We have concentrated on coordination mechanisms but have not treated the actors who are involved in coordination as a contingency in our research. And while we have described the coordination mechanisms between headquarters, service offshoring center, and other international subsidiaries, we have not addressed how an MNC can coordinate a set of (potentially diverse) service offshoring subsidiaries or how different subsidiaries – of which the service offshoring subsidiary is but one – are coordinated. We have also seen that the different setup as a profit center or a cost center can impact on the coordination of a service offshoring center but have not explicitly considered this factor in our typology. These topics could be included as variables in a quantitative analysis to measure their impact on service offshoring centers or provide the basis for more in-depth analysis to better understand the organizational arrangements that are made with regard to service offshoring.

- *No inclusion of performance aspects:* We have described and evaluated our typology, but our research cannot serve normative purposes since we have not evaluated the performance of the different types. We do not know if a specialized contributor is – especially in the long term – more successful than a support center, for instance. To enhance lessons for practitioners and researchers, future studies could include performance implications of the different types we derived and establish whether or not one type always performs better than another type. This kind of research could also show how much performance improvement (in the form of cost savings or additional revenues) can be typically expected from service offshoring.

- *Simplification through typology research:* Of course, some of the typical criticism of typology research can be applied to our research. We have discussed in more detail how we have overcome several weaknesses of this research stream,[1359] but we needed to limit our typology to two dimensions, thereby excluding other, potentially valuable, approaches from our considerations. We still believe that the selection of the resource-based view and network approaches is

---

[1359] See section 4.1.2.

8 – Conclusions   375

well grounded and suitable. There is little that future research can do to overcome this. One could include more dimensions and more types in a study, however, to derive results that are even more precise.[1360]

- *Limited geographical scope and neglect of potential cultural differences:* We have only considered MNCs of German origin and focused on their Eastern European service offshoring subsidiaries. Our cases cover only four countries in Eastern Europe and we have no basis for determining the impact on coordination of country culture in different Eastern European countries. In addition, we cannot judge on potential differences from a German MNC to MNCs of other nationalities. It would be especially interesting to find out how Indian MNCs such as Tata Consulting coordinate the Eastern European subsidiaries that they have set up to provide offshore services to MNCs from Continental Europe. New research could cover additional geographical areas and could allow for a comparison between different geographical regions such as, for instance, between Eastern Europe and India. To compare our results to findings with offshoring to more distant regions is another avenue that could provide important insights. This more detailed comparison on the differences of offshoring to nearby locations versus very remote locations could also be carried out with special focus on coordination and find out in more detail what impact physical distance has upon coordination. The same applies to the extension to functional areas other than IT, such as, for instance, R&D or finance.

- *Limited functional scope:* We restricted our empirical analysis to the IT function. It is known that the functional area can impact on coordination. Thus, the extension of our findings to other functions will need separate consideration.

- *Potential bias due to reliance on a single researcher for interviews, coding, and analysis:* While a research design with a single researcher has advantages, it also causes potential bias during the interviewing and analysis process. A team of interviewers could potentially reduce bias and provide an additional quality control.

All research seems to raise as many questions as it has answered – or indeed new ones. Our study is no exception. Already during interviews and even more so during data

---

[1360] See, however, the discussion in section 4.1.1.

analysis, we came across several interesting questions that we need to leave for future research efforts. While we have dealt with the possibilities of a direct extension of our study, there are additional avenues for future research that go beyond the focus of our own research.

These refer to the topics (1) coordination of several service offshoring centers in a single MNC, (2) offshoring in born-globals, (3) local network of a service offshoring center, (4) comparison of newly-established versus acquired subsidiaries, (5) role of transfers in service offshoring and other types of international subsidiary, (6) longitudinal studies, (7) perception gaps, and (8) additional influencers on coordination.

(1) For the time being, offshoring decisions are mostly taken as individual events that do not necessarily alter the way an MNC looks. However, as offshoring is set to grow, more and more of these decisions will take place and change companies and the way they operate. Even though estimates of the magnitude of service offshoring may vary, the question that an increasing number of MNCs will face is how they can use service offshoring. As the number of offshoring centers grows, it will become more likely that an MNC will have to cope with several service centers and new coordination challenges. It seems a promising avenue for future research to assess how an MNC incorporates several service offshoring centers into its worldwide network and how it coordinates these – possible interdependent – centers.

(2) Some companies are no longer "offshoring" parts of their operations in the sense of relocating them, but rather they start out as "born globals" or "micro MNCs" – firms that internationalize very early in their development. These companies do not have to go through the often complicated process of actually moving tasks but design their operations globally right from the start.[1361] It will be interesting to compare global distribution in a born global to that of a more traditional MNC that grew out of one home market.

(3) Another topic worthy of further investigation could be how the most advanced service offshoring centers make better use of their local networks, for instance, to access additional local resources and how the importance of the local network changes over

---

[1361] Hopkins (2005). For recent contributions on born global firms, see Hashai/Almor (2004), Knight/Cavusgil (2004).

8 – Conclusions   377

time. We have found some indications of this in the case of Delta and would expect to see more as centers grow and mature.

(4) International business research has often dealt only with acquired subsidiaries[1362] or with newly-built subsidiaries – often neglecting the latter.[1363] Other contributions have assessed entry mode decisions.[1364] However, it could be worthwhile to go beyond the initial decision and discuss how the differences between the two types develop and to compare their development and performance in longitudinal studies.

(5) Research on transfers has focused on many different aspects of the phenomenon. For instance, the adjustment of the expatriate to the foreign country[1365] and his or her satisfaction[1366] have been evaluated, as have the selection of appropriate persons for a transfer,[1367] and the success of expatriation,[1368] aspects of repatriation,[1369] and their relevance for different functions, such as coordinating a subsidiary.[1370] However, it seems that the actual decision of why to send employees abroad is less discussed.[1371] Our findings indicate that transfers might not play an unimportant role or in fact no role at all in service offshoring. To evaluate in more detail the situations in which transfers are still needed and which role they (should) play, could both advance this stream of research and help MNCs to make better decisions with regard to sending employees abroad.

(6) Future studies could also take a longitudinal perspective. The process from the decision to the setup and eventually the operation of a service offshoring subsidiary is also of major concern to practitioners and academics.[1372] For instance, there is a need to evaluate how companies go through the location selection process, especially when more than one center is to be built.

[1362] See for some examples Uhlenbruck/De Castro (1998), Rondinelli/Black (2000), Uhlenbruck/De Castro (2000), Piske (2002), Meyer/Lieb-Dóczy (2003), Uhlenbruck et al. (2003), Uhlenbruck (2004).
[1363] Kutschker/Schmid (2005), p. 882.
[1364] Harzing (2002), Sharma/Erramilli (2004), Eicher/Kang (2005).
[1365] Lee/Liu (2006). For the adjustment of the expatriates' spouses see Mohr/Klein (2004).
[1366] McCaughey/Bruning (2005).
[1367] Zeira/Banai (1985), Anderson (2005), Tye/Chen (2005).
[1368] Edmond (2002), McNulty/Tharenou (2004), Toh/DeNisi (2005).
[1369] Napier/Peterson (1991), Suutari/Brewster (2003).
[1370] Delios/Björkman (2000), Harzing (2001).
[1371] For recent exceptions, see however Belderbos/Heijltjes (2005), Tan/Mahoney (2006).
[1372] Wiedenhofer (2003), p. 22.

(7) Such research could also "drill deeper" on perception gaps in the relationships between different units of an MNC that can provide a wide field of research opportunities.[1373] Further research on the reasons for and effects of perception gaps – especially with regard to service offshoring – could also be helpful for practitioners.

(8) As further addition to research design, more influencers on coordination could be included. We only considered the influences of subsidiary characteristics on coordination mechanisms. There are, however, other levels of influence such as "characteristics of multinational corporation and management's global philosophy"[1374] that we did not include in our analysis. While we believe that our findings are relevant for the coordination of service offshoring subsidiaries, they obviously need to be put in the context of general characteristics of the MNC.

Finally, our study has delivered only one perspective on the phenomenon of service offshoring that seems to have the potential to engage for some years to come the minds of researchers and corporate decision makers alike. We hope the topic will generate the necessary interest and wish those who become involved in service offshoring, from a research or from a practitioners' perspective, much success.

[1373] See for recent contributions, Birkinshaw et al. (2000), Chini et al. (2005), Li (2005).
[1374] Garnier (1982), p. 896.

APPENDICES

1. RESULTS OF LITERATURE REVIEW ON NETWORK EMBEDDEDNESS 380
2. OVERVIEW OF INTERVIEWS 388
3. EVALUATION GUIDE 390
4. INTERVIEW GUIDE 391
5. TRANSCRIPTION RULES 401

1. RESULTS OF LITERATURE REVIEW ON NETWORK EMBEDDEDNESS

For the development of an operationalization for network embeddedness, we have carried out a literature review on embeddedness literature as discussed in section 3.3. While we present the results in the text section, we here – in the appendix – display the overview of all the contributions we reviewed in the table below (Table Appendix 1). In this table, we show the authors' names of the respective publication accompanied by a symbol that stands for the type of publication (C – conceptual; Quant – quantitative; Qual – qualitative case study). In parentheses, we include the network level that the embeddedness concept refers to (intra-organizational, inter-organizational and local). Then, we indicate the definition of embeddedness the authors give (with the main terms in bold letters). We also summarize in a concise way the application of each contribution, before providing the operationalization that is used by the author(s). We highlight the term(s) that best represent the dimension that the author(s) refer(s) to (in bold letters). We also inform about the number of dimensions that the operationalizations contain and present the result in parentheses right after the operationalization. The operationalization is followed by a display of measures (indicating the scale, if available) and finally by a brief result of the study). We decided to present the embeddedness operationalizations and measures that were used in the study as exactly as possible. In accordance with literature on methodology, operationalization is the construct that a study deploys to adapt a concept – in our case embeddedness – to the subject under analysis.[1375] Measures in turn represent concrete questions and/or formulas that are used in questionnaires, structured interviews or database queries to generate a value or values for the concept in question, in our case for making the concept of embeddedness measurable.[1376] In our table, we have indicated in brackets if a scale was given and what kind of scale has been used. If authors do not present an operationalization or measure, we use the symbol "(not provided)". Where authors include several types of embeddedness (such as Rowley et al. (2000); Andersson et al. (2002)), we report only on the structural embeddedness.

[1375] Bryman (1989), p. 6, Creswell (2003), p. 159.
[1376] Bryman (1989), p. 34, Creswell (2003), p. 157.

Table Appendix 1: Definitions and uses of embeddedness in a network context

Article	C: Gulati (1998) (inter)	C: Jones et al. (1997) (inter)	Quant: Andersson/Forsgren (1996) (intra, local)
Definition	Embeddedness refers to the **influence of social relations on economic activity** (p. 295).	Embeddedness refers to the fact that **economic action and outcomes are affected by network relationships and structure** (p. 922). Structural embeddedness is the degree to which a dyad's mutual contacts are connected to each other (p. 924).	"A subsidiary's embeddedness is defined as the **total sum of interdependencies** it has as a consequence of its position in a business network" (p. 490).
Application	Author applies a network perspective to the evaluation of alliance formation, choice of governance structure in alliances, dynamic evolution of alliances, alliance performance, and performance consequences for firms entering alliances.	Authors want to synthesize the transaction cost view and network perspectives by including more than the dyadic relationship in the analysis.	Authors evaluate how a subsidiary's network embeddedness correlates with the degree of control that headquarters have. Authors distinguish external (e.g., with customers) and corporate embeddedness (with sister units).
Operationalization	Not provided but author argues that embeddedness is positively related to **centrality**, the **frequency** of adding new ties and the **likelihood** of adding new ties.	(not provided)	A subsidiary's embeddedness is operationalized as the degree of **adaptation** of resources to other network actors (1 dimension).
Measure	(not provided)	(not provided)	Respondents were asked to what extent the relation with a given customer/supplier/other counterpart caused adaptation for the subsidiary concerning product technology and production technology (5-point scale).
Results	Structural embeddedness can influence the partner choice in alliances and is positively connected to the reputation an organization has in the network.	Authors propose to enhance transaction cost theory by a governance form that is between market and hierarchy - networks. In this governance form, embeddedness can influence access to exchanges, culture, sanctions and reputation.	If subsidiaries' relationships are dominated by corporate relations to their sister units, headquarters can exert more control. Conversely, with high external embeddedness, external units have a higher degree of control.

Article	Quant: Rowley et al. (2000) (inter)	Quant: Andersson/Forsgren (2000) (local)	Quant: Gulati (1999) (inter)
Definition	Embeddedness refers to **how networks facilitate or impede firm's behavior** and performance (p. 369).	Embeddedness refers to the **degree of mutual adaptation between counterparts** (p. 335).	Embeddedness refers to the **influence of social structure of ties on economic activity** (p. 398).
Application	Authors study how structural embeddedness as a mediator variable affects the relationship between strong ties and firm performance (which is expected to be positive). They also test the effect of structural embeddedness on firm performance in industries with high demand for exploration (versus exploitation).	Authors want to test the effects of a subsidiary's external embeddedness on a) the subsidiary's possibility to influence MNC strategy and b) the MNC's managers' perception of the subsidiary's importance.	Author studies the role of network resources in alliance formation. Network resources are informational advantages that come through a network of interfirm ties.
Operationalization	A firm's embeddedness is operationalized as the **density** of its network, i.e. the interconnectedness of the firm's direct partners (1 dimension).	A subsidiary's external embeddedness is operationalized as the degree of **adaptation** to its partners (such as suppliers, customers) (1 dimension).	A firm's embeddedness is operationalized as the **centrality** of the focal firm in its network (1 dimension).
Measure	Density is measured as the number of existing ties in a firm's network, divided by the total number of possible ties in that network (no scale given, data obtained from databases, not through survey).	Respondents were asked to evaluate the subsidiary's degree of adaptation to the requirements of the specific customer/supplier concerning product and process technology (5-point scale).	Embeddedness is measured as the clique size (number of cliques a firm belongs to) and the closeness (number of firms to go through to reach another firm) (no scale given, data obtained from databases, not through survey).
Results	With low structural embeddedness, strong ties have a stronger impact on firm performance than for high structural embeddedness. High structural embeddedness has a negative effect on firm performance in industries with high demand for exploration.	External embeddedness has significant and positive effects on the subsidiary's strategic influence and on MNC's managers' perception of the importance.	Firms that are centrally located in a network (highly embedded) are more likely to form new alliances.

Article	Quant: Håkanson/Nobel (2001) (local)	C: Gnyawali/Madhavan (2001) (inter)	Quant: Andersson/Forsgren/Pedersen (2001) (local)
Definition	Embeddedness refers to the fact that "the effectiveness and outcome of technical exchange are determined not only by the **nature of individual, pairwise interactions** but also by the **overall structure** and characteristics of a larger network of relations of which they are part" (p. 398).	Embeddedness refers to the effect that the **network of relationships** influences the competitive behavior of firms (p. 431).	Technology embeddedness "is **dependencies between firms** in a business network related to, for example, product development or production process development" (p. 9).
Application	Authors evaluate the impact of subsidiaries' local embeddedness with customers, suppliers, competitors, etc. on their innovativeness.	Authors intend to explain how the embeddedness of a firm in a network of cooperative linkages to competitors influences their behavior of the firm and its competitors.	Authors evaluate the effect of technology embeddedness on a subsidiary's market performance and a subsidiary's organizational performance.
Operationalization	Embeddedness is operationalized as **frequent and significant interactions** with local organizations (customers, suppliers, competitors, etc.) (1 dimension).	(not provided)	A subsidiary's technology embeddedness is operationalized as the degree to which it **adapts** to its customers and how **important** a given customer relationship is and the degree to which it **adapts** to its suppliers and how **important** a given supplier relationship is (2 dimensions).
Measure	Embeddedness is measured as a) frequency of face-to-face contacts, b) frequency of other types of contacts (letter, phone, data link, etc.), c) number of ongoing corporative projects with local universities and research institutions, customers and suppliers in local market (no scale given).	(not provided)	Respondents were asked for a) the counterpart's importance for the product and production process development and b) the adaptation of the product and production process development to the specific relationship (5-point scale).
Results	Strong local embeddedness positively influences the innovativeness of subsidiaries.	The conceptual model derives several propositions that explain how different network properties affect the likelihood of competitive action of the focal firm and the likelihood of responses by its competitors.	Technology embeddedness has a significant and positive impact on subsidiary market performance. However, no impact on organizational performance could be identified.

Article	C: Karamanos (2003) (inter)	Quant: Andersson et al. (2002) (local)	Quant: Newburry (2001) (local)
Definition	Embeddedness refers to the fact that economic action and outcomes are affected by **actors' dyadic relations** and by the **structure of the network of relations** (p. 1872).	"[E]mbeddedness can be looked upon as a **strategic resource influencing the firm's future capability** and expected performance" (p. 980).	Embeddedness is defined as how the **quality of relationships and the network structure relationships** affect economic activity (p. 499).
Application	Author evaluates the effect of network embeddedness (structural embeddedness) on the value of a firm.	Authors analyze how a subsidiary's local technical embeddedness impacts firm performance and competence development.	Authors analyze the effect of local embeddedness on how employees in an MNC subsidiary judge global integration as beneficial for their career.
Operationalization	(not provided)	Technical embeddedness is operationalized as **adaptation** between firms in terms of their product and production development processes (1 dimension).	Embeddedness is operationalized as the **strength** of ties to the local environment (1 dimension).
Measure	(not provided)	Respondents were asked to what degree a specific relationship with a customer or supplier had caused the subsidiary's product and production process to be adapted (5-point scale).	Subsidiary's embeddedness is measured as the number of years employees have spent in the office and whether the office joined the MNC by acquisition (no scale given).
Results	Structural embeddedness can facilitate learning. This in turn can help the creation of complex capabilities which can finally lead to sustainable competitive advantages.	Technical embeddedness has a positive and significant effect on subsidiary's performance and competence.	Employees in MNC subsidiaries judge global integration of their subsidiary as negative if the subsidiary is locally embedded.

Appendices

Article	Quant: Schmid/Schurig (2003) (intra, local)	Qual: Hardy et al. (2003) (inter)
Definition	Embeddedness refers to the characteristic of units that have **close, intense and frequent relationships** in their network (p. 759).	Embeddedness in networks is the fact that **facilitates and constrains action** of network actors (p. 327).
Application	Authors evaluate the impact of a subsidiary's corporate and external network on the development of critical capabilities.	Authors explore which characteristics of an inter-organizational collaboration lead to collaboration results (such as strategic effects, knowledge effects, political effects).
Operationalization	Embeddedness is operationalized as the **degree of influence** that a relationship to a partner in the corporate and the external network has (1 dimension).	The operationalization of embeddedness is derived from the evaluation of cases. It is operationalized as a **broad scope of interactions** (involving third parties), as a **representative network structure** (where one actor represents the interests of another one) and with a **multi-directional flow of information** (3 dimensions).
Measure	Respondents were asked to evaluate the influence of the relationship of several network partners on the development of critical capabilities within the subsidiary (7-point scale).	(not provided – study identifies embeddedness as a factor and does not measure it)
Results	Relationships are important for the development of critical capabilities - on the corporate level especially to the parent company, and on the external level, especially to market customers. Differences are found according to the value activity in question.	Study reveals that embeddedness is one differentiating characteristic of collaborations. It is positively correlated with political effects (influence) and under specific circumstances also with knowledge effects (creation of knowledge).

Article	C: Young/Tavares (2004) (intra, local)	Quant: Venkatraman/Chi-Hyon (2004) (inter)	Quant: Fischer/Pollock (2004) (inter)
Definition	Embeddedness refers to **"close, intense and frequent intra-organizational relationships"** and can be corporate (company-internal) or external (to suppliers, customers or R&D units) (p. 219).	"Embeddedness refers to the fact that exchanges within a group ... have an **ongoing social structure** [that operates] by **constraining the set of actions** available to the individual actors and by changing the dispositions of those actors toward the actions they make" (p. 878).	Embeddedness refers to a **dense network of social ties** that impact actors' behavior p. 469).
Application	Authors review research that report on the influence of external and corporate embeddedness on the control mechanisms between headquarters and subsidiaries.	Authors tests the impact of network structures (measured among others by structural embeddedness) on interorganizational coordination of product launches in the U.S. video game industry by analyzing the relationships between game development firms and the video game platforms the games are developed for.	Authors analyze the embeddedness of IPO firms in a network of investors and its influence on the after-IPO performance of the firm.
Operationalization	(not provided)	Embeddedness is operationalized as the **pattern of distribution** of video game titles offered by the different developer companies for the different platforms (1 dimension).	Embeddedness is operationalized by the **frequency** and the **concentration** of transactions between actors (2 dimensions).
Measure	(not provided)	Embeddedness is measured by a) platform embeddedness (the proportion of video games for one platform from one development company compared to all of the platform's titles) and b) developer embeddedness (the proportion of video games for one platform compared to all the developments of one development company) (calculated as index from 0 to 1).	Embeddedness is measured as a) frequency of acting together as lead underwriter and institutional investor in an IPO and b) the degree of concentration of transaction among the same group of lead underwriter and institutional investors (no scale given, data obtained from databases, not through survey).
Results	After reviewing existing literature, the authors conclude that corporate embeddedness has a negative correlation with subsidiary autonomy. Findings for external embeddedness are equivocal.	Study shows that a platform embeddedness has a significant effect and that "developers were unlikely to release titles to a platform that was already tightly connected to few developers" (p. 885).	Results show that embeddedness has a significant, negative relationship with IPO failure.

Article	Quant: Andersson et al. (2005) (local)	Quant: Echols/Tsai (2005) (inter)
Definition	Embeddedness is **"closeness in the relationships**, in terms of trust, adaptation of resources and frequency of interaction" (p. 522).	"Network embeddedness describes the **structure of a firm's relationships** with other firms" (p. 221).
Application	Authors evaluate influence of headquarters' control mechanisms on subsidiaries' local embeddedness and on subsidiary knowledge creation.	Authors analyze the effect of network embeddedness on the performance of a firm that is either in a product or a process niche.
Operationalization	Embeddedness is operationalized as degree of mutual **adaptation** of resources/activities. Authors also mention frequency as a common operationalization for embeddedness.	Embeddedness is operationalized as the "extent to which a firm is surrounded by other firms in such a way that its network structure is **redundant** or not." (p. 221) (1 dimension).
Measure	Respondents were asked how much adaptations their local business relationships had caused for a) product technology, b) production technology, c) standard operating procedures, d) business practice (7-point scale).	Embeddedness is measured as network redundancy (redundancy measures how many different connections a firm has to another firm) divided by network size to adjust for size effects (calculated as percentage from 0% to 100%).
Results	Control systems that include knowledge development as criteria have positive effects on local embeddedness and lead to more knowledge creation.	When a firm is in a product or process niche, its performance is positively related to network embeddedness.

Note: A first version of this table has been published in Schmid/Daub (2007).

2. Overview of Interviews

No.	Case	Position	Unit	Language	Recording
1	Support center	Head of Consulting Finance Department	German HQ	English	Yes
2	Support center	Quality manager for software department	German HQ	German	Yes
3	Support center	Relationship manager, quality manager, project manager (3 persons)	Hungarian SOS	German	Yes
4	Internal Competence Center	Head of German Offshoring	German HQ	German	No
5	Internal Competence Center	Vice Head of German Offshoring	German HQ	German	Yes
6	Internal Competence Center	Head of IT Help Desk	Russian SOS	English	Yes
7	Internal Competence Center	Head of Software Development	Russian SOS	English	Yes
8	Internal Competence Center	Business Director	Russian SOS	German	Yes
9	Internal Competence Center	Customer	Austrian subsidiary	German	Yes
10	Specialized contributor	Former managing director	German HQ	German	Yes

No.	Case	Position	Unit	Language	Recording
11	Specialized contributor	Current relationship manager	German HQ	German	Yes
12	Specialized contributor	Senior software architect	German HQ	English	Yes
13	Specialized contributor	Center Vice President, Software Architect, Project Manager (3 persons)	Bulgarian SOS	English	Yes
14	Specialized contributor	Center CEO	Bulgarian SOS	English	Yes
15	Service Factory	Center CEO	Czech SOS	English	Yes
16	Service Factory	Center Vice President for Infrastructure	Czech SOS	English	Yes
17	Service Factory	Relationship Manager	Czech SOS	English	Yes
18	Service Factory	Manager for Infrastructure	Czech SOS	English	Yes
19	Service Factory	Director of IT Governance	German HQ	German	Yes
20	Service Factory	Customer	German subsidiary	German	Yes

HQ – headquarters   SOS – service offshoring subsidiary

3. Evaluation Guide

This guide was used in an initial contact with an MNC to determine the appropriateness for taking part in our study:

I would like to understand if your organization lends itself for inclusion in the research project we are working on. To do so, it would be helpful if you could answer some initial questions. I will evaluate these and would then come back to you so that we can decide together on the continuation of the research in your organization.

1. How large is your unit and how many people are there in the entire company?[1377] Is the number of ... [to be filled in for each interview] people correct and can I use the revenue figure of ... [to be filled in for each interview] million EUR that I took from your annual report?

2. Would you mind telling me a little more about your service offshoring subsidiary? For example, I would be interested in the kind of services it provides and how these are used in the larger corporate context of your organization. To whom do you provide services? Would you consider the services your subsidiary provides to be "strategic"?

3. Please elaborate on the other international subsidiaries that you interact with. It would be helpful for me to know how many units you deal with, how often you have interactions with them and how "close" you are to them.

4. Where in the overall organization is your unit located? Do you have a chart of the organization for me to look at?

[1377] The number of employees is a frequent measurement for the size of the unit as is the number of years in existence for its age (Gates/Egelhoff (1986)).

4. INTERVIEW GUIDE

Opening

After the introduction it was explained to the interviewees that the interview would consist of three major segments but that additional comments would be very much appreciated. The segments were outlined as follows:

1. *Offshoring setting*: This section aims at a description of the offshoring setting to allow the researcher to gain a broader perspective. The interviewee will be asked about the history and the development of the setting, the initial goals for the setup and the achievement of those goals.

2. *Type of service offshoring subsidiary*: The aim of this section is to identify the position of the service offshoring subsidiary on the two dimensions network embeddedness and strategic relevance. To that end, the interviewee will be asked to give details on the relationships with other units in the MNC network and on the type of service that the service offshoring subsidiary provides.

3. *Coordination mechanisms*: This section will identify which coordination mechanisms are in place between the service offshoring subsidiary and (a) the MNC headquarters and (b) other international subsidiaries. Therefore, the researcher will ask questions on the use of structural, technocratic and personal coordination mechanisms.

4. *Additional topics*: To conclude and to allow for a more open discussion, the researcher will ask about future plans for the service offshoring subsidiary and about other new topics that might arise in the course of the interview.

Identification

Category	Value
Name of organization	
Interviewee's name	
Interviewee's position	
Number of years in current position/with company	

Category	Value
Date and time of interview	

Offshoring situation

I would like to learn more about the service offshoring setting.

1. Could you tell me about the history of your current offshoring situation? When did you decide to set the subsidiary up, who was involved in that decision and how has it developed so far?

2. What were the reasons for the initial setup? Have these changed?

3. Have you achieved the goals that you had originally set?

Type of service offshoring subsidiary – strategic relevance

I would like to understand more about the role of the service offshoring subsidiary in the wider context of the entire corporation. Therefore, I would first like to ask you to explain the services you provide.

1. What kind of services does the service offshoring subsidiary provide?

2. Are there any other services that are soon to be provided? Have you provided other services in the past?

3. What function/unit/hierarchy deals with the service offshoring subsidiary at the headquarters level and at other international subsidiaries?

VALUE

4. Does the service that the service offshoring subsidiary provides meet a key need of its customer(s)?

5. Imagine you lost the center all of a sudden for political or other unforeseeable reasons. What effect would that have on the firm?

6. How valuable would it be for your competitor to gain access to your service offshoring subsidiary?

7. What does the service offshoring subsidiary bring you: monetary advantages, quality advantages and/or flexibility advantages?

RARENESS

8. Are these services "marketable", i.e. could you have bought them from a third party? If so, why did you decide to have them in-house? What are the reasons for your "make" instead of "buy" decision.

9. Is the service that is provided by the "service offshoring subsidiary" a commodity?

10. Are the services specific to your company, i.e. something that only your company has or needs? Or, alternatively, are the services something that every other company (in your industry) would also need?

11. Would your competitors be interested in finding out more about the service offshoring subsidiary or having such a subsidiary as well? Do you know of competitors that engage in service offshoring as well? If so, what kind?

INIMITABILITY

12. How difficult would it be for your competitors/other firms to establish a service offshoring subsidiary similar to yours?

13. How long would it take a competitor to build up a similar center?

14. Are there external providers that can build up a center like yours?

15. How easy would it be to transfer the knowledge that you have here to another unit in the firm or outside the firm?

NON-SUBSTITUTABILITY

16. When the service offshoring subsidiary was set up, what were the alternatives that you had considered?

17. Could you have found another solution for the service that the service offshoring subsidiary provides? For instance, could you have decided to automate the process?

Type of service offshoring subsidiary – network embeddedness

NETWORK STRUCTURE & NUMBER OF RELATIONSHIPS

I would now like to learn more about the relationships between the service offshoring subsidiary and other international subsidiaries. I understand a relationship as a connection between two or more parties that is made up of a series of interactions that represent the exchange of information and resources.

1. How many international subsidiaries have a relationship with the service offshoring subsidiary? Just include those relationships that have regular interactions (i.e. at least once per month).

2. Can you describe the structure of the relationship (for instance, one-to-one relationship, one-to-many, many-to-many, ...)?

3. Can you draw a picture of the relationship for me?

4. Where are these international subsidiaries located? If there are too many, please just name the continents.

FREQUENCY

5. Does the service offshoring subsidiary connect to new units within the firm?

6. How often does that take place?

7. How many units will the service offshoring subsidiary be eventually connected to?

8. How often can these relationships change?

CLOSENESS

9. What kind of resources (capital, human resources, information) is exchanged between the service offshoring subsidiary and the other units in the firm?

10. How much did the partners in the service offshoring setting have to adapt to the new situation?

11. Would you consider the exchange between service offshoring subsidiary and other units to be a complex exchange or is it more like to a market relationship?

12. Do you know if the relationship that you have with your partner differs from other relationships between the service offshoring subsidiary and another international unit?

Coordination mechanisms

1. How do you coordinate the delivery of services?

2. Which governance regime best characterizes the offshoring subsidiary, e.g. profit center, cost center, shared service?

3. How many resources (time, financial resources) are required to coordinate the delivery of services? For instance, have you employed a person whose only task is the management of the interface between the receiving and the providing end of the service delivery?

4. By which means does coordination take place? Are there people traveling back and forth, do people talk on the phone, are there very specific instructions for everybody about how to behave? What about video and phone conferences? What are the expectations from one party to another?

AUTONOMY

5. To what extent is the service offshoring subsidiary autonomous in its decisions, e.g., with regard to recruiting, sourcing, accounting, budgeting, service delivery, service portfolio, information systems, service quality, etc.? In how many functional areas does the service offshoring subsidiary have autonomy?

	Very low	Low	Medium	High	Very high
Number of functions involved	One	Two-three	Four-five	Six-seven	Eight or more

6. In case of conflict who makes the final decision?

7. Does the service offshoring subsidiary have the freedom to choose which way it wants to do things? Does the job that the service offshoring subsidiary carries out involve creativity?

STANDARDIZATION

8. How standardized is the relationship between the service offshoring subsidiary and other units, for instance, in policies and procedures?

9. Does every unit receive the same treatment or are there differences?

10. What happens if a new unit is added to the list of internal clients of the service offshoring subsidiary? Is there a standardized process?

FORMALIZATION

11. How well documented is the service delivery process?

12. Do people talk on the phone, write each other emails or is there an automated, computerized process in place (for instance, a workflow management system)?

13. How often are documents such as, for instance, work plans and schedules used?

Appendices

Never	Rarely	Sometimes	Often	Very often

OUTPUT CONTROL

14. How well can the output of the service offshoring subsidiary be described upfront? Is it possible to exactly specify results or are these specifications difficult to create and subject to frequent changes?

15. When the service offshoring subsidiary is evaluated, to what extent is evaluation based on performance measured against predetermined service levels?

DIRECT PERSONAL COORDINATION

16. Do people from the headquarters or other international subsidiaries directly supervise people in the service offshoring subsidiary?

17. Are there personal relationships between people in the service offshoring subsidiary and people from other units? If so, how many and on which management levels?

18. How often do the parties interact with each other (regular meetings, exchange of reports, phone calls, email, etc.)?

	Very low (every 6 months)	Low (quarterly)	Medium (monthly)	High (weekly)	Very high (daily)
Phone calls					
Phone conferences					
Video conferences					
Email					

	Very low (every 6 months)	Low (quarterly)	Medium (monthly)	High (weekly)	Very high (daily)
Visits					
Electronic exchange					

19. How intense are these interactions?

	Very low (one person from each side)	Low (one person from one side, small group (2-4 persons) on the other)	Medium (small groups from each side)	High (small groups from three or more parties)	Very high (large groups (> 4 persons) from three or more parties)
Phone calls					
Phone conferences					
Video conferences					
Email					
Visits					
Electronic exchange					

20. How long do the interactions typically last?

	Very short (a few minutes)	Short (lees than an hour)	Medium (some hours)	Long (full day)	Very long (several days)
Phone calls					

	Very short (a few minutes)	Short (lees than an hour)	Medium (some hours)	Long (full day)	Very long (several days)
Phone conferences					
Video conferences					
Email					
Visits					
Electronic exchange					

TRANSFERS

21. Are there transferees from the headquarters or international subsidiaries working in the service offshoring subsidiary? Out of all the employees, how many transferees work in the service offshoring subsidiary?

VISITS

22. Are there personal visits from other units to the service offshoring subsidiary? If so, how many, how often and how long?

CULTURAL COORDINATION

23. How important are possible language differences across locations?

24. Is there a team spirit across the different locations?

25. Do people share values and goals across locations? Do the managers share values and goals across locations?

26. Is there the possibility for people across locations to get to know each other? For instance, are there trainings or events that are held across locations?

27. Do you provide training for your new employees? If so, does this training teach technical skills, or does it focus more on soft skills, or both?

Discussion of additional topics

Lastly, I would like to take the opportunity of asking you about other important aspects relating to the service offshoring subsidiary. For example, can you say something about the plans for the future? For instance, are there plans to extend the service portfolio?

5. TRANSCRIPTION RULES

The interviews were transcribed by two external transcribers, one for German and one for English. The following instructions were provided to them to guide the transcription process.

"I do not need any 'aehm' or other kind of intonations to be transcribed. Only the content counts.

Interruptions by the interviewer 'I understand', 'go on', etc. should not be transcribed.

Parts of the interviews that you do not understand should be listened to three times. If the part is still not understandable, single words should be replaced by ??; several missing words by ???. Words or expressions where you are not sure if you understand them correctly should be followed by (??)

Please use #1 for interviewer and #2 for interviewee. Every time the speaker changes there should be a new line in the transcription (without blank lines in between). For more than two speakers the speaker's initial should be added (initials will be provided for each interview). Should there be the need to add any notes from the transcriber please indicate this by #5.

The output should be plain text that I can analyze going forward in other programs.

Please add a time mark every two minutes (for example, after two minutes, set a mark (#3 02:00), after four minutes (#3 04:00), after six minutes (#03 06:00) and so on)."

LITERATURE

Aaker, David A. (1989): Managing Assets and Skills: The Key to a Sustainable Competitive Advantage. California Management Review. Vol. 31, No. 2, 1989, pp. 91-106.

Abramovsky, Laura/Griffith, Rachel (2005): Outsourcing and Offshoring of Business Services: How Important Is ICT? IFS Working Papers, No. 22, The Institute for Fiscal Studies, 2005.

Adam Jr., Everett E. (1983): Towards a Typology of Production and Operations Management Systems. Academy of Management Review. Vol. 8, No. 3, 1983, pp. 365-375.

Agarwal, Sanjeev (1993): Influence of Formalization on Role Stress, Organizational Commitment, and Work Alienation of Salespersons: A Cross-National Comparative Study. Journal of International Business Studies. Vol. 24, No. 4, 1993, pp. 715-739.

Agrawal, Vivek/Farrell, Diana (2003): Who Wins in Offshoring. McKinsey Quarterly. No. 4, 2003, pp. 36-41.

Agrawal, Vivek/Farrell, Diana/Remes, Jaana K. (2003): Offshoring and Beyond. McKinsey Quarterly. No. 4, 2003, pp. 24-33.

Akintoye, Akintola/Hardcastle, Cliff/Beck, Matthias/Chinyio, Ezekiel/Asenova, Darinka (2003): Achieving Best Value in Private Finance Initiative Project Procurement. Construction Management & Economics. Vol. 21, No. 5, 2003, pp. 461-470.

Albach, Horst (1989): Dienstleistungsunternehmen in Deutschland. Zeitschrift für Betriebswirtschaft (ZfB). Vol. 59, No. 4, 1989, pp. 397-420.

Alguire, Mary S./Frear, Carl R./Metcalf, Lynn E. (1994): An Examination of the Determinants of Global Sourcing Strategy. Journal of Business & Industrial Marketing. Vol. 9, No. 2, 1994, pp. 62-76.

Amit, Raphael/Schoemaker, Paul J. H. (1993): Strategic Assets and Organizational Rent. Strategic Management Journal. Vol. 14, No. 1, 1993, pp. 33-46.

Amshoff, Bernhard (1993): Controlling in deutschen Unternehmungen: Realtypen, Kontext und Effizienz. 2 edition. Gabler, Wiesbaden, 1993.

Anderson, Barbara A. (2005): Expatriate Selection: Good Management or Good Luck? International Journal of Human Resource Management. Vol. 16, No. 4, 2005, pp. 567-583.

Anderson, Joan B. (1983): Factor Substitution and Adaptation in the 'Off-Shore' Assembly Plants of Baja California. Annals of Regional Science. Vol. 17, No. 2, 1983, pp. 29-44.

Andersson, Maria/Holm, Ulf/Holmström, Christine (2001): Relationship Configuration and Competence Development in MNC Subsidiaries, in: Håkansson, Håkan/Johanson, Jan (Eds., 2001): Business Network Learning. Pergamon, Amsterdam et al., pp. 185-205.

Andersson, Ulf (2003): Managing the Transfer of Capabilities within Multinational Corporations: The Dual Role of the Subsidiary. Scandinavian Journal of Management. Vol. 19, No. 4, 2003, pp. 425-442.

Andersson, Ulf/Forsgren, Mats (1995): Using Networks to Determine Multinational Parental Control of Subsidiaries, in: Paliwoda, Stanley J./Ryans Jr., John K. (Eds., 1995): International Marketing Reader. Routledge, London, New York, pp. 72-87.

Andersson, Ulf/Forsgren, Mats (1996): Subsidiary Embeddedness and Control in the Multinational Corporation. International Business Review. Vol. 5, No. 5, 1996, pp. 487-508.

Andersson, Ulf/Forsgren, Mats (2000): In Search of Centre of Excellence: Network Embeddedness and Subsidiary Roles in Multinational Corporations. Management International Review. Vol. 40, No. 4, 2000, pp. 329-350.

Andersson, Ulf/Forsgren, Mats/Holm, Ulf (2001): Subsidiary Embeddedness and Competence Development in MNCs: Multi-level Analysis. Organization Studies. Vol. 22, No. 6, 2001, pp. 1013-1034.

Andersson, Ulf/Forsgren, Mats/Pedersen, Torben (2001): Subsidiary Performance in Multinational Corporations: The Importance of Technology Embeddedness. International Business Review. Vol. 10, No. 1, 2001, pp. 3-23.

Andersson, Ulf/Forsgren, Mats/Holm, Ulf (2002): The Strategic Impact of External Networks: Subsidiary Performance and Competence Development in the Multinational Corporation. Strategic Management Journal. Vol. 23, No. 11, 2002, pp. 979-996.

Andersson, Ulf/Björkman, Ingmar/Forsgren, Mats (2005): Managing Subsidiary Knowledge Creation: The Effect of Control Mechanisms on Subsidiary Local Embeddedness. International Business Review. Vol. 14, No. 5, 2005, pp. 521-538.

Angelos, Terry N. (2004): The Impact of Offshoring on the Venture Capital Industry. Journal of Private Equity. Vol. 7, No. 4, 2004, pp. 36-47.

Anonymous (2003): Lufthansa Accountancy to Be Placed in Krakow. Polish News Bulletin. Date: 27.03.2003.

Anonymous (2004a): Point-Counterpoint Edith Penrose and the Resource-Based View of Strategic Management. Journal of Management Studies. Vol. 41, No. 1, 2004a, pp. 181-182.

Anonymous (2004b): Trade Disputes. Vol. 372. No. 8393, 2004b, p. 80.

Anonymous (2005): Outsourcing bringt noch Probleme. Handelsblatt. Vol. 42. Date: 01.03.2005, p. 18.

Anonymous (2006): Deutsche Bank verlagert Jobs nach Indien. Handelsblatt. Vol. 62. Date: 28.03.2006, p. 22.

Araujo, Luis/Rezende, Sergio (2003): Path Dependence, MNCs and the Internationalisation Process: A Relational Approach. International Business Review. Vol. 12, No. 6, 2003, pp. 719-737.

Argyres, Nicholas (1996): Capabilities, Technological Diversification and Divisionalization. Strategic Management Journal. Vol. 17, No. 5, 1996, pp. 395-410.

Arndt, Sven W. (1997): Globalization and the Open Economy. North American Journal of Economics & Finance. Vol. 8, No. 1, 1997, pp. 71-79.

Aubert, Benoit A./Rivard, Suzanne/Patry, Michel (2004): A Transaction Cost Model of IT Outsourcing. Information & Management. Vol. 41, No. 7, 2004, pp. 921-932.

Auster, Ellen R. (1994): Macro and Strategic Perspectives on Interorganizational Linkages: A Comparative Analysis and Review with Suggestions for Reorientation, in: Shrivastava, Paul/Huff, Anne S./Dutton, Jane E. (Eds., 1994): Interorganizational Relations and Interorganizational Strategies. JAI Press, Greenwich, London, pp. 3-40.

Ayers, Douglas J./Gordon, Geoffrey L./Schoenbachler, Denise D. (2001): Integration and New Product Development Success: The Role of Formal and Informal Controls. Journal of Applied Business Research. Vol. 17, No. 2, 2001, pp. 133-148.

Baily, Martin Neil/Lawrence, Robert Z. (2004): What Happened to the Great U.S. Job Machine? The Role of Trade and Electronic Offshoring. Brookings Papers on Economic Activity. No. 2, 2004, pp. 201-260.

Baldauf, Artur/Cravens, David W./Piercy, Nigel F. (2005): Sales Management Control Research - Synthesis and an Agenda for Future Research. Journal of Personal Selling & Sales Management. Vol. 25, No. 1, 2005, pp. 7-26.

Baliga, B. Ram/Jaeger, Alfred M. (1984): Multinational Corporations: Control Systems and Delegation Issues. Journal of International Business Studies. Vol. 15, No. 2, 1984, pp. 25-40.

Bamberger, Ingolf/Wrona, Thomas (1996): Der Ressourcenansatz und seine Bedeutung für die strategische Unternehmensführung. Zfbf: Schmalenbachs Zeitschrift für betriebswirtschaftliche Forschung. Vol. 48, No. 2, 1996, pp. 130-153.

Barner-Rasmussen, Wilhelm/Björkman, Ingmar (2005): Surmounting Interunit Barriers. International Studies of Management & Organization. Vol. 35, No. 1, 2005, pp. 28-46.

Barney, Jay B. (1986): Organizational Culture: Can It Be a Source of Sustained Competitive Advantage? Academy of Management Review. Vol. 11, No. 3, 1986, pp. 656-665.
Barney, Jay B. (1991): Firm Resources and Sustained Competitive Advantage. Journal of Management. Vol. 17, No. 1, 1991, pp. 99-120.
Barney, Jay B. (2001a): Is the Resource-Based 'View' a Useful Perspective for Strategic Management Research? Yes. Academy of Management Review. Vol. 26, No. 1, 2001a, pp. 41-56.
Barney, Jay B. (2001b): Resource-Based Theories of Competitive Advantage: A Ten-Year Retrospective on the Resource-Based View. Journal of Management. Vol. 27, No. 6, 2001b, pp. 643-650.
Barney, Jay B./Arikan, Asli M. (2001): The Resource-Based View: Origins and Implications, in: Hitt, Michael A./Freeman, R. Edward/Harrison, Jeffrey S. (Eds., 2001): The Blackwell Handbook of Strategic Management. Blackwell Publishers, Cambridge, Oxford, pp. 124-188.
Barney, Jay B./Wright, Mike/Ketchen Jr., David J. (2001): The Resource-Based View of the Firm: Ten Years After 1991. Journal of Management. Vol. 27, No. 6, 2001, pp. 625-641.
Bartlett, Christopher A./Ghoshal, Sumantra (1986): Tap Your Subsidiaries for Global Reach. Harvard Business Review. Vol. 64, No. 6, 1986, pp. 87-94.
Bartlett, Christopher A./Ghoshal, Sumantra (1988): Organizing for Worldwide Effectiveness: The Transnational Solution. California Management Review. Vol. 31, No. 1, 1988, pp. 54-74.
Bartlett, Christopher A./Ghoshal, Sumantra (1989): Managing Across Borders: The Transnational Solution. Harvard Business School Press, Boston, 1989.
Baum, Joel A. C./Dutton, Jane E. (1996): Introduction: The Embeddedness of Strategy, in: Baum, Joel A. C./Dutton, Jane E. (Eds., 1996): The Embeddedness of Strategy. JAI Press, Greenwich, London, pp. 1-15.
Beachboard, John C./Beard, David V. (2005): Innovation in Information Systems Education-II Enterprise IS Management: A Capstone Course for Undergraduate IS Majors. Communications of AIS. Vol. 2005, No. 15, 2005, pp. 315-330.
Beechler, Schon/Yang, John Zhuang (1994): The Transfer of Japanese-Style Management to American Subsidiaries: Contingencies, Constraints, and Competencies. Journal of International Business Studies. Vol. 25, No. 3, 1994, pp. 467-491.
Belderbos, Rene/Heijltjes, Marie (2005): The Determinants of Expatriate Staffing by Japanese Multinationals in Asia: Control, Learning and Vertical Business Groups. Journal of International Business Studies. Vol. 36, No. 3, 2005, pp. 341-354.
Bensaou, Bob M./Venkatraman, N. (1995): Configurations of Interorganizational Relationships: A Comparison between U.S. and Japanese Automakers. Management Science. Vol. 41, No. 9, 1995, pp. 1471-1492.
Berger, Ulrike/Bernhard, Mehlich (2002): Die Verhaltenswissenschaftliche Entscheidungstheorie, in: Kieser, Alfred (Ed., 2002): Organisationstheorien. Kohlhammer, Stuttgart, pp. 133-168.
Berggren, Christian/Bengtsson, Lars (2004): Rethinking Outsourcing in Manufacturing: A Tale of Two Telecom Firms. European Management Journal. Vol. 22, No. 2, 2004, pp. 211-223.
Berry, John (2006): Offshoring Opportunities: Strategies and Tactics for Global Competitiveness. John Wiley & Sons, Hoboken, 2006.
Bhagwati, Jagdish/Panagariya, Arvind/Srinivasan, T. N. (2004): The Muddles over Outsourcing. Journal of Economic Perspectives. Vol. 18, No. 4, 2004, pp. 93-114.
Bhambal, Juhi (2005): From Gecis to Genpact. 2005. URL: http://www.GlobalOutsourcing.org/content/Companies/1899/105120501.asp (accessed 04.05.2006).
Bigio, David/Edgeman, Rick L./Ferleman, Thomas (2004): Six Sigma Availability Management of Information Technology in the Office of the Chief Technology Officer of Washington, DC. Total Quality Management & Business Excellence. Vol. 15, No. 5/6, 2004, pp. 679-687.

Biles, James J. (2004): Export-Oriented Industrialization and Regional Development: A Case Study of Maquiladora Production in Yucatán, Mexico. Regional Studies. Vol. 38, No. 5, 2004, pp. 517-532.

Birkinshaw, Julian M. (1996): How Multinational Subsidiary Mandates Are Gained and Lost. Journal of International Business Studies. Vol. 27, No. 3, 1996, pp. 467-495.

Birkinshaw, Julian M. (1998): Corporate Entrepreneurship in Network Organizations: How Subsidiary Initiative Drives Internal Market Efficiency. European Management Journal. Vol. 16, No. 3, 1998, pp. 355-364.

Birkinshaw, Julian M./Morrison, Allen J. (1995): Configurations of Strategy and Structure in Subsidiaries of Multinational Subsidiaries. Journal of International Business Studies. Vol. 26, No. 4, 1995, pp. 729-753.

Birkinshaw, Julian M./Nobel, Robert/Ridderstråle, Jonas (2002): Knowledge as a Contingency Variable: Do the Characteristics of Knowledge Predict Organization Structure? Organization Science. Vol. 13, No. 3, 2002, pp. 274-289.

Birkinshaw, Julian M./Holm, Ulf/Thilenius, Peter/Arvidsson, Niklas (2000): Consequences of Perception Gaps in the Headquarters-Subsidiary Relationship. International Business Review. Vol. 9, No. 3, 2000, pp. 321-344.

Björkman, Ingmar/Barner-Rasmussen, Wilhelm/Li, Li (2004): Managing Knowledge Transfer in MNCs: The Impact of Headquarters Control Mechanisms. Journal of International Business Studies. Vol. 35, No. 5, 2004, pp. 443-455.

Blakley, D./Doyle, B./Murray, W. (1987): Improving the Effectiveness of Offshore Production Agreements in Dynamic Product Markets. Management International Review. Vol. 27, No. 3, 1987, pp. 26-37.

Blau, Peter M./Scott, W. Richard (1963): Formal Organizations: A Comparative Approach. Routledge, London, New York, 1963.

Blinder, Alan S. (2006): Offshoring: The Next Industrial Revolution? Foreign Affairs. Vol. 85, No. 2, 2006, pp. 113-128.

Blunden, Bill (2004): Offshoring IT: The Good, the Bad, and the Ugly. Apress, Berkeley, 2004.

BMF (2004): Monatsbericht 08.2004. Bundesministerium der Finanzen. Berlin, 2004.

Boddewyn, Jean J./Halbrich, Marsha Baldwin/Perry, Andrew C. (1986): Service Multinationals: Conceptualization, Measurement and Theory. Journal of International Business Studies. Vol. 17, No. 3, 1986, pp. 41-57.

Boes, Andreas/Schwemmle, Michael (2005): Was ist Offshoring? in: Boes, Andreas/Schwemmle, Michael (Eds., 2005): Bangalore statt Böblingen? Offshoring und Internationalisierung im IT-Sektor. VSA-Verlag, Hamburg, pp. 9-12.

Boes, Andreas/Schwemmle, Michael/Becker, Ellen (2004): Herausforderung Offshoring: Internationalisierung und Auslagerung von IT-Dienstleistungen. Hans-Böckler-Stiftung, Düsseldorf, 2004.

Bogner, Alexander/Menz, Wolfgang (2002): Expertenwissen und Forschungspraxis: Die modernisierungstheoretische und die methodische Debatte um die Experten. Zur Einführung in ein unübersichtliches Problemfeld, in: Bogner, Alexander/Littig, Beate/Menz, Wolfgang (Eds., 2002): Das Experteninterview: Theorie, Methode, Anwendung. Leske + Budrich, Opladen, pp. 7-29.

Bollen, Kenneth A. (1984): Multiple Indicators: Internal Consistency or No Necessary Relationship? Quality and Quantity. Vol. 18, No. 4, 1984, pp. 377-385.

Böttcher, Roland (1996): Global Network Management: Context - Decision-Making - Coordination. Gabler, Wiesbaden, 1996.

Bottino, Susan J. (2004): Perspective on Offshoring and New Jersey. 2004. URL: http://www.offshoringforum.com/article_read.asp?id=42 (accessed 11.08.2005).

Bowman, Cliff/Collier, Nardine (2006): A Contingency Approach to Resource-creation Processes. International Journal of Management Reviews. Vol. 8, No. 4, 2006, pp. 191-211.

Brass, Daniel J./Burkhardt, Marlene E. (1992): Centrality and Power in Organizations, in: Nohria, Nitin/Eccles, Robert G. (Eds., 1992): Networks and Organizations: Structure, Form, and Action. Harvard Business School Press, Boston, pp. 191-215.

Brass, Daniel J./Butterfield, Kenneth D./Skaggs, Bruce C. (1998): Relationships and Unethical Behavior: A Social Network Perspective. Academy of Management Review. Vol. 23, No. 1, 1998, pp. 14-31.

Brass, Daniel J./Galaskiewicz, Joseph/Greve, Henrich R./Tsai, Wenpin (2004): Taking Stock of Networks and Organizations: A Multilevel Perspective. Academy of Management Journal. Vol. 47, No. 6, 2004, pp. 795-817.

Brouthers, Lance Eliot/McCray, John P./Wilkinson, Timothy J. (1999): Maquiladoras: Entrepreneurial Experimentation to Global Competitiveness. Business Horizons. Vol. 42, No. 2, 1999, pp. 37-44.

Brown, Steven P./Evans, Kenneth R./Mantrala, Murali K./Challagalla, Goutam (2005): Adapting Motivation, Control, and Compensation Research to a New Environment. Journal of Personal Selling & Sales Management. Vol. 25, No. 2, 2005, pp. 156-167.

Bruhn, Manfred (2000): Qualitätssicherung im Dienstleistungsmarketing - eine Einführung in die theoretischen und praktischen Probleme, in: Bruhn, Manfred/Stauss, Bernd (Eds., 2000): Dienstleistungsqualität: Konzepte - Methoden - Erfahrungen. 3 edition. Gabler, Wiesbaden, pp. 21-48.

Bruhn, Manfred (2005): Internationalisierung von Dienstleistungen - eine Einführung in den Sammelband, in: Bruhn, Manfred/Stauss, Bernd (Eds., 2005): Internationalisierung von Dienstleistungen - Forum Dienstleistungsmanagement. Gabler, Wiesbaden, pp. 3-42.

Brumagim, Alan L. (1994): A Hierarchy of Corporate Resources, in: Shrivastava, Paul/Huff, Anne S./Dutton, Jane E. (Eds., 1994): Resource-Based View of the Firm. JAI Press, Greenwich, London, pp. 81-112.

Bryman, Alan (1989): Research Methods and Organization Studies. Unwin Hyman, London, 1989.

Buckley, Peter J./Casson, Mark (1991): The Future of the Multinational Enterprise. 2 edition. Macmillan, Houndmills, Basingstoke, Hampshire, 1991.

Bufka, Jürgen (1997): Auslandsgesellschaften internationaler Dienstleistungsunternehmen: Koordination - Kontext - Erfolg. Gabler, Wiesbaden, 1997.

Bunyaratavej, Kraiwinee/Hahn, Eugene D./Doh, Jonathan P. (2007): International Offshoring of Services: A Parity Study. Journal of International Management. Vol. 13, No. 1, 2007, pp. 7-21.

Burgmaier, Stefanie/Handschuch, Konrad/Ramthum, Christian/Sprothen, Vera (2004): Mit einem Mausklick. Wirtschaftswoche. No. 39, 2004, pp. 20-30.

Burrell, Gibson/Morgan, Gareth (1979): Sociological Paradigms and Organisational Analysis: Elements of the Sociology of Corporate Life. Heinemann, London, 1979.

Busse, C./Hennes, M. (2004): Stunden für den Standort. Handelsblatt. Vol. 121. Date: 25.06.2004, p. 2.

Calori, Roland/Melin, Leif/Atamer, Tugrul/Gustavsson, Peter (2000): Innovative International Strategies. Journal of World Business. Vol. 35, No. 4, 2000, pp. 333-354.

Campenhausen, Claus von/Rudolf, Andreas (2001): Shared Services - Profitabel für vernetzte Unternehmen. Harvard Business Manager. Vol. 23, No. 1, 2001, pp. 82-94.

Cardinal, Laura B./Sitkin, Sim B./Long, Chris P. (2004): Balancing and Rebalancing in the Creation and Evolution of Organizational Control. Organization Science. Vol. 15, No. 4, 2004, pp. 411-431.

Carmel, Erran/Tjia, Paul (2005): Offshoring Information Technology: Sourcing and Outsourcing to a Global Workforce. Cambridge University Press, Cambridge, 2005.

Carper, William B./Snizek, William E. (1980): The Nature and Types of Organizational Taxonomies: An Overview. Academy of Management Review. Vol. 5, No. 1, 1980, pp. 65-75.

Cassell, Catherine/Symon, Gillian (1994): Qualitative Research in Work Contexts, in: Cassell, Catherine/Symon, Gillian (Eds., 1994): Qualitative Methods in Organizational Research - A Practical Guide. Sage Publications, Thousand Oaks, London, New Delhi, pp. 1-13.

Cavusgil, S. Tamer/Shaoming, Zou/Naidu, G. M. (1993): Product and Promotion Adaptation in Export Ventures: An Empirical Investigation. Journal of International Business Studies. Vol. 24, No. 3, 1993, pp. 479-506.

Chatterjee, Savan/Wernerfelt, Birger (1991): The Link between Resources and Type of Diversification: Theory and Evidence. Strategic Management Journal. Vol. 12, No. 1, 1991, pp. 33-48.

Chen, Tain-Jy/Chen, Homin/Ku, Ying-Hua (2004): Foreign Direct Investment and Local Linkages. Journal of International Business Studies. Vol. 35, No. 4, 2004, pp. 320-333.

Cheng, Joseph L. C./Miller, Edwin L. (1985): Coordination and Output Attainment in Work Units Performing Non-Routine Tasks: A Cross-National Study. Organization Studies. Vol. 6, No. 1, 1985, pp. 23-39.

Cheon, Myun J./Grover, Varun/Teng, James T. C. (1995): Theoretical Perspectives on the Outsourcing of Information Systems. Journal of Information Technology. Vol. 10, No. 4, 1995, pp. 209-219.

Chi, Tailan (1994): Trading in Strategic Resources: Necessary Conditions, Transaction Cost Problems, and Choice of Exchange Structure. Strategic Management Journal. Vol. 15, No. 4, 1994, pp. 271-290.

Child, John (1972): Organization Structure and Strategies of Control: A Replication of the Aston Study. Administrative Science Quarterly. Vol. 17, No. 2, 1972, pp. 163-177.

Child, John/Faulkner, David (1998): Strategies of Cooperation: Managing Alliances, Networks, and Joint Ventures. Oxford University Press, Oxford et al., 1998.

Chini, Tina/Ambos, Björn/Wehle, Katrin (2005): The Headquarters-Subsidiaries Trench: Tracing Perception Gaps within the Multinational Corporation. European Management Journal. Vol. 23, No. 2, 2005, pp. 145-153.

Choi, Chong Ju/Manoj, Raman/Usoltseva, Olga/Lee, Soo Hee (1999): Political Embeddedness in the New Triad: Implications for Emerging Economies. Management International Review. Vol. 39, No. 3, 1999, pp. 257-275.

Christensen, Jens Frøslev (2000): Building Innovative Assets and Dynamic Coherence, in: Foss, Nicolai J. (Ed., 2000): Resources, Technology, and Strategy: Explorations in the Resource-Based Perspective. Routledge, London, New York, pp. 123-152.

Clark, Don P./Sawyer, W. Charles/Sprinkle, Richard L. (1993): Determinants of Offshore Assembly in Developing and Developed Countries. Social Science Quarterly. Vol. 74, No. 4, 1993, pp. 771-782.

Clark, Terry/Rajaratnam, Daniel/Smith, Timothy (1996): Toward a Theory of International Services: Marketing Intangibles in a World of Nations. Journal of International Marketing. Vol. 4, No. 2, 1996, pp. 9-28.

Clott, Christopher B. (2004): Perspectives on Global Outsourcing and the Changing Nature of Work. Business & Society Review. Vol. 109, No. 2, 2004, pp. 153-170.

Colbert, Barry A. (2004): The Complex Resource-Based View: Implications for Theory and Practice in Strategic Human Resource Management. Academy of Management Review. Vol. 29, No. 3, 2004, pp. 341-358.

Colling, Trevor/Ferner, Anthony (1992): The Limits of Autonomy: Devolution, Line Managers and Industrial Relations in Privatized Companies. Journal of Management Studies. Vol. 29, No. 2, 1992, pp. 209-227.

Collis, David J. (1991): A Resource-Based Analysis of Global Competition: The Case of the Bearings Industry. Strategic Management Journal. Vol. 12, No. 4, 1991, pp. 49-68.

Collis, David J. (1994): Research Note: How Valuable Are Organizational Capabilities? Strategic Management Journal. Vol. 15, No. 8, 1994, pp. 143-152.

Collis, David J./Montgomery, Cynthia A. (1995): Competing on Resources: Strategy in the 1990s. Harvard Business Review. Vol. 73, No. 4, 1995, pp. 118-128.

Colquhoun, Grant/Edmonds, Keith/Goodger, David (2004): "Offshoring": How Big an Issue? Economic Outlook. Vol. 28, No. 3, 2004, pp. 9-15.

Combs, James G./Ketchen Jr., David J. (1999): Explaining Interfirm Cooperation and Performance: Toward a Reconciliation of Predictions from the Resource-Based

View and Organizational Economics. Strategic Management Journal. Vol. 20, No. 9, 1999, pp. 867-888.
Connell, Regina (1996): Learning to Share. Journal of Business Strategy. Vol. 17, No. 2, 1996, pp. 55-58.
Contractor, Farok J./Lorange, Peter (2002): Cooperative Strategies in International Business: Joint Ventures and Technology Partnerships between Firms. 2 edition. Pergamon, Amsterdam, 2002.
Coronado, Roberto/Fullerton Jr., Thomas M./Clark, Don P. (2004): Short-Run Maquiladora Employment Dynamics in Tijuana. Annals of Regional Science. Vol. 38, No. 4, 2004, pp. 751-763.
Coyne, Kevin P. (1986): Sustainable Competitive Advantage - What It Is, What It Isn't. Business Horizons. Vol. 29, No. 1, 1986, pp. 54-61.
Cray, David (1984): Control and Coordination in Multinational Corporations. Journal of International Business Studies. Vol. 15, No. 2, 1984, pp. 85-98.
Creswell, John W. (2003): Research Design: Qualitative, Quantitative, and Mixed Methods Approaches. 2 edition. Sage Publications, Thousand Oaks, London, New Delhi, 2003.
D'Cruz, Joseph R. (1986): Strategic Management of Subsidiaries, in: Etemad, Hamid G./Séguin, Dulude (Eds., 1986): Managing the Multinational Subsidiary: Response to Environmental Changes and to Host Nation R&D Policies. Croom Helm, London, pp. 75-89.
D'Cruz, Joseph R./Rugman, Alan M. (1994): Business Network Theory and the Canadian Telecommunications Industry. International Business Review. Vol. 3, No. 3, 1994, pp. 275-288.
Dacin, M. Tina/Ventresca, Marc J./Beal, Brent D. (1999): The Embeddedness of Organizations: Dialogue & Directions. Journal of Management. Vol. 25, No. 3, 1999, pp. 317-356.
Dagnino, Giovanni Battista (2004): Complex Systems as Key Drivers for the Emergence of a Resource- and Capability-Based Interorganizational Network. Emergence: Complexity & Organization. Vol. 6, No. 1/2, 2004, pp. 61-69.
Das, T. K./Bing-Sheng, Teng (2000): A Resource-Based Theory of Strategic Alliances. Journal of Management. Vol. 26, No. 1, 2000, pp. 31-62.
Davidson, William H. (1980): The Location of Foreign Direct Investment Activity: Country Characteristics and Experience Effects. Journal of International Business Studies. Vol. 11, No. 2, 1980, pp. 9-22.
Davies, Paul (2004): What's this India Business? Offshoring, Outsourcing, and the Global Services Revolution. Nicholas Brealey Publishing, London, 2004.
Davis, Lee N./Meyer, Klaus E. (2004): Subsidiary Research and Development, and the Local Environment. International Business Review. Vol. 13, No. 3, 2004, pp. 359-382.
Davis, Tim R. V. (1991): Information Technology and White-Collar Productivity. Academy of Management Executive. Vol. 5, No. 1, 1991, pp. 55-67.
Day, George S./Wensley, Robin (1988): Assessing Advantage: A Framework for Diagnosing Competitive Superiority. Journal of Marketing. Vol. 52, No. 2, 1988, pp. 1-20.
De Looff, Leon A. (1995): Information Systems Outsourcing Decision Making: A Framework, Organizational Theories and Case Studies. Journal of Information Technology. Vol. 10, No. 4, 1995, pp. 281-297.
Dedoussis, Vagelis (1995): Simply a Question of Cultural Barriers? The Search for New Perspectives in the Transfer of Japanese Management Practices. Journal of Management Studies. Vol. 32, No. 6, 1995, pp. 731-745.
Delios, Andrew/Björkman, Ingmar (2000): Expatriate Staffing in Foreign Subsidiaries of Japanese Multinational Corporations in the PRC and the United States. International Journal of Human Resource Management. Vol. 11, No. 2, 2000, pp. 278-293.
Deloitte (2004): The Titans Take Hold - How Offshoring has Changed the Competitive Dynamic for Global Financial Services Institutions. Deloitte. New York, 2004.

Dess, Gregory G./Newport, Stephanie/Rasheed, Abdul M. A. (1993): Configuration Research in Strategic Management: Key Issues and Suggestions. Journal of Management. Vol. 19, No. 4, 1993, pp. 775-795.

DeVault, James M. (1997): Offshore Assembly and the Dominican Republic. World Economy. Vol. 20, No. 7, 1997, pp. 951-966.

Dhanaraj, Charles/Lyles, Marjorie A./Steensma, H. Kevin/Tihanyi, Laszlo (2004): Managing Tacit and Explicit Knowledge Transfer in IJVs: The Role of Relational Embeddedness and the Impact on Performance. Journal of International Business Studies. Vol. 35, No. 5, 2004, pp. 428-442.

Diamantopoulos, Adamantios/Winklhofer, Heidi M. (2001): Index Construction with Formative Indicators: An Alternative to Scale Development. Journal of Marketing Research. Vol. 38, No. 2, 2001, pp. 269-277.

Dierickx, Ingemar/Cool, Karel (1989): Asset Stock Accumulation and the Sustainability of Competitive Advantage. Management Science. Vol. 35, No. 12, 1989, pp. 1504-1511.

Dittrich, Jörg/Braun, Marc (2004): Business Process Outsourcing: Ein Entscheidungsleitfaden für das Out- und Insourcing von Geschäftsprozessen. Schäffer-Poeschel, Stuttgart, 2004.

Doh, Jonathan P. (2005): Offshore Outsourcing: Implications for International Business and Strategic Management Theory and Practice. Journal of Management Studies. Vol. 42, No. 3, 2005, pp. 695-704.

Donnely, Michael (2005): Avaya's Journey to Global HR Shared Service. Strategic HR Review. Vol. 4, No. 2, 2005, pp. 20-23.

Dorestani, Alireza (2004): Transfer Price and Equilibrium in Multidivisional Firms: An Examination of Divisional Autonomy and Central Control. Applied Economics. Vol. 36, No. 17, 2004, pp. 1899-1906.

Dossani, Rafiq/Kenney, Martin (2003): "Lift and Shift": Moving the Back Office to India. Information Technologies & International Development. Vol. 1, No. 2, 2003, pp. 21-37.

Dossani, Rafiq/Kenney, Martin (2006): Reflections upon "Sizing the Emerging Global Labor Market." Academy of Management Perspectives. Vol. 20, No. 4, 2006, pp. 35-41.

Doty, D. Harold/Glick, William H. (1994): Typologies as a Unique Form of Theory Building: Toward Improved Understanding and Modeling. Academy of Management Review. Vol. 19, No. 2, 1994, pp. 230-251.

Dowlatshahi, Shad (2005): An Operational Perspective of the Relationships between the Headquarters and the Maquiladoras. International Journal of Production Research. Vol. 43, No. 14, 2005, pp. 2949-2975.

Downey, Kirk H./Ireland, Duane R. (1979): Quantitative versus Qualitative: Environmental Assessment in Organizational Studies. Administrative Science Quarterly. Vol. 24, No. 4, 1979, pp. 630-637.

Doz, Yves L./Prahalad, Coimbatore K. (1984): Patterns of Strategic Control within Multinational Corporations. Journal of International Business Studies. Vol. 15, No. 2, 1984, pp. 55-72.

Doz, Yves L./Prahalad, Coimbatore K. (1991): Managing DMNCs: A Search for a New Paradigm. Strategic Management Journal. Vol. 12, No. 4, 1991, pp. 145-164.

Doz, Yves L./Hamel, Gary (1998): Alliance Advantage: The Art of Creating Value through Partnering. Harvard Business School Press, Boston, 1998.

Drechsler, Wolfgang (2006): Lufthansa findet billige Logistiker am Kap. Handelsblatt. Vol. 9. Date: 12.01.2006, p. 7.

Dubie, Denise (2005): A Closer Look at ITIL. Network World. Vol. 22, 2005, pp. 27-30.

Dunning, John H. (1973): The Determinants of International Production. Oxford Economic Papers. Vol. 25, No. 3, 1973, pp. 289-336.

Dunning, John H. (1979): Explaining Changing Patterns of International Production: In Defense of the Eclectic Theory. Oxford Bulletin of Economics & Statistics. Vol. 41, No. 4, 1979, pp. 269-295.

Dunning, John H. (1988): The Eclectic Paradigm of International Production: A Restatement and Some Possible Extensions. Journal of International Business Studies. Vol. 19, No. 1, 1988, pp. 1-31.

Dunning, John H. (1989): Multinational Enterprises and the Growth of Services: Some Conceptual and Theoretical Issues. Service Industries Journal. Vol. 9, No. 1, 1989, pp. 5-39.

Dunning, John H. (1994): Re-Evaluating the Benefits of Foreign Direct Investment. Transnational Corporations. Vol. 3, No. 1, 1994, pp. 23-39.

Dunning, John H. (1995): Reappraising the Eclectic Paradigm in an Age of Alliance Capitalism. Journal of International Business Studies. Vol. 26, No. 3, 1995, pp. 461-491.

Dunning, John H. (2000): The Eclectic Paradigm as an Envelope for Economic and Business Theories of MNE Activity. International Business Review. Vol. 9, No. 2, 2000, pp. 163-190.

Dunning, John H./Rugman, Alan M. (1985): The Influence of Hymer's Dissertation on the Theory of Foreign Direct Investment. American Economic Review. Vol. 75, No. 2, 1985, pp. 228-232.

Dunning, John H./Narula, Rajneesh (1995): The R&D Activities of Foreign Firms in the United States. International Studies of Management & Organization. Vol. 25, No. 1/2, 1995, pp. 39-73.

Dunning, John H. (2003): The Contribution of Edith Penrose to International Business Scholarship. Management International Review. Vol. 43, No. 1, 2003, pp. 3-19.

Dutta, Amitava/Roy, Rahul (2005): Offshore Outsourcing: A Dynamic Causal Model of Counteracting Forces. Journal of Management Information Systems. Vol. 22, No. 2, 2005, pp. 15-35.

Dutta, Shantanu/Narasimhan, Om/Rajiv, Surendra (2005): Conceptualizing and Measuring Capabilities: Methodology and Empirical Application. Strategic Management Journal. Vol. 26, No. 3, 2005, pp. 277-285.

Dyer, Jeffrey H./Chu, Wujin (2000): The Determinants of Trust in Supplier-Automaker Relationships in the U.S., Japan, and Korea. Journal of International Business Studies. Vol. 31, No. 2, 2000, pp. 259-285.

Ebstrategy (2005): Offshore Outsourcing Failure Case Studies. Ebstrategy, 2005. URL: http://www.ebstrategy.com/outsourcing/cases/failures.htm (accessed 13.10.2005).

Echols, Ann/Tsai, Wenpin (2005): Niche and Performance: The Moderating Role of Network Embeddedness. Strategic Management Journal. Vol. 26, No. 3, 2005, pp. 219-238.

Eckhaus, Jill (2005): ITIL: The First Stepping Stone to Standardization. DM Review. Vol. 15, No. 2, 2005, p. 43.

Edmond, Steven (2002): Exploring the Success of Expatriates of U.S. Multinational Firms in Mexico. International Trade Journal. Vol. 16, No. 3, 2002, pp. 233-255.

Edwards, Ron/Ahmad, Adlina/Moss, Simon (2002): Subsidiary Autonomy: The Case of Multinational Subsidiaries in Malaysia. Journal of International Business Studies. Vol. 33, No. 1, 2002, pp. 183-191.

Egelhoff, William G. (1984): Patterns of Control in U.S., UK, and European Multinational Corporations. Journal of International Business Studies. Vol. 15, No. 2, 1984, pp. 73-83.

Eicher, Theo/Kang, Jong Woo (2005): Trade, Foreign Direct Investment or Acquisition: Optimal Entry Modes for Multinationals. Journal of Development Economics. Vol. 77, No. 1, 2005, pp. 207-228.

Eisenhardt, Kathleen M. (1985): Control: Organizational and Economic Approaches. Management Science. Vol. 31, No. 2, 1985, pp. 134-149.

Eisenhardt, Kathleen M. (1989): Building Theories from Case Study Research. Academy of Management Review. Vol. 14, No. 4, 1989, pp. 532-550.

Eisenhardt, Kathleen M./Schoonhoven, Claudia Bird (1996): Resource-Based View of Strategic Alliance Formation: Strategic and Social Effects in Entrepreneurial Firms. Organization Science. Vol. 7, No. 2, 1996, pp. 136-150.

Eisenhardt, Kathleen M./Martin, Jeffrey A. (2000): Dynamic Capabilities: What Are They? Strategic Management Journal. Vol. 21, No. 10/11, 2000, pp. 1105-1121.

Eschen, Erik (2002): Der Erfolg von Mergers & Acquisitions: Unternehmungszusammenschlüsse aus der Sicht des ressourcenbasierten Ansatzes. Deutscher Universitätsverlag, Wiesbaden, 2002.

Espino-Rodríguez, Tomás F./Padrón-Robaina, Víctor (2006): A Review of Outsourcing from the Resource-Based View of the Firm. International Journal of Management Reviews. Vol. 8, No. 1, 2006, pp. 49-70.

Etzioni, Amitai (1975): A Comparative Analysis of Complex Organizations: On Power, Involvement, and Their Correlates. The Free Press, New York, 1975.

Fahy, John (1996): Competitive Advantage in International Services: A Resource-Based View. International Studies of Management & Organization. Vol. 26, No. 2, 1996, pp. 24-37.

Farrell, Diana (2004): Can Germany Win from Offshoring? McKinsey Global Institute. 2004.

Farrell, Diana (2005): Offshoring: Value Creation through Economic Change. Journal of Management Studies. Vol. 42, No. 3, 2005, pp. 675-683.

Farrell, Diana/Zainulbhai, Adil S. (2004): A Richer Future for India. McKinsey Quarterly. No. Special Edition: What Global Executives Think, 2004, pp. 50-59.

Farrell, Diana/Laboissière, Martha A./Rosenfeld, Jaeson (2006): Sizing the Emerging Global Labor Market: Rational Behavior from Both Companies and Countries Can Help It Work More Efficiently. Academy of Management Perspectives. Vol. 20, No. 4, 2006, pp. 23-34.

Farrell, Diana/Laboissière, Martha A./Pascal, Robert/Rosenfeld, Jaeson/De Segundo, Charles/Stürze, Sascha (2005): The Emerging Global Labor Market: Part I - The Demand for Offshore Talent in Services. McKinsey Global Institute. 2005.

Feinberg, Martin/Rydl, Lester/Vinaja, Roberto/Flores, Oscar (2003): An Empirical Comparison of Maquiladoras with Mexican Service Firms Regarding Compliance to the International Quality Standard ISO 900. International Journal of Management. Vol. 20, No. 2, 2003, pp. 209-214.

Feinberg, Susan E./Gupta, Anil K. (2004): Country Risk and Network Linkages within Multinationals. Academy of Management Proceedings. 2004, pp. P1-P6.

Ferdows, Kasra (1989): Mapping International Factory Networks, in: Ferdows, Kasra (Ed., 1989): Managing International Manufacturing. North-Holland/Elsevier, Amsterdam, pp. 3-21.

Ferdows, Kasra (1997): Making the Most of Foreign Factories. Harvard Business Review. Vol. 75, No. 2, 1997, pp. 73-86.

Fischer, Harald M./Pollock, Timothy G. (2004): Effects of Social Capital and Power on Surviving Transformational Change: The Case of Initial Public Offerings. Academy of Management Journal. Vol. 47, No. 4, 2004, pp. 463-481.

Fischer, William A./Behrman, Jack N. (1979): The Coordination of Foreign R&D Activities by Transnational Corporations. Journal of International Business Studies. Vol. 10, No. 3, 1979, pp. 28-35.

Fladmoe-Lindquist, Karin/Tallman, Stephen B. (1994): Resource-Based Strategy and Competitive Advantage among Multinationals, in: Shrivastava, Paul/Huff, Anne S./Dutton, Jane E. (Eds., 1994): Resource-Based View of the Firm. JAI Press, Greenwich, London, pp. 45-72.

Flick, Uwe (2002): Qualitative Sozialforschung: Eine Einführung. 6 edition. Rowohlt, Reinbek bei Hamburg, 2002.

Flick, Uwe (2004): Zur Qualität qualitativer Forschung - Diskurse und Ansätze, in: Kuckartz, Udo/Grunenberg, Heiko/Lauterbach, Andreas (Eds., 2004): Qualitative Datenanalyse: Computergestützt - Methodische Hintergründe und Beispiele aus der Forschungspraxis. VS, Wiesbaden, pp. 43-63.

Flick, Uwe/Kardorff, Ernst von/Steinke, Ines (2003): Was ist qualitative Forschung? in: Flick, Uwe/Kardorff, Ernst von/Steinke, Ines (Eds., 2003): Qualitative Forschung - ein Handbuch. Rowohlt, Reinbek bei Hamburg, pp. 13-29.

Forsgren, Mats/Holm, Ulf (1990): Internationalization of Division Management in Swedish International Firms. Working Paper, No. 5, Företagsekonomiska Institutionen, Uppsala Universitet, 1990.
Forsgren, Mats/Pedersen, Torben (1997): Centres of Excellence in Multinational Companies: The Case of Denmark. Working Paper, No. 2, Institute of International Economics and Management, Copenhagen Business School Denmark, 1997.
Forsgren, Mats/Pedersen, Torben/Foss, Nicolai J. (1999): Accounting for the Strengths of MNC Subsidiaries: The Case of Foreign-Owned Firms in Denmark. International Business Review. Vol. 8, No. 2, 1999, pp. 181-196.
Forst, Leland I. (2001): Shared Services Grows Up. Journal of Business Strategy. Vol. 22, No. 4, 2001, pp. 13-15.
Foss, Nicolai J./Robertson, Paul L. (2000): Introduction - Resources, Technology and Strategy, in: Foss, Nicolai J. (Ed., 2000): Resources, Technology, and Strategy: Explorations in the Resource-Based Perspective. Vol. 11. Routledge, London, New York, pp. 1-10.
Foss, Nicolai J./Pedersen, Torben (2002): Transferring Knowledge in MNCs: The Role of Sources of Subsidiary Knowledge and Organizational Context. Journal of International Management. Vol. 8, No. 1, 2002, pp. 49-67.
Freiling, Jörg (2001): Resource-Based View und ökonomische Theorie: Grundlagen und Positionierung des Ressourcenansatzes. Deutscher Universitätsverlag, Wiesbaden, 2001.
Friedman, Walter F. (1975): Physical Distribution: The Concept of Shared Services. Harvard Business Review. Vol. 53, No. 2, 1975, pp. 24-31.
Friedrich von den Eichen, Stephan A. (2002): Kräftekonzentration in der diversifizierten Unternehmung: Eine ressourcenorientierte Betrachtung der Desinvestition. Deutscher Universitätsverlag, Wiesbaden, 2002.
Frost, Tony S./Birkinshaw, Julian M./Ensign, Prescott C. (2002): Centers of Excellence in Multinational Corporations. Strategic Management Journal. Vol. 23, No. 11, 2002, pp. 997-1018.
Garner, C. Alan (2004): Offshoring in the Service Sector: Economic Impact and Policy Issues. Economic Review. Vol. 89, No. 3, 2004, pp. 5-37.
Garnier, Gerard H. (1982): Context and Decision Making Autonomy in the Foreign Affiliates of U.S. Multinational Corporations. Academy of Management Journal. Vol. 25, No. 4, 1982, pp. 893-908.
Gates, Stephen R./Egelhoff, William G. (1986): Centralization in Headquarters-Subsidiary Relationships. Journal of International Business Studies. Vol. 17, No. 2, 1986, pp. 71-92.
Ge, Ling/Konana, Prabhudev/Tanriverdi, Huseyin (2004): Global Sourcing and Value Chain Unbundling. University of Texas at Austin, 2004.
Gençtürk, Esra F./Aulakh, Preet S. (1995): The Use of Process and Output Controls in Foreign Markets. Journal of International Business Studies. Vol. 26, No. 4, 1995, pp. 755-786.
Gençtürk, Esra F./Aulakh, Preet S. (2007): Norms- and Control-Based Governance of International Manufacturer-Distributor Relational Exchanges. Journal of International Marketing. Vol. 15, No. 1, 2007, pp. 92-126.
Ghauri, Pervez N. (2004): Designing and Conducting Case Studies in International Business Research, in: Marschan-Piekkari, Rebecca/Welch, Catherine (Eds., 2004): Handbook of Qualitative Research Methods for International Business. Elgar, Cheltenham, Northampton, pp. 109-124.
Ghoshal, Sumantra/Bartlett, Christopher A. (1988): Creation, Adoption, and Diffusion of Innovations by Subsidiaries of Multinational Corporations. Journal of International Business Studies. Vol. 19, No. 3, 1988, pp. 365-388.
Ghoshal, Sumantra/Nohria, Nitin (1989): Internal Differentiation within Multinational Corporations. Strategic Management Journal. Vol. 10, No. 4, 1989, pp. 323-337.
Ghoshal, Sumantra/Bartlett, Christopher A. (1990): The Multinational Corporation as an Interorganizational Network. Academy of Management Review. Vol. 15, No. 4, 1990, pp. 626-645.

Ghoshal, Sumantra/Bartlett, Christopher A. (1993): The MNC as Interorganizational Network, in: Ghoshal, Sumantra/Westney, D. Eleanor (Eds., 1993): Organization Theory and the Multinational Corporation. Macmillan, Houndmills, Basingstoke, Hampshire, pp. 77-104.

Ghoshal, Sumantra/Westney, D. Eleanor (1993): Organization Theory and the Multinational Corporation. Macmillan, Houndmills, Basingstoke, Hampshire, 1993.

Ghoshal, Sumantra/Westney, D. Eleanor (2005): Organization Theory and the Multinational Corporation. 2 edition. Macmillan, Houndmills, Basingstoke, Hampshire, 2005.

Gilbert, Linda S. (2002): Going the Distance: 'Closeness' in Qualitative Data Analysis Software. International Journal of Social Research Methodology. Vol. 5, No. 3, 2002, pp. 215-228.

Gilley, K. Matthew/Rasheed, Abdul A. (2000): Making More by Doing Less: An Analysis of Outsourcing and Its Effects on Firm Performance. Journal of Management. Vol. 26, No. 4, 2000, pp. 763-790.

Gimeno, Javier (2004): Competition within and between Networks: The Contingent Effect of Competitive Embeddedness on Alliance Formation. Academy of Management Journal. Vol. 47, No. 6, 2004, pp. 820-842.

Gittell, Jody Hoffer (2000): Paradox of Coordination and Control. California Management Review. Vol. 42, No. 3, 2000, pp. 101-117.

Glaister, Keith W. (2004): The Rationale for International Equity Joint Ventures. European Management Journal. Vol. 22, No. 5, 2004, pp. 493-507.

Glaser, Barney G./Strauss, Anselm Leonard (1980): The Discovery of Grounded Theory. Strategies for Qualitative Research. 11 edition. Aldine Publications, New York, 1980.

Glass, Robert L. (2004): Matching Methodology to Problem Domain. Communications of the ACM. Vol. 47, No. 5, 2004, pp. 19-21.

Gnyawali, Devi R./Madhavan, Ravindranath (2001): Cooperative Networks and Competitive Dynamics: A Structural Embeddedness Perspective. Academy of Management Review. Vol. 26, No. 3, 2001, pp. 431-445.

Gong, Yaping (2003): Subsidiary Staffing in Multinational Enterprises: Agency, Resources, and Performance. Academy of Management Journal. Vol. 46, No. 6, 2003, pp. 728-739.

Gordon, Joseph D. (1998): Maquiladoras: The First World Abusing the Third World? Business Ethics: A European Review. Vol. 7, No. 1, 1998, pp. 7-11.

Grandori, Anna (1997): An Organizational Assessment of Interfirm Coordination Modes. Organization Studies. Vol. 18, No. 6, 1997, pp. 897-925.

Grandori, Anna/Soda, Giuseppe (1995): Inter-Firm Networks: Antecedents, Mechanisms and Forms. Organization Studies. Vol. 16, No. 2, 1995, pp. 183-214.

Granovetter, Mark S. (1985): Economic Action and Social Structure: The Problem of Embeddedness. American Journal of Sociology. Vol. 91, No. 3, 1985, pp. 481-510.

Grant, Robert M. (1996): Prospering in Dynamically-Competitive Environments: Organizational Capability as Knowledge Integration. Organization Science. Vol. 7, No. 4, 1996, pp. 375-387.

Gresov, Christopher (1989): Exploring Fit and Misfit with Multiple Contingencies. Administrative Science Quarterly. Vol. 34, No. 3, 1989, pp. 431-453.

Griffith, David A./Hu, Michael Y./Ryans Jr., John K. (2000): Process Standardization across Intra- and Inter-cultural Relationships. Journal of International Business Studies. Vol. 31, No. 2, 2000, pp. 303-324.

Grote, Michael H./Täube, Florian A. (2007): When Outsourcing Is Not an Option: International Relocation of Investment Bank Research - Or Isn't it? Journal of International Management. Vol. 13, No. 1, 2007, pp. 57-77.

Grunenberg, Heiko (2004): Empirische Befunde zur Qualität qualitativer Sozialforschung, in: Kuckartz, Udo/Grunenberg, Heiko/Lauterbach, Andreas (Eds., 2004): Qualitative Datenanalyse: Computergestützt - Methodische Hintergründe und Beispiele aus der Forschungspraxis. VS, Wiesbaden, pp. 65-80.

Gulati, Ranjay (1998): Alliances and Networks. Strategic Management Journal. Vol. 19, No. 4, 1998, pp. 293-317.
Gulati, Ranjay (1999): Network Location and Learning: The Influence of Network Resources and Firm Capabilities on Alliance Formation. Strategic Management Journal. Vol. 20, No. Issue 5, 1999, pp. 397-420.
Gummesson, Evert (2000): Qualitative Methods in Management Research. 2 edition. Sage Publications, Thousand Oaks, London, New Delhi, 2000.
Gupta, Amar/Seshasai, Satwik (2004): Toward the 24-Hour Knowledge Factory. MIT Sloan Working Paper, No. 4455-04, 2004.
Gupta, Anil K./Govindarajan, Vijay (1991): Knowledge Flows and the Structure of Control within Multinational Corporations. Academy of Management Review. Vol. 16, No. 4, 1991, pp. 768-792.
Gupta, Anil K./Govindarajan, Vijay (2000): Knowledge Flows within Multinational Corporations. Strategic Management Journal. Vol. 21, No. 4, 2000, pp. 473-496.
Hadjikhani, Amjad/Thilenius, Peter (2005): Non-Business Actors in a Business Network - A Comparative Case on Firms' Actions in Developing and Developed Countries. Elsevier, Amsterdam et al., 2005.
Hage, Jerald/Aiken, Michael (1967): Relationship of Centralization to Other Structural Properties. Administrative Science Quarterly. Vol. 12, No. 1, 1967, pp. 72-92.
Hage, Jerald/Aiken, Michael (1969): Routine Technology, Social Structure, and Organization Goals. Administrative Science Quarterly. Vol. 14, No. 3, 1969, pp. 366-377.
Hagel III, John (2004): Offshoring Goes on the Offensive. McKinsey Quarterly. No. 2, 2004, pp. 82-91.
Hagel, John/Brown, John Seely (2005): The Only Sustainable Edge: Why Business Strategy Depends on Productive Friction and Dynamic Specialization. Harvard Business School Press, Boston, 2005.
Håkanson, Lars/Nobel, Robert (2001): Organizational Characteristics and Reverse Technology Transfer. Management International Review. Vol. 41, No. 4, 2001, pp. 395-420.
Håkansson, Håkan/Snehota, Ivan (1995): Developing Relationships in Business Networks. Routledge, London, New York, 1995.
Håkansson, Håkan/Johanson, Jan (2001): Business Network Learning - Basic Considerations, in: Håkansson, Håkan/Johanson, Jan (Eds., 2001): Business Network Learning. Pergamon, Amsterdam et al., pp. 1-13.
Halinen, Aino/Törnroos, Jan-Åke (1997): The Role of Embeddedness in the Evolution of Business Networks. Scandinavian Journal of Management. Vol. 14, No. 3, 1997, pp. 187-2005.
Hall, Richard (1993): A Framework Linking Intangible Resources and Capabilities to Sustainable Competitive Advantage. Strategic Management Journal. Vol. 14, No. 8, 1993, pp. 607-618.
Hambrick, Donald C. (1983): An Empirical Typology of Mature Industrial-Product Environments. Academy of Management Journal. Vol. 26, No. 2, 1983, pp. 213-230.
Hambrick, Donald C. (1984): Taxonomic Approaches to Studying Strategy: Some Conceptual and Methodological Issues. Journal of Management. Vol. 10, No. 1, 1984, pp. 27-41.
Hambrick, Donald C. (1994): What if the Academy Actually Mattered? Academy of Management Review. Vol. 19, No. 1, 1994, pp. 11-16.
Hamel, Gary/Prahalad, Coimbatore K. (1994): Competing for the Future. Harvard Business Review. Vol. 72, No. 4, 1994, pp. 122-128.
Hansen, Morten T. (1999): The Search-Transfer Problem: The Role of Weak Ties in Sharing Knowledge across Organization Subunits. Administrative Science Quarterly. Vol. 44, No. 1, 1999, pp. 82-111.
Hansen, Morten T./Nohria, Nitin (2004): How to Build Collaborative Advantage. MIT Sloan Management Review. Vol. 46, No. 1, 2004, pp. 22-30.

Hansen, Morten T./Nohria, Nitin/Tierney, Thomas (1999): What's Your Strategy for Managing Knowledge? Harvard Business Review. Vol. 77, No. 2, 1999, pp. 106-116.

Hansen, Niles (1981): Mexico's Border Industry and the International Divison of Labor. Annals of Regional Science. Vol. 15, No. 2, 1981, pp. 1-12.

Hardy, Cynthia/Phillips, Nelson/Lawrence, Thomas B. (2003): Resources, Knowledge and Influence: The Organizational Effects of Interorganizational Collaboration. Journal of Management Studies. Vol. 40, No. 2, 2003, pp. 321-347.

Harrison, Ann E./McMillan, Margaret S. (2006): Dispelling Some Myths About Offshoring. Academy of Management Perspectives. Vol. 20, No. 4, 2006, pp. 6-22.

Hartley, Jean F. (1994): Case Studies in Organizational Research, in: Cassell, Catherine/Symon, Gillian (Eds., 1994): Qualitative Methods in Organizational Research - A Practical Guide. Sage Publications, Thousand Oaks, London, New Delhi, pp. 208-229.

Harzing, Anne-Wil Käthe (1999): Managing the Multinationals: An International Study of Control Mechanisms. Elgar, Cheltenham, Northampton, 1999.

Harzing, Anne-Wil Käthe (2000): An Empirical Analysis and Extension of the Bartlett and Ghoshal Typology of Multinational Companies. Journal of International Business Studies. Vol. 31, No. 1, 2000, pp. 101-119.

Harzing, Anne-Wil Käthe (2001): Of Bears, Bumble-Bees, and Spiders: The Role of Expatriates in Controlling Foreign Subsidiaries. Journal of World Business. Vol. 36, No. 4, 2001, pp. 366-379.

Harzing, Anne-Wil Käthe (2002): Acquisitions versus Greenfield Investments: International Strategy and Management of Entry Modes. Strategic Management Journal. Vol. 23, No. 3, 2002, pp. 211-227.

Harzing, Anne-Wil Käthe/Noorderhaven, Niels (2006): Knowledge Flows in MNCs: An Empirical Test and Extension of Gupta and Govindarajan's Typology of Subsidiary Roles. International Business Review. Vol. 15, No. 3, 2006, pp. 195-214.

Hashai, Niron/Almor, Tamar (2004): Gradually Internationalizing 'Born Global' Firms: An Oxymoron? International Business Review. Vol. 13, No. 4, 2004, pp. 465-483.

Hatch, Mary Jo (1997): Organization Theory: Modern, Symbolic, and Postmodern Perspectives. Oxford University Press, Oxford et al., 1997.

Hedlund, Gunnar (1981): Autonomy of Subsidiaries and Formalization of Headquarters-Subsidiary Relationships in Swedish MNCs, in: Otterbeck, Lars (Ed., 1981): The Management of Headquarters-Subsidiary Relationships in Multinational Corporations. Gower, Aldershot/Hampshire, pp. 25-78.

Hedlund, Gunnar (1984): Organization In-Between: The Evolution of the Mother-Daughter Structure of Managing Foreign Subsidiaries in Swedish MNCs. Journal of International Business Studies. Vol. 15, No. 2, 1984, pp. 109-123.

Hedlund, Gunnar (1986): The Hypermodern MNC - a Heterarchy? Human Resource Management. Vol. 25, No. 1, 1986, pp. 9-35.

Hedlund, Gunnar/Rolander, Dag (1990): Action in Heterarchies - New Approaches in Managing the MNC, in: Bartlett, Christopher A./Doz, Yves L./Hedlund, Gunnar (Eds., 1990): Managing the Global Firm. Routledge, London, New York, pp. 15-46.

Heise Online News (2004): J.P. Morgan holt sich ausgelagerte IT zurück. 2004. URL: http://www.heise.de/newsticker/meldung/51125 (accessed 03.10.2005).

Heise Online News (2006): Microsoft und Google wollen in Bulgarien investieren. 2006. URL: http://www.heise.de/newsticker/meldung/74995 (accessed 03.07.2006).

Henderson, Rebecca/Cockburn, Iain (1994): Measuring Competence? Exploring Firm Effects in Pharmaceutical Research. Strategic Management Journal. Vol. 15, No. Special Issue, 1994, pp. 63-74.

Herbert, Theodore T. (1984): Strategy and Multinational Organization Structure: An Interorganizational Relationships Perspective. Academy of Management Review. Vol. 9, No. 2, 1984, pp. 259-271.

Hill, Peter (1999): Tangibles, Intangibles and Services: A New Taxonomy for the Classification of Output. Canadian Journal of Economics. Vol. 32, No. 2, 1999, pp. 426-446.

Hill, T. P. (1977): On Goods and Services. Review of Income & Wealth. Vol. 23, No. 4, 1977, pp. 315-338.

Hillebrand, Bas/Kok, Robert A. W./Biemans, Wim G. (2001): Theory-Testing Using Case Studies: A Comment on Johnston, Leach, and Liu. Industrial Marketing Management. Vol. 30, No. 8, 2001, pp. 651-657.

Holm, Ulf/Pedersen, Torben (Eds., 2000): The Emergence and Impact of MNC Centres of Excellence: A Subsidiary Perspective. Macmillan, Houndmills, Basingstoke, Hampshire.

Holtbrügge, Dirk/Kittler, Markus G./Rygl, David (2004): Konfiguration und Koordination internationaler Dienstleistungsunternehmen, in: Gardini, Marco A./Dahlhoff, H. Dieter (Eds., 2004): Management internationaler Dienstleistungen: Kontext, Konzepte, Erfahrungen. Gabler, Wiesbaden, pp. 159-179.

Homburg, Christian/Workman Jr., John P./Jensen, Ove (2002): A Configurational Perspective on Key Account Management. Journal of Marketing. Vol. 66, No. 2, 2002, pp. 38-60.

Hopkins, Jim (2005): To Start Up Here, Companies Hire Over There - In New Type of Offshoring, Jobs Aren't Leaving USA: They Were Never Here. USA Today. Date: 11.02.2005, p. B.1.

Hoskisson, Robert E./Eden, Lorraine/Lau, Chung-Ming/Wright, Mike (2000): Strategy in Emerging Economies. Academy of Management Journal. Vol. 43, No. 3, 2000, pp. 249-267.

Hung, R. (1997): Shiftwork Scheduling Algorithms with Phase-Delay Feature. International Journal of Production Research. Vol. 35, No. 7, 1997, pp. 1961-1968.

Hymer, Stephan H. (1976): The International Operations of National Firms: A Study of Direct Foreign Investment. The MIT Press, Cambridge, 1976.

Inside Market Data (2004): Offshoring: Not Just About Saving Costs. 2004. URL: http://www.capco.com/capco.aspx?id=475 (accessed 11.08.2005).

Jacobson, Carol K./Lenway, Stefanie A./Ring, Peter S. (1993): The Political Embeddedness of Private Economic Transactions. Journal of Management Studies. Vol. 30, No. 3, 1993, pp. 453-478.

Jaeger, Alfred M. (1983): The Transfer of Organizational Culture Overseas: An Approach to Control in the Multinational Corporation. Journal of International Business Studies. Vol. 14, No. 2, 1983, pp. 91-114.

Jaeger, Alfred M./Baliga, B. Ram (1985): Control Systems and Strategic Adaptation: Lessons from the Japanese Experience. Strategic Management Journal. Vol. 6, No. 2, 1985, pp. 115-134.

Jarillo, J. Carlos/Martinez, Jon I. (1990): Different Roles for Subsidiaries: The Case of Multinational Corporations in Spain. Strategic Management Journal. Vol. 11, No. 7, 1990, pp. 501-512.

Jarvenpaa, Sirkka J./Leidner, Dorothy E. (1998): An Information Company in Mexico: Extending the Resource-Based View of the Firm to a Developing Country. Information Systems Research. Vol. 9, No. 4, 1998, pp. 342-361.

Jeannet, Jean-Pierre/Liander, Bertil (1978): Some Patterns in the Transfer of Technology within Multinational Corporations. Journal of International Business Studies. Vol. 9, No. 3, 1978, pp. 108-118.

Jensen, Robert/Szulanski, Gabriel (2004): Stickiness and the Adaptation of Organizational Practices in Cross-Border Knowledge Transfers. Journal of International Business Studies. Vol. 35, No. 6, 2004, pp. 508-523.

Jolly, Dominique R. (2005): The Exogamic Nature of Sino-Foreign Joint Ventures. Asia Pacific Journal of Management. Vol. 22, No. 3, 2005, pp. 285-306.

Jones, Candace/Hesterly, William S./Borgatti, Stephen P. (1997): A General Theory of Network Governance: Exchange Conditions and Social Mechanisms. Academy of Management Review. Vol. 22, No. 4, 1997, pp. 911-945.

Jones, Gareth R. (2001): Organizational Theory: Text and Cases. 3 edition. Prentice Hall, Upper Saddle River, 2001.

Jones, Gary K./Davis, Herbert J. (2000): National Culture and Innovation: Implications for Locating Global R&D Operations. Management International Review. Vol. 40, No. 1, 2000, pp. 11-39.

Jones, Marc T. (2005): The Transnational Corporation, Corporate Social Responsibility and the 'Outsourcing' Debate. Journal of American Academy of Business, Cambridge. Vol. 6, No. 2, 2005, pp. 91-97.

Kabanoff, Boris/Waldersee, Robert/Cohen, Marcus (1995): Espoused Values and Organizational Change Themes. Academy of Management Journal. Vol. 38, No. 4, 1995, pp. 1075-1104.

Kacmar, K. Michelle/Hochwarter, Wayne A. (1996): Rater Agreement Across Multiple Data Collection Media. Journal of Social Psychology. Vol. 136, No. 4, 1996, pp. 469-475.

Kagelmann, Uwe (2001): Shared Services als alternative Organisationsform - am Beispiel der Finanzfunktion im multinationalen Konzern. Deutscher Universitätsverlag, Wiesbaden, 2001.

Kapur, Devesh/Ramamurti, Ravi (2001): India's Emerging Competitive Advantage in Service. Academy of Management Executive. Vol. 15, No. 2, 2001, pp. 20-33.

Karamanos, Anastasios G. (2003): Complexity, Identity and the Value of Knowledge-Intensive Exchanges. Journal of Management Studies. Vol. 40, No. 7, 2003, pp. 1871-1890.

Karmarkar, Uday (2004): Will You Survive the Services Revolution? Harvard Business Review. Vol. 82, No. 6, 2004, pp. 100-107.

Karnøe, Peter (1995): Competence as Process and the Social Embeddedness of Competence Building. Academy of Management Proceedings. 1995, pp. 427-431.

Karsatos, James G. (1988): Shared Services: A Growing Trend. Management Review. Vol. 77, No. 11, 1988, pp. 35-37.

Kedia, Ben L./Lahiri, Somnath (2007): International Outsourcing of Services: A Partnership Model. Journal of International Management. Vol. 13, No. 1, 2007, pp. 22-37.

Keeling, Bette (1999a): How to Allocate the Right Staff Mix Across Shifts, Part 1. Nursing Management. Vol. 30, No. 9, 1999a, pp. 16-17.

Keeling, Bette (1999b): How to Allocate the Right Staff Mix Across Shifts, Part 2. Nursing Management. Vol. 30, No. 10, 1999b, pp. 16-18.

Kelle, Udo/Kluge, Susann (1999): Vom Einzelfall zum Typus - Fallvergleich und Fallkontrastierung in der qualitativen Sozialforschung. Leske + Budrich, Opladen, 1999.

Kenter, Michael E. (1985): Die Steuerung ausländischer Tochtergesellschaften: Instrumente und Effizienz. Peter Lang, Frankfurt am Main et al., 1985.

Kerry, John (2004): The Hope Is There - Looking toward the Next Horizon. Vital Speeches of the Day. Vol. 70, No. 20, 2004, pp. 610-615.

Ketchen Jr., David J./Thomas, James B./Snow, Charles C. (1993): Organizational Configurations and Performance: A Comparison of Theoretical Approaches. Academy of Management Journal. Vol. 36, No. 6, 1993, pp. 1278-1313.

Ketchen Jr., David J./Combs, James G./Russell, Craig J./Shook, Chris/Dean, Michelle A./Runge, Janet/Lohrke, Franz T./Naumann, Stefanie E./Haptonstahl, Dawn Ebe/Baker, Robert/Beckstein, Brenden A./Handler, Charles/Honig, Heather/Lamoureux, Stephen (1997): Organizational Configurations and Performance: A Meta-Analysis. Academy of Management Journal. Vol. 40, No. 1, 1997, pp. 223-240.

Khandwalla, Pradip N. (1973a): Effect of Competition on the Structure of Top-Management Control. Academy of Management Journal. Vol. 16, No. 2, 1973a, pp. 285-295.

Khandwalla, Pradip N. (1973b): Viable and Effective Organizational Designs of Firms. Academy of Management Journal. Vol. 16, No. 3, 1973b, pp. 481-495.

Khandwalla, Pradip N. (1977): The Design of Organizations. Harcourt Brace Jovanovich, New York, 1977.
Kieser, Alfred (2002): Organisationstheorien. 5 edition. Kohlhammer, Stuttgart, 2002.
Kim, Kwangsoo/Park, Jong-Hun/Prescott, John E. (2003): The Global Integration of Business Functions: A Study of Multinational Businesses in Integrated Global Industries. Journal of International Business Studies. Vol. 34, No. 4, 2003, pp. 327-344.
King, William R. (2005): Innovation in Responding to the "Threat" of IT Offshoring. Information Systems Management. Vol. 22, No. 4, 2005, pp. 80-81.
Kirkman-Liff, Bradford/Mondragón, Delfi (1991): Language of Interview: Relevance for Research of Southwest Hispanics. American Journal of Public Health. Vol. 81, No. 11, 1991, pp. 1399-1404.
Klein, Heinz H. (2002): On the Theoretical Foundations of Current Outsourcing Research, in: Hirschheim, Rudy/Heinzl, Armin/Dibbern, Jens (Eds., 2002): Information Systems Outsourcing: Enduring Themes, Emergent Patterns and Future Directions. Springer, Berlin et al., pp. 24-44.
Kluge, Susann (1999): Empirisch begründete Typenbildung: Zur Konstruktion von Typen und Typologien in der qualitativen Sozialforschung. Leske + Budrich, Opladen, 1999.
Knight, Gary (1999): International Services Marketing: Review of Research, 1980-1998. Journal of Services Marketing. Vol. 13, No. 4/5, 1999, pp. 347-360.
Knight, Gary A./Cavusgil, S. Tamer (2004): Innovation, Organizational Capabilities and the Born-Global Firm. Journal of International Business Studies. Vol. 35, No. 2, 2004, pp. 124-141.
Kobayashi-Hillary, Mark (2004): Outsourcing to India: The Offshore Advantage. Springer, Berlin et al., 2004.
Kochan, Anna (2002): D/C Expertise, Influence Helps Cut Smart costs. Vol. 7. No. 12, 2002, p. 31.
Kogut, Bruce/Zander, Udo (1993): Knowledge of the Firm and the Evolutionary Theory of the Multinational Corporation. Journal of International Business Studies. Vol. 24, No. 4, 1993, pp. 625-645.
Kogut, Bruce/Zander, Udo (2003): Knowledge of the Firm and the Evolutionary Theory of the Multinational Corporation. Journal of International Business Studies. Vol. 34, No. 6, 2003, pp. 516-529.
Kor, Yasemin Y./Mahoney, Joseph T. (2004): Edith Penrose's (1959) Contributions to the Resource-Based View of Strategic Management. Journal of Management Studies. Vol. 41, No. 1, 2004, pp. 183-191.
Kostova, Tatiana (1999): Transnational Transfer of Strategic Organizational Practices: A Contextual Perspective. Academy of Management Review. Vol. 24, No. 2, 1999, pp. 308-324.
Kotabe, Masaaki (1990): The Relationship between Offshore Sourcing and Innovativeness of U.S. Multinational Firms: An Empirical Investigation. Journal of International Business Studies. Vol. 21, No. 4, 1990, pp. 623-638.
Kotabe, Masaaki/Swan, K. Scott (1994): Offshore Sourcing: Reaction, Maturation, and Consolidation of U.S. Multinationals. Journal of International Business Studies. Vol. 25, No. 1, 1994, pp. 115-140.
Kotabe, Masaaki/Murray, Janet Y. (2004): Global Procurement of Service Activities by Service Firms. International Marketing Review. Vol. 21, No. 6, 2004, pp. 615-633.
Kotha, Suresh/Rindova, Violina P./Rothaermel, Frank T. (2001): Assets and Actions: Firm-Specific Factors in the Internationalization of U.S. Internet Firms. Journal of International Business Studies. Vol. 32, No. 4, 2001, pp. 769-791.
Kranz, Patricia (2005): Sitting Pretty in Prague: DHL's Tech Triumph. 2005. URL: http://www.businessweek.com/print/magazine/content/05_50/b3963033.htm?chan=gl (accessed 24.04.2006).
Kratochwill, Thomas R./Levin, Joel R. (1992): Single-Case Research Design and Analysis: New Directions for Psychology and Education. Lawrence Erlbaum Associates, Hillsdale, 1992.

Kreikebaum, Hartmut (2004): Innovation Processes in Pharmaceutical Companies - Organizational Determinants, in: Albers, Sönke/Brockhoff, Klaus (Eds., 2004): Cross-functional Innovation Management: Perspectives from Different Disciplines - To Klaus Brockhoff for His 65. Birthday. Gabler, Wiesbaden, pp. 71-83.

Kreikebaum, Hartmut/Gilbert, Dirk Ulrich (2003): Neue Organisationsformen Multinationaler Unternehmungen - Besonderheiten einer Strukturation strategischer Unternehmensnetzwerke, in: Holtbrügge, Dirk (Ed., 2003): Management multinationaler Unternehmungen: Festschrift zum 60. Geburtstag von Martin K. Welge. Physica, Heidelberg, pp. 141-160.

Kreikebaum, Hartmut/Gilbert, Dirk Ulrich/Reinhardt, Glenn O. (2002): Organisationsmanagement internationaler Unternehmen: Grundlagen und moderne Netzwerkstrukturen. 2 edition. Gabler, Wiesbaden, 2002.

Kreisel, Henning (1995): Zentralbereiche: Formen, Effizienz und Integration. Gabler, Wiesbaden, 1995.

Kriegmeier, Jochen Ralph (2003): Professional Service Firms: Koordination im Spannungsfeld von globaler Integration und lokaler Differenzierung. Difo-Druck, Bamberg, 2003.

Kshetri, Nir (2007): Institutional Factors Affecting Offshore Business Process and Information Technology Outsourcing. Journal of International Management. Vol. 13, No. 1, 2007, pp. 38-56.

Kubicek, Herbert/Welter, Günter (1985): Messung der Organisationsstruktur: Eine Dokumentation von Instrumenten zur quantitativen Erfassung von Organisationsstrukturen. Enke, Stuttgart, 1985.

Kuemmerle, Walter (1997): Building Effective R&D Capabilities Abroad. Harvard Business Review. Vol. 75, No. 2, 1997, pp. 61-70.

Kuemmerle, Walter (1999): The Drivers of Foreign Direct Investment into Research and Development: An Empirical Investigation. Journal of International Business Studies. Vol. 30, No. 1, 1999, pp. 1-24.

Kulkarni, Subodh P. (2000): The Influence of Information Technology on Information Asymmetry in Product Markets. Journal of Business & Economic Studies. Vol. 6, No. 1, 2000, pp. 55-71.

Kumra, Gautam/Sinha, Jayant (2003): The Next Hurdle for Indian IT. McKinsey Quarterly. No. 4, 2003, pp. 42-53.

Kutschker, Michael/Schmid, Stefan (2005): Internationales Management. 4. edition. Oldenbourg, München, Wien, 2005.

Kutschker, Michael/Bäurle, Iris/Schmid, Stefan (1997): Quantitative und qualitative Forschung im Internationalen Management: Ein kritisch-fragender Dialog. Diskussionsbeiträge der Wirtschaftswissenschaftlichen Fakultät, No. 82, Katholische Universität Eichstätt, 1997.

Kutschker, Michael/Schurig, Andreas/Schmid, Stefan (2001): The Existence of Centers of Excellence in Multinational Corporations: Results from an International Research Project. Diskussionsbeiträge der Wirtschaftswissenschaftlichen Fakultät, No. 154, Katholische Universität Eichstätt, 2001.

Kutschker, Michael/Schurig, Andreas/Schmid, Stefan (2002): The Influence of Network Partners on Critical Capabilities in Foreign Subsidiaries. Diskussionsbeiträge der Wirtschaftswissenschaftlichen Fakultät, No. 158, Katholische Universität Eichstätt, 2002.

Kvale, Steinar (1996): InterViews: An Introduction to Qualitative Research Interviewing. Sage Publications, Thousand Oaks, London, New Delhi, 1996.

Lamnek, Siegfried (1995): Qualitative Sozialforschung - Bd. 1 Methodologie. 3 edition. Beltz, Weinheim, 1995.

Lapid, Karen (2006): Outsourcing and Offshoring under the General Agreement on Trade in Services. Journal of World Trade. Vol. 40, No. 2, 2006, pp. 341-364.

Lawrence, Paul R./Lorsch, Jay W. (1967): Differentiation and Integration in Complex Organizations. Administrative Science Quarterly. Vol. 12, No. 1, 1967, pp. 1-47.

Leavitt, Harold Jack (1964): Applied Organization Change in Industry: Structural, Technical, and Human Approaches, in: Cooper, William W./Leavitt, Harold Jack

(Eds., 1964): New Perspectivies in Organization Research. John Wiley & Sons, New York, London, Sydney, pp. 55-71.

Lee, Hung-Wen/Liu, Ching-Hsiang (2006): Determinants of the Adjustment of Expatriate Managers to Foreign Countries: An Empirical Study. International Journal of Management. Vol. 23, No. 2, 2006, pp. 302-311.

Lee, Jae-Nam/Kim, Young-Gul (2005): Understanding Outsourcing Partnership: A Comparison of Three Theoretical Perspectives. IEEE Transactions on Engineering Management. Vol. 52, No. 1, 2005, pp. 43-58.

Lee, Jae-Nam/Miranda, Shaila M./Kim, Yong-Mi (2004): IT Outsourcing Strategies: Universalistic, Contingency, and Configurational Explanations of Success. Information Systems Research. Vol. 15, No. 2, 2004, pp. 110-131.

Lee, Soo Hoon/Phan, Phillip H./Chan, Elaine (2005): The Impact of HR Configuration on Firm Performance in Singapore: A Resource-Based Explanation. International Journal of Human Resource Management. Vol. 16, No. 9, 2005, pp. 1740-1758.

Lee, Thomas W. (1999): Using Qualitative Methods in Organizational Research. Sage Publications, Thousand Oaks, London, New Delhi, 1999.

Lee, Thomas W./Mitchell, Terence R./Sablynski, Chris J./Burton, James P./Holtom, Brooks C. (2004): The Effects of Job Embeddedness on Organizational Citizenship, Job Performance, Volitional Absences, and Voluntary Turnover. Academy of Management Journal. Vol. 47, No. 5, 2004, pp. 711-722.

Leeds, Christopher A. (1998): A Study of Communitarianism as a Feature of Contemporary Capitalist Societies and Management. International Business Review. Vol. 7, No. 1, 1998, pp. 51-67.

Leong, Siew Meng/Tan, Chin Tiong (1993): Managing Across Borders: An Empirical Test of the Bartlett and Ghoshal (1989) Organizational Typology. Journal of International Business Studies. Vol. 24, No. 3, 1993, pp. 449-464.

Levy, David L. (2005): Offshoring in the New Global Political Economy. Journal of Management Studies. Vol. 42, No. 3, 2005, pp. 685-693.

Levy, David L./Egan, Daniel (2003): A Neo-Gramscian Approach to Corporate Political Strategy: Conflict and Accommodation in the Climate Change Negotiations. Journal of Management Studies. Vol. 40, No. 4, 2003, pp. 803-829.

Lewin, Arie Y./Peeters, Carine (2006): Offshoring Work: Business Hype Or the Onset of Fundamental Transformation? Long Range Planning. Vol. 39, No. 3, 2006, pp. 221-239.

Li, Li (2005): The Effects of Trust and Shared Vision on Inward Knowledge Transfer in Subsidiaries' Intra- and Inter-organizational Relationships. International Business Review. Vol. 14, No. 1, 2005, pp. 77-95.

Lindstrom, Lowell/Jeffries, Ron (2004): Extreme Programming and Agile Software Development Methodologies. Information Systems Management. Vol. 21, No. 3, 2004, pp. 41-52.

Lockett, Andy/Thompson, Steve (2004): Edith Penrose's Contributions to the Resource-Based View: An Alternative Perspective. Journal of Management Studies. Vol. 41, No. 1, 2004, pp. 193-203.

Logan, Mary S. (2000): Using Agency Theory to Design Successful Outsourcing Relationships. International Journal of Logistics Management. Vol. 11, No. 2, 2000, pp. 21-32.

London, Ted/Hart, Stuart L. (2004): Reinventing Strategies for Emerging Markets: Beyond the Transnational Model. Journal of International Business Studies. Vol. 35, No. 5, 2004, pp. 350-370.

Lory, Rolf (2005): Outsourcing der Banken-IT - Differenzierungen. Schweizer Bank. Date: 20.07.2005, p. 52.

Lovelock, Christopher H. (1983): Classifying Services to Gain Strategic Marketing Insights. Journal of Marketing. Vol. 47, No. 3, 1983, pp. 9-20.

Lundberg, Craig C. (1972): Planning the Executive Development Program. California Management Review. Vol. 15, No. 1, 1972, pp. 10-15.

Luo, Yadong (1997): Partner Selection and Venturing Success: The Case of Joint Ventures with Firms in the People's Republic of China. Organization Science. Vol. 8, No. 6, 1997, pp. 648-662.

Luo, Yadong (2000): Dynamic Capabilities In International Expansion. Journal of World Business. Vol. 35, No. 4, 2000, pp. 355-378.

Macdonald, Stuart/Hellgren, Bo (2004): The Interview in International Business Research: Problems We Would Rather Not Talk About, in: Marschan-Piekkari, Rebecca/Welch, Catherine (Eds., 2004): Handbook of Qualitative Research Methods for International Business. Elgar, Cheltenham, Northampton, pp. 264-281.

Madhok, Anoop/Tallman, Stephen B. (1998): Resources, Transactions and Rents: Managing Value Through Interfirm Collaborative Relationships. Organization Science. Vol. 9, No. 3, 1998, pp. 326-339.

Madhok, Anoop/Phene, Anupama (2001): The Co-Evolutional Advantage: Strategic Management Theory and the Eclectic Paradigm. International Journal of the Economics of Business. Vol. 8, No. 2, 2001, pp. 243-256.

Madureira, Ricardo (2004): The Role of Managerial Dependence and Uncertainty in Foreign Subsidiary Coordination, in: Larimo, Jorma/Rumpunen, Sami (Eds., 2004): European Research on Foreign Direct Investment and International Human Resource Management. Vol. 112. Vaasa/Finland, pp. 276-294.

Mahon, John F./Heugens, Pursey P. M. A. R./Lamertz, Kai (2004): Social Networks and Non-Market Strategy. Journal of Public Affairs. Vol. 4, No. 2, 2004, pp. 170-189.

Mahoney, Joseph T./Pandian, J. Rajendran (1992): The Resource-Based View within the Conversation of Strategic Management. Strategic Management Journal. Vol. 13, No. 5, 1992, pp. 363-380.

Maister, David H./Lovelock, Christopher H. (1982): Managing Facilitator Services. Sloan Management Review. Vol. 23, No. 4, 1982, pp. 19-29.

Makadok, Richard (1999): Interfirm Differences in Scale Economies and the Evolution of Market Shares. Strategic Management Journal. Vol. 20, No. 10, 1999, pp. 935-952.

Makadok, Richard (2001): Toward a Synthesis of the Resource-Based and Dynamic-Capability Views of Rent Creation. Strategic Management Journal. Vol. 22, No. 5, 2001, pp. 387-401.

Makadok, Richard/Walker, Gordon (2000): Identifying a Distinctive Competence: Forecasting Ability in the Money Fund Industry. Strategic Management Journal. Vol. 21, No. 8, 2000, pp. 853-864.

Maleri, Rudolf (1997): Grundlagen der Dienstleistungsproduktion. 4 edition. Springer, Berlin et al., 1997.

Maleri, Rudolf (2004): Zur Relevanz der Dienstleistungsbesonderheiten für das internationale Dienstleistungsmanagement, in: Gardini, Marco A./Dahlhoff, H. Dieter (Eds., 2004): Management internationaler Dienstleistungen: Kontext, Konzepte, Erfahrungen. Gabler, Wiesbaden, pp. 37-62.

Malnight, Thomas W. (1996): The Transition from Decentralized to Network-Based MNC Structures: An Evolutionary Perspective. Journal of International Business Studies. Vol. 27, No. 1, 1996, pp. 43-65.

Manwar, Ali/Johnson, Bruce D./Dunlap, Eloise (1994): Qualitative Data Analysis with Hypertext: A Case of New York City Crack Dealers. Qualitative Sociology. Vol. 17, No. 3, 1994, pp. 283-292.

Marcati, Alberto (1989): Configuration and Coordination - The Role of US Subsidiaries in the International Network of Italian Multinationals. Management International Review. Vol. 29, No. 3, 1989, pp. 35-50.

Marin, Dalia (2006): A New International Division of Labor in Europe: Outsourcing and Offshoring to Eastern Europe. Journal of the European Economic Association. Vol. 4, No. 2/3, 2006, pp. 612-622.

Marino, Kenneth E. (1996): Developing Consensus on Firm Competencies and Capabilities. Academy of Management Executive. Vol. 10, No. 3, 1996, pp. 40-51.

Markides, Constantinos C./Williamson, Peter J. (1994): Related Diversification, Core Competences and Corporate Performance. Strategic Management Journal. Vol. 15, No. 5, 1994, pp. 149-165.
Marquardt, Gernot (2003): Kernkompetenzen als Basis der strategischen und organisationalen Unternehmensentwicklung. Deutscher Universitätsverlag, Wiesbaden, 2003.
Marschan-Piekkari, Rebecca/Reis, Cristina (2004): Language and Languages in Cross-Cultural Interviewing, in: Marschan-Piekkari, Rebecca/Welch, Catherine (Eds., 2004): Handbook of Qualitative Research Methods for International Business. Elgar, Cheltenham, Northampton, pp. 224-243.
Martin, Andrew (2003): What Drives the Configuration of Information Technology Projects? Exploratory Research in 10 Organizations. Journal of Information Technology. Vol. 18, No. 1, 2003, pp. 1-15.
Martinez, Jon I./Jarillo, J. Carlos (1989): The Evolution of Research on Coordination Mechanisms in Multinational Corporations. Journal of International Business Studies. Vol. 20, No. 3, 1989, pp. 489-514.
Martinez, Jon I./Jarillo, J. Carlos (1991): Coordination Demands of International Strategies. Journal of International Business Studies. Vol. 22, No. 3, 1991, pp. 429-444.
Mascarenhas, Briance (1984): The Coordination of Manufacturing Interdependence in Multinational Companies. Journal of International Business Studies. Vol. 15, No. 3, 1984, pp. 91-106.
Mascarenhas, Briance/Baveja, Alok/Jamil, Mamnoon (1998): Dynamics of Core Competencies in Leading Multinational Companies. California Management Review. Vol. 40, No. 4, 1998, pp. 117-132.
Maskell, Peter/Pedersen, Torben/Petersen, Bent/Dick-Nielsen, Jens (2007): Learning Paths to Offshore Outsourcing: From Cost Reduction to Knowledge Seeking. Industry & Innovation. Vol. 14, No. 3, 2007, pp. 239-257.
Mason, Jennifer (2002): Qualitative Researching. 2 edition. Sage Publications, Thousand Oaks, London, New Delhi, 2002.
Mathews, John A. (2002): A Resource-based View of Schumpeterian Economic Dynamics. Journal of Evolutionary Economics. Vol. 12, No. 1/2, 2002, pp. 29-54.
Mayring, Philipp (2002): Einführung in die qualitative Sozialforschung: Eine Anleitung zu qualitativem Denken. 5 edition. Beltz, Weinheim, Basel, 2002.
Mayshar, Joram/Halevy, Yoram (1997): Shiftwork. Journal of Labor Economics. Vol. 15, No. 1, 1997, pp. 198-222.
McCarthy, John C. (2003): Users' Offshore Evolution and Its Governance Impact. Forrester Research Consultancy. 2003.
McCarthy, John C. (2004): Near-Term Growth of Offshoring Accelerating. Forrester Research Consultancy. 2004.
McCaughey, Deirdre/Bruning, Nealia S. (2005): Enhancing Opportunities for Expatriate Job Satisfaction: HR Strategies for Foreign Assignment Success. Human Resource Planning. Vol. 28, No. 4, 2005, pp. 21-29.
McClintock, Charles C./Brannon, Diane/Maynard-Moody, Steven (1979): Applying the Logic of Sample Surveys to Qualitative Case Studies: The Case Cluster Method. Administrative Science Quarterly. Vol. 24, No. 4, 1979, pp. 612-629.
McCormack, Coralie (2004): Storying Stories: A Narrative Approach to In-depth Interview Conversations. International Journal of Social Research Methodology. Vol. 7, No. 3, 2004, pp. 219-236.
McGrath, Rita Gunther/MacMillan, Ian C. (2000): The Entrepreneurial Mindset: Strategies for Continuously Creating Opportunity in an Age of Uncertainty. Harvard Business School Press, Boston, 2000.
McKelvey, Bill (1975): Guidance for the Empirical Classification of Organizations. Administrative Science Quarterly. Vol. 20, No. 4, 1975, pp. 509-525.
McLaughlin, Kevin (2005): ITIL Catches On. Computerworld. Vol. 39, No. 44, 2005, pp. 39-42.
McNulty, Yvonne M./Tharenou, Phyllis (2004): Expatriate Return on Investment. International Studies of Management & Organization. Vol. 34, No. 3, 2004, pp. 68-95.

Meilich, Ofer (2005): Are Formalization and Human Asset Specificity Mutually Exclusive? - A Learning Bureaucracy Perspective. Journal of American Academy of Business, Cambridge. Vol. 6, No. 1, 2005, pp. 161-169.

Merchant, Hemant (2005): Efficient Resources, Industry Membership, and Shareholder Value Creation: The Case of International Joint Ventures. Canadian Journal of Administrative Sciences. Vol. 22, No. 3, 2005, pp. 193-205.

Meyer, Alan D./Tsui, Anne S./Hinings, C. R. (1993): Configurational Approaches to Organizational Analysis. Academy of Management Journal. Vol. 36, No. 6, 1993, pp. 1175-1195.

Meyer, Klaus E./Lieb-Dóczy, Enese (2003): Post-Acquisition Restructuring as Evolutionary Process. Journal of Management Studies. Vol. 40, No. 2, 2003, pp. 459-482.

Miles, Matthew B./Huberman, A. Michael (1994): Qualitative Data Analysis: An Expanded Sourcebook. 2 edition. Sage Publications, Thousand Oaks, London, New Delhi, 1994.

Miles, Raymond E./Snow, Charles C. (1978): Organizational Strategy, Structure, and Process. McGraw-Hill, New York et al., 1978.

Miller, Danny (1981): Toward a New Contingency Approach: The Search for Organizational Gestalts. Journal of Management Studies. Vol. 18, No. 1, 1981, pp. 1-26.

Miller, Danny/Friesen, Peter H. (1977): Strategy-Making in Context: Ten Empirical Archetypes. Journal of Management Studies. Vol. 14, No. 3, 1977, pp. 253-280.

Miller, Danny/Friesen, Peter H. (1978): Archetypes of Strategy Formulation. Management Science. Vol. 24, No. 9, 1978, pp. 921-933.

Miller, Danny/Friesen, Peter H. (1980): Archetypes of Organizational Transition. Administrative Science Quarterly. Vol. 25, No. 2, 1980, pp. 268-299.

Miller, Danny/Shamsie, Jamal (1996): The Resource-Based View of the Firm in Two Environments: The Hollywood Film Studios from 1936 to 1965. Academy of Management Journal. Vol. 39, No. 3, 1996, pp. 519-543.

Minbaeva, Dana B. (2005): HRM Practices and MNC Knowledge Transfer. Personnel Review. Vol. 34, No. 1, 2005, pp. 125-144.

Minbaeva, Dana B./Pedersen, Torben/Björkman, Ingmar/Fey, Carl F./Park, Hyeon Jeong (2003): MNC Knowledge Transfer, Subsidiary Absorptive Capacity, and HRM. Journal of International Business Studies. Vol. 34, No. 6, 2003, pp. 586-599.

Miner, John B. (1984): The Validity and Usefulness of Theories in an Emerging Organizational Science. Academy of Management Review. Vol. 9, No. 2, 1984, pp. 296-306.

Miner, John B. (2003): The Rated Importance, Scientific Validity, and Practical Usefulness of Organizational Behavior Theories: A Quantitative Review. Academy of Management Learning & Education. Vol. 2, No. 3, 2003, pp. 250-268.

Mintzberg, Henry (1977): Policy as a Field of Management Theory. Academy of Management Review. Vol. 2, No. 1, 1977, pp. 88-103.

Mintzberg, Henry (1989): Mintzberg on Management: Inside Our Strange World of Organizations. The Free Press, New York, 1989.

Mitchell, Terence R./Holtom, Brooks C./Lee, Thomas W./Sablynski, Chris J./Erez, Miriam (2001): Why People Stay: Using Job Embeddedness to Predict Voluntary Turnover. Academy of Management Journal. Vol. 44, No. 6, 2001, pp. 1102-1121.

Mohr, Alexander T./Klein, Simone (2004): Exploring the Adjustment of American Expatriate Spouses in Germany. International Journal of Human Resource Management. Vol. 15, No. 7, 2004, pp. 1189-1206.

Moingeon, Bertrand/Ramanantsoa, Bernard/Métais, Emmanuel/Orton, J. Douglas (1998): Another Look at Strategy-Structure Relationships: The Resource-Based View. European Management Journal. Vol. 16, No. 3, 1998, pp. 297-305.

Mol, Michael J./van Tulder, Rob J. M./Beije, Paul R. (2005): Antecedents and Performance Consequences of International Outsourcing. International Business Review. Vol. 14, No. 5, 2005, pp. 599-617.

Mol, Michael J./Pauwels, Pieter/Matthyssens, Paul/Quintens, Lieven (2004): A Technological Contingency Perspective on the Depth and Scope of International Outsourcing. Journal of International Management. Vol. 10, No. 2, 2004, pp. 287-305.

Monteiro, L. Felipe/Arvidsson, Niklas/Birkinshaw, Julian M. (2004): Knowledge Flows within Multinational Corporations: Why Are Some Subsidiaries Isolated? Academy of Management Proceedings. 2004, pp. B1-B6.

Moore, Karl J. (2001): A Strategy for Subsidiaries: Centres of Excellences to Build Subsidiary Specific Advantages. Management International Review. Vol. 41, No. 3, 2001, pp. 275-290.

Moore, Karl J./Birkinshaw, Julian M. (1998): Managing Knowledge in Global Service Firms: Centers of Excellence. Academy of Management Executive. Vol. 12, No. 4, 1998, pp. 81-92.

Moore, Marguerite (2005): Towards a Confirmatory Model of Retail Strategy Types: An Empirical Test of Miles and Snow. Journal of Business Research. Vol. 58, No. 5, 2005, pp. 696-704.

Moran, Peter (2005): Structural vs. Relational Embeddedness: Social Capital and Managerial Performance. Strategic Management Journal. Vol. 26, No. 12, 2005, pp. 1129-1151.

Morash, Edward A./Lynch, Daniel F. (2002): Public Policy and Global Supply Chain Capabilities and Performance: A Resource-Based View. Journal of International Marketing. Vol. 10, No. 1, 2002, pp. 25-51.

Morecroft, John D. W. (2002): Resource Management under Dynamic Complexity, in: Morecroft, John D. W./Sanchez, Ron/Heene, Aimé (Eds., 2002): Systems Perspectives on Resources, Capabilities and Management Processes. Pergamon, Amsterdam et al., pp. 19-39.

Morecroft, John D. W./Sanchez, Ron/Heene, Aimé (2002): Integrating Systems Thinking and Competence Concepts in a New View of Resources, Capabilities and Management Processes, in: Morecroft, John D. W./Sanchez, Ron/Heene, Aimé (Eds., 2002): Systems Perspectives on Resources, Capabilities and Management Processes. Pergamon, Amsterdam et al., pp. 3-16.

Moreira, Charles F. (2004): IT Grads in Demand at BPO Centres. 2004. URL: http://www.cyberjaya-msc.com/cgi-bin/news.cgi?action=display&id=1088926820 (accessed 31.01.2005).

Mößlang, Angelo M. (1995): Internationalisierung von Dienstleistungsunternehmen: Empirische Relevanz - Systematisierung - Gestaltung. Gabler, Wiesbaden, 1995.

Nagengast, Johann (1997): Outsourcing von Dienstleistungen industrieller Unternehmen: Eine theoretische und empirische Analyse. Kovač, Hamburg, 1997.

Nair, K. G. K./Prasad, P. N. (2004): Offshore Outsourcing: A Swot Analysis of A State in India. Information Systems Management. Vol. 21, No. 3, 2004, pp. 34-40.

Napier, Nancy K./Peterson, Richard B. (1991): Expatriate Re-Entry: What Do Repatriates Have to Say? Human Resource Planning. Vol. 14, No. 1, 1991, pp. 19-28.

Nelson, Richard R./Winter, Sidney G. (1982): An Evolutionary Theory of Economic Change. Belknap Press, Cambridge, London, 1982.

Newburry, William (2001): MNC Interdependence and Local Embeddedness Influences on Perceptions of Career Benefits from Global Integration. Journal of International Business Studies. Vol. 32, No. 3, 2001, pp. 497-507.

Ngwenyama, Ojelanki K./Bryson, Noel (1999): Making the Information Systems Outsourcing Decision: A Transaction Cost Approach to Analyzing Outsourcing Decision Problems. European Journal of Operational Research. Vol. 115, No. 2, 1999, pp. 351-367.

Nielsen, Richard P. (1984): Arendt's Action Philosophy and the Manager as Eichmann, Richard III, Faust, or Institution Citizen. California Management Review. Vol. 26, No. 3, 1984, pp. 191-201.

Nobel, Robert/Birkinshaw, Julian M. (1996): Patterns of Control and Communication in International Research and Development Units. Academy of Management Proceedings. 1996, pp. 166-170.

Nobel, Robert/Birkinshaw, Julian M. (1998): Innovation in Multinational Corporations: Control and Communication Patterns in International R&D. Strategic Management Journal. Vol. 19, No. 5, 1998, pp. 479-496.

Nohria, Nitin/Ghoshal, Sumantra (1997): The Differentiated Network: Organizing Multinational Corporations for Value Creation. Jossey-Bass, San Francisco, 1997.

Nonaka, Ikujiro/Takeuchi, Hirotaka (1995): The Knowledge-Creating Company: How Japanese Companies Create the Dynamics of Innovation. Oxford University Press, New York et al., 1995.

Noordegraaf, Mirko/Stewart, Rosemary (2000): Managerial Behaviour Research in Private and Public Sectors: Distinctiveness, Disputes and Directions. Journal of Management Studies. Vol. 37, No. 3, 2000, pp. 427-443.

O'Donnell, Sharon Watson (2000): Managing Foreign Subsidiaries: Agents of Headquarters, or an Interdependent Network? Strategic Management Journal. Vol. 21, No. 5, 2000, pp. 525-548.

Offshore Outsourcing (2005): Offshore Outsourcing. Journal of Management Studies. Vol. 42, No. 3, 2005, pp. 673-674.

Oliver, Daniel G./Serovich, Julianne M./Mason, Tina L. (2005): Constraints and Opportunities with Interview Transcription: Towards Reflection in Qualitative Research. Social Forces. Vol. 84, No. 2, 2005, pp. 1273-1289.

Ouchi, William G. (1977): The Relationship between Organizational Structure and Organizational Control. Administrative Science Quarterly. Vol. 22, No. 1, 1977, pp. 95-113.

Ouchi, William G. (1978): The Transmission of Control through Organizational Hierarchy. Academy of Management Journal. Vol. 21, No. 2, 1978, pp. 173-192.

Ouchi, William G. (1979): A Conceptual Framework for the Design of Organizational Control Mechanisms. Management Science. Vol. 25, No. 9, 1979, pp. 833-848.

Ouchi, William G. (1980): Markets, Bureaucracies, and Clans. Administrative Science Quarterly. Vol. 25, No. 1, 1980, pp. 129-131.

Ouchi, William G./Maguire, Mary Ann (1975): Organizational Control: Two Functions. Administrative Science Quarterly. Vol. 20, No. 4, 1975, pp. 559-569.

Özsomer, Ayşegül/Gençtürk, Esra F. (2003): A Resource-Based Model of Market Learning in the Subsidiary: The Capabilities of Exploration and Exploitation. Journal of International Marketing. Vol. 11, No. 3, 2003, pp. 1-29.

Pahlberg, Cecilia (2001): Creation and Diffusion of Knowledge in Subsidiary Business Networks, in: Håkansson, Håkan/Johanson, Jan (Eds., 2001): Business Network Learning. Pergamon, Amsterdam et al., pp. 169-181.

Paik, Yongsun/Teagarden, Mary B. (1995): Strategic International Human Resource Management Approaches in the Maquiladora Industry: A Comparison of Japanese, Korean, and US Firms. International Journal of Human Resource Management. Vol. 6, No. 3, 1995, pp. 568-587.

Paik, Yongsun/Sohn, J. H. Derick (1998): Confucius in Mexico: Korean MNCs and the Maquiladoras. Business Horizons. Vol. 41, No. 6, 1998, pp. 25-33.

Pain, Nigel/Van Welsum, Desirée (2004): International Production Relocation and Exports of Services. OECD Economic Studies. Vol. 2004, No. 1, 2004, pp. 67-94.

Palek, Bohumil (1997): Typology: Prototypes, Item Orderings and Universals - Proceedings of LP '96. Karolinum, Prague, 1997.

Papalexandris, Nancy/Kramar, Robin (1997): Flexible Working Patterns: Towards Reconciliation of Family and Work. Employee Relations. Vol. 19, No. 6, 1997, pp. 581-595.

Parker, Andrew (2004): Two-Speed Europe: Why 1 Million Jobs Will Move Offshore. Forrester Research Consultancy. 2004.

Peng, Mike W. (2001): The Resource-Based View and International Business. Journal of Management. Vol. 27, No. 6, 2001, pp. 803-829.

Penrose, Edith Tilton (1959): The Theory of the Growth of the Firm. Blackwell Publishers, Cambridge, Oxford, 1959.

Perks, Helen (2004): Exploring Processes of Resource Exchange and Co-Creation in Strategic Partnering for New Product Development. International Journal of Innovation Management. Vol. 8, No. 1, 2004, pp. 37-61.

Perlmutter, Howard V. (1969): The Tortuous Evolution of the Multinational Corporation. Columbia Journal of World Business. Vol. 4, No. 1, 1969, pp. 9-18.

Perrow, Charles (1967): A Framework for the Comparative Analysis of Organizations. American Sociological Review. Vol. 32, No. 2, 1967, pp. 194-208.

Peteraf, Margaret A. (1993): The Cornerstones of Competitive Advantage: A Resource-Based View. Strategic Management Journal. Vol. 14, No. 3, 1993, pp. 179-191.

Peterson, Mark F. (1985): Attitudinal Differences among Work Shifts: What do They Reflect? Academy of Management Journal. Vol. 28, No. 3, 1985, pp. 723-732.

Pfannenstein, Laura L./Tsai, Ray J. (2004): Offshore Outsourcing: Current and Future Effects on American IT Industry. Information Systems Management. Vol. 21, No. 4, 2004, pp. 72-80.

Pinder, Craig C./Moore, Larry F. (1979): The Resurrection of Taxonomy to Aid the Development of Middle Range Theories of Organizational Behavior. Administrative Science Quarterly. Vol. 24, No. 1, 1979, pp. 99-118.

Piske, Reiner (2002): German Acquisitions in Poland: An Empirical Study on Integration Management and Integration Success. Human Resource Development International. Vol. 5, No. 3, 2002, pp. 295-312.

Pitelis, Christos N. (2004): Edith Penrose and the Resource-Based View of (International) Business Strategy. International Business Review. Vol. 13, No. 4, 2004, pp. 523-532.

Podolny, Joel M./Page, Karen L. (1998): Network Forms of Organizations. Annual Review of Sociology. Vol. 24, No. 1, 1998, pp. 57-76.

Polanyi, Michael (1962): Personal Knowledge: Towards a Post-Critical Philosophy. 2 edition. Routledge, London, New York, 1962.

Poon, Jessie P. H./MacPherson, Alan (2005): Technology Acquisition among Korean and Taiwanese Firms in the United States. International Business Review. Vol. 14, No. 5, 2005, pp. 559-575.

Popović, Tobias (2004): Customer Capital: Die Wertschöpfung von E-Commerce-Unternehmen und ihre zweckadäquate Bewertung aus Perspektive des Aktienresearch. Verlag Wissenschaft und Praxis, Sternenfels, 2004.

Poppo, Laura (2003): The Visible Hands of Hierarchy within the M-Form: An Empirical Test of Corporate Parenting of Internal Product Exchanges. Journal of Management Studies. Vol. 40, No. 2, 2003, pp. 403-430.

Poppo, Laura/Zenger, Todd (1998): Testing Alternative Theories of the Firm: Transaction Cost, Knowledge-based, and Measurement Explanations for Make-or-Buy Decisions in Information Services. Strategic Management Journal. Vol. 19, No. 9, 1998, pp. 853-877.

Porter, Michael Eugene (1980): Competitive Strategy: Techniques for Analyzing Industries and Competitors. The Free Press, New York, 1980.

Porter, Michael Eugene (1985): Competitive Advantage: Creating and Sustaining Superior Performance. The Free Press, New York, 1985.

Porter, Michael Eugene (1990): The Competitive Advantage of Nations. Macmillan, London, Basingstoke, 1990.

Potter, Andrew/Breite, Rainer/Naim, Mohamed/Vanharanta, Hannu (2004): The Potential for Achieving Mass Customization in Primary Production Supply Chains via a Unified Taxonomy. Production Planning & Control. Vol. 15, No. 4, 2004, pp. 472-481.

Powell, Thomas C. (1995): Total Quality Management As Competitive Advantage: A Review and Empirical Study. Strategic Management Journal. Vol. 16, No. 1, 1995, pp. 15-37.

Prahalad, Coimbatore K./Hamel, Gary (1990): The Core Competence of the Corporation. Harvard Business Review. Vol. 68, No. 3, 1990, pp. 79-91.

Priem, Richard L./Rosenstein, Joseph (2000): Is Organization Theory Obvious to Practitioners? A Test of One Established Theory. Organization Science. Vol. 11, No. 5, 2000, pp. 509-524.

Priem, Richard L./Butler, John E. (2001): Is the Resource-Based 'View" a Useful Perspective for Strategic Management Research? Academy of Management Review. Vol. 26, No. 1, 2001, pp. 22-40.

Pugh, Derek S./Hickson, David J./Hinings, C. R./Turner, C. (1969): The Context of Organization Stuctures. Administrative Science Quarterly. Vol. 14, No. 1, 1969, pp. 91-114.

Pugh, S./Hickson, David J./Hinings, C. R./Turner, C. (1968): Dimensions of Organization Structure. Administrative Science Quarterly. Vol. 13, No. 1, 1968, pp. 65-105.

Quelch, John A./Hoff, Edward J. (1986): Customizing Global Marketing. Harvard Business Review. Vol. 64, No. 3, 1986, pp. 59-68.

Quinn, Barbara/Cooke, Robert/Kris, Andrew (2000): Shared Services: Mining for Corporate Gold. Financial Times Prentice Hall, London, 2000.

Ramachandran, K./Voleti, Sudhir (2004): Business Process Outsourcing (BPO): Emerging Scenario and Strategic Options for IT-Enabled Services. Vikalpa: The Journal for Decision Makers. Vol. 29, No. 1, 2004, pp. 49-52.

Ramamurti, Ravi (2004): Developing Countries and MNEs: Extending and Enriching the Research Agenda. Journal of International Business Studies. Vol. 35, No. 4, 2004, pp. 277-283.

Randoy, Trond/Li, Jiatao (1998): Global Resource Flow and MNE Netwok Integration, in: Birkinshaw, Julian M./Hood, Neil (Eds., 1998): Multinational Corporate Evolution and Subsidiary Development. St. Martin's Press, New York, pp. 76-101.

Rathmell, John M. (1974): Marketing in the Service Sector. Winthrop, Cambridge, 1974.

Ray, Gautam/Barney, Jay B./Muhanna, Waleed A. (2004): Capabilities, Business Processes, and Competitive Advantage: Choosing the Dependent Variable in Empirical Tests of the Resource-Based View. Strategic Management Journal. Vol. 25, No. 1, 2004, pp. 23-37.

Reed, Kevin (2006): Research Predicts Finance Is Offshoring's Next Big Thing. Accountancy Age. Date: 09.03.2006.

Reed, Richard/DeFillippi, Robert J. (1990): Causal Ambiguity, Barriers to Imitation, and Sustainable Competitive Advantage. Academy of Management Review. Vol. 15, No. 1, 1990, pp. 88-102.

Reger, Guido (1997): Koordination und strategisches Management internationaler Innovationsprozesse. Physica-Verlag, Heidelberg, 1997.

Regnér, Patrick (2003): Strategy Creation in the Periphery: Inductive versus Deductive Strategy Making. Journal of Management Studies. Vol. 40, No. 1, 2003, pp. 57-82.

Reichert, Christian (2005): Business Process Offshoring in the Indo-German Context. Difo-Druck, Bamberg, 2005.

Reinhardt, Andy (2004): Forget India, Let's Go to Bulgaria. 2004. URL: http://www.businessweek.com/magazine/content/04_09/b3872010_mz001.htm (accessed 10.07.2006).

Renz, Timo (1998): Management in internationalen Unternehmensnetzwerken. Gabler, Wiesbaden, 1998.

Reppesgaard, Lars (2004): Outsourcing nimmt neue Formen an. Handelsblatt. Vol. 202. Date: 18.10.2004, p. B1.

Ricardo, David (1817/1970): On the Principles of Political Economy and Taxation. Part of the Works and Correspondence of David Ricardo edited by Piero Sraffa. University Press for the Royal Economic Society, Cambridge, 1817/1970.

Rich, Philip (1992): The Organizational Taxonomy: Definition and Design. Academy of Management Review. Vol. 17, No. 4, 1992, pp. 758-781.

Ritter, Ronald C./Sternfels, Robert A. (2004): When Offshore Manufacturing Doesn't Make Sense. McKinsey Quarterly. No. 4, 2004, pp. 124-127.

Robinson, Marcia/Kalakota, Ravi (2004): Offshore Outsourcing - Business Models, ROI and Best Practices. Mivar Press, Alpharetta, 2004.

Roland Berger/UNCTAD (2004): Service Offshoring - Service Offshoring Takes Off in Europe - In Search of Improved Competitiveness. Roland Berger, UNCTAD. Geneva, Munich, 2004.
Rondinelli, Dennis A./Black, Sylvia Sloan (2000): Multinational Strategic Alliances and Acquisitions in Central and Eastern Europe: Partnerships in Privatization. Academy of Management Executive. Vol. 14, No. 4, 2000, pp. 85-98.
Ronen, Joshua/MacKiney III, George (1970): Transfer Pricing for Divisional Autonomy. Journal of Accounting Research. Vol. 8, No. 1, 1970, pp. 99-112.
Rose, Howard (1991): Case Studies, in: Allan, Graham/Skinner, Chris (Eds., 1991): Handbook for Research Students in the Social Sciences. Falmer, London, pp. 190-202.
Rose, Peter M. (2000): Analyse ausgewählter Methoden zur Identifikation dynamischer Kernkompetenzen. Hampp, München, Mering, 2000.
Roth, Kendall/Nigh, Douglas (1992): The Effectiveness of Headquarters-Subsidiary Relationships: The Role of Coordination, Control, and Conflict. Journal of Business Research. Vol. 25, No. 4, 1992, pp. 277-301.
Rouse, Michael J./Daellenbach, Urs S. (1999): Rethinking Research Methods for the Resource-Based Perspective: Isolating Sources of Sustainable Competitive Advantage. Strategic Management Journal. Vol. 20, No. 5, 1999, pp. 487-494.
Rowley, Tim/Behrens, Dean/Krackhardt, David J. (2000): Redundant Governance Structures: An Analysis of Structural and Relational Embeddedness in the Steel and Semiconductor Industries. Strategic Management Journal. Vol. 21, No. 3, 2000, pp. 369-386.
Rugman, Alan M./Girod, Stéphane (2003): Retail Multinationals and Globalization: The Evidence Is Regional. European Management Journal. Vol. 21, No. 1, 2003, pp. 24-37.
Rugman, Alan M./Verbeke, Alain (2004): A Final Word on Edith Penrose. Journal of Management Studies. Vol. 41, No. 1, 2004, pp. 205-217.
Rumelt, Richard P. (1984): Towards a Strategic Theory of the Firm, in: Lamb, Robert B. (Ed., 1984): Competitive Strategic Management. Prentice Hall, Englewood Cliffs, pp. 556-570.
Rutten, Roel (2004): Inter-Firm Knowledge Creation: A Re-Appreciation of Embeddedness from a Relational Perspective. European Planning Studies. Vol. 12, No. 5, 2004, pp. 659-673.
Samuelson, Paul A. (2004): Where Ricardo and Mill Rebut and Confirm Arguments of Mainstream Economists Supporting Globalization. Journal of Economic Perspectives. Vol. 18, No. 3, 2004, pp. 135-146.
Sanchez, Julio C. (1993): The Long and Thorny Way to an Organizational Taxonomy. Organization Studies. Vol. 14, No. 1, 1993, pp. 73-92.
Sanchez, Ron (2000): Product and Process Architectures in the Management of Knowledge Resources, in: Foss, Nicolai J. (Ed., 2000): Resources, Technology, and Strategy: Explorations in the Resource-Based Perspective. Vol. 11. Routledge, London, New York, pp. 100-122.
Schaaf, Jürgen (2004): Offshoring: Globalisierungswelle erfasst Dienstleistungen. Deutsche Bank Research. 2004.
Scherer, Andreas Georg (2002): Kritik der Organisation oder Organisation der Kritik? Wissenschaftstheoretische Bemerkungen zum kritischen Umgang mit Organisationstheorien, in: Kieser, Alfred (Ed., 2002): Organisationstheorien. 5 edition. Kohlhammer, Stuttgart, pp. 1-37.
Schmid, Stefan (1994): Orthodoxer Positivismus und Symbolismus im internationalen Management: Eine kritische Reflexion situativer und interpretativer Ansätze. Diskussionsbeiträge der Wirtschaftswissenschaftlichen Fakultät, No. 49, Katholische Universität Eichstätt, 1994.
Schmid, Stefan (1999): Centres of Competence in MNCs: Do Japanese MNCs Differ from German MNCs? Diskussionsbeiträge der Wirtschaftswissenschaftlichen Fakultät, No. 121, Katholische Universität Eichstätt, 1999.

Schmid, Stefan (2000): Foreign Subsidiaries as Centres of Competence - Empirical Evidence from Japanese Multinationals, in: Larimo, Jorma/Kock, Sören (Eds., 2000): Recent Studies in Interorganizational and International Business Research. Vol. 58. Vaasan Yliopiston Julkaisuja, Vaasa, pp. 182-204.

Schmid, Stefan (2004): The Roles of Foreign Subsidiaries in Network MNCs - A Critical Review of the Literature and Some Directions for Future Research, in: Larimo, Jorma/Rumpunen, Sami (Eds., 2004): European Research on Foreign Direct Investment and International Human Resource Management. Vol. 112. Vaasa, pp. 237-255.

Schmid, Stefan (2005): Kooperation: Erklärungsperspektiven interaktionstheoretischer Ansätze, in: Zentes, Joachim/Swoboda, Bernhard/Morschett, Dirk (Eds., 2005): Kooperationen, Allianzen und Netzwerke: Grundlagen - Ansätze - Perspektiven. 2 edition. Gabler, Wiesbaden, pp. 237-256.

Schmid, Stefan/Gouthier, Matthias (1999): Dienstleistungskunden: Ressourcen im Sinne des resource-based-view des Strategischen Managements? Diskussionsbeiträge der Wirtschaftswissenschaftlichen Fakultät, No. 131, Katholische Universität Eichstätt, 1999.

Schmid, Stefan/Schurig, Andreas (2003): The Development of Critical Capabilities in Foreign Subsidiaries: Disentangling the Role of the Subsidiary's Business Network. International Business Review. Vol. 12, No. 6, 2003, pp. 755-782.

Schmid, Stefan/Kutschker, Michael (2003): Rollentypologien für ausländische Tochtergesellschaften in Multinationalen Unternehmungen, in: Holtbrügge, Dirk (Ed., 2003): Management multinationaler Unternehmungen: Festschrift zum 60. Geburtstag von Martin K. Welge. Physica, Heidelberg, pp. 161-182.

Schmid, Stefan/Machulik, Mario (2004): Die Bedeutung von Tochtergesellschaften bei der Erschließung mittel- und osteuropäischer Märkte, in: Zschiedrich, Harald (Ed., 2004): Internationales Management in den Märkten Mittel- und Osteuropas. Hampp, München, Mering, pp. 21-43.

Schmid, Stefan/Daub, Matthias (2005): Service Offshoring Subsidiaries - Towards a Typology. Working Paper, No. 12, ESCP-EAP Europäische Wirtschaftshochschule Berlin, 2005.

Schmid, Stefan/Daub, Matthias (2007): Embeddedness in International Business Research - The Concept and Its Operationalization. Working Paper, No. 23, ESCP-EAP Europäische Wirtschaftshochschule Berlin, 2007.

Schmid, Stefan/Bäurle, Iris/Kutschker, Michael (1998): Tochtergesellschaften in international tätigen Unternehmungen: Ein "State-of-the-Art" unterschiedlicher Rollentypologien. Diskussionsbeiträge der Wirtschaftswissenschaftlichen Fakultät, No. 104, Katholische Universität Eichstätt, 1998.

Schmid, Stefan/Schurig, Andreas/Kutschker, Michael (2002): The MNC as a Network: A Closer Look at Intra-Organizational Flows, in: Lundan, Sarianna M. (Ed., 2002): Network Knowledge in International Business. Elgar, Cheltenham, Northampton, pp. 45-72.

Schoonhoven, Claudia Bird (1981): Problems with Contingency Theory: Testing Assumptions Hidden within the Language of Contingency 'Theory.' Administrative Science Quarterly. Vol. 26, No. 3, 1981, pp. 349-377.

Schott, Eberhard (1997): Markt und Geschäftsbeziehung beim Outsourcing: Eine marketingorientierte Analyse für die Informationsverarbeitung. Deutscher Universitätsverlag, Wiesbaden, 1997.

Schreyögg, Georg (1995): Umwelt, Technologie und Organisationsstruktur: Eine Analyse des kontingenztheoretischen Ansatzes. 3 edition. Haupt, Bern, Stuttgart, Wien, 1995.

Schulman, Donniel S. (1999): Shared Services: Adding Value to the Business Units. John Wiley & Sons, New York et al., 1999.

Schurig, Andreas (2002): Centers of Excellence: Darstellung und Ergebnisse eines internationalen Forschungsprojektes. Peter Lang, Frankfurt am Main et al., 2002.

Scott-Kennel, Joanna/Enderwick, Peter (2004): Inter-Firm Alliance and Network Relationships and the Eclectic Paradigm of International Production: An Exploratory

Analysis of Quasi-Internalisation at the Subsidiary Level. International Business Review. Vol. 13, No. 4, 2004, pp. 425-445.

Scott, Susanne G./Lane, Vicki R. (2000): A Stakeholder Approach to Organizational Identity. Academy of Management Review. Vol. 25, No. 1, 2000, pp. 43-62.

Seo, Myeong-Gu/Creed, W. E. Douglas (2002): Institutional Contradictions, Praxis, and Institutional Change: A Dialectical Perspective. Academy of Management Review. Vol. 27, No. 2, 2002, pp. 222-247.

Sharma, Varinder M./Erramilli, M. Krishna (2004): Resource-Based Explanation of Entry Mode Choice. Journal of Marketing Theory & Practice. Vol. 12, No. 1, 2004, pp. 1-18.

Siegel, Karolynn (1982): Shift Work: The Wave of the Future. SAM Advanced Management Journal. Vol. 47, No. 4, 1982, pp. 42-48.

Simon, Herbert Alexander (1997): Administrative Behavior: A Study of Decision Making Processes in Administrative Organizations. The Free Press, New York, 1997.

Skaggs, Bruce C./Huffman, Tammy Ross (2003): A Customer Interaction Approach to Strategy and Production Complexity Alignment in Service Firms. Academy of Management Journal. Vol. 46, No. 6, 2003, pp. 775-786.

Slater, Joanna (2004): For India's Youth, New Money Fuels a Revolution. Wall Street Journal. Date: 27.01.2004, pp. 1-2.

Smith, Adam (1775/1976): Der Wohlstand der Nationen. Eine Untersuchung seiner Natur und seiner Ursachen. Aus dem Englischen übertragen und mit einer Würdigung von Horst Claus Recktenwald. Beck, München, 1775/1976.

Smith, Calvin/Short, Patricia M. (2001): Integrating Technology to Improve the Efficiency of Qualitative Data Analysis - A Note on Methods. Qualitative Sociology. Vol. 24, No. 3, 2001, pp. 401-407.

Snell, Scott A. (1992): Control Theory in Strategic Human Resource Management: The Mediating Effect of Administrative Information. Academy of Management Journal. Vol. 35, No. 2, 1992, pp. 292-327.

Srivastava, Shirish C. (2005): Managing Core Competence of the Organization. Vikalpa: The Journal for Decision Makers. Vol. 30, No. 4, 2005, pp. 49-63.

Stack, Martin/Gartland, Myles/Keane, Timothy (2007): The Offshoring of Radiology: Myths and Realities. SAM Advanced Management Journal. Vol. 72, No. 1, 2007, pp. 44-51.

Streitz, Matthias (2005): Dow Jones stoppt Übersetzer-Dienste aus Ungarn. Spiegel Online, 2005. URL: http://www.spiegel.de/wirtschaft/0,1518,388614,00.html (accessed 05.12.2005).

Sullivan, Dan (2004): Exploring Text with Qualitative Data Analysis. DM Review. Vol. 14, No. 5, 2004, p. 58.

Surlemont, Bernard (1996): Types of Centers within Multinational Corporations: An Empirical Investigation, in: Business, Institute of International (Ed., 1996): Innovation and International Business. Proceedings of the 22nd Annual Conference of the European International Business Acadamy (December 15 - 17, 1996). Stockholm, pp. 745-765.

Suutari, Vesa/Brewster, Chris (2003): Repatriation: Empirical Evidence from a Longitudinal Study of Careers and Expectations among Finnish Expatriates. International Journal of Human Resource Management. Vol. 14, No. 7, 2003, pp. 1132-1151.

Swartz, Nikki (2004): Offshoring Privacy. Information Management Journal. Vol. 38, No. 5, 2004, pp. 24-26.

Sweeney, Michael T. (1994): A Methodology for the Strategic Management of International Manufacturing and Sourcing. International Journal of Logistics Management. Vol. 5, No. 1, 1994, pp. 55-58.

Sydow, Jörg/Windeler, Arnold (1994): Über Netzwerke, virtuelle Integration und Interorganisationsbeziehungen, in: Sydow, Jörg/Windeler, Arnold (Eds., 1994): Management interorganisationaler Beziehungen: Vertrauen, Kontrolle und Informationstechnik. Westdeutscher Verlag, Opladen, pp. 1-21.

Symon, Gillian/Cassell, Catherine (1998): Reflections on the Use of Qualitative Methods, in: Symon, Gillian/Cassell, Catherine (Eds., 1998): Qualitative Methods and

Analysis in Organizational Research: A Practical Guide. Sage Publications, Thousand Oaks, London, New Delhi, pp. 1-9.

Szulanski, Gabriel (1996): Exploring Internal Stickiness: Impediments to the Transfer of Best Practice within the Firm. Strategic Management Journal. Vol. 17, No. Winter 1996 Special Issue, 1996, pp. 27-43.

Taggart, James H. (1997): Autonomy and Procedural Justice: A Framework for Evaluating Subsidiary Strategy. Journal of International Business Studies. Vol. 28, No. 1, 1997, pp. 51-76.

Tahai, Alireza/Meyer, Michael J. (1999): A Revealed Preference Study of Management Journals' Direct Influences. Strategic Management Journal. Vol. 20, No. 3, 1999, pp. 279-296.

Tallman, Stephen B. (1991): Strategic Management Models and Resource-Based Strategies among MNEs in a Host Market. Strategic Management Journal. Vol. 12, No. 4, 1991, pp. 69-82.

Tallman, Stephen B. (2003): The Significance of Bruce Kogut's and Udo Zander's Article, 'Knowledge of the Firm and the Evolutionary Theory of the Multinational Corporation'. Journal of International Business Studies. Vol. 34, No. 6, 2003, pp. 495-497.

Tallman, Stephen B./Fladmoe-Lindquist, Karin (2002): Internationalization, Globalization, and Capability-Based Strategy. California Management Review. Vol. 45, No. 1, 2002, pp. 116-135.

Tan, Danchi/Mahoney, Joseph T. (2006): Why a Multinational Firm Chooses Expatriates: Integrating Resource-Based, Agency and Transaction Costs Perspectives. Journal of Management Studies. Vol. 43, No. 3, 2006, pp. 457-484.

Teece, David J. (1981): The Market for Know-How and the Efficient International Transfer of Technology. Annals of the American Academy of Political and Social Science. Vol. 458, No. Technology Transfer: New Issues, New Analysis, 1981, pp. 81-96.

Teece, David J./Pisano, Gary/Shuen, Amy (1997): Dynamic Capabilities and Strategic Management. Strategic Management Journal. Vol. 18, No. 7, 1997, pp. 509-533.

Tesch, Peter (1980): Die Bestimmungsgründe des internationalen Handels und der Direktinvestition: Eine kritische Untersuchung der außenwirtschaftlichen Theorien und Ansatzpunkte einer standorttheoretischen Erklärung der leistungswirtschaftlichen Auslandsbeziehungen der Unternehmen. Duncker & Humblot, Berlin, 1980.

Thibodeau, Patrick (2005): Execs Use Services Model to Reshape IT Units. Computerworld. Vol. 39, No. 42, 2005, pp. 71-72.

Thompson, James D. (1967): Organizations in Action: Social Science Bases of Administrative Theory. McGraw-Hill, New York et al., 1967.

Tichy, Noel M./Tushman, Michael L./Fombrun, Charles (1979): Social Network Analysis for Organizations. Academy of Management Review. Vol. 4, No. 4, 1979, pp. 507-519.

Toh, Soo Min/DeNisi, Angelo S. (2005): A Local Perspective to Expatriate Success. Academy of Management Executive. Vol. 19, No. 1, 2005, pp. 132-146.

Trampel, Julia (2004): Offshoring oder Nearshoring von IT-Dienstleistungen? - Eine transaktionskostentheoretische Analyse. ARBEITSPAPIERE des Instituts für Genossenschaftswesen der Westfälischen Wilhelms-Universität Münster, No. 39, Westfälische Wilhelms-Universität Münster; Institut für Genossenschaftswesen, 2004.

Trent, Robert J./Monczka, Robert M. (2002): Pursuing Competitive Advantage through Integrated Global Sourcing. Academy of Management Executive. Vol. 16, No. 2, 2002, pp. 66-80.

Trevino, Len J./Grosse, Robert (2002): An Analysis of Firm-Specific Resources and Foreign Direct Investment in the United States. International Business Review. Vol. 11, No. 4, 2002, pp. 431-451.

Tsai, Wenpin (2001): Knowledge Transfer in Intra-Organizational Networks: Effects of Network Position and Absorptive Capacity on Business Unit Innovation and Performance. Academy of Management Journal. Vol. 44, No. 5, 2001, pp. 996-1004.

Tsikriktsis, Nikos (2004): A Technology Readiness-Based Taxonomy of Customers: A Replication and Extension. Journal of Service Research. Vol. 7, No. 1, 2004, pp. 42-52.
Tsurumi, Yoshi (1979): Two Models of Corporation and International Transfer of Technology. Columbia Journal of World Business. Vol. 14, No. 2, 1979, pp. 43-50.
Tu, Qiang/Vonderembse, Mark A./Ragu-Nathan, T. S./Ragu-Nathan, Bhanu (2004): Measuring Modularity-Based Manufacturing Practices and their Impact on Mass Customization Capability: A Customer-Driven Perspective. Decision Sciences. Vol. 35, No. 2, 2004, pp. 147-168.
Türk, Klaus (2000): Hauptwerke der Organisationstheorie. Westdeutscher Verlag, Wiesbaden, 2000.
Turner, Karynne L./Makhija, Mona V. (2006): The Role of Organizational Controls in Managing Knowledge. Academy of Management Review. Vol. 31, No. 1, 2006, pp. 198-217.
Tye, Mary G./Chen, Peter Y. (2005): Selection of Expatriates: Decision-Making Models Used by HR Professionals. Human Resource Planning. Vol. 28, No. 4, 2005, pp. 15-20.
Uhlenbruck, Klaus (2004): Developing Acquired Foreign Subsidiaries: The Experience of MNEs in Transition Economies. Journal of International Business Studies. Vol. 35, No. 2, 2004, pp. 109-123.
Uhlenbruck, Klaus/De Castro, Julio O. (2000): Foreign Acquisitions in Central and Eastern Europe: Outcomes of Privatization in Transitional Economies. Academy of Management Journal. Vol. 43, No. 3, 2000, pp. 381-402.
Uhlenbruck, Klaus/Meyer, Klaus E./Hitt, Michael A. (2003): Organizational Transformation in Transition Economies: Resource-Based and Organizational Learning Perspectives. Journal of Management Studies. Vol. 40, No. 2, 2003, pp. 257-282.
Uhlenbruck, Nikolaus/De Castro, Julio O. (1998): Privatization from the Acquirer's Perspective: A Mergers and Acquisitions Based Framework. Journal of Management Studies. Vol. 35, No. 5, 1998, pp. 619-640.
Ulrich, Dave (1995): Shared Services: From Vogue to Value. Human Resource Planning. Vol. 18, No. 3, 1995, pp. 12-23.
UNCTAD (2004a): Trade in Services and Manufacturing. United Nations Conference on Trade and Development. New York, Geneva, 2004a.
UNCTAD (2004b): World Investment Report 2004 - The Shift towards Services. United Nations Conference on Trade and Development. New York, Geneva, 2004b.
UNCTAD (2005): World Investment Report 2005 - Transnational Corporations and the Internationalization of R&D. United Nations Conference on Trade and Development. New York, Geneva, 2005.
Uzzi, Brian (1996): The Sources and Consequences of Embeddedness for the Economic Performance of Organizations: The Network Effect. American Sociological Review. Vol. 61, No. 4, 1996, pp. 674-698.
Uzzi, Brian (1997): Social Structure and Competition in Interfirm Networks: The Paradox of Embeddedness. Administrative Science Quarterly. Vol. 42, No. 1, 1997, pp. 37-69.
Uzzi, Brian/Gillespie, James J. (2002): Knowledge Spillover in Corporate Financing Networks: Embeddedness and the Firm's Debt Performance. Strategic Management Journal. Vol. 23, No. 7, 2002, pp. 595-618.
Van De Ven, Andrew H./Delbecq, André L./Koenig Jr., Richard (1976): Determinants of Coordination Modes within Organizations. American Sociological Review. Vol. 41, No. 2, 1976, pp. 322-338.
Vandermerwe, Sandra/Chadwick, Michael (1989): The Internationalisation of Services. Service Industries Journal. Vol. 9, No. 1, 1989, pp. 79-93.
Vandermerwe, Sandra/Gilbert, Douglas (1989): Making Internal Services Market Driven. Business Horizons. Vol. 32, No. 6, 1989, pp. 83-89.

Venkatraman, N./Grant, John H. (1986): Construct Measurement in Organizational Strategy Research: A Critique and Proposal. Academy of Management Review. Vol. 11, No. 1, 1986, pp. 71-87.

Venkatraman, N./Chi-Hyon, Lee (2004): Preferential Linkage and Network Evolution: A Conceptual Model and Empirical Test in the U.S. Video Game Sector. Academy of Management Journal. Vol. 47, No. 6, 2004, pp. 876-892.

Venkatraman, N. Venkat (2004): Offshoring without Guilt. Sloan Management Review. No. Spring, 2004, pp. 14-16.

Villalonga, Belén/McGahan, Anita M. (2005): The Choice among Acquisitions, Alliances, and Divestitures. Strategic Management Journal. Vol. 26, No. 13, 2005, pp. 1183-1208.

Wagstyl, Stefan (2004): We Speak Your Language and We Are nearby. Financial Times. Date: 21.09.2004, p. 4.

Walsh, James P./Dewar, Robert D. (1987): Formalization and the Organizational Life Cycle. Journal of Management Studies. Vol. 24, No. 3, 1987, pp. 215-231.

Wan, William P. (2005): Country Resource Environments, Firm Capabilities, and Corporate Diversification Strategies. Journal of Management Studies. Vol. 42, No. 1, 2005, pp. 161-182.

Warner, Jeremy (2005): Outlook: Offshoring Is a Fact of Life: Get Used to It. The Independent. Date: 16.07.2005, p. 45.

Warren, Kim (2002): Operationalizing the Impact of Competence-Building on the Performance of Firms' Resource Systems, in: Morecroft, John D. W./Sanchez, Ron/Heene, Aimé (Eds., 2002): Systems Perspectives on Resources, Capabilities and Management Processes. Pergamon, Amsterdam et al., pp. 41-55.

Weber, Ron (1997): Ontological Foundations of Information Systems. Coopers & Lybrand, Blackburn, 1997.

Weick, Karl E. (1974): Middle Range Theories of Social Systems. Behavioral Science. Vol. 19, No. 6, 1974, pp. 357-367.

Weik, Elke/Lang, Reinhart (2001): Moderne Organisationstheorien: Eine sozialwissenschaftliche Einführung. Gabler, Wiesbaden, 2001.

Weik, Elke/Lang, Reinhart (2003): Moderne Organisationstheorien 2: Strukturorientierte Ansätze. Gabler, Wiesbaden, 2003.

Welch, Denice/Welch, Lawrence/Piekkari, Rebecca (2005): Speaking in Tongues. International Studies of Management & Organization. Vol. 35, No. 1, 2005, pp. 10-27.

Welge, Martin K./Holtbrügge, Dirk (2003): Internationales Management: Theorien, Funktionen, Fallstudien. 3 edition. Schäffer-Poeschel, Stuttgart, 2003.

Wernerfelt, Birger (1984): A Resource-Based View of the Firm. Strategic Management Journal. Vol. 5, No. 2, 1984, pp. 171-180.

Wernerfelt, Birger (1995): The Resource-Based View of the Firm: Ten Years After. Strategic Management Journal. Vol. 16, No. 3, 1995, pp. 171-174.

Westerhoff, Thomas (2006): Corporate-Shared-Services - Das Geschäftsmodell aus strategischer Unternehmenssicht, in: Keuper, Frank/Oecking, Christian (Eds., 2006): Corporate Shared Services - Bereitstellung von Dienstleistungen im Konzern. Gabler, Wiesbaden, pp. 55-74.

Weston, Cynthia/Gandell, Terry/Beauchamp, Jacinthe/McAlpine, Lynn/Wiseman, Carol/Beauchamp, Cathy (2001): Analyzing Interview Data: The Development and Evolution of a Coding System. Qualitative Sociology. Vol. 24, No. 3, 2001, pp. 381-400.

Whaley, Lindsay J. (1997): Introduction to Typology: The Unity and Diversity of Language. Sage Publications, Thousand Oaks, London, New Delhi, 1997.

White, Roderick E./Poynter, Thomas A. (1984): Strategies for Foreign-Owned Subsidiaries in Canada. Business Quarterly. Vol. 49, No. 2, 1984, pp. 59-69.

White, Roderick E. /Poynter, Thomas A. (1989): Achieving Worldwide Advantage with the Horizontal Organization. Business Quarterly. Vol. 54, No. 2, 1989, pp. 55-60.

Whiteman, Gail/Cooper, William H. (2000): Ecological Embeddedness. Academy of Management Journal. Vol. 43, No. 6, 2000, pp. 1265-1282.

Widener, Sally K./Selto, Frank H. (1999): Management Control Systems and Boundaries of the Firm: Why do Firms Outsource Internal Auditing Activities? Journal of Management Accounting Research. Vol. 11, 1999, pp. 45-73.
Wiedenhofer, Marco (2003): Bewertung von Kernkompetenzen: Strategische Ressourcen als Realoption. Deutscher Universitätsverlag, Wiesbaden, 2003.
Wildemann, Horst (1997): Koordination von Unternehmensnetzwerken. Zeitschrift für Betriebswirtschaft (ZfB). Vol. 67, No. 4, 1997, pp. 417-439.
Wildemann, Horst (2005): Outsourcing - Offshoring - Verlagerung: Leitlinien und Programme. Transfer-Centrum GmbH&Co. KG, München, 2005.
Willenbrock, Harald (2004): Wo der Pfeffer wächst. McK Wissen. No. 9, 2004, pp. 64-71.
Williams, Kathy (2003): Is Offshoring for You? Strategic Finance. Vol. 85, No. 1, 2003, pp. 19-20.
Williamson, Oliver E. (1994): Transaction Cost Economics and Organization Theory, in: Smelser, Neil J./Swedberg, Richard (Eds., 1994): The Handbook of Economic Sociology. Princeton University Press, Princeton, pp. 77-107.
Williamson, Oliver E. (1999): Strategy Research: Governance and Competence Perspectives. Strategic Management Journal. Vol. 20, No. 12, 1999, pp. 1087-1108.
Winstanley, Graham (2004): Distributed and Developed Work Allocation Planning. Applied Artificial Intelligence. Vol. 18, No. 2, 2004, pp. 97-115.
Winter, Sidney G. (1987): Knowledge and Competence as Strategic Assets, in: Teece, David J. (Ed., 1987): The Competitive Challenge: Strategies for Industrial Innovation and Renewal. Ballinger, Cambridge, pp. 159-184.
Wolf, Joachim (1994): Internationales Personalmanagement: Kontext - Koordination - Erfolg. Gabler, Wiesbaden, 1994.
Woodward, Joan (1965): Industrial Organizaton: Theory and Practice. Oxford University Press, London, 1965.
Wrona, Thomas (2005): Die Fallstudienanalyse als wissenschaftliche Forschungsmethode. Working Paper, No. 10, ESCP-EAP Europäische Wirtschaftshochschule Berlin, 2005.
Yeung, Henry Wai-Chung (1995): Qualitative Personal Interviews in International Business Research: Some Lessons from a Study of Hong Kong Transnational Corporations. International Business Review. Vol. 4, No. 3, 1995, pp. 313-339.
Yin, Robert K. (1981): The Case Study Crisis: Some Answers. Administrative Science Quarterly. Vol. 26, No. 1, 1981, pp. 58-65.
Yin, Robert K. (1993): Applications of Case Study Research. Sage Publications, Newbury Park, 1993.
Yin, Robert K. (2003): Case Study Research - Design and Methods. 3 edition. Sage Publications, Thousand Oaks, London, New Delhi, 2003.
Young, Stephen/Tavares, Ana Teresa (2004): Centralization and Autonomy: Back to the Future. International Business Review. Vol. 13, No. 2, 2004, pp. 215-237.
Zaheer, Akbar/Zaheer, Srilata (1997): Catching the Wave: Alertness, Responsiveness, and the Market Influence in Global Electronic Networks. Management Science. Vol. 43, No. 11, 1997, pp. 1493-1509.
Zahra, Shaker A./Pearce II, John A. (1990): Research Evidence on the Miles-Snow Typology. Journal of Management. Vol. 16, No. 4, 1990, pp. 751-768.
Zatolyuk, Sergiy/Allgood, Bridget (2004): Evaluating a Country for Offshore Outsourcing: Software Development Providers in the Ukraine. Information Systems Management. Vol. 21, No. 3, 2004, pp. 28-33.
Zedeck, Sheldon/Jackson, Susan E./Summers, Elizabeth (1983): Shift Work Schedules and Their Relationship to Health, Adaptation, Satisfaction, and Turnover Intention. Academy of Management Journal. Vol. 26, No. 2, 1983, pp. 297-310.
Zeffane, Rachid (1989): Computer Use and Structural Control: A Study of Australian Enterprises. Journal of Management Studies. Vol. 26, No. 6, 1989, pp. 621-648.
Zeira, Yoram/Banai, Moshe (1985): Selection of Expatriate Managers in MNCs: The Host-Environment Point of View. International Studies of Management & Organization. Vol. 15, No. 1, 1985, pp. 33-51.

Zimmermann, Udo (1992): Planung von Service-Centern in Industriekonzernen unter besonderer Berücksichtigung des Instandhaltungsbereiches. Ferber, Giessen, 1992.
Zukin, Sharon/DiMaggio, Paul (1990): Structures of Capital: The Social Organization of the Economy. Cambridge University Press, Cambridge, 1990.